SPACE AND SPATIAL ANALYSIS IN ARCHAEOLOGY

edited by Elizabeth C. Robertson,
Jeffrey D. Seibert, Deepika C. Fernandez,
and Marc U. Zender

Space and Spatial Analysis in Archaeology

New Mexico

UNIVERSITY OF CALGARY PRESS

Published by the University of Calgary Press
2500 University Drive NW, Calgary, Alberta, Canada
T2N 1N4 www.uofcpress.com

LIBRARY AND ARCHIVES CANADA CATALOGUING IN PUBLICATION

University of Calgary. Archaeological Association. Conference (34th : 2002 : University of Calgary)
Space and spatial analysis in archaeology / edited by Elizabeth C. Robertson ... [et al.].

Co-published by the University of New Mexico Press.
Papers originally presented at the Conference: Space and spatial analysis in Archaeology held at the University of Calgary, Nov. 18th., 2002.

Includes bibliographical references and index.
ISBN 10: 1-55238-168-4 (University of Calgary Press)
ISBN 13: 978-1-55238-168-7 (University of Calgary Press)
ISBN 10: 0-8263-4022-9 (University of New Mexico Press)
ISBN 13: 978-0-8263-4022-1 (University of New Mexico Press)

1. Social archaeology—Congresses. 2. Spatial systems—Congresses. 3. Archaeological geology—Congresses. 4. Landscape archaeology—Congresses. 5. Archaeoastronomy—Congresses. I. Robertson, Elizabeth C., 1971- II. Title.

CC72.4.U56 2005 930.1 C2005-902763-0

We acknowledge the financial support of the Government of Canada through the Book Publishing Industry Development Program (BPIDP), the Alberta Foundation for the Arts and the Canada Council for the Arts for our publishing program.

Printed and bound in Canada by
∞ This book is printed on 55 lb. Eco book Natural.
Cover design by Mieka West.

Canada Council for the Arts | Conseil des Arts du Canada

Canada

TABLE OF CONTENTS

PREFACE

Kathryn V. Reese-Taylor

Kathryn V. Reese-Taylor, Department of Archaeology, University of Calgary, 2500 University Drive N.W., Calgary, Alberta T2N 1N4, Canada.

Each year the undergraduate and graduate students of the Chacmool Archaeological Association and the Department of Archaeology, University of Calgary, sponsor the Chacmool Conference. The first Chacmool Conference, held in 1967, was a one-day workshop focused on the topic "Early Man and Environments in Northern North America." Five papers were presented at the workshop. Over the next few years other workshops were organized, again dealing with topics relevant to the early peopling of North America.

In the ensuing years, the event, which is organized around a central theme, has attained the status of a major conference on both a national and international level. Scholars from all regions of Canada, the United States, and throughout the world regularly attend and present papers, and as a result the conference has become the largest thematic archaeological and cross-disciplinary conference in North America.

The papers from these conferences were published as proceedings, edited by graduate student members of the Chacmool Association. These publications have proven to be extremely successful endeavours and have included many volumes that have become classics, such as *The Archaeology of Gender* (Walde and Willows 1989) and *Debating Complexity* (Meyer et al. 1993). However, the Chacmool Conferences and the subsequent publications have become victims of their own success. Because of the growth in the number of papers submitted for both the conference and the proceedings, the Chacmool Association and the Department of Archaeology decided to seek outside help with the publication and distribution of the Chacmool series.

Therefore, in 2002, the executive members of the Chacmool Association and the editors of the 2001 Chacmool Conference volume approached the University of Calgary Press. The resulting partnership has lead to a new publication series in association with the Chacmool Conference, a series that continues to be guided and edited by members of the Chacmool Association, but also undergoes a rigorous process of peer review. Consequently, it is our hope that this, the inaugural volume, will reflect the underlying spirit of the previous Chacmool Association publications, as well as the professionalism that can be afforded by a university press.

The papers included in this volume reflect the breadth of the 2001 Chacmool Conference, which addressed four areas of investigation under the rubric of spatial studies: archaeoastronomy, geoarchaeology, landscape studies and spatial analysis. These topics are united by their focus on understanding humanity's interaction with the environment, both physically, as well as cognitively. Significantly, this was one of the first conferences to address the issue of spatial studies from a multiplicity of perspectives. Other thematic conferences have chosen to limit their focus to one, or at most two, of the topics addressed during the 2001 Chacmool Conference. However, by choosing to contextualize the question of spatial analysis broadly, the conference organizers sought to engender a cross-disciplinary discussion.

In conclusion, we anticipate that this volume, like the conference, will be an important resource for scholars of many disciplines to explore a multiplicity of perspectives regarding space and spatial studies – ancient people's relationship with their environment, however they choose to conceive of it.

Kathryn Reese-Taylor
Faculty advisor for the 2001 Chacmool Conference

REFERENCES CITED

Meyer, D. A., P. C. Dawson, and D. T. Hanna (editors)
|1996| *Debating Complexity: Proceedings of the 26th Annual Chacmool Conference.* Chacmool Archaeological Association, University of Calgary, Calgary, Alberta.

Walde, D., and N. D. Willows (editors)
|1989| *The Archaeology of Gender: Proceedings of the 22nd Annual Chacmool Conference.* Chacmool Archaeological Association, University of Calgary, Calgary, Alberta.

ACKNOWLEDGMENTS

Elizabeth C. Robertson, Jeffrey D. Seibert, Deepika C. Fernandez, and Marc U. Zender

Elizabeth C. Robertson, Department of Archaeology, University of Calgary, 2500 University Drive N.W., Calgary, Alberta T2N 1N4, Canada.
Jeffrey D. Seibert, Department of Archaeology, University of Calgary, 2500 University Drive N.W., Calgary, Alberta T2N 1N4, Canada.
Deepika C. Fernandez, Department of Archaeology, University of Calgary, 2500 University Drive N.W., Calgary, Alberta T2N 1N4, Canada.
Marc U. Zender, Peabody Museum, Harvard University, 11 Divinity Avenue, Cambridge, Massachusetts 02138, U.S.A.

This volume could not have happened without the contributions of many individuals and organizations. Based on papers originally presented at the 34th Annual Chacmool Conference, held at the University of Calgary from November 14 to 18, 2001, it would not exist without the tremendous efforts of all those who helped organize, run and fund the conference. In particular, we would like to thank the conference chairs, Christine Cluney, Janet Blakey and Andrew White, and their faculty advisers, Dr. William Glanzman and Dr. Kathryn Reese-Taylor, for putting together an extremely successful conference that featured an array of fascinating and thought-provoking presentations that formed the nuclei of the papers that we have the honour of publishing in this volume.

We also would like to express our thanks to Dr. Kathryn Reese-Taylor for her ongoing contributions as faculty adviser to the 2001 Chacmool editorial committee and to Dr. J. Scott Raymond for his invaluable assistance as general editor of Chacmool publications. This volume marks the first Chacmool publication to be issued by the University of Calgary Press, an endeavour which would not have happened without their guidance. For this, we would like to like to express our appreciation to everyone at the Press, with special thanks to Walter Hildebrandt, John King, Wendy Stephens, and Joan Barton for their patience and assistance with our many questions. We would also like to thank the reviewers to whom the Press forwarded our initial manuscript; their thoughtful and insightful comments have made it a much stronger volume. We also owe special thanks to the administrative staff of the University of Calgary's Department of Archaeology, Lesley Nicholls, Nicole Ethier and Anna Nicole Skierka, for all their help putting the volume together, and to the 2001, 2002, 2003 and 2004 executive committees of the Chacmool Archaeological Association for their assistance.

We would like to acknowledge the Social Science and Humanities Research Council of Canada, the University of Calgary's Research Grant Committee, the Department of Archaeology and the Chacmool Archaeological Association for their financial assistance with the organization of the 2001 Chacmool Conference and the production of this volume.

Last but certainly not least, we want to express our appreciation to everyone who contributed papers to the volume. It is entirely a reflection of their tremendous patience and effort, and we cannot thank them enough.

Elizabeth C. Robertson
Jeffrey D. Seibert
Deepika C. Fernandez
Marc U. Zender
2001 Chacmool Conference editorial committee

INTRODUCTION

Jeffrey Seibert

Jeffrey Seibert, Department of Archaeology, University of Calgary, 2500 University Drive N.W., Calgary, Alberta T2N 1N4, Canada.

Spatial analysis has long been an important aspect of the archaeological endeavour and has provided numerous insights into the behaviour, social organization and cognitive structures of past cultures. Spatial analyses of archaeological materials have become quite varied as diverse methods and theoretical approaches have emerged, making the concept of space somewhat nebulous. The theme for the 2001 Chacmool Conference was chosen to serve as a forum to discuss these diverse approaches.

The response to this proposed theme was enormous, and the 2001 Chacmool Conference was one of the largest conferences in this annual series of meetings, both in terms of the number of papers presented and the number of conference attendees. While this was no doubt due in part to the breadth of this topic, it was also due to the fact that spatial analysis of archaeological materials has been recognized as being one of the most important ways of gaining insights into past forms of social and cultural organization.

One of the attractive aspects of a conference organized around this theme is that space, both as a theoretical and methodological concern, is not constrained by any of the grand theoretical paradigms or meta-narratives of the social sciences (see Johnson 1999:162–163) or what Trigger (1989:19–25) refers to as "High Theory." Spatial analyses and approaches to space in archaeology are instead what Trigger (1989) refers to as "Middle Level Theory," because it attempts to explain and account for patterning in the archaeological record. In short, spatial analysis in archaeology is relevant to scholars pursuing all sorts of "higher level" theoretical questions, insofar as the spatial analysis of archaeological materials allows for the generalizations to be drawn that fuel the higher level theoretical inferences.

As Kroll and Price (1991) note, spatial analyses of archaeological remains are as old as the discipline itself, as the context and provenience of artifacts have been recorded in excavations of archaeological sites since the beginnings of modern archaeology. While Kroll and Price (1991:1) make this assertion with particular reference to Paleolithic archaeology, this early focus on spatial approaches to archaeology is also true of archaeologists working in the Scandinavian tradition, such as Thomsen and Worsae (see Trigger 1989:76–86). In these early examples of archaeological research concerned with space, the spatial arrangements of artifacts, features and architecture were recorded with functional interpretations in mind, but were not conceived of as being the key to either sociocultural systems, as the later functionalist and processualist archaeologists believed, or imbued with multifaceted sociocultural meanings, as many postprocessual archaeologists believe. The influence of the Scandinavian archaeologists on scholars working in other areas of Europe and in North America in the late eighteenth and early nineteenth centuries meant the spread of this increasingly spatial view of archaeology, and the transformation of earlier antiquarian studies of artifacts into systematic analyses of artifacts in context (Trigger 1989).

The techniques employed in these early excavations of archaeological sites were often crude by modern standards with regards to their recording of the spatial arrangements of these sites (Trigger 1989:196). It was not until the late nineteenth century that methods of recording the provenience of artifacts were comparable to modern "scientific" archaeological standards. The improvement of these methods has often been attributed to A. Pitt-Rivers (see Daniel 1967:225–233), although there were other scholars that were employing similarly meticulous methods at roughly the same time as Pitt-Rivers (Trigger 1989:196–199).

Despite these early studies of the spatial layout of archaeological sites, most scholars would concede that explicitly spatial approaches to archaeology developed in conjunction with the functional approach to archaeology, pioneered by scholars such as Clark (1954) in Europe, and Willey (1948) in North America (see Trigger 1989:264–274). These analyses sought to explain the correlation between spatial patterning of artifacts and architecture in sites and the way that past societies functioned as systems. The importance of spatial analysis was further underscored by Walter Taylor (1948) in his discussion of his conjunctive approach to archaeology, which emphasized the importance of the analysis of all forms of material and ecological evidence recovered from archaeological sites and the spatial relationships between these lines of evidence.

As ecological concerns became increasingly important in archaeology, spatial approaches to the analysis of archaeological remains expanded to include settlement studies. These studies sought to examine the relationship between the spatial patterning of settlements on the natural landscape and ecological determinants of settlement (Willey and Sabloff 1993:172–176). The first of the studies, and the most influential, was Willey's (1953) study of settlement patterns in the Viru Valley in Peru. This study sought to explain the relationship between settlement, environment and sociocultural systems over time (and obviously space), and sparked considerable interest in this aspect of spatial analyses of the material remains of past cultures.

As functionalism gave way to processualism as the prevailing paradigm in archaeology in the Americas, spatial analyses continued to be important, and indeed blossomed as archaeologists sought to explain intercultural regularities through the analysis of the spatial patterning of architecture and artifacts in a number of contexts (see Trigger 1989:289–326 and Willey and Sabloff 1993:214–305 for a discussion of processualism). Settlement studies, discussed above, became an important part of any archaeological project (Willey and Sabloff 1993:216–219), and archaeologists sought increasingly to draw cross-cultural generalizations regarding the relationship between past behaviours and modern ethnographic observations.

The work of Lewis Binford (1968:27) perhaps best exemplifies this approach, with his assertions that one of archaeology's main goals should be to develop "laws of cultural dynamics." This was done by comparing ethnoarchaeological observations about the spatial patterning of artifacts with the archaeological past and attempting to discern regularities between past and present societies. This is exemplified by Binford's (1980) famous discussion of the relationship between ethnoarchaeology and the archaeological past entitled "Willow Smoke and Dogs' Tails: Hunter-Gather Settlement Systems and Archaeological Site Formation." In this paper, he asserts that observations about various contemporary hunter-gatherer groups' mobility patterns and internal site arrangements can serve as direct analogies by which to explain spatial patterning in the archaeological record. By doing this, Binford effectively projects the present onto the past, and asserts that the patterns seen in present times are representative of broader reaching behavioural patterns that transcend temporal and cultural differences.

In a related vein is the work of Susan Kent (1983), Nicolas David (1971), Carol Kramer (1979) and other ethnoarchaeologists who were working on similar problems regarding the spatial organization of present societies and their relevance to archaeological interpretation in the 1960s and 1970s. Kent's (1983) work regarding the spatial organization of residences in various cultural groups in the United States is a fine example of the processual approach to the ethnoarchaeology of space. She conducted ethnoarchaeological studies of Navajo, Euroamerican and what she terms "Spanish-American" households in order to examine how they were organized spatially. She proceeded, in turn, to compare these spatial patterns to Navajo archaeological sites in order to test hypotheses regarding the organization of Navajo households over time. This is an example of Binford's (1980) approach to ethnoarchaeology, outlined above, being applied to a broader study. It is interesting to note, and will be discussed in further detail below, that ethnoarchaeologists, despite the strongly processual genesis of their approach to archaeology, were instrumental in bringing postprocessual archaeology into the spotlight in the U.K. and subsequently North America.

In a less nomothetic albeit equally processual vein is the work of Kent Flannery and his students, who often employ overtly spatial approaches in their studies of Mesoamerican archaeology. This approach is perhaps best exemplified in *The Early Mesoamerican Village* (Flannery 1976a), an edited volume that examines the study of early Mesoamerican villages from an explicitly spatial standpoint. Much of this volume is devoted to the analysis of settlement patterns and systems (e.g., Flannery 1976b, 1976c; Earle 1976; Rossmann 1976 to name just three examples), community organization (e.g., Flannery 1976d; Marcus 1976; Whalen 1976) and the organization of households (e.g., Flannery 1976e; Flannery and Winter 1976; Winter 1976). In effect, this book is an archaeological how-to manual about the spatial analysis of small scale agrarian societies, complete with amusing anecdotes regarding the follies of pseudo-fictitious Mesoamerican archaeologists.

During the processual era settlement studies also began to develop in a more ecologically driven and often narrowly materialist (referred to as "vulgar materialism" by many scholars of a Marxist bent) views of past human societies. Sanders et al.'s (1979) study of central Mexico, entitled *The Basin of Mexico: Ecological Processes in the Evolution of a Civilization*, exemplifies this symbiosis between ecological process, cultural evolution and settlement study quite well. Sanders et al. (1979) discuss the development of civilization in the Basin of Mexico in direct reference to changing relationships between people and their natural environment, and the influence of demographic pressures on social organization. The volume is concerned largely with settlement patterns and systems, and their relationship to the natural landscape, and the authors tend to couch most of their discussion of this relationship in the very processual terms, and employ ethnographic and ethnohistoric analogies extensively to the subsistence systems of the distant past. This study is truly impressive because of the vast amount of labour invested in it, and the grand theoretical conclusions of the authors, but is quite limited in its theoretical scope, and in many ways can be seen as exemplifying the marriage between cultural ecology and processualism that typified much of the work in the 1970s in the Americas. Many of the aforementioned settlement and settlement system studies in *The Early Mesoamerican Village* (Flannery 1976a; also see Flannery 1976b, 1976c; Earle 1976; Rossmann 1976) also are overtly focused on cultural evolution and ecology, although perhaps with less of an ecologically deterministic strain than Sanders et al. (1979).

Household archaeology as a particular focus of research can be seen in many ways to have originated with the advent of processual archaeology in the 1960s and 1970s, crossbred with the activity area studies of the functionalist archaeologists and early cultural ecology (Steadman 1996:52). Household archaeology in this time period can be seen in many ways as an outgrowth of settlement archaeology: it is interested in the spatial components of a system and their interrelated nature, but focuses on a much smaller spatial area. That is not to argue that there was not archaeological research being conducted on houses prior to this time; instead it was through the development of processual archaeology that the archaeology of the spatial and social organization of past households crystallized into what we now call household archaeology. As was alluded to previously, the work of Flannery (1976a) and his students truly revolutionized household archaeology, and developed it into a separate field of inquiry. Indeed, as Steadman (1996:56) notes, much of the early work in household archaeology was conducted in Mesoamerica (also see Rathje 1983; Wilk 1983; Wilk and Rathje 1982). Recent developments in spatial approaches to household archaeology will be discussed in more detail below.

In Great Britain a number of approaches to the spatial analysis of archaeological materials also developed, in many ways in a parallel fashion to developments in the Americas. The volume entitled *Man, Settlement and Urbanism* (Ucko et al. 1972) was based on a symposium held at the Institute of Archaeology, University College London, and in many ways represents a watershed in the study of settlement patterns and the development of urbanism in the U.K. While a number of the participants in the symposium came from outside of the U.K. (mostly from the U.S.A. and Canada), which suggests a degree of international "cross-pollination" of ideas, the majority of participants were British, suggesting that by 1970 spatial approaches to archaeology had become important in Britain as well as the Americas. Later in the 1970s an overtly "scientific" approach to spatial analysis in archaeology was championed by David Clarke and his students (Hodder and Orton 1976; Clarke 1977). Hodder and Orton (1976) called for a more explicitly quantitative approach to the study of spatial patterning, and applied statistical methods to all levels of spatial analysis.

As this normative approach to spatial analysis became dominant in Anglo-American archaeology (and in certain branches of European archaeology as well [Johnson 1999]), some scholars began to question the relevance of such an approach to the spatial analysis of past cultures. As Ashmore (2002:1175) notes, the late 1970s saw increasing interest in overtly social approaches to spatial questions in archaeology. The development of postprocessual archaeology (or archaeologies as many scholars have argued) resulted in a number of scholars questioning the normative assumptions made by the processualists, and beginning to examine aspects of human behaviour in a less deterministic and rigid light (Patterson 1986:20). Scholars started to examine less "tangible" aspects of human culture, such as ideology, and began to critically analyze power relations and social structures in past societies (e.g., Hodder 1984; Leone 1986; Miller and Tilley 1984; Shanks and Tilley 1987a, 1987b).

This new theoretical focus affected the ways in which archaeologists analyzed spatial relations between archaeological materials (whether artifacts, features, or sites) by introducing aspects of analysis that began to focus more on the social and cultural implications of spatial relations in past societies. This thread was present in both the functional and processual approaches to spatial archaeology (see for example Clark 1954; Flannery 1976a), but the development of postprocessual archaeology effectively gave the social, cognitive and cultural aspects of spatial analyses centre stage.

Some scholars, influenced by cultural geographers and anthropologists such as Amos Rapoport (1968, 1982, 1990), Lawrence and Low (1990) and Hillier and Hanson (1984; also Hillier 1996; Hanson 1998), sought to analyze the built environment constructed by past peoples, looking at the social, cultural and ideological aspects of past buildings and cities (e.g., Blanton 1994; Hodder 1984; Martin 2001; Trigger 1990). Some of the more recent work by Flannery (1998) has begun to address questions such as these, although many of his earlier, more processual ideas still remain in this more recent literature.

Analysis of the spatial arrangements of the built environment has been approached form the standpoint of space syntax analysis, developed by Bill Hillier and Julienne Hanson (Hillier and Hanson 1984; Hillier 1996; Hanson 1998). Space syntax analyses of the built environment seek to analyze the ways in which the built environment constructs and constrains space, and how this construction of space can be described using a standardized lexicon, and represented through a series of standardized visual conventions. Through these standardized forms of visual representation and description, it becomes possible to analyze the social relationships inherent in space as it is constructed through the built environment. Markus (1993:13) notes that this perspective is inherently social insofar as it assumes that all space is shaped and defined by social relationships, and that social relations define and constrain the makeup of spatial relations in the built environment. He also notes that *The Social Logic of Space* (Hillier and Hanson 1984) has inherently Durkheimian underpinnings by conceiving of the organization of space in terms of organic and mechanical solidarity.

In archaeology, the work of scholars such as Ferguson (1996), Grahame (1997), Stuardo (2003) and A. Smith (2003), all of whom employ some form of space syntax analysis in their work, represent the growing importance of this approach in the field. It is important to note that many of these scholars reject the functionalist undertones of Hillier and Hanson's (1984) theoretical approach, and instead modify the theoretical perspective of space syntax analysis while maintaining the methodology (see Ferguson 1996:21–22 for a discussion of this paradigm shift). Most of the studies employing space syntax analyses in archaeology use Hillier and Hanson (1984) as their theoretical inspiration. As Dawson (personal communication 2004) points out, however, this text is out of date, and space syntax analysis has progressed significantly since 1984 in terms of the methods employed, as well as changing significantly in the ensuing years theoretically.

Another related field that developed out of these new interests in the less physically tangible aspects of human culture is the study of archaeological landscapes, influenced strongly by human geography (see Gamble 1987; also see Muir 1999 for a discussion of the development of landscape studies among human geographers) and sociocultural anthropology (see Basso 1996). Interest in archaeological landscapes can be seen, in many ways, as an outgrowth of studies of settlement patterns and systems because of the relationship between the natural environment and settlement that is seen in a number of these studies. As was discussed previously, the study of settlement patterns and settlement systems grew out of the functional approach to archaeology, and in particular cultural ecological approaches to anthropology and archaeology. Settlement studies blossomed through the New Archaeology, and became a standard component of all large-scale archaeological projects (see Flannery 1976a; Trigger 1989). Interest in the ideological and symbolic components of societies and cultures, and the increasing importance that was placed on the constitution of social relations in past societies, which can largely be seen as an outgrowth of the postprocessual approach to archaeology, resulted in the more humanistic approach of landscape archaeology.

Landscape archaeology, by its very nature, is often concerned with the perception and experience of landscape, and the relationship between the empirically observable material components of the landscape and how people and cultures navigate these landscapes, both conceptually and through lived experience. As Knapp and Ashmore (1999:6) note, landscape archaeology recognizes a dialectical relationship between society and culture on one hand and the natural environment on the other: namely, people's perceptions shape how they see the environment, and the environment, in turn, shapes the prevailing cultural perceptions of landscape in a given society. A related concept is the relationship between space, as an empirically neutral series of relationships between objects and the environment, and place, which is the meaningfully constituted and culturally constructed space that people dwell in. Landscapes as culturally constructed and experienced "spaces" are effectively "places" because of the culturally and socially determined understandings that people have of them (Tilley 1994). Space exists merely as an abstraction according to this perspective, because people's personal, cultural and social experiences in space reconstitute spaces as places through experience.

These themes have been taken up by a number of archaeologists and has developed into a vibrant field of inquiry (see Daniels and Cosgrove 1988; Tilley 1994; Ashmore and Knapp 1999; and A. Smith 2003 for examples of landscape archaeology). A healthy debate exists in the discipline regarding the nature of landscape archaeology, both regarding the content of landscape studies and the theoretical approaches advocated by landscape archaeologists. Tilley (1994) offers an important discussion of the varying theoretical approaches to landscape archaeology, and highlights his own interest in phenomenological approaches to this line of inquiry.

An important aspect of landscape archaeology is the study of settled landscapes, an area of inquiry also heavily influenced by human geography. The study of archaeological urban landscapes has been taken up by a number of scholars interested in the sociopolitics of urbanism, as well as the evolution of the built environment. In his recent *magnum opus* entitled *Understanding Early Civilizations: A Comparative Study*, Bruce Trigger (2003) discusses both the urban landscapes of cities in early civilizations, as well as various aspects of monumental architecture in these cities. Trigger's analysis focuses on the urban landscapes of the so-called primary civilizations of the world, and draws on both archaeological and historical material (where available). This book is especially significant because urban landscapes and city planning are portrayed in this book as both being constituted by, and constituting, the nature of power in early civilizations. Similar concepts are explored by Adam Smith (2003) who postulates that the very nature of power in what he refers to as "early complex societies" are linked to the construction and maintenance of urban landscapes. Smith (2003:202–231) explicitly discusses the importance of urban landscapes in the constitution of society, and using the example of ancient Mesopotamian cites discusses how power was idealized and realized through the urban landscapes of ancient Mesopotamian cities. The work of Wendy Ashmore (1991, 1992; also see Brady and Ashmore 1999; Ashmore and Sabloff 2002) has also explored the connections between urban built forms and social organization. Ashmore's work suggests that urban landscapes in the Maya area reflect broader political affiliations, and that site plans among lower order centres often emulate the site plans of major players in Classic period power politics, such as Tikal and Calakmul. Recent work by Timothy Pugh (2003) has examined the social landscape of the highly nucleated and densely settled centre of Mayapan, a Late Postclassic Maya city from the Yucatan Peninsula, by examining statistical correlates of proposed social groupings in the city. He ultimately concludes that some of the social divisions at the site that have been proposed to have existed through previous archaeologists' qualitative analyses can be demonstrated statistically, offering a more nuanced approach to the study of this urban landscape by articulating social inference to statistical methods (Pugh 2003:951).

In a related vein, Canuto and Yaeger (2000) have recently published a volume of papers discussing community organization in a number of different cultural and archaeological settings in the New World. Most of these papers deal with settlements smaller than cities, but larger than individual homesteads, hence the designation "community." Most of these papers are explicitly spatial in their orientation, and look at the arrangement of non-urban settlements on the landscape, as well as their internal organization. Other scholars (e.g., Snead and Preucel 1999) have also approached non-urban settlements from a landscape perspective, making the landscape analysis of non-urban settlements a vibrant field of inquiry.

This by no means represents an exhaustive survey of approaches to landscape approaches to settlement in archaeology. As recent edited volumes concerning the nature of urbanism in early civilizations have illustrated, scholars working on a number of topics in various culture regions are interested in the spatial composition of urban landscapes in the archaeological past (see various papers in Aufrecht et al. 1997; Manzanilla 1997; M. Smith 2003). This relationship between the study of "natural," urban and non-urban settled areas from a landscape perspective is interesting because it illustrates the power of this approach to archaeology: landscape as a concept can be used to describe the phenomenological and ideological relationship between people, cultures and their respective environments (both natural and built).

Archaeological approaches to the study of households have also been influenced by the critiques of postprocessual archaeologists and the increasingly eclectic and interdisciplinary nature of archaeology. Household archaeology has become increasingly influenced by studies conducted in archaeology's sister disciplines of social anthropology and sociology (see Wilk and Ashmore 1988). In particular the ethnographic work carried out by Netting et al. (1984) is an important source of ethnographic analogy and theoretical inspiration for much of the work conducted by household archaeologists since the 1980s. The question of the relationship between spatial organization and domestic architecture from an interdisciplinary perspective is also explored in volume edited by Susan Kent (1990) entitled *Domestic Architecture and the Use of Space.* This volume draws together work conducted by sociocultural anthropologists, archaeologists and geographers to examine questions regarding the spatial analysis of residential architecture from a number of cultural contexts. Blanton's (1994) cross-cultural study entitled *Houses and Households* examines the nature of domestic architecture and its influence on household organization from a number of contexts, both ethnographic and archaeological. In Classical archaeology, recent scholarship has addressed similar questions regarding the relationship between domestic architecture, household units and space (Laurence and Wallace-Hadrill 1997). This volume is, by the very nature of Classical archaeology, interdisciplinary in scope, but what is surprising about this volume is the amount of influence from other disciplines, particularly anthropology and human geography. All of these volumes represent an attempt to examine the domestic architecture and household organization from an interdisciplinary and cross-cultural perspective.

The Encyclopedia of Vernacular Architecture of the World (Oliver 1997) also represents an important resource for the archaeologist interested in cross-cultural studies of domestic architecture and its relationship to household archaeology. Fedick's (1997) discussion of archaeological approaches to households and domestic architecture in the *Encyclopedia* highlights the importance of cross-cultural research driven by ethnographic observations in the study of archaeological households, and in turn underscores the importance of the chronological depths that archaeological studies can add to the investigation of the vernacular architecture of the world. Fedick's (1997:9) discussion also notes the importance of explicitly spatial studies of architecture and households in archaeology, and the interdisciplinary nature of these spatial approaches. These studies take this perspective in order to look for similarities between cultures, but also in order to highlight differences between them. These studies also represent the cross-pollination of ideas between archaeology and related disciplines in recent years and the diversity of approaches that could be focused on a single topic.

As with the other sections of this paper it is beyond the scope of this paper to discuss recent developments in household archaeology in greater detail. Suffice it to say that many other contributions have been made to the study of space in domestic archaeology in recent years by other scholars (e.g., Parker Pearson and Richards 1994). For a more in depth discussion of the development of household archaeology and current approaches, see Steadman (1996).

An interesting historical footnote with regards to both the aforementioned studies of household and community concerns the 1988 Chacmool Conference, which was focused on precisely this topic. Many of the papers contained in the proceedings of the conference (MacEachern et al. 1989) dealt specifically with the spatial patterning of archaeological remains, and how these remains could be used to reconstruct household organization. The 1988 Chacmool Conference can be seen in many ways as a precursor to many of the studies detailed above that deal with the social and ideological components of household and community organization that became characteristic of the late 1980s and continue today. The 1988 Chacmool Conference and its proceedings (MacEachern et al. 1989) effectively represent a watershed effort in the study of the relationship between the spatial and the socio-ideological at the level of the household and community.

The new concern with humanistic approaches to archaeology also influenced ethnoarchaeological studies of spatial organization. As was mentioned previously, the work of many ethnoarchaeologists was influenced by, and in turn strongly influenced developments in postprocessual archaeology (see David and Kramer

2001:59–61). Archaeologists employing ethnoarchaeological evidence, such as Hodder (1982) and Shanks and Tilley (1987a), began to note that ethnoarchaeological studies of material culture underscore the degree to which material culture is meaningfully constituted by sociocultural factors, and in turn influences culture (see David and Kramer 2001 for a discussion of this concept). This is a far cry from the ethnoarchaeology of the processual period that sought to explain the past by employing analogies from the anthropological present. Space and spatial organization was, of course, vital to this understanding of the relationship between material culture and meaning. David and Kramer's (2001:278–283) discussion of ethnoarchaeological approaches to gendered spaces is a good example of these new ways in which ethnoarchaeology is incorporating postprocessual approaches to spatial organization.

The application of geographical information systems (GIS) to archaeological data is another relatively recent development. GIS is defined by Wheatley and Gillings (2002) as being a "spatial database" which allows for the manipulation and analysis of data, as well as visualization and reporting of the results of the manipulation and analysis of the data. It is this combination of elements that differentiates GIS from both other forms of data bases as well as other cartographic programs utilized by scholars. The first GIS in the world was developed by the Canadian Department of Forestry and Rural Development 1964 in order to deal with an inventory of available natural resources in the country and develop a strategic and sustainable plan for their development and exploitation (Wheatley and Gillings 2002:14–15). Kvamme (1995) notes that the first application of a GIS to archaeological material was conducted between 1979 and 1982 as a part of the Granite Reef archaeological project in the American Southwest. While the term GIS was not used in the report itself, Kvamme (1995:2) suggests that the approach employed in this study was not substantively different from what we now refer to as GIS. Early approaches employing GIS in archaeology were explicitly concerned with developing predictive models for distribution (Kvamme 1995:2–3). Predictive modeling, of course, represents a strongly processual theoretical inclination, as it explains to chart and model regularity, and explain away variation in data.

These approaches were not extremely influential on either side of the Atlantic, however, because of the lack of communication regarding the technology, and the expense and inaccessibility of the technology itself (Kvamme 1995:5). The seminal volume entitled *Interpreting Space: GIS and Archaeology* (Allen et al. 1990) marked the first published volume of collected papers from a number of different culture areas and research projects, dealing explicitly with GIS applications to archaeology, and also represented the first exposure of the approach to a wider audience. Because of this volume's emphasis on the Americas (see Kvamme 1995), a volume was assembled dealing with GIS and archaeology from an Old World perspective entitled *Archaeology and Geographical Information Systems* (Lock and Stančič 1995). In the following year, Aldenderfer and Maschner (1996) published a volume dealing with anthropological approaches to GIS, with a particular emphasis being placed on GIS's methodological importance for archaeology. These three volumes represented a breakthrough for GIS studies in archaeology, as they exposed GIS to a wider audience. GIS is considered increasingly important by archaeologists, and has very much become part of the mainstream of the discipline, fulfilling an important niche in the archaeologist's methodological tool kit (see Wheatley and Gillings 2002:20).

While GIS does represent an important methodological tool for archaeologists seeking to examine materials in a spatial context, it is important to note that GIS does not represent a theoretical approach in and of itself. As Claxton (1995) notes, there are important theoretical implications for archaeological theory that stem from the increasing use of GIS in the discipline. This accords with the observations of Hodder (1999) concerning the hermeneutic relationship between theory, data and praxis in archaeology. This does not make GIS a theoretical perspective in and of itself, however, because GIS does not seek to explain social or cultural phenomena in the same way that functionalist or processualist (to name only two theoretical schools) approaches do.

Many of these newer approaches to archaeology represent a departure from the logico-positivist approaches of the processualists to spatial archaeology and introduce a much more interpretative aspect to the whole endeavour. As Adam Smith (2003) cogently notes, however, archaeologists' notions of space are in many cases still tied to ideas of social evolution which give temporal and chronological concerns in archaeology centre stage in archaeology at the expense of space. The purpose of this volume is not to divorce time from space (which is not Smith's intent, but a possible reading of his text) but instead to highlight the various ways that archaeologists approach the study of space. This volume represents a combination of various approaches to spatial analysis in archaeology, and it is the opinion of the editors that this diversity is the strength of the volume.

It is worth noting that this volume deals largely with applications of spatial approaches to space and theoretical perspectives on the topic, and is not a volume devoted to either discussions of statistical approaches of space or the prospect of developing new ways of modeling archaeological space quantitatively. This is in large part due to the fact that this volume represents the collected work of a number of the participants in the 2001 Chacmool Conference. Papers dealing with the quantification of spatial data and the development of new statistical techniques for dealing with this data were simply not among papers submitted for publication in this volume. While this may be seen by some as a flaw in the structure of this volume, the editors instead see it as one of the volume's strengths, as many of the earlier volumes to be released that deal with the spatial analysis of archaeological materials are explicitly quantitative and statistical in their focus, and conversely many volumes dealing with the quantification and statistical analysis of archaeological data are explicitly spatial in their approach (Hodder and Orton 1976; Clarke 1977; Buck et al. 1996). The editors of this volume believe that this volume represents a balanced view of spatial approaches to archaeology at the beginning of the new millennium, which is more concerned with meaningfully constituted social and cultural organization in a spatial context than with the abstract and methodologically driven approach of the processual archaeologists to space.

In this book, a variety of topics are covered in a series of thematic sections. These sections differ from the general overarching themes identified throughout this introduction in terms of the categories employed for a number of reasons. The first, and most immediate, relates to the nature of the submissions. Many of the papers employ multiple forms of spatial analysis to address very specific questions, and as such could not be easily put into a single one of the aforementioned categories. In addition to this consideration many of the sections were chosen with the express purpose of preserving the integrity of the sessions that the papers were presented in. The "In Transit" section of this book is the clearest example of this approach, whereby the entire session was kept intact and presented as a single section of the volume.

The first section of this volume consists of theoretical discussions about the concept of space and spatial approaches to archaeology. Sections two through five of the book have been organized to deal with progressively larger scales of spatial analysis, whereas sections six and seven deal with specialized approaches and topics that fall under the rubric of spatial analysis in archaeology. Section eight, which consists of a modified version of the banquet address from the conference effectively serves as a summation of previous approaches to spatial archaeology and a prospectus for the future. We believe that organizing sections two through five based on scale of analysis as opposed to based on methods of analysis allows us to highlight the variability of methodological approaches that can be used to approach similar data sets.

As was alluded to above, section one of this volume is concerned with theoretical approaches to space, and is comprised of papers that focus primarily on theories concerning spatial analysis in archaeology (e.g., Holmberg et al., Owoc). This section of the book effectively serves to frame the remainder of the volume, by offering a theoretical overview from which to view the remaining sections. Many of the papers in other sections of this volume make important theoretical contributions to the study of space (e.g., Lominy, Fisher) in archaeology, but fit more snugly into other sections of the book because of what was being studied, instead of the theoretical approach that was employed.

The second section of the volume is comprised of analyses of intrasite artifact and architectural distributions, many of which draw heavily from the theoretical approaches of the processual era, but in many cases seek meaning in addition to pattern (e.g., Greenfield and Jongsma, Greenfield and van Schalkwyk). The third section of the book consists of discussions of architectural analyses of single structures and architectural complexes (e.g., Fisher, Glanzman, Loten), and serves in many ways as the bridge between the spatial analysis of small groups of people and larger social aggregations.

The fourth section is made up of discussions of urban spaces and urban configurations (e.g., Child, Dawson, Iannone). This section of the book deals with spatial and social inference on a larger scale than the previous ones, and in many cases represents spatial patterning and analysis at the societal scale. The fifth section of the volume consists of a variety of papers concerning both landscape archaeology and the natural environment (e.g., Haynes, Schreyer), two topics which are considered either to be directly related or dichotomous, depending on the theoretical perspective that one adopts in their analysis.

The sixth section of papers is contributed from the "In Transit" session from the conference, organized by Heather Miller, which is presented here as a complete package, in order to preserve the intellectual integrity of the session. This session's theme was one of movement across space, which is an avenue of archaeological inquiry that has often been overlooked in the past. The last section of contributed papers is comprised of papers that use textual and iconographic representations of architecture and landscape to examine the importance of emic presentations of landscape (e.g., Allison, McCafferty and McCafferty). Finally, as was mentioned previously, we have placed Carole Crumley's banquet address from the conference in a section entitled "Framework for the Future." Crumley's paper assesses the current state of archaeology from an interdisciplinary perspective, and underscores the role that archaeology can have in effecting positive change in society.

This overview of the volume is by no means comprehensive, and is instead merely being presented to illustrate the diversity of its contents, and place them in a theoretical context. It is hoped that the theoretical, methodological and topical variety seen in this volume will highlight the wide array of approaches employed by conference presenters. As archaeologists we are currently at a theoretical crossroads, as postprocessual approaches to the discipline become part of the theoretical mainstream, and a new synthesis of processual and postprocessual theories emerges (Johnson 1999:176–187). As Levinson (2003) has suggested, notions of space and spatial reckoning are inextricably culture- (and language-) bound, and a better understanding of space and the experience of living in space should be one of the primary goals of the behavioural and social sciences, as well as the humanities. We believe that this volume is firmly ensconced in this new theoretical milieu, as it contains a variety of opinions and approaches to spatial analysis in archaeology, and underscores the cultural construction of the very concept of space itself.

REFERENCES CITED

Allen, K. M. S., S. W. Green, and E. Zubrow (editors)
|1990| *Interpreting Space: GIS and Archaeology*. Taylor and Francis, London.

Aldenderfer, M., and H. D. G. Maschner (editors)
|1996| *Anthropology, Space and Geographical Information Systems*. Oxford University Press, Oxford.

Ashmore, W.
|1991| Site Planning Principles and Concepts of Directionality among the Ancient Maya. *Latin American Antiquity* 2:199–226.
|1992| Deciphering Maya Site Plans. In *New Theories on the Ancient Maya*, edited by E. C. Danien, and R. J. Sharer, pp. 173–184. Museum Monographs 77. University Museum, University of Pennsylvania, Philadelphia.
|2002| "Decisions and Dispositions": Socializing Spatial Archaeology. *American Anthropologist* 104:1172–1183.

Ashmore, W., and B. Knapp (editors)
|1999| *Archaeologies of Landscape*. Blackwell, Oxford.

Ashmore, W., and J. Sabloff
|2002| Spatial Orders in Maya Civic Plans. *Latin American Antiquity* 13:201–216.

Aufrecht, W. E., N. A. Mirau, and S. W. Gauley (editors)
|1997| *Urbanism in Antiquity: From Mesopotamia to Crete*. Journal for the Study of the Old Testament Supplement Series 244. Sheffield Academic Press, Sheffield.

Basso, K. H.
|1996| *Wisdom Sits in Places: Landscape and Language among the Western Apache*. University of New Mexico Press, Albuquerque.

Binford, L. R.
|1968| Archaeological Perspectives. In *New Perspectives in Archaeology*, edited by S. R. Binford, and L. R. Binford, pp. 5–32. Aldine, Chicago.
|1980| Willow Smoke and Dog's Tails: Hunter-Gather Settlement Systems and Archaeological Site Formation. *American Antiquity* 45:4–20.

Blanton, R. E.
|1994| *Houses and Households: A Comparative Study*. Plenum Press, New York.

Brady, J., and W. Ashmore
|1999| Mountains, Caves, Water: Ideational Landscapes of the Ancient Maya. In *Archaeologies of Landscape*, edited by W. Ashmore, and B. Knapp, pp. 124–145. Blackwell, Oxford.

Buck, C. E., W. G. Cavanaugh, and C. D. Litton
|1996| *Bayesian Approach to Interpreting Archaeological Data*. John Willey and Sons, Toronto.

Canuto, M., and J. Yaeger (editors)
|2000| *The Archaeology of Communities: A New World Perspective*. Routledge, London.

Clark, J. G. D.
|1954| *Excavations at Starr Carr*. Cambridge University Press, Cambridge.

Clarke, D. L. (editor)
|1977| *Spatial Archaeology*. Academic Press, New York.

Claxton, J. B.
|1995| Future Enhancements to GIS: Implications for Archaeological Theory. In *Archaeology and Geographical Information Systems*, edited by G. Lock, and Z. Stančič, pp. 335–348. Taylor and Francis, London.

Daniel, G.
|1967| *The Origins and Growth of Archaeology*. Thomas Y. Crowell, New York

Daniels, S., and D. Cosgrove
|1988| Introduction: Iconography and Landscape. In *The Iconography of Landscape*, edited by D. Cosgrove, and S. Daniels, pp 1–10. Cambridge University Press, Cambridge.

David, N.
|1971| The Fulani Compound and the Archaeologist. *World Archaeology* 3:111–131.

David, N., and C. Kramer
|2001| *Ethnoarchaeology in Action*. Cambridge University Press, Cambridge.

Earle, T. K.
|1976| A Nearest-Neighbor Analysis of Two Formative Settlement Systems. In *The Early Mesoamerican Village*, edited by K. V. Flannery, pp. 196–221. Academic Press, Toronto.

Fedick, S.
|1997| Archaeological. In *Encyclopedia of Vernacular Architecture of the World: Volume 1, Theories and Principles*, edited by P. Oliver, pp 9–11. Cambridge University Press, Cambridge.

Ferguson, T. J.
|1996| *Historic Zuni Architecture and Society: An Archaeological Application of Space Syntax*. Anthropological Papers of the University of Arizona, no. 60. University of Arizona Press, Tucson.

Flannery, K. V. (editor)
|1976a| *The Early Mesoamerican Village*. Academic Press, Toronto.

Flannery, K. V.
|1976b| Evolution of Complex Settlement Systems. In *The Early Mesoamerican Village*, edited by K. V. Flannery, pp. 162–173. Academic Press, Toronto.
|1976c| Linear Stream Patterns and Riverside Settlement Rules. In *The Early Mesoamerican Village*, edited by K. V. Flannery, pp.173–180. Academic Press, Toronto.
|1976d| Sampling by Intensive Surface Collection. In *The Early Mesoamerican Village*, edited by K. V. Flannery, pp.51–62. Academic Press, Toronto.
|1976e| The Early Mesoamerican House. In *The Early Mesoamerican Village*, edited by K. V. Flannery, pp.16–25. Academic Press, Toronto.
|1998| The Ground Plan of the Archaic State. In *Archaic States*, edited by G. Feinman, and J. Marcus, pp. 15–58, School of American Research Press, New Mexico.

Flannery, K. V., and M. Winter
|1976| Analyzing Household Activities. In *The Early Mesoamerican Village*, edited by K. V. Flannery, pp. 34–45. Academic Press, Toronto.

Gamble, C.
|1987| Archaeology, Geography and Time. *Progress in Human Geography* 11:227–246.

Grahame, M.
|1997| Public and Private in the Roman House: The Spatial Order of the *Casa del Fauno*. In *Domestic Space in the Roman World: Pompeii and Beyond*, edited by R. Laurence, and A. Wallace-Hadrill, pp. 137–164. Journal of Roman Archaeology Supplementary Series No. 22. Journal of Roman Archaeology, Portsmouth, Rhode Island.

Hanson, J.
|1998| *Decoding Houses and Homes*. Cambridge University Press, Cambridge.

Hillier, B.
|1996| *Space is the Machine*. Cambridge University Press, Cambridge.

Hillier, B., and J. Hanson
|1984| *The Social Logic of Space*. Cambridge University Press, Cambridge.

Hodder, I.
|1982| *Symbols in Action: Ethnoarchaeological Studies of Material Culture*. Cambridge University Press, Cambridge.
|1984| Burials, Houses, Women and Men in the European Neolithic. In *Ideology, Power and Prehistory*, edited by D. Miller, and C. Tilley, pp. 51–68. Cambridge University Press, Cambridge.
|1999| *The Archaeological Process: An Introduction*. Blackwell, Oxford.

Hodder, I., and C. Orton
|1976| *Spatial Analysis in Archaeology*. Cambridge University Press, Cambridge.

Johnson, M.
|1999| *Archaeological Theory: An Introduction*. Blackwell, Oxford.

Kent, S.
|1983| *Analyzing Activity Areas: An Ethnoarchaeological Study of the Use of Space*. University of New Mexico Press, Albuquerque.
|1990| *Domestic Architecture and the Use of Space: An Interdisciplinary Cross-Cultural Study*. Cambridge University Press, Cambridge.

Knapp, A. B., and W. Ashmore.
|1999| Archaeological Landscapes: Constructed, Conceptualized, Ideational. In *Archaeologies of Landscape*, edited by W. Ashmore, and B. Knapp, pp. 1–30. Blackwell, Oxford.

Kramer, C. (editor)
|1979| *Ethnoarchaeology: Implications of Ethnography for Archaeology*. Columbia University Press, New York.

Kroll, E., and D. Price (editors)
|1991| *The Interpretation of Archaeological Spatial Patterning*. Plenum Press, New York.

Kvamme, K. J.
|1995| A View from across the Water: The North American Experience in Archaeological GIS. In *Archaeology and Geographical Information Systems*, edited by G. Lock, and Z. Stančič, pp. 1–14. Taylor and Francis, London.

Laurence, R., and A. Wallace-Hadrill (editors)
|1997| *Domestic Space in the Roman World: Pompeii and Beyond*. Journal of Roman Archaeology Supplementary Series No. 22. Journal of Roman Archaeology, Portsmouth, Rhode Island.

Lawrence, D. L., and S. M. Low
|1990| The Built Environment and Spatial Form. *Annual Review of Anthropology* 19:453–505.
Leone, M. P.
|1986| Symbolic, Structural and Critical Archaeology. In *American Archaeology Past and Future: A Celebration of the Society for American Archaeology (1935–1985)*, edited by D. Meltzer, D. Fowler, and J. Sabloff, pp. 415–438. Smithsonian Institution, Washington, D.C.
Levinson, S.
|2003| *Space in Language and Cognition: Explorations in Cognitive Diversity*. Cambridge University Press, Cambridge.
Lock, G., and Z. Stančič
|1995| *Archaeology and Geographical Information Systems*. Taylor Francis Inc., New York.
MacEachern, S., D. J. W. Archer, and R. D. Garvin
|1989| *Households and Communities: Proceedings of the 21st Annual Chacmool Conference*. Archaeological Association of the University of Calgary, Calgary, Alberta.
Manzanilla, L. (editor)
|1997| *Emergence and Change in Early Urban Societies*. Plenum Press, New York.
Marcus, J.
|1976| The Size of the Early Mesoamerican Village. In *The Early Mesoamerican Village*, edited by K. V. Flannery, pp. 79–88. Academic Press, Toronto.
Markus, T. A.
|1993| *Buildings and Power: Freedom and Control in the Origin of Modern Building Types*. Routledge, London.
Martin, S.
|2001| Court and Realm: Architectural Signatures in the Southern Maya Lowlands. In *Royal Courts of the Ancient Maya*, vol. 1, edited by T. Inomata and S. Houston, pp. 168–194. Westview Press, Boulder, Colorado
Miller, D., and C. Tilley (editors)
|1984| *Ideology, Power and Prehistory*. Cambridge University Press, Cambridge.
Muir, R.
|1999| *Approaches to Landscape*. MacMillan Press, London.
Netting, R. McC., R. Wilk, and E. Arnould
|1984| *Introduction*. In *Households*, edited by R. McC. Netting, R. Wilk, and E. Arnould, pp. xi–xxxviii. University of California Press, Berkeley.
Oliver, P. (editor)
|1997| *Encyclopedia of Vernacular Architecture of the World*. Cambridge University Press, Cambridge.
Parker Pearson, M., and C. Richards (editors)
|1994| *Architecture and Order: Approaches to Social Space*. Routledge, London.
Patterson, T. C.
|1986| The Last Sixty Years: Toward a Social History of Americanist Archaeology in the United States. *American Anthropologist* 88:7–23.
Pugh, T.
|2003| A Cluster and Spatial Analysis of Ceremonial Architecture at Late Postclassic Mayapan. *Journal of Archaeological Science* 30:941–953.
Rapoport, A.
|1968| *House Form and Function*. Foundation of Cultural Geography Series. Prentice Hall, Englewood Cliffs, New Jersey.
|1982| Vernacular Architecture and the Cultural Determinants of Form. In *Buildings and Society*, edited by A. D. King, pp. 283–305. Routledge and Keagan Paul, London.
|1990| *Thirty Three Papers in Environment-Behaviour Research*. Urban International Press, Pune, India.
Rathje, W. L.
|1983| The Salt of the Earth: Some Comments on Household Archaeology among the Maya. In *Prehistoric Settlement Patterns: Essays in Honor of Gordon R. Willey*, edited by E. Vogt, and R. M. Leventhal, pp. 23–34. University of New Mexico Press, Albuquerque.
Rossmann, D. L.
|1976| A Site Catchment Analysis of San Lorenzo, Veracruz. In *The Early Mesoamerican Village*, edited by K. V. Flannery, pp. 95–103. Academic Press, Toronto.
Sanders, W. T., J. R. Parsons, and R. S. Santley
|1979| *The Basin of Mexico: Ecological Processes in the Evolution of a Civilization*. Academic Press, New York.
Shanks, M., and C. Tilley
|1987a| *Reconstructing Archaeology*. Cambridge University Press, Cambridge.
|1987b| *Social Theory and Archaeology*. Polity Press, Cambridge.
Smith, A.
|2003| *The Political Landscape: Constellations of Authority in Early Complex Polities*. University of California Press, Berkeley.
Smith, M. (editor)
|2003| *The Social Construction of Ancient Cities*. Smithsonian Books, Washington, D.C.
Snead, J. E., and R. Preucel
|1999| The Ideology of Settlement: Ancestral Keres Landscapes in the Northern Rio Grande. In *Archaeologies of Landscape*, edited by W. Ashmore, and B. Knapp, pp. 169–200. Blackwell, Oxford.
Steadman, S.
|1996| Recent Research in the Archaeology of Architecture: Beyond the Foundations. *Journal of Archaeological Research* 4:51–93.
Stuardo, R. L.
|2003| Access Patterns in Maya Royal Precincts. In *Maya Palaces and Elite Residences: An Interdisciplinary Approach*, edited by J. J. Christie, pp. 184–203. University of Texas Press, Austin.
Taylor, W. W.
|1948| *A Study of Archeology*. American Anthropological Association Memoir 69. American Anthropological Association, Menasha, Wisconsin.
Tilley, C.
|1994| *A Phenomenology of Landscape*. Berg, Oxford.

Trigger, B. G.
|1989| *A History of Archaeological Thought*. Cambridge University Press, Cambridge.
|1990| Monumental Architecture: A Thermodynamic Explanation of Symbolic Behaviour. *World Archaeology* 22:119–131.
|2003| *Understanding Early Civilizations: A Comparative Study*. Cambridge University Press, Cambridge.

Ucko, P. J., R. Tringham, and G. W. Dimbleby
|1972| *Man, Settlement and Urbanism: Proceedings of a Meeting of the Research Seminar in Archaeology and Related Subjects Held at the Institute of Archaeology, London University*. Research Seminar in Archaeology and Related Subjects, 1970. Duckworth, London.

Whalen, M. E.
|1976| Zoning within an Early Formative Community in the Valley of Oaxaca. In *The Early Mesoamerican Village*, edited by K. V. Flannery, pp. 75–78. Academic Press, Toronto.

Wheatley, D., and M. Gillings
|2002| *Spatial Technology and Archaeology: The Archaeological Applications of GIS*. Taylor and Francis, London.

Wilk, R. R.
|1983| Little House in the Jungle: The Causes of Variation in House Size among the Kekchi Maya. *Journal of Anthropological Research* 2:99–116

Wilk, R. R., and W. Ashmore
|1988| *Household and Community in the Mesoamerican Past*. University of New Mexico Press, Albuquerque.

Wilk, R. R., and W. L. Rathje
|1982| Household Archaeology. *American Behavioral Scientist* 25:617–639.

Willey, G. R.
|1948| A Functional Analysis of "Horizon Styles" in Peruvian Archaeology. In *A Reappraisal of Peruvian Archaeology*, edited by W. C. Bennett, pp. 8–15. Society for American Archaeology Memoir 4. Society for American Archaeology, Menasha, Wisconsin.
|1953| *Prehistoric Settlement Patterns in the Viru Valley, Peru*. Bureau of American Ethnology, Bulletin No. 155. Bureau of American Ethnology, Washington, D.C.

Willey, G. R., and J. A. Sabloff
|1993| *A History of American Archaeology*. 3rd ed. Thames and Hudson, London.

Winter, M. C.
|1976| The Archaeological Household Cluster in the Valley of Oaxaca. In *The Early Mesoamerican Village*, edited by K. V. Flannery, pp. 25–30. Academic Press, Toronto.

PART I: THEORETICAL AND CONCEPTUAL APPROACHES

BEYOND GEOARCHAEOLOGY: PRAGMATIST EXPLORATIONS OF ALTERNATIVE VIEWSCAPES[1] IN THE BRITISH BRONZE AGE AND BEYOND

Mary Ann Owoc

Mary Ann Owoc, Department of Anthropology/Archaeology, Mercyhurst College, 501 E 38th Street, Erie, Pennsylvania 16546, U.S.A.

ABSTRACT

Viewscapes are historically constructed and socially reproduced conceptions of the world that go beyond our present notions of "landscape." Significant contrasts exist between the viewscapes of archaeologists/geoarchaeologists and native peoples concerning the geomorphic landscape. These differences are important, since they highlight the shortcomings of traditional descriptions in coming to terms with the fullness of human-environment relations in the past. It is argued that a practice-centred, phenomenological approach to past human-environment relations may bear more interpretive fruit than current totalizing and specular perspectives. An overview of some alternative ways in which traditional societies make sense of their buried landscapes is presented. This is followed by several archaeological case studies from the southwestern British Bronze Age which suggest that multifaceted viewscapes linking time, space, the living and the dead were objectified and reproduced through soils, sediments and rocks.

> "All we need to know is whether some competing description might be more useful for some of our purposes" (Rorty 1999:xxvi).

This contribution arose from an interest in the somewhat peculiar practices involved in the construction of a number of southwestern British Bronze Age funerary/ritual sites (Owoc 2000). The sites belong to the general class of monuments known as "barrows" or "cairns," and formed an integral part of the British later prehistoric funerary landscape between ca. 2500–1400 cal B.C. The monuments are generally circular, constructed of earth and/or stone, and take the form of mounds, cairns, ditches, and/or ring banks/cairns. These constructions, in turn, often overlay or underlay the physical remains of a series of performative activities. Such practices generally include but are not limited to: the deposition of human remains, feasting, processing, trampling, stone or stake circle erection, fire setting, charcoal depositions, pit excavation/filling, and the deliberate deposition of material culture items. Although the burial/deposition of inhumed or cremated human remains within, under, or adjacent to one of these structures is the norm, construction and activities at these sites do not appear to have required the on-site presence of human remains in all cases.

The central focus in this paper with regard to these monuments is the constructional materials comprising them. These generally consist of a variety of local lithologies and/or their overlying sediments and soils. These materials occur singly (as in the case of a turf mound) or more often in various combinations. While detailed descriptions of the origin, composition, and stratigraphic/temporal arrangement of these components exist for these sites, traditional archaeological/geoarchaeological accounts do little to illuminate why certain materials were chosen over others, or why materials were employed in particular temporal or spatial configurations. Some questions then, might be raised about the adequacy of the conceptual tools favored by archaeologists in dealing with human-earth relations, particularly when the complexity of particular practices are taken into account.

After a consideration of the respective "technologies" which define how both geoarchaeology/archaeology and non-Western traditional societies give meaning to the environment, it is suggested that earth-science-based, and non-Western/prehistoric descriptions of the natural geomorphic environment represent two very different sorts of utilitarian projects with contrasting goals and outcomes. Specifically, the manner in which many communities give meanings to their buried landscapes involves an idealized meaningful encounter that extends *beyond* the identification of objective or functional qualities of individual materials. As an alternative to more traditional disciplinary approaches to site contexts and geomorphic landscapes, a practice-centred approach to lithospheric engagement is forwarded that employs a phenomenological view of the relations between humans and their environments. Such an approach is argued to have greater potential for providing a better understanding of the rationale behind human-landscape relations in both the ethnographic present, and the southwestern Bronze Age past.

ALTERNATIVE VIEWSCAPES?

A "view" implies some sense of seeing, but what one sees or perceives is entirely a function of phenomenological perspective, which, while physically grounded in the body, is also historically and culturally situated (see Classen 1993). Views of land, or the environment then, can take many forms (Bender 1993). Our own Western view may be understood through an examination of the "landscape" concept. Our contemporary notion of "landscape" has its roots in a particular way of seeing (itself based upon a visual paradigm) that developed in Europe during the Renaissance and was codified during the nineteenth century (Classen 1993; Olwig 1993; Thomas 1993). This sort of view, which Thomas (1993:22, 25), drawing on Foucault (1977:201–226) describes as "specular," is also a totalizing one, which involves a simultaneous perspective achieved through an intellectual and physical separation of subject from object. It therefore relies upon a variety of individualizing or differentiating techniques such as classification, cataloguing, and partitioning. It is thus a uniquely modern and Western view, which moreover, is linked with the emergence of the techniques of investigation, and later, the empirical sciences (Foucault 1977). As Thomas (1993:25) notes, the particular viewpoint which structures our modern archaeological representation of place is the historical descendent of this construction. As our attempts to explore the rationalities which informed past human-environment relations increase in breadth and therefore, interpretative endeavor, it becomes necessary to critically evaluate the extent to which this viewpoint structures other facets of our practice.

As a philosophical doctrine that addresses the relationship of theory to effective action, pragmatism provides a particularly useful standpoint for evaluating the theories and disciplinary tools and technologies we employ to describe our subject matter and the outcomes of those descriptions. Though historically variable in its constructions, lying at the core of philosophical pragmatism is a rejection of the dualistic platonic tradition that rests upon a split between the found and the made, fact and theory, and so on. Instead, pragmatists argue that "interpenetration" or holism best describes the relation between the observer and what is observed (Putnam 1995:7). From the position of this tradition then, descriptions do not serve as reliable, truthful means of knowing the world. Instead, they are a function of practice, or *utility* (Rescher 2000; Rorty 1999:xxvi). In other words, descriptions are relative to purposes. Therefore, borrowing from Richard Rorty (1999:xxiii) for the present discussion, just as words should be seen as not representing the intrinsic nature of the environment, but instead, only as tools to deal with it; the creation of particular viewscapes should be seen as a construct of and related to particular utilitarian concerns.

These observations become important if we are to judge the effectiveness of the historically situated viewscapes of archaeology/geoarchaeology for engaging with the past through the archaeological matrix or the geomorphic landscape. What pragmatic goals do the study of rocks, sediments, and soils address within the discipline of archaeology? What is the historical/disciplinary context of the formation of this discourse? Finally, what are the products of these studies and are they adequate for engaging with past rationalities to the extent that our practice increasingly demands?

THE "TECHNOLOGY" OF GEOARCHAEOLOGY

The integration of geoscience techniques and archaeological questions culminating in the creation of the discipline of geoarchaeology emerged in the mid-twentieth century within an archaeological environment increasingly receptive both to the methods and techniques of the natural sciences. Further, this emergence paralleled a particular view of scientific practice that privileged a neutral, generalizing, and explanatory framework over a hermeneutic, particularistic, and historical one. As a result of these circumstances, the discipline of geoarchaeology has produced a particular set of products and a distinctive viewscape that merits some attention.

Geoarchaeology involves the application of a variety of descriptive techniques and classificatory principles that aim to objectively distinguish and classify various components of the site matrix and the geomorphic site context on the basis of their observed, physical characteristics. The outcome of this process is acknowledged to yield meaningful categories (e.g., particular lithostratigraphic units) useful in making statements about a site's temporal context, stratigraphy, formation, surrounding landscape development, and so on (Waters 1996). The "technology" and objectives of geoarchaeology then, parallel those found within the broader geoscientific discourse, which has a totalizing perspective,[2] adopts a "specular" gaze, and privileges objective description over subjective interpretation. This totalizing agenda and the results it has produced however, cannot be described as either neutral or all encompassing. First, as a practice and discipline aimed at making statements about the world, it has much in common with other fields of study, like archaeology, that employ an interpretative discourse.[3] For example, the delineation of meaningful categories of description is itself a value-dependent process, partly self confirming and more hermeneutic than explanatory. Second, the practice of geoarchaeology should be understood as taking place in a historical, disciplinary context that defines the broader goals of its practice in line with specific ideas about the world beforehand.

In addition to addressing traditional goals such as the identification of soils and sediments, and the establishment of site stratigraphy and temporal sequences, a large amount of the methodological and technological repertoire of contemporary geoarchaeology is directed towards producing data that informs on larger questions concerning the morphology of noncultural past landscapes and the nature of the formation processes that acted upon them (Rapp and Hill 1998; Renfrew 1976; Waters 1996:88). This is due to the fact that temporally, the development of the modern discipline of geoarchaeology paralleled the development of a theoretical framework in archaeology that incorporated a processual view (Rapp and Hill 1998). The analysis of the natural world via soils, sediments, and landforms within archaeology then, has primarily contributed to a broader human ecology and/or systems theory project (Waters 1996). In such a project, the relations between humans and the geomorphic landscape are depicted as causal, determinant, and systemic ones, in which humans act in response to or are affected by wider environmental conditions/earth processes. Such an endeavour presupposes a split between humans and their environments, producing a view of the past and of people in the past, that is materialist, functionalist, and adaptive, rather than interpretative, reflexive or dialectical.

If we follow Thomas (1993:25) on landscape from the perspective of *this* critique, there are dangers in relying entirely on a geoarchaeological appropriation of the past that employs an objective, all-encompassing (but actually quite situated) set of descriptions. These dangers may be summarized by the following. First, by privileging an objectifying methodology, we may well unconsciously represent the geoarchaeological/archaeological "viewpoint" as the whole story, effectively erasing the possibility for there to be other stories or "viewpoints" (Bender 1993). Another concern is that this "outsider's" viewpoint, though meaningful to us, represents a totally modern fabrication of the physical world that would most likely be unrecognizable and insensible to the communities who inhabited it.

It is at this point that a pragmatist like Rorty might wonder (as he does in the opening quote to this paper) whether or not the sorts of geoarchaeological viewscapes we routinely use to appropriate the past are really the most useful in our quest for exploring the complexities of the relationship between humans and their worlds. Ethnographic analyses of the relationships between humans, their physical environments, and the soils, rocks, and sediments which comprise those environments suggest that they may indeed fall short, and that some other way of describing/seeing both that world, and how people interact with it might be more desirable.

PHENOMENOLOGY AND VIEWSCAPES

Recently, archaeologists have begun to employ a phenomenological perspective for conceptualizing how communities understood and acted within their environment (e.g., Thomas 1993, 1998, 2001; Tilley 1994). The phenomenological tradition emphasizes experiential perspective or "being-in-the-world" over empiricist objectivism. From this perspective, descriptions of the world are understood as historically formed by embodied, social subjects, and conditioned and guided by tradition, memory, myth, and the time-space paths of individuals and communities. A phenomenological perspective then provides an alternative to the Western objectifying, totalizing tradition that has framed our appropriation of the three-dimensional landscape. It therefore raises our awareness of the possibility of alternative viewscapes and the process of their creation and renewal through action in relation to soils, stones and sediments. Such alternative viewscapes may be characterized by mythical spaces, incorporate both horizontal and vertical axes, integrate nature and the body, unite the social and the physical, merge time and space, and link the cosmos to the land (Bender 1993; Tuan 1977). Examples of ways in which non-western societies create such viewscapes via stones, soils and sediments may serve to introduce an analysis of similar processes in the southwestern British Bronze Age.

ALTERNATIVE VIEWSCAPES IN THE ETHNOGRAPHIC PRESENT

Numerous ethnographic studies and commentaries overwhelmingly indicate that non-Western cultural constructions of the environment and its components are often at variance with the sorts we ourselves produce. While a great deal of recent anthropological literature exists concerning the human construction of the biological environment, only a small portion of it addresses the manner in which humans engage with the lithospheric elements of the environment (see Boivin and Owoc n.d.). Extrapolating from this material, it appears that other societies also perceive vertical stratigraphy, differentiate between good and bad agricultural soils, and are sensitive to mineral texture, colour and consistency. However, comparisons break down when the particulars, strengths and importance of these dimensions of variation are taken into account. For instance, whilst doing fieldwork amongst the Baruya of Womenara, New Guinea, Ollier et al. (1971:36) noticed that across the board, subjects' definitive identification of soil colours in a Munsell book did not match their "real" appearance, which was always "less glamorous" (of diminished hue). Additionally, they pointed out that their own arrangement and description of the Baruya soil repertoire/nomenclature was at variance with that of their informants who, among other things, separated limestone from other rocks, but did not distinguish soils and rocks as definitively different materials. For the Baruya however, these idealized, or imaginative constructions were no less real than the ones which Ollier, Drover and Godlier employed, yet we might fail to perceive them as archaeologists operating exclusively through our own objectifying methodologies.

Several other examples may serve to illustrate the existence of alternative and rich descriptive regimes for the geomorphic landscape. Additionally, the extent to which such regimes form part of meaningful traditions of knowledge that both structure and respond to particular practices in those landscapes should be addressed.

Soils for the Kogi Indians of Northern Colombia are intimately related to their creation myth, in which the Great Mother created a nine-layered universe. Each layer of this universe has a place in a vertical scheme that is characterized by a variety of physical attributes (e.g., world of the sun, world of trees, world of stones and sand and wet clay), and has dual associations with particular agricultural soil types and each of the Mother's daughters (Reichel-Dolmatoff 1987). The significance and division of soils for the Kogi, then, does not rest solely on their agricultural potential, but arises from the way in which each objectifies the primordial act of creation and a number of mythical personages.

Many South Asian communities display considerable interest in the various qualities of soil and sediment, including colour, texture, taste, and amount and type of coarse fraction (Boivin 2000a, 2000b; McDougall 1971). The particular significance, if any, of each of these attributes may be understood through an examination of the ways in which particular soils are used or chosen during activities like land clearance, house building and floor plastering. Each of these activities is conditioned and dictated by concerns for present or future prosperity, health or well-being. The selection of certain soils, building sites containing such soils and the alteration of the landscape to ensure the presence of such soils is therefore related to the *invisible* qualities these materials contain (e.g., auspiciousness, sacredness), and by the sort of future their presence will guarantee (e.g., a life free from hardship). Accounting for human/environmental relationships in these communities through the medium of the geomorphic landscape then clearly requires some sort of engagement with the alternative logic of landscape "construction" present in each case.

The viewscape of the inhabitants of Eastern Arnhem Land in Australia involves a cosmological vision which links the mythological past, the social present, the ancestors and the physical world through the importance of quartzite. Quartzite, its colour and its location in the landscape are intimately bound up with patrilineal kinship, historical human/land relations, gender and wider cosmological constructions of the physical and biological environment (Jones and White 1988; Taçon 1991). Quarries, because of their associations with totemic beings and patrilineal lines of descent, are viewed as sacred and often restricted places. The power and significance of these sites are produced and reproduced by restricted access, myths and timely visits by lineage members. The classification mechanisms employed in the selection and reduction of stone from these quarries rely on a cosmological construction which relates some of the stone's physical properties to both biological and sacred referents. The appearance and amount of weathered cortex surrounding quartzite used for flaking, for example, is understood through analogies to cooking (overcooked or burnt). Additionally, the inner white sparkling quartzite reserved for stone tool production is compared to kidney fat and is believed to possess power, influencing the effectiveness of the projectiles it is made from. Community visits to quarries, reduction practices, and other human-earth relations for Aborigines can be understood as arising from, and further contributing to, this phenomenological construction of the environment.

Finally, returning again to the Baruya, the importance of limestone in their nomenclature rests on the belief that it represents the bones of the original mythological inhabitants of their region (Ollier et al. 1971). Further, elements like soil colour are often of more importance than texture, consistency or geographical location, since particular soil colours have the ability to produce certain effects when used as pigments. For the Baruya, the invisible origin of the world and its visible structure are intimately linked, and one cannot be properly understood without some recognition of the other (Ollier et al. 1971).

The point to be made here is that cultural constructions of the geomorphic environment for any group do not emerge from the viewpoint of a detached objective viewer, but instead on an experiential interaction with the world. Moreover, this interaction is meaningful and always bound up with mythical cosmologies, disciplinary, group, and individual histories, and symbolic power. Acknowledging this entails some additional responsibilities for us in our attempts to responsibly address the relations between humans and their physical environments. First, we should be sensitive to the potential shortcomings of our own systems of categorization in our descriptions of those environments. Second, we must begin to take into account the intimate connection between the landscape and the people who inhabited it as we search for possible alternatives to those systems. Humans do not merely react to their physical surroundings; they *construct* them, and those constructions further influence their actions. Failure to appreciate the contextual particularities of these encounters, and to act on them in crafting our observations and interpretations of human-environment relations will surely involve us in a reproduction of *our own* particular viewscape and toward the production of pasts unrecognizable to their inhabitants (Thomas 1993). Such a product will surely fall short in its attempt to address those relations to the fullness that our practice demands.

A PHYSICAL CONTEXT FOR SOUTHWESTERN BRONZE AGE FUNERARY PRACTICE

An examination of several funerary/ritual monuments of the British southwestern Bronze Age may serve to both illustrate the shortcomings of traditional earth-science-based constructions of the lithosphere, and evaluate the utility of a phenomenological approach to the geomorphic landscapes of the past. As noted above, these sites incorporate a variety of stony materials we

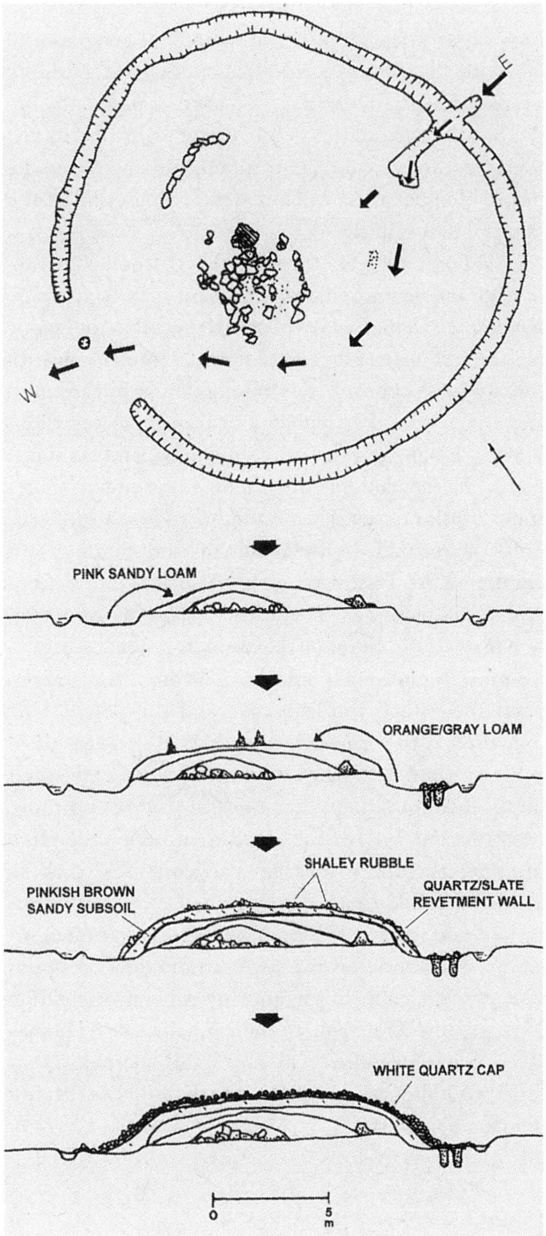

Figure 1. Crig-a-Mennis funerary enclosure and mound construction. (Plan view reproduced with changes from Christie 1960:79 with permission of The Prehistoric Society.)

define as variously coloured granites, quartzes, slates and flints. Additionally, orange, yellow, gray, pink and reddish subsoils, and a number of brown and black surface units of various textures were also employed in constructions. Most of these components were either derived from local lithologies and their overlying sediments and soils, or from specially selected materials brought from a distance. The overall diversity of these materials may be explained by the complex geological composition of southwest Britain (Rayner 1981; Selwood et al. 1998). While the particular arrangement and use of these materials on the sites is generally a function of localized building traditions, the details of construction cannot be entirely explained by this observation.

The use of these material components in the monuments displays a departure from our sense of the practical, the expedient or the necessary. It is clear the disposal of human remains in the Bronze Age did not physically necessitate the construction of a complex barrow, cairn, or ring of stone or soil, since alternative and simpler forms of disposal have been demonstrated from the Neolithic onwards. Further, the manner in which the materials for these monuments were obtained and used suggests a very particular and localized view, or meaningful "construction" of these elements. For example, turf and topsoil were carefully stripped from portions of the sites to reveal subsoil components (e.g., Christie 1988). Additionally, various geomorphic elements displaying contrasting textures, colours, and consistencies initially stripped from the sites were retained separately, then used differentially during monument building stages (e.g., Christie 1960; Pollard and Russell 1969). Interestingly, soil and stones were frequently separated out and/or used in an alternating fashion (e.g., Grimes 1960; Williams 1950). Given the nature of this evidence, all indications are that soil, sediments and stones were used during the funerary rituals of the southwestern Bronze Age as *material cultural* elements (Owoc 2000) in deliberate and knowledgeable ways that were designed to create and perpetuate particular schemes of perception. These schemes formed the basis for a variety of local and regional viewscapes.

Although useful as a starting point, standard archaeological/geoarchaeological analyses of both the anthropogenic materials used to construct these sites and the natural geomorphic context of the sites themselves at some point fall short when attempting to address the local, meaningful significance of these components, and thus their appearance, selection and use in the monuments. To explain and interpret the varied construction techniques and material selection represented on the sites requires an engagement with the alternative logics that informed and were reproduced by these sites' constructions. In short, it necessitates a reconstruction of the phenomenological links between these communities and their geomorphic environments, which goes beyond the adaptive and the systemic. This entails a departure from our disciplinary understanding of the categories and qualities of these materials and a search for new, historically situated possibilities of meaningful classification and construction. Such a departure begins by revisiting the qualities and understandings of these materials in light of their particular use contexts. This approach is *practice* centred, since, as noted above, it is only through embodied experiential perception (Tuan 1977) that the natural world is categorized and made meaningful.

BRONZE AGE SCHEMES OF PERCEPTION

Crig-a-Mennis is an Early Bronze Age funerary/ritual site in central Cornwall (Christie 1960). It was built sometime between 2042 and 1680 cal B.C. directly over a geological break between soft, pink sandstone and a harder greenish slate, which enabled its builders to employ local materials of contrasting textures, colours and consistencies. The site began as a causewayed ditch that served to demarcate the remains of the deceased from the community of mourners through a technique of enclosure, and relate the rite of passage to the rising and setting of the equinoctial sun (Owoc 2000) (Figure 1).

This demarcation between the living and the deceased took on a vertical aspect, as the cremated remains of at least three individuals were slowly incorporated in a multiphase mound of contrasting turf, subsoil and stony elements. The particular use order of these components in light of their characteristics and natural positions in the local environment are of interest. The construction of the monument was accomplished over a period of some months or years, during which time mourners returned to the site to perform a number of activities as part of a timely, protracted rite of passage for themselves and their dead. As this rite progressed, the form and appearance of the mound changed. It began as a simple causewayed ditch, and later, became a complex multicomponent mound. Examining the both the progression of mound construction and its components in terms of their contrasting qualities, a general trend from looser or more friable to harder materials can be discerned, as well as a general reversal of their natural stratigraphic positions. A final milky white quartz cap further indicates that material colour or reflective brilliance was recognized as a significant dimension of variation (Owoc 2002). I have suggested elsewhere (Owoc 2000) that by employing certain classificatory principles of enclosure, time, and stratigraphy (or verticality), the builders of Crig-a-Mennis created and renewed the particular meanings of both horizontal and vertical space and, the natural geomorphic components of their environment. By so doing, they objectified a taxonomic scheme that allowed for living and dying to be rationalized by the community of mourners, and further, meaningfully understood via a number of natural events and processes. This was accomplished by establishing oppositional relationships between mound materials, objects, persons/movements and cosmic events/movements within ritually established domains of *enclosure*, *axial alignment*, *temporality*, and *verticality*. In this way, the viewscape of the builders may be seen to have meaningfully linked the community with the physical earth and the cosmos. For example, by creating an initial ditch *enclosing* the burial area, the builders separated categories of living and dead, and established a space and a place for each. Giving this circular space and any entry/egress from it a dominant *alignment* on the equinoctial sunrise and sunset, the builders related the rite of passage to this cosmic daily and seasonal transition. They further linked this passage and the alignments to qualities of wetness and dryness via an east wet ditch passage into the enclosure, and a dry causewayed passage out of it. This enabled an analogous link to be made between the solstial, quotidian qualities of beginning/ending and the physical states of the deceased during their lives (wet birth/dry death). Finally, the dead became locked in a world "under ground" *below* the living by the mound construction, and over *time*, the qualities of their objective visible (and presumably conceptual) representation became harder and lighter with each new mound addition. Such a taxonomic scheme may be partially represented here in the form of the following pairs of analogous oppositions:

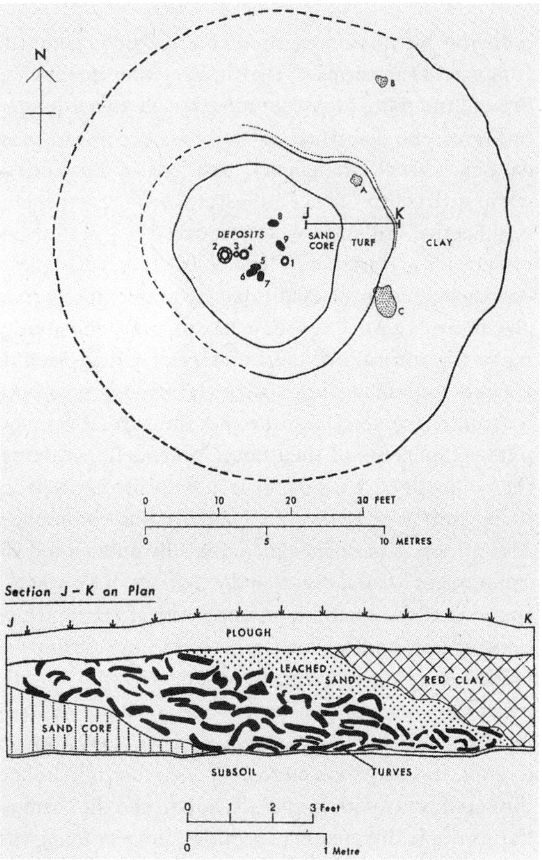

Figure 2. Mound construction and stratigraphy at Upton Pyne 284b. (Pollard and Russell 1969: Figures 3, 4c; reproduced with permission from the Devon Archaeological Society).

Enclosure	Axial	Vertical/ Stratigraphic	Temporal
inside/ outside	east/west (sun)	above/below	above/ below
dead/ living	birth-living/ death living/ dead soft/hard	wet/dry	dark/light

The extent to which the mourners themselves may have been able to represent the totality of such a generative scheme is debatable (see Bourdieu 1977:109–114). However two things seem certain. The first is that particular qualities of the geomorphic landscape were both recognized and highlighted in ways that suggest particular metaphorical understandings or meanings of them existed and were being reproduced. Second, the directed employment of particular mound materials combined with other ritual elements appears to have served as a reference guide for establishing meaningful ways to comprehend death, the dead, and the everyday world of the living.

A similar concern with stratigraphy and time is also apparent at the site of Upton Pyne 284b, which was built sometime between 1749 and 1495 cal B.C. in East Devon (Pollard and Russell 1969, 1976) (Figure 2). The site is unusual among barrows since it contained the cremated remains of at least three infants who were accompanied by or contained within inverted urns. Many Bronze Age communities segregated or treated infants differently in death (Mizoguchi 1992; Owoc 2000), and it is suggested here that the existence of this site, and its particular form were a response to the death of what may have been uncategorized liminal personages. The preparation of a platform for the deposition of the cremations involved the removal and separate retention of three stratigraphic components on the site: the turf and upper A horizon, a white leached A horizon lying directly below it, and a portion of the deeper reddish sandy subsoil. The latter formed the platform upon which the infants were deposited and their covering mound. The builders then covered this soil and the cremations with the stripped turves and the leached portion of the A horizon, allowing the latter material to harden and weather for some time. Then, basket load by basket load, over the course of some weeks or months, they encased the site in an outer envelope of orange-red clay subsoil, which they obtained from a particular subsoil location near the site. The construction of the mound itself reversed the natural *stratigraphy* of the landscape and placed the infants in a *remade inverted world.* During this process, a *temporality* for the rite of passage was defined for both the infants and the mourners, which was associated with particular colour elements (hues and values) and qualities (texture and consistency) of the geomorphic landscape. As time progressed the site became harder, lighter and/or brighter, likely signaling some change of status and ritual stage for the infants and/or the community.[4] It is notable that the cremations burials are initially placed in direct association with the redder stratigraphic members. As the rite progressed, and the community returned to normal, the site became harder and whiter, perhaps signaling some change in the liminality, power, or danger of the deceased. Further, if the reddish stratigraphic member embodied powerful symbolic associations, such as liminality or danger, etc., the final completion of the mound with a harder and brighter subsoil component may have made a statement about the significance of the infant burials within. The bright final subsoil cap to the mound is paralleled at other sites in the southwest where brighter subsoil members have solar associations, and entire ceremonies reference or correspond with certain solar transitions.

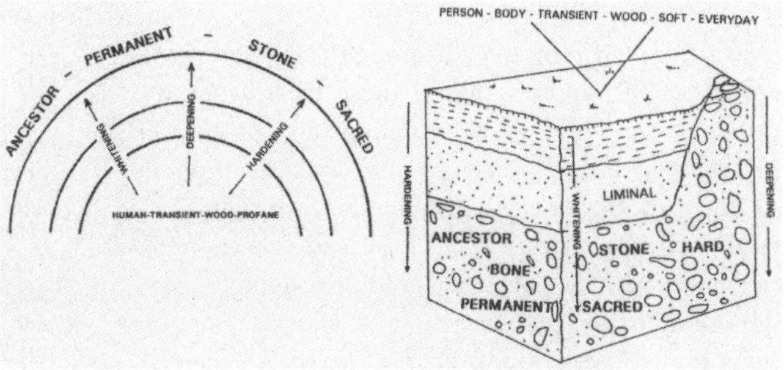

Figure 3. A suggested "vertical" southwestern Bronze Age viewscape as objectified in a funerary mound, and perceived in particular local buried landscapes.

By constructing the site in this way then, the particular symbolic associations of the geomorphic landscape may have served to construct a reading of the rite for all present, particularly since the site itself was situated so as to be visible from some distance. In this way, the symbolic associations of the lithospheric materials themselves would also have been reproduced in action.

A partial scheme that may have been mobilized and reproduced by the construction activities on the sites follows below in the form of analogous pairs of oppositions:

Vertical/Stratigraphic	Temporal
above/below	soft/firm
soft/firm	dark/bright
dark/bright	below/above

At Upton Pyne and Crig-a-Mennis, principles of enclosure, verticality and carefully timed actions served to differentiate between persons and materials on the basis of one or more of their qualities. This process of differentiation was local and contingent upon cultural constructions of the immediate geomorphic environment. In each case, different understandings of life, death, the qualities or states of the dead, the mourners and the elements of the natural world would have been created through operations of analogy and metaphor, culminating in particular traditions of knowledge or viewscapes of the world. An attempt to translate such a cultural perception of the mineral world and its "construction" in a funerary site of the southwestern British Bronze Age is offered in Figure 3.

CONCLUSION

Increasing attempts to understanding the fullness of the human-environment relationship by the earth and human sciences necessitate a critical evaluation of the theories and disciplinary tools which inform their practices. It has been suggested that traditional earth-science-based constructions of sites and their geomorphic landscapes fall short in their attempts to address the fullness of human-environment relations. Although productive of an enormous descriptive taxonomy and methodological repertoire, the situated geoscience approach employs a totalizing and "specular" view, typical of western scientific modes of discourse, and is therefore limited in its ability to address alternative views and experiences of the physical environment.

Consideration of a number of ways in which non-Western groups make sense of their worlds indicates that a phenomenological approach, and a practice-based investigation of past human-landscape encounters may bear more interpretative fruit. With this in mind, an analysis of two particular cultural constructions of the physical environment in the southwestern British Bronze Age revealed alternative past viewscapes that were both complex and multifaceted, incorporating a variety of overlapping understandings of space, time, life, death, and the cosmos that were objectified and reproduced through soils, sediments and rocks. An appreciation of these viewscapes was primarily facilitated by an attention toward repeated practices, deliberate engagements with the mineral world, embodied experiences in the local landscape (and with respect to the cosmos), and the appreciation and structuring of time by builders and mourners. The complexities of these practices, and the constructions they engendered, suggests that the conceptual tools we conventionally use in our descriptions of the mineral world and its larger context might be fruitfully augmented by being situated within a broader theoretical repertoire centred on the human experience of being in the world.

ACKNOWLEDGMENTS

A number of people past and present contributed directly or indirectly to this paper. David Pedler at the Mercyhurst Archaeological Institute provided graphic and editorial assistance. Don Thieme and Jim Adovasio engaged in many long discussions about geoarchaeology and archaeological recording with me. Nikki Boivin's research on soil significance in India/Neolithic Turkey was informative and inspiring. Matt Jelacic suggested I take another look at pragmatism, and Mike Parker Pearson encouraged me to pursue my initial observations about contrasting barrow materials. Special thanks go to the Prehistoric Society and the Devon Archaeological Society for permission to reproduce a portion of Figure 1 and Figure 2, respectively.

REFERENCES CITED

Bender, B. (editor)
|1993| *Landscape: Politics and Perspectives.* Berg, Oxford.

Boivin, N.
|2000a| Life Rhythms and Floor Sequences: Excavating Time in Rural Rajasthan and Neolithic Çatalhöyük. *World Archaeology* 31:367–388.
|2000b| Divine Soils and Auspicious Floors: Bridging the Science-Theory Gap in a Rural Rajasthani Village. Paper presented at the 22nd Annual Theoretical Archaeology Group Conference, Oxford.

Boivin, N., and Owoc, M. A.
|n.d.| *Soils, Stones and Symbols: Archaeological and Anthropological Perspectives on the Mineral World.* UCL Press, London.

Bourdieu, P.
|1977| *Outline of the Theory of Practice.* Cambridge University Press, Cambridge.

Christie, P.
|1960| Crig-a-Mennis: A Bronze Age Barrow at Liskey, Perranzabuloe, Cornwall. *Proceedings of the Prehistoric Society* 26:76–97.
|1988| A Barrow Cemetery on Davidstow Moor, Cornwall, Wartime Excavations by C. K Croft Andrew. *Cornish Archaeology* 27:27–169.

Classen, C.
|1993| *Worlds of Sense: Exploring the Senses in History and Across Cultures.* Routledge, London.

Foucault, M.
|1977| *Discipline and Punish.* Pantheon Books, New York.

Frodeman, R.
|1995| Geological Reasoning: Geology as an Interpretive and Historical Science. *GSA Bulletin* 107(8):960–968.
|2003| *Geo-Logic: Breaking Ground Between Philosophy and the Earth Sciences.* SUNY Press, Albany.

Grimes, W. F.
|1960| *Excavations on Defense Sites 1939–1945 I: Mainly Neolithic – Bronze Age.* Ministry of Works Archaeological Reports No. 3. Her Majesty's Stationary Office, London.

Jones, R., and White, N.
|1988| Point Blank: Stone Tool Manufacture at the Ngilitji Quarry, Arnhem Land, 1981. In *Archaeology With Ethnography: An Australian Perspective*, edited by B. Meehan and R. Jones, pp. 51–87. Research School of Pacific Studies, The Australian National University, Canberra.

McDougall, R. D.
|1971| Domestic Architecture among the Kandyan Sinhalese. Unpublished Ph.D. dissertation, Department of Anthropology, University of Michigan, Ann Arbor, Michigan.

Mizoguchi, K.
|1992| A Historiography of a Linear Barrow Cemetery: A Structurationists's Point of View. *Archaeological Review from Cambridge* 11:39–49.

Ollier, C. D., D. P. Drover, and M. Godlier
|1971| Soil Knowledge amongst the Baruya of Womenara, New Guinea. *Oceania* 42:33–41.

Olwig, K.
|1993| Sexual Cosmology: Nation and Landscape at the Conceptual Interstices of Nature and Culture: Or What Does Landscape Really Mean? In *Landscape: Politics and Perspectives*, edited by B. Bender, pp. 307–343. Berg, Oxford.

Owoc, M. A.
|2000| Aspects of Ceremonial Burial in the Bronze Age of Southwest Britain. Unpublished Ph.D. thesis, Department of Prehistory and Archaeology, Sheffield University, Sheffield, England.
|2002| Munselling the Mound: The Use of Soil Colour as Metaphor in British Bronze Age Funerary Ritual. In *Colouring the Past: the Significance of Colour in Archaeological Research*, edited by A. Jones and G. McGregor, pp. 127–140. Berg, London.
|n.d.| A Phenomenology of the Buried Landscape: Soil and Material Culture in the Bronze Age of Southwest Britain. In *Soils, Stones and Symbols: Archaeological and Anthropological Perspectives on the Mineral World*, edited by N. Boivin, and M. A. Owoc. UCL Press, London.

Parker Pearson, M.
|n.d.| Earth, Chalk, Wood, and Stone: Materiality and Stonehenge. In *Soils, Stones and Symbols: Archaeological and Anthropological Perspectives on the Mineral World* edited by N. Boivin, and M. A. Owoc. UCL Press, London.

Pollard, S. H. M., and P.M.G. Russell
|1969| Excavation of Round Barrow 284b, Upton Pyne, Exeter. *Proceedings of the Devon Archaeological Society* 27:49–78.
|1976| Radiocarbon Dating. Excavation of Round Barrow 284b, Upton Pyne, Exeter. *Proceedings of the Devon Archaeological Society* 34:95.

Putnam, H.
|1995| *Pragmatism: An Open Question*. Blackwell, Oxford.

Rapp, Jr., G., and C. L. Hill
|1998| *Geoarchaeology: The Earth Science Approach to Archaeological Interpretation*. Yale University Press, New Haven.

Rayner, D. H.
|1981| *The Stratigraphy of the British Isles*. Cambridge University Press, Cambridge.

Reichel-Dolmatoff, G.
|1987| The Great Mother and the Kogi Universe: A Concise Overview. *Journal of Latin American Lore* 13(1): 73–113.

Renfrew, C.
|1976| Archaeology and the Earth Sciences. In *Geoarchaeology: Earth Sciences and the Past*, edited by D. A. Davidson and M. L. Shackley, pp.1–5. Duckworth, London.

Rescher, N.
|2000| *Realistic Pragmatism: An Introduction to Pragmatic Philosophy*. State University of New York Press, Albany.

Rorty, R.
|1999| *Philosophy and Social Hope*. Penguin, London.

Selwood, E. B., E. M. Durrance, and C. M. Bristow
|1998| *The Geology of Cornwall and the Isles of Scilly*. University of Exeter Press, Exeter.

Stein, J. K.
|1993| Scale in Archaeology, Geosciences, and Geoarchaeology. In *Effects of Scale on Archaeological and Geoscientific Perspectives*, edited by J. K. Stein, and A. R. Linse, pp. 1–10. Geological Society of America Special Paper 283. Geological Society of America, Boulder.

Taçon, P.
|1991| The Power of Stone: Symbolic Aspects of Stone Use and Tool Development in Western Arnhem Land, Australia. *Antiquity* 65:192–207.

Thomas, J.
|1993| The Politics of Vision and the Archaeologies of Landscape. In *Landscape: Politics and Perspectives*, edited by B. Bender, pp. 19–48. Berg, Oxford.
|1998| *Time, Culture and Identity*. Routledge, London.
|2001| Archaeologies of Place and Landscape. In *Archaeological Theory Today*, edited by I. Hodder, pp. 165–186. Polity Press, Oxford.

Tilley, C.
|1994| *A Phenomenology of Landscape: Places, Paths and Monuments*. Berg, London.

Tuan, Y-F.
|1977| *Space and Place: The Perspective of Experience*. University of Minnesota Press, Minneapolis.

Waters, M. R.
|1996| *Principles of Geoarchaeology: A North American Perspective*. University of Arizona Press, Tucson.

Williams, A.
|1950| Bronze Age Barrows on Charmy Down, Landsdowne, Somerset. *The Antiquaries Journal* 30:34–46.

NOTES

1 The 2001 Chacmool session for which this contribution was originally prepared was entitled "Viewscapes." Although the subject for this paper is ostensibly the buried landscape of the earlier Bronze Age, I have chosen to retain the term viewscape in the title of the present contribution because it bypasses the historical and perhaps limiting associations of the world "landscape," and further, admits the possibility of more than one "viewpoint" from which the world may be constructed (Bender 1993).

2 The totalizing character of geoarchaeology has been addressed by Stein (1993) within an important call for rethinking the scale and resolution at which geoarchaeology should operate.

3 This point is powerfully made by Frodeman (1995, 2003) in examining the epistemological character of geology, which he argues is a hermeneutic endeavor – informed by concepts and conditioned by history.

4 This progression can be observed on other funerary and ritual sites of the region and period, and likely relates to a metaphorical understanding of the process of hardening that was objectified through a variety of media in various contexts (see Owoc 2000, n.d.; Parker Pearson n.d.).

PERCEPTIONS OF LANDSCAPES IN UNCERTAIN TIMES: CHUNCHUCMIL, YUCATÁN, MEXICO AND THE VOLCÁN BARÚ, PANAMA

Karen G. Holmberg, Travis W. Stanton, and Scott R. Hutson

Karen G. Holmberg, Department of Anthropology, Columbia University, New York, New York, U.S.A.
Travis W. Stanton, Departamento de Antropología, Universidad de las Américas, Puebla, Sta. Catarina Mártir, S/N, Cholula, Puebla, C.P. 72820, Mexico.
Scott R. Hutson, Department of Anthropology, University of California at Berkeley, Berkeley, California, U.S.A.

ABSTRACT

Space cannot be conceived without the simultaneous consideration of time. Using two complementary contexts from Middle America, the authors seek to highlight the conceptions of landscape with an awareness of space-time. In conceptualizing these landscapes the theories of Henri Bergson – who viewed time as a fluid and strongly experiential element that is heavily imbued with perception – are considered particularly useful to the study of past spaces. While we easily see our contemporary landscapes as richly filled with experience, it is important to remember that the past was just as perceptively complex and that past peoples did not live in sterile worlds of objects and environments that can always be neatly lined up in Cartesian order.

In the first example, the Classic-period northern Maya lowland centre of Chunchucmil is examined within the context of growing urbanism and its impact upon two groups, the Muuch and 'Aak, in their perception of the built environment over time. In the second, the Volcán Barú region of western Panamá is discussed in regards to the volcano's role as a landscape monument both in the contemporary and possible past contexts. The petroglyphs which are common in the Barú area are invoked both in their context within the archaeological landscape and in regards to their perception within modern archaeological interpretation. For both cases discussed, a tension exists for the authors between interpretations of the archaeological past and the contemporary context.

The two archaeological contexts are not offered for means of comparison, but instead to address their differing space-time contexts while musing over the perception of landscapes in periods of "uncertain" times. While this easily refers to the time period in which this paper was originally presented – immediately post-September 11, 2001 and the dramatic changes that day wrought upon the home city, New York, of two of the authors – it also refers to landscapes in which strict chronometric controls are not possible. Though the two study areas discussed are quite different, the authors come to the same conclusion for each, which is that the non-artifactual, non-tangible elements of past perceptions may be just as important as any artifact assemblage and possibly more important than rigid temporal placement of past events or set definitions of spatial radii.

TIME IN THE STUDY OF SPACE

Time is as elusive as it is pervasive. In the Western perspective, from Greek philosophers to Einstein and contemporary theorists, the reality of the true form of time has been extensively debated. Despite the recent attempts of scientific gurus such as Stephen Hawking to determine the profound clockwork of the universe, the mechanics of its nature remain in a Cimmerian darkness. Definitive explanations of time remain more the domain of fiction writers like Michael Crichton (1999) in his scientific thriller novel, *Timeline*, while non-fiction writers tend towards more inchoate descriptions. Unfortunately, our primitive understanding of the cerebral mechanics of spatio-temporal perception in the hippocampus and other brain regions does not provide insights that can resolve such matters (Bostock et al. 1991; Foster et al. 1989; Jung and McNaughton 1993). Therefore, we are left with the conundrum of how to conceptualize time.

Time can be seen as the other self of space (Hägerstrand 1976, 1985; Munn 1992; Pred 1977). Together they embody all forms of movement and passage. The two pervade our unconscious and are nearly translucent to daily perception, yet they maintain the very foundations of human experience. In anthropological thought, however, these siblings are often studied in disembodied isolation. We either focus on the temporal rhythms of calendars, daily routines and flux of social institutions, or we focus on cultural construction of the body, house or settlement. As the title of this volume indicates, the "odyssey of space" has reached greater academic prominence, enticing a focus on activity areas, landscapes and other spatial topics among varied theoretical traditions. As Kwinter (2001:11) states, however, "The problematization of *time* entails a challenge to the primacy of the role of space, and the reintroduction of the classical problem of *becoming* in opposition to that of Being."

A varied number of authors grapple with the concept of an intertwined time-space, although no true consensus exists. Quantum physics and related fields continue to raise questions concerning the uniformity of time, and thus how it manifests in the physical realm. Einstein's theory of relativity, of course, is the best known of these. Kwinter (2001:4) describes time as having a "relentless fluidity" and "irreducible materiality" through its association with space that is somehow repellent for the modern mind to conceive. The idea of multiplicity in time arises from the fact that different societies maintain different rhythms of life (despite the steady encroachment of one particular rhythm: the measured time of the capitalist workplace). These rhythms are produced by daily practice, such that the multiplicity of rhythms inheres in the multiplicity of forms of practice (Giddens 1984). The combination of a physical, temporally placed landscape and an envisionment of it as active and dynamic invoke what Soja (1996) terms the "Thirdspace," or lived space. Soja draws on the works of LeFebvre (1996) to incorporate both the individual and the collective experience of the landscape, which are a combination of both the physical and the perceived or imagined elements of space. Likewise, we might conceive of a lived time as the conflation of what Shanks and Tilley (1987) term substantial (experiential) and abstract (measured) time, although the "physicality" of time may be more multifaceted than what we traditionally measure. The commonality in these various conceptions is the incorporation of space "so deeply into the body of time as to change its nature," as Kwinter (2001:69) states. With these varied conceptions and questionings in mind, we propose that the intersection of experiential time and space is an important consideration in the archaeology of landscape.

A useful starting point for identifying aspects of time that we should remain sensitive to when studying space can be found in Hägerstrand's (1976, 1985) idea of the corporeality of the body. This viewpoint allows us to acknowledge our bodily existence and the personal timescale created by it. Movement in space is movement in time. Even Aristotelians who see space and time as mere containers for human action must admit that two bodies cannot occupy the same space at the same time. Yet bodies are not simply in time, occupying time. Since human practice creates our lived senses of time, time is in the body, durably inculcated as Bourdieu argued (1977). Although Hägerstrand's argument that movement in time is movement in space is argued against by some cognitive scientists (Elitzur 1996), the *perception* of time's movement cannot be denied by those debating the physics of time. We all share this perception, although the nature of that perception may vary from culture to culture or individual to individual. Van der Leeuw's (1994) point that space and time always intersect in our experiences of them and that each perception is unique as actors constantly resituate themselves mentally from moment to moment is germane here.

Yet time is not only personal: the work of Martin Heidegger allows a distinction between private time and public time. Heidegger (1996[1927]) argues that every person has an authentic, personalized state of being, whose only certainty is death. Dwelling on this primordial state of being and its inevitable mortality is unsettling, so people instead tend to "fall" into a more superficial, public, state of being, absorbing themselves in gossip, idle talk, and social structures that outlast the lifetime of any single human being (see also Dreyfus 1991). Personal time is short, limited by one's authentic, mortal state, whereas public time endures beyond the individual subject.

The conception of time provided by Henri Bergson (2001) is perhaps most useful for the context of this paper in apprehending the human experience of space in the past, or at least the authors' use of present contexts to better understand the past. According to Bergson, imposed designations of time are artificial, as for the human being time operates as a continuous flow in which past and present are inseparable from elements such as memory and consciousness. Rather than living in a series of single, discrete moments, memories and experiences from the past weigh upon action in the present, which in turn shapes the possibilities for the future (Heidegger 1996[1927]). Bergson touches upon the consideration that states of consciousness are alive and changing. They are processes, not things. In this context, time is a qualitative, dynamic process that intersects with space. Space, in turn, is not a homogenous and static container, but a mobile, rich, and heterogeneous phenomenon (Mullarkey 2000:10).

With these conceptions in mind, we turn to explore the meanings of two spatio-temporal landscapes in Middle America. In this paper, we will discuss a built landscape from Chunchucmil, Yucatán, Mexico and a more "natural" landscape surrounding the Volcán Barú in western Panamá. In both cases, a tension exists for the authors between the present and the past in their interpretations of the archaeological landscape. While at points we walk the fine line between exposing the actors of and imposing faces upon the past, this study should be viewed as a heuristic exercise designed to enrich the flavour of an often dry and stale perception of the past in the study areas.

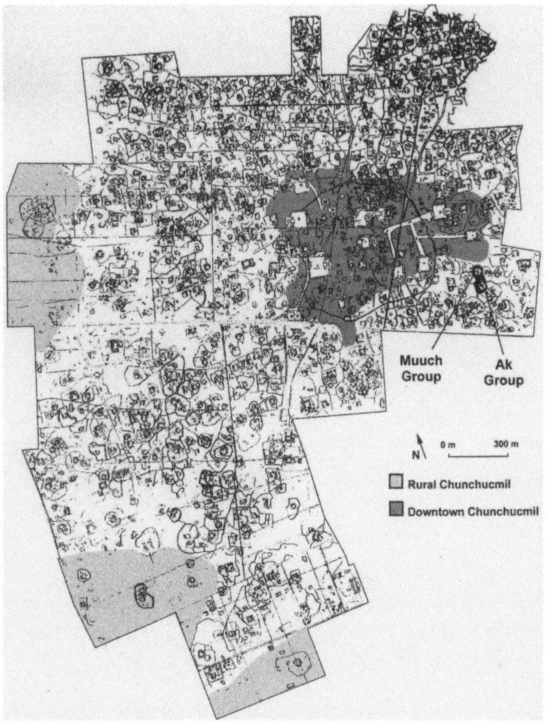

Figure 1. A portion of the Chunchucmil site map showing relative locations of sampled houselots.

CHUNCHUCMIL

Chunchucmil is a sprawling Precolumbian centre situated on the northwestern coastal plain of the Yucatán peninsula (Figure 1). Located in a flat, low-lying karst environment with very thin soils and a reduced rainfall regime (Beach 1998), this centre exhibits a palimpsest of transforming settlement patterns spanning at least the last two and a half millennia (Ardren 1999; Hutson et al. 2004; Magnoni 1995; Magnoni et al. 2002; Stanton et al. 2000; Vlcek et al. 1978). Whether all of these manifestations of settlement were conceived of, in some general sense, as the same place by their inhabitants is open to question. Certainly the modern and historic pueblos built on the outskirts of the site are not viewed as an extension of the Precolumbian settlement by their inhabitants. In fact, the remains of the ancient city have quite varied meanings for the local modern Maya. Regardless, towards the end of the Early Classic period (ca. A.D. 400–650), Chunchucmil was one of the largest demographic centres in the Maya lowlands. It does not appear, however, to be *like* other Classic Maya centres. During this period, Chunchucmil is characterized by a redundancy of monumental architectural forms we term quadrangles, instead of the common palace, temple and acropolis arrangements found at other sites. Furthermore, the domestic settlement is inordinately dense with stone walls encircling even the smallest of patio groups. These walls not only define houselot boundaries, but also often form pathways through the sites that, in conjunction with raised causeways, provide an extraordinary opportunity to study spatial relations. From 1999 to 2002, excavations were performed by Scott Hutson and Travis Stanton in two small adjacent domestic groups (Figure 2) , 'Aak and Muuch (Hutson 2000a, 2000b; Hutson and Forde 2003; Hutson and Stanton 2001; Hutson et al. 2003; Stanton 2001). We draw from these data to explore the perceptions of time and space among the Classic Maya.

Although we focus on a discussion of only two groups, it is important to view the 'Aak and Muuch

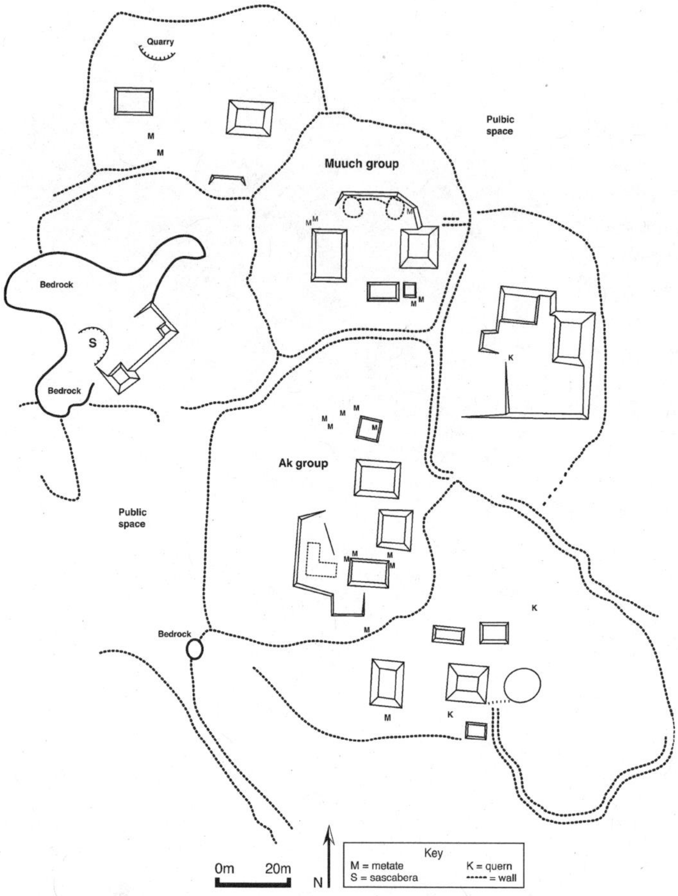

Figure 2. The 'Aak and Muuch groups, showing their neighborhood contexts.

groups not just as discreetly bounded residential locales, but as segments of an integrated local and regional network. Profound similarities in material culture such as architecture and ceramics extend to large centres such as Oxkintok located 16 km to the east (see Varela 1998; Vidal 1999). In this regional context, the 'Aak and Muuch groups are composed of small masonry structures situated around central patios near the site core of Chunchucmil.

Three structures in the 'Aak group and two structures in the Muuch group were subjected to extensive horizontal and vertical exposure. Functioning artifacts appear to have been taken by the residents when both groups were abandoned. Although the chemical analyses of the soils are still in process, macroartifact data yielded distinct areas of houselot use and insights into refuse disposal patterns (Hutson and Stanton 2001). Unfortunately, these data are difficult to analyze in regards to changing perceptions of time for two reasons. First, the soils are very thin and, given millennia of post-depositional disturbance, intact stratigraphy is virtually nonexistent. Second, our ceramic chronology for the period in question is not yet fine grained enough to distinguish the temporal relations among the disturbed deposits. Thus, our analysis here primarily relies on the architectural data. These data yield some interesting suggestions of changing perceptions of time and space, especially in regards to modifications of domestic ritual structures.

A general pattern in Maya domestic groups is for the eastern or northern structure on the patio to be the locus for ancestor rituals (see Ashmore 1991; Becker 1971; McAnany 1995). This pattern is borne out in the 'Aak and Muuch groups where excavations revealed the presence of relatively high status burials that are interpreted as the remains of important ancestors for corporate groups (Hutson et al. 2004). Briefly, the eastern structure in the 'Aak group revealed at least five construction events and several unusual architectural features. This structure was first built as a very low platform, but reached over 1 m in height during its final phase of construction. Two rich burials were located at its centre, and three unusual compartments were appended to its southern edge (Ardren 2001; Ardren and Hutson 2002; Hutson 2000a). These compartments contained three broken pottery vessels, including one serving plate with modeled tripod feet; one greenstone bead; a grooved stone; and polished fragments of greenstone and hematite (possibly pieces of a mosaic). One of the compartments was constructed over a circular cist filled with specially deposited soil. If analogies to similar archaeological and ethnographic features from Guatemala are valid, they may likely have contained ritual paraphernalia or bundles that were removed upon abandonment. These data suggest that the structure began as a residence but functioned as a locus of ritual activity for most of its life history.

In contrast, in the eastern structure in the Muuch group, excavations revealed that the structure was built in a single event and that its front had been covered with a red-painted stucco façade with geometric designs, possibly breath imagery marking the structure as symbolically alive. Facing the patio, the staircase is flanked by sloping walls that jog before reaching their northern and southern extents. At its centre, several faced stone compartments were located in the construction fill. The central compartment contained the only burial, a poorly preserved secondary burial placed in a large unslipped *olla*. Two matching pairs of serving bowls were the only artifacts recovered with this individual. In the main residential structure of the Muuch group, located on the west side of the patio, directly across from the ritual structure, excavations documented two stages of construction. In the first stage, the structure consisted of two long rooms and a broad entranceway flanked by freestanding stone column drums. In the second stage of construction, the Muuch occupants divided one of the rooms into two, added a back patio, and reduced the size of the entryway (Hutson and Forde 2003). Excavations at the Muuch group therefore succeeded in revealing evidence for multiple construction stages, but these construction stages are dramatically fewer than those documented for the 'Aak group. These data suggest two things about this part of the transforming landscape at Chunchucmil. First, the continual elaboration of the burial monument in 'Aak likely provided both stasis and transformation in the perception of local space. Throughout the multiple modifications to its form, the structure remained the ritual focus of the group, a constant, durable monument on the east side of the patio. If we equate each modification with the passage of a new generation of leadership in the 'Aak group (Hutson et al. 2004), then the ritual structure lasted through four generations of occupations. The continuity of the ritual structure, the oldest structure in the group, created a "public" time. As discussed above, public time is a social time, a kind of institutional time that outlasts the private time scales of any specific individuals.

In contrast to the stable aspects of this structure (its long tenure as the ritual focus of the group), manipulation of burial monuments provide not only the opportunity to break with and transform the past, but they facilitate the renegotiation of the present (Humphreys 1981; see also Tarlow 1992). The famous multigenerational manipulation of the "founder" of the ancient Maya kingdom of Copán, Honduras, Yax-Kuk-Mo, is an elegant example of how short-, medium- and long-term rituals based around the founding ancestor mobilized the renegotiation of political, social, and religious life (Fash 1998). The ancient Maya used the built environment to engender such renegotiations. As the residents of 'Aak continued to modify the burial shrine, the conceptions of the house or compound likely changed (Hutson et al. 2004). Again it is difficult to understand the perceptions of individuals long dead, but such activity likely reinforced ideas of place, as residents who continued to live in the group grew older there. At Muuch, where evidence suggests a shorter occupation and fewer phases of construction, these perceptions of the landscape were likely different from the range of perceptions that existed in the 'Aak household. The local-scale passage of time likely impacted the perceptions of place and landscape at all spatial scales.

Excavation data suggest that the Muuch Group was occupied for a shorter period of time than the 'Aak Group. The public time of the ritual monument of the 'Aak group can be perceived as a counterbalance to the rapid processes of urbanization occurring around 'Aak during the Early Classic period. The boundary walls of Muuch were likely appended to those of 'Aak. Muuch appears to have been built as a new settlement encroaching on the vacant area to the north. Although the exact timing of this event is unclear, it indicates that at least the older residents of 'Aak may have witnessed a drastic change to their local landscape as the site became more populous and this "barrio" increased in residential density. The idea that the 'Aak folk "witnessed" a drastic change to their landscape is perhaps too passive. Recent excavations provide evidence that a splinter group from 'Aak settled Muuch: the floor plans and many of the details of the major residential structure in both groups are suspiciously identical (Hutson and Forde 2003, Hutson et al. 2003). We suspect that as 'Aak residents with this spatio-temporal knowledge grew older, the settlement of the Muuch group impacted their short- and long-term perceptions of their local space. Residents born after the construction of Muuch may have had a very different spatio-temporal perception of the local landscape, although they may have been conditioned in some ways to the descriptions of the previous state of the landscape by their elders. In this way, older group members can influence the perception of younger group members in attempts to transcend the personal time scales engendered by the corporality of the body. In transcending the personal time scales, these elders create public time. Understanding exactly what these perceptions were is difficult and necessitates speculation, but without making specific assumptions, we believe that a general sense of urbanism was likely impacting the changing perceptions of the local landscape. This sense was certainly perceived differently by individuals operating with different experiences of time-depth within this space, but common ground may have been found in the likely increasing political, social, and economic importance of this rapidly growing metropolis.

At the time Muuch was built, Chunchucmil appears to have reached its maximum population, most likely at a time when trade networks were successfully supplying the site with subsistence resources that could not be locally acquired. The fact that a large demographic centre could expand in such a poor resource zone suggests that the end of the Early Classic was a time of prosperity for the inhabitants of Chunchucmil. Rich burials in the 'Aak Group corroborate this idea. Thus, the inhabitants of the Muuch Group were establishing a residential compound replete with a founding ancestor during a positive growth period for the site. They prepared the eastern structure to accommodate a number of burials by constructing a series of internal compartments with dressed stone. Although only the founding ancestor was placed in the central compartment, this planning suggests that the inhabitants of Muuch anticipated a longer occupation. In this context, we can imagine that the founders of the Muuch group, unlike the founders of the 'Aak group, might have perceived the landscape as urban without ever having experienced the site before it became crowded and extensive. Their perception of the landscape at the time of the onset of decline at Chunchucmil was likely one characterized by noise, movement, and growth. If the residents of Muuch used the concept of cyclical time, they did not anticipate the cycle of rise and decline at Chunchucmil. Like the stock traders of New York in the late 1990s, they appear to have anticipated further growth and prosperity that would have furthered the urban construction of the landscape. This was not, however, to pass.

At the turn of the Late Classic period (ca. A.D. 600), domestic groups were slowly abandoned at Chunchucmil. For unknown reasons, the Muuch and 'Aak groups, among others, were left to fall into ruins. Other groups survived for another hundred years or so (Magnoni et al. 2002), but by A.D. 700 the site was virtually abandoned. Reoccupation would occur several hundred years later, but the landscape of this centre would never regain a sense of urban occupation. The younger inhabitants of groups that continued to occupy the space during the seventh century might have viewed the decaying structures as normal. As these residents grew older and still more groups were abandoned, the ruined structures may have begun to symbolize economic hardship, depopulation and failure, which is a reversal of the ideas that this aspect of the built landscape could have invoked for the inhabitants of these groups 100 years before.

In a current example of such a shifting of perceptions in our own landscape, it is interesting to note a November 3, 2001, *New York Times* article entitled "It's savings over sorrow as apartment hunters consider Battery Park." This article discusses the demographic shift currently going on around the site where the twin towers of the World Trade Center stood until September 11, 2001. Those moving out of the area cannot bear to be in the vicinity as they see it as a graveyard and "are unwilling to deal with the lingering psychological effects of living so close to ground zero." Those moving in, however, are drawn by the plummeting prices; as they did not physically witness the event from close range and do not have as much personal time invested in the area, the newcomers are able to view the site as though it were one of construction rather than destruction. We bring this example in to the discussion not to essentialize or rationalize past actors or landscapes from an empathetic vantage or parallel present, but instead to simply remind us all that we, too, have deeply seated time and space perceptions invoked in our contemporary urbanism. Our perceptions of such issues in the past are most certainly tempered or prompted by our awareness and experience of them in the present, and yet it is important not to oversimplify past actors and place them in sterile, physical settings devoid of the complex networks of memories and experience that time creates.

For Neolithic England, Chris Gosden (1994) discusses a contrast between the public time of long-lasting, immobile, socially integrating monuments (henges, barrow mounds) and the more short-lived private times created by shifting, individualized subsistence practices scattered across the landscape. At Chunchucmil we similarly see interplay between public and private time. While landscape perceptions may be partially conditioned by habitus and follow some gross schedule (Bourdieu 1977), they may shift rapidly by chance events in an individual's daily life. Similar processes impact the perception of collective time. While the archaeological remains cannot offer sufficient data to view rapid changes in perception, we may acknowledge their presence and search for the general types of past perceptions that potentially existed.

THE VOLCÁN BARÚ AREA OF WESTERN PANAMÁ

At an elevation of 3,477 m asl, the Volcán Barú of western Panamá dominates the landscape of which it is a part (Figure 3). Though both frequent tremors and hot springs emanate from the volcano, proving that it is not seismically dead, it is its monumentality that provides the symbolic importance of the Volcán Barú in its modern context. The volcano has a strongly evident social impact within its contemporary landscape; it exists both as an imposing physical presence and as a conceptual symbol of place and regional identity. This is most striking and tangible in its everyday embodiments. In the small town of Boquete, nestled along the volcano's skirt at 1,200 m asl, the pizzeria, "*La Volcanica*," is marked by a sign with a handle-bar mustached Italian kissing his fingers and winking in front of an image of Barú's crater. A local breakfast nook operated out of a home announces itself as a friendly meeting place, "*Punto de Encuentro*," with a drawing of the volcano surrounded by images of the omnipresent and invasive impatience flowers that blanket the area and are called a plague. The ice machines found at any gas station in Boquete proclaim themselves to contain "*Hielo Barú*" (Barú Ice), and like the pizzeria also picture a cloud-topped image of the volcano. A nearby nightspot is named simply "*Erupcion 81*," marking the year it opened with the discotheque-worthy connotations of a fiery eruption. Even a local supermarket incorporates the volcano into its stylized neon logo and into its name, the "*Super Barú*." The t-shirts that the grocery store employees wear proclaim under a stylized image of the volcano that the store is "*Chiricano*

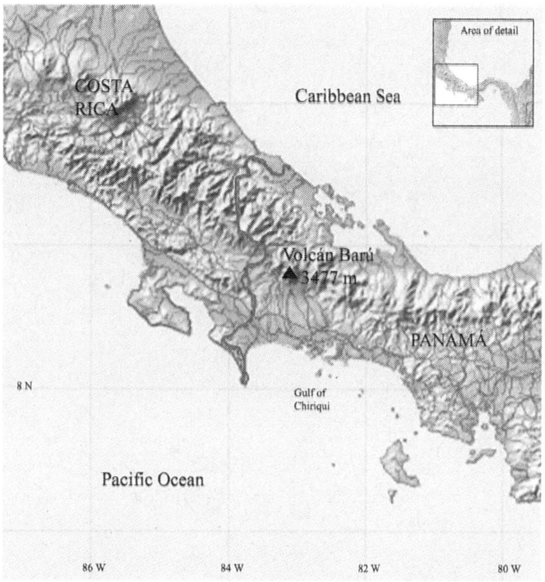

Figure 3. A sample of petroglyph designs from the Volcán Barú study area.

como tu" (Chiricano like you); the store, like the volcano, is a part of the community and shares something in common with the shoppers from the Panamanian province of Chiriqui. Each of these uses of the volcano embodies a sense of community and identity that is tied to the landscape through the volcano. These examples are given not to provide direct analogy to ways in which Barú may have been conceived of in the past, but only to entice one's mind to begin thinking in a direction that allows for more than a simple environmental role for the volcano. It is important to reiterate that the Volcán Barú has not erupted during the memory of current residents. It is not viewed as a destructive element, but one of both local and national pride as it is the highest point on the isthmus and the most distinctive element of both the natural and social landscape.

While the social role of the Volcán Barú is easily seen in its modern context, through both its domination of the landscape and its eruptive history it is also evident that the volcano played an important role in the archaeological past. Current interpretations of the archaeology of this cultural region, known as Gran Chiriqui, propose that settlers first entered the highlands around Barú ca. 300 B.C. (Linares and Ranere 1980).

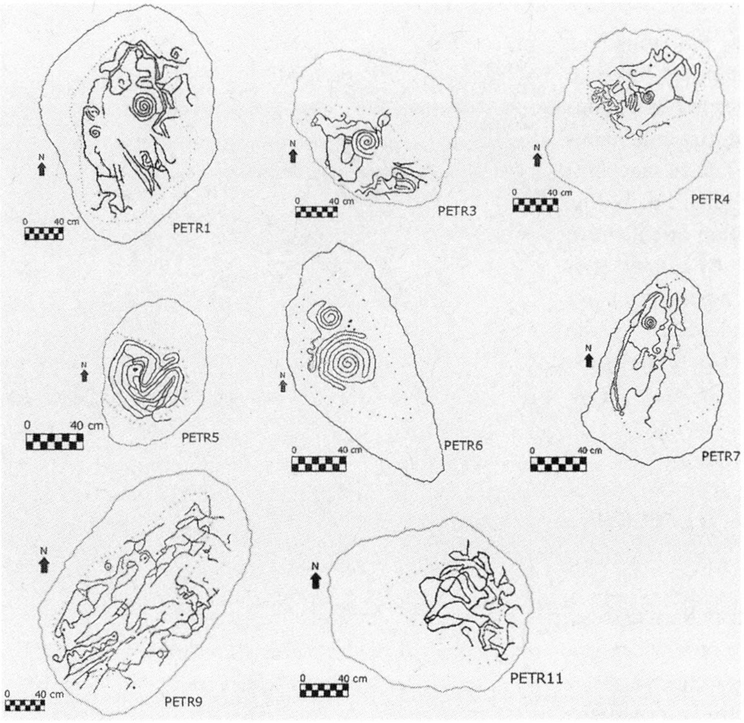

Figure 4. A schematic of the Caldera petroglyph boulder and "passageway" rock

cano outside of its environmental impact. One of these roles is as a monument within the landscape.

Landscape monuments, whether built or natural, are frequently referenced over long spans of time to create tradition and to evoke a sense of continuity (Edmonds 1993:107). Mountain peaks and volcanoes are especially prone to symbolism (Whitley 2001:22). This is not relegated solely to prehistoric contexts, and is very much a part of the modern, global experience of volcanic regions. Though exact meanings or interpretations imbued to landscape monuments may change, the commonality that is assumed by many interpretive studies of monuments is that of a shared physical perception (e.g., Edmonds 1999; Thomas 1993; Tilley 1994). Though it is not possible to enter the minds of the past people in the Barú landscape and divine their perceptions, it is at least certain that they were aware of the presence of the volcano's form.

Since the time period of the initial settlement in the area, evidence exists for a number of volcanic eruptions. A geological study examined a 2,860-year pollen and charcoal record from a lake coring done 20 km to the southwest of the Volcán Barú, and identified eruptions from A.D. 250, A.D. 1030, and A.D. 1380 (Behling 2000). Historical reports from the nineteenth century additionally mention an A.D. 1550 eruption of Barú (Montessus de Ballore 1884, 1888), and colonial era paintings further support this date. Most significantly, archaeological survey in the early 1970s, 8 km to the west of the caldera, determined that an eruption ca. A.D. 600 forced a migration from the area to the previously uninhabited Caribbean coast of the isthmus (Linares and Ranere 1980; Linares et al. 1975). In all archaeological discussions of the Chiriqui highlands, it is striking that the volcano is only considered in its role as an eruptive device. This is not to say that it is considered only as a destructive element, as multiple publications cite the boon of fertile soils from volcanic eruption (Linares and Sheets 1980). What is missing, however, is a conception of the social role of the vol-

To better understand the prehistoric landscape, an intensive survey of a 48 km^2 area to the southeast of the Barú crater was initiated by Karen Holmberg in 1999 and is ongoing. One of the more striking landscape elements encountered by the survey project is the petroglyphs that can be found pecked and chiseled into boulders in the area. Each boulder can have anywhere from one to hundreds of abstract designs, predominantly comprised of spirals, irregular lines, and cupules. These designs are found on basaltic and andesitic boulders averaging 6.75 m in length.

Twenty-six petroglyph sites have been identified per the 2004 field season (Figure 4). This adds to a tally of seven sites identified by Harte in 1959 in the study area, and two described by recent CRM work (Brizuela 2000). It is certain that numerous additional petroglyphs exist.

Lacking carbon-based pigmentation or a stylistic dating method, it is currently impossible to know when the petroglyphs were created. Regardless, what cannot be denied is that rock art is a direct material expression of human thought and action (Hartley and

Wolley Vawser 1998). Petroglyphs were not created in a cultural vacuum; they are disembodied elements of an entire cultural context rather than isolated anomalies. In the case of the Barú petroglyphs, time has directly impacted our perception of the Barú space. Though obviously intentionally created to mark their space, over time the meaning of the petroglyphs has been forgotten. The memory of their intended purpose is mislaid. Additionally, the trajectory of archaeological thought and fashion has conspired against analysis of the petroglyphs. While they were the object of debate for both amateur archaeologists and mainstream researchers in the earlier part of the twentieth century (e.g., Harte 1959), the prevalence of processual studies following the rise of New Archaeology relegated rock art to the category of non-data due to the slipperiness of their dating and the impossibility of a literal "translation" of their symbols. Given the ephemeral nature and poor preservation of material culture in this region, the dismissal of such a purposefully created artifact class as rock art creates a vacuum for understanding of the overall landscape.

When analyzed for location within the landscape, it is striking that many of the petroglyphs examined are within a direct and clear line-of-sight to the volcano. Despite the height of the volcano, the many deep valleys in this area do not make this as mundane an observation as it might at first appear. The majority of rock art sites are also found in close association with water. The most striking petroglyph site is that of Caldera, containing numerous of stylized designs on a 10 m long boulder. This rock art site is within direct line-of-sight to the volcano, but even more strikingly has a naturally formed, culturally appropriated "passageway" rock beside a stream that aligns the field of vision of a spectator directly at both the petroglyphic designs and the crater of the volcano in one field of vision (Figure 5). This is a very tangible and visceral linkage of the petroglyphs within the natural landscape and the volcano which dominates it. Line-of-sight relation to a volcano is also noted for petroglyphs in other areas, such as the Ometepe volcano in Nicaragua (Baker 2001). Those petroglyphs in the Barú study area that do not have a direct vantage of the volcano are located in places where there is a direct vantage to distinctive mountain peaks. Some of these even seem to mimic the outline of visible landscape forms.

One way in which the rock art of highland Chiriqui can be conceived of operating in the past, which does not require either a definitive time or a literal "translation" of the designs – is that of mimesis (see Taussig 1993). Mimetic landscapes appropriate power or meaning through their reference to distinctive elements of the natural world. Though theories of many local residents in the Volcán Barú area today state that the petroglyph designs are stylized landscape sketches with the volcano itself represented by spirals, less debatable is the proposition that the petroglyphs are intentionally located in places that are intended to create a socialized space within the landscape. As a monument within this socialized space, the volcano becomes linked to the petroglyphs through their mutual creation of the landscape.

Figure 5. A petroglyph in its landscape.

The presence of petrolyphs in areas of western Panamá far from the Volcán Barú – and worldwide for that matter – provide that, obviously, not all petroglyphs are to be considered linked indelibly to a volcano. Rather, it is their position as creators and markers of their social landscape, and the volcano's domination of that landscape in the Barú example, that we are most interested in teasing out. While it may not be possible to know the exact time period of the petroglyphs' creation or their explicit "interpretation," if one should even exist, their placement shows a perception of the landscape and a relational correspondence with the volcano as the most distinct monument within the landscape. This is not as direct a correlation as the identity and community association seen in the contemporary pizzeria or grocery store signs. Such a parallel would indeed be surprising given intrusions such as colonialism, Christianity, and modernity between the disparate time periods. It is obvious, however, that perception of Barú formed an element of the cognition and life of people in the past landscape and does in the present. The possible linkage of petroglyphs within a location that is referenced by the volcano hint at a role for it that is more encompassing than that of an eruptive, environmental object, and begin to reposition the Volcán Barú as a member and component of a lived archaeological space. In conjunction with the volcano, the petroglyphs provide the sole remnants from the archaeological landscapes of the past due to the ephemeral nature of the material culture from the area as well as the poor level of preservation inherent to volcanic soils. Far more work will be required to determine the lengths to which interpretations can responsibly be taken regarding the petroglyphs, but the openness to examine them despite the "uncertain time" of their original creation is a marked departure from prior studies conducted in this area. The modern context and use of the volcano as a symbol reminds us that the volcanic landscape is inextricably social, not just environmental, and the petroglyphs that marked past landscapes hint at webs of lost meanings that crisscross space and time.

DISCUSSION

Like all actors, archaeologists do not just conceive of or perceive time; we are in it. How do we as archaeologists conceptualize time in the present and past? Free flowing? Stochastic? Deep? Today we have complex time systems that range from daily to global (Gosden 1994). Does this suggest that current perceptions of time are not appropriate for analyses of ancient time, or much more the relationship of time to people's perceptions of landscape? As Heidegger (1996 [1927]) and Hägerstrand (1976, 1985) point out, our bodily existence gives us a personal time scale, but people and societies construct their own "local" conceptions of time (Gurvitch 1964; Hall 1983; Pocock 1967). Are comparisons or inspirations from our modern time applicable to interpretations of archaeological landscapes? More importantly, is it possible to remove our contemporary landscape experience from the interpretations we impose upon the past?

Amidst all of these questions, for which we are not capable of proffering definitive answers, we are grappling with the uncertainties of chronological sequences within the dating of our two field projects. In the case of Chunchucmil, we have a rough outline of when the 'Aak and Muuch groups were built, modified, and abandoned, but, as in most archaeological sites, the chronological data do not allow us to focus on individual perceptions of landscape. Therefore, we focus on generational changes that would have impacted individuals' perceptions of their landscape. In this context, we talk about some of the likely perceptions that would have been felt by many members of these residential groups. We contrast a monolithic public time, created through a durable, multigenerational monument, to multiply varied private times, lived in the throes of urban landscape transformations. The Chunchucmil example also underlines a second central idea presented at the beginning of this paper: the inseparability of time and space. Different actors will have different perceptions of the space depending on the different times they live and create, regardless of any stability forged through burial monuments or other enduring features of the landscape.

In the case of the Volcán Barú area, it is uncertain exactly what the petroglyphs prevalent in the area were created to "do," or the timing of their creation. Additionally, the passage of time has erased both the meaning of petroglyphs and archaeological willingness in the region to engage in interpretation of them. What seems evident, however, is that the perception of the petroglyphs is inextricably linked to the entire landscape, including their relationship to the volcano as a monument within their landscape. The further examination of such linkages will be useful for further understanding of this rather understudied archaeological region.

What is most obvious about the "odyssey of space" is that it is our perception of time and how it intersects with space that provides much of the fodder for archaeological interpretation. Despite this, no consensus exists for exactly how time and space interplay.

Taking cue from Bergson (2001), perhaps the intersection of time and space in both the Chunchucmil and the Volcán Barú contexts should be viewed more as a process that is alive and changing and open for perception than as a concrete entity. In such a case, the "uncertain times" of the archaeological contexts matter less than is often expected in archaeological discourse, while the uncertain times of the authors while penning their interpretations of those contexts potentially matters more than is frequently considered. In attempting to focus on landscape perception in uncertain times, do we have faceless blobs and sterile landscapes, or do we impose faces and create speculative landscapes? Do such heuristic exercises advance our understanding of the past? These are all questions not for conclusion, but for continued discourse.

REFERENCES CITED

Ardren, T.

|1999| Chunchucmil: A Preliminary Chronology and Summary of Research. Paper presented at the 98th Annual Meeting of the American Anthropological Association, Philadelphia.

|2001| Ancient Maya Religious Practices: Textual and Archaeological Voices. In *Religious Texts and Material Contexts*, edited by J. Neusner, and J. F. Strange, pp. 251–274. University Press of America, Lanham, Maryland.

Ardren, T., and S. Hutson

|2002| Ancient Maya Religious Practices at Chunchucmil and Yaxuna: Using Evidence from Epigraphy and Excavation. *Pre-Columbian Art Research Institute Journal* 2(4):5–11.

Ashmore, W.

|1991| Site-Planning Principles and Concepts of Directionality among the Ancient Maya. *Latin American Antiquity* 2:199–225.

Baker, S.

|2001| *The Petroglyphs of Ometepe Island, Nicaragua*. Paper presented at the 66th Annual Meeting of the Society for American Archaeology, New Orleans.

Beach, T.

|1998| Soil Constraints on Northwest Yucatan, Mexico: Pedoarchaeology and Maya Subsistence at Chunchucmil. *Geoarchaeology* 13:759–791.

Becker, M.

|1971| Identification of a Second Plaza Plan at Tikal, Guatemala, and Its Implications for Ancient Maya Social Complexity. Unpublished Ph.D. Dissertation, Department of Anthropology, University of Pennsylvania, Philadelphia.

Behling, H.

|2000| A 2860-Year High-Resolution Pollen and Charcoal Record from the Cordillera de Talamanca in Panama: A History of Human and Volcanic Forest Disturbance. *The Holocene* 10(3):387–393.

Bergson, H.

|2001|[1913] *Time and Free Will: An Essay on the Immediate Data of Consciousness*. Translated by F. L. Pogson. Dover Publications, Mineola.

Bostock, E., R. Muller, and J. Kubie

|1991| Experience-Dependent Modifications of Hippocampal Place Cell Firing. *Hippocampus* 1:193–206.

Bourdieu, P.

|1977| *Outline of a Theory of Practice*. Cambridge University Press, Cambridge.

Brizuela, A.

|2000| *Proyecto de Rescate Arqueologicao Esti, Informe Final, Primera Temporado de Excavacion*. Arqueología S.A., Panamá.

Crichton, M.

|1999| *Timeline*. Ballantine Books, New York.

Dreyfus, Hubert L.

|1991| *Being-in-the-World*. MIT Press, Cambridge, Massachusetts.

Edmonds, M.

|1993| Interpreting Causewayed Enclosures in the Past and the Present. In *Interpretive Archaeology*, edited by C. Tilley, pp. 99–142. Berg, Providence.

|1999| *Ancestral Geographies of the Neolithic: Landscapes, Monuments and Memory*. Routledge, London.

Elitzur, A.

|1996| Time and Consciousness: The Uneasy Bearing of Relativity Theory on the Mind-Body Problem. In *Toward a Science of Consciousness: The First Tucson Discussions and Debates*, edited by S. R. Hameroff, A. W. Kaszniak, and A. C. Scott, pp. 543–550. MIT Press, Cambridge.

Fash, W., Jr.

|1998| Dynastic Architectural Programs: Intention and Design in Classic Maya Buildings at Copan and Other Sites. In *Function and Meaning in Classic Maya Architecture*, edited by S. D. Houston, pp. 223–270. Dumbarton Oaks Research Library and Collection, Washington, D.C.

Foster, T., C. Castro, and B. McNaughton

|1989| Spatial Selectivity of Rat Hippocampal Neurons: Dependence on Preparedness for Movement. *Science* 244:1580–1582.

Giddens, A.

|1984| *The Constitution of Society*. University of California Press, Berkeley

Gosden, C.

|1994| *Social Being and Time*. Blackwell, Oxford.

Gurvitch, G.

|1964| *The Spectrum of Social Time*. Reidel, Dordrecht.

Hägerstrand, T.

|1976| *Innovation as a Spatial Process*. University of Chicago Press, Chicago.

|1985| Time-Geography: Focus on the Corporeality of Man, Society, and Environment. In *The Science and Praxis of Complexity*, edited by S. Aida et al., pp. 193–216. The United Nations University, Tokyo.

Hall, E.
|1983| *The Dance of Life: The Other Dimension of Time.* Doubleday, New York.

Harte, E.
|1959| Petroglyphs in Panama. *Panama Archaeologist* 2:58–69.

Hartley, R., and A. Wolley Vawser
|1998| Spatial Behavior and Learning in the Prehistoric Environment of the Colorado River Drainage (South-Eastern Utah), Western North America. In *The Archaeology of Rock Art, New Directions in Archaeology*, edited by C. Chippendale, and P. Tacon, pp. 185–206. Cambridge University Press, Cambridge.

Heidegger, M.
|1996|[1927] *Being and Time.* Translated by J. Stambaugh. SUNY Press, Albany.

Humphreys, S.
|1981| Death and Time. In *Mortality and Immortality: The Anthropology and Archaeology of Death*, edited by S. C. Humphreys, and H. King, pp. 261–283. Academic Press, London.

Hutson, S.
|2000a| Excavation at Residential Groups 'Aak and Chiwo'ol. In *Chunchucmil Regional Economy Program: Report of the 1999 Field Season*, edited by T. Ardren, pp. 24–30. Department of Anthropology, Florida State University, Tallahassee.
|2000b| Excavations at the 'Aak Group. In *Pakbeh Regional Economy Program: Report of the 2000 Field Season*, edited by T. W. Stanton, pp. 18–45. Social Science and Business Division, Jamestown Community College, New York.

Hutson, S., and J. Forde
|2003| Horizontal Excavations of Structure 13 of the Muuch Group. In *Pakbeh Regional Economy Program: Report of the 2002 Field Season*, edited by B. Dahlin, and D. Mazeau. Department of Anthropology and Sociology, Howard University, Washington, D.C.

Hutson, S., A. Magnoni, and T. Stanton
|2004| House Rules? Practice of Social Organization in Classic-Period Chunchucmil, Yucatan, Mexico. *Ancient Mesoamerica* 15:73–90.

Hutson, S., and T. Stanton
|2001| *Espacios Domesticos y la Vida Cotidiana del Sitio Arqueológico de Chunchucmil, Yucatán.* Paper presented at the Congreso Internacional de Cultura Maya, Mérida, Mexico.

Hutson, S., C. West, J. Forde, and B. Moore
|2003| Horizontal Excavations of Structure 22 of the 'Aak Group. In *Pakbeh Regional Economy Program: Report of the 2002 Field Season*, edited by B. Dahlin, and D. Mazeau. Department of Anthropology and Sociology, Howard University, Washington, D.C.

Jung, M., and B. McNaughton
|1993| Spatial Selectivity of Unit Activity in the Hippocampal Granular Layer. *Hippocampus* 3: 165–182.

Kwinter, S.
|2001| *Architectures of Time: Toward a Theory of the Event in Modernist Culture.* MIT Press, Cambridge, Massachusetts.

LeFebvre, H.
|1996| *Writings on Cities/Henri Lefebvre.* Blackwell, Oxford.

Linares, O., and A. Ranere (editors)
|1980| *Adaptive Radiations in Prehistoric Panamá.* Peabody Museum Monographs Vol. 5. Harvard University Press, Cambridge.

Linares, O., P. Sheets, and J. Rosenthal
|1975| Prehistoric Agriculture in Tropical Highlands. *Science* 187:137–145.

Linares, O., and P. Sheets
|1980| Highland Agricultural Villages in the Volcán Barú Region. In *Adaptive Radiations in Prehistoric Panama*, vol. 5, edited by O. Linares, and A. Ranere, pp. 44–55. Harvard University Press, Cambridge.

Magnoni, A.
|1995| *Albarradas at Chunchucmil and in the Northern Maya Area.* Unpublished bachelors thesis, University College London, Institute of Archaeology, London.

Magnoni, A., S. Hutson, and T. Stanton
|2002| *Urban Landscape Transformations and Perceptions at Chunchucmil, Yucatan.* Paper presented at the 101st Annual Meeting of the American Anthropological Association, New Orleans.

McAnany, P.
|1995| *Living with the Ancestors.* University of Texas Press, Austin.

Montessus de Ballore, F.
|1884| *Temblores y Erupciones Volcanicas en Centro-America.* F. Sagrini, San Salvador.
|1888| *Tremblements de terre et éruptions volcaniques au Centre-Amérique depuis la conquête espagnole jusqu'à nos jours.* E. Jobard, Dijon.

Mullarkey, J.
|2000| *Bergson and Philosophy.* University of Notre Dame Press, Notre Dame.

Munn, N.
|1992| The Cultural Anthropology of Time: A Critical Essay. *Annual Review of Anthropology* 21:93–123.

Pocock, D.
|1967| The Anthropology of Time Reckoning. In *Myth and Cosmos*, edited by J. Middleton, pp. 303–314. Natural History Press, New York.

Pred, A.
|1977| The Choreography of Existence: Comments of Hägerstrand's Time-Geography. *Economic Geography* 53: 207–221.

Shanks, M., and C. Tilley
|1987| *Re-Constructing Archaeology.* Cambridge University Press, Cambridge.

Soja, E.
|1996| *Thirdspace: Journeys to Los Angeles and Other Real-and-Imagined Places.* Blackwell, Oxford.

Stanton, T.
|2001| Horizontal Excavations at the Muuch Group. In *Pakbeh Regional Economy Program: Report of the 2001 Season*, edited by B. H. Dahlin, and D. Mazeau, pp. 82–106. Department of Sociology and Anthropology, Howard University, Washington, D.C.

Stanton, T., T. Ardren, and T. Bond
|2000| *Chunchucmil as a Specialized Trade Center in Western Yucatan.* Paper presented at the 65th Annual Meeting of the Society for American Archaeology, Philadelphia.

Tarlow, S.
|1992| Each Slow Dawn a Drawing Down of Blinds. *Archaeological Review from Cambridge* 11:125–140.
Taussig, M.
|1993| *Mimesis and Alterity: A Particular History of the Senses*. Routledge, New York.
Thomas, J.
|1993| The Hermeneutics of Megalithic Space. In *Interpretive Archaeology*, edited by C. Tilley, pp. 73–97. Berg, Providence.
Tilley, C.
|1994| *A Phenomenology of Landscape: Places, Paths and Monuments*. Berg, Oxford.
van der Leeuw, S.
|1994| Cognitive Aspects of "Technique." In *The Ancient Mind: Elements of Cognitive Archaeology*, edited by C. Renfrew and E. B. W. Zubrow, pp. 135–142. Cambridge University Press, Cambridge.
Varela, C.
|1998| *El Clasico Medio en el Noroccidente de Yucatán*. Paris Monographs in American Archaeology No. 2, British Archaeological Reports International Series 739. British Archaeological Reports, Oxford.
Vidal, C.
|1999| *Arte, Arquitectura y Arqueologia en el Grupo Ah Canul de la Ciudad Maya Yucateca de Oxkintok*. British Archaeological Reports International Series 779. British Archaeological Reports, Oxford.
Vlcek, D., S. Garza, and E. Kurjack
|1978| Contemporary Farming and Ancient Maya Settlements: Some Disconcerting Evidence. In *Pre-Hispanic Maya Agriculture*, edited by P. D. Harrison, and B. L. Turner II, pp. 211–223. University of New Mexico Press, Albuquerque.
Whitley, D. (editor)
|2001| *Handbook of Rock-Art Research*. AltaMira, Walnut Creek.

SPECIALIZATION, SOCIAL COMPLEXITY AND VERNACULAR ARCHITECTURE: A CROSS-CULTURAL STUDY OF SPACE CONSTRUCTION

Elizabeth A. Bagwell

Elizabeth Bagwell, Department of Anthropology, University of New Mexico, Albuquerque, New Mexico 87131, U.S.A.

ABSTRACT

The archaeological study of the organization of production has long been understood to provide information about the nature of social hierarchies in prehistoric societies. In particular, the adoption and increasing levels of specialized production have been associated with increasing complexity. Very little is known, however, about the relationship between specialized architectural production – the production of space – and social complexity. Clark and Parry (1990) argue that this relationship is dominated by the amount of time spent in production and variations in relationships between the producer and the consumer. Further, in the specific case of architecture, McGuire and Schiffer (1983) argue that changes in social complexity or social differentiation are associated with changing relationships to three primary activity sets in the built environment – production (including material collection, material preparation and construction), use and maintenance. In this study, a cross-cultural sample of non-industrial societies from the Human Area Relations Files (HRAF), were examined in order to test these two arguments using architectural data. Architectural production has some distinct differences from other kinds of craft production, which suggest that standard assumptions about the relationship between specialized production and social complexity may not apply to this data set. Results suggest that these hypotheses can indeed predict the patterns of spatial production in simple and complex societies, but that middle-range societies show some patterns that need to be explored more fully.

One of the most basic precepts of the study of architecture is that the relationship between humans and the built environment is a reflexive one, where human behaviour influences the organization of built space and built space influences human behaviour (Lawrence and Low 1990; Rapoport 1969). Most archaeologists are interested in studying the second half of this relationship – space that is created by and for human actions. The archaeological study of space takes three main forms. The first kind of spatial study is the exploration of what that space contains. This is the examination of room contents in order to determine activity areas or room function that allows the identification of households, and in turn allows archaeologists to make inferences about the nature of prehistoric social organization (Bawden 1989; Donley-Reid 1990; Flannery 1976; Morgan 1965), and perhaps even level of complexity (Kent 1990). The second kind of spatial study is the examination of the shape of an architectural container. Shape is usually argued to reflect the function of a space (Hunter-Anderson 1977; Wilcox 1975). The third kind of spatial study is the examination of the nature of the connections between spaces and how the built environment functions as a boundary that contains or excludes certain kinds of information. Boundaries have two main functions in this context. First, they physically differentiate space by providing information about the function and/or structure of a space. Second, they provide interpersonal regulation, encouraging and limiting both social and physical contact (Lavin 1981). The studies described above are focused toward understanding what sort of human behaviours took place *in* these spaces.

The first half of this relationship, the human behaviour involved in the *creation* of built space, has rarely been studied by archaeologists. Examining this relationship requires the study of built space as an artifact, to determine among other things, who and by what methods built space was produced. Archaeological

Simple: Groups 0 and 1
Little or no specialized production.
Middle: Groups 1 and 2
Part-time production of utilitarian implements and patronized production.
Complex: Group 3
Full-time production of utilitarian implements and attached production.

Figure 1. Clark and Parry's (1990) levels of complexity.

knowledge of how prehistoric architectural production was organized is still in its most preliminary stages. The following is a presentation of the preliminary results of a cross-cultural study based on the Human Area Relations Files (or HRAF files) undertaken with the hope of finding ethnographic examples to provide models of one part of architectural production – specialization – and how it varies with changes in social complexity. This study attempts to clarify two key issues. First, how did non-industrial architectural specialists organize themselves? Second, were architectural specialists only a part of state-level societies or were they found in less complex societies as well, where some parts of the production process were specialized and others were not? We must understand these relationships in order to determine what the signals of variability in architectural craft production look like in the archaeological record.

In this study, a re-analysis of Clark and Parry's more specific work (1990), a cross-cultural sample of 38 ethnographic reports of non-industrial societies from the Human Area Relations Files (HRAF) were re-examined in order to test two arguments regarding the relationship between craft specialization and social complexity. First, Clark and Parry (1990) suggest that changes in social complexity are reflected by changes in the amount of time spent in production and variations in relationships between the producer and the consumer. Their study included but did not focus on architectural data, and so the original sources were re-examined for this study. Second, McGuire and Schiffer (1983) argue that in the specific case of architecture changes in social complexity are associated with changing relationships to three primary activity sets in the built environment – production (including material collection, material preparation and construction), use and maintenance. The results of my cross-cultural analysis suggest that architectural production has some distinct differences from other kinds of craft production, and therefore standard assumptions about the relationship between specialized production and social complexity may not apply to this data set. Further, this research shows that the arguments tested here can indeed be used to predict the patterns of architectural production in simple and complex societies, but that middle-range societies show some patterns that need to be explored more fully.

CRAFT SPECIALIZATION AND COMPLEXITY

Anthropologists have a long tradition of connecting increasing specialization with increasing social complexity. Boas (1940:285), for example, argues that "a surplus food supply is liable to bring about an increase of population and an increase in leisure, which gives opportunity for occupations that are not absolutely necessary for the needs of everyday life." Ultimately, craft specialization that is permitted by this surplus (or any number of other factors) is associated with the appearance of social differentiation and related attempts to demonstrate power and prestige. As Clark and Parry (1990:290) have noted, "archaeologists commonly rely on the presence of craft specialization to infer aspects of cultural complexity." Architecture has the potential to be useful to archaeologists in this same way if the organization of architectural production is better understood.

For the purposes of this study the definition of complexity used here is limited by the underlying perspectives of the scholars who developed the codes through which the HRAF files organize ethnographic information. While most scholars today are more comfortable with the idea of complexity as a continuum based on a large number of factors, these scholars were in the business of classifying and quantifying everything, including "levels of complexity" which they broke down into the well-known categories – band, tribe, chiefdom and state. Since this study is also a re-analysis of Clark and Parry's original more general work, it is also restricted by their definition of complexity. Therefore complexity is based on five indices originally defined by Murdock and Provost (1973) and Murdock and Wilson (1972). These indices – level of political integration, social stratification, density of population, community size and agricultural dependence – measure complexity based on a five-point scale. Clark and Parry then grouped the sample societies into four general categories or levels of cultural complexity based on a Principal Components Analysis. These same levels, from 0 to 3, were used in this analysis (Figure 1).

This study follows Costin and Hagstrum's (1995:620) definition that views specialization not as a single kind of organization but a "broad concept encompassing several distinctive types of organization." They identify four parameters that can be used to describe these distinctive organizational types. First, the *context* of production involves the "nature of the demand for a particular good," particularly the distinction between specialists who are "attached" to elite patrons and produce at their demand, and "independent" specialists who produce for the generalized subsistence economy. Second, the *concentration* of production involves the spatial distance between the producer and the consumer, and by association has implications for transportation time and cost. The third parameter is the *constitution* of the production unit; in other words the number of people who produce the product and the nature of their social relationships. The fourth parameter, the *intensity* of production, involves the amount of time a producer spends on their craft in comparison to other duties such as agricultural production. Although these parameters are reasonably effective for describing most kinds of specialization, there are some aspects of architectural production that Costin and Hagstrum's system does not account for.

First, architecture is consistently produced by groups rather than individuals. Costin and Hagstrum's (1995) model of the "constitution of the production unit" is not quite capable of dealing with this situation. This parameter assumes that the craft item can be made by an individual and that working in household or factory groups is a sign of increasing specialization. Architectural production at its simplest almost always includes a group, yet this is not an automatic sign of craft specialization. For example, among the Azande the men of the household cut and shape the poles, dig and fix the poles, tie the poles together into walls, thatch the roof and dig the mud for the adobe. The women of the household, on the other hand, cut and carry the thatch grass, carry the water, puddle the mud, and carry the mud to the men making the walls (DeSchlippe 1956:146). No single individual could complete the house without the others.

Level	Intensity	Context
Simple	Non-specialized	Non-specialized
Middle	Part-time	Patronized
Complex	Full-time	Attached

Figure 2. Clark and Parry's (1990) expectations

Second, as a result of group-oriented production, architectural production appears to involve more kinds of specialist activities. Specifically, there is the case of the professional house-building supervisor. In several ethnographies, especially from the Pacific Islands, part-time-specialist house-builders supervise the occupants as they build their own house, only occasionally doing work themselves, such as the difficult fitting or decorative work. Rather than contributing labour, this kind of specialization primarily contributes knowledge in the form of advice and an organizational structure. This kind of division of labour is frequently explained as complexity rather than craft specialization, where researchers have suggested that supervisors are primarily specialized members of an elite hierarchy rather than primarily craft specialists. Ultimately, this research suggests that supervisors can be *both* members of the elite and craft specialists and therefore operate in multiple hierarchies simultaneously.

ETHNOGRAPHIC CASE STUDY – HRAF FILES

My study tests Clark and Parry's (1990) arguments regarding the relationship between specialization and social complexity, and McGuire and Schiffer's (1993) more specific argument regarding changes in social complexity that are associated with changing relationships to three primary activity sets in the built environment – production, maintenance, and use.

Clark and Parry

Clark and Parry (1990) argue that simple societies have little or no specialized production. Middle-range

O – Occupants
FR – Friends
P1 – Part-time work only for elites
P2 – Part-time work for elites and commoners
F1 – Full-time work only for elites
F2 – Full-time work for elites and commoners

Figure 3. Six kinds of production intensity.

societies are associated with part-time production of utilitarian implements and "patronized" production. Specialization in complex, highly stratified states with urban centres and intensive agriculture, on the other hand, has been consistently characterized as involving the full-time production of utilitarian implements and "attached" production. Patronized production is similar to the more commonly discussed "attached" production, except that the producers are not formally in the service of a particular elite and do not produce full-time. This kind of production creates value through the amount of time and effort put into an artifact rather than its material type or amount of decoration (Clark and Parry 1990). These expectations are summarized in Figure 2.

In order to evaluate Clark and Parry's hypothesis I re-used their standard cross-cultural sample of 53 non-industrial societies from the HRAF files. Only 38 societies of Clark and Parry's (1990) sample of 53 had enough information about the production of architecture to be part of this study. Using the four levels of cultural complexity developed by Clark and Parry, I considered Level 0 societies to be simple, Level 1 and 2 societies to be middle range, and Level 3 societies to be complex (Figure 1). These societies were re-examined to see if middle-range societies are indeed characterized by the part-time patronized production of architecture. This re-examination should clarify the usefulness of this model for architectural analyses relating to social complexity.

Results

In my evaluation of Clark and Parry's (1990) expectations for the intensity and context of production, I determined six kinds of production intensity relating to who produced the architecture and their relationship to the occupants of the final product (Figure 3). Full- and part-time work for both elites and commoners were also distinguished by elements of patronized production, i.e., elaboration of an object beyond utilitarian needs but without the "attachment" of the producer to an elite group. This study had mixed results (Figure 4). In simple societies (Level 0), these authors expected non-specialized production. My study supported this expectation, with 1 out of 7 societies sampled with part-time architectural production. Middle-range societies (Levels 1 and 2) were expected to have part-time production, and my results support this hypothesis with 12 of 28 of the societies demonstrating some kind of part-time production. One interesting pattern is that 10 of these 12 had part-time production for both elites and commoners (P2). This result contradicts Clark and Parry's (1990) argument that specialized production for commoners is associated with the most complex societies. Complex societies (Level 3) were expected to have full-time production, and in two of the three cases this sort of production was present. Overall, these results suggest that house building may rarely be a full-time occupation.

My evaluation of the context of production had mixed results as well (Figure 5). Simple societies (Level 0), were expected to have non-specialized production. My results for this level were the same as above: 1 of 7 societies was specialized, and the small sample size suggests this may be a fluke. Middle-range societies (Levels 1–2), were expected to have patronized production. In this case, Levels 1 and 2 showed distinct patterns of their own. Level 1 had 7 of 8 societies with non-specialized production, while Level 2 societies were equally divided between non-specialized and patronized production. This pattern suggests that middle-range architectural production has several distinct patterns which Clark and Parry (1990) did not predict. The complex societies in this sample (Level 3) showed evidence of both attached and patronized production, as expected, but attached house-builders appeared to be rare.

McGuire and Schiffer

McGuire and Schiffer (1983) have argued that in the simplest societies, the built environment is produced, used and maintained by the same people. On the other hand, middle-range societies often have groups who specialize in production while the occupants use

Figure 4. The intensity of production at each level of complexity.

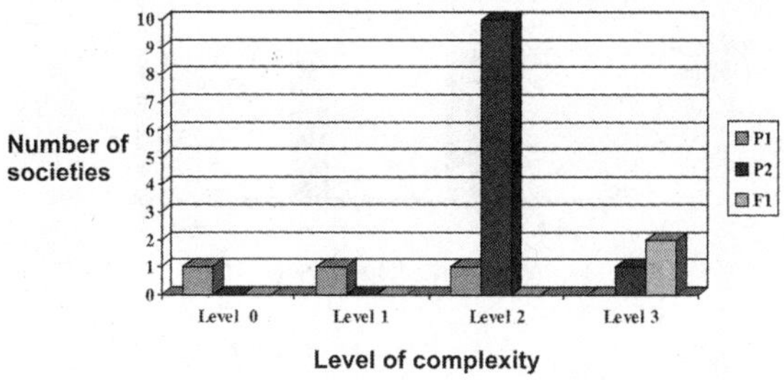

Figure 5. The context of production at each level of complexity.

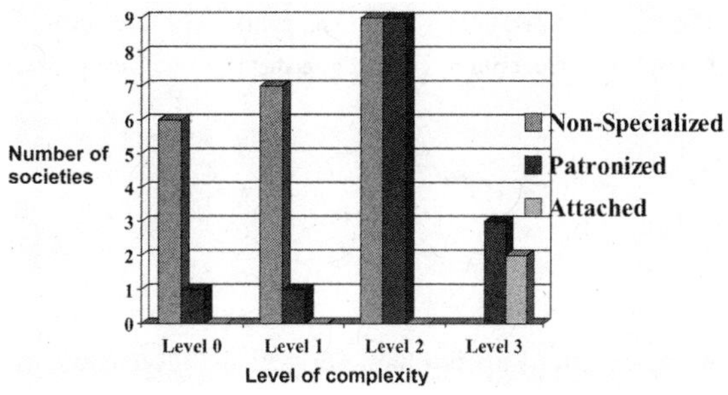

and maintain the structure. In the most complex societies, separate groups specialize in all of these activity sets, often partitioning them into smaller pieces such as design and demolition (Figure 6). Since the production process is very complex, and often the focus of specialization analyses, I further divided the category of "production" into material collection, material preparation and construction.

In order to test McGuire and Schiffer's (1983) expectations, I used the same set of 38 societies and levels of complexity used by Clark and Parry (1990) in their cross-cultural analysis. The 38 HRAF societies were then examined to get a more detailed understanding of the intensity of architectural production in each of the six categories described above (Figure 3). McGuire and Schiffer's (1983) arguments lead me to examine the intensity of production in ways in which Clark and Parry (1990) never considered. Again, the evaluation of this hypothesis will determine if McGuire and Schiffer's ideas are appropriate for examining the relationship between prehistoric architectural production and social complexity.

Results

My study found McGuire and Schiffer's hypothesis to be primarily correct (Figures 7 and 8) . In most simple societies production and maintenance were performed by the occupants. In nearly half (12 of 28) of the middle-range societies, houses were constructed by part-time specialists, while they were used and maintained by the occupants. In the complex societies, full-time specialization in production *and* maintenance was noted in 2 of 3 of the societies. Particularly interesting were the results of my three-part breakdown of production – material procurement, material preparation, and construction. Contrary to a more general argument by Clark and Parry (1990) that the construction of the craft item is the key element of analysis, part-time specialization in material preparation came hand in hand with part-time specialization in construction. Material procurement, however, was largely an unskilled job except in the most complex societies. Finally, maintenance is a promising but difficult-to-uncover data set. The majority of the ethnographies I read did not mention the process of architectural maintenance, possibly because they did not observe any or it was not as dramatic as the construction of a new house. Nevertheless, it was my impression that part-time producers in middle-range societies probably repaired houses as well as built them, especially if the buildings were very large or of ritual importance.

CONCLUSION

In this study I have used a cross-cultural analysis of HRAF file data for 38 societies to get a better understanding of the relationship between specialized architectural production and social complexity. In an attempt to understand how non-industrial architectural specialists organize themselves and how this specialization varies in relation of social complexity, two sets of expectations were tested. First I tested the arguments of Clark and Parry (1990), who suggest that the

Figure 6. McGuire and Schiffer's (1983) expectations.

Level	Production	Maintenance	Use
Simple	Occupants	Occupants	Occupants
Middle	Specialists	Occupants	Occupants
Complex	Specialists	Specialists	Occupants

above relationship is characterized by increasing intensity of production (towards full-time) and changes in the context of production (towards attached specialization) are associated with increasing complexity. Second, McGuire and Schiffer (1983) argue that changes in social complexity are associated with changing relationships to who produces and maintains the built environment – occupants as opposed to specialists. By testing these premises I hoped to determine their suitability for use as models in the interpretation of prehistoric architecture and the social complexity of the societies that built them. The results of this study suggest that overall the architectural data examined matched the patterns predicted by these two sets of expectations. In particular their predictions for the simplest and the most complex societies were supported. Predictions for middle-range architectural production were not nearly as accurate. These problems may also be the result of analyzing the production of a product that is built by large groups rather than individuals. This suggests that archaeologists need to take a closer look at specialized craft production and the categories used to describe this process such as standardization in material composition, size and shape. The research described here implies that for the study of architecture, the examination of attributes related to maintenance may be especially fruitful in future analyses.

Acknowledgments

This research was supported by a Latin American and Iberian Institute Title VI Grant from the University of New Mexico. The insightful comments of Todd VanPool, Christine VanPool, Ana Steffen and Patricia Crown on earlier drafts of this paper are gratefully acknowledged.

Figure 7. Specialization in architectural maintenance.

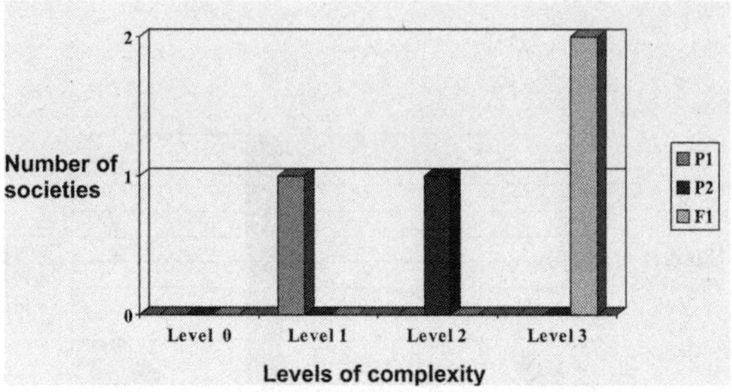

Figure 8. Specialization in production and maintenance

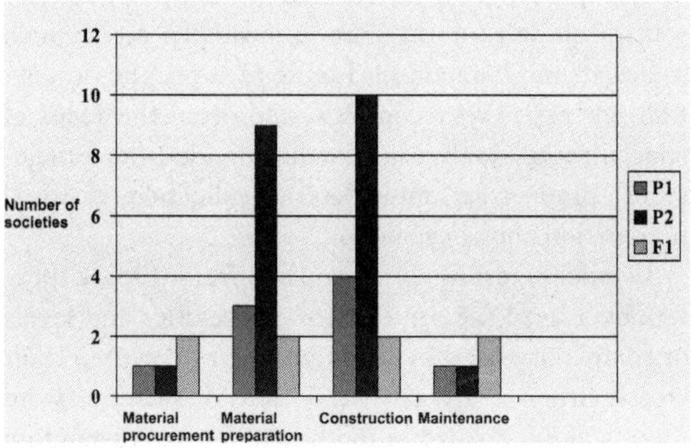

REFERENCES CITED

Bawden, G.
|1989| The Andean State as a State of Mind. *Journal of Anthropological Research* 45:327–333.

Boas, F.
|1940| *Race, Language and Culture.* The Free Press, London.

Clark, J. E., and W. J. Parry
|1990| Craft Specialization and Cultural Complexity. *Research in Economic Anthropology* 12:289–346.

Costin, C. L., and M. B. Hagstrum
|1995| Standardization, Labor Investment, Skill, and the Organization of Ceramic Production in Late Prehispanic Highland Peru. *American Antiquity* 60:619–639.

DeSchlippe, P.
|1956| *Shifting Cultivation in Africa: The Zande System of Agriculture.* Routledge and Kegan Paul, London.

Donley-Reid, L.W.
|1990| A Structuring Structure: The Swahili House. In *Domestic Architecture and the Use of Space,* edited by S. Kent, pp. 114–126. Cambridge University Press, Cambridge.

Flannery, K. V.
|1976| *The Early Mesoamerican Village*. Academic Press, New York.
Hunter-Anderson, R. L.
|1977| A Theoretical Approach to the Study of House Form. In *For Theory Building in Archaeology*, edited by L. R. Binford, pp. 287–315. Academic Press, New York.
Lawrence, D. L., and S. M. Low
|1990| The Built Environment and Spatial Form. *Annual Review of Anthropology* 19:453–505.
Lavin, M. W.
|1980| Boundaries in the Built Environment: Concepts and Examples. *Man-Environment Systems* 11:195–206.
McGuire, R. H., and M. B. Schiffer
|1983| A Theory of Architectural Design. *Journal of Anthropological Archaeology* 2:277–303.
Morgan, L. H.
|1965| *Houses and House-Life of the American Aborigines*. University of Chicago Press, Chicago.
Murdock, G. P., and C. Provost
|1973| Measurement of Cultural Complexity. *Ethnology* 12:379–392.
Murdock, G. P., and S. F. Wilson
|1972| Settlement Patterns and Community Organization: Cross-Cultural Codes 3. *Ethnology* 2:254–295.
Rapoport, A.
|1969| *House Form and Culture*. Prentice Hall, Engelwood Cliffs.
Wilcox, D. R.
|1975| A Strategy for Perceiving Social Groups. *Fieldiana* 65:121–159.

MAYA MORTUARY SPACES AS COSMOLOGICAL METAPHORS

Pamela L. Geller

Pamela L. Geller, American University, Department of Anthropology, Battelle-Tompkins, Room T-21, 4400 Massachusetts Avenue, NW, Washington, D.C. 20016–8003, U.S.A.

ABSTRACT

Precolumbian peoples physically recreated their cosmos on different spatial scales. Grand-scale research treats regional and community settlement patterns; for the Maya, orientation and purposeful layout of architecture served as cosmological simulacra. I argue that at an individual scale, burials from commoner contexts functioned in a similar manner. The Maya imbued landscape features with sacred meaning. Using nature as their template, the Classic Maya designed mortuary settings as metaphorical caves and mountains. As the deceased were buried near or in residences, built spaces replicated cosmological and religious meanings at a mundane level. Research conducted in northwestern Belize supports this argument.

The selection of an appropriate spatial scale is an essential first step in the process of archaeological reconstruction. Investigations that highlight regional interactions direct one's gaze to expansive spaces. Alternatively, scalar designs may be further reduced to consider single sites. Descending in grandeur, but not importance, small scales can treat the spaces encompassed by individual burials. This discussion will integrate different levels of spatial organization – from landscapes to sites to houses to burial spaces to individual bodies – to offer an interpretation of Precolumbian Maya people's emic conception of space.

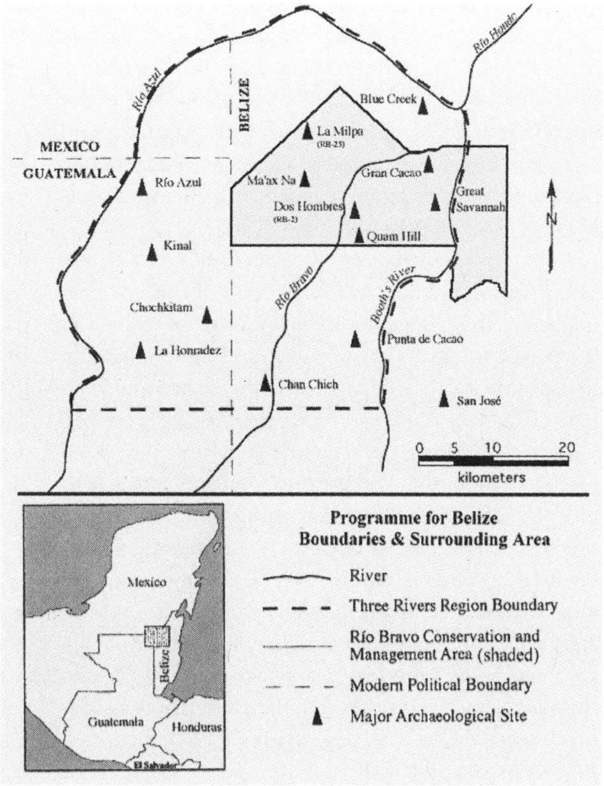

Figure 1. Map illustrating the Rio Bravo Conservation Area's boundaries, which is managed and owned by the Programme for Belize. (Reproduced courtesy Brett Houk)

In this discussion, I will first address Maya sanctification of natural landscapes. In particular, I will consider the way that specific mortuary rituals reflect broader cosmological beliefs associated with caves and mountains. I will do this by discussing burials as built spaces and the ways in which such spaces are structured and given meaning. While scholars have addressed these issues for Maya elite burials, seemingly less sensational commoner burials have received far less attention. Giving prominence to commoner burials, the bulk of the populace, expands our understanding of Maya society. What is important about this research is that it identifies parallels between elite and commoner mortuary phenomena and the messages they convey.

Published literature treating ancestor veneration and sacred landscapes provides key points of reference for my research concerned with bodies and spaces. This rich corpus has expanded understandings of the functional, ritual, and symbolic roles that sacred features, such as caves and mountains, play in Maya society. I also draw on my own investigations of Classic period burials from sites interspersed throughout the 250,000 acres owned and managed by the Programme for Belize, hereafter referred to as PfB.[1] While the boundaries of PfB's conservation area (Figure 1) are a modern creation, this corner of northwestern Belize represents a sizeable subregion in which the Classic Maya conducted their lives (and deaths).

Karen Bassie-Sweet (1996:3) identifies cosmology as "explain[ing] not only the creation of the universe but the birth of humankind, the ordering of the world, the place of humans in that order, and their obligation to maintain it." I would argue that the design and location of mortuary spaces and treatment of decedents' bodies, in addition to signaling practical and ritual concerns about dying and death, reaffirm Maya peoples' beliefs about and place within their world. In this discussion, I stress that closer consideration of architectural, material and osteological dimensions reveals information about individuals' interactions with and conceptions of their natural environments, sacred landscapes and built features. Cross-culturally, societies have conceived of their domestic settings as replications of the cosmos (e.g., Blanton 1994; Bourdieu 1973; Griaule 1965; Kus 1997; Yates 1989). The Precolumbian Maya are no exception. An examination of Maya burials associated with residential settings argues for smaller-scale recreation of pervasive natural features and replication of these features' sacred overtones. The Maya ritually and physically reproduced elements of their cosmos in mundane settings. Such an analysis highlights the often underexplored symbolic and social dimensions of Maya burials.

NATURAL SPACES MADE SACRED

For Precolumbian peoples, intimate and enduring interactions with the land have produced the sanctification of certain natural elements. Sanctified, natural spaces, such as caves and mountains, play a significant role in structuring cultural practices and beliefs throughout the Precolumbian world (e.g., Benson 1981; Brady and Ashmore 1999; Carrasco 1991; Kolata 1996; Soafer 1997). In Mesoamerica, caves serve as the location for creation, purification, and cessation of human lives. The connection between ritually charged activities and sacred spaces is an enduring and pan-Mesoamerican one designed to maintain world orders (Heyden 1981).

A variety of ethnographic, iconographic and archaeological sources highlight the sacred meanings that the Maya have attached to natural spaces. Scholars (e.g., Brady and Ashmore 1999) have demonstrated that the landscape triad of caves, mountains, and bodies of water represent sacred elements of the Maya cosmos. As components of the quadripartite system, caves and mountains emblematize *axes mundi* (Ashmore 1991; Brady and Ashmore 1999; Coggins 1980). Fraught with liminal connotations, *axes mundi* mediate between past and present, natural and supernatural arenas. Thus, these sacred spaces are ideal areas for situating and transforming ambiguous elements of society, such as dead bodies. Mountains – and caves within them[2] – facilitate transformation from a socially liminal decedent to a socially viable ancestor, thereby functioning as powerful venues for rites of passage (Stone 1997; Vogt 1970:5–6).

It is important to digress for a moment to define what I mean by a "cave," since the formal geological understanding of caves does not fit with an emic conception of these features. Caves, for the Maya, comprise a number of topographical features. In his ethnographic case study of highland Chiapas, Vogt (1981:120, 126) translates the Tzotzil word *ch'en* not only as "cave" but also as "a limestone sink…a waterhole, a spring, or a ravine" and a "hole in the ground." An understanding of the cave as an unassuming "hole in the ground" is underlined, since most Maya commoner burials fit such a description; this idea will be revisited later in the paper.

Mesoamerican societies have long linked caves and mountains with death and bodies. Fortunately, preservation in cavernous environs is excellent, and much information can be gleaned from the excavation of burials in these settings. Archaeological evidence suggestive of elaborate mortuary ritual and body processing from the Tehuacán Valley's Coxcatlán Cave dates to approximately 5000 B.C. (MacNeish et al. 1972:266–270). For the Maya, natural caves, ubiquitous in the karstic Yucatan Peninsula, served as ready-made and final resting places as early as the Middle Preclassic (ca. 900–400 B.C.) (e.g., Cueva del Rio Taluga[3] [Brady 1997]; Copán [Brady 1995]; Cuyamel Caves [Healy 1974]). Rockshelters containing ceramic vessels dating to the Classic period have also been identified within the PfB conservation area; however, these features have yet to be fully explored for evidence of skeletal materials and formal mortuary practices (Sagebiel, personal communication 2000). Future investigations might prove fruitful in establishing these spaces as ossuaries. As confirmed by ethnohistoric and ethnographic literatures, religious and ritual cave use evocative of ancestor veneration survived the Conquest and continues into contemporary times (e.g., Vogt 1970; Wagley 1949).

BUILT SPACES AND SACRED TEMPLATES

In Mesoamerica, native peoples' built spaces were often designed to reproduce sacred landscape features in structure and meaning. As evidenced by monumental architecture, a considerable amount of effort was expended to create elaborate and visually prominent edifices. At the Olmec center of La Venta, the 30-m-high, artificially constructed pyramid typifies a mountain-like structure, in spite of its resemblance to a bakery good. At Teotihuacan, the imposing Pyramid of the Sun, framed by the surrounding mountains, and the artificially constructed cave beneath it emphasize the importance of architecturally replicating natural features in ceremonial and political arenas (Heyden 1981).

Specific royal cases of this architectural replication can be found at several Maya centers, just two of which will be detailed in this discussion. The site of Copán in northwestern Honduras offers a royal example of architectural duplication. Natural caves are located within the southern section of the site's core (Brady 1995). It is possible that these geological formations were used as a template in the design of the dynastic founder's tomb, whose death, or burial, dates to A.D. 437. Yax Kuk Mo's final resting place is located deep within and beneath a series of monumental buildings; an argument can be made for this burial space as emblematic of a metaphoric cave internalized within a metaphoric mountain.

Monumental architecture and iconography from the Chiapas highland site of Palenque testify to replication of sacred spaces (Brady and Ashmore 1999). Situated atop bedrock, Pacal's tomb is located at the bottom of the Temple of the Inscriptions, which was constructed in a single building episode following the ruler's death in A.D. 683. As evidenced by iconography on his sarcophagus lid, Pacal's descent into the mouth of the Earth Monster, a metaphoric cave opening, indicates the ruler's entrance into the Underworld (Bassie-Sweet 1996). Elsewhere, Ashmore and I (2001) have argued that by mirroring the alignment of the World Tree displayed on his sarcophagus lid, Pacal's body position – extended with head to north and feet to south – embodies this symbol's complex meanings and fortifies his dynasty's authority and longevity.

Mayanists' fascination with elite burials and related monumental architecture, what Coe (1988:235) refers to as "house-sepulchers writ large," has provided a valuable contribution to investigators' understanding of Maya society. Burials within the PfB conservation area have been excavated at urban sites, such as La Milpa and Dos Hombres, as well as rural, agricultural groups interspersed between these large centers; the sample, therefore, represents a cross-section of society with regard to sex, age, status and occupation. Burials excavated from commoners' residential spaces, as opposed to elites' tombs housed within temple-pyramids, are highlighted in this discussion.

Though the case might not be so pronounced in contemporary Western society, Pre- and Postcolumbian houses serve as arenas for major lifecycle events – births, initiation rites, marriages and deaths. Wagley's (1949:23; see also Vogt 1970:62) ethnography about Chimaltenango, a highland Guatemalan community, details the contemporary Maya practice of burying afterbirths underneath the floors of patios and sweathouses, which are ancillary, residential structures. Despite Chimalteco syncretism of indigenous and Christian religions, such evidence may point to

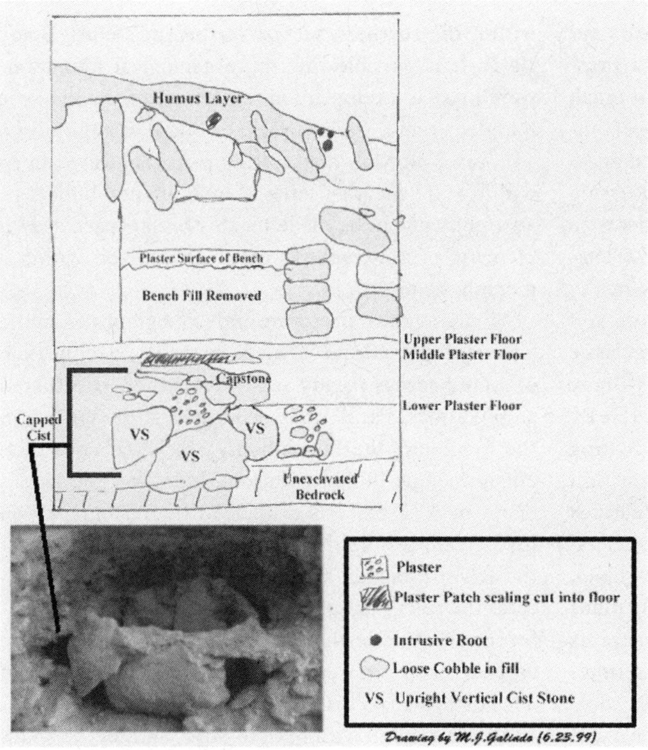

Figure 2. Cist burial from a site located within the *bajo* periphery of La Milpa. This burial was interred beneath a bench within a structure's room. The cist contained a tightly flexed body placed on the individual's left side. The decedent's head was placed to the south and the pelvis to the north. In this photograph, the capstone had been removed to access the interred burial and does not appear in the photograph. (Photograph by author, 2000; drawing by M. J. Galindo 1999)

a certain degree of continuity in the structuring and meaning of Precolumbian lifecycle activities. The binary opposition of death and life (or birth) is not as evident in Maya society as it is in our own Western one. Biological death does not necessitate social death (Hallam et al. 1999); ancestor veneration testifies to social life despite biological death. As rites of passage, per van Gennep, mortuary rituals initiate the decedent's transformation, allowing the individual to be reborn as an ancestor. For the Maya, McAnany (1995, 1998) has recognized that as ancestors the dead maintained an active presence for the living, especially in regard to the legitimation and maintenance of a lineage's resource rights. This notion is reinforced by the physical nearness of decedents' bodies. No formal cemeteries dating to the Classic period have been found in the Maya area. Instead, residential structures often served as the final resting places for a family's deceased kin, rather than the monumental temples of ruling groups. The sixteenth-century Friar Diego de Landa recounts,

> They were buried inside of their own houses, or at the back of them... Usually they deserted the house and left it abandoned after the burial, except when there were many people living there, in whose company they lost some of the fear which the death had caused them [Pagden 1975:93–94].

Interment of the dead beneath house floors emphasizes the intimate connection and enduring dialogue between the biologically dead/socially alive and living family members.[4] In light of Maya peoples' conception of the fluid boundary between life and death, Precolumbian interment of decedents' bodies underneath domestic structures perhaps represents a variation on an enduring burial theme pertaining to lifecycle events.

Aside from political and socioeconomic factors, what else contributed to the placement and significance of Precolumbian Maya commoners' burials? And, what sets ancestral transformation in motion? These questions are not mutually exclusive. Scholars have cross-culturally argued that houses and their internal ordering represent and reproduce the cosmos (e.g., Blanton 1994; Bourdieu 1973; Griaule 1965; Kus 1997; Yates 1989). For the Maya, houses are constructed by referencing the spatial and directional symbols in quadrilateral frameworks (Bassie-Sweet 1996:4; Vogt 1970). As built spaces, these architectural features physically expressed cosmological concepts, such as the quadrilateral world model, and mythological narratives, as well as reinforced ideological structures (for an example of this on a larger scale see Ashmore 1989, 1991, 1992; Coggins 1980; Houk 1996).

Heyden's (1981) discussion of Aztec funerary practices provides great insight into a Maya case study and supports the notion that certain aspects of mortuary rituals represent larger Mesoamerican patterns. According to Heyden (1981:22),

> mummy bundles placed in the mouth of the earth often represent cave burials... A burial under the floor of a house must have had the same significance. The ancient custom of placing skeletal remains [especially a fetus] or the aches of a person in a jar, which was then buried, can be interpreted as a return to the womb; the jar could symbolize the cave as well as the uterus. This is an artificial cave, as a box is, or a chamber in the interior of a pyramid.

Drawing on my earlier discussion of the relationship between sacred spaces and ancestors, I contend that for the Maya in specific, though not all instances: 1) houses for non-ruling peoples, similar to royal temples, replicated sacred mountains in structure and meaning; 2) burial spaces – comprised of graves, architectural features and bedrock modifications – artificially reproduced caves; and 3) commoners' bodies – their processing, position, alignment and associated goods – communicated symbolic information, practical concerns and social roles, much as their elite counterparts did. Construction of mortuary spaces and processing of decedents' bodies facilitated the rebirth of ancestors. Burial evidence from PfB substantiates this argument.

For the purposes of this discussion, the term burial refers to unproblematic "primary interments," which Becker (1992) identifies as interments in small, residential structures. Secondary, or intentionally disarticulated, deposits, which comprise a smaller portion of the PfB sample, also speak of the importance of skeletal partibility in conducting rituals related to ancestor veneration (Becker 1992; McAnany 1995). Multiple PfB sites contain evidence of commoner burials placed underneath households' floors or near residential architecture. Careful reconstruction of building phases often ascertains continuing habitation of these structures following interment of the decedent's body; a similar phenomenon has been documented at Tikal (Becker 1992; Haviland 1981; Haviland et al. 1985). In fact, several structures in house groups contain multiple interments of presumed family members capped by subsequent construction episodes. For instance, Structure 11 at the small Maya community of Dos

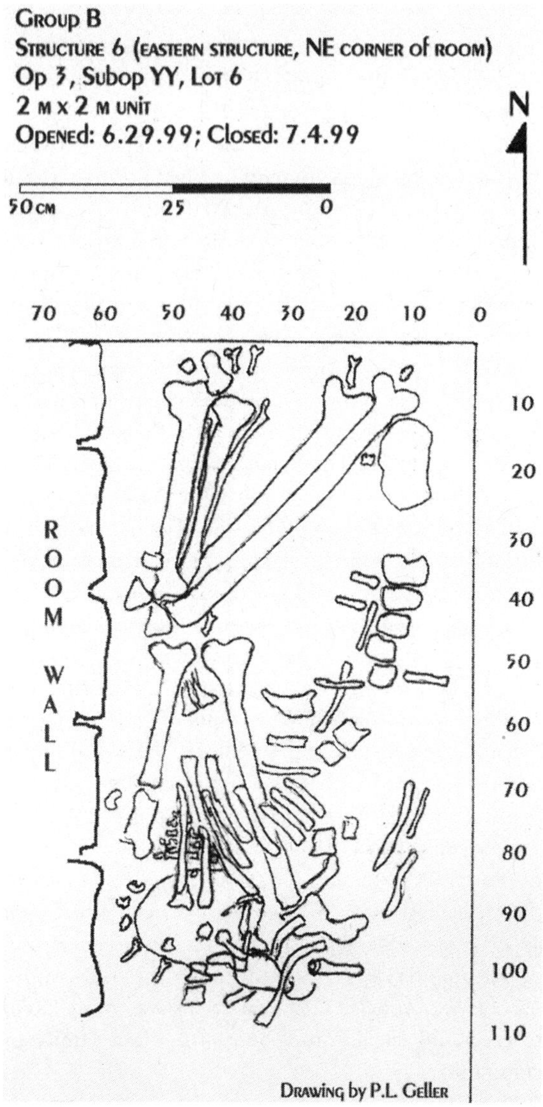

Figure 3. Drawing of a tightly flexed burial at Dos Barbaras; skull is pointing towards the south, feet are towards the north, and body is lying on its left side. (Drawing by author, 2004)

Barbaras[5] within PfB's boundaries contained at least eight separate interments of decedents' bodies.

Grave types found within PfB's domestic structures take two forms – those that precede and provide a catalyst for building episodes and those that are intrusive to construction phases. Cists and burials that are intermixed with construction fill constitute the former type (Figure 2). Cists are roughly hewed from limestone slabs; these slabs are irregular in shape and were placed standing on their long axis. An additional irregular limestone slab often capped these grave types. In some cists, the spaces in between stones were filled in with mortar. The bottom of these cists contained a loosely packed layer of soft marl. The formal demarcation of these burial spaces suggests that they were constructed prior to subsequent building episodes. The second, and more prevalent, grave type is an unassuming hole in the ground, or informal hole punched into the plaster or earth-packed floors of house. These occur even when bedrock is less than 10 cm beneath the plaster floor; often this type of burial is accompanied by bedrock modification. Fill in direct association with skeletal remains is distinguishable from fill outside of the burial space. Both cists and informal holes are oval shaped, measuring approximately 50 ±10 cm from east to west and 70 ±10 cm from north to south. Often concomitant with the latter grave types are evidence of re-plastering events, which not only seal the hole, but also often function to resurface floors. Adults of both sexes are placed in these grave types; children are never found within these spaces.[6] Rather, children nine years of age and younger, a rather small percentage of the PfB sample (less than 15 per cent), were usually found interred within structures' walls or floors, as if part of the construction fill. Though highly speculative, such an occurrence perhaps speaks to a Maya conception of personhood, regardless of whether the deaths were natural or sacrificial; ancestral status was most likely reserved for specific members of a Maya family or community.

Atop floors' resurfacing episodes, PfB investigators have unearthed plastered benches comprised of cobble fill. Burials have also been located within benches at PfB sites. Benches are unique architectural features as they served as spaces for both ordinary and extraordinary activities. Deal's (1987) ethnoarchaeological study of Maya highland peoples considers the ritual aspects of household altars; household altars are conceived of as spaces for appeasing, petitioning and venerating ancestors. These altars were constructed of perishable wood and stone masonry, and often take the form of tables or benches positioned against the back wall of domestic structures (see also Thompson and Thompson 1955). In light of burials' stratigraphic locations beneath and within these benches, I would argue that benches from PfB sites functioned as spaces for ritual performances such as bloodletting, divination and ancestral communication, as well as the more quotidian activities of sleeping and food preparation.

Detection of the intentional positioning of whole bodies within burial spaces augments our understanding of ancestor veneration's material reflections. There is ubiquitous evidence for tightly flexed positioning of decedents' bodies at PfB's commoner sites (Figure 3). The seasonally wet and humid Maya lowlands dramatically accelerate corpse decomposition (rigor mortis, algor mortis, livor mortis and blotation) and insect infestation[7] (Goff 2001). Therefore, this position requires immediate bundling as a result of environmental factors. Brady (1988) has argued that interment in natural caves engenders a return to the womb, a rebirth of sorts located in the sphere of the dead. Placing an individual tightly bundled, reminiscent of the fetal position, in the metaphoric cave of the burial space reinforces the decedent's rebirth as an ancestor. The majority of bodies were placed in a north-south alignment, though as far as placement of the head to either the north or south, no consistency has been observed. The connection between body alignments at PfB and symbolically important cardinal directions remains unclear (Figure 3).

CONCLUSION

Architectural and mortuary evidence from the Programme for Belize suggests that the Classic Maya referenced sacred spaces as templates in their designing of elite and commoner mortuary contexts. By creating metaphoric mountains and caves, artificial constructions were meant to convey similar cosmological and religious messages as their geological counterparts. Likewise, consideration of mortuary contexts as metaphoric caves and mountains emphasizes the role that these spaces had in transforming decedents' bodies to ancestors. The selection of residential settings as final resting places for commoners facilitated ancestral processing and rituals, sustained familial rhythms, and reinforced long-standing cosmological beliefs in a manner similar to that of elite decedents, their tombs, and funerary temples. Continuing habitation of residential structures suggest an ongoing dialogue between living family members and their ancestors. Analysis of the PfB sample has established a base for comparison, so that future investigations of commoner burials may isolate larger Maya and Mesoamerican patterns related to the structure and meaning of burial spaces. It is important that future excavations and analyses of commoner burials simultaneously consider bodies, their associations and their architectural contexts. While more research on commoner burials throughout the Maya area is needed, the physical expression of a world view at any level of society underscores the shared cultural affiliation of lowland Maya peoples.

ACKNOWLEDGMENTS

In the Programme for Belize, I am grateful to Fred Valdez, Brandon Lewis, Julie Saul and Frank Saul who have offered invaluable encouragement and guidance for my ongoing research. Much gratitude to Clark Erickson, Wendy Ashmore and Miranda Stockett for their comments on earlier versions of this draft. I would also like to thank Kathryn Reese-Taylor for her initial suggestion that I present at the 2001 Chacmool Conference and the editors of this volume for all of their hard work seeing it through to publication.

REFERENCES CITED

Ashmore, W.
|1989| Construction and Cosmology: Politics and Ideology in Lowland Maya Settlement Patterns. In *Word and Image in Maya Culture: Explorations in Language, Writing, and Presentation*, edited by W. F. Hanks, and D. S. Rice, pp. 272–286. University of Utah Press, Salt Lake City.
|1991| Site Planning Principles and Concepts of Directionality among the Ancient Maya. *Latin American Antiquity* 2:199–226.
|1992| Deciphering Maya Architectural Plans. In *Theories on the Ancient Maya*, edited by E. C. Danien, and R. J. Sharer, pp. 173–184. University Museum Monograph 77. The University Museum, Philadelphia.

Ashmore, W., and P. L. Geller
|2001| Social Dimensions of Mortuary Space. Paper presented at the 66th Annual Meeting of the Society for American Archaeology, New Orleans.

Bassie-Sweet, K.
|1996| *At the Edge of the World: Caves and Late Classic Maya World View*. University of Oklahoma Press, Norman, Oklahoma.

Becker, M. J.
|1992| Burials as Caches, Caches as Burials: A New Interpretation of the Meaning of Ritual Deposits among the Classic Period Lowland Maya. In *New Theories on the Ancient Maya*, edited by E. C. Danien, and R. J. Sharer, pp. 185–196. University Museum, University of Pennsylvania, Philadelphia.

Benson, E. P. (editor)
|1981| *Mesoamerican Sites and Worldviews*. Dumbarton Oaks Research Library and Collections, Washington, D.C.

Blanton, R.
|1994| *Houses and Households: A Comparative Study*. Plenum Press, New York.

Bourdieu, P.
|1973| The Berber House. In *Rules and Meanings: The Anthropology of Everyday Knowledge*, edited by M. Douglas, pp. 98–110. Penguin Education, Harmondsworth, England.

Brady, J. E.
|1988| The Sexual Connotation of Caves in Mesoamerican Ideology. *Mexicon* 10(3):51.
|1995| A Reassessment of the Chronology and Function of Gordon's Cave #3, Copán, Honduras. *Ancient Mesoamerica* 6:29–38.
|1997| Places of the Dead: Glimpses of the Afterlife from a Middle Preclassic Cave Ossuary. In *Proceedings of the 1995 and 1996 Latin American Symposia*, edited by A. Cordy-Collins, and G. Johnson, pp. 21–32. San Diego Museum of Man, San Diego.

Brady, J. E., and W. Ashmore
|1999| Mountains, Caves, Water: Ideational Landscapes of the Ancient Maya. In *Archaeologies of Landscape: Contemporary Perspectives*, edited by W. Ashmore, and A.B. Knapp, pp. 124–145. Blackwell Publishers, Malden, Massachusetts.

Butler, J.
|1990| *Gender Trouble: Feminism and the Subversion of Identity*. Routledge, New York.
|1993| *Bodies that Matter: On the Discursive Limits of "Sex."* Routledge, New York.

Carrasco, D. (editor)
|1991| *To Change Place: Aztec Ceremonial Landscapes*. University of Colorado Press, Boulder.

Chase, D. Z., and A. F. Chase
|1998| The Architectural Context of Caches, Burials, and Other Ritual Activities for the Classic Period Maya (as Reflected at Caracol, Belize). In *Function and Meaning in Classic Maya Architecture*, edited by S. Houston, pp. 299–332. Dumbarton Oaks Research Library and Collections, Washington, D.C.

Coe, M. D.
|1988| Ideology of the Maya Tomb. In *Maya Iconography*, edited by E. P. Benson and G. G. Griffen, pp. 222–235. Princeton University Press, Princeton.

Coggins, C.
|1980| The Shape of Time: Some Political Implications of a Four-Part Figure. *American Antiquity* 45:727–739.

Deal, M.
|1987| Ritual Space and Architecture in the Highland Maya Household. In *Mirror and Metaphor: Material and Social Constructions of Reality*, edited by D.W. Ingersoll, Jr., and G. Bronitsky, pp. 171–198. University Press of America, Lanham, Maryland.

Goff, A.
|2001| Body Decomposition: An Influencing Factor on Ancient Maya Burials. Unpublished undergraduate senior thesis, Department of Anthropology, University of California, Los Angeles.

Griaule, M.
|1965| *Conversations with Ogotemmêli: An Introduction to Dogon Religious Ideas*. Oxford University Press, London.

Hallam, E., J. Hockey, and G. Howarth
|1999| *Beyond the Body: Death and Social Identity*. Routledge, London.

Haviland, W.
|1981| Dower Houses and Minor Centers at Tikal, Guatemala: An Investigation into the Identification of Valid Units in Settlement Hierarchies. In *Lowland Maya Settlement Patterns*, edited by W. Ashmore, pp. 89–117. University of New Mexico Press, Albuquerque.

Haviland, W. A., M. J. Becker, A. Chowning, K. A. Dixon, and K. Heider
|1985| *Excavations in Small Residential Groups of Tikal: Groups 4F-1 and 4F-2*. Tikal Report No. 19. The University Museum Monograph 58. The University Museum, Philadelphia.

Healy, P.
|1974| The Cuyamel Caves: Preclassic Sites in Northeast Honduras. *American Antiquity* 39:435–447.

Heyden, D.
|1981| Caves, Gods, and Myths: World-View and Planning in Teotihuacan. In *Mesoamerican Sites and World-Views*, edited by E. P. Benson, pp. 1–40. Dumbarton Oaks Research Library and Collections, Washington, D.C.

Houk, B.
|1996| The Archaeology of Site Planning: An Example from the Maya Site of Dos Hombres. Unpublished Ph.D. dissertation, Department of Anthropology, The University of Texas, Austin.

Kolata, A.
|1996| *Valley of the Spirits: A Journey into the Lost Realm of the Aymara*. John Wiley & Sons, New York.

Kus, S.
|1997| Archaeologist as Anthropologist: Much Ado about Something after All? *Journal of Archaeological Method and Theory* 4(3/4):199–213.

Laqueur, T.
|1990| *Making Sex: Body and Gender from the Greeks to Freud*. Harvard University Press, Cambridge, Massachusetts.

MacNeish, R. S., M. L. Fowler, A. García Cook, F. A. Peterson, A. Nelken-Terner, and J. A. Neely
|1972| *The Prehistory of the Tehuacán Valley*, Vol. 5: *Excavations and Reconnaissance*. University of Texas Press, Austin.

McAnany, P.
|1995| *Living with the Ancestors*. University of Texas Press, Austin.
|1998| Ancestors and the Classic Maya Built Environment. In *Form and Meaning in Classic Maya Architecture*, edited by S. Houston, pp. 271–298. Dumbarton Oaks Research Library and Collection, Washington, D.C.

Pagden, A. R.
|1975| *The Maya: Diego de Landa's Account of the Affairs of Yucatan*. J. Philips O'Hara, Chicago.

Saul, F.P., and J.M. Saul
|1991| The Preclassic Population of Cuello. In *Cuello: An Early Maya Community in Belize*, edited by N. Hammond, pp. 134–158. Cambridge University Press, Cambridge.

Sofaer, A.
|1997| The Primary Architecture of the Chacoan Culture: A Cosmological Expression. In *Anasazi Architecture and American Design*, edited by B.H. Morrow and V.B. Price, pp. 88–132. University of New Mexico Press, Albuquerque.

Stone, A.
|1997| Precolumbian Cave Utilization in the Maya Area. In *The Human Use of Caves*, edited by C. Bonsall and C. Tolan-Smith, pp. 201–206. British Archaeological Reports International Series 667. British Archaeological Reports, Oxford.

Stuart, D.
|1987| *Ten Phonetic Syllables*. Research Reports on Ancient Maya Writing 14. Center for Maya Research, Washington, D.C.

Thompson, D. E., and J. E. S. Thompson
|1955| A Noble's Residence and its Dependencies at Mayapan. *Carnegie Institution of Washington, Current Reports* 2(25):225–251.

Vogt, E. Z.
|1970| *The Zinacantecos of Mexico: A Modern Maya Way of Life*. Case Studies in Cultural Anthropology. Holt, Rinehart and Winston, New York.
|1981| Some Aspects of Sacred Geography of Highland Chiapas. In *Mesoamerican Sites and World Views*, edited by E. P. Benson, pp. 119–142. Dumbarton Oaks Research Library and Collections, Washington, D.C.

Wagley, C.
|1949| *The Social and Religious Life of a Guatemalan Village*. Memoirs of the American Anthropological Association, no. 71. American Anthropological Association, Menasha, Wisconsin.

Yates, T.
|1989| Habitus and Social Space: Some Suggestions about Meaning in the Saami (Lapp) Tent ca. 1700–1900. In *The Meaning of Things: Material Culture and Symbolic Expression*, edited by I. Hodder, pp. 249–260. Unwin Hyman, London.

NOTES

1 Fieldwork was conducted under the aegis of Fred Valdez, Jr., Director of the Programme for Belize Archaeological Project (PfBAP). Frank and Julie Saul conducted and trained me in analysis of PfB's

skeletal sample. The burial sample from PfB contains roughly 100 individuals. The majority of these date to the Late and Terminal Classic periods; burials dating to the Late Preclassic comprise a small portion of the overall sample.

2 In Mesoamerica, native peoples believe that mountains possess internal caves even in the absence of a visible opening (Bassie-Sweet 1996; Vogt 1981).

3 The cultural affiliation of the interred individuals is in question. Brady and his colleagues (1995, 1997) assert that the deceased are ethnically non-Maya. The cave's location in northeastern Honduras places the site out of the Maya cultural sphere, though such evidence points to the general Mesoamerican pattern of associating sacred landscapes, cosmology and mortuary rituals.

4 Continuing interaction with royal decedents occurs throughout the Maya area, as well. At Caracol in western Belize, Diane and Arlen Chase (1998) have detailed the repeated re-entry of several tombs housed within pyramidal structures. Such evidence reinforces these decedents' active social roles.

5 As a small center, Dos Barbaras is comprise of between five and six courtyards, containing anywhere from two to eight structures. Dr. Brandon Lewis has conducted ongoing research at Dos Barbaras, which includes mapping and intensive excavations, since 1992.

6 Saul and Saul (1991) have subdivided adults' ages into five phases, young adult (20–34 years), young/middle adult (30–40 years), middle adult (35–54 years), middle/old adult (45–55 years), and old adult (55+ years); subadult age cohorts range from birth to 4 years; 5 to 9 years; 10 to 14 years; and 15 to 19 years. However, it is important to remember that these age ranges are convenient diagnostic tools created and deployed by investigators. It is quite possible that such age cohorts bear no resemblance to Maya designations and experiences of lifecycle events. Constructions or understandings of childhood or adulthood are historically and culturally contingent. The same can be said for categorizations of sex; recent theorizing highlights gender *and* sex as socioculturally constructed (e.g., Butler 1990, 1993; Laqueur 1990).

7 By experimenting on immature pigs, Goff (2001) has found that full skeletonization of unburied corpses occurs within two weeks in the Maya lowlands.

PART II: INTRASITE SPATIAL ANALYSIS

THE BEHAVIOURAL ECOLOGY OF EARLY PLEISTOCENE HOMINIDS IN THE KOOBI FORA REGION, EAST TURKANA BASIN, NORTHERN KENYA

S. M. Cachel and J. W. K. Harris

S. M. Cachel, Department of Anthropology, Rutgers University, New Brunswick, New Jersey 08901–1414, U.S.A.

J. W. K. Harris, Department of Anthropology, Rutgers University, New Brunswick, New Jersey 08901–1414, U.S.A.

ABSTRACT

The geological context and distribution of stone artifacts and/or hominid modified bone across ancient landscapes provide means for reconstructing early hominid foraging and ranging behaviour. We discuss the distribution of archaeological sites from previous research, along with two new bone modification sites east of Lake Turkana, in the Koobi Fora region of northern Kenya. The sites are in Okote Member deposits (1.64–1.39 mya) in the Koobi Fora Formation. These sites are FwJj 14 in Collecting Area 1A at Ileret and GaJi 14 in Area 103 at the Koobi Fora Ridge. These sites are separated by about 40 km. It is possible that the new sites were located in areas that were being newly exploited by hominids. Hominids may have been foraging not only for food, but also for critical lithic resources. Zones of exploitation within the ancient landscape must have included areas where prospecting for lithic resources could take place. This evidence therefore implies complex foraging for dispersed resources.

Living hunter-gatherers are dependent upon the natural distribution of resources in their environment. These modern humans are characterized by mobility, specialized foraging groups, transport and sharing of resources, the ability to predict the localized abundance and depletion of resources, and hoarding of seasonally scarce resources like food and fuel for future consumption (Winterhalder 2001). These behaviours epitomize the behavioural ecology of modern humans; they can be considered species-specific. Hence, the nature of the very first traces of human interaction with the landscape has implications for fundamental ideas about human origins, such as the evolution of human social structure, activity patterns, resource acquisition, and intelligence. These ideas can be tested by paleoanthropologists using the Plio-Pleistocene archaeological record.

Potts (1994) discusses four major concepts about Plio-Pleistocene land use. Central place foraging is Isaac's (1978) revision of the home base model that he originally developed and then discarded. In central place foraging, researchers do not assume complex sociality among Plio-Pleistocene hominids, which was implicit when a home base was treated as analogous to a campsite maintained by modern hunter-gatherers. In central place foraging, there is a core area on the landscape (a "central place") to which hominids regularly return because of special local resources. They transport food or other resources (e.g., wood, lithics) to the central place. Food sharing may occur here. In routed foraging (Binford 1984), a social group traverses a landscape with no set plan. Resources are foraged for whenever the group encounters them, and resources are accessed in the same proportion that they are encountered in the landscape. Particular resources are not deliberately sought and collected in higher proportions than they would naturally occur within a particular habitat, and these resources are not hoarded. The riverine woodland scavenging model argues that Plio-Pleistocene hominids searched in dense woodland that fringed rivers as they scavenged for carcasses abandoned by large carnivores. In the multiple place foraging model, Plio-Pleistocene hominids are foraging at several centers on the landscape, but their activities are tethered to certain areas (stone caches) where the hominids have previously transported and collected crucial lithic raw materials (Potts 1994). In this paper, we will assess two of these models: central place foraging and routed foraging.

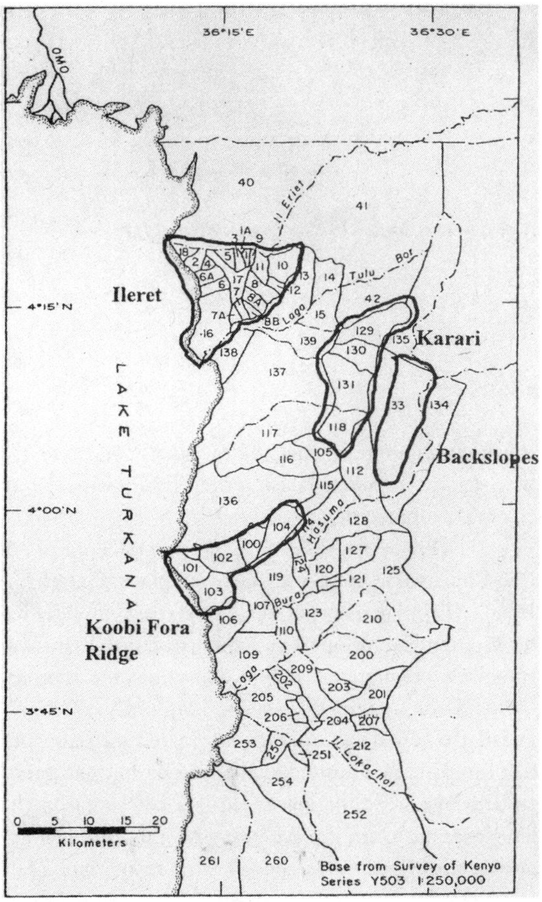

Figure 1. Location of the new Okote Member sites within the paleontological collecting areas of the Koobi Fora region, from Rogers (1997: Figure 2.3). The collecting areas are formally numbered, and their boundaries are indicated on the map. FwJj 14 is in area 1A at Ileret; GaJi 14 is in area 103 at the Koobi Fora Ridge. The sites are separated by about 40 km.

One of the major concerns of Plio-Pleistocene paleoanthropological research is to document early hominid ranging and foraging behaviour from archaeological traces. The Koobi Fora region, in northern Kenya, contains a record of such behaviour in sediments that are discontinuously preserved in the eastern part of the Turkana Basin. Members of the Koobi Fora Formation are defined by tuffs at the base of the member; these tuffs indicate a time span of 4.35–0.6 mya for the sequence. This stratigraphic sequence is well studied. It is unequivocally correlated by the sequence of unique volcanic tuffs (tephrostratigraphy) to sediments in the western half of the Turkana Basin, to the lower Omo Basin sediments in southern Ethiopia, and to deep-sea core sediments off the African and Arabian coasts (Brown 1995). The Okote Member of the Koobi Fora Formation dates from 1.64–1.39 mya, and preserves both paleontological and archaeological records of Plio-Pleistocene hominids. Here we report on two new bone modification sites in Okote Member deposits. These sites are FwJj 14 in Paleontological Collecting Area 1A at Ileret and GaJi 14 in Collecting Area 103 at the Koobi Fora Ridge. The sites are separated by about 40 km (Figure 1). Excavation has been carried out by the Koobi Fora Field School, which, from 1997 to 2004, has been jointly run through collaboration between Rutgers University and the National Museums of Kenya.

Paleoanthropological debate about Early Pleistocene hominid foraging and ranging behaviour has been intense. Debate concerns whether hominid ranging and foraging abilities were at the level of other higher primates (e.g., chimpanzees), or whether hominids were already beginning to demonstrate a more sophisticated knowledge of crucial resources that were localized in time and space. The occurrence of modified bone at these two sites is the first new source of data on hominid ranging and foraging to emerge from this region during the last 20 years (Rogers et al. n.d.). Previously excavated sites in the Koobi Fora region greatly influenced models of early hominid ranging and foraging behaviour. In particular, evidence garnered during the 1970s at sites like FxJj 1 and FxJj 50 influenced the late Glynn Isaac's interpretation of these sites as being home bases, and his subsequent theory that complex hominid sociality was generated by food sharing at a central place (Isaac 1971, 1975, 1978). Isaac's reconstruction subsequently exerted a powerful and lasting effect on ideas about Plio-Pleistocene hominid behaviour.

Using data from Koobi Fora excavations, Glynn Isaac also introduced a new landscape or regional perspective into Plio-Pleistocene archaeology. He argued that any reconstruction of hominid behaviour in the Koobi Fora region must analyze the distribution of hominid fossils, discarded tools, and hominid-modified animal bones within a landscape in order to reveal ancient patterns of land use (Isaac 1975). This approach resembles the catchment area analysis of much more recent time ranges, in which researchers document the zones of resource exploitation around a site (Hodder and Orton 1976). However, in contrast to later periods, the very definition of a site is equivocal in the Plio-Pleistocene. Instead, Isaac wrote of concentrated "patches" of material on a landscape that might yield evidence of foraging and ranging behaviour, as well as ancient sociality. During the Plio-Pleistocene, the relative paucity of archaeological materials, the lack of obvious landscape modification, smaller relative brain size in hominids, and the presence of multiple hominid species mandate that any analysis be conducted on a landscape or regional scale. The pattern of "scatters" and "patches" of material distributed through a landscape occupied by Plio-Pleistocene hominids might indicate the relative importance of certain behaviours (Isaac 1975:Figure 3). Work in the early Pleistocene of the Olorgesailie Basin in Kenya has utilized this approach (Potts et al. 1999), and has revealed differences in hominid land use between two members within the Olorgesailie Formation.

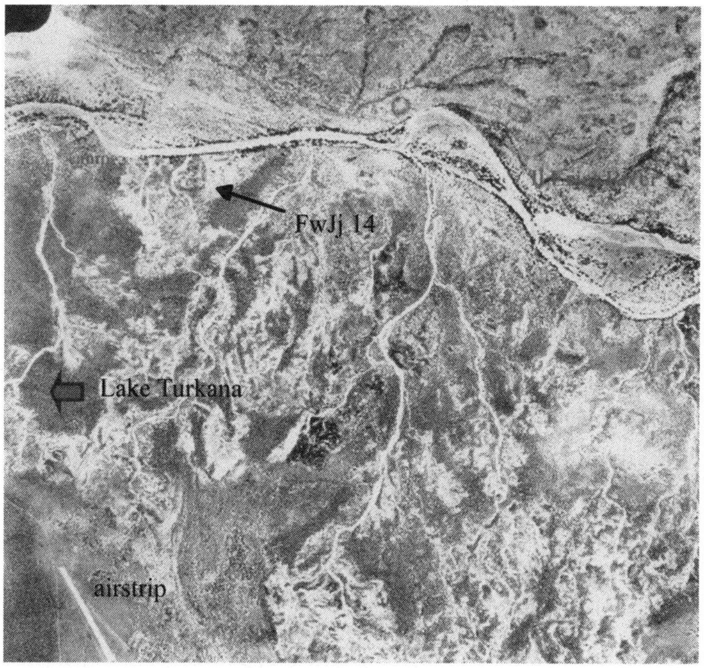

Figure 2. Aerial photograph of the Ileret region, east of Lake Turkana, showing the location of FwJj 14. The dry sand channel of the Il Eriet (Ileret) River is located immediately to the north of the site.

In this paper, we discuss how lithic raw material may have been a critical factor in influencing hominid movements. Hominids may have been prospecting for sources of large stone clasts suitable for flaking. This search was important by itself, and was not simply incidental to foraging activities related to food. Stone sources, hominid acquisition and transport of stone clasts, flaking localities or reduction areas, the scatter of discarded flakes across a region, and the curation of stone artifacts all document lithic movement or flow across a landscape. The dynamic interaction of hominids and stone can reveal behavioural aspects of the hominid niche that are otherwise invisible to human paleontologists. For example, it can reveal that stone was transported across longer distances and into a wider variety of habitats. Artifact curation can record the degree to which hominids had become obligate tool users. Hominid dispersal into novel or disturbed habitats can indicate a tolerance of environmental disruption and seasonal perturbation that is not found in non-human primates.

During the 1998 survey at Koobi Fora, we discovered GaJi 14 in Collecting Area 103 near the site where the *Homo erectus* fossil mandible KNM-ER 730 was found in 1970. The new site is near GaJi 5, a previously documented archaeological locality. In 1997 we discovered FwJj 14 in Collecting Area 1A near Ileret, when we found several cut-marked bones on a gently sloping low ridge within Okote Member deposits (Figure 2). In situ modified bones and unmodified bones were found in both sites during the 1999–2001 field seasons. A single core fragment was excavated in situ from FwJj 14B in 2000 – the only artifact recovered from either of these sites.

The Koobi Fora Formation is a succession of Pliocene to Pleistocene fluvial and lacustrine sediments deposited in the Turkana continental rift basin in northern Kenya. Okote Member sediments are dominated by sandy, fluvially reworked tephra and tuffaceous mudstones, with local channel formation. These deposits represent a perennial fluvial regime in which sediments of the Proto-Omo River are punctuated by influxes of volcaniclastic material brought down

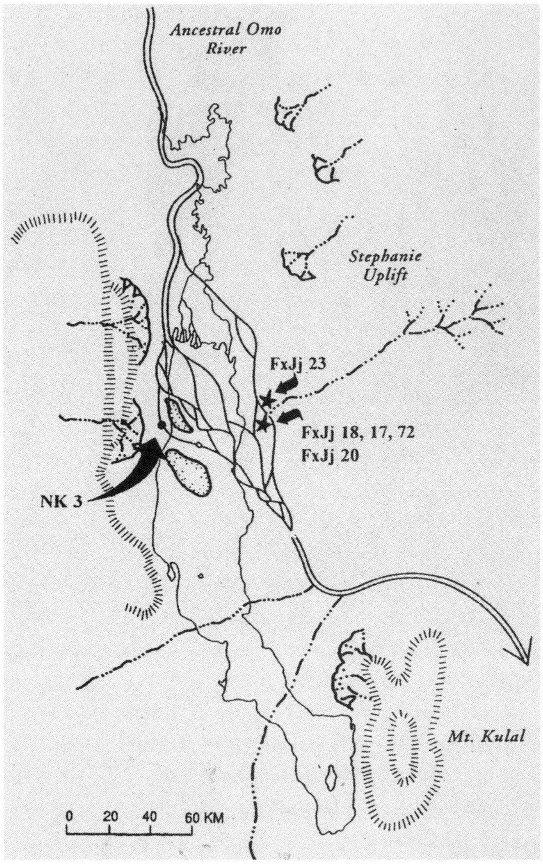

Figure 3. Paleogeography of the Turkana Basin during Okote Member times (1.65–1.39 mya), from Rogers (1997:Figure 2.10). Note the absence of a lake, and the existence of a braided river system, with complex, anastomosing channels. Some archaeological sites in the Karari Escarpment are shown in the eastern part of the basin. NK 3, in the western part of the basin, is the site where the Nariokotome *Homo erectus* specimen was discovered.

from the highlands of Ethiopia. Many small channels branch and then recombine into a braided river system. Complexly fingering, discontinuous tuff lenses occur (Figure 3). This river system was frequently choked by the 20 or more tephra that were dumped in short episodes, which quickly followed each other.

THE MODIFIED BONES

Specimens are located in the Division of Archaeology, Kenya National Museums, Nairobi. About 350 of the catalogued specimens are identifiable to skeletal element, although analysis of the 2000–2003 collections is not completed. Taxa represented are diverse. Four bovid tribes are present, signifying that the zooarchaeological remains are sampling different habitats. Reduncines, for example, are indicators of closed habitats, while alcelaphines are indicators of arid, open-country habitats. A reduncine bovid, a tragelaphine bovid, a possible hippotragine bovid, an alcelaphine bovid, a large suid (*Metridiochoerus*), other suid remains, an equid, large hippo (*Hippopotamus gorgops*), pygmy hippo (*Hippopotamus aethiopicus*), and several small fish, including catfish (*Clarias*), are each represented by several bones and teeth. Crocodile teeth, tortoise fragments, and an elephant tooth are also present. The nature and the character of the modified bone at FwJj 14 and GaJi 14 are discussed in the following sections. We now have a sample size of 151 modified specimens from both surface collections and in situ excavation (Table 1). The bones are generally fragmentary. Teeth are isolated, or occur in jaw fragments. Bones are not articulated. However, there is no preferred orientation to the bones plotted in situ, and no apparent concentration. The preservation of fragile specimens and the ability to conjoin some broken specimens confirms the sedimentary analysis of the geological sections, which indicates that the fossils were not subject to fluvial transport. The newly reported modified bones number 151 out of a total of 220 modified bones reported from all Koobi Fora subregions. Hence, research conducted at sites excavated by the Koobi Fora Field School during 1997–2000 accounts for 68.64 per cent of the hominid-modified bones from all Koobi Fora subregions.

Artifacts are virtually absent. Only a single bifacially flaked core fragment (#5032-2000) and a cobble fragment (#5020-2000) were recovered in situ. Hence, it is particularly important to distinguish hominid modification from natural taphonomic processes that may mimic hominid alteration of bone. The quality of surface bone preservation is also important, because poor surface preservation or adhering matrix can obscure the signatures of hominid behaviour. Surface preservation is generally very good, and ranges from fair to excellent. Approximately 80 per cent of the

Table 1. Number of Hominid-Modified Bones from Koobi Fora Subregions.

Subregion	Previously Reported	Newly Reported
Karari	19	–
KF Ridge	43	26
Ileret	7	125
Total	69	151
Total of all modified bones = 220		
Total of newly reported modified bones = 151		

bone surfaces are suitable for mark inspection. Limb elements and long-bone shafts are most common, but there are also cut-marked skull and axial elements. The high number of modified limb elements relative to axial elements probably reflects their greater density and their greater likelihood of preservation, rather than hominid behaviour and selectivity. Percussion marks, which are not caused by natural effects, and which therefore indicate hominid marrow exploitation, were also discovered in 1999. Carnivore tooth marks are rare. Pending completion of analyses, we estimate the relative frequency of modified bones to be about 6 per cent of the specimens. This is comparable to the FLK Zinjanthropus site at Olduvai, where about 10 per cent of all skeletally identifiable specimens exhibit modification. Modifications occur on the bones of a number of different taxa (bovid, suid, hippo), through a range of different body sizes – size 2 animals (e.g., impala-sized bovid [20–115 kg]) through size 5 animals (e.g., hippo [900–3000 kg]). The elements that are modified are diverse, as are mark locations. The description of animal size in terms of a range of general body categories was initiated during taphonomic research by Brain (1981), in order to estimate the likelihood of carcass persistence after death.

Hominid activity is discernable on some of the mammal bones recovered from FwJj 14 during the 1997–2000 field seasons (Table 2). These bones are located in the collections of the Division of Archaeology, National Museums of Kenya, Nairobi. Table 2 demonstrates three interesting points. First, the ratio of total percussion-marked to total cut-marked bones is 20.80 per cent (26/125). Cut marks are therefore nearly five times more numerous than percussion marks. Removal of vertebrate meat is occurring at a far higher rate than is marrow extraction. Second, the ratio of total carnivore-tooth-marked to total hominid-modified bones is 27.61 per cent (37/134). Hominid modifications are therefore more than two-thirds more numerous than carnivore tooth marks. Carnivores are present and are altering the bones, but signs of their behaviour are far less abundant than are signs of hominid behaviour. Third, the ratio of excavated to surface tool-marked bone is 34 per cent (34/100), while the ratio of excavated to surface carnivore-tooth-marked bone is 12.12 per cent (4/33). Tool-marked bone is therefore almost three times more numerous than carnivore tooth-marked bone in the excavated sample. If one considers the excavated sample to be a more pristine data set than surface samples are, then hominid modification is much more abundant than carnivore modification in the original condition or data set.

A Rutgers University graduate student, Briana Pobiner, is studying the traces of hominid butchery on some of the mammal bones recovered from FwJj 14. The anatomical location and detailed examination of the cut-marked bones collected from FwJj 14 during the 1997 and 1998 seasons yields evidence of probable hominid disarticulation or dismembering, skinning, and defleshing of carcasses. A number of the specimens have groups of fine cut marks in a number of different locations. The density of cut marks on single specimens can be interpreted either as potential evidence of a leisurely episode of defleshing, or as evidence of hasty, imprecise butchery. The answer hinges on the results of laboratory experimentation. A delicately cut-marked bovid hyoid was excavated in 1999 from FwJj 14B (#3124-1999), and another cut-marked hyoid fragment was also recovered in situ in 2000. The two cut-marked hyoids from FwJj 14B may demonstrate that hominids had primary access to a carcass, because mammalian carnivores with initial access to a carcass routinely target and fully consume the tongue – a large mass of tissue that is completely unprotected by bone.

Another Rutgers graduate student, Stephen Merritt, is analyzing stone tool cut marks produced by controlled butchery of goat hind limbs (Merritt 2000).

Table 2. Tool-Marked Bone Counts from FwJj 14 (1997–2000).

	Cut marked	Percussion-marked	Total tool-marked	Tooth marked
Surf	96	13	100	33
Excavation	29	13	34	4
Total	125	26	134	37
Total tool-marked elements	Head bones (including hyoids)	Axial bones	Limb bones	Unidentifiable
134	6	16	58	54

Statistically significant differences in surface width, bottom width, and depth separate core versus flake cut-mark classes. Henry Bunn (1994) hypothesized that curation of large flaked pieces at Ileret and the Koobi Fora Ridge created different signatures of hominid behaviour in the Koobi Fora region during Okote Member times. Curation would require less frequent trips to raw material sources. Sites at the Karari Escarpment were closer to these sources. Future analysis of FwJj 14 and GaJi 14 material will test Bunn's hypotheses.

DISCUSSION

Laboratory experimentation at Rutgers University has already yielded some insight into tool type and the structure of cut marks on animal bone (see above). Future Rutgers research on hominid bone modification will involve laboratory analysis of cut marks to examine the critical question of the rapidity of hominid carcass processing. In particular, we propose tentatively to assess the nature of sympatric carnivore and hominid interaction by identifying qualitative and quantitative signatures of leisurely versus hasty carcass processing. Persistent carnivore interference with hominid carcass processing will generate the hasty processing category. Carcass processing time is critical to resolving the question of the character of the hominid niche within an East African Plio-Pleistocene ecosystem that also contains many living and extinct carnivore species. Desperately quick carcass processing, taking place under the threat of carnivore interference, might result in a jumble of disorderly or untidy cut marks, not necessarily made in the optimal position for skinning, dismembering, or defleshing. However, multiple, parallel and orderly fine lines produced at multiple locations on the same element might indicate leisurely behaviour.

Henry Bunn (1994:262) reconstructs a "more ape-like, feed-as-you-go strategy" for hominid foraging behaviour using evidence from the Koobi Fora Ridge. This is identical to Lewis Binford's (1984) idea of routed foraging behaviour. Because limb bones were defleshed without breaking them to extract marrow, Bunn infers that hominids needed to butcher carcasses in lightning-like forays, in order to avoid dangerous predators. Hominids abandoned the bone marrow, which would need more time and intense labour to extract. Alternatively, Bunn considers that hippo carcasses, which he presumes were a primary focus of hominid butchering, yield a glut of meat; hominids might choose quantity over quality (meat over fat) in processing these carcasses. However, at FwJj 14 and GaJi 14, the high prevalence of cut marks, the density of the marks on individual bones, and the careful motor control of hands and fingers necessary to produce such dense, fine marks all indicate that a relatively long time was spent processing individual pieces. Hence, one might infer hominid safety and protection during the butchery process. We consequently reject the routed foraging model of behaviour for the hominid species modifying animal bones during Okote Member times. We assume that this species was *Homo erectus*.

It is now widely recognized that hominid evolutionary ecology changes drastically with the advent of early African *Homo erectus* specimens (Cachel and Harris 1995, 1996, 1998). In fact, some taxonomists argue that changes in hominid functional morphology imply that African *Homo erectus* is the first member of genus *Homo*. Bipedalism is a very energy-efficient mode of locomotion. This consideration, along with increased body size, implies both a necessary dietary shift and energy-efficient ranging abilities during Okote Member times. The Nariokotome *Homo erectus* specimen (KNM-WT 15000) clearly demonstrates a marked increase in body size. This specimen comes from the Okote time interval, although it was found in the western part of the Turkana Basin (Figure 3). This specimen has the linear body build (ectomorphy) associated with arid heat adaptation in modern hominids. Ectomorphy is, in fact, exaggerated; this individual falls at the uppermost range of ectomorphy seen in living people adapted to arid heat. Access to abundant, fresh, potable water would have been critical to the survival of hominids in arid climates. Significantly, in terms of hominid activity, all of the Koobi Fora subregions have paleoenvironmental indications of fresh water during Okote Member times, although Ileret may have been wetter than the other two regions. The primacy of fresh water in determining hominid presence and activity patterns is confirmed at an earlier time range (1.8 mya) in the Olduvai Basin, Tanzania. Note, however, that artifact curation is not as visible at Olduvai as at FwJj 14 and GaJi 14. This is an apparent reflection of proximity to lithic source areas at Olduvai, and easier access to suitable clast sizes.

Wrangham et al. (1999) argue that the large body size of KNM-WT 15000 could not be sustained by a diet of vertebrate meat – *Homo erectus* individuals must therefore have ingested considerable amounts of other dietary items, such as invertebrates or cooked tubers. O'Connell et al. (1999) question whether archaeological evidence supports hominid big game hunting and confrontational scavenging in the Lower Paleolithic. Alternatively, they argue for the nutritional importance of essential plant foods, especially tubers, which were gathered principally by post reproductive females. Ethnographic evidence suggests that these plant foods would have been shared within matrilines. Behavioural data from living mammalian carnivores can contribute to these debates. For example, modern humans can successfully engage in confrontational scavenging with large carnivores, even if the humans are armed only with simple weapons (Treves and Naughton-Treves 1999).

What can be inferred about diet and ranging behaviour in Plio-Pleistocene hominids from the biology of living mammals? A marked increase in body size in *Homo erectus*, particularly among females, argues for a dietary shift and a significant improvement in nutrition. Plant foods are unable to account for this. The nutrient quality of plant foods is too low – even if massive ingestion of cooked tubers took place, as some argue (O'Connell et al. 1999, Wrangham et al. 1999). Foraging for insects or other invertebrates is also unlikely, because diet has a major impact on body size as well as foraging behaviour. The maximum body mass of living terrestrial mammalian carnivores is highly constrained by diet (Carbone et al. 1999). At a predator mass of 21.5–25 kg, a transition occurs from feeding on small prey (less than half predator mass) to feeding on large prey (near the mass of the predator). Predators with a body mass above 21.5 kg cannot be sustained on an invertebrate diet, because ingestion rates are too low and foraging time is too costly (Carbone et al. 1999). Insectivorous mammals achieving a larger body size begin to specialize in eating social insects, with concomitant loss of teeth, elaborate tongue and tongue muscle adaptations, and a lowered metabolic rate, because of detritus that is inescapably ingested (Nowak 1999). The most parsimonious conclusion from increased hominid body size – and one that agrees with the archaeological evidence – is that vertebrate meat and fat were important and reliable components of the diet of *Homo erectus*. At an earlier date (1.7 mya) in the Koobi Fora region, an adult female specimen of *Homo erectus* (KNM-ER 1808) with skeletal pathologies indicating hypervitaminosis A may support early access to a carcass, or perhaps even hunting (Walker and Shipman 1996). This is because liver, and especially carnivore liver, appears to be the only natural source for the toxic overdose of vitamin A that caused the system-wide cortical bone pathologies seen in the ER 1808 specimen. Because viscera and abdominal organs are the first items targeted by mammalian carnivores, hominid ingestion of liver seems to indicate that hominids had early access to a carcass, and may even have hunted the animal, rather than scavenging it.

It is possible that home range size can be reconstructed for *Homo erectus* during Okote Member times in the Koobi Fora region. Because stone tools were strongly retained or curated, lithic raw material was apparently a critical resource. Lithic transport data might therefore be productively used to infer range use. Critical lithic transport from known source areas could be used to reconstruct the home range of fossil hominid species during Okote Member times. Lithic resources would not be as ephemeral as food resources. Stones, unlike food, would not degrade through time. The presence of stone clasts of a useful size for knapping might depend on water transport during seasonal floods, but, once transported to a particular area, these clasts would be permanent resources, and would not degrade like food resources. Field biologists have developed software to estimate the home range of animals from a series of discontinuous sightings that document the presence of the animals in a certain area. Home ranges are generated when the software creates either minimum convex polygons or Jennrich-Turner ellipses (Jennrich and Turner 1969). Lithic transport data could be used in a similar manner to estimate home range sizes for Okote Member hominids.

Furthermore, body size, diet, and home range size all affect the dispersal abilities of a species. It is now clear from multiple dating techniques at the site of Dmanisi, Republic of Georgia, that *Homo erectus* dispersed from Africa and established a presence in Eurasia as early as 1.7 mya (Gabunia et al. 2000). This dispersal was accomplished by hominids using Oldowan technology. The ability of hominids to cross large geographic expanses and penetrate novel environments is fundamentally a matter of evolutionary biology, rather than a product of acquiring novel Acheulean lithic technology (Cachel and Harris 1995, 1996, 1998).

However, the rules for ranging behaviour and home range size are significantly different for bipedal hominids than for other terrestrial mammals. Detailed biomechanical analysis of bipedalism in living humans clearly demonstrates the following: bipedalism imposes low travel speeds, although humans expend very little energy at normal walking speeds (Cachel and Harris 1995, 1996, 1998). Humans travel slowly, but exhibit only minor amounts of muscle activity during normal walking. Bipedalism is very cost effective. In general, normal human walking uses only about 87 per cent of the energy used by a generalized quadrupedal mammal of the same size moving at the same rate. The energy saved by bipedal hominids is even more striking when compared to the locomotion costs incurred by other primates. Primates in general exhibit less efficient locomotion than other quadrupeds of the same body size. Chimpanzees are especially inefficient. Hence, the transport costs incurred by moving body weight alone are low in hominids. Bipedal hominids incur transport costs only when objects are carried (e.g., when carrying infants or juveniles, lithic raw materials, or carcass parts). By virtue of locomotion efficiency alone, one would expect that home range size would be larger in hominids than in other primates. One would also expect farther ranging and foraging behaviour in hominids. In comparison to chimpanzees, for example, hominid home range size would be larger, and ranging for food or other resources would traverse greater distances away from core areas inside the home range. Furthermore, in comparison to earlier hominids, *Homo erectus* may have been characterized by increased mobility, and the capacity to transport significant burdens such as food or lithic raw materials across the landscape. Comparative anatomy and biomechanical analysis indicate that changing body proportions would make *Homo erectus* better at long-distance endurance walking than earlier hominids, and would also enable this species to transport heavy loads across the landscape (Carrier 2004).

The availability of raw material may significantly affect tool manufacture. For example, recent study of artifacts from the Bose Basin in China implies that the presence or absence of Acheulean artifacts is dependent upon lithic raw material of a certain clast size (Yamei et al. 2000). Although patch size of food items in time and space has often been considered a significant variable in paleoanthropological reconstruction, it is possible that limited availability of lithic raw materials in suitable clast sizes had a major impact on Plio-Pleistocene hominid foraging and ranging behaviour.

Archaeological survey which demonstrates alternative foraging strategies and complex foraging for dispersed resources implies intimate knowledge of the regional environment, and the ability to locate and predict the abundance of resources which fluctuate widely in space and time. We are here arguing that *Homo erectus* populations in the Koobi Fora region were dispersing into novel environments during Okote times. The geographic range of this species may have been expanding in the Horn of Africa, as well. With the documentation that this species occurs at the Georgian site of Dmanisi, dated to 1.7 mya (Gabunia et al. 2000), the dispersal ability or vagility of this species apparently exceeds that of earlier hominids. We propose that this species was able to exploit novel resources even in disturbed environments. In fact, the species may have flourished in disturbed environments, in the manner of "weed" species today (Cachel and Harris 1995, 1996, 1998).

This idea can be tested. It is well known that certain species are more sensitive to short-term climatic oscillations or to seasonal perturbations or increased seasonality; other species are more resistant to these changes. Species also have different sensitivities when they are located in an ecotone. Mountainous areas obviously incorporate a series of habitats within a relatively compressed area. Because of exaggerated topography, the ecotones are dramatically juxtaposed. The obvious strategy for testing an early hominid preference for ecotones is to sample synchronous localities along a transect that rises through a mountainous area. Unfortunately, relief is very low in the Koobi Fora region. However, relief becomes higher immediately to the north of the Turkana Basin, in Ethiopia. If we were to study a series of archaeological sites in the Ethiopian highlands during this time range and survey along a transect that samples different altitudes during the same time range, we would then be sampling a series of ecotones in space. Comparisons could be made to contemporary transects of similar length in the Koobi Fora Basin. This strategy would be a good way to identify whether *Homo erectus* populations truly did possess less sensitivity to habitat differences than earlier or sympatric hominid species. It might establish that members of the taxon *Homo erectus* were particularly adept at exploiting disturbed environments, as well.

SUMMARY

Recent discoveries of hominid-modified bone at the new sites of FwJj 14 and Gaji 14 have nearly tripled the known, published sample size of this category of archaeological data from the Koobi Fora region. These discoveries include both surface and in situ (excavated) finds. They now account for over 65 per cent of the modified bones from all Koobi Fora subregions.

Zooarchaeological analysis documents a high prevalence of cut marks, on about 6 per cent of the specimens. Modification occurs on bones from diverse taxa, and from a range of body sizes, from size 2 (20–115 kg [e.g., impala]) up to size 5 animals (900–3000 kg [e.g., hippo]). The elements modified are diverse. The modifications occur in a variety of locations. Taken all together, this evidence implies a certain degree of hominid behavioural complexity.

Detailed examination of the cut-marked bones collected from FwJj 14 during the 1997 and 1998 seasons yields evidence of hominid disarticulation or dismembering, skinning, and defleshing of carcasses. In 1999–2001, excavated cut-marked bones were collected from both FwJj 14 and GaJi 14. Percussion marks indicating marrow exploitation were found in 1999. Carnivore tooth marks are rare; there are only a few identified specimens.

Some researchers argue that Plio-Pleistocene hominids needed to locate and scavenge a carcass in a cheetah-like mode of enhanced mobility, rapid processing behaviour, and hurried flight before the arrival of large carnivores. At FwJj 14 and Gaji 14, however, we see some evidence of carcass processing occurring in a leisurely fashion, with little apparent threat from predators. This may result either from increasing hominid sophistication in acquiring or processing carcasses, or from increasing social complexity. New technology (shelter or control of fire) may also have played a role in affording protection to hominids.

Laboratory experimentation demonstrates that the morphology of experimentally produced cut marks is significantly correlated with tool type (core versus flake). These actualistic data can be applied to the zooarchaeological assemblages in order to test previously proposed hypotheses about hominid behavioural ecology.

The modified bones are found in concentrations without stone tools. We excavated only one artifact (a basalt, bifacially flaked probable core fragment) from FwJj 14. Concentrations of modified bones may possibly imply the transport of carcasses or repeated site visits. Although hominids engaged in focused carcass processing in these areas, they did not discard stone tools. The tools were carefully retained or curated. This behaviour may be explained by the lack of adjacent suitable raw material for stone tools.

Raw material for stone tool manufacture may have been a crucial resource for hominids. In fact, the proximity of lithic raw material sources of a suitable clast size may have profoundly affected hominid ranging and foraging behaviour. Complex foraging for dispersed resources implies intimate knowledge of the regional environment, and the ability to locate and predict the abundance of resources that fluctuate widely in space and time.

Evidence presented here does not support Lewis Binford's (1984) routed foraging model for hominids, with its ape-like, "feed-as-you-go" behaviour. Bunn (1994) had used Binford's routed foraging model in reconstructing Early Pleistocene hominid foraging in the Koobi Fora region, but our analysis suggests much more complex hominid foraging behaviour. *Homo erectus* individuals presumably created the zooarchaeological data. Profound alterations in behaviour may have occurred with the advent of this hominid species. Earlier or sympatric hominid taxa may have been unlike *Homo erectus* in terms of behaviour and may have been distinctly different in niche structure and behavioural ecology.

REFERENCES CITED

Binford, L. R.
|1984| *Faunal Remains from Klasies River Mouth.* Academic Press, London.

Brain, C. K.
|1981| *The Hunters or the Hunted? An Introduction to African Cave Taphonomy.* University of Chicago Press, Chicago.

Brown, F. H.
|1995| The Potential of the Turkana Basin for Paleoclimatic Reconstruction in East Africa. In *Paleoclimate and Evolution, with Emphasis on Human Origins*, edited by E. S. Vrba, G. H. Denton, T. C. Partridge, and L. G. Burckle, pp. 319–330. Yale University Press, New Haven

Bunn, H. T.
|1994| Early Pleistocene Hominid Foraging Strategies along the Ancestral Omo River at Koobi Fora, Kenya. *Journal of Human Evolution* 27:247–266.

Cachel, S. M., and J. W. K. Harris
|1995| Ranging Patterns, Land-Use and Subsistence in *Homo erectus* from the Perspective of Evolutionary Ecology. In *Proceedings of the Pithecanthropus Centennial, 1893–1993; Vol. I, Palaeoanthropology: Evolution & Ecology of Homo erectus*, edited by J. R. F. Bower, and S. Sartono, pp. 51–66. Leiden University Press, Leiden.
|1996| The Paleobiology of *Homo erectus*: Implications for Understanding the Adaptive Zone of this Species. In *Aspects of African Archaeology: Papers from the 10th Congress of the PanAfrican Association for Prehistory and Related Studies*, edited by G. Pwiti, and R. Soper, pp. 3–9. University of Zimbabwe Publications, Harare.
|1998| The Lifeways of *Homo erectus* Inferred from Archaeology and Evolutionary Ecology: A Perspective from East Africa. In *Early Human Behaviour in Global Context: The Rise and Diversity of the Lower Palaeolithic Record*, edited by M.D. Petraglia, and R. Korisettar, pp. 108–132. One World Archaeology Series. Routledge Press, London.

Carbone, C., G. M. Mace, S. C. Roberts, and D. W. Macdonald
|1999| Energetic Constraints on the Diet of Terrestrial Carnivores. *Nature* 402:286–288.

Carrier, D.
|2004| The Running-Fighting Dichotomy and the Evolution of Aggression in Hominids. In *From Biped to Strider: The Emergence of Modern Human Walking, Running, and Resource Transport*, edited by D. J. Meldrum, and C. E. Hilton, pp. 135–162. Kluwer Academic, New York.

Gabunia, L., A. Vekua, D. Lordkipanidze, C. C. Swisher, III, R. Ferring, A. Justus, M. Nioradze, M. Tvalchrelidze, S. C. Antón, G. Bosinski, O. Jöris, M.-A. de Lumley, G. Majsuradze, and A. Mouskhelishvili
|2000| Earliest Pleistocene Hominid Cranial Remains from Dmanisi, Republic of Georgia: Taxonomy, Geological Setting, and Age. *Science* 288:1019–1025.

Hodder, I., and C. Orton
|1976| *Spatial Analysis in Archaeology*. Cambridge University Press, Cambridge.

Isaac, G. L.
|1971| The Diet of Early Man: Aspects of Archaeological Evidence from Lower and Middle Pleistocene Sites in Africa. *World Archaeology* 2:278–298.
|1975| Early Hominids in Action: A Commentary on the Contribution of Archeology to Understanding the Fossil Record in East Africa. *Yearbook of Physical Anthropology* 19:19–35.
|1978| The Food-Sharing Behavior of Proto-Human Hominids. *Scientific American* 238:90–108.

Jennrich, R. I., and F. B. Turner
|1969| Measurement of Noncircular Home Range. *Journal of Theoretical Biology* 22:227–237.

Merritt, S.
|2000| *Quantitative Analysis of Cut Marks Experimentally Produced by Large Bifacial Tools and Small Flakes.* Unpublished undergraduate honors thesis, Department of Anthropology, Rutgers University, New Brunswick, New Jersey.

Nowak, R. M.
|1999| *Walker's Mammals of the World.* 6th ed. 2 vols. Johns Hopkins University Press, Baltimore.

O'Connell, J. F., K. Hawkes, and N. G. Blurton Jones
|1999| Grandmothering and the Evolution of *Homo erectus*. *Journal of Human Evolution* 36:461–485.
Potts, R.
|1994| Variables Versus Models of Early Pleistocene Hominid Land Use. *Journal of Human Evolution* 27:7–24.
Potts, R, A. K. Behrensmeyer, and P. Ditchfield
|1999| Paleolandscape Variation and Early Pleistocene Hominid Activities: Members 1 and 7, Olorgesailie Formation, Kenya. *Journal of Human Evolution* 37:747–788.
Rogers, M. J.
|1997| A Landscape Archaeological Study at East Turkana, Kenya. Unpublished Ph.D. dissertation, Department of Anthropology, Rutgers University, New Brunswick, New Jersey.
Rogers, M. J., J. W. K. Harris, S. M. Cachel, S. Merritt, B. L. Pobiner, and D. R. Braun
|n.d.| Early Pleistocene Hominid Behavioral Adaptations in the Koobi Fora Region, East of Lake Turkana, Northern Kenya. In *Proceedings of the 11th Congress of the PanAfrican Association for Prehistory and Related Studies*, edited by T. Togola. Bamako, Mali, in press.
Treves, A., and L. Naughton-Treves
|1999| Risk and Opportunity for Humans Coexisting with Large Carnivores. *Journal of Human Evolution* 36:275–282.
Walker, A. C., and P. Shipman
|1996| *The Wisdom of the Bones: In Search of Human Origins*. Knopf, New York.
Winterhalder, B.
|2001| The Behavioural Ecology of Hunter-Gatherers. In *Hunter-Gatherers: An Interdisciplinary Perspective*, edited by C. Panter-Brick, R. H. Layton, and P. Rowley-Conwy, pp. 12–38. Cambridge University Press, Cambridge.
Wrangham, R. W., J. H. Jones, G. Laden, D. Pilbeam, and N. Conklin-Brittain
|1999| The Raw and the Stolen: Cooking and the Ecology of Human Origins. *Current Anthropology* 40:567–594.
Yamei, H., R. Potts, Y. Baoyin, G. Zhengtang, A. Deino, W. Wei, J. Clark, X. Guangmao, and H. Weiwen
|2000| Mid-Pleistocene Acheulean-like Stone Technology of the Bose Basin, South China. *Science* 287:1622–1626.

SPATIAL MODELS OF INTRASETTLEMENT SPATIAL ORGANIZATION IN THE EIA OF SOUTHERN AFRICA: A VIEW FROM NDONDONDWANE ON THE CENTRAL CATTLE PATTERN

Haskel Greenfield and Len O. van Schalkwyk

Haskel Greenfield, University of Manitoba, Department of Anthropology, Fletcher Argue 435, Winnipeg, Manitoba R3T 5V5, Canada.
Len O. van Schalkwyk, eThembini, #7 Deli Crescent, Pietermaritzberg, KwaZulu-Natal 3201, South Africa.

ABSTRACT

Over the years, competing explanations have been proposed for the spatial organization of Early Iron Age (EIA) villages in southern Africa. Until recently, no EIA village was investigated in a manner that allowed rigorous testing of the various models. Recently, an international team from Canada and South Africa has completed its investigation of the EIA site of Ndondondwane, the type site for the EIA phase of the same name in KwaZulu-Natal, South Africa. The site appears to be of short-term occupation (50–100 years), and thus has the potential to reveal a great deal about settlement layout and the intrasite spatial dynamics of an Early Iron Age community. The research demonstrated that there were two major areas of occupation: 1) the central area, which included a livestock kraal, iron forges, ivory workshop, large central huts, and ritual objects; and 2) a peripheral area consisting of a series of domestic complexes. This pattern is corroborated by research at two other sites in the region that have been spatially investigated. In its generalities, the data supports the theoretical model known as the Central Cattle Pattern to predict the spatial organization of Iron Age villages in southern Africa. However, many of the specific behavioural correlates of the model are not supported. This paper will present new data from the Early Iron Age (ca. eighth century A.D.) village site of Ndondondwane (KwaZulu-Natal, South Africa) as a test of the Central Cattle Pattern model.

Until recently, relatively little effort has been expended to reconstruct the intrasite (or community) social and economic organization of Early Iron Age (EIA) society in southern Africa. This is the phase of earliest farming communities in the region. Various and often contradictory models have been proposed to explain the nature of EIA community organization. Hall (1987) and others argue that EIA communities were organized at a household or domestic level of production, while Huffman (1993, 2001), Denbow (1984), and others argue for more community-wide modes of production. However, the internal economic and social organization of EIA settlements and households remains inadequately understood. The goal of this article is to increase our understanding of the intrasettlement economic and social organization of the EIA communities in southeastern Africa through the study of an EIA village site.

MODELS OF EIA INTRASETTLEMENT SPATIAL ORGANIZATION

While the models that have been proposed to explain the nature and distribution of activities within southern African EIA sites may be placed along a behavioural continuum, the most diametrically opposed are the Central Cattle Pattern and the Household (Domestic) Mode of Production.

Huffman's (1993, 2001) model, known as the Central Cattle Pattern (CPP), is based upon Kuper's (1982) ethnographic study of the Eastern Bantu Cattle Pattern. It postulates that certain social institutions (a cattle-based bride wealth institution) are associated with specific features of the social and economic organization of eastern Bantu society. Kuper discusses the division of social and economic space in eastern Bantu society. He notes the fundamental division between public (male) and private (female) space, and its

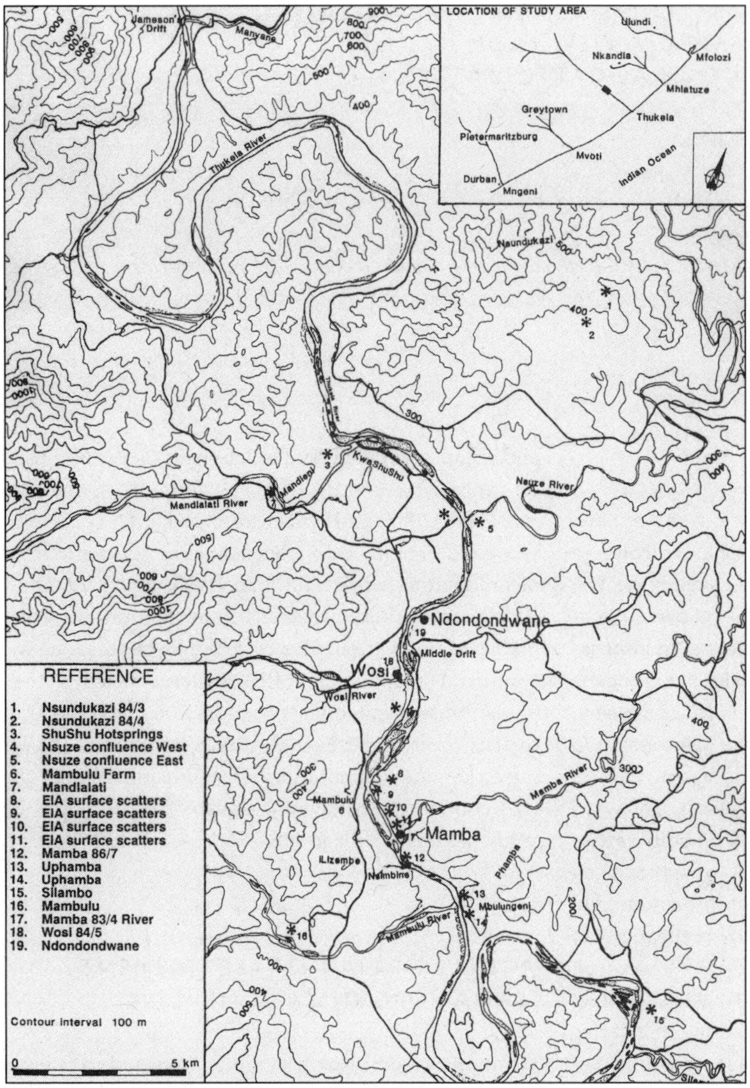

Figure 1. Map of Thukela region, showing location of site.

in a site if the archaeological correlates are present – an outer zone of circular huts with central fire places, associated with burials and grain storage and processing facilities; and an inner zone of livestock byres associated with grain storage facilities and burials, and large middens formed by the residues of specialist (traditionally male) activities (e.g., iron production, ivory working, etc.). If behaviour is spatially organized along these lines, the distribution of activities (and consequent residues) should be differentially clustered between the peripheral and central zones. For example, iron production and stock keeping should be limited to the inner zone, and there should be a single cattle byre for any given phase of occupation. On the basis of their excavations, Huffman (1993, 2001) and Whitelaw (1993) argue that the CPP and its concomitant socioeconomic organization were in place by the sixth century A.D. in southern Africa. However, neither study conclusively demonstrated its presence. Both sites are characterized by multiple-period occupations resulting in a blurring of the nature and extent of diagnostic activity areas. Neither study was able to demonstrate more than the presence of some of the individual elements of the CCP model (as archaeological features). Isolated elements were present (e.g., cattle byre, pits, burials, houses), but their distribution often did not meet the test implications of the model. The mere presence of elements of the model on a site does not demonstrate that the model is supported. They could just at easily represent other patterns of behaviour.

manifestation in the distribution of activities within a settlement. Huffman proposed that this ethnographically observable pattern be used as a model to infer the social and economic organization of Iron Age communities and evolution of the bride wealth system. "While it is generally accepted that the exchange of cattle for wives was well established by A.D. 1000, it is unclear whether this institution was introduced by the first agropastoralists in southern Africa or whether it evolved in situ a few centuries later" (Huffman 1993:220). Huffman considers the model validated

The alternative model is more implicit – the Household (Domestic) Mode of Production (HHMP). It argues that EIA communities were organized at the household or coresident extended family level (Godelier 1972; Meillasoux 1972; Sahlins 1972). Maggs (1984c) proposed that EIA villages were large (10–15 ha), housing 100–150 people; economically self-sufficient; located in nodes of the woodland-savannah environment that provided good arable soil, and year-round sweet *veld* (grass) grazing, water, wood for building, forging, and domestic consumption; only a few kilometres apart; and politically autonomous. Loubser (1993) proposed that residences and activity areas within the Ndondondwane site were linearly distributed along river terraces. The implication, hence, is that there was a repetition of activity areas (including iron production) linearly within EIA sites, implying that each residential unit was economically self-sufficient. This is contrary to the LIA where iron forging is found in more restricted contexts. Hall (1987) argues that the CCP only appeared in the LIA and that EIA communities were organized at the household or coresident extended family level. While the archaeological correlates of this model include many of the same features as the CCP (cattle byres, grain bins, burials, special activity areas), they are in a different spatial distribution. They should be more evenly distributed across a site (e.g., iron smelting and stock keeping may occur at multiple locations).

Neither model deals with the essential variability of human behaviour. Both are essentially normative in their perspective, trying to impose their limits upon what may be a more complex, more regionally variable, and complementary phenomenon (see Godelier 1972 versus Terray 1972). Tests implications of both models need to be applied against appropriately recovered and analyzed data. The CCP predicts cultural continuity from the beginning of the Iron Age to the ethnographic present. In contrast, the HHMP predicts a dramatic change in the organization of communities and therefore space. Fundamentally, the two models predict differing distributions of activity areas. The CCP predicts an inner-outer zoning of activities, while the HHMP predicts a more randomized or linear distribution.

RESULTS – THE SITE

In order to subject the above models to archaeological testing, the EIA site at Ndondondwane was chosen. It is a single phase site in the Lower Thukela valley of KwaZulu-Natal, South Africa (Figure 1). The environment, with its rich and easily tillable soils, must

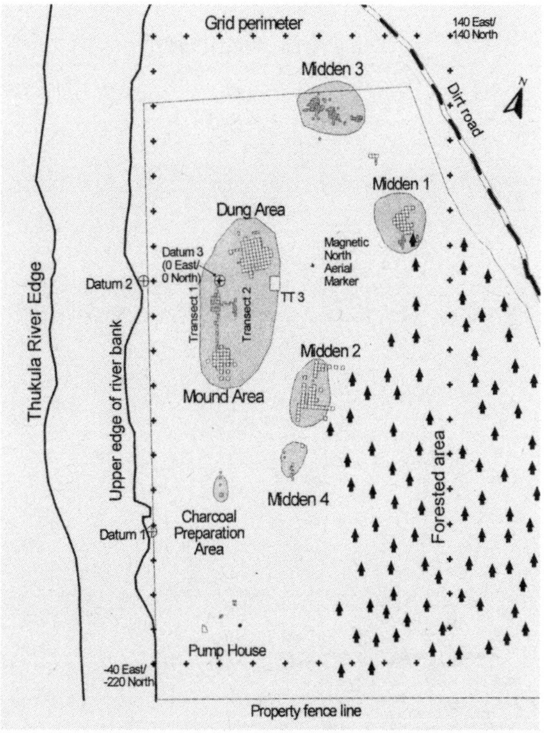

Figure 2. Map of Ndondondwane, showing location of major activity areas.

have been very attractive for the earliest agriculturalists (Maggs 1984c; van Schalkwyk 1992). Excavations at the site were initiated by Maggs (1984a) in 1978, continued by Loubser (1993) in 1982 and 1983, and completed by van Schalkwyk and Greenfield in 1995 to 1997 (van Schalkwyk et al. 1997; Greenfield 1997, 1998; Greenfield et al. 1997, 2001). The site is relatively small (ca. 5 ha), has little overburden, good preservation of bone and plant remains, and relatively soft soils. The culture historical sequence of the region has been worked out. Chronological control of ceramic phases has been achieved and is based on a radiocarbon chronology. The site is dated to ca. A.D. 750 during the Ndondondwane phase of the EIA (A.D. 700–900) (Maggs 1984a).

There is firm evidence that the site was organized into a series of spatially discrete activity areas, divided into two major zones: a central and a peripheral zone (Figure 2). The central zone comprises three activity areas, arranged in a line from north to south: a livestock enclosure (Dung Area); a large hut floor (Transect 1); and an area reserved for specialized activities associated with iron forging, ivory working,

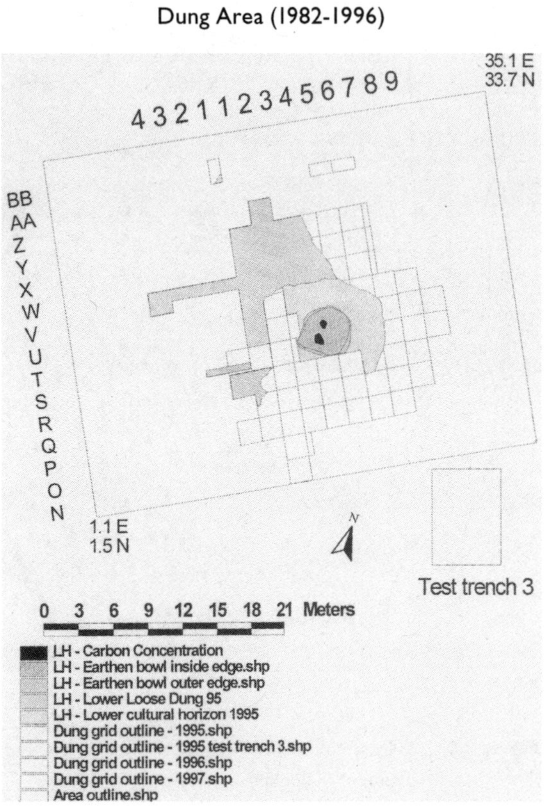

Figure 3. Map of Dung Area.

and various rituals (Mound Area). Each of these major activity areas is within 40 m of each other. The peripheral zone is a series of middens distributed in an arc around the central zone and separated from it by a large open space. The two zones are separated by approximately 100 m.

The first major activity area in the central zone is the Mound Area. It appears to be reserved for specialized activities associated with iron forging (with furnaces and slag pits), ivory working (bangle manufacture), and various rituals. The latter are inferred from the presence of numerous clay mask fragments (Loubser 1993:141–148). The mound accumulated through a shifting series of these activities. Almost all the wild fauna from the site came from this area.

The second major activity area in the central zone is a large circular burnt hut floor, ca. 10 cm thick and with a diameter of ca. 10 m. An ashy depression filled with charcoal towards the centre of the floor suggests the presence of a possible hearth. A large quantity of pottery sherds were found scattered on the floor, but the remains of both large and small vessels were clustered along the north and northeastern extremity of the floor. A number of small pots (fine finish) and bowls were also present. Associated with the floor were a number of typical EIA flat lower and upper grinding stones. The flat grinding stones had a polished surface and a shape implying they were not used for grinding grain (i.e., *muti* grinder). A large flat stone, suitable for sharpening iron tools and weapons, was found in the centre of the floor.

The third major activity area in the central zone of the site is the livestock enclosure (Dung Area) (Figure 3). Inside of the Dung Area, it is possible to recognize two spatially contiguous zones of activity: animal and human. The two zones are differentiated on the basis of quantities of ash and dung in the deposits and were divided by a palisade around the animal zone. The animal zone has multiple layers of compact and loose dung strata, mixed with some ash and fewer artifacts. The human zone is represented by a high quantity of ash and much less dung, with far higher quantities of artifacts (bone, ceramic). Within the human zone, there are discrete micro-activity areas (e.g., iron forging, meat preparation, etc.). Discrete micro-activity areas could not be defined within the animal zone.

The peripheral zone can be divided into a series of domestic activity areas and other specialized activity areas. These formed an arc around the central zone. The space between domestic middens, just as the space between peripheral and central zones, is largely empty of cultural activity loci. No features or artifact accumulations were found in these areas in spite of intensive systematic surface collections, geophysical survey, and coring of the areas. Four of the peripheral middens (1–4) were the remains of domestic household complexes. A fifth peripheral midden in the southern end of the arc was a specialized charcoal and raw ore preparation area.

The nature of domestic household compounds has been defined. The pattern repeats itself from midden to midden across the entire site. Each domestic household complex contained at least one hut, a food preparation and storage area, and a discard area. The only burial found on the site was an infant burial in a pot placed in Pit 3 of Midden 1. These are the essential elements of the EIA household cluster. The best-preserved domestic compound is Midden 1 (Figure 4). Several features were excavated in this area. The floor of a living structure was found in the south end of the area. It was a very hard, compact, but thin (less than 5 cm) horizon with no cultural debris associated with it. It could be traced over an area of 4 m by 2 m, but may have been larger. The base of a small hearth was identified inside of the floor.

Midden 1 is a palimpsest of ash deposits. The largest, Ash 1, was an ash deposit dumped into a shallow depression within the sterile base. All of the others were above the sterile base, and were relatively thin and ephemeral. It appears that the each of the ash concentrations was associated with a micro-activity locus. For example, Ash 5 is probably associated with the forging locus in trench 3b, while Ash 6 surrounds the ash-filled Pit 2. Ash 4 is probably related to another feature that has been destroyed by erosion and ploughing to the immediate west of the excavated area. Ash 1 was the best preserved. It was deposited within a shallow depression that was dug down into the pre-EIA rocky substrate. The deposits in the depression represent an activity that may have included cooking, pottery firing, and the cleaning of domestic activity areas, such as hearth and cooking areas, through the collection of ash, ceramics, bone, and calcium carbonate concretions which was subsequently deposited here. It may also represent the cleaning up possibly of a storage pit or the area around one, since large numbers of calcium carbonate nodules from the pits were dumped here.

Three storage pits, subsequently filled with midden and other remains, were found in Midden 1. They are distributed in a semi-circle to the north of the hut floor. All three are cut into the underlying Pleistocene deposits and calcium carbonate rock basement. They tend to be circular in shape, with a diameter of ca. 1 m, were 1 m to 2 m deep, and were dung lined. The nature of the lining supports the interpretation of its original function as a grain storage pit. The pits were rapidly filled immediately after their use as storage facilities was finished. One of the pits, Pit 2, was capped by several large stones. Stone caps are rare, but not uncommon coverings for EIA grain storage pits. The stone cap is indication the special nature of Pit 2. It is interesting that a cap was not discovered over Pit 3, used as a burial, indicating the absence of any special significance to the use of pits for burials. The basal horizon contained ceramics, bones, beads, grinding stones, charcoal in a random distribution, and a concentration of four large cattle long bones

Midden I (1995-1996): Plan

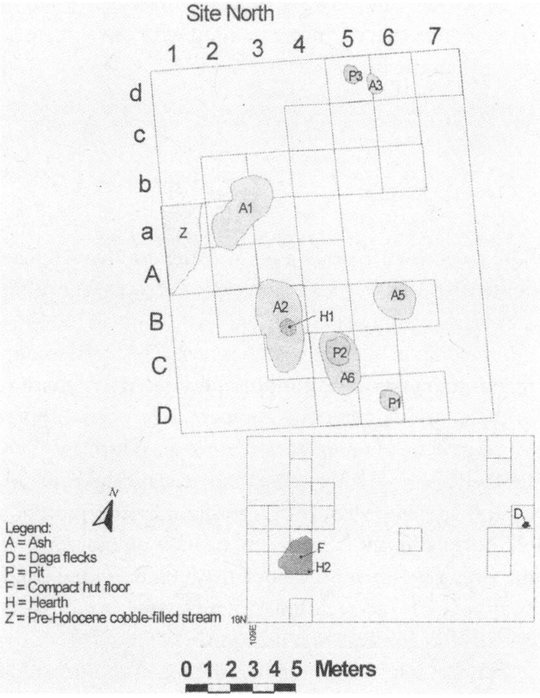

Figure 4. Map of Midden 1.

arranged in a cruciform pattern in the centre of the pit. The upper fill of Pit 2 contained ash, charcoal, and large and small upper and lower grooved grindstones. The stones appear to be deposited as if they were all thrown into the pit at the same time. Dung linings are not unusual in EIA pits. It was dung lining which indicated its prior function as a grain storage pit. The dung seals the pit from moisture to protect the stored grain. The grain was probably placed in baskets and would have been placed in the pit for a short time only.

Pit 3 was much shallower (ca. 40 cm from the preserved mouth) than the other pits and contained three major horizons. Above the thin basal horizon, a large fragmented inverted globular ceramic pot was found. The pot contained the burial of a complete articulated skeleton of a three-month-old human infant. The infant was found face down in the deposit, implying that it was originally lying on its back in the base of the pot with its face up toward the mouth of the pot, as the pot was being carried to the pit. The pot was inverted into pit and the infant fell forward against the upper wall and shoulder of the pot. There is no indication that the pot was thrown into the pit since it is not shattered. It was carefully placed when inverted. There is no evidence that the pot was filled with anything else other than the infant.

CONCLUSION

The combined excavations at Ndondondwane have confirmed that it was a single-period site, whose occupation possibly spanned only a few decades. Most other comparable large and intact EIA settlements in the region exhibit multiple periods of occupation, often spanning more than one ceramic period representing several hundreds of years (e.g., Whitelaw 1994, 1996). This invariably results in a juxtaposition of cultural evidence, which often confounds interpretation of the relationships between various phenomena on the site. The situation is obviously compounded when dealing with more complex issues, such as intrasite social and economic organization.

For the first time, there is evidence of the nature of the EIA intrasettlement spatial organization. Because of the short time span of occupation (less than 50 years), there is no question as to which features are contemporary. Ndondondwane was organized into a series of spatially discrete activity areas, divided into two major zones: a central and a peripheral zone. The central zone comprises three activity areas, arranged in a line from north to south: a livestock enclosure (Dung Area), a large hut floor (Transect 1), and an area reserved for specialized activities associated with iron forging, ivory working, and various rituals (Mound Area). Each of these major activity areas is within 40 m of each other. The peripheral zone is distributed in an arc around the central zone and separated from it by a large open space. The two zones are separated by a distance of approximately 100 m. The peripheral zone can be divided into a series of domestic activity areas and other specialized activity areas. The domestic activity areas (Middens 1–4) were located to the north, east and southeast of the central zone. A fifth peripheral activity area, a specialized charcoal and raw ore preparation area, was found in the southern end of the arc.

The preliminary results of the excavation indicate the existence of a well-ordered community. At the centre of the community lay structures and activity areas associated with a variety of what are considered to be male-associated activities in traditional eastern Bantu culture (a large men's hut, a livestock byre, iron furnaces, and iron and ivory working areas). Around this core area, moving upslope from the river, was a large open area, with very little debris and no evident features.

At the north end of the site, relatively isolated from the domestic complexes, lay a charcoal preparation (pre-forging) area. Using ethnographic analogies, it was also associated with male activities, given its isolation and the ethnographic association of males with iron production.

At least three domestic household complexes were found in a large semi-circle (northwest, west, and southwest) around the central open area. They are equidistant from the activity areas at the centre of the site. The three domestic midden deposits are areas where household activities took place (viz. food processing and storage, sleeping, tool repair, ceramic production, etc.). Such domestic complexes are the traditional domain of women in eastern Bantu ethnographic contexts.

This spatial distribution of activity areas appears to tentatively support Huffman's (1993, 2001) Central Cattle Pattern model for the Early Iron Age in its broad outlines – with a central area dominated by male activities (cattle keeping, iron production), surrounded by a plethora of domestic (female-focused) compounds. The domestic compounds are distributed in an arc from the central area of the site and are almost equidistant from the central hut. On the surface, this pattern appears to fit that predicted by the Central Cattle Pattern model. However, there are some important differences that remain, such as the absence of any evidence for grain storage in the central area of the site. Grain storage, both short and long term, is found in the peripheral domestic middens. Iron smelting is taking place in the centre of the site, rather than off-site as occurs in the LIA and ethnographic present. Iron forging is occurring everywhere, even in the domestic areas. There is also an evident lack of male burials in the centre (especially the livestock enclosure). This is compounded by the lack of adult burials anywhere on the site. As a result, it is difficult to make conclusions concerning the respective role of men and women without resorting to direct ethnographic analogy (Kent 1998; Lane 1996; Wadley 1997).

As Lane cogently argued (1996), to assume that settlement space is structured by a single symbolic scheme (such as that proposed by Kuper 1982 and extended archaeologically by Huffman 1993, 2001) is questionable. There remain hypotheses that must be tested by the archaeological data. If they are not supported, then either the hypothesis must be modified or discarded. To argue that if the material correlates of the spatial pattern are present, then the symbolic scheme must also be present is a structured tautology. This is particularly true among the proponents of the Central Cattle Pattern model.

At the same time, the spatial pattern from Ndondondwane does not fit the models proposed by Hall (1987), Maggs (1984c) and Loubser (1993), each of who argued for a more domestic mode of production. Instead, there appears to be a subtle interplay of activity features, which suggests that EIA culture is organized in a fundamentally different manner than during the LIA and ethnographic present. Domestic animal resources are pooled together, while grain is kept separately in each compound. The exact relationship between each compound is an issue to be investigated more closely at a future time.

During the last two decades, research on the EIA of southern Africa has been increasingly directed at trying to obtain greater insights into the social dynamics of the earliest agricultural communities (Hall 1987; Lane 1996; Loubser 1993; Maggs 1984b, 1984c; Maggs and Ward 1984; Prins 1993; 1994; van Schalkwyk 1992, 1994a, 1994b, 1996; Whitelaw 1993, 1996). The socio-economic organization of these communities, however, is still poorly understood (van Schalkwyk 1992; Whitelaw 1994). The arrival of the first food producing communities lays the foundation for the evolution of complex societies in the region during the following 1,500 years. By collecting data in order to reconstruct the internal social and economic organization of the first farming communities, we can better understand the origins and evolution of the LIA cultures in the region, the precolonial indigenous societies, and those recorded in the ethnographic present.

ACKNOWLEDGMENTS

The authors are indebted to the many participants of the field research, but in particular to the permanent field staff, including Tina Jongsma, Themba Nogwaza, and the late Bheki Mazibuko. Any errors are our sole responsibility.

REFERENCES CITED

Denbow, J.
|1984| Cows and Kings: A Spatial and Economic Analysis of a Hierarchical Early Iron Age Settlement System in Eastern Botswana. In *Frontiers: Southern African Archaeology Today*, edited by M. Hall, G. Avery, D. M. Avery, M. L. Wilson, and A. J. B. Humphreys, pp. 24–39. British Archaeological Reports International Series 207. Monographs in African Archaeology No. 10. British Archaeological Reports, Oxford.

Godelier, M.
|1972| *Rationality and Irrationality in Economics*. New Left Books, London.

Greenfield, H. J.
|1997| Research Report on Activities during the Summer of 1996. *University of Manitoba Anthropology Newsletter* 7:11–12.
|1998| Preliminary Report on the 1997 Summer Field Season at Ndondondwane. *University of Manitoba Anthropology Newsletter* 9:6–8.

Greenfield, H. J., L. O. van Schalkwyk, and T. L. Jongsma
|1997| Ndondondwane: Preliminary Report on the 1995 Survey and Excavations. *Nyame Akuma* 47(June):42–52.

Greenfield, H. J., L. O. van Schalkwyk, and T. L. Jongsma
|2001| Surface and Subsurface Reconnaissance at Ndondondwane: Preliminary Results of the 1995–97 Field Seasons. *Southern African Field Archaeology* 9:5–16.

Hall, M.
|1987| Archaeology and Modes of Production in Pre-Colonial Southern Africa. *Journal of Southern African Studies* 14(1):1–17.

Huffman, T. N.
|1993| Broederstroom and the Central Cattle Pattern. *South African Journal of Science* 89:220–226.
|2001| The Central Cattle Pattern and Interpreting the Past. *Southern African Humanities* 13:1–16.

Kent, Susan
|1998| *Gender in African Archaeology*. Altamira Press, Walnut Creek, California.

Kuper, A.
|1982| *Wives for Cattle: Bridewealth and Marriage in Southern Africa*. Routledge and Kegan Paul, London.

Lane, P.
|1996| The Use and Abuse of Ethnography in Iron Age Studies of Southern Africa. *Azania* 29–30:51–64.

Loubser, J. H. N.
|1993| Ndondondwane: The Significance of Features and Finds from a Ninth-Century Site on the Lower Thukela River, Natal. *Natal Museum Journal of Humanities* 5:109–151.

Maggs, T.
|1984a| Ndondondwane: A Preliminary Report on an Early Iron Site on the Lower Tugela River. *Annals of the Natal Museum* 26:71–94.
|1984b| The Iron Age South of the Zambezi. In *Southern African Prehistory and Paleoenviroments*, edited by R. E. Klein, pp. 329–360. Balkema, Rotterdam.
|1984c| Iron Age Settlement and Subsistence Patterns in the Tugela River Basin, Natal. In *Frontiers – Southern African Archaeology Today*, edited by M. Hall, G. Avery, D. M. Avery, M. L. Wilson, and A. J. B. Humphreys. British Archaeological Reports International Series 207. Monographs in African Archaeology No. 10. British Archaeological Reports, Oxford.
Maggs, T., and V. Ward
|1984| Early Iron Age Sites in the Muden Area of Natal. *Annals of the Natal Museum* 26:95–138.
Meillassoux, C.
|1972| From Reproduction to Production, a Marxist Approach to Economic Anthropology. *Economy and Society* 1:93–104
Prins, F.
|1993| Early Farming Communities in Northern Transkei: The Evidence from Ntsitsana and Adjacent Areas. *Natal Museum Journal of Humanities* 5:153–174.
|1994| Climate, Vegetation and Early Agricultural Communities in Natal and Transkei. *Azania* 29–30:179–186.
Sahlins, M.
|1972| *Stone Age Economics*. Chicago University Press, Chicago.
Terray, E.
|1972| *Marxism and Primitive Society*. Monthly Review Press, New York.
van Schalkwyk, L. O.
|1992| Society in Transformation: Early Iron Age Mixed Farming Communities in the lower Thukela Basin – Zululand. Unpublished master's thesis, University of Cape Town, Cape Town, South Africa.
|1994a| Mamba Confluence – a Preliminary Report on an Early Iron Age Industrial Centre in the Lower Thukela Basin, Zululand. *Natal Museum Journal of Humanities* 6:119–144.
|1994b| Wosi, an Early Iron Age Agriculturist Village in the Lower Thukela Basin, Zululand. *Natal Museum Journal of Humanities* 6:64–96.
|1996| Settlement Shifts and Socio-Economic Transformations in Early Farming Communities in the Lower Thukela Basin, Zululand. A Revisionist Model. *Azania* 29–30:187–198.
van Schalkwyk, L. O., H. J. Greenfield, and T. L. Jongsma
|1997| Ndondondwane: Preliminary Report on the 1995 Survey and Excavations. *South African Field Archaeology* 6:61–79.
Wadley, L.
|1997| *Our Engendered Past: Archaeological Studies of Gender in Southern Africa*. University of Witwatersrand Press, Johannesburg.
Whitelaw, G.
|1993| Customs and Settlement Patterns in the First Millennium AD: Evidence from Nanda, an Early Iron Age Site in the Mngeni Valley, Natal. *Natal Museum Journal of Humanities* 5:47–81.
|1994| KwaGandaganda: Settlement Patterns in the Natal Early Iron Age. *Natal Museum Journal of Humanities* 6:1–64.
|1996| Toward an Early Iron Age Worldview: Some Ideas from KwaZulu-Natal. *Azania* 29–30:37–50.

THE INTRASETTLEMENT SPATIAL STRUCTURE OF EARLY NEOLITHIC SETTLEMENTS IN TEMPERATE SOUTHEASTERN EUROPE: A VIEW FROM BLAGOTIN, SERBIA

Haskel Greenfield and Tina Jongsma

Haskel J. Greenfield, University of Manitoba, Department of Anthropology, Fletcher Argue 435, Winnipeg, Manitoba R3T 5V5, Canada.
Tina Jongsma, University of Manitoba, Department of Anthropology, Fletcher Argue 435, Winnipeg, Manitoba R3T 5V5, Canada.

ABSTRACT

This paper will examine the spatial organization of Early Neolithic settlements in temperate southeastern Europe. As early agricultural settlement moves north from the Mediterranean into a more temperate central European climate, the nature of sites and by implication settlement and economy change. In the southern or Mediterranean half of the Balkan Peninsula (Greece, Macedonia, and southern Bulgaria), most Early Neolithic settlements are represented by tell-like deposits, with rectilinear above-ground and free-standing architecture. In the northern or temperate half of the peninsula and extending across the rest of southeastern Europe, Early Neolithic tell-like settlements are almost non-existent. Instead, most sites appear to be composed of laterally displaced horizontal deposits associated with pit house deposits. For almost 100 years, archaeologists have been arguing about whether the pits in such sites represents the remains of pit houses or borrow pits for free-standing houses that have subsequently been destroyed by ploughing and other disturbance processes. In this paper, we will present the results of our research at the Early Neolithic Starčevo culture site of Blagotin to demonstrate that the pits are the remains of pit houses. A

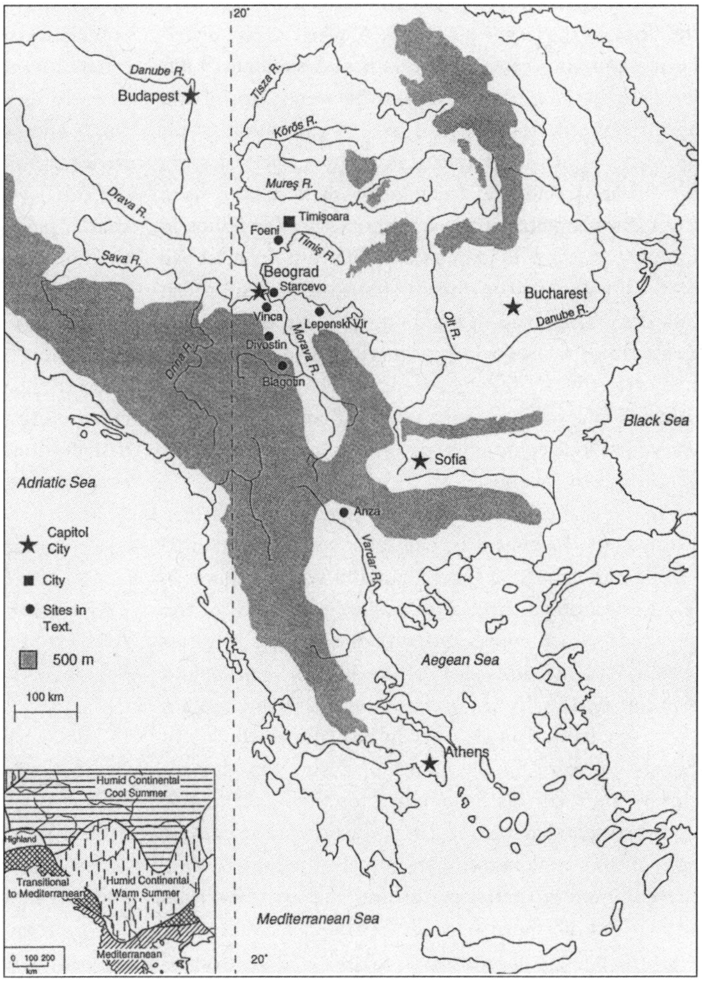

Figure 1. Map of northern Balkans showing location of Early Neolithic sites in the region mentioned in the text. Insert map shows climatic divisions of the Balkan Peninsula (cf. Pounds, 1969).

new and unexpected spatial distribution of remains are discernible from the archaeological record at Blagotin with the recognition of the location of Early Neolithic. Two types of pit houses are distinguishable. A smaller and shallower set of pit houses is distributed in a circle around a large open space. The second larger and deeper type is found at the centre of the large open space. This pattern has now been recognized at three sites in the region (Blagotin, Foeni-Salač, and Vinča-Belo Brdo). The function of the central pit house is clearest at Blagotin because of the nature of preservation at the site. It is clearly very different from those surrounding it. Two large (30 cm) idols were found on the floor of the larger pit house. Analysis of the distribution of animal remains also indicates substantial differences in the types of remains between central and peripheral structures. The spatial organization of pit houses, the heavily domesticated fauna, lack of storage facilities, and low frequencies of domestic flora from the site imply that early agricultural societies in this region were fundamentally different from those of the Mediterranean littoral (Greece and southern Bulgaria). These represent short-term occupations by a relatively mobile society, primarily relying upon their domestic animals for subsistence. This analysis is another step towards a more systematic investigation of Early Neolithic community patterning in the temperate southeastern Europe.

Archaeological research in temperate southeastern Europe (also known as the central or northern Balkans) has been ongoing for more than 100 years (Figure 1). Most research on the Early Neolithic societies of the region has been concerned with the intra- and inter-regional chronologies and culture history (Ehrich and Bankoff 1991). While many issues of this nature remain to be resolved, enough is known to allow scholars to begin to investigate the nature of Early Neolithic societies. Yet relatively little of this research has focused upon the spatial nature and organization of the earliest agricultural settlements. Attempts at reconstructing the community spatial patterning of Early Neolithic sites in the northern Balkans has been frustrated by both the paucity of large-scale excavations and the inability to define houses. A few large-scale excavations of Early Neolithic sites have been undertaken over the course of the last century (Divostin, Vinča, Foeni-Salač, and Blagotin). These yielded a wealth of spatial data that is only beginning to be absorbed into the literature. Most importantly, they have allowed comparison of the spatial distribution of features on sites, both within and between regions. These large scale excavations have allowed for the recognition of differences in the nature and distribution of architectural features between southern Balkans and central Europe, on the one hand, and the northern Balkans, on the other. It is clear that, as early agricultural settlement moves north from the Mediterranean into a more temperate central European climate, the nature of structures and their spatial structure changes. These differences have implications for the settlement and economy. Not only are the types of structure difficult to identify and appear different, but also their nature or function is subject to controversy.

In order to increase our understanding of the nature of early agricultural societies in southeastern Europe, this paper will undertake the following tasks: 1) to review the differing nature of Early Neolithic site deposits, types of structures, and the evidence for spatial patterns in the distribution of structures from the southern Balkans, northern Balkans, and central Europe; and 2) to attempt to reconstruct the spatial structure of Early Neolithic settlements in the northern Balkans (of temperate southeastern Europe). Data from the excavations at the Early Neolithic Starčevo culture site of Blagotin will be used to demonstrate the distribution and nature of structures in Early Neolithic sites from temperate southeastern Europe.

EARLY NEOLITHIC SITES AND ARCHITECTURE IN THE SOUTHERN BALKANS

In the southern or Mediterranean half of the Balkan Peninsula (Greece, Macedonia, and southern Bulgaria), most Early Neolithic settlements are represented by tell-like deposits, with vertically superimposed deposits. On the basis of archaeological features and clay model structures recovered from archaeological contexts, researchers have described the dwellings as rectilinear surface dwellings, often organized in rows. The structures are timber-frame dwellings with wattle-and-daub walls and clay-plastered floors. Surface houses are generally small in size, with a single room, and without any evidence for internal divisions. Most surface houses are single story. However, some structures appear to have two floors. The second floor may not have been a full storey, but may have been used as a loft or granary. The average size appears to be 7–10 m long and 4–6 m wide. In general, the shape of surface houses is rectangular or square in shape. All surface houses have postholes in and around the floors to support the wattle-and-daub walls. The roofs either were thatch or gabled (Chapman 1989; Gimbutas 1976, 1991; Gimbutas et al. 1989; Runnels and Murray 2001).

EARLY NEOLITHIC SITES AND ARCHITECTURE IN CENTRAL EUROPE

Very different kinds of archaeological deposits are found in the major Early Neolithic archaeological culture (Linearbandkeramik or LBK) of central Europe. Most sites are very shallow, with little if any vertical superposition of deposits. They are largely characterized by laterally displaced deposits. The architectural forms in LBK sites tend to be very rectangular surface structures. Characteristically, they are extremely long and easily identifiable by the distribution of post molds in the soil. In LBK sites where settlement has been short term and the distribution of features is visible, long houses are placed parallel to each other, although it is difficult to perceive the presence of any clear rows (Bogucki 1988, 1996; Milisauskas and Kruk 1989).

EARLY NEOLITHIC SITES AND ARCHITECTURE IN THE NORTHERN BALKANS

The northern half of the Balkans has a more temperate continental climate, and takes on characteristics of a central European regime (Figure 1) (Greenfield 1991; Pounds 1969). It extends across northern Bulgaria, Serbia, southern Hungary, eastern Bosnia, and southern Romania. This is the spatial extent of the Early Neolithic Starčevo-Criş-Körös culture (Dumitrescu 1983; Garašanin 1983; Tringham 1971). Recent research has indicated the presence of similar sites in Greek Macedonia, as well (Halstead 1999).

In the northern or temperate half of the Balkans and extending across the rest of southeastern Europe, Early Neolithic tell-like settlements are extremely rare. Instead, most sites appear to be composed of laterally displaced horizontal deposits.

The architecture in the northern half of the Balkans stands in contrast to the regions to the north and south. The evidence for surface rectilinear houses, such as those found in the Mediterranean cultures, disappears as one moves inland across the mountainous divide into the northern Balkans. What appears in its place is less clear. Instead of surface houses, an abundance of pits are found. There are no unambiguous surface architectural features until the end of the Early Neolithic period (Bogdanović 1988; Horvath 1989).

For almost 100 years, archaeologists have been arguing about whether the pits in these sites represent the remains of pit houses or borrow pits for free-standing houses. Borrow pits have been identified in southern Balkan sites, such as Achilleion (Gimbutas et al. 1989), and in central European sites, such as Olszanica (Milisauskas 1986). But they are always immediately adjacent to surface houses. There is no such obvious spatial relationship from northern Balkan Early Neolithic sites. Most local prehistorians assume that these pits were domestic dwellings or were semisubterranean dwellings (e.g., Bogdanović 1988; Garašanin 1979, 1983; Lazarovici 1979; Makkay 1978, 1992; Srejović 1988). Some, however, attempt to demonstrate the evidence for such dwellings, rather than make the assumption (Greenfield and Draşovean 1994; Jongsma 1997; Jongsma and Greenfield 2000).

A small, but vocal minority of prehistorians advocate that occupation was in the form of surface houses. Those who argue against the presence of pit houses in these sites have offered a variety of explanations to account for the absence of surface houses. The absence of surface houses is usually explained to be either a function of destruction by later ploughing or erosion of sites, or result of poor and unsystematic excavations that have failed to uncover architectural evidence for either surface or pit occupation (Ehrich 1977; Tringham 1971). The presence of many pits on sites is explained to be a result of their use for a variety of non-habitation functions, such as refuse, storage, or borrow pits (e.g., Horvath 1989:85–86; Tringham 1971, 2000). Until the nature of dwellings has been established, however, it is difficult to progress to more behavioural levels of analysis, such as household and community pattern studies, and issues of colonization.

It is impossible and inaccurate to begin a study of community patterns, including activity areas and

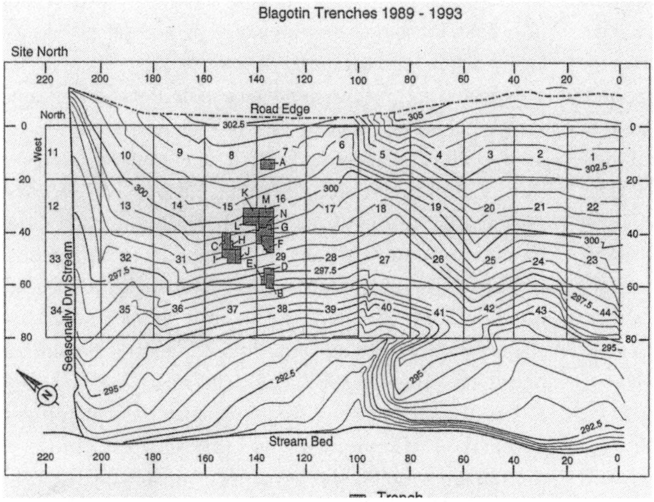

Figure 2. Topographic map of the Blagotin site, showing grid system and location of trenches.

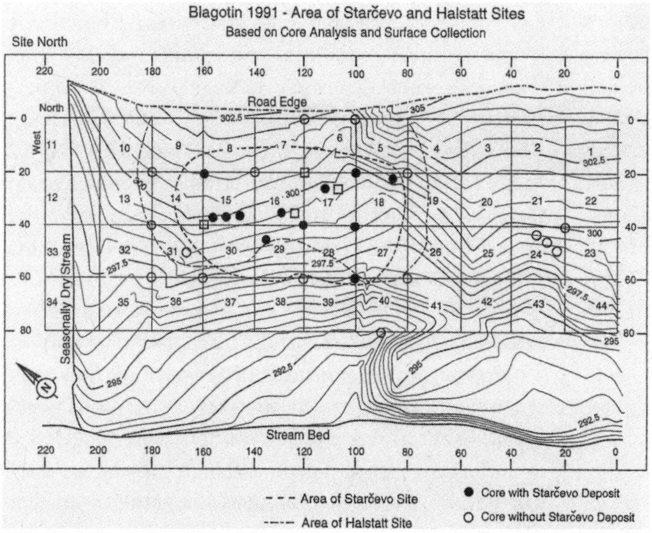

Figure 3. Topographic map of site showing location of auger holes and extent of Starčevo and Halstatt sites at Blagotin.

household clusters (Winter 1976), until it is understood what an Early Neolithic house is composed of. Are houses surface structures made of wattle-and-daub walls or semisubterranean pit dwellings? Are these pits simply refuse areas? The general opinion until now has been not to discuss these issues in too much detail because of the uncertainty of the function of these pits. However, until these questions are answered it is impossible to accurately reconstruct the community organization on a sociopolitical or economic level.

A few scholars have attempted to look at the spatial organization of Early Neolithic communities. Srejović attempted to look at the social organization of the Mesolithic and Early Neolithic horizons from Lepenski Vir (Srejović 1972) and Vlasac (Srejović and Letica 1978) by examining the layout of the houses across the site. Unfortunately, the excavation and recovery techniques were not systematic enough to yield an accurate picture of the site. More recently, Chapman (1989) examined the spatial arrangement of structures in Early Balkan villages (Serbia, Bulgaria, and Romania) to determine the social organization of sites. But, most research on the spatial organization of Early Neolithic communities has been hampered by the lack of systematic and extensive excavations of single sites.

Greenfield has attempted to rectify this problem in the overall database through extensive excavations at two Early Neolithic sites: one in central Serbia – Blagotin (Greenfield 2000), and one in the Banat section of southwestern Romania – Foeni-Salaş (Greenfield and Draşovean 1994). At both sites, the excavations have been systematic and over a large enough area that it is possible for the first time to determine community organization and household clusters. It was finally possible to determine house location and the surrounding features that can be associated with these Early Neolithic houses. In the rest of this paper, some of the data from Blagotin will be presented.

BLAGOTIN, AN EARLY NEOLITHIC SITE

The site

Blagotin is located in the heart of Serbia, in an area known as Šumadija. The region is characterized by a

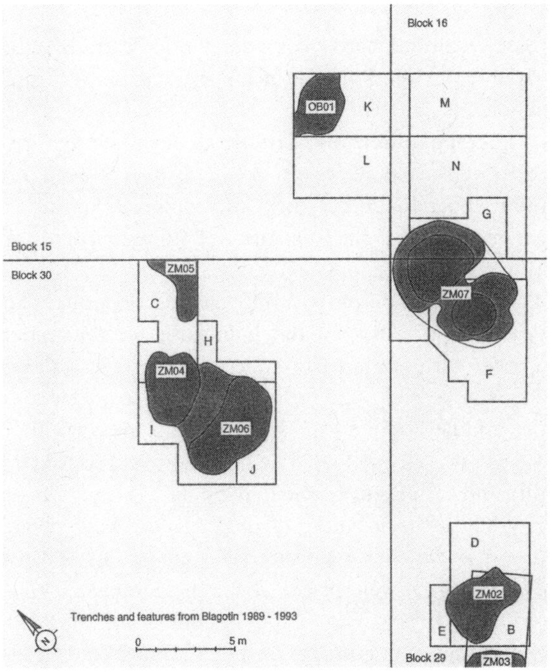

Figure 4. Map of center of site showing the distribution of 1989-1993 excavated trenches and Early Neolithic pit-structures. Light shading represents the basal level and the dark shading represents the upper edge of the pit structures. Trench A with ZM 1 is not shown on the map.

Figure 5. Photograph of the fill deposits of the pit feature profile (ZM 2).

southern variant of the Central European temperate climatic regime (Pounds 1969). The site is located on the northern outskirts of the village of Poljna, 12 km north of the slightly larger village of Velika Drenova, and about 50 km northeast of the town of Trstenik (in the county or *opština* of Trstenik). It is on a gently sloping terrace, above an incised stream valley at the base of a mountain (Figure 2). The surface of the site was entirely cultivated during the period of field research.

Blagotin is a multi-period and stratigraphically complex site. It was initially inhabited during the Early Neolithic (Starčevo culture, ca. 6100–5100 B.C.), reoccupied during the Eneolithic (Baden-Kostolac culture, ca. 3300–2500 B.C.), and occupied again during the Early Iron Age (Halstatt culture, ca. 1000–700 B.C.). It was not occupied again until modern times. Each of the occupations only partially overlapped the other, resulting in both lateral displacement and vertical superposition of cultural stratigraphy. Recent radiocarbon dates place it among the earliest sites in the Starčevo culture – ca. 6100 B.C., cal. (Whittle et al. 2002).

On the basis of the magnetometer, coring, and surface collection, the dimensions of the Early Neolithic Starčevo occupation at Blagotin was determined (Figure 3). It was limited to an ellipse with maximum dimensions of ca. 80 m east to west by 50 m north to south. Blagotin was a relatively small and insignificant settlement (Greenfield 2000).

Systematic excavations at Blagotin were opened by Svetozar Stanković of the University of Beograd in 1989. In 1991, a joint team from the Universities of Manitoba and Beograd applied a variety of systematic surface and subsurface reconnaissance techniques to the site and excavated additional trenches (Greenfield 1995, 2000; Radoman 1994; Redzić and Zečević 1996; Stanković and Greenfield 1992; Stanković and Leković

Figure 6. Photograph of distribution of postholes around ZM 2.

1994; Stanković and Runić 1990). These trenches were extended in 1992 and 1993 by the Stanković team during the period of the embargo against Yugoslavia. Excavation of a deep trench in the northeastern corner of the site occurred in 1994 and 1995, but there is little information about the exact location and information derived from this trench (not shown on the maps). Research at the site came to a halt with the premature death of the director, Svetozar Stanković, in 1996.

Excavation results

Excavations of the Early Neolithic horizon at the site uncovered a series of small pit features (ZM 1 through 6 and OB 1) (Figure 4) encircling a larger and more centrally located semisubterranean structure Early Neolithic pit house feature and clay platform (ZM 7)[1]. The features can be divided into secular and ceremonial types.

Secular Starčevo architecture

Several depressions filled with and covered over by dense concentrations of Starčevo cultural remains were excavated (ZM 1 through 7, and OB 1 and 2). They were dug during the initial occupation of the site, into the sterile substrates formed during the later Pleistocene and subsequently during the early Holocene.

The Starčevo pit feature internal horizons

The fill deposits of the depressions can always be divided into three major horizons (Figure 5): a thin lower (basal) cultural horizon, a sterile middle horizon of variable thickness, and a thick upper (capping) cultural horizon – each of which was described above.

The upper horizons of nearly all of the pit features excavated have relatively dense artifact concentrations, about 10–20 cm thick, and composed mostly of ceramics, with a small quantity of stone (normally of a mica schist composition), and a few animal bones. They seem to be purposefully created deposits. The synchroneity between the boundaries of the upper level(s) with the artifact concentrations and the pit edges is very close. The near absence of artifacts in the middle horizon would argue for its creation after the site was abandoned. The basal horizon tends to be thin and appears to be the living floor.

What is the meaning of the concentrations above the pits? Do they represent the foundations of later dwellings that were placed above the earlier semisubterranean structure or simply middens? The simplest explanation is one that is seen on pit house sites from the Canadian British Columbia area (Hayden 1997). There, it appears that the durable rubbish was often added to the roof of the structure in order to better insulate it or waterproof it. Objects, such as bones, stone, and ceramics could easily be added to the roof structure, slowly throughout its lifetime. Otherwise, it would be necessary to hypothesize that the artifact concentrations in the capping horizons reflect a habit on the part of the occupants of the earlier horizon to throw their garbage into open pits and periodically clean their living floors of accumulated debris. However, there is always an intervening low artifact density horizon within the pit. This would imply that the pits were abandoned for a period of time, and the roof subsequently collapsed.

Superstructure

Is there any evidence for roofing over the depressions? Postholes were found around and inside of several of the pit features during excavation (Figure 6). The surrounding postholes were largely vertical in orientation, and narrow in dimensions. This would imply that the walls were mostly upright, and the roofs were not substantial. The walls were probably made of the branches of small saplings and the roofs were probably covered by light-weight materials, such as thatch or brush.

This is the kind of reconstruction that has been proposed for sites such as Lepenski Vir and Divostin, and

Figure 7. Photograph of ZM 7. Note division between daub floor and depression.

Figure 8. Photograph of idols from ZM 7.

which can be found used through the region today. This reconstruction is supported by the type of wattling evident in the daub from Blagotin. At Blagotin, we find only parallel wattle impressions, implying that the complex interweaving of substantial vertical and insubstantial horizontal wattle structure of later Vinča (Late Neolithic) period houses was not in use. The kinds of superstructure suggested for other semi-subterranean houses (e.g., Bogdanović 1988; Srejović 1972) may be appropriate models – thin branches or thatch leaning over the pits and occasionally being covered by daub. The daub would preserve only if the structure burnt down. Only the central depression shows evidence for final burning and daub preservation. Otherwise, few daub remains were found, reinforcing indications that there was little investment in the construction of substantial superstructure architecture. Hence, the presence of architectural features would indicate that these were residential structures of some sort.

Size of pit house features and population estimates

The pit features at Blagotin can be divided into groups: the central depression versus those distributed around the edge of the site. The pit features around the periphery tend to be relatively small. On average, they are 3 m wide and 6 m long. The central pit feature is much larger. It is approximately 10 m wide and 8 m long. They are all shaped in the form of an ellipse or rough trapezoid.

Floor areas of pit houses (*zemunicas*) can be used to predict population size of each household (LeBlanc 1971; Narroll 1962). While there is no ethnographic data on population/m^2 of floor area for *zemunicas*, the standard formula for agriculturalists is 10 m^2/person. Using this quotient yields an unacceptably low value (2.5 persons/structure). But, the formula is 3 m^2/person for mobile hunter-gatherers, which would yield a nuclear family sized unit (5 persons/structure). At present, 5 pit house features have been excavated around the large central structure. In addition, integrated surface survey indicates the presence of others. If a total of 10 structures are assumed to be occupied contemporaneously, then the total population of the site would be in the range of 50 persons.

Starčevo ritual space

In the area beneath trenches F and G, a large structure called ZM 7 was excavated. It was also covered by the thick capping horizon. Beneath the capping horizon, the feature was divided into a northern and southern zone (Figure 7). The southern zone was a thick daub platform at the entrance of the structure. On the floor, two large (30 cm high) figurines and altars were found (Figure 8). The northern zone was the core of the depression. It contained a variety of artifacts, including ceramics, figurines, animal bones, grain-shaped offerings, and an early example of a map of the site. The map would represent one of the earliest, if not the earliest map in Europe. Beneath the daub floor, a thick ash deposit and pit were found. In the ash, the remains of a human infant were interred. The remains from the pit also included extremely large numbers of the bones of young animals. The presence of the large figurines, thick bone deposits of very young animals, and a human internment reinforce the interpretation of this depression as a ritually oriented structure or shrine (Stanković 1993, 1995).

Open space

The space between the central pit feature (ZM 7) and surrounding pit house features had extremely low Early Neolithic artifactual densities on the surface and had extremely low subsurface densities of artifacts. It would argue that rubbish was not simply thrown out into the open space between depressions. Instead, this surface was kept relatively clean of debris. This pattern is seen in other sites from the region. Most of the remains are found in or immediately around the pit features.

DISCUSSION – HOUSE SPACING IN OTHER STARČEVO-KÖRÖS-CRI SITES

Are the pits all contemporary?

Superficially, it would appear that the spatial pattern of Early Neolithic features is a circular one. But in order to determine if this spatial pattern corresponds to behavioural correlates, it must be demonstrated that the features are contemporary. A program to systematically date each of the pit features with absolute dating techniques was interrupted by the Balkan wars and consequent embargo. In its absence, other sources of evidence have to be used. Based on the following evidence, it would appear that the structures are indeed contemporary:

1) They are arranged in a circular pattern and not randomly placed around the site.
2) There is no disturbance by contemporary deposits (earlier pits do not cut into later pits).
3) All of the peripherally positioned pits are of a similar depth and contain similar deposits (three horizons).
4) There is at least one ceramic join between two pit houses.

All of the features contain similar ceramic types, and all date to the same ceramic subperiod of the culture (Starčevo IIB) (Stanković and Greenfield 1992). Given all of the above, it would be logical to conclude that the structures at Blagotin are all contemporary.

Spatial structure of Early Neolithic sites

Due to the dearth of large-scale horizontal excavations, there is little detailed information on the spatial distribution of features within Starčevo-Körös-Criş sites. Only a few sites have been spatially excavated. These enable us to better understand the internal structure of these sites and to interpret areas of activities. At each of these sites, almost all of the structures excavated were semisubterranean.

One of the sites, presented above, is Blagotin. It reveals a circular distribution of structures around a larger centrally positioned structure. Another site, Foeni-Salaş, has also been spatially excavated (Jongsma 1997; Jongsma and Greenfield 2001). Five small structures were found distributed in a semicircle around a larger structure. The distance between each of the small structures was more or less the same (about 20 m), and the distance between the central and peripheral structures was about 10 m. Such a distribution of Early Neolithic features was found long before this, albeit it was not recognized as such. Vasić (1936:Tabla VI and LVIII, Slika 8 and 209) in his early excavations in the basal levels at Vinča found a similar distribution of Starčevo pit features – a large central pit house surrounded by an open space of about 10 m and a ring of peripheral smaller pit houses.

EXPLANATION FOR DIFFERENCES IN ARCHITECTURE BETWEEN THE NORTH AND SOUTH BALKANS – WHY PIT HOUSES AND NOT SURFACE HOUSES?

House form is not simply the result of physical forces or any single causal factor, but is the consequence of a whole range of sociocultural factors seen in their broadest terms. Form is in turn modified by climatic conditions (the physical environment which makes some things impossible and encourages others) and by methods of construction, materials available, and the technology (the tools for achieving the desired environment). Rapoport considers the sociocultural forces to be primary, and the others secondary or modifying (1969:47).

All of the Early Neolithic cultures of the southern Balkans and central Europe have surface houses. The appearance of pit houses in the intervening Starčevo-Criş-Körös culture area obviously is not related to the particulars of the environment of this culture because the environment is essentially similar to that of the neighbouring cultures.

The essential reason that pit houses appear and become the common architectural form for the northern Balkan Early Neolithic cultures must be sought in the nature of occupation, not the environment. Short occupation spans seem to generally be the rule based on the thickness of deposits (characteristically thin horizons), the lack of overlapping deposits, and lower frequencies of internal features (i.e., ovens, hearths, etc.) (Jongsma 1997; Jongsma and Greenfield 2000). If environment is not a sufficient reason to explain the differences, then other reasons must be considered.

One hypothesis is that the architectural form is a function of mobility. Pit houses are cross-culturally associated with cultures that have high mobility (Jongsma and Greenfield 2000). If this is accepted, then the question becomes why did the cultures of the northern Balkans have higher mobility patterns than those to the north or south? This leads to the second hypothesis, which is that the occupants of the Early Neolithic sites would be considered similar to or descendants of the indigenous hunter-gatherers of the Balkans. How else can one explain the penchant toward mobile house patterns, the lack of evidence for cultivated crops, and the reliance upon a mixture of domestic and wild stock? The rapidity with which the Early Neolithic cultures of the northern Balkans spread would be a testimonial to the widespread adoption of the trappings of an agricultural lifestyle by indigenous hunter-gatherers rather than the simple migration of sedentary agriculturalists from the south.

CONCLUSION

In summary, a new and unexpected spatial distribution of remains is discernible from the archaeological record at Blagotin with the recognition of the location of Early Neolithic. The remains of nine pit house features were excavated across the site. Two types of pit houses are distinguishable. A smaller and shallower set of pit houses is distributed in a circle around a large open space. The second larger and deeper type is found at the centre of the large open space (ZM 7) and is associated with a daub platform and large idols. Surrounding this feature was a large open space, approximately 10 m wide. A ring of smaller pit house features surrounded the central pit house and plaza. Based on the differences in artifactual contents, it would appear that the function of the central and peripheral pit house features differed. Suggestions have been made that the peripheral features were domestic in nature, while the central pit house was a shrine (Stanković 1993, 1995). Analysis of the distribution of animal remains also indicates substantial differences in the types of remains between central and peripheral structures (Greenfield and Jongsma 2003).

In conclusion, there is no evidence for Starčevo surface houses at Blagotin. Nor from the study of surface remains and distribution of artifacts is there any evidence that they were eroded downslope. It can be safe to state that they never existed. The only evidence for architectural elements in the Starčevo horizon is associated with the large pits. In the face of this evidence, we cannot simply continue to maintain that the pits on Starčevo sites are the borrow pits for above ground wattle-and-daub houses. Enough sites have been excavated to be able to conclude that if surface houses were present, they would have been found. The fact is that they have not been found. Similar structures in similar spatial patterns have also been identified at Vinča and Foeni-Salaş. All of this leads to the conclusion that we are indeed dealing with semisubterranean dwellings or pit houses.

It would appear that we are only beginning to identify the spatial nature of Early Neolithic sites. Archaeologists have been looking for a pattern that did not exist. Instead of rectilinear surface structures, we have found circular distribution of subsurface dwellings. Linear arrangements of structures do not appear until the end of the Early Neolithic in Starčevo-Criş sites.

This pattern has now been recognized at three sites in the region (Blagotin, Foeni-Salaş, and Vinča-Belo Brdo). The function of the central pit house is clearest at Blagotin because of the nature of preservation at the site. It is clearly very different from those surrounding it. Two large (30 cm) idols were found on the floor of the larger pit house. Analysis of the distribution of animal remains also indicates substantial differences in the types of remains between central and peripheral structures. The spatial organization of pit houses, the heavily domesticated fauna, lack of storage facilities, and low frequencies of domestic flora from the site imply that early agricultural societies in this region were for the most part fundamentally different from those of the Mediterranean littoral (Greece and southern Bulgaria). These represent short-term occupations by a relatively mobile society, primarily relying upon their domestic animals for subsistence. This analysis is another step towards a more systematic investigation of Early Neolithic community patterning in the temperate regions of southeastern Europe.

REFERENCES CITED

Bogdanović, M.
|1988| Architecture and Structural Features at Divostin. In *Divostin and the Neolithic of Central Serbia*, edited by A. McPherron and D. Srejović, pp. 35–142. Ethnology Monographs No. 10. University of Pittsburgh, Department of Anthropology, Pittsburgh.

Bogucki, P.
|1988| *Forest Farmers and Stockherders: Early Agriculture and its Consequences in North-Central Europe*. Cambridge University Press, Cambridge.
|1996| The Spread of Farming in Europe. *American Scientist* 84(3):242–253.

Chapman, J. C.
|1989| The Early Balkan Village. In *Varia Archaeologica Hungarica I: Neolithic of Southeastern Europe and its Near Eastern Connections*, pp. 33–53. Archaeological Institute, Budapest.

Dumitrescu, V.
|1983| The Prehistory of Romania from the Earliest Times to 1000 B.C. In *The Cambridge Ancient History*, vol. 3, part 1, 2nd ed., pp. 1–74. Cambridge University Press, Cambridge.

Ehrich, R.
|1977| Starčevo Revisited. In *Ancient Europe and the Mediterranean*, edited by Vladimir Markotić, pp. 59–67. Aris and Phillips, Warminster, England.

Ehrich, R., and H. A. Bankoff
|1991| East-Central Europe. In *Chronologies in Old World Archaeology*, vol. 1, 3rd ed., edited by R. Ehrich, pp. 375–394. University of Chicago Press, Chicago.

Garašanin, M.
|1979| Centralbalkanska zona. In *Praistorija Jugoslavenskih Zemalja II: Neolitsko Doba*, edited by D. Basler, A. Benac, S. Gabrovec, M. Garašanin, N. Tasić, B. Čović, and K. Vinska-Gasparini, pp. 79–212. Akademija Nauka i Umjetnosti Bosne i Hercegovine, Sarajevo.
|1983| The Stone Age in the Central Balkans. In *The Cambridge Ancient History*, vol. 3, part 1, 2nd ed., pp. 75–135. Cambridge University Press, Cambridge.

Gimbutas, M.
|1976| *Neolithic Macedonia*. University of California, Institute of Archaeology, Los Angeles.
|1991| *The Civilization of the Goddess: The World of Old Europe*. Harper Collins, New York.

Gimbutas, M., S. Winn, and D. Shimabuku
|1989| *Achilleion: A Neolithic Settlement in Thessaly, Greece, 6400–5600 BC*. Monumenta Archaeologica 14. Institute of Archaeology, University of California, Los Angeles.

Greenfield, H. J.
|1991| Fauna from the Late Neolithic of the Central Balkans: Issues in Subsistence and Land Use. *Journal of Field Archaeology* 18:161–186.
|1995| Systematic Surface Collection from Blagotin. *Glasnik Srpska Arheološka Društvo (Journal of the Serbian Archaeological Society)* (Belgrade, Yugoslavia) 10:89–99.
|2000| The Application of Integrated Surface and Subsurface Reconnaissance Techniques to Later Prehistoric SE European Sites: Blagotin Serbia. *Geoarchaeology* 15:167–201.

Greenfield, H. J., and F. Draşovean
|1994| An Early Neolithic Starčevo-Criş Settlement in the Romanian Banat: Preliminary Report on the 1992 Excavations at Foeni-Salaş. *Annale Banatului: Journal of the Museum of the Banat* (Timişoara, Romania) 3:45–85.

Greenfield, H. J., and T. L. Jongsma
|2003| Preliminary Report on the Faunal Remains from Blagotin. Unpublished manuscript on file in the Department of Anthropology, University of Manitoba.

Halstead, P.
|1999| *Neolithic Society in Greece*. Sheffield Academic Press, Sheffield, England.

Hayden, B.
|1997| *The Pithouses of Keatley Creek: Complex Hunter-Gatherers of the Northwest Plateau*. Harcourt Brace College Publishers, Fort Worth, Texas.

Horvath, F.
|1989| A Survey on the Development of Neolithic Settlement Pattern and House Types in the Tisza Region. In *Neolithic of Southeastern Europe and its Near Eastern Connections*, pp. 85–103. Varia Archaeologica Hungarica 2. Institute of Archaeology, Academy of Sciences, Budapest.

Jongsma, T. L.
|1997| Distinguishing Pits from Pit Houses through Daub Analysis: The Nature and Location of Early Neolithic Starčevo-Criş Culture Houses at Foeni-Salaş, Romania. Unpublished master's thesis, Department of Anthropology, University of Manitoba, Winnipeg, Manitoba.

Jongsma, T. L., and H. J. Greenfield
|2000| Architectural Technology and the Spread of Early Agricultural Societies in Temperate Southeastern Europe. In *On Being First: Cultural Innovation and Environmental Consequences of First Peopling*, edited by J. Gillespie, S. Tupakka, and C. de Mille, pp. 181–200. Chacmool Archaeological Association, University of Calgary, Calgary, Alberta.

Lazarovici, G.
|1979| *Neoliticul Banatului*. Bibliotheca Musei Napocensis, Cluj-Napoca, Romania.

Leblanc, S.
|1971| An Addition to Naroll's Suggested Floor Area and Settlement Population Relationship. *American Antiquity* 36:210–211.

Makkay, J.
|1978| Excavations at Bicske I. The Early Neolithic – The Earliest Linear Band Ceramic. *Alba Regia* (Szekesfehervar, Hungary) 16:9–60.
|1992| Excavations at the Körös Culture Settlement of Endröd-Öregszölök 119 in 1986–1989. In *Cultural and Landscape Changes in South-East Hungary: Report on the Gyomaendröd Project*, edited by S. Bökönyi, pp. 121–194. Archaeolingua, Budapest.

Milisauskas, S.
|1986| *Early Neolithic Settlement and Society at Olszanica*. Memoirs of the Museum of Anthropology No. 19. University of Michigan, Ann Arbor.

Milisauskas, S., and J. Kruk
|1989| Neolithic Economy in Central Europe. *Journal of World Prehistory* 3:403–446.

Naroll, R.
|1962| Floor Area and Settlement Population. *American Antiquity* 27:587–589.

Pounds, N.
|1969| *Eastern Europe*. University of Chicago Press, Chicago.

Radoman, A.
|1994| Blagotin, the Configuration of Features: Microdrillings, Geomagnetometer – Measurements and Excavation. *Glasnik Srpskog Arheološkog Društvo (Journal of the Serbian Archaeological Society)* (Belgrade, Yugoslavia) 10:100–103.

Rapoport, A.
|1969| *House Form and Culture*. Prentice Hall, New Jersey.

Redžić, M., and Zečević, J.
|1996| The Neolithic Settlement Blagotin: 1993 Excavations. *Glasnik Srpskog Arheološkog Društvo (Journal of the Serbian Archaeological Society)* (Belgrade, Yugoslavia) 10:169–180.

Runnels, C., and P. M. Murray
|2001| *Greece Before History: An Archaeological Companion and Guide*. Stanford University Press, Stanford

Srejović, D.
|1972| *Europe's First Monumental Sculpture: New Discoveries at Lepenski Vir*. Stein and Day, New York.
|1988| *Neolithic of Serbia*. Centre for Archaeological Research, University of Belgrade, Belgrade.

Srejović, D., and Z. Letica
|1978| *Vlasac*. Sprski Akademija Nauka i Umetnosti, Belgrade.

Stanković, S.
|1993| Ritual Places and Artifacts in Early Neolithic Cultures of the Central Balkans. Unpublished Ph.D. dissertation, University of Belgrade, Belgrade, Yugoslavia.
|1995| Anthropomorphic Sculptures from Blagotin, *Glasnik Srpskog Arheološkog Društvo (Journal of the Serbian Archaeological Society)* (Belgrade, Yugoslavia) 10:7–14.

Stanković, S., and H. J. Greenfield
|1992| Arheološka istraživanja višeslojnog praistorijskog lokaliteta Blagotin u selu Poljna (iskopovanja 1991 godine). *Glasnik Srpsko Arheološko Društvo (Journal of the Serbian Archaeological Society)* (Belgrade, Yugoslavia) 8:46–50.

Stanković, S., and V. Leković
|1994.| Neolithic Settlement at Blagotin. *Glasnik Srpsko Arheološko Društvo (Journal of the Serbian Archaeological Society)* (Belgrade, Yugoslavia) 9:177–179.

Stanković, S., and D. Runić
|1990| Višeslojno naselje u Poljni (iskopovanja u 1988 godini). *Glasnik Srpsko Arheološko Društvo (Journal of the Serbian Archaeological Society)* (Yugoslavia, Belgrade) 6:64–67.

Tringham, R.
|1971| *Hunters, Fishers, and Farmers of Eastern Europe, 6000–3000 BC*. Hutchinson University Library, London.
|2000| Southeastern Europe in the Transition to Agriculture. In *Europe's First Farmers*, edited by T. D. Price, pp. 19–56. Cambridge University Press, Cambridge.

Vasić, M. M.
|1932–1936.| *Prehistoriska Vinča*, vol. 2. Državne Štamparija Kraljevine Yugoslavije, Beograd.

Whittle, A., L. Bartosiewicz, D. Borić, P. Pettitt, and M. Richards
|2002.| In the Beginning: New Radiocarbon Dates for the Early Neolithic in Northern Serbia and South-East Hungary. *Antaeus* 25:63–117.

Winter, M.
|1976| The Household Cluster. In *The Mesoamerican Village*, edited by K. V. Flannery, pp. 25–31. Academic Press, New York.

NOTES

1 ZM and OB is an abbreviation for the Serbian words, *zemunica* and *objekat*. They are commonly translated as semisubterranean or pit house feature and an archaeological feature, respectively. OB 1, in this case, turned out to be another semisubterranean dwelling.

PART III: ARCHITECTURAL COMPLEXES

THE INHABITATION OF RÍO VIEJO'S ACROPOLIS

Arthur A. Joyce

Arthur A. Joyce, Department of Anthropology, University of Colorado at Boulder, Boulder, Colorado 80903, U.S.A.

ABSTRACT

This article examines the life history of the acropolis at Río Viejo, Oaxaca, Mexico, from the perspective of what John Barrett (1999) calls the "archaeology of inhabitation." Río Viejo's acropolis went through a complex history of construction, use, modification, abandonment, and reuse beginning in the Terminal Formative and continuing until at least the Postclassic. I argue that changes in the use and meaning of the acropolis embodied in important ways political changes of the Río Viejo polity. In particular, during the Terminal Formative and again in the Late Classic the acropolis went through periods of construction and use that expressed sacred authority and political power. During the Early Classic and Early Postclassic Periods, however, the acropolis evinced a very different dialectic between spatial structure and agency, reflecting the collapse of political institutions and rulership and the emergence of alternative or foreign ideologies.

This chapter examines the life history of the acropolis at Río Viejo on the Pacific Coast of Oaxaca, Mexico. The acropolis was a monumental architectural complex that was first constructed during the late Terminal Formative Period (A.D. 100–250) as the ceremonial precinct of the Río Viejo state. I trace the subsequent use, modification, abandonment and reuse of the acropolis until the decline of the Río Viejo polity during the Early Postclassic Period (A.D. 800–1100). I argue that, like other monumental spaces in Mesoamerica, the acropolis went through a complex history that embodied in important ways political transformations of the Río Viejo polity including incorporation, domination, resistance, negotiation, and perhaps conquest. In particular, during the Terminal Formative and again in the Late Classic the acropolis went through periods of construction and use that expressed sacred authority and political power. During the Early Classic and Early Postclassic Periods, however, the acropolis evinced a very different dialectic between spatial structure and agency, reflecting the collapse of political institutions and rulership and the emergence of alternative or foreign ideologies. In each period, however, the symbolism of the acropolis was informed in important ways by the broader context of its earlier uses and the meanings embodied therein. Before examining the archaeology of Río Viejo, I will briefly discuss the theoretical perspective through which I examine the inhabitation of the acropolis.

THEORETICAL BACKGROUND

Following recent developments in landscape archaeology (Alcock 2002; Ashmore 2002; Ashmore and Knapp 1999; Bradley 1998; Koontz et al. 2001), I argue that the way in which people organize space, including how they conceptualize and alter landscapes, are important aspects of structure that both shape and are shaped by social action. In complex societies, constructed landscapes, especially monumental spaces, are important in reinforcing power within the established social order (Ashmore 1991; Couture 2002; Joyce 2000; Koontz et al. 2001; Love 1999; Van Dyke 2003; Wheatley 1971). Monumental spaces embody politico-religious beliefs that legitimate authority. The physical arrangement and symbolism of buildings, plazas, courtyards, roads and other architectural

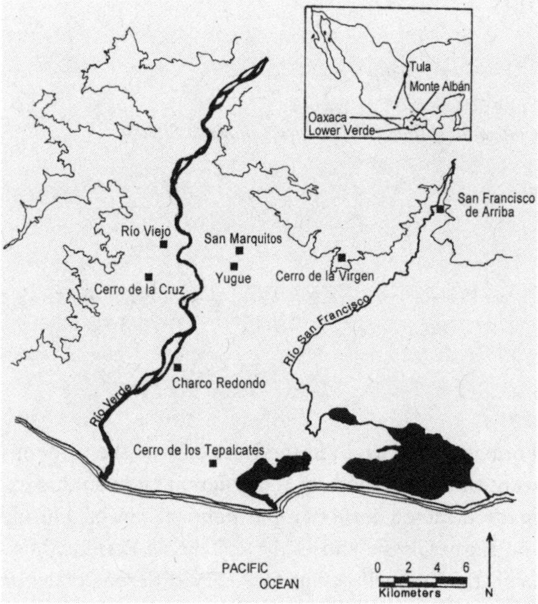

Figure 1. The lower Río Verde Valley, Oaxaca.

features channel the movement and experiences of actors.

In Mesoamerica, archaeological research has shown that the architectural arrangement of ceremonial precincts at cities like Monte Albán, Teotihuacan, Copán, and Tikal materialized a shared view of the cosmos, although one that was shaped by local political history (Ashmore 1991; Ashmore and Sabloff 2002; Joyce 2000, 2004; Sugiyama 1993). Mesoamerican ceremonial precincts, like those in many ancient cities, served as *axes mundi* where cosmic planes like earth, sky, and underworld intersected. Pyramids, in particular, were viewed as sacred mountains (Schele and Freidel 1990:71–72). These centres were also often viewed as places of cosmic creation (Schele and Guernsey Kappleman 2001; Sugiyama 1993:120–121).

A common pattern among Mesoamerican ceremonial centres was to construct a symbolic vision of the cosmos in the layout and symbolism of buildings, plazas, courtyards, and art. While patterns varied through time and among peoples of different regions (Ashmore 2003; Ashmore and Sabloff 2002; Grove 1999; Joyce 2004), this sacred geography usually involved rotating the cosmos onto the surface of the site's ceremonial centre such that north represented the celestial realm and south the earth or underworld (Ashmore 1991; Ashmore and Sabloff 2002; Joyce 2000, 2004; Sugiyama 1993). In addition, at least in the Maya lowlands and especially during the Late Preclassic (300 B.C.–A.D. 300), the east-west axis of ceremonial centres represented the rising and setting points of the sun. For example, at Tikal in the Peten lowlands of Guatemala, the Great Plaza is bounded to the south by Structure 5D-120 with its nine doorways symbolizing the underworld and to the north by the North Acropolis with its royal tombs and stelae depicting rulers, while the east-west axis is defined by Temples I and II (Ashmore 1991:200–203, 2003; Coggins 1980). Furthermore, at Tikal this architectural template seems to be repeated at varying spatial scales from Twin Pyramid Complexes up to the layout of the entire site core. At Monte Albán in the Oaxaca Valley the Main Plaza complex includes representations of the celestial realm on the North Platform and images of sacrifice, warfare, and the underworld to the south (Joyce 2000; Masson and Orr 1998). While significant architectural changes occurred in the Main Plaza at Monte Albán, this basic pattern of cosmic symbolism persisted from the time of the site's founding at 500 B.C. until about A.D. 500 when new patterns emerged (Joyce 2004).

This sacred geography cosmically sanctified authority by positioning nobles as powerful intermediaries between commoners and the divine forces that created and maintained the cosmos. The iconography of carved stones and painted murals and pottery often depict nobles performing important rituals in ceremonial precincts. Nobility was often associated with the northern end of ceremonial precincts through the placement of their residences, their tombs, or their depictions in monumental art, which symbolically associated them with the celestial realm (Ashmore 1991:200–203; Joyce 2000, 2004).

The power of monumental spaces, however, does not derive just from the ideas that they embody, but is produced and experienced through the practices that take place within these places (Ashmore and Knapp 1999; Bradley 1998). Rituals in temples and public plazas involving sacrifice, shamanism, ancestor veneration, processions, divination, and dance communicated aspects of the dominant ideologies of Mesoamerican states. Many of the ceremonies performed by nobles reenacted the cosmic creation and were means of petitioning supernaturals for fertility and prosperity on behalf of their people (Ashmore 2003; Freidel et al. 1993; Joyce 2000). In Prehispanic Mesoamerican written texts, including creation myths and dynastic histories, nobles were seen as fundamentally different from common people, with distinct origins and with special powers to contact the supernatural realm (Freidel et al. 1993; Schele and Freidel 1990). Religious beliefs and practices were, therefore, in part ideological, creating a social contract where nobles performed the most important rituals that petitioned supernaturals for fertility and prosperity, while commoners provided allegiance and tribute in return (Joyce 2000, 2004). By participating in emotionally charged ritual performances, often invoking the cosmic creation, people came to identify with and incorporate in their dispositions messages about their place in the social and cosmic order, including social constructions of class, gender, faction, and polity.

The ongoing use and alteration of monumental space transformed the meanings they embodied, although in ways that reflected the past, creating a life history of place (Ashmore 2002:1177–1179; Barrett 1999; Bradley 1998; Couture 2002:16–29; Knapp and Ashmore 1999). Recently, John Barrett (1999) has described the creation of these life histories of place as involving the inhabitation of landscapes. Transformations of inhabited landscapes, including constructed monuments, involve the reworking of established meanings and the politics of their control. For example, by manipulating space through the erection of physical or symbolic barriers, elites restrict interaction between members of different groups to times and places of their choosing so as to control both the content and presentation of social discourse (Hegmon et al. 2000; Hillier and Hanson 1984). In Mesoamerica, the creation of civic-ceremonial precincts and the sacred calendar were ways in which nobles controlled access to monumental spaces and ritual performances (Love 1999). For example, during the Classic Period, Monte Albán's Main Plaza was transformed from a largely public ceremonial space to an increasingly private elite residential area with a trend towards ritual performances involving a more restricted audience of nobles (Joyce 2004). The increasing exclusion of commoners from the Main Plaza may have alienated them from the rulers and ruling institutions of the Monte Albán state since commoners would have had a social memory of the Main Plaza as a more public and inclusive place as well as a symbol of communal identity.

Monumental spaces, however, were also sites of social negotiation and resistance to authority such as when Native American forced labourers incorporated Prehispanic carved stones or architectural elements into Early Colonial buildings constructed under Spanish rule. The creation, use, and alteration of monumental space, therefore, embodied changes in power and domination in the complex polities of ancient Mesoamerica. Even after their primary period of construction and use, monuments continued to hold meanings that were informed by their earlier histories (also see Bender 1998; Bradley 1998; Sinopoli 2003) as exemplified by the Aztecs' performance of rituals at Teotihuacan, which they viewed as the place of the gods where time began (Hamann 2002).

INHABITING RÍO VIEJO'S ACROPOLIS

The inhabitation of Río Viejo's acropolis has been examined as part of a long-term interdisciplinary project in the lower Río Verde Valley, Oaxaca (Barber and Joyce 2004; Joyce 1991a, 1991b, 1999, 2003; Joyce et al. 1998, 2001; Workinger 2002). This research has included horizontal and/or block excavations at the sites of Río Viejo, Cerro de la Cruz, San Francisco de Arriba, Cerro de la Virgen and Yugüe as well as test excavations at 13 other sites (Figure 1). The entire region has been the focus of a non-systematic surface reconnaissance, while full-coverage surveys have systematically studied an area of 152 km^2. The research has focused on understanding the origins, development, and collapse of the Río Viejo polity.

The acropolis at Río Viejo, designated Mound 1, was a huge architectural complex consisting of a platform measuring approximately 350 m by 200 m along its base and rising at least 5 m above the floodplain (Figure 2). The platform supports two large substructures, reaching heights of 15 m above the floodplain. The large substructure on the northwestern end of the acropolis we designated Mound 1-Structure 1 and the one on the eastern end of the platform was Mound 1-Structure 2. The acropolis also supported five smaller structures, a plaza, and a sunken patio. With an estimated volume of 395,000 m^3, the Mound 1 acropolis is one of the largest structures in Prehispanic Oaxaca (Levine et al. 2004).

Excavations in Mound 1-Structure 2 during the 2000 field season yielded architectural data from the eastern end of the acropolis (Joyce 2003; Joyce et al.

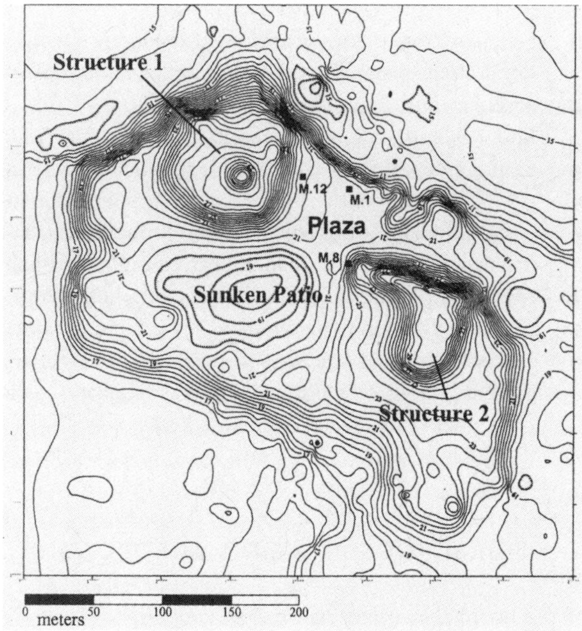

Figure 2. The acropolis at Río Viejo (■ = location of carved stone monuments).

2001; Levine et al. 2004). Mound 1-Structure 2 is an L-shaped monumental substructure that rises approximately 8 m above the surface of the acropolis plaza and 15 m above the surrounding floodplain. Excavations exposed an area of 242 m^2 on Structure 2 and penetrated in places to a depth of 3.2 m below the current surface of the mound. The data indicate that all but the upper 1.1 m of the structure were built during the late Terminal Formative and probably during the latter part of that phase. A small number of redeposited early Terminal Formative sherds in the structure's fill, however, suggest the possibility that there might be an earlier building phase beneath our excavations. While the acropolis was apparently abandoned at the beginning of the Early Classic (A.D. 250–500), construction and occupation resumed during the Late Classic (A.D. 500–800) and continued during the Early Postclassic (A.D. 800–1100).

The Terminal Formative acropolis: Embodying incorporation

Excavations in the acropolis show that it was probably constructed largely during the late Terminal Formative Chacahua phase from A.D. 100 to 250. Excavation and survey data show that the Terminal Formative in the lower Río Verde Valley was a time of increasing social complexity with Río Viejo emerging as an urban centre and probably the capital of a state polity (Joyce 1999:137–138, 2003). By the late Terminal Formative Río Viejo covered 200 ha and was the first-order centre in a five-tiered settlement hierarchy. People from Río Viejo and several other communities in the lower Verde region began constructing monumental buildings during the early Terminal Formative Miniyua phase (150 B.C.–A.D. 100), while Late Formative Minizundo Phase (400–150 B.C.) monumental architecture has been excavated by Workinger (2002) at San Francisco de Arriba. The acropolis at Río Viejo was the largest building constructed in the region during the Formative and was the civic-ceremonial centre of the city.

The evidence indicates that during the late Terminal Formative, Structure 2 consisted of a large stepped platform reaching approximately 14 m above the floodplain that supported a public building. An unusual feature of the structure was that it was constructed of adobe blocks with almost no stone, despite the fact that granite was locally available and was used during the Formative Period for the construction of building foundations. Excavation stratigraphy and results of a preliminary micromorphological study provide data on construction methods (Levine et al. 2004). Excavations indicate that the platform consisted of at least two levels that were retained by walls made from fired earthen blocks and chunks. Platform fill consisted of unfired adobe blocks probably made by pouring a mud-slurry into a mold. After drying, the bricks were set into a silty, perhaps slightly calcareous mortar of coarser composition. On the summit of the platform, excavations revealed remnants of a poorly preserved adobe building. Only a few short sections of the base of the wall were preserved. The recovery of pieces of faced stucco that apparently covered portions of the building as well as one piece of painted adobe indicates that it was an architecturally elaborate building. The pieces of architectural stucco constitute the only examples of this material found thus far in the lower Verde region. The low density of artifacts and lack of domestic debris indicates that the structure was a public building.

The poor preservation of the Terminal Formative building limits inferences about architectural form and associated activities. In addition, our excavations on Mound 1 are limited to Structure 2 so we do not know the overall configuration of the acropolis at this time and are unable at present to develop a model of the ceremonial centre's sacred geography. Based on the available architectural data along with the regional archaeological record and comparative data from other Mesoamerican centres, it is possible, however, to suggest something of the sociopolitical significance of Structure 2. As in many parts of Mesoamerica, the Terminal Formative in the lower Verde region was a time of political centralization and the emergence of urbanism. In the lower Verde, Río Viejo increased from 20 ha in the Late Formative to 200 ha by the end of the Terminal Formative, while the regional settlement hierarchy increased from three to five levels (Joyce 2003).

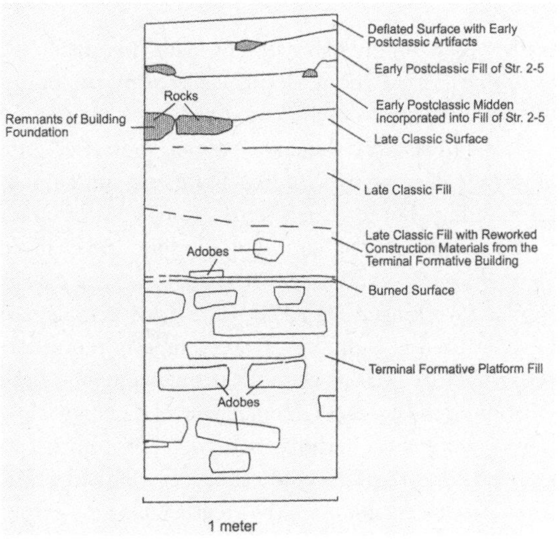

Figure 3. Representative excavation profile (Unit 6C75) showing the building stages of the acropolis at Río Viejo.

At this time throughout much of Mesoamerica people were building monumental public buildings and plazas like those on the acropolis at Río Viejo that became symbols of emerging state polities (Joyce 2000; Laporte and Fialko 1995; Sharer 1994; Sugiyama 1993). Some of the more impressive examples include the Pyramids of the Sun and Moon at Teotihuacan, the Main Plaza at Monte Albán, the El Tigre and Danta complexes at El Mirador, and the North Acropolis and Mundo Perdido Complex at Tikal. Archaeological, iconographic, and epigraphic research shows that the ceremonial precincts of these Terminal Formative cities were constructed according to the principles of sacred geography discussed above and therefore operated as *axes mundi*, creating a point of communication and mediation between the human world and the supernatural otherworld (Ashmore 1991; Ashmore and Sabloff 2002; Joyce 2000; Sugiyama 1993). The dramatic public ceremonies organized and led by nobles in ceremonial precincts would have created powerful psychological forces that bound commoners to the rulers, the symbols, and the new social order centred at these emerging political centres. Public plazas built at major political centres of the Terminal Formative were far larger than those of previous periods and imply a scale of performance that would have engaged larger populations and people from broader territories.[1] These public ritual performances produced larger-scale corporate identities internalized in people's dispositions and externalized in social practices like contributing tribute, allegiance, and labour to the state. Monumental buildings like Río Viejo's acropolis were also visible for great distances so that their power as sacred mountains and political centres would have been present in the everyday lived experiences of people throughout the region. Even the initial construction of monumental buildings would have engaged people in emerging corporate structures since it appears likely that labour was contributed voluntarily. Evidence suggests that warfare may have increased in scale at this time, which could also have acted to unite people behind rulers and ruling institutions (Clark et al. 1998; Freidel 1986:101–106; Joyce and Winter 1996; Webster 1977). While people were increasingly incorporated into larger-scale political formations, which in most cases can probably be described as states, there undoubtedly were different degrees of compliance and involvement with unifying rulers, institutions, and practices (Joyce et al. 2001). In some cases, commoners and nobles outside the centre may have actively resisted emerging political structures (Joyce 2000:85; Joyce 2004).

Given the poor condition of the Terminal Formative architecture at Río Viejo, I am primarily drawing on analogies with other monumental spaces in Mesoamerica to argue for the importance of the acropolis in the creation of larger-scale corporate identities. One available source of data for the sociopolitical significance of the acropolis, however, is its technique of construction.

Rather than simply using basket loads of earthen fill or rubble to raise the Structure 2 platform, the builders made thousands of fired earthen bricks and unfired adobes and secured them with a mud mortar (Figure 3). Other excavated Terminal Formative monumental buildings in the region were constructed of either basket loads of earthen fill (Gillespie 1987; Joyce 1991a:367–371; Workinger 2002:163–234) or rarely, rubble (Workinger 2002:171). The time and labour invested in the building of the acropolis represents active and uncoerced commoner involvement in the creation of the civic-ceremonial centre. The participation of commoners in the construction of the civic-ceremonial centre as well as the rituals carried out there, would have contributed to the creation of a new corporate identity centred on the symbols, institutions, and rulers at Río Viejo. Monumental buildings have also been excavated at second-order and third-order sites in the lower Verde region such as Charco Redondo, San Francisco de Arriba, and Yugüe (Barber and Joyce 2004; Gillespie 1987; Workinger 2002).

Political power during the Terminal Formative in the lower Verde may have reflected a corporate pattern as described by Blanton and his colleagues (1996). In polities with corporate forms of political organization, the exclusionary power of nobles is restricted by an ideology that limits self-aggrandizing impulses of leaders. In the lower Verde, the communal labour invested in the construction of monumental architecture and the relative lack of evidence of inequality expressed in mortuary ritual as well as the absence of monumental art are consistent with corporate forms of political organization, which have been described as "group oriented" and "faceless" (Blanton 1998). The Terminal Formative acropolis at Río Viejo, therefore, may have been as much a symbol of community and its relationship to the supernatural realm as of the power of individual rulers or royal families.

A more corporate/communal form of political organization is supported by Stacy Barber's recent excavation of a portion of a late Terminal Formative cemetery at the third-order site of Yugüe (Barber and Joyce 2004). Barber's excavations recovered the remains of at least 33 individuals, both male and female and of varying status levels and ages buried within a public platform. In contrast, excavation of a high-status residence at the site of Cerro de la Virgen recovered no burials. The dense placement of burials in the Yugüe cemetery as well as the frequent disturbance and movement of the bones of earlier interments by later ones can be interpreted as an assertion of the collective and a denial of the individual and perhaps of differences among individuals (see Shanks and Tilley 1982; however, see below). Similar collective mortuary practices were found with a Late Formative (400–150 B.C.) cemetery at the site of Cerro de la Cruz (Joyce 1991a, 1994).

The Early Classic acropolis: Embodying collapse/conquest

The architectural complex on the acropolis as well as the politico-religious institutions that it housed had a short-lived prominence, probably lasting less than 100 years. At about A.D. 250 the elaborate adobe building on Structure 2 was abandoned. Burned adobes and floor areas suggest that the structure may have been destroyed by fire. The summit of the Structure 2 platform, however, lay exposed to the elements for perhaps as long as 250 years, resulting in erosion and disintegration of most of the building. Two AMS dates have been obtained from the remains of the adobe structure. A date of 1573 ± 40 B.P. or A.D. 377 (AA40036) was obtained from charcoal associated with adobe building materials. A second date of 1696 ± 43 B.P. or A.D. 254 (AA40037) was recovered from charcoal lying directly on a section of burned floor and sealed by overlying adobes. I consider the second sample to be more reliable in dating the abandonment and possible destruction of the building because of the latter's more secure context and because a date of A.D. 254 is more consistent with the ceramic evidence from the underlying platform.

The abandonment of the acropolis was part of a regional disruption in sociopolitical organization (Joyce 2003). Río Viejo experienced a major decrease in size going from 200 ha in the late Terminal Formative to 75 ha in the Early Classic, while the settlement hierarchy declined from five to four levels. The full-coverage survey data indicate that during the Early Classic Coyuche Phase (A.D. 250–500), the lower Verde region contained multiple first-order centres with perhaps as many as eight sites of roughly equivalent size. The systematic survey data show that the percentage of the occupational area in the piedmont increased from 38 per cent in the late Terminal Formative to 63 per cent in the Early Classic, suggesting a shift to defensible locations. Several other large Terminal Formative floodplain sites with mounded architecture, including Yugüe, declined significantly in size or were abandoned.

The data suggest that some form of conflict led to Early Classic political fragmentation in the lower Verde. It is not clear whether this conflict involved local political factions or if an outside power conquered the region. Excavation data suggest that the Early Classic disruption in settlement patterns and sociopolitical organization may have had something to do with the powerful central Mexican polity of Teotihuacan located about 400 km northwest of the lower Verde (Barber and Joyce 2002; Joyce 2003). Two high-status Early Classic burials excavated at Río Viejo have elaborate offerings including green obsidian from the Pachuca source, controlled by Teotihuacan, and imported or local imitations of thin-orange vessels, suggesting interaction with Central Mexico and probably Teotihuacan. Obsidian studies, including neutron activation analyses (Joyce et al. 1995), have shown that 80 per cent of the 356 pieces of obsidian excavated from Early Classic contexts in the region was from Pachuca. This is the highest proportion known for a region outside of the central Mexican highlands (Joyce et al. 1995; Workinger 2002). While the data for Teotihuacan contacts are intriguing, at present plausible models of Early Classic interaction range from conquest to increased reciprocal exchange (Joyce 2003; Workinger 2002).

I would like to suggest, however, that not only the abandonment of the acropolis, but the fact that it was left to disintegrate for at least 250 years, should be seen as having political significance. The 250 years during which the acropolis was left in ruin should be viewed from the perspective of the inhabitation of the site, such that its political importance during the Terminal Formative informed the significance of the ruins during the Early Classic (see Ashmore 2002:1178; Barrett 1999; Bradley 1987). This important political and religious building, which had taken considerable communal labour to construct, and which presumably was an important symbol of the Terminal Formative state, was left to slowly disintegrate. Like its architecturally impressive, intact predecessor, the ruined building would have been visible to the remaining occupants of the site as well as to people in surrounding communities. It is interesting to speculate why Structure 2 was not rebuilt or reoccupied since flat elevated surfaces are ideal locations on which to live in the hot, lowland climate of the Oaxaca Coast. If the Terminal Formative state collapsed due to factional competition it could have symbolized a failed political system. Another possibility is that foreign conquerors could have seen the acropolis as a symbol of a defeated enemy, and its reoccupation, a potential expression of resistance.

The Late Classic acropolis: Embodying domination

During the Late Classic Yuta Tiyoo Phase (A.D. 500–800) Río Viejo returned to prominence as the regional centre in the lower Verde (Joyce et al. 2001:349–354). Río Viejo grew to 250 ha, and the regional settlement hierarchy increased from four to seven levels. The survey data show that in the Late Classic people left defensible piedmont sites and returned to the floodplain. In the full-coverage survey zone, the percentage of settlement in the floodplain increased from its Early Classic level of 22 to 56 per cent by the Late Classic. Río Viejo was the first-order capital of a state polity given its large size, monumental architecture, and numerous carved stone monuments. The rulers of Río Viejo may have dominated areas to the east and west along the Pacific Coast and had exchange relations with regions as distant as the central Mexican highlands and the Gulf Coast (Joyce 1993:75–76; Joyce et al. 1995:11–12).

In the Late Classic, the huge acropolis at Mound 1 once again became the civic-ceremonial centre of Río Viejo. Evidence that Mound 1 was a locus of important public ceremonies, and probably the ruler's palace, includes the presence of three Late Classic carved stone monuments depicting rulers (Urcid and Joyce 2001), a plaza spatially situated for public gatherings, and a sunken patio probably for elite-restricted activities. A test excavation 50 m south of Mound 1 recovered thick deposits of Late Classic sherds from fancy serving vessels, suggesting elite domestic activities or perhaps feasting (Joyce 1991a:480). Excavations during the 2000 field season in Structure 2, demonstrate that this part of the acropolis was reoccupied during the Late Classic, although the architecture from this period was very poorly preserved, due to reuse of foundation stones during the Early Postclassic (A.D. 800–1100). Excavation and surface collections suggest that the entire acropolis was occupied during the Late Classic.

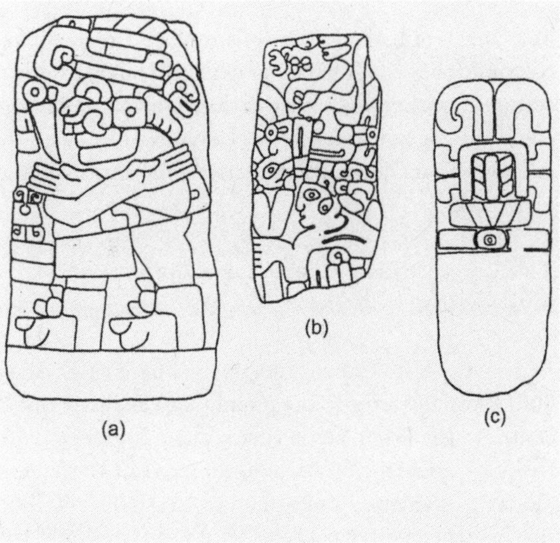

Figure 4. Carved stone monuments from Río Viejo: (a) Monument 8; (b) Monument 11; (c) Monument 14.

Evidence from Río Viejo indicates that the Late Classic polity was no longer characterized by the corporate political organization and communal building projects that occurred during the Terminal Formative. Excavations at Río Viejo indicate that rather than large-scale building projects, construction of public buildings during the Late Classic involved only minor renovations of earlier structures that would not have required large labour forces. For example, Structure 2 on the acropolis was rebuilt by laying down a 0.6 m thick deposit of fill over the ruins of the Terminal Formative building and then constructing another building on this surface, this time with a stone foundation and perishable walls (see Figure 3).

Iconography from Late Classic carved stone monuments in the lower Río Verde Valley suggests a more exclusionary form of political power legitimated through the aggrandizement of individual rulers, their ancestors, and their place in the line of dynastic succession. A total of 13 carved stone monuments have been dated stylistically to the Late Classic at Río Viejo (Urcid and Joyce 2001). They are carved in low relief and are made of the local granite. Many of the carved stones depict nobles, probably rulers of Río Viejo, dressed in elaborate costumes and sometimes accompanied by a glyph that represents their name in the 260-day ritual calendar (Figure 4). For example, Río Viejo Monument 8, located on the acropolis, depicts a noble wearing an elaborate headdress and the profile head of a jaguar. The personage also wears a jaguar buccal mask with prominent fangs and earspools. To the left of the figure is the individual's hieroglyphic name, "10 Eye." Río Viejo Monument 11 depicts a noble holding a zoomorphic staff. The person is wearing a composite pendant and an elaborate headdress that has a jaguar head protruding from its back. Above the figure are the glyph "2 Jaguar" and the "blood" glyph, probably a reference to the autosacrificial letting of blood. Human sacrifice may be referred to on Monument 15 where a noble is shown with several glyphs including those for heart and blood. In addition to actual depictions of rulers, two carved stones (Monuments 1 and 14) each include only a single glyph, which we hypothesize to be the calendrical name of a ruler.

The aggrandizement of nobles as well as their physical and symbolic separation from commoners is indicated by data from the hilltop ceremonial site of Cerro de los Tepalcates that overlooks the ocean and estuaries about 2.5 km north of the coast. At Cerro de los Tepalcates, hieroglyphic inscriptions are carved into boulders. The inscriptions appear to be calendrical names of nobles. The names often occur in pairs, suggesting that they may represent marital pairs. The site also included a probable looted tomb. Since no tombs have been discovered elsewhere in the region, these data suggest that lower Verde nobles may not have been interred in their communities, but rather in sacred non-residential sites.

The reoccupation of the acropolis during the Late Classic, the rebuilding of temples, and the erection of carved stone monuments would have symbolized and embodied the resurgence of lower Verde nobles following the polity's fragmentation and perhaps subjugation during the Early Classic. The acropolis once again became the centrepiece of the Río Viejo state. The Late Classic acropolis was a monument expressing the sacred authority and political power of the nobility. It was easily visible to commoners living at Río Viejo and nearby communities, symbolically reinforcing the dominant position of the nobility, especially in their role as intermediaries between people and the sacred (Joyce et al. 2001). Public rituals on the acropolis, including sacrifice and ancestor veneration, would have even more forcefully enacted the dominant ideology. Presumably, nobles positioned on the monumental buildings of the acropolis would have led public ceremonies with commoners in attendance on the plaza below amongst the carved stone monuments of their rulers. In contrast to the Terminal Formative, however, commoners seem to have been less involved in state projects such as the construction of public buildings. While lower Verde nobles expressed their power in monumental art and architecture, the focus on individual rulers in monumental art and the decrease in state building projects suggest a less communal, more exclusionary ideology. Commoners may have been less actively engaged in the kinds of dramatic ritual performances and shared experiences that created a sense of belonging and identity with state symbols, rulers, and institutions (Joyce and Weller n.d.; Kertzer 1988). At present, we have no evidence for Late Classic expressions of resistance by commoners. Developments during the Early Postclassic suggest, however, that there may have been a hidden transcript of resistance (see Scott 1990) that only became public once the state, and its coercive powers, had collapsed (Joyce et al. 2001).

The Early Postclassic acropolis: Embodying resistance

The data from the lower Río Verde demonstrate that a major change in settlement patterns and sociopolitical organization occurred during the Early Postclassic Yugüe Phase (A.D. 800–1100). Río Viejo continued as a first-order centre, although settlement at the site declined from 250 to 140 ha. At the same time, another first-order centre emerged at San Marquitos, which grew from 7 ha in the Late Classic to 191 ha in the Early Postclassic. The regional settlement hierarchy declined from seven to four levels. There was a settlement shift to higher elevations with piedmont sites increasing from 34 per cent of the occupational area recorded in the survey during the Late Classic to 62 per cent by the Early Postclassic. Excavation and survey projects have found no evidence for the construction of monumental architecture at Río Viejo and other sites during the Early Postclassic. The lack of monumental building activities is mirrored by a reduction in monumental art with only three carved stone monuments recorded at Río Viejo that are tentatively dated stylistically to the Early Postclassic (Urcid and Joyce 2001). The regional data, therefore, suggest a fragmentation of political centres, more decentralized political control, a decrease in social stratification, changes in ideology, and perhaps a shift to a more corporate pattern of political organization (Joyce et al. 2001).

Explanations for the collapse of Río Viejo's ruling institutions are difficult to demonstrate given the available data (Joyce et al. 2001). Population decline resulting from environmental factors like landscape degradation or drought are not indicated at present. Some form of conflict seems to be a more likely factor in the collapse. The dramatic settlement shift into the piedmont would be consistent with the movement of people to defensive locations. In addition, Early Postclassic settlement is concentrated in a very small area of the piedmont with 58 per cent of the total occupational area in the full-coverage survey located within a radius of 3 km from the first-order centre of San Marquitos. This settlement nucleation could have been for defensive purposes. Excavations and surface survey at Early Postclassic sites have recovered large numbers of chert projectile points. For example, ten projectile point fragments were recovered from the Early Postclassic residences on the acropolis, while only two have been recovered from all earlier excavated contexts in the region. These data could indicate greater conflict in the region. It is unclear whether conflict was intraregional, involving factions of the fragmented Río Viejo polity, or if it involved incursions by people from outside the region.

Excavations at Río Viejo show that by the Early Postclassic, the acropolis was no longer the civic-ceremonial centre of the site, but instead was a locus of commoner residences. Large-scale horizontal excavations exposed two areas of Río Viejo with the remains of Early Postclassic houses (Joyce and King 2001). One area with Early Postclassic residences was on Structure 2 of the acropolis where excavations exposed the remains of five residences surrounding a central patio (Joyce et al. 2001). The residences consisted of low (ca..5 m) platforms, which provided a base on which wattle-and-daub structures were built (Figure 5). Carbon samples associated with the Early Postclassic residences yielded dates of 899 ± 44 B.P., or A.D. 1051 (AA40034), and 997 ± 47 B.P., or A.D. 953 (AA37669). Excavations recovered burials, utilitarian artifacts, and middens that demonstrate the domestic function of these buildings. While inhabitants had access to a variety of local and imported goods, the relatively modest architecture and burial offerings indicate commoner status.

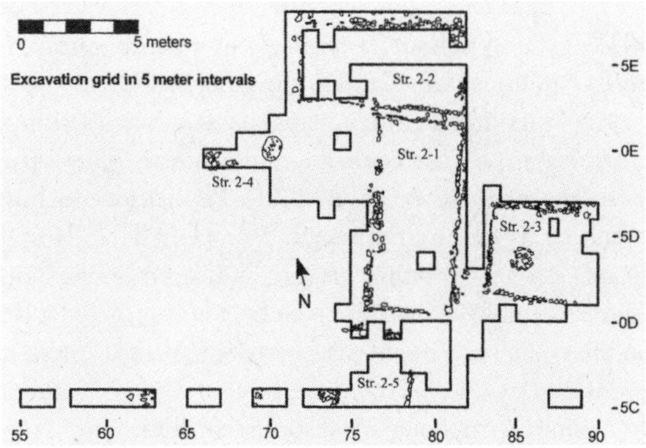

Figure 5. Early Postclassic low-status residences on Río Viejo's acropolis.

The presence of commoner residences on the acropolis at Río Viejo show that Early Postclassic people did not treat the earlier sacred spaces, objects, and buildings with the same reverence they had been afforded in the Late Classic and before (Joyce et al. 2001). A dramatic example of this disjunction between Late Classic and Early Postclassic political organization and ideology is marked by the discovery of a fragment of a Late Classic carved stone monument re-utilized in an Early Postclassic structure wall exposed in excavations 180 m southeast of Structure 2. The carved stone, recovered in an Early Postclassic residence excavated by Stacie King (Joyce and King 2001:5), depicted an elite individual with an elaborate feathered headdress. Prior to its placement in the wall of a commoner residence, this monument had first been re-utilized as a *metate*. At least four other Classic Period carved stones were also re-set in walls during terminal, presumably Early Postclassic, occupations (Urcid and Joyce 2001). It is unlikely that only a few generations after the collapse that these carved stones were simply reused opportunistically for the construction of walls and a *metate* and that Early Postclassic people exhibited ignorance of or indifference to the earlier meanings of sacred objects and spaces. Both areas where Early Postclassic residences were excavated exhibited stratigraphic continuity between Late Classic and Early Postclassic deposits and there are no indications of a hiatus in the occupation of these areas (Joyce and King 2001). Evidence from Mesoamerica and throughout the world shows that earlier meanings of monumental art and architecture continue to inform their reuse and reinterpretation for hundreds and sometimes thousands of years after their creation and initial use (Barrett 1999; Bender 1998; Bradley 1998; Hamann 2002; Masson and Orr 1998; Schele and Freidel 1990:195–196).

The Early Postclassic occupation of the acropolis by commoners, the dismantling of public buildings, and the reuse of carved stone monuments for utilitarian purposes suggests the active denigration of earlier sacred spaces, objects, and buildings rather than simply the transformation of those institutions by rulers (Joyce et al. 2001; Joyce and Weller n.d.). The Early Postclassic acropolis, therefore, evinces a very different dialectic between spatial structure and agency, though one informed by earlier meanings. During the Early Postclassic, the collapse of ruling institutions would have been manifest on a continuous basis as commoners, some living on the acropolis and dismantling its buildings, looked out onto the deteriorating remains of the once sacred space that had been the centrepiece of the Late Classic state.

The way in which state symbols were treated in the Early Postclassic suggests that commoners increasingly penetrated and perhaps actively resisted the dominant ideology in the years prior to the political collapse. Although the collapse in the lower Verde probably did not involve a commoner rebellion, allegiance to the nobility may have been weak during the Late Classic such that non-elites would not have supported their leaders in the face of external military incursions or internal factional competition. By the Early Postclassic, people were free of the coercive power of Late Classic nobles and were able to publicly oppose and subvert the meanings of traditional symbols of state power via actions such as the reuse of carved stones, the dismantling of public buildings, and the occupation of previously sacred spaces. The destruction, denigration, and reuse of these material symbols of the Late Classic state were based on a collective memory of the experiences of having lived under elite domination. This Early Postclassic transformation suggests that a hidden transcript of Late Classic resistance had become public (Joyce et al. 2001).

CONCLUSIONS

The life history of Río Viejo's acropolis embodied transformations in political power and ideologies from the Terminal Formative through the Postclassic. The initial construction of the acropolis occurred during a period of political centralization and increasing social inequality with the development of the Río Viejo state. Political power at this time appears to have exhibited a more corporate pattern such that the acropolis was probably a symbol of communal identity and the community's relationship to the supernatural realm as well as a symbol of emerging rulers and ruling institutions. The acropolis as well as the ritual and political practices that occurred therein embodied new systems of social relations, but also contributed to the production of those social systems. These new social relations included the incorporation of people into a larger-scale, politically centralized state polity at Río Viejo.

It is important to acknowledge, however, that Terminal Formative social change would not have been driven simply by emerging elites or the new corporate structures of the Río Viejo state. In addition to cooperative social practices such as the construction of monumental buildings and ritual performances, social change at this time was undoubtedly also an outcome of struggle, negotiation, and perhaps conflict that should be considered in the life history of Río Viejo's acropolis. One possible point of tension may have been between the emerging institutions of rulership and traditional structural principles that were more egalitarian and community based. This tension is suggested by Late/Terminal Formative mortuary data from the cemeteries at Cerro de la Cruz and Yugüe (Barber and Joyce 2004; Joyce 1991a, 1994). The majority of skeletons recovered in the cemeteries were interred in dense concentrations where individual bodies were often rearranged and piled together as a result of successive burial events, thereby losing their individuality and becoming incorporated into the social group at death. Some burials, however, especially high-status ones, were left as intact skeletons, suggesting a more individualized form of authority linked perhaps to emerging state institutions as symbolized, for example, by Río Viejo's acropolis. While the overall pattern of rulership at this time may appear to be corporate, it was not necessarily the result of a structural unity, but was instead in part an outcome of negotiation among those people that identified with traditional communal authority and those that were aligned with newer more individualized and unequal forms of power. The potential conflict between traditional and state forms of authority also highlights the different meanings that the acropolis no doubt had for people depending on their position relative to these divergent ideas and institutions.

The tension between traditional and state forms of authority could have been a factor contributing to the abandonment and possible destruction of Río Viejo's acropolis within only 150 years of its construction. While this scenario is speculative given the available data, social tension over divergent ideologies and forms of authority could have led to the rejection of state rulers and ruling institutions. The construction of the acropolis may have been an attempt by Río Viejo's rulers to consolidate state power, which instead became the spark that triggered the rejection of the state and the resulting political fragmentation of the Early Classic Period. Of course, other factors such as interaction with Teotihuacan could also have played a part in social change at this time (Joyce 2003; cf. Workinger 2002:394–402).

Throughout the Early Classic Period Structure 2 on the acropolis at Río Viejo was left to disintegrate. The Early Classic was a time of political fragmentation and possibly conflict. The impression is that the region was characterized by multiple, perhaps competing polities (Joyce 2003; Workinger 2002). Río Viejo had decreased in size and political importance, and no community in the region approached the scale that had been reached by Río Viejo during the Terminal Formative. The ruins of the acropolis would have persisted, however, as a reminder of the people, institutions and ideas that sponsored its construction during the Terminal Formative.

Ironically, Early Classic burials at Río Viejo occur most often as individual interments, and there is no evidence of the dense cemeteries of the Formative. Two high-status burials have been recovered with offerings of up to 29 ceramic vessels as well as greenstone, shell, and obsidian artifacts (Joyce 1991a:779, 784). The data suggest that Early Classic social organization involved a decrease in the scale of political control, but with more individualized forms of authority perhaps closer to the network pattern of Blanton and his colleagues (1996). Nobles may have been more successful in consolidating power, developing new forms of rulership within smaller more traditional community-level scales of control.

By the Late Classic Period, Río Viejo again grew into an urban centre and capital of a state polity that dominated the lower Río Verde region. While additional research is needed to examine the sacred geography of

Río Viejo, the Late Classic acropolis was undoubtedly a monument expressing the sacred authority and political power of the nobility. The rebuilding of the acropolis during the Late Classic can be viewed as more than a simple reflection of the administrative institutions of a state, it represented the regional reemergence of Río Viejo's nobles and ruling institutions from the ruins of earlier monuments and the political orders that they symbolized. Political power in the Late Classic exhibited a more exclusionary form than previously, which was legitimated through the aggrandizement of individual rulers, their ancestors, and their place in the line of dynastic succession.

The current data from the Late Classic do not directly suggest the earlier structural contradictions and resulting tensions between more communal and more individualistic forms of authority, although there seems to have been less public participation in state projects relative to the Terminal Formative. The fragmentation of political centres and the return to more decentralized political control during the Early Postclassic (A.D. 800–1100) indicates that these tensions may have continued to be present. Regardless of the conditions that triggered the political collapse, the Early Postclassic evidence from Río Viejo's acropolis indicate that shortly after the collapse people were no longer treating the earlier sacred spaces, objects, and buildings with the same reverence they had been accorded previously. I argue that the dismantling of public buildings and the reuse of carved stones during the Early Postclassic represent more than just a political collapse, these were expressions of a previously hidden transcript of resistance by the inhabitants of Río Viejo made possible by the removal of the coercive forces of the state.

In conclusion, the history of monuments like the acropolis at Río Viejo must be understood as more than static reflections of successive forms of sociopolitical organization (also see Ashmore 2002; Barrett 1999; Bradley 1987, 1998). The acropolis was an inhabited place that went through a complex history of transformations that embodied broader political and ideological relations involving incorporation, domination, resistance, negotiation, and perhaps conquest. The life history of the construction, use, modification, abandonment, and reuse of the acropolis must be understood as transformations achieved by practices that reworked previous meanings embodied in spatial organization, architecture, and iconography. By examining the inhabitation of monuments such as Río Viejo's acropolis, it is possible to go beyond functional explanations to examine a life history of place that considers the ways in which monumental spaces both shape and were shaped by social action.

Acknowledgments

I would like to thank the Instituto Nacional de Antropología e Historia, especially the President of the Consejo de Arqueología, Joaquín García-Bárcena, and the director of the Centro INAH Oaxaca, Eduardo López Calzada, who have supported the research in the lower Río Verde Valley, Oaxaca. Funding for the 2000 field season in the lower Verde was provided by grants from the National Science Foundation (SBR-9729763), the Foundation for the Advancement of Mesoamerican Studies (#99012) and the University of Colorado. I appreciate comments on the manuscript by Doug Bamforth, Cathy Cameron, Linda Cordell, Steve Lekson, and Payson Sheets. I would also like to thank the 2001 Chacmool editorial committee for their comments on this chapter.

REFERENCES CITED

Alcock, S. E.
|2002| *Archaeologies of the Greek Past.* Cambridge University Press, Cambridge.

Ashmore, W.
|1991| Site-Planning Principles and Concepts of Directionality among the Ancient Maya. *Latin American Antiquity* 2:199–226.
|2002| "Decisions and Dispositions": Socializing Spatial Archaeology. *American Anthropologist* 104:1172–1183.
|2003| The Idea of a Maya Town. In *Structure and Meaning in Human Settlement*, edited by T. Atkin and J. Rykwert. University of Pennsylvania Museum Publications, Philadelphia, in press.

Ashmore, W., and A. B. Knapp (editors)
|1999| *Archaeologies of Landscape: Contemporary Perspectives.* Blackwell, Oxford.

Ashmore, W., and J. Sabloff
|2002| Spatial Orders in Maya Civic Plans. *Latin American Antiquity* 13:201–216.

Barber, S., and A. A. Joyce
|2002| Interaction between the Oaxaca Coast and the Valley of Mexico in the Early Classic Period: Preliminary Evidence. Paper presented at the 67th Annual Meeting of the Society for American Archaeology, Denver.

|2004| First among Equals? Elite Status Groups in Terminal Formative Coastal Oaxaca. Paper presented at the 69th Annual Meeting of the Society for American Archaeology, Montreal.

Barrett, J. C.
|1999| The Mythical Landscapes of the British Iron Age. In *Archaeologies of Landscape: Contemporary Perspectives*, edited by W. Ashmore, and A. B. Knapp, pp. 253–265. Blackwell, Oxford.

Bender, B.
|1998| *Stonehenge: Making Space*. Berg, Oxford

Blanton, R. E.
|1998| Beyond Centralization: Steps Toward a Theory of Egalitarian Behavior in Archaic States. In *Archaic States*, edited by G. M. Feinman, and J. Marcus, pp. 135–172. School of American Research Press, Santa Fe.

Blanton, R. E., G. M. Feinman, S. A. Kowalewski, and P. N. Peregrine
|1996| A Dual-Processual Theory for the Evolution of Mesoamerican Civilization. *Current Anthropology* 37:1–14.

Bradley, R.
|1987| Time Regained: The Creation of Continuity. *Journal of the British Archaeological Association* 140:1–17.
|1998| *The Significance of Monuments*. Routledge, London.

Clark, J. E., R. D. Hansen, and T. Pérez
|1998| Maya Genesis: Towards an Origin Narrative of Maya Civilization. Ms. in possession of author.

Coggins, C. C.
|1980| The Shape of Time: Some Political Implications of a Four-Part Figure. *American Antiquity* 45:727–739.

Couture, N. C.
|2002| *The Construction of Power: Monumental Space and Elite Residence at Tiwanaku, Bolivia*. Ph.D. dissertation, Department of Anthropology, University of Chicago. University Microfilms, Ann Arbor.

Freidel, D. A.
|1986| Maya Warfare: An Example of Peer-Polity Interaction. In *Peer Polity Interaction and Socio-Political Change*, edited by C. Renfrew, and J. F. Cherry, pp. 93–108. Cambridge University Press, Cambridge.

Freidel, D. A., L. Schele, and J. Parker
|1993| *Maya Cosmos: Three Thousand Years on the Shaman's Path*. William Morrow, New York.

Gillespie, S. D.
|1987| *Excavaciones en Charco Redondo 1986*. Submitted to the Centro Regional de Oaxaca, Instituto Nacional de Antropología e Historia, Oaxaca, Mexico.

Grove, D. C.
|1999| Public Monuments and Sacred Mountains: Observations on Three Formative Period Sacred Landscapes. In *Social Patterns in Pre-Classic Mesoamerica*, edited by D. C. Grove, and R. A. Joyce, pp. 255–299. Dumbarton Oaks Research Library and Collection, Washington, D.C.

Hamann, B.
|2002| The Social Life of Pre-Sunrise Things. *Current Anthropology* 43:351–382.

Hegmon, M., S. G. Ortman, and J. L. Mobley-Tanaka
|2000| Women, Men, and the Organization of Space. In *Women & Men in the Prehispanic Southwest: Labour, Power, & Prestige*, edited by Patricia L. Crown, pp. 43–90. School of American Research Press, Santa Fe.

Hillier, B., and J. Hanson
|1984| *The Social Logic of Space*. Cambridge University Press, Cambridge.

Joyce, A. A.
|1991a| *Formative Period Occupation in the Lower Río Verde Valley, Oaxaca, Mexico: Interregional Interaction and Social Change*. Ph.D. dissertation, Department of Anthropology, Rutgers University. University Microfilms, Ann Arbor.
|1991b| Formative Period Social Change in the Lower Río Verde Valley, Oaxaca, Mexico. *Latin American Antiquity* 2:126–150.
|1993| Interregional Interaction and Social Development on the Oaxaca Coast. *Ancient Mesoamerica* 4:67–84.
|1994| Late Formative Community Organization and Social Complexity on the Oaxaca Coast. *Journal of Field Archaeology* 21:147–168.
|2000| The Founding of Monte Albán: Sacred Propositions and Social Practices. In *Agency in Archaeology*, edited by M. Dobres, and J. Robb, pp. 71–91. Routledge, London.
|2003| Imperialism in Pre-Aztec Mesoamerica: Monte Albán, Teotihuacan, and the Lower Río Verde Valley. In *Ancient Mesoamerica Warfare*, edited by M. K. Brown, and T. M. Stanton, pp.49–72. AltaMira Press, Walnut Creek, California.
|2004| Sacred Space and Social Relations in the Valley of Oaxaca. In *Mesoamerican Archaeology*, edited by J. Hendon, and R. Joyce, pp.192–216. Blackwell, Oxford.

Joyce, A. A. (editor)
|1999| *El Proyecto Patrones de Asentamiento del Río Verde*. Submitted to the Consejo de Arqueología, Instituto Nacional de Antropología e Historia, Mexico.

Joyce, A. A., and S. M. King
|2001| *Household Archaeology in Coastal Oaxaca, Mexico*. Submitted to the Foundation for the Advancement of Mesoamerican Studies, Inc., Crystal River, Florida.

Joyce, A. A., and E. Weller
|n.d.| Commoner Rituals, Resistance, and the Classic-to-Postclassic Transition. In *Commoner Ritual, Commoner Ideology: Evidence from Households and Beyond across Ancient Mesoamerica*, edited by N. Gonlin, and J. C. Lohse. University of Colorado Press, Boulder, under review.

Joyce, A. A., and M. Winter
|1996| Ideology, Power, and Urban Society in Prehispanic Oaxaca. *Current Anthropology* 37:33–86.

Joyce, A. A., J. M. Elam, M. D. Glascock, H. Neff, and M. Winter
|1995| Exchange Implications of Obsidian Source Analysis from the Lower Río Verde Valley, Oaxaca, Mexico. *Latin American Antiquity* 6:3–15.

Joyce, A. A., M. Winter, and R. G. Mueller
|1998| *Arqueología de la costa de Oaxaca: Asentamientos del periodo Formativo en el valle del Río Verde inferior*. Estudios de Antropología e Historia No. 40. Centro INAH Oaxaca. Oaxaca, Mexico.

Joyce, A. A., L. Arnaud Bustamante, and M. N. Levine
|2001| Commoner Power: A Case Study from the Classic Period Collapse on the Oaxaca Coast. *Journal of Archaeological Method and Theory* 8:343–385.

Kertzer, D.
|1988| *Ritual, Politics and Power.* Yale University Press, New Haven.
Knapp, A. B., and W. Ashmore
|1999| Archaeological Landscapes: Constructed, Conceptualized, Ideational. In *Archaeologies of Landscape: Contemporary* Perspectives, edited by W. Ashmore and A. B. Knapp, pp. 1–30. Blackwell, Oxford.
Koontz, R., K. Reese-Taylor, and A. Headrick
|2001| *Landscape and Power in Ancient Mesoamerica.* Westview Press, Boulder.
Laporte, J. P. and V. Fialko
|1995| Reencuentro con Mundo Perdido, Tikal, Guatemala. *Ancient Mesoamerica* 6:41–94.
Levine, M. N., A. A. Joyce, and P. Goldberg
|2004| Earthen Mound Construction at Río Viejo on the Pacific Coast of Oaxaca, Mexico. Poster presented at the 69th Annual Meeting of the Society for American Archaeology, Montreal, Canada.
Love, M.
|1999| Ideology, Material Culture, and Daily Practice in Pre-Classic Mesoamerica: A Pacific Coast Perspective. In *Social Patterns in Pre-Classic Mesoamerica*, edited by D. C. Grove and R. A. Joyce, pp. 127–154. Dumbarton Oaks Research Library and Collection, Washington, D.C.
Kertzer, D.
|1988| *Ritual, Politics, and Power.* Yale University Press, New Haven.
Masson, M. A., and H. Orr
|1998| The Writing on the Wall: Political Representation and Sacred Geography at Monte Albán. In *The Sowing and the Dawning*, edited by S. B. Mock, pp. 165–175. University of New Mexico Press, Albuquerque.
Schele, L., and D. A. Freidel
|1990| *A Forest of Kings: The Untold Story of the Ancient Maya.* William Morrow, New York.
Schele, L., and J. Guernsey Kappelman
|2001| What the Heck's Coatépec? The Formative Roots of an Enduring Mythology. In *Landscape and Power in Ancient Mesoamerica*, edited by R. Koontz, K. Reese-Taylor, and A. Headrick, pp. 29–53. Westview Press, Boulder.
Scott, J. C.
|1990| *Domination and the Arts of Resistance.* Yale University Press, New Haven.
Shanks, M., and C. Tilley
|1982| Ideology, Symbolic Power and Ritual Communication: A Reinterpretation of Neolithic Mortuary Practices. In *Symbolic and Structural Archaeology*, edited by I. Hodder, pp. 129–154. Cambridge University Press, Cambridge.
Sharer, R. J.
|1994| *The Ancient Maya.* 5th ed. Stanford University Press, Stanford.
Sinopoli, C. M.
|2003| Echos of Empire: Vijayanagara and Historical Memory, Vijayanagara as Historical Memory. In *Archaeologies of Memory*, edited by R. M. Van Dyke, and S. E. Alcock, pp. 17–33. Blackwell, Oxford.
Sugiyama, S.
|1993| Worldview Materialized in Teotihuacán, Mexico. *Latin American Antiquity* 4:103–129.
Urcid, J., and A. A. Joyce
|2001| Carved Monuments and Calendrical Names: The Rulers of Río Viejo, Oaxaca. *Ancient Mesoamerica* 12:199–216.
Van Dyke, R. M.
|2003| Memory and the Construction of Chacoan Society. In *Archaeologies of Memory*, edited by R. M. Van Dyke, and S. E. Alcock, pp. 180–200. Blackwell, Oxford.
Webster, D. L.
|1977| Warfare and the Evolution of Maya Civilization. In *The Origins of Maya Civilization*, edited by R. E. W. Adams, pp. 335–372. University of New Mexico Press, Albuquerque.
Wheatley, P.
|1971| *The Pivot of the Four Quarters.* Aldine, Chicago.
Workinger, A.
|2002| *Coastal/Highland Interaction in Prehispanic Oaxaca, Mexico: The Perspective from San Francisco de Arriba.* Ph.D. Dissertation, Department of Anthropology, Vanderbilt University, University Microfilms, Ann Arbor.

NOTES

1 An exception to this generalization is the Middle Formative (800–400 B.C.) Olmec centre of La Venta, which appears to have had large performance spaces probably reaching the scale of some of those of the Late/Terminal Formative (400 B.C.–A.D. 250).

WHO PUT THE "ḤARAM" IN THE MAḤRAM BILQĪS?

William D. Glanzman

William D. Glanzman, Department of Archaeology, University of Calgary, 2500 University Drive N.W., Calgary, Alberta T2N 1N4, Canada.

ABSTRACT

The results of recent excavation and subsurface survey at the pre-Islamic sanctuary complex known today as the Maḥram Bilqīs in Mārib, shed light on the notion of sacred space in pre-Islamic Arabia. The sanctuary belongs to a special class of sacred structures known as *ḥaram* in modern Arabic, ḤRM in Ancient South Arabian. Special relationships are found with in situ ancient texts, enhanced by other forms of material culture, shedding light on the cult's participants and the site's activity areas. Conforming to pan-Semitic concepts in pre-Islamic times, various prohibitions were in place within the *maḥram*. Recycling of materials within the boundaries of the site, however, was common. Faunal remains, their identity and their condition, coupled with their associations, enable activity areas to be defined, especially in the western sector of the site. Subsurface survey has detected buried structures buried under massive accumulations of aeolian sediments, again in the western part of the site. Access to the site has changed through time, as have its spatial arrangements. Several structural and functional parallels can now be invoked with early Islamic religious monuments and notions of sacred space, demonstrating strong currents of continuity between ancient South Arabia and early Islam.

SACRED SPACE OR PLACE: THE PROBLEM FOR SOUTH ARABIA AND THE EVIDENCE

The notion of a "sacred space" is one that has caught the attention of archaeologists, anthropologists, sociologists and linguists the world over. Within each of those disciplines there are different meanings applied by researchers, just as in each culture area today there are found differing views of what constitutes a sacred space. The definition of a sacred space for prehistoric sites is particularly difficult, and reliance must be on traditional archaeological data and in some cases ethnoarchaeology. The situation is different for historic period sites, as more lines of evidence may be present. In the ancient Near East in particular, besides evidence derived from archaeological and ethnoarchaeological research, we often have relevant data from folklore, the perpetuation of toponyms, and historical sources such as inscriptions. Even with these sources in mind, the problem for archaeologists is how any sanctuary can be defined in terms of spatial analysis (e.g., Friedland and Hecht 1991:21–28).

A sacred place or space for historic period sites within South Arabia is partially known from archaeological evidence. It usually consists of a rectilinear temple, often with a forecourt and stepped access points, sometimes surrounded by a wall or located in a specially designated part of a site (e.g., Breton and Darles 1998; Daum 2000; de Maigret and Robin 1993; Jung 1988; Schmidt 1997/1998; Sedov and Bâtâyi‘ 1994:184–187; Vogt 2000). However, few details are published pertaining to the spatial extent of any temple or sanctuary and its associated activity areas. The question of whether or not the archaeological data conform to an ancient recognition of a sacred space has, until now, remained unexplored. The site of the Maḥram Bilqīs located in Mārib, Republic of Yemen, has the potential to resolve some of these issues.[1]

The Maḥram Bilqīs is an extramural sanctuary complex located several kilometres distant from the ancient city of Mārib, the capital of the kingdom of Saba' (Figure 1).[2] A modern fence arbitrarily delimits the

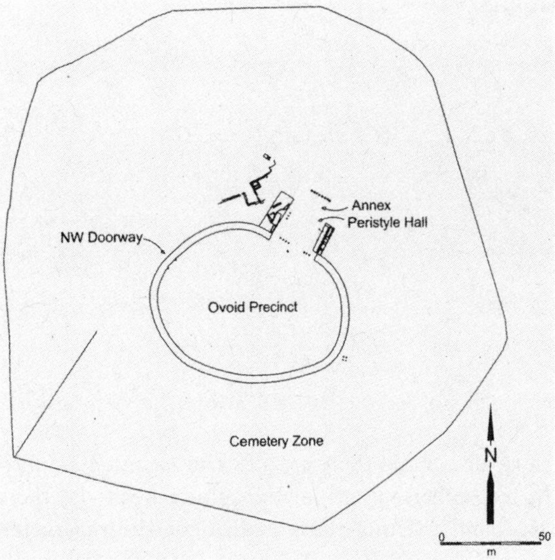

Figure 1. Plan of the site as defined by the fence enclosure.

site based on access roads and tribal farming plots, and ancient irrigation field systems surround it (see Müller 1991). This sanctuary was composed of a number of structures and was once the largest within the Arabian Peninsula (Glanzman 1999:84, 86, no. 14). The major components of the site are: the Ovoid Precinct with its northwestern Doorway, the Peristyle Hall and its Annex in the north, and a Cemetery zone covering much of the south part of the site (Figure 1). Our excavations outside of the Peristyle Hall have yielded some potsherds that date back to ca. 1500–1200 B.C., and the latest evidence demonstrates the sanctuary complex went out of use between the fourth and sixth centuries A.D. Unpublished linguistic analysis of the site's name suggests its function as a pilgrimage centre and is reinforced by inscriptions bearing the names of many individuals and their hometowns recovered in the Cemetery. As a result of our explorations, there are six lines of evidence that are now available for review: the relevant folkloric, historic, ethnographic, linguistic, epigraphic and archaeological evidence.

THE FOLKLORIC, HISTORIC, AND ETHNOGRAPHIC EVIDENCE

The site's name, the Maḥram Bilqīs, is Arab folklore's name for the otherwise nameless Queen of Sheba, who is first encountered in the Old Testament in I Kings 10 and the parallel chapter in II Chronicles 9. In those passages the nameless queen pays a visit, for unclear reasons, to an equally mysterious figure, King Solomon in Jerusalem. Biblical historians usually place Solomon's reign around 970/960–930/920 B.C. (Tomoo 1992:105).

The word "Sheba" in biblical Hebrew is linguistically identical to the South Semitic word *Saba'*, an ancient place name. None of the early religious stories concerning the Queen of Sheba provide her name, and all point to her homeland somewhere within the Arabian Peninsula. The account from the seventh century A.D. Qur'an has the queen's home town as Mārib, the capital of Saba', the kingdom famous for its dam that watered the "two gardens" (or "oases") until its demise in the sixth century A.D. By the ninth century A.D. or perhaps a little earlier, Arab folklore provides the queen's name for the first time, "Bilqīs" (Pritchard 1974; Robin 1996).

Arab folklore's name for the site, the *Maḥram Bilqīs*, literally means "sanctuary of Bilqīs" (Glanzman 1999), with *maḥram* being the Arabic word for "sanctuary" (Beeston et al. 1982:70; Chelhod 1978:372). Folk memory therefore preserves the ancient function of the site. Such functionally correct associations in toponymy for the Near East are not common. Graffiti found on the site demonstrate that respect for its sacred character ceased at least by the twelfth century A.D. and probably earlier, as historical and archaeological evidence indicate extensive plundering of the site may have occurred as early as the sixth century A.D. (Glanzman 1997, 1999:83–84, no.14). Today, the indigenous folk refer to the site also as the *ma'abad*, which in Arabic means "shrine" or "place of service/servitude [to a deity]"; in Islam, the reference is to 'Allah, while for pre-Islamic times the reference is to any deity. This appellation colloquially reinforces the modern toponym as well as the ancient function of the site.

THE LINGUISTIC EVIDENCE: ḤARAM AND MAḤRAM

In the Middle East there are several Arabic terms used to designate a place that is "sacred" or that has some degree of inviolability associated with it, and their meanings cover a spectrum of prohibited activities. The relevant terms are *ḥawṭah*, *ḥima*, and *ḥaram*.

The term *ḥawṭah* refers to an easily defensible enclosure where certain activities are prohibited, such as hunting. Its root also gives rise to the notion of "enclosure," as in the derived word for a woman's "belt" or "girdle." The sanctity of the place is always the result of swearing oaths invoking a tribal deity – and in Islam, 'Allah – as the overseer of the guaranty (Chelhod 1971; Serjeant 1987). Hence, the deity becomes associated with the place by human agency.

The word *ḥima* refers to a territory that is under the protection of the head of a tribe or other elite, in which certain activities such as hunting of animals and the cutting of trees are prohibited. In function, it is essentially no different than *ḥaram*, and during the Islamic period it gradually replaces that older term (Chelhod 1964:230–232; Serjeant 1987).

In Arabic the root meaning of *ḥaram* refers to anything that is not permitted – an object, activity, or thought – in contrast to that which is permitted, or *halāl* (Al-Qaradawi 1994). When referring to a place, the form *maḥram* or *muḥarrem* is used and refers to any place that is inviolable and under the protection of a deity (Chelhod 1978:372; Jamme 1962:193).

Both *maḥram* and *ḥawṭah* have a high degree of parallelism in meaning and application, and for this reason occasionally the terms have become confused and in some cases even interchangeable in practice (Serjeant 1987). For example, piles of stones, called *anṣāb*, can spatially delineate both (Fahd 1993:154). Both entities also have behavioural restrictions, such as a prohibition of cutting of trees or hunting within them (Chelhod 1964:50–52, 210; Schimmel 1991:164–166; Serjeant 1987:196). And both are considered as places of safe haven for the refugee and criminal alike (Chelhod 1971; Farah 1994:32–34).

There is one essential difference, however. At each *maḥram* there is always a divine presence. The deity is felt to be present or reside within a *bayt*, a "temple" or "shrine" that may take a variety of forms. It is always located within the *maḥram*, and the territory that surrounds it is placed under the protection of a deity (Chelhod 1964:213). Further, a *maḥram* is and always has been associated with a pre-Islamic deity, and in modern times transfers to 'Allah as in the case of the Ḥaram al-Masjīd in Mecca, the centre of Islam (Glanzman 1999:85, no. 2). In all cases, the association is of divine origin, not an appointed role involving human agency.

In pre-Islamic times and during the dawn of Islam within the Arabian Peninsula we find a number of uses of the Old South Arabian term ḤRM, from which the Arabic term *ḥaram* derives (Biella 1982:189–190). Many other texts reveal that animal sacrifice was common within many of those sanctuaries (Allouche 1987:366; Gawlikowski 1982; Ryckmans 1992:173–174). At the Maḥram Bilqīs our fieldwork has made the meaning of ḤRM and its associated activities clearer. While animal sacrifices are as yet not specified in the texts recovered, the primary deity worshipped here, 'Almaqah, did receive agricultural products as tithes in kind from which he provided a banquet (Serjeant 1987:197; cf. Beeston 1984:261, 262, 264; Jamme 1962:55–56).

PREVIOUSLY RECOVERED EPIGRAPHIC EVIDENCE

Between 1951 and 1952 the site yielded several Old South Arabian texts that attest the usage of MḤRM, a noun derived from ḤRM (Biella 1982:74, 505, 507; Jamme 1962:192–193). In one of these texts, known by its *siglum* as Ja 702, we receive our first clue to spatial functions on the site. One clause (line 10) reads: "it is forbidden to herd [sc. pasture] animals within the MḤRM of the dead" (Biella 1982:74, 505, 507). This passage clearly refers to the "sacred space" of the recently uncovered Cemetery complex at the site (Glanzman 1999:85, no. 2, 2002:187–188, Figure 1). It is juxtaposed with the term BT (line 7) in the phrase BBT 'LMQH, "in the temple of 'Almaqah," a reference to the area enclosed by the massive curving wall. This juxtaposition of BT and MḤRM is deliberate, and reflects a spatial reality for the Sabaeans. That is, there were at least two separate yet contiguous sacred spaces on the site: one is the temple proper, 'WM (*'Awām*), the ancient name for the BT 'LMQH (*bayt 'Almaqah*); the other is the Cemetery.

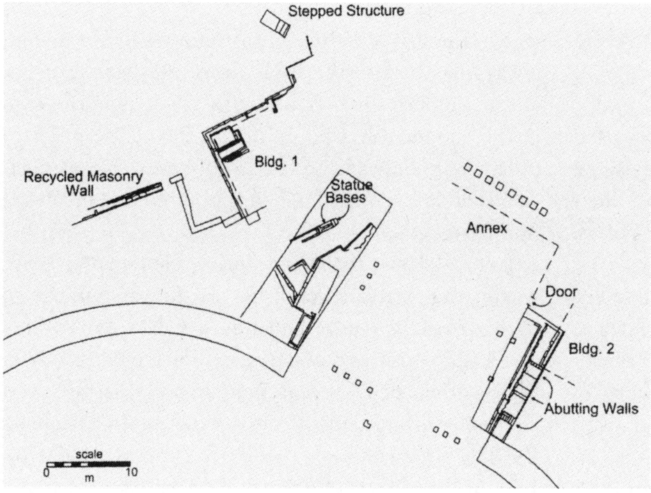

Figure 2. Detail of the architecture exposed around the Peristyle Hall in 2001.

THE MAḤRAM BILQĪS (MB) PROJECT: ARCHAEOLOGICAL, EPIGRAPHIC AND SUBSURFACE SURVEY EVIDENCE IN AREA B

In 2001 we exposed the earliest known in situ inscription so far recovered from the sanctuary complex. It begins about 2.9 m beyond the abutment of the wall with the Peristyle Hall and continues for approximately 11 m (Glanzman 2002:189). Its large letter size, approximately 25 cm in height, and prominence indicate that the viewer was meant to see it at a distance upon approaching this part of the wall from the northeast.

An important relationship is found at the beginning of the text: "Yada''il Dhariḥ, son of Sumhu'alay, the *mukarrib* [confederator] of Saba', has built 'Awām, the temple of 'Almaqah" (see Glanzman 2003:186; Maraqten 2002:211–212). The ruler, who reigned sometime before 620 B.C. (Glanzman 1994:85, 1999:82, 2003:186–192), claims only to have built up the *bayt* or "temple" of the deity, not the entire sanctuary or *maḥram*. Here, the *bayt* is either defined by or contained within the Ovoid Precinct's enclosure wall, conforming to known pre-Islamic and Islamic period practices, and is certainly the *bayt* encountered in the text recovered during the 1950s that juxtaposes the MḤRM of the Cemetery with the temple proper.

In the 1999 field season we employed a ground-penetrating radar (GPR) survey to investigate the extent and complexities of the site beneath the massive accumulations of wind-blown sediment, which in some places exceeds 6.0 m. We found evidence of a Processional Way as well as numerous other structures, evidence of several floors within the Peristyle Hall, and some erratic anomalies flanking either side of the hall (Moorman et al. 2001). During the last two field seasons one of our goals was to investigate those erratic GPR anomalies. In the area beyond the southeast flank of the Peristyle Hall we found a parallel wall face of Building 2, made of nicely dressed limestone blocks, with a passageway approximately 1.2 m wide between them. Several parallel walls, built of dressed limestone and hewn basalt blocks, are also found here and abut the hall at a right angle, creating a series of rooms. One of these abuts both Building 2 and the hall and blocks the passageway (Figure 2). The passageway and rooms were filled with masonry and other debris.

The artifacts found in the passageway and within the rooms are mixed from ancient looting activities. The latest datable pottery form is the Wavy Rim Bowl, spanning the third century B.C. through the third century A.D. or a little later (Glanzman 1994:215–229, 2002:189–191). Architectural details demonstrate that the early stage of the Ovoid Precinct's enclosure wall, bearing the monumental inscription, and Building 2 are roughly contemporary and coincide with other early construction activities on the site. Some encroachment of this area may have taken place with the construction of Building 2; the Peristyle Hall was built shortly thereafter, around 500 B.C., coinciding with the beginning of a later stage of the enclosure wall (Glanzman 1999:82).

Further to the east during our first field season we discovered a new genre of inscription, a small two-line text known by the *siglum* as MB 98 I-10. In summary, it prohibits the erection and placement of any structure or monument from the location of the text and beyond. Paleographically it belongs to the Middle Sabaic period, spanning roughly the first century B.C. through the third century A.D. (Glanzman 2002:191–192, Figure 5, 2003:188, Figure 4; Maraqten 2002:210).

According to the published information and archival photo data from the 1950s (Glanzman 1998:Figure 4), the latest access into the Peristyle Hall – and thus the temple proper – was via a circuitous route from the northeast, within our Area B and adjacent to Building 2, through a small doorway in the Annex because the other doors were blocked up in antiquity (Figure 2).

Therefore, the space in front of the long inscription changed radically by some relatively late point in time, up to and possibly beyond the third century A.D., with the erection of Building 2 and finally with the placement of the abutting walls. Once those walls were put in place, before or by the end of the Middle Sabaic period in the third century A.D., the orientation and function of this space had changed dramatically. It became very crowded, requiring a prohibition against further encroachment within the MḤRM.

ARCHAEOLOGICAL, EPIGRAPHIC AND SUBSURFACE SURVEY DATA IN AREA A

During 2001 in Area A we concentrated our efforts between the Peristyle Hall and Building 1. Here we uncovered a series of structures (Figure 2): several rooms; a series of late walls built against the northwest flank of the Peristyle Hall; and a sequence of abutting structures. These latter are a division wall abutted by a statue base, both with an inscription on their northern face, and a final abutting statue base with an inscription on its eastern face. The inscriptions mention a succession of three Sabaean kings reigning from the late first century B.C. through the late second century A.D., whose dates are in the same sequence as their structural abutments. These structures successively restricted traffic flow coming toward the Peristyle Hall from the west during the Middle Sabaic period (Glanzman 2002:192–195; Maraqten 2002:210, 213–214, Figures 3, 5, 6).

Beyond Building 1 a number of structures can be seen (Figure 2): a wall composed of recycled masonry, a stepped structure that further delineates the space near Building 1, and a crude stone wall and a curved structure immediately west of the stepped structure.[3]

This year we also employed three subsurface survey techniques: GPR, an electromagnetic resistivity survey, and a magnetometer survey, together with hand auger verification of anomalies at various locations. These survey data complement one other and are still under analysis, but some preliminary results are revealing (Maillol et al. 2002).

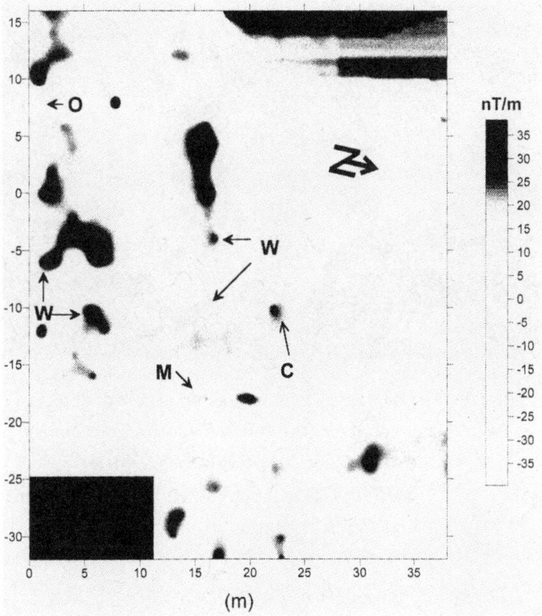

Figure 3. Magnetometer results in Area A, showing relationships with Building 1 (lower left) and other exposed architecture: o = ovoid enclosure wall, w = walls, m = mud and stone wall, c = circular structure.

The magnetometer results highlight the partially exposed architecture, as well as other structures invisible from the surface (Figure 3). Buried and partly buried structures, seen here as magnetic highs of 15 nT/m (nanotesla per metre) or higher (indicated by the gray scale), appear to direct eastbound traffic moving from the west toward the Peristyle Hall, such as a rectilinear structure that seems to articulate with our recycled masonry wall and forms a corner. The curved structure is further delineated, suggesting it is circular in form.

Building 1 is a large structure with many construction phases, uncovered during the 2000 and 2001 field seasons. Along its west wall there is the remnant of a long, Middle Sabaic inscription (*siglum* MB 2000 I-7) stating that whoever brings a series of animals – camels, caravan camels, donkeys, etc. – to the sanctuary and allows them to wander inside must pay a penalty to the king (Glanzman 2002:192–195, 2003:Figure 2; Maraqten 2002:210, Figures 2, 3).

Around Building 1, where the subsurface survey revealed buried structures, are massive deposits of

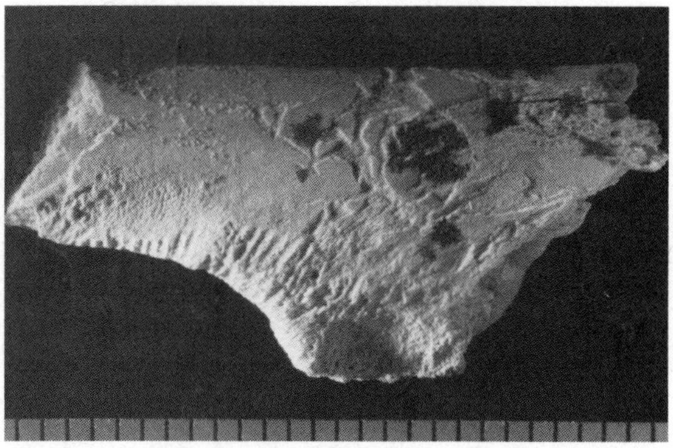

Figure 4. Ovi-caprid fragment showing a rodent's gnawing marks and meandering root marks (MB Project 2001 Registry No. MCR-287.100, General Organization for Antiquities and Museum, Republic of Yemen).

loose silty soil with abundant fragments of animal bone, often burnt. Beneath this deposit and north of the recycled masonry wall is a thick accumulation of small undulating deposits composed of very hard-packed silty soils (see Maraqten 2002:Figure 2). Some of these contain ash and numerous artifacts. Once again, the latest datable artifacts within them seem to be the Wavy Rim Bowl.

Given the placement and details of inscription MB 2000 I-7, and the architectural relationships we uncovered in the 2001 field season, the reader of the text was meant to have seen it when approaching from the west. The different activity areas within this portion of the site, as demonstrated by the exposed architecture and the subsurface survey data, are still untested yet suggest the presence of an animal reception and processing area.

POST-FIELD LABWORK

The faunal remains from the 2000 field season retain traces of butchery patterns on many examples. Some of the bones have minute gnawing marks and others have root marks; occasionally, both features appear on the same bone fragment (Figure 4). Some specimens are also burnt.

The animals mentioned in inscription MB 2000 I-7 correspond to many of the species identified in the corpus. According to well-known ancient Near Eastern practices, some of the animals were brought to this sanctuary as animal offerings or property transfers to the deity 'Almaqah. Also according to ancient Near Eastern practices, the butchered animal was prepared for the deity or cooked for the temple staff within the sacred complex. Once consumed, the remains were discarded within a designated dump zone in some as yet unexplored part of the site. While there, rodent exploitation and plant colonization would occur because of the proximity of the nearby ancient field systems (Glanzman 2002:195–197).

These animal bone fragments were found within wall fill of Building 1 in Area A, where they were associated with numerous artifacts. Their features enable us to reconstruct at least six archaeological contexts, and consequently spatial functions, relating to animals on the site: reception, sacrifice or butchery, burnt and other offerings, consumption, discard, and recycling.

SYNTHESIS

We now have a better understanding of the sacred space occupied by the Mahram Bilqis. We have many different kinds of religious buildings as determined by architectural details, inscriptions and contextually related items. The sanctuary is unique when compared to all other known religious complexes within the region, so we must be cautious in our interpretations.

As yet, we do not know the limits of our sanctuary complex, although it is clear that it extends beyond the modern fence. We can anticipate, on analogy to the *anṣāb* of Islamic shrines and sanctuaries, that formal boundary markers, or inscriptional evidence of them, may be present.

In the northwest part of the site, the subsurface survey has detected what seems to be the remains of a Processional Way facilitating access to the site by pilgrims. From analogy to ancient Mesopotamian, Egyptian and early Christian pilgrimage sites, we must anticipate that some of the remains are facilities that cater to their needs, for example, places to stay, eat, make and sell offerings suitable for the sanctity of the site and the prestige of the deity.

Once inside, there were at least two contiguous sacred spaces: the area of the Cemetery, and the area containing the *bayt 'Almaqah*. For each such space we must keep in mind that a series of ritual taboos and prohibitions exist to restrict access of practitioners of the cult and their offerings in ancient Semitic cultures and in Islam. The inscriptions here are of immense value, as some indicate by whom and how access could be gained into parts of the sanctuary. Hence, there were status-related places within sacred spaces.

Access to parts of the sanctuary changed through time, as did the functions of the spaces they created. During the later stages of use of the sanctuary complex, especially during the Middle Sabaic period, the spaces around the northern part of the site became very crowded with monuments left behind by the pious – so much so that formal decrees served to prohibit further crowding and violations of sanctity. The subsurface survey demonstrates that, as the complex grew through time, major reorientations in spatial function occurred before the abandonment of the sanctuary complex.

All of the evidence from Area A suggests that part of it was once a zone into which animals were brought as property transfers to the deity for sacrifice and subsequent processing. The animals and other offerings became *ḥaram* once the sanctuary personnel accepted them. The contextual associations demonstrate that several ancient deposits were exploited in antiquity and were recycled as wall fill and other purposes. The value of reused and recycled objects, and remnants of offerings, was primarily that they were still considered property of the deity. That is, their removal from the sanctuary was *ḥaram*.

The sanctity of the artifacts and buildings within the complex did not prevent their alteration as the sanctuary grew and reorientations became necessary. Use, reuse and recycling of building materials in or for other facilities within the *maḥram* were acceptable activities to the Sabaeans. However, it was *ḥaram* to remove them from the sacred space, constituting yet another parallel to Islamic practice.

The parallels to Islamic sacred places are so strong that we can assert that the origins of many Islamic practices within religious complexes of the Middle East can be found in pre-Islamic times within South Arabia. At the Maḥram Bilqīs that origin extends back in time at least to the late second millennium B.C. Once the historical period of South Arabia begins, before 1200 B.C., the Sabaeans are known to dwell in the area of Mārib to at least the fourth century A.D., when site abandonment and looting took place. It was during that time that the monarchs of Saba', first the *mukarribs* and later the kings, and their subjects worshipped at the site. Following the introduction of Islam into the region during the early seventh century A.D., Arab folklore and linguistic evidence preserve the site's religious function.

Acknowledgments

I gratefully acknowledge Dr. Yusuf Muḥammad 'Abdullah, former President of the General Organization for Antiquities and Museums (GOAM) and his representatives for making the first four field seasons possible and for permission to take artifacts out of the country for further study. The Maḥram Bilqīs (MB) Project was an American Foundation for the Study of Man (AFSM) field project initiated by Mrs. Merilyn Phillips Hodgson, President of the AFSM. Funding and support for it has been provided by the AFSM, International Tourism Inc. of Yemen, Yemenia Airlines, the Foundation for Ancient Research and Mormon Studies (FARMS), the University of Calgary, and Nexen Inc. of Calgary. Computer graphics for Figures 1 and 2 were compiled by Mr. Mitch Hendrickson, Cadd-Fu Archaeological Drafting Services, Calgary. Dr. Jean-Michel Maillol, Department of Geology and Geophysics, University of Calgary, created Figure 3. Dr. Gerry Newlands, technician for the Department of Archaeology, University of Calgary, took the photograph used as Figure 4.

REFERENCES CITED

Allouche, A.

|1987| Arabian Religions. In *AARO–AUST*, edited by C. J. Adams, J. M. Kitagawa, M. E. Marty, R. P. McBrien, J. Needleman, A. Schimmel, R. M. Seltzer, and V. Turner, pp. 363–367. The Encyclopaedia of Religion, vol. 1, M. Eliade, general editor, Macmillan Publishing Company, New York.

Al-Qaradawi, Y.

|1994| *The Lawful and the Prohibited in Islam (Al-Halal Wal Haram Fil Islam).* Translated by K. El-Helbawy, M. M. Siddiqui, and S. Shukry. American Trust Publications, Plainfield, Indiana.

Beeston, A. F. L.
|1984| The Religions of Pre-Islamic Yemen. In *L'Arabie du Sud: Histoire et civilization: I. Le peuple yéménite et ses raciness*, edited by J. Chelhod, R. de Bayle des Hermens, A. F. L. Beeston, G. Garbini, H. Labrousse, P. Marthelot, L. Ricci, P. Richard, C. Robin, and M. Rodinson, pp. 259–269. Islam d'hier et d'aujourd'hui, tome 21, A. M. Turki, general editor, Editions G.-P. Maisonneuve et Larose, Paris.

Beeston, A. F. L., M. A. Ghul, W. W. Müller, and J. Ryckmans
|1982| *Sabaic Dictionary (English-French-Arabic)*. Publications of the University of Sanaa, YAR. Éditions Peeters, Louvain-la-Neuve.

Biella, J. C.
|1982| *Dictionary of Old South Arabic: Sabaean Dialect*. Harvard Semitic Studies, no. 25, Frank Moore Cross, Jr., general editor, Scholars Press, Chico, California.

Breton, J.-F., and C. Darles
|1998| Le grand temple. In *Fouilles de Shabwa III: Architecture et techniques de construction*, edited by J.-F. Breton, pp. 95–151. Institut français d'archéologie du proche-orient, Beyrouth-Damas-Amman, Bibliothèque archéologique et historique Tome CLIV. IFAPO, Beyrouth.

Chelhod, J.
|1964| *Les structures du sacré chez les Arabes*. Islam d'hier et d'aujourd'hui, vol. XIII, R. Brunschvig, general editor, G.-P. Maisonneuve et Larose, Paris.
|1971| Ḥawṭa. In *H–IRAM*, edited by B. Lewis, V.L. Ménage, C. Pellat, and J. Schacht, p. 294. The Encyclopaedia of Islam, new edition, vol. III. E. J. Brill, Leiden.
|1978| Ḳadāsa. In *IRAN–KHA*, edited by C. E. Bosworth, E. van Donzel, B. Lewis, and C. Pellat, p. 372. The Encyclopaedia of Islam, new edition, vol. IV. E. J. Brill, Leiden.

Daum, W.
|2000| Der heilige Berg Arabiens. In *Im Land der Königin von Saba. Kunstschätze aus dem antiken Jemen*, edited by W. Daum, W. W. Müller, N. Nebes, and W. Raunig, pp. 223–232. Staatlichen Museum für Völkerkunde München, IP, München.

de Maigret, A., and C. Robin
|1993| Le temple de Nakraḥ à Yathill (aujourd'hui Barāqish), Yémen, resultats des deux premières campagnes de fouilles de la mission italienne. *Académie des inscriptions et belles-lettres, compte-rendus* avril–juin:427–496.

Fahd, T.
|1993| Nuṣub. In *NEDĪM–NŪR AL-DĪN MAHMŪD B. ZANKĪ, Fascicles 131–146*, edited by C. E. Bosworth, E. van Donzel, W. P. Heinrichs, and G. Lecomte, pp.154–155. The Encyclopaedia of Islam, new edition, vol. VIII. E. J. Brill, Leiden.

Farah, C. E.
|1994| *Islam: Beliefs and Observances*. 5th ed. Barron's, Hauppauge, New York.

Friedland, R., and Hecht, R. D.
|1991| The Politics of Sacred Place: Jerusalem's Temple Mount/*al-haram al-sharif*. In *Sacred Places and Profane Spaces: Essays in the Geographics of Judaism, Christianity, and Islam*, edited by J. Scott, and P. Simpson-Housley, pp 21–61. Contributions to the Study of Religion, no. 30, Henry Warner Bowden, general editor, Greenwood Press, New York.

Gawlikowski, M.
|1982| The Sacred Space in Ancient Arab Religions. In *Studies in the History and Archaeology of Jordan*, vol. I, edited by A. Hadidi, pp. 301–303. Department of Antiquities, Amman.

Glanzman, W. D.
|1994| *Typology and Chronology of the Pottery from Hajar ar-Rayḥāni, Republic of Yemen*. Ph.D. Thesis, University of Pennsylvania, Philadelphia. University Microfilms, Ann Arbor.
|1997| Les temple de Mârib: Awwâm (aujourd'hui Maḥram Bilqîs) grand temple d'Almaqah. In *Yémen, au pays de la reine de Saba': Exposition présentée à l'Institut du monde arabe du 25 octobre 1997 au février 1998*, p. 145. Flammarion, Paris.
|1998| Digging Deeper: The Results of the First Season of Activities of the AFSM on the Maḥram Bilqīs, Mārib. *Proceedings of the Seminar for Arabian Studies* 28:89–104.
|1999| Clarifying the Record: the Bayt 'Awwām Revisited. *Proceedings of the Seminar for Arabian Studies* 29:73–88.
|2002| Some Notions of Sacred Space at the Maḥram Bilqīs in Mārib. *Proceedings of the Seminar for Arabian Studies* 32:187–201.
|2003| An Examination of the Building Campaign of Yada''il Dharīḥ bin Sumhu'alay, *mukarrib* of Saba', in Light of Recent Archaeology. *Proceedings of the Seminar for Arabian Studies* 33:183–198.

Jamme, A.
|1962| *Sabaean Inscriptions from Maḥram Bilqîs (Mârib)*. Publications of the American Foundation for the Study of Man, vol. III, edited by W. F. Albright, R. L. Cleveland, and G. W. Van Beek. Johns Hopkins Press, Baltimore.

Jung, M.
|1988| The Religious Monuments of Ancient Southern Arabia: A Preliminary Typological Classification. *Annali dell'Istituto orientali di Napoli* 48:177–218.

Maillol, J. M., B. J. Moorman, W. D. Glanzman, F. S. Walter, and J. L. Williams
|2002| Multi-Method Geophysical Investigations at Mahram Bilqis, Yemen – Unveiling the Temple of the Queen of Sheba. In *Proceedings of SAGEEP (Symposium on the Application of Geophysics to Engineering and Environmental Problems) 2002*. CD-ROM, Environmental and Engineering Geophysical Society, Denver, Colorado.

Maraqten, M.
|2002| New Inscriptions from the Maḥram Bilqīs. *Proceedings of the Seminar for Arabian Studies* 32:209–216.

Moorman, B., W. D. Glanzman, J.-M. Maillol, and A. L. Lyttle
|2001| Imaging Beneath the Surface at Mahram Bilqīs. *Proceedings of the Seminar for Arabian Studies* 31:179–187.

Müller, W. W.
|1991| Mārib. In *MAHK–MID*, edited by C. E. Bosworth, E. van Donzel, W. P. Heinrichs, and C. Pellat, pp. 559–567. The Encyclopaedia of Islam, new edition, vol. VI. E. J. Brill, Leiden.
Pritchard, J. B. (editor)
|1974| *Solomon & Sheba*. Phaidon, London.
Robin, C.
|1996| Sheba. In *Sexualité–Sichem*, edited by J. Briend and É. Cothenet, cols. 1043–1254. Supplément au dictionnaire de la Bible, fascicle 70, H. Cazelles and A. Feuillet, general editors, Letouzey & Ané, Paris.
Ryckmans, J.
|1992| South Arabia, Religions of. In *Si–Z*, edited by G. A. Herion, D. F. Graf, and J. D. Pleins, pp. 171–176. The Anchor Bible Dictionary, vol. 6, D. N. Freedman, general editor, Doubleday, New York.
Schimmel, A.
|1991| Sacred Geography in Islam. In *Sacred Places and Profane Spaces: Essays in the Geographics of Judaism, Christianity, and Islam*, edited by J. Scott, and P. Simpson-Housley, pp. 163–175. Contributions to the Study of Religion, no. 30, H. W. Bowden, general editor, Greenwood Press, New York.
Schmidt, J.
|1997/1998| Tempel und Heiligtümer in Südarabien. Zu den materiellen und formalen Strukturen der Sakralbaukunst. *Nürnberger Blätter zur Archäologie* 14:10–40.
Sedov, A. V., and A. Bâtâyi'
|1994| Temples of Ancient Hadramawt. *Proceedings of the Seminar for Arabian Studies* 24:183–196.
Serjeant, R. B.
|1987| Ḥaram and Ḥawṭah. In *GOD–ICHI*, edited by C. J. Adams, J. M. Kitagawa, M. E. Marty, R. P. McBrien, J. Needleman, A. Schimmel, R. M. Seltzer, and V. Turner, pp. 196–198. The Encyclopedia of Religion, vol. 6, M. Eliade, general editor, Macmillan Publishing Company, New York.
Tomoo, I.
|1992| Solomon. In *Si–Z*, edited by G. A. Herion, D. F. Graf, and J. D. Pleins, pp. 105–113. The Anchor Bible Dictionary, vol. 6, D. N. Freedman, general editor, Doubleday, New York.
Vogt, B.
|2000| Der Almaqah-Tempel von Bar'ân ('Arsh Bilqîs). In *Im Land der Königin von Saba: Kunstschätze aus dem antiken Jemen*, edited by W. Daum, W. W. Müller, N. Nebes, and W. Raunig, pp. 106–109. Staatlichen Museum für Völkerkunde München, IP, München.

NOTES

1 The Maḥram Bilqīs (MB) Project was initiated in 1996 by the American Foundation for the Study of Man (AFSM) and directed by the author for its first four field seasons (1998–2001).

2 The site came to the attention of the western world in 1843 and was first explored in detail during 1888. The first archaeological exploration took place between November 1951 and February 1952 by the American Foundation for the Study of Man (AFSM) and consisted of clearance work. No further explorations took place on the site until 1997. In 1998 the AFSM renewed its exploration of the site (Glanzman 1997, 1999), and the fourth season was completed in 2001 (Glanzman 2002).

3 These last two structures are only partially exposed and were thus not plotted on the site plan.

THE FORM, STYLE AND FUNCTION OF STRUCTURE 12A, MINANHÁ, BELIZE

Jeffrey Seibert

Jeffrey Seibert, Department of Archaeology, University of Calgary, 2500 University Drive N.W., Calgary, Alberta T2N 1N4, Canada.

ABSTRACT

This paper seeks to examine how public architecture can serve as a means of understanding political structure among the ancient Maya. This paper will present information concerning the form and style of Structure 12A, located in the site epicentre of Minanhá, Belize. This type of structure, classified as a range structure by Mayanists, is believed to have served as a locus of administration in Classic period Maya polities. This assumption will be examined by looking at the form of the excavated portions of the structure. In addition, stylistic attributes of the architecture itself, especially the benches, will be examined in order to enhance these functional inferences.

Much attention has been focused recently on the problem of assessing the nature of ancient Maya palaces and royal courts (e.g., Inomata and Houston 2001). While different authors, most notably Webster (2001), have postulated that the entire architectural assemblage found in the epicentre of a site constitutes the space the royal court would have utilized, most recent investigations have focused on the dwellings of the rulers themselves. This paper seeks to expand the scope of these inquiries by examining the role that another type of public structure found in a site's epicentre would have played. This type of building is the public range structure. In this paper I am attempting to examine the role that a particular range structure, Structure 12A from Minanhá, Belize, would have fulfilled. This is being done through an analysis of the form of the building, focusing on its spatial characteristics as well as its stylistic attributes. This, in turn, will allow for comparisons with structures from other sites in the Maya area.

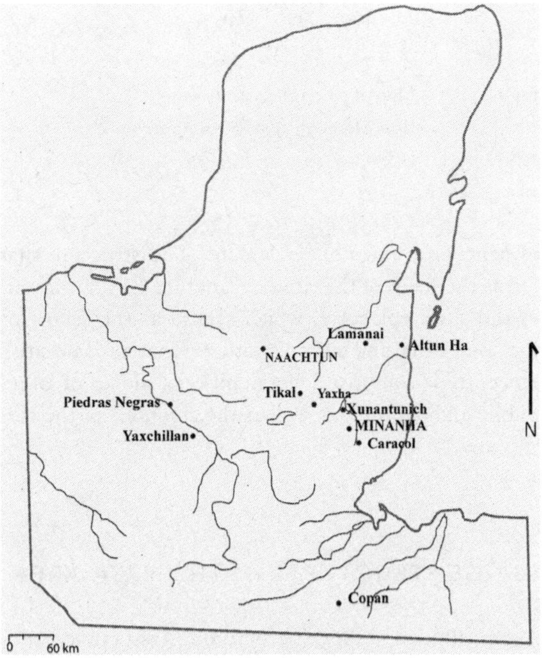

Figure 1. Map of the Maya area, showing the location of Minanhá

MINANHÁ

The site of Minanhá is located in the North Vaca plateau in western Belize (Figure 1). Excavations have been conducted at the site since 1999 by Trent University's Social Archaeology Research Program, under the direction of Professor Gyles Iannone. As Iannone (1999) has outlined elsewhere, this site is located in what was a politically volatile area during the Classic period, and as such is an ideal place to study sociopolitical organization and integration. Minanhá is a medium-sized major centre composed of a number

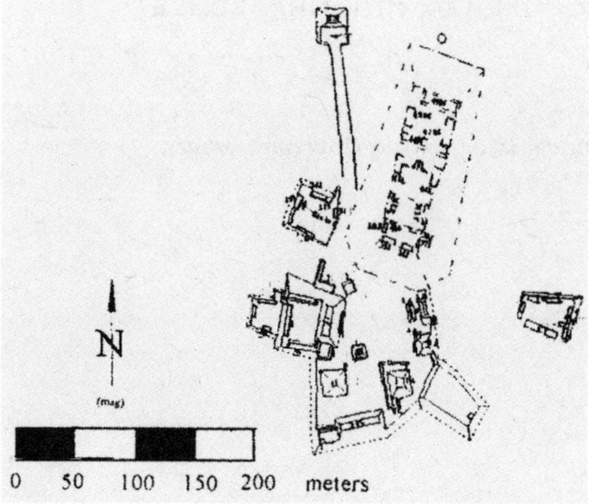

Figure 2. Map of Minanhá site epicentre. (Map courtesy G. Iannone)

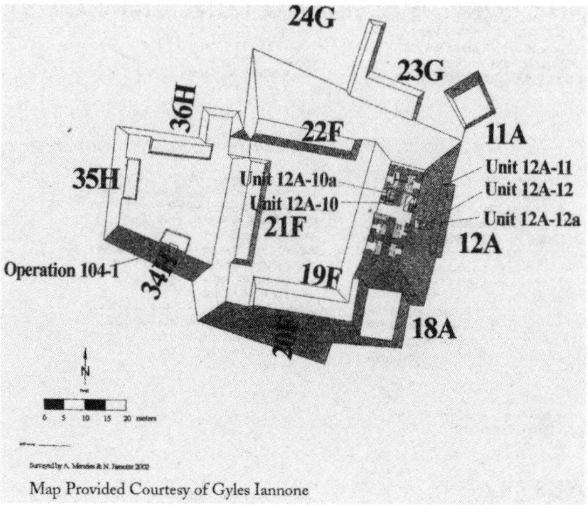

Figure 3. Map of Structure 12A and Courtyard F. (Map courtesy G. Iannone)

of concentric rings of settlement. The structure that forms the focus of this study, Structure 12A, is located in the site's epicentre, which served as the focus for the site's ritual and administrative activities. The site's epicentre is comprised of a number of pieces of large, public architecture, as well as the acropolis of the site (Figure 2).

RANGE STRUCTURES IN THE MAYA AREA

As was alluded to above, Structure 12A is a range structure, meaning that it is a long, multiroomed building. Range structures are remarkably heterogeneous as structural types, as is outlined by Harrison (1971, 2001). A range structure is composed of rows, or "ranges" of rooms, organized in variable arrangements. Harrison (1999:185–186) makes a primary distinction in range structure types in his discussion of the central acropolis at Tikal. The distinction is made between range structures where the ranges of rooms face in the same direction, and range structures where the ranges of rooms face in opposite directions. This second general type of range structure is often characterized by a central passageway that transects the building. One range of rooms typically faces into a public space, whereas the other range faces into a spatially discrete courtyard or courtyard complex (i.e., a palace). The passageway that transects these buildings serves as liminal spaces between these public and "private" areas. It is worth noting that range structures can be found as isolated buildings that are part of plazas or in association with courtyard groups or complexes. Indeed, the variety of spatial arrangements of these buildings truly underscores the potential functional variability of range structures.

THE FORM OF STRUCTURE 12A

Structure 12A is located on the western side of Plaza A in the epicentre of the site. Structure 12A is one of the larger structures in the site, being 6.47 m tall, approximately 40 m long and 20 m wide (Figure 3). The front of the structure faced directly onto the main plaza of the site, and was accessible through a staircase excavated in the 2003 field season (Figure 4). Excavations in the 2000 field season revealed that there was also a staircase that led from the back of the structure into Courtyard F.

The general form of Structure 12A conforms to the second of the two general types of range structures outlined by Harrison (1999:185–186), meaning that it was a public building with at least two ranges of rooms that were separated by a spine-wall. Excavations conducted in the structure in the 2000 and 2001

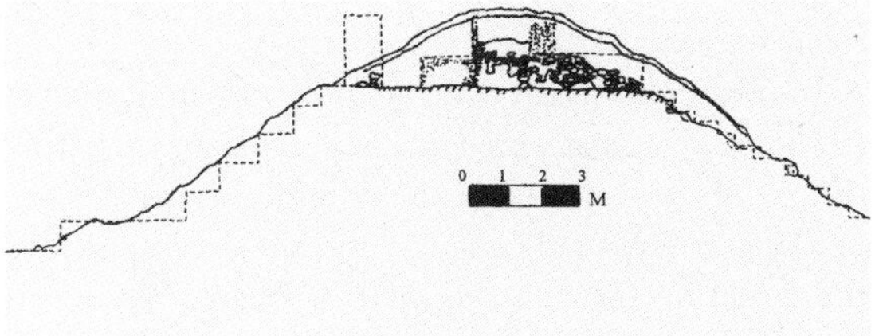

Figure 4. Profile of Structure 12A, showing excavated architecture.

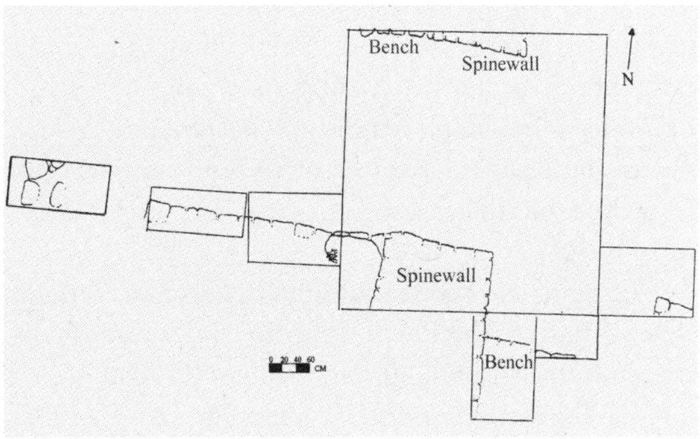

Figure 5. Plan of units excavated in 2000 field season, illustrating the central passageway and benches.

field seasons (Seibert 2000, 2001) have revealed that Structure 12A was composed of two ranges of rooms, which faced in opposite directions, and which were bisected by a central passageway. This building serves as a boundary between Plaza A, one of the principal public plazas at the site and Courtyard F, which lies directly behind Structure 12A. The passageway running through Structure 12A, as such, would have served to channel traffic between these two spaces, as will be discussed in more detail below. This general form of structural configuration is seen in a number of sites in the immediate vicinity of Minanhá, including Caracol (Chase and Chase 2001), Cahal Pech (Awe and Campbell 1989; Ball 1993), Buenavista del Cayo (Ball and Taschek 2001), as well as being present throughout the Peten (Harrison 1970, 1999) (see Seibert 2004 for an overview of the distribution and variability in this type of structure in the Belize Valley and Vaca Plateau).

The two ranges of rooms, mentioned above, are separated by a spine wall approximately a metre and a half thick, and all exposed rooms contain masonry benches. These benches are low (approximately 1 m high), and appear to be linear benches. Excavations in one of these benches suggest that it was constructed at the same time as the terminal phase of the structure itself, based on the inferred construction sequence of the structure. Dividing walls, approximately 75 cm thick, separate the rooms of Structure 12A. The walls of this structure, as well as the benches, were plastered in antiquity as is evidenced by extant patches of plaster on the walls, and the presence of plaster on the benches. The benches in this structure are undecorated and non-ornate, which is suggestive of certain broad stylistic affiliations, as will be discussed below. The central passageway discussed above is lined with benches, with two on each side of the passageway. These benches run parallel to the passageway, and appear to be rectangular, although the backs of the benches were not exposed. All of these benches lack the arm and head rests seen at many other sites in the lowlands (Figure 5).

The exterior walls of this structure have largely collapsed, with relatively low portions of the walls (at most four to five courses high) remaining intact in sections adjacent to room doors. These wall sections are likely piers or supports for the superstructure of the building and roof, which were entirely masonry. The roof was made of vaulted masonry, as is evidenced by the large number of corbelled vault stones (see Loten and Pendergast 1984:23 for a discussion of vault form) and capstones recovered from the excavations and the sheer mass of structural debris that formed the overburden. The floors of the structure are made of durable plaster, which in areas of heavy overburden are extremely well preserved. This plaster is difficult to penetrate with a pick to this day, suggesting its durability and the high quality of its manufacture.

THE STYLE OF STRUCTURE 12A

As was discussed previously, the frontal and rear façades of this structure have long since collapsed, and at best only a few courses of these walls remain. As such, one of the best stylistic indicators from this structure is the benches that are seen in the rooms, and the central passage.

The benches of this structure display characteristics that conform to the Peten style of architecture, as discussed by Harrison (2001) and Kubler (1990:207–215). This architectural style is typified by its austerity, which is in contrast to much of the architecture from the rest of the Maya lowlands. Harrison (2001) emphasizes the plain design of the benches from Tikal, which is the site that best exemplifies this Peten style, and in many ways defined it. The benches from Structure 12A would not be out of place at Tikal, owing to their plain design elements. As was discussed above, these benches are notable for their lack of sculpted or molded stucco decoration, and lack such simple decoration as superior or basal moldings (see Loten and Pendergast 1984). This designation is tentative, however, as the façade of the building has collapsed.

THE FUNCTION OF STRUCTURE 12A

For the most part, past research on these structures has tended to emphasize their elite residential function through their roles as components of palace groups. Although the potentially administrative function of some of these structures has been recognized (e.g., Harrison 1970; Martin 2001; McAnany and Plank 2001), this aspect of their usage has received little scholarly attention. The functional attributes of residential and administrative range structures can be distinguished by examining a number of architectural and artifactual criteria. The criteria indicative of an administrative function for a range structure, as postulated by Kowalski (1987:85; see also Iannone 1999), include: their orientation towards a public plaza; the presence of a large, easily accessible staircase; and the presence of a throne or bench situated on the central axis of the structure. Residential range structures, conversely, would be organized into courtyard groups or multicourtyard complexes with restricted access and associated elite domestic artifactual assemblages. The key to assessing the function of a given range structure relies on applying these criteria. As Flannery (1998) notes, examination of the public architecture of archaic states can yield valuable information concerning social organization.

In relation to the general architectural indicators of administration that were laid out previously, this structure fulfils at least two of the criteria, through its orientation towards public space and the accessibility of the structure through the main staircase. While this structure does not have a bench or throne on its primary axis, there are a number of rooms in the front of this structure that contain benches that are oriented towards the public plaza. As was discussed numerous times throughout this paper, the central axis of this structure is situated in the central passageway that transects the building and leads to Courtyard F. The rooms that form the rest of the public focus of this building, however, would have provided ample space to carry out administrative duties.

Both Harrison (1970, 2001) and Valdez (2001) note the importance of benches in "palace structures" for social interaction and administration, and Reents-Budet (1994, 2001) illustrates the importance of benches for administration based on the iconography of polychrome cylinder vases. As both Reents-Budet (2001) and Martin (2001:178) note, these polychrome vases clearly illustrate members of the "royal courts" of various sites accepting tribute. These individuals are typically seated on benches, and the pictures on the vases often illustrate so-called "palace-type" (or range structure) architecture, in the form of benches or thrones, broad staircases and palace rooms. In Structure 12A, the large size of the benches, both in the public and more restricted rooms would have facilitated such administrative activities by allowing for relatively large and concentrated gatherings of people. It seems likely, based on the spatially discrete nature of the rooms in the "back" of the structure that they would have fulfilled a slightly different function than the front rooms, as will be discussed below.

Webster (2001:150) postulates, conversely, that these public-oriented rooms would have likely served as viewing areas where important symbols of power, such as jade artifacts, would have been displayed to impress the populace at large and maintain the power of the theatre state. In the case of Structure 12A, this seems like an unlikely conclusion, because the height of the structure (roughly 6.5 m) would have precluded easy visual access into these rooms from the plaza. In addition, it seems likely that the structure itself would have been more of a symbol of power than mere artifacts and performance would have been, because of the labour invested in it (see Abrams 1994; Trigger 1990).

There would have likely been a differentiation in the activities being carried out in the more public and restricted (i.e., facing towards the courtyard) sides of this structure, owing to the large degree of architectural investment that was made in defining these spaces. The fact that the passageway was the only entrance into the courtyard and the back of the structure, in addition to the possibility that the benches along the passageway controlled traffic, makes it seem likely that the back section of the structure was a more private location. Without artifactual indicators of function it is extremely difficult to delimit the nature of the activities that were carried out in this structure, except in very general terms. The only artifactual indicator of structure function is a small grinding stone found at the front of the passageway that might have served as a pigment grinder (see Inomata 1997:346) or a bark paper smoother (see Coe and Kerr 1998:152). As no other artifacts that would indicate function have been found, discussions of possible room function must rely primarily on architectural data.

The question of the role of the benches that face inward toward the central passageway of the structure is also an important one. Comparisons of the form of Structure 12A to the range structures located on the front of the Caana architectural complex from Caracol yield interesting insights into its possible function. Chase and Chase (2001:112) note the presence of benches that face inward towards the central passageway of the structure in question and postulate that these benches were seats for guards or other individuals who restricted access to the upper portions of the complex. As was discussed above, there are similar benches in Structure 12A at Minanhá, and the prospect that they served a similar function is intriguing and reinforces the notion that Courtyard F is a more private locus than Plaza A. Even without "guard posts," however, the fact that the passageway in the centre of Structure 12A is the only clear entranceway into the back of the structure, and Courtyard F, says a great deal about the spatial restrictions regarding access into the "private" portions of the group.

As was alluded to above, the location of the structure in relation to the rest of the site also yields insights into its role. Structure 12A, as is mentioned above, in many ways serves as a barrier between Plaza A and Courtyard F. Hillier and Hanson (1984) postulate that one of the primary functions of architecture is to define and structure the space that it contains. In a cultural context where outdoor space is defined by architecture, such as courtyards and plazas among the Maya (Andrews 1975), the role of architecture as a barrier between these spaces becomes increasingly important. As such, in addition to serving as a public edifice, Structure 12A served as an important spatial barrier between outdoor activity areas. In addition to this, the public nature and relative accessibility of the front portions of this structure strongly suggest that it fulfilled a public function. Access from Plaza A into this portion of the structure would have been much more highly restricted if it was a private structure.

The fact that Structure 12A faces onto a public plaza is instructive regarding this proposed public function because, as numerous scholars (e.g., Ashmore 1987; Kubler 1985; Low 1995, 2000) note, the public plaza is one of the most important public spaces in Mesoamerican cities, in both Precolumbian and colonial times. Instead of simply serving as the empty space between buildings, plazas in Mesoamerica serve as important public areas, which served both sacred and secular functions. Indeed plazas, such as Plaza A and the other public plazas of Maya sites, were effectively nuclei of public activity, and in many ways more important than the buildings that surrounded them. It is important to note, however, that, although this plaza is public, this does not mean that access to it was entirely unrestricted. As Webster (2001) asserts, the epicentre of a site likely constitutes the built environment of the royal court. As such, this structure is best thought of as being public, but in terms that were strongly circumscribed by the elites of the site. This is reinforced by an examination of the site plan of Minanhá (see Figure 2), which clearly illustrates that the site epicentre itself was an area that was spatially circumscribed, and therefore possibly spatially restricted.

CONCLUSION

The form of Structure12A, as discussed throughout this paper, conforms to the general designation of a range structure, and more specifically to Harrison's (1999) "type two" designation, meaning that it is organized in two ranges of rooms, which face in opposite directions and were transected by a central passageway. Based on the evidence recovered so far, this structure seems likely to have been an administrative building differentiated into public and more restricted spaces. The style of this structure, based on the benches that have been excavated, seems linked to the Peten style seen throughout the region, which is hardly surprising. If the structural façade had remained intact, this would be a much more definite statement. An important functional aspect of Structure 12A, in addition to its posited role as a public structure, is its role as a spatial barrier. Not only do buildings contain space in the Maya area, they also structure outdoor space. This structure is no exception, as it effectively serves as a boundary between Plaza A and Courtyard F, thereby separating and creating public and private space.

Acknowledgments

I would like to thank Professor Gyles Iannone for his continuing support of my own research interests, his leadership of the project, and also for being a good friend for a number of years. I would like to thank the members of the Belize Department of Archaeology, especially George Thompson, Brian Woodeye, Jaime Awe, Alan Moore and John Morris for continuing to support this project. Funding for my research came from a number of sources including Trent University, the Social Sciences and Humanities Research Council of Canada, and the University of Calgary. My supervisor, Dr. Kathryn Reese-Taylor, also deserves many thanks, both for her support and for making me examine the data employed in this paper from a number of standpoints. Dr. Peter Dawson, also of the University of Calgary, has also been extremely helpful in helping me think about the organization of space in society. I would like to thank all of my fellow staff members, too many to mention here, and in particular Sonja Schwake, Amy Seibert, James Stemp, Nadine Gray, Joelle Chartrand and Adam Menzies, for everything. All of this work would have been impossible without the help of the great students that I have had the pleasure of working with, also too many to mention in this context. My Belizean colleagues, Jose Martinez, Lazaro Martinez, Efrain Martinez, Rosa Martinez, David Valencia and Everald Tut, are also thanked for their help and efforts. I would also like to thank my mother, father and sister for their ongoing support, and Laura Roskowski for putting up with me, and just for being her.

REFERENCES CITED

Abrams, E.
|1994| *How the Maya Built their World.* University of Texas Press, Austin.

Andrews, G.
|1975| *Maya Cities: Placemaking and Urbanization.* University of Oklahoma Press, Norman.

Awe, J., and M. Campbell
|1988| *Site Core Investigations at Cahal Pech, Cayo District, Belize: Preliminary Report of the 1998 Season.* Ms. on file with author.

Ball, J.
|1993| *Cahal Pech, the Ancient Maya, and Modern Belize: The Story of an Archaeological Park.* San Diego State University Press, San Diego

Ball, J., and J. Taschek
|2001| The Buenavista Cahal-Pech Royal Court: Multi Palace Court Mobility and Usage in a Petty Lowland Maya Kingdom. In *Royal Courts of the Ancient Maya*, vol. 2, edited by T. Inomata, and S. Houston, pp. 165–200. Westview Press, Boulder, Colorado.

Chase, A., and D. Chase
|2001| The Royal Courts of Caracol, Belize: Its Places and People. In *Royal Courts of the Ancient Maya*, vol. 2, edited by T. Inomata, and S. Houston, pp. 102–137. Westview Press, Boulder, Colorado.

Coe, M., and J. Kerr
|1998| *The Art of the Maya Scribe.* Thames and Hudson, London.

Flannery, K.
|1998| The Ground Plan of the Archaic State. In *Archaic States*, edited by G. Feinman, and J. Marcus, pp. 15–58. School of American Research, New Mexico.

Harrison, P.
|1970| *The Central Acropolis: A Preliminary Study of the Functions of its Structural Components during the Late Classic Period.* Ph.D. dissertation, University of Pennsylvania. University Microfilms, Ann Arbor.
|1999| *The Lords of Tikal.* Thames and Hudson, New York.
|2001| Thrones and Throne Structures from the Central Acropolis, Tikal as an Expression of the Royal Court. In *Royal Courts of the Ancient Maya*, vol. 2, edited by T. Inomata, and S. Houston, pp. 74–101. Westview Press, Boulder, Colorado.

Hillier, B., and J. Hanson
|1984| *The Social Logic of Space.* Cambridge University Press, Cambridge.
Iannone, G.
|1999| Archaeological Investigations at Minanhá, Belize. In *Archaeological Investigations in the North Vaca Plateau, Belize: Progress Report of the First (1999) Field Season*, edited by G. Iannone, J. Seibert, and N. Gray, pp. 1–28. Department of Anthropology, Trent University, Peterborough.
Inomata, T.
|1997| The Last Day of a Fortified Classic Maya Center: Archaeological Investigations at Aguateca, Guatemala. *Ancient Mesoamerica* 8:337–351.
|2001| The King's People: Classic Maya Courtiers in a Comparative Perspective. In *Royal Courts of the Ancient Maya*, vol. 1, edited by T. Inomata, and S. Houston, pp. 27–53. Westview Press, Boulder, Colorado.
Inomata, T., and S. Houston
|2001| Opening the Royal Maya Court. In *Royal Courts of the Ancient Maya*, vol. 1, edited by T. Inomata, and S. Houston, pp. 3–23. Westview Press, Boulder, Colorado.
Kowalski, J.
|1987| *The House of the Governo*r. University of Oklahoma Press, Norman.
Kubler, G.
|1985| [1958] The Design of Space in Maya Architecture. In *The Collected Essays of George Kubler*, edited by T. F. Reese, pp. 242–250. Yale University Press, New Haven.
|1990| *The Art and Architecture of Ancient America.* Yale University Press, New Haven.
Loten, S., and D. Pendergast
|1984| *A Lexicon for Maya Architecture.* Royal Ontario Museum, Toronto.
Low, S.
|1995| Indigenous Architecture and the Spanish American Plaza in Mesoamerica and the Caribbean. *American Anthropologist* 97(4):748–762.
|2000| *On the Plaza: the Politics of Public Space and Culture.* University of Texas Press, Austin.
McAnany, P., and S. Plank
|2001| Perspectives on Actors, Gender Roles and Architecture at Classic Maya Courts and Households. In *Royal Courts of the Ancient Maya*, vol. 1, edited by T. Inomata, and S. Houston, pp. 84–129. Westview Press, Boulder, Colorado.
Martin, S.
|2001| Court and Realm: Architectural Signatures in the Southern Maya Lowlands. In *Royal Courts of the Ancient Maya*, vol. 1, edited by T. Inomata, and S. Houston, pp. 168–194. Westview Press, Boulder, Colorado.
Reents-Budet, D.
|1994| *Painting the Maya Universe: Royal Ceramics of the Classic Period.* Duke University Press, Durham.
|2001| Classic Maya Concepts of the Royal Court: An Analysis of Rendering on Pictorial Ceramics. In *Royal Courts of the Ancient Maya*, vol. 1, edited by T. Inomata, and S. Houston, pp. 195–233. Westview Press, Boulder, Colorado.
Seibert, J.
|2000| Preliminary Excavations in Structure 12A at Minanhá, Belize. In *Archaeological Investigations in the North Vaca Plateau, Belize: Progress Report of the Second (2000) Field Season*, edited by G. Iannone, L. McFarland, A. Menzies, and R. Primrose, pp. 35–50. Department of Anthropology, Trent University, Peterborough.
|2001| Continuing Excavations of Structure12A, Minanhá, Belize. In *Archaeological Investigations in the North Vaca Plateau Belize: Progress Report of the Third (2001) Field Season*, edited by G. Iannone, L. McParland, A. Menzies, and R. Primrose. Department of Anthropology, Trent University, Peterborough.
|2004| Functional Analysis of Structure 12A, Minanhá. *Research Reports in Belizean Archaeology, Volume 1. Archaeological Investigations in the Eastern Maya Lowlands: Papers of the 2003 Belize Archaeology Symposium*, edited by J. Awe, J. Morris, and S. Jones, pp. 165–171. Institute of Archaeology, National Institute of Culture and History, Belmopan, Belize.
Taschek, J., and J. Ball
|1999| Las Ruinas de Arenal. Preliminary Report on a Sub-Regional Center in the Upper Belize Valley. *Ancient Mesoamerica* 10:215–235.
Trigger, B.
|1990| Monumental Architecture: A Thermodynamic Explanation of Symbolic Behavior. *World Archaeology* 22:119–131.
Valdez, J.
|2001| Palaces and Thrones Tied to the Destiny of the Royal Courts of the Ancient Maya. In *Royal Courts of the Ancient Maya*, vol. 2, edited by T. Inomata, and S. Houston, pp. 138–154. Westview Press, Boulder, Colorado.
Webster, D.
|2001| Spatial Dimensions of Courtly Life: Problems and Issues. In *Royal Courts of the Ancient Maya*, vol. 1, edited by T. Inomata, and S. Houston, pp. 130–167. Westview Press, Boulder, Colorado.

THE MACHINE IN THE CEREMONIAL CENTRE

H. Stanley Loten

H. Stanley Loten, 24 Springfield Road # 203, Ottawa, Ontario K1M 1C9, Canada.

ABSTRACT

The North Acropolis at the ancient Maya site of Tikal, Guatemala, is an example of a monumental architectural complex at the centre of a major urban development that eventually attained regional power status. Digital modeling shows how building forms and plan arrangements evolved and changed over at least eight centuries. This diachronic pattern is interpreted as a process of continual redesign aimed at increasing the effectiveness of the installation as a support for Tikal's ruling elite. Insofar as investment in architectural development was motivated by material considerations, the complex can be equated with a major industrial development in modern western culture. The final developmental episode confirms epigraphic evidence that a new dynastic line took power at Tikal in the fourth century A.D.

The primary objective of this paper is simply to illustrate architectural development of the North Acropolis at Tikal from the late Preclassic Period through the Early Classic Period so that it can be appreciated visually. The report presenting results and findings of the University of Pennsylvania 1955–1959 excavation project (Coe 1990) provides copious plans, sections, elevations and details, but does not include three-dimensional illustrations. Perspective views show the character of the architecture in a way that plans, sections and elevations do not. Ability to see the architecture in three-dimensional projection allows for a kind of judgment that may be difficult to obtain from two-dimensional drawings. What direction such judgment might take will naturally vary with individuals. The text that follows presents my own interpretations. Hopefully, the images accompanying the text will enable readers to form independent opinions.

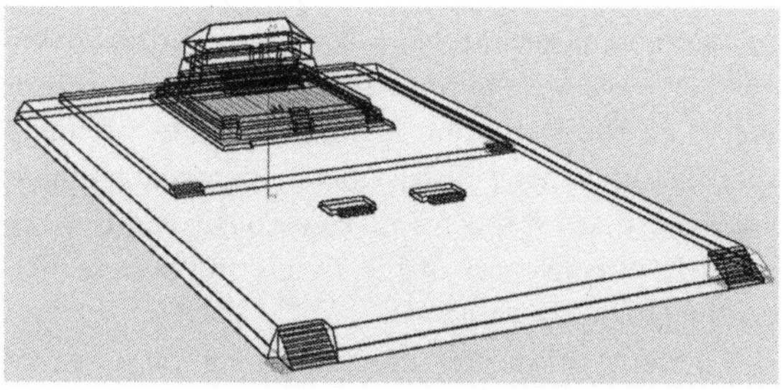

Figure 1. Wire frame model of the North Acropolis, Tikal, Guatemala. View from southwest (after Coe 1990:Figure 6a).

The metaphor of the machine was proposed by Lewis Mumford (Mumford 1966) in his assessment of early technical development. He saw the institution of divine rulership as a kind of tool, a "megamachine," enabling ancient societies to achieve many new things, among them, monumental architectural projects that can themselves be thought of as very large machines. Mumford's context was ancient Egypt and Mesopotamia but I suspect that his insight may apply equally well to Mesoamerica, as indeed, Mumford himself suggested (Mumford 1966:191).

The machine in the ceremonial centre, in this case, is the North Acropolis at Tikal, Guatemala. I assume that this complex of monumental architecture provided a setting for ritual activities intended to mediate with the non-material forces that, according to ancient Maya animistic belief, affected all natural phenomena and all human affairs. Due to the fact that the acropolis was more or less continuously modified and rebuilt over more than half a millennium, the developmental sequence can be seen as a series of architectural experiments that I interpret as aimed at improving

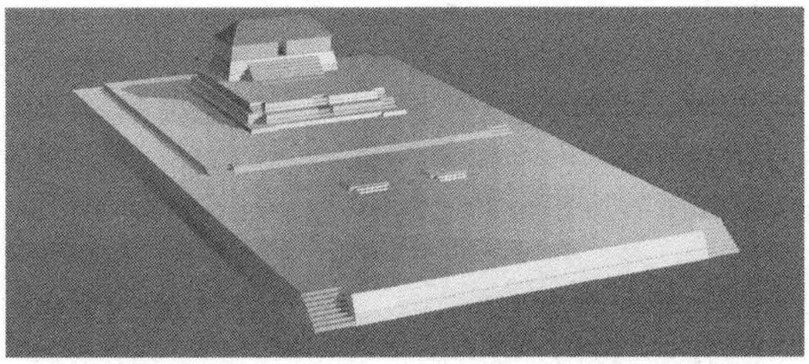

Figure 2. Rendered model of the North Acropolis, Tikal, Guatemala. View from southwest (after Coe 1990:Figure 6a).

Figure 3. North Acropolis, Tikal, Guatemala. View from southwest (after Coe 1990:Figure 6b).

productivity in such things as victory in battle, health, good crops, success in trade and in all state enterprises including the institution of rulership. The architectural features that I discuss in the paragraphs below are those that I suspect were consciously contrived to improve effectiveness of the rituals and ceremonials conducted on the acropolis.

The illustrations are based on excavation data produced by the University of Pennsylvania Tikal Project (Coe 1990).[1] Three-dimensional models were made in FormZ version 3.6 Renderzone Radiozity (autodessys). They were first set up as wire frames, and then rendered (Figures 1 and 2) . The character of the rendering is intended to show how the structures looked when they were freshly built and their plaster finish was shiny and reflective. Surviving plasters, where protected, were distinctly smooth as though rubbed and burnished, and I imagine that when newly finished the surfaces were somewhat glossy. Many surfaces were unpainted and had the creamy tint of natural plaster; others were painted a strong vibrant red. However, in the illustrations below I have employed a uniform rendering to emphasize architectural form rather than colour.

Although the acropolis evolved and functioned from at least 600 B.C. into the ninth century A.D., the architectural development presented here covers only the period from the late second century B.C. to the early fifth century A.D. During this time, from Late Preclassic through most of the Early Classic, the architectural development, as I hope will be evident from the series of models, is a very consistent one. That is, initial forms were retained through major changes. At no time was the entire fabric of an earlier acropolis completely concealed beneath later additions. Certainly, as will be evident, very marked changes were regularly introduced by new construction but in a context of renewing the previous fabric, which more or less inadvertently got larger and larger. Then, at the end of the series described here, in the fifth century A.D., the pattern of development changed abruptly. The "arrival of strangers" (Stuart 1999) may have precipitated this change. Indeed, the pattern of architectural development described here may actually provide support for the epigraphic evidence.

Figure 2 shows the earliest recovered acropolis, dating to the late second century B.C. It rested partly on bedrock and partly on debris of earlier totally razed structures. Its somewhat residential appearance seems inconsistent with the size and complexity of the lower substructure platforms. The thatch roof shown is conjectural. Monumentality was modest but maybe intentional and may indicate a ceremonial function, although monumentality as such certainly would not rule out residence as primary function. On the other hand, residential form could be appropriate for ceremonial functioning. It has been suggested that ceremonial structures were places where the gods came to receive their offerings (Bassie-Sweet 1996:18). For this purpose, a house form might serve well. Features that appear non-residential include expansiveness of the substructure platforms, their complex mix of very low and somewhat higher units, doubled lower stairs, tripled mid-level stairs, and the twin frontal units that might be small platforms or altars.

In Figure 3, which probably dates to the first half of the first century B.C., the earlier building had been kept while all substructure units were changed. A vaulted roof shown here is, again, conjectural. The lower substructure was transformed into a two-platform system repeated in the rebuilt mid-level platform, each with a very low basal unit. Twin stairs were

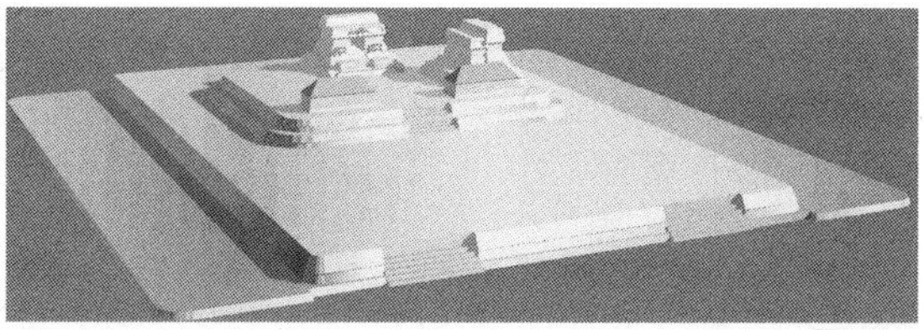

Figure 4. North Acropolis, Tikal, Guatemala. View from southwest (after Coe 1990:Figure 6c).a

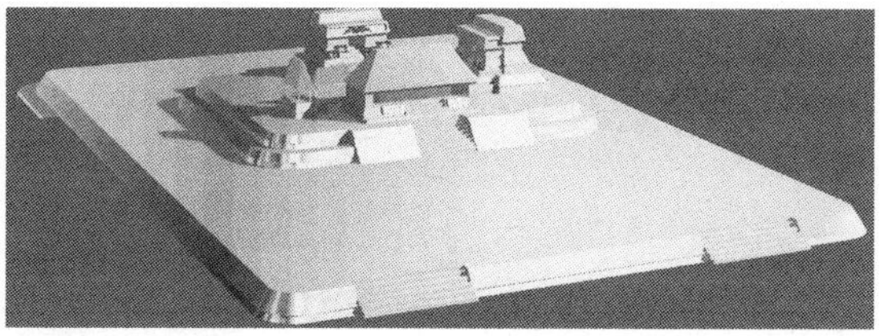

Figure 5. North Acropolis, Tikal, Guatemala. View from southwest (after Coe 1990:Figure 6d).

retained as in the previous structure. The mid-level substructure had no front stair; access to the upper level was from east and west sides. The north building, its building platform partly submerged, was now the dominant element of an open-cornered quadrangle. Unfortunately, only basal stubs of the three other units remained. The quadrangular format of upper units again suggests residential function, and again, I interpret this as use of residential form for non-residential purposes, primarily because of the strict axiality on the quadrangle on cardinal lines.

The acropolis that followed (Figure 4), still in the first century B.C., left lower substructure features substantially unchanged while completely reworking the upper parts. A two-terraced upper substructure platform with generously rounded corners now had a central axial stair. At the summit, flanking this stair, were two thatched buildings that acted as a threshold, or gateway, to the space behind, defined by two identical units of distinctly non-residential form. These had high building platforms with mask panels and were almost certainly vaulted. By Mesoamerican conventions they are "temples" presumably built to serve ceremonial purposes. This change either indicates a new function for the acropolis, or confirms the previous function as ceremonial despite the residential character of the earlier architecture.

Two features seem puzzling: absence of a single dominant element, and imbalance between east and west. The former may have been met by the whole upper ensemble including the round-cornered, two-terraced platform with central stair; indeed this may be the explanation for the positioning of this stair, as if the stair of the north axial building platform in the earlier acropolis had been transferred to the two-terraced upper substructure of this one. East-west imbalance is harder to interpret. Perhaps the west side of the upper complex was reserved for ceremonial activities that required open space.

The approximate time of construction and use of this acropolis appears to coincide with initial paving of the Great Plaza, though of relatively modest extent (Coe 1990:818). This development would seem to indicate a general increase in size and impressiveness of the whole ceremonial centre at Tikal, perhaps reflecting growth in importance of the city, or alternatively, power and status of the folks using the centre.

In the early first century A.D. changes were made at all levels, yet the two "temples" from the earlier arrangement were retained unaltered (Figure 5). The lateral lower substructure platform was now eliminated and wide "alfardas" flanked the axial stair at the middle level. Entry to the acropolis summit was now formalized by a thatched building with rear doorways allowing through circulation. This now became the dominant element as seen from the Great Plaza. Intentional opening of the west side at the summit level seems to be confirmed by small thatched units placed awkwardly to avoid closure on that side. Elaborate burials with mural painting suggest that by this time rulership was an aspect of acropolis function. Alternatively, royal burials may indicate royal residence, since burial beneath residence is not uncommon in Mesoamerican contexts. I am inclined to reject this interpretation on the grounds that this acropolis seems to lack any unit that could conceivably function residentially.

Not much later, around the middle of the first century A.D., plan proportions previously developed for the middle substructure, were applied to the lower platform so that all major platform units now had the same near square format (Figure 6). This move made axial non-alignment of upper and lower units more

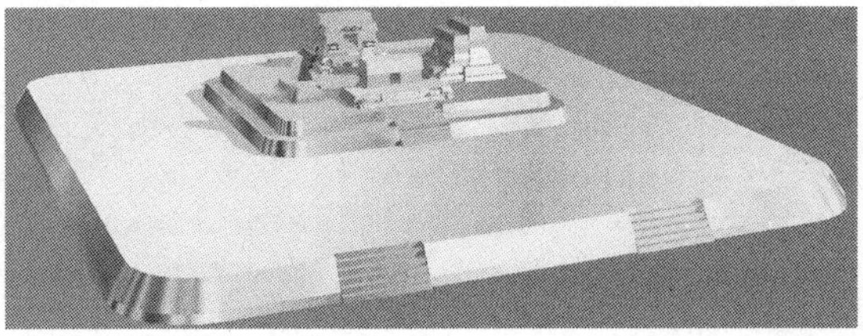

Figure 6. North Acropolis, Tikal, Guatemala. View from southwest (after Coe 1990:Figure 6e).

Figure 7. North Acropolis, Tikal, Guatemala. View from southwest (after Coe 1990:Figure 6f).

obvious, something that would seem to be a defect. Possibly this was a kind of homage to earlier fabrics even though development had shifted toward the east. The twin stairs of the lower platform were themselves archaic features perhaps also making explicit reference to an earlier axial line.

At the top of the mid-level stair a new portal structure was built. It is shown here only partly vaulted because ancient demolition had removed evidence. The two "temple" structures behind it had by this time survived as summit defining features through three sequent acropolis formats.

The mid-first century A.D. saw a major development; the whole upper ensemble was rebuilt much higher, possibly in response to the scale demanded for a powerful presence on the Great Plaza (Figure 7). But it was only the rear part of the upper complex that was elevated; the front part, with its portal building, remained in place, although rebuilt, now mid-way up the central stairway. A second portal building at the head of the upper stair, with flanking wings, and beam-and-mortar roof, effectively closed the upper surface and shut it off from the frontal and Great Plaza areas.

This acropolis was functioning at the time the Tikal dynastic "founder," Yax Ehb' Xook, took power according to much later inscriptions (Martin and Grube 2000:26), and it continued in use long after his demise, through nearly the whole second century A.D. It is the second longest used acropolis in the whole Early Classic series. Its amplified height, which must have increased its visual impact, may have reflected a particularly robust political status enjoyed by Tikal at this time. This may be why later rulers claimed legitimacy from this particular reign. Architectural forms appear unfinished as compared with other major works because finished surfaces were inaccessible and therefore are shown as unresolved.

The long duration of the preceding acropolis was followed by one used for only about ten years at the end of the second century A.D. (Figure 8). The importance of this acropolis lies in its monumental stairway that greatly increased its visual impact. The magnitude of the stair suggests it may have been built for ritual or ceremony involving vertical movement, rather than merely for access to the summit, but once in place it showed the kind of strong monumentality that was possible. Perhaps this is why it was left in use for only a relatively short time.

New twin stairs on the lower platform now centred on this stair defined a single axial line noticeably off-centred. The middle body terraces, lacking apron mouldings, and in some cases defined on the front only, subtract from the effect of the great stair. This may again indicate that the visual effect of the stair was unanticipated. The summit features also now seem dwarfed.

Toward the end of the second century the middle platform was made a little higher and much more imposing by the installation of large mask panels flanking the axial stair (Figure 9). New versions of the portal structure at the head of the stair and the east summit structure were built, but the old north axial structure was retained with its building platform almost totally obscured. The decisive change here was the installation of very large mask panels flanking the stair. I interpret this as recalling much earlier summit structures (Figure 3) which had displayed stair-side mask panels some three centuries earlier. As I suggested above, such features appear as parts of a "temple" format. In this later development the masks may indicate that the whole upper complex of the acropolis had come

Figure 8. North Acropolis, Tikal, Guatemala. View from southwest (after Coe 1990:Figure 6g).

Figure 9. North Acropolis, Tikal, Guatemala. View from southwest (after Coe 1990:Figure 6h).

to be understood as a "temple," that is, a place habitable by supernatural powers. Presumably this would accord with and support the association of rulers with the acropolis. Deceased rulers buried within the fabric of the acropolis would have been numbered among the supernatural powers addressed by ceremonial functions. Placement of the masks on the middle platform might have linked them to rituals conducted on the stair they flank, and might indicate that, in ancient Maya thinking, the body of the platform was the focus of the "temple" identification, since that was where the burials were located.

Two features support my inference that earlier ideas were being invoked in this acropolis: the east-west lateral stairs and the new single stair to the basal platform. This latter, although new, was placed on the older, more westerly axial line, noticeably offset from the powerful axis projected by the upper features. The lateral stairs had appeared briefly in the first century B.C. (Figure 3) and subsequently had been omitted. Their restoration at the end of the second century A.D. can hardly have been coincidental.

In use through most of the third century and into the fourth, the next acropolis constituted a restatement of the preceding arrangement with significant revisions (Figure 10). The middle platform now had two terraces each formed with apron mouldings, and a summit complex of four structures on cardinal axes. This, again, may have been a restoration of the earlier format (Figure 3) recalled in the preceding acropolis.

Curiously, although the north axial summit structure was rebuilt along with the other three, it was the smallest. The portal structure at the head of the stair appeared as the dominant element, although the open space behind it, defined by three "temples" may have been the prime focus of ritual events.

On the second terrace of the middle platform, new secondary stairs were added flanking the mask panels and formalizing the path up from the lateral stairs which previously had required treading directly on top of the masks. This would seem to our eyes like a violation of sanctity, but may simply have emphasized that access to the summit was highly restricted, perhaps limited to those participating in ceremonial activities. The path from east and west sides, rebuilt for this acropolis, may have been the path of access, while the central, monumental stair may have been primarily for ceremonial use, perhaps for the descending bodies of sacrificial offerings.

The acropolis of longest duration (Figure 11) was used from early in the fourth century to the latter part of the fifth. As it turned out, except for one final refinement (below), this form of the acropolis established its maximum point of development, at least in terms of visual impact and monumentality. The middle level platform now had three terraces; three stairways lead up to the summit; three "temple" structures occupied the summit; and the whole was formed by three main bodies, basal platform, mid-level platform and upper assemblage. Three structures faced on to the Great Plaza, and major interior spaces were accessed by triple doorway openings. The lower stair had been moved eastward to align with the upper axis, and the acropolis as a whole now had a sense of unity as though it had been designed as one structure. This kind of itemization, however, does not account for the effect of monumentality that this acropolis must have projected, which I would guess was much stronger than in any previous version. Multiple triadic elements would no doubt embody theological correctness to satisfy initiates, but the overall effect would have been felt by all. My guess is the effect of embodied power, or

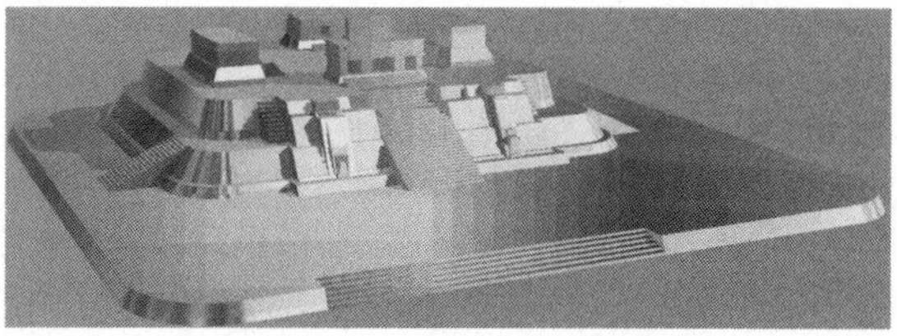

Figure 10. North Acropolis, Tikal, Guatemala. View from southwest (after Coe 1990:Figure 6i).

Figure 11. North Acropolis, Tikal, Guatemala. View from southwest (after Coe 1990:Figure 6j).

monumentality, might have been understood as palpable proof that supernatural entities really were present in the fabric, or at least could be, at times of ceremonial activity. Presence of a single dominant element, the north axial "temple" would have increased the effect of monumentality while at the same time recalling a much earlier acropolis form (Figure 2).

One more feature remains to be considered in relation to this acropolis (Figure 12). At some point a new set of outsets on the rear, east, and west facades was added (Coe 1990:133). Coe placed these in the succeeding acropolis (Figure 14) on stratigraphic grounds, because they clearly were built as modifications to the earlier fabric. However, the evidence of stratigraphy does not demand that these features also precede drastic changes made to the south front, and since they constitute a consistent development of the old acropolis while the frontal changes discussed below do not, I have shown them here as a distinct substage, stratigraphically possible though not absolutely necessary.

The effect of this addition is more apparent from the rear (Figure 13). From this viewpoint, the rear and west side outsets are both visible. They were large features with major visual impact, yet they accomplished nothing in any functional sense that one can readily imagine. In visual terms, they carried the lines of the three major upper features down to the bottom of the mid-level platform, as though the identity of these entities was not confined to the summit but was embodied as well in the fabric of the platform. They very strongly reinforced the cardinal directionality of the upper features. As many scholars have observed, cardinal directions are associated with supernatural forces (Ashmore 1992:174; Aveni 1980:135; Bassie-Sweet 1996:21; Carlson 1981:146; Dunning 1992:137; Freidel et al. 1993:129; Justeson et al. 1988:143; Kelley 1976:53; Paxton 2001:15; Schele and Mathews 1998:26; Sharer 1994:531; Thompson 1960:10, 1970:198). My guess is these outsets served a function similar to that of the royal tombs, as elements intended to induce greater presence of these powers. That they were added by themselves, and not as parts of some larger entity, suggests that they were thought about separately. It is clear stratigraphically that outsets in this form had been initially introduced in the substructure of the north axial summit "temple" (5D-22-3rd, Figure 12) and then subsequently applied to the platform sustaining this structure. Therefore it seems reasonable to infer that the significance attached to the upper feature was shared by the platform below it. Whatever the term "temple" may signify, it was not just the building with interior space, but equally the solid body that elevated it to a commanding height. Presumably the primary function of installations like the North Acropolis was that of negotiating with supernatural forces, and rulership was based on the claimed ability to use this instrument of power effectively for the good of the whole community.

In other words, these outsets may have completed a process started earlier by the positioning of mask panels to flank the monumental front, axial stair, marking the large body of the middle level platform as a feature of the landscape formed by presence of supernaturals. "Witz" masks are commonly understood in this way (Schele and Mathews 1998:43).

The end point of the sequence described here was initiated by a political event that took place during use of the preceding acropolis, the well-known "arrival of strangers" at A.D. 378 (Stuart 1999:471). I am assuming the radical change in the pattern of North

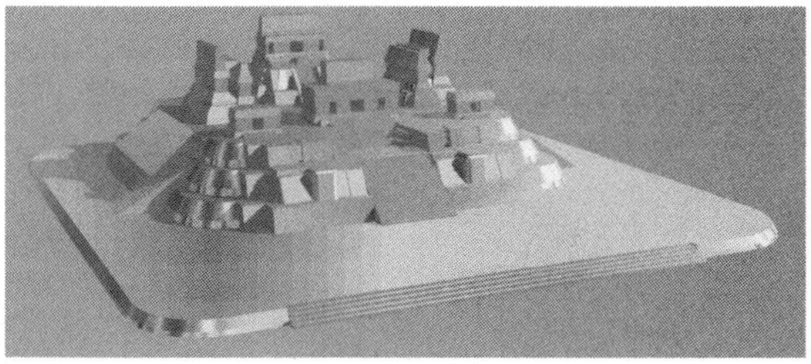

Figure 12. North Acropolis, Tikal, Guatemala. View from southwest (after Coe 1990:Figure 6j and k).

Figure 13. North Acropolis, Tikal, Guatemala. View from northwest (after Coe 1990:Figure 6j and k).

Acropolis architectural development that appeared in the succeeding acropolis (Figure 14) reflected this event. In Figure 14 we see that the old acropolis actually ceased to develop and instead new additions came to be placed across its front. These structures contained tombs of rulers put into office by the "strangers" who had or claimed some kind of connection to Teotihuacan (Mathews 2001). These rulers may have wanted to be entombed at the site of the acropolis, they numbered themselves in succession from the same "founder," but they either were not interested, or were unable to continue its architectural development along lines previously followed. Indeed, the North Acropolis may not have been their instrument of power at all. This may have been the Mundo Perdido complex (Laporte and Fialko 1990) in the southwest of the site centre, where Teotihuacan architectural forms were displayed conspicuously.

Side and rear outsets applied to the acropolis that was functioning when "strangers" arrived (Figures 12 and 13) provide clearest evidence for a materialistic function aimed at achieving practical results, since these elements relate so directly to the action of supernatural forces. The abrupt shift in pattern of architectural development following their arrival may perhaps confirm the textual evidence that they were indeed strangers, and may further imply that these new rulers claimed to be able to gain advantages for the people of Yax Mutal, as the traditional North Acropolis users had, but now by other methods, elsewhere (Mundo Perdido), and associated with different architectural forms.

REFERENCES CITED

Ashmore, W.
|1992| Deciphering Maya Architectural Plans. In *New Theories on the Ancient Maya*, edited by E. C. Danien, and R. J. Sharer, pp. 173–184. University Museum, University of Pennsylvania, Philadelphia.

Aveni, A. F.
|1980| *Skywatchers of Ancient Mexico*. University of Texas Press, Austin.

Carlson, J.
|1981| A Geomantic Model for the Interpretation of Mesoamerican Sites: An Essay in Cross-Cultural Comparison. In *Mesoamerican Sites and World Views*, edited by E. P. Benson. Dumbarton Oaks Research Library and Collection, Washington, D.C.

Coe, W. R.
|1990| *Tikal Report 14: Excavations in the Great Plaza, North Terrace and North Acropolis of Tikal*. University Museum, University of Pennsylvania, Philadelphia.

Bassie-Sweet, K.
|1996| *At the Edge of the World*. University of Oklahoma Press, Oklahoma.

Dunning, N. P.
|1992| *Lords of the Hills: Ancient Maya Settlement in the Puuc Region, Yucatán, Mexico*. Prehistory Press, Madison.

Freidel, D., L. Schele, and J. Parker
|1993| *Maya Cosmos*. William Morrow, New York.

Justeson, J. S., W. M. Norman, and N. Hammond
|1988| The Ponoma Flare: A Preclassic Maya Hieroglyphic Text. In *Maya Iconography*, edited by E. P. Benson, and G. G. Griffin. Princeton University Press, Princeton.

Kelley, D. H.
|1976| *Deciphering the Maya Script*. University of Texas Press, Austin.

Laporte, J. P., and V. Fialko C.
|1990| New Perspectives on Old Problems: Dynastic References for the Early Classic at Tikal. In *Vision and Revision in Maya Studies*, edited by F. S. Clancy, and P. D. Harrison, pp. 33–66. University of New Mexico Press, Albuquerque.

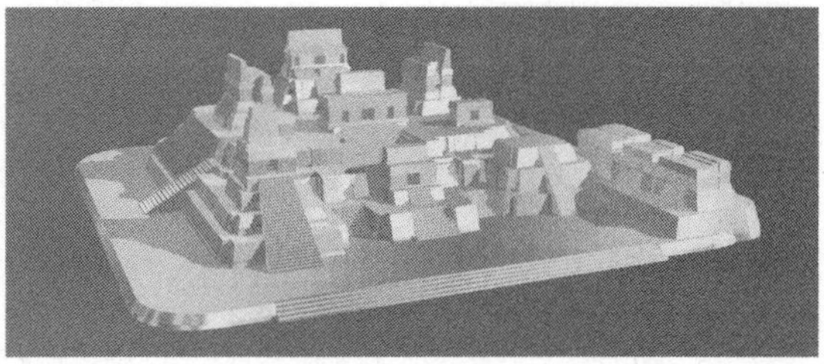

Figure 14. North Acropolis, Tikal, Guatemala. View from southwest (after Coe 1990:Figure 6k).

Martin, S., and N. Grube
|2000| *Chronicle of the Maya Kings and Queens*. Thames and Hudson, London.
Mathews, P.
|2001| Space among the Maya. Paper presented at the 34th Annual Chacmool Conference, Calgary, Alberta.
Mumford, Lewis
|1966| *The Myth of the Machine: Technics and Human Development*. Harcourt, Brace and World, New York
Paxton, M.
|2001| *The Cosmos of the Yucatec Maya*. University of New Mexico Press, Albuquerque.
Schele, L., and P. Mathews
|1998| *The Code of Kings*. Scribner, New York.
Sharer, R. J.
|1994| *The Ancient Maya*. Stanford University Press, Stanford.
Stuart, D.
|1999| The Arrival of Strangers: Teotihuacan and Tollan in Classic Maya History. In *Mesoamerica's Classic Heritage: From Teotihuacan to the Aztecs*, edited by D. Carrasco, L. Jones, and S. Sessions. University Press of Colorado, Boulder.
Thompson, J. E. S.
|1960| *Hieroglyphic Writing*. University of Oklahoma Press, Norman.
|1970| *Maya History and Religion*. University of Oklahoma Press, Norman.

NOTES

1 Computer models are based on data contained in *Tikal Report 14* (Coe 1990). The 13 acropolis formats illustrated here represent only a fraction of all the structures described in *Tikal Report 14*.

MESSAGES IN STONE: CONSTRUCTING SOCIOPOLITICAL INEQUALITY IN LATE BRONZE AGE CYPRUS

Kevin D. Fisher

Kevin Fisher, Department of Anthropology, University of Toronto, 100 St. George Street, Toronto, Ontario M5S 3G3, Canada

ABSTRACT

The presence of "public" and domestic architecture utilizing ashlar (cut-stone) masonry has often been cited as an indicator of sociopolitical inequality in Cyprus during the Late Cypriot Bronze Age (ca. 1650–1050 B.C.E.). Instead of seeing this architecture as a passive reflection of social and political structures, however, my work investigates the active role that the built environment played in shaping sociopolitical interrelationships among the constituents of Late Cypriot society. Specifically, I employ space syntax analysis to examine aspects of publicity and privacy in the layout of the Ashlar Building at Enkomi in order to shed light on the use of architectural design and embellishment by Late Cypriot elites as a means of encoding messages of power.

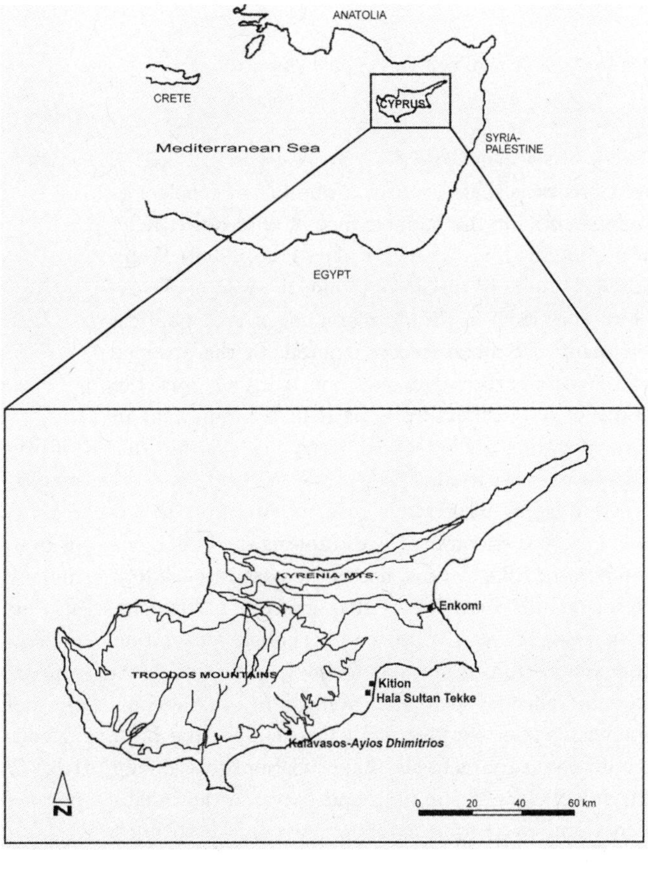

Figure 1. Cyprus in its regional context with the Late Bronze Age sites mentioned in the text.

The Late Bronze Age (LBA) in Cyprus (ca. 1650–1050 B.C.E.) witnessed a number of significant developments that marked the island's transition from a relatively secluded, village-based culture to an urban-oriented complex society with extensive international contacts. This process was intimately linked to the emergence of ruling elites whose power was established and maintained through a combination of economic control and ideological legitimization (see Knapp 1986, 1988a, 1990). The primary foci of elite power were the various urban centres that arose on Cyprus during the LBA (Figure 1). Sites such as Enkomi, Kition, Hala Sultan Tekke and Kalavasos-Ayios Dhimitrios, with their impressive administrative, religious and residential architecture, are among the most enduring testimonials of the ability of these emergent elites to control resources and mobilize labour. As well, the events which took place within these buildings, whether administrative activities or

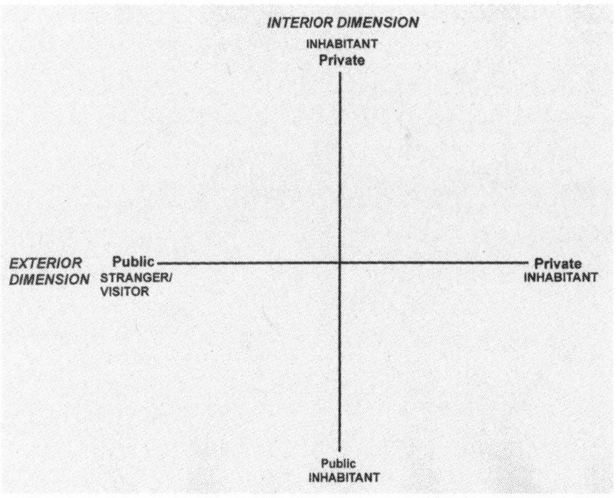

Figure 2. Two dimensions of publicity-privacy (after Grahame 1997:Figure 4).

religious rituals, are seen by a number of scholars as being central to the maintenance of elite power (e.g., Karageorghis 1982:101–106; Knapp 1986, 1988b; Webb 1999). In spite of this recognition, the role of the architecture itself in the development of sociopolitical inequality has been largely ignored. In the absence of translated written records from LBA Cyprus, the study of its architecture is particularly important in understanding sociopolitical dynamics during this transformative period.

My ongoing dissertation research attempts to address these shortcomings by examining the built environment of LBA Cyprus, not as the passive backdrop to sociopolitical activities, but as an active participant. This perspective is based on an explicit recognition that architecture is more than simply a physical location, but encodes sociopolitical meanings that it communicates and reproduces. In this manner the built environment can actively shape relationships among the inhabitants of buildings and between the inhabitants and those who enter (or pass by) as visitors. Architecture can therefore serve as a mechanism for the maintenance and expansion of elite power and sociopolitical inequality.

ARCHITECTURE AND POWER

In discussing the relationship between power and architecture, architect Kim Dovey (1999:1) notes that "Placemaking is an inherently elite practice. This does not suggest that built form is inherently oppressive. However, it does suggest that places are necessarily programmed and designed in accord with certain interests – primarily the pursuit of amenity, profit, status and political power." Furthermore, he suggests that power is not inertly embedded in built form, but instead is actively mediated through it and expressed in several possible dimensions (1999:15–16). The following dimensions are particularly relevant to the present discussion:

1) *publicity/privacy*: Built form can segment space in a manner that places certain kinds of people and action under conditions of surveillance while privileging other kinds of people and action as private.
2) *segregation/access*: Boundaries and pathways can segregate places by status, gender, race, culture, class or age, creating privileged enclaves of access, amenity and community.
3) *identity/difference*: Places can symbolize socially constructed identities and differences of individuals, cultures, institutions and nations.

Of primary concern to archaeologists is how these dimensions manifest themselves materially in the remains of ancient structures. While certain correlates of power (e.g., the monumentality of the Giza pyramids) might be quite obvious, messages of power can also be encoded in more subtle ways that may not be evident from a cursory look at site plans or the material remains themselves. Isolating the material manifestations of these meanings and determining the manner in which they were employed in the architecture of LBA Cyprus requires the use of a variety of analytical methods developed outside of archaeology.

SPACE SYNTAX AND VISITOR-INHABITANT RELATIONS

The use of space syntax as developed by Hillier and Hanson in *The Social Logic of Space* (1984) provides a starting point for examining spatial configurations in built form. In particular, their *gamma analysis* (also called *access analysis*) is useful for identifying how spaces within a structure are arranged and related to one another, and how a building mediates the relationship between its occupants and visitors. The first part of such an analysis involves translating a building into an access graph or "gamma map" in which each room is represented as a circle, with access between rooms represented as lines linking them together (e.g., Figures 5 and 6). The access graph can be "justified" by arranging it such that each room that is the same depth from the outside is depicted on the same level.

Space syntax works on the assumption that the space around buildings is structured such that strangers can move about, but only inhabitants and certain strangers (visitors) are allowed inside structures. Inhabitants have an investment of power and are the controllers, while visitors enter or stay as subjects of the system and are therefore the controlled (Markus 1993:13). Typically, the deeper spaces of a building are occupied by the inhabitants and the shallower spaces by visitors. The depth of an inhabitant and the degree to which visitors are allowed to penetrate into a structure are seen as indicators of their status (Dovey 1999:22). This allows us to examine the dimensions of publicity/privacy and segregation/access noted above.

In examining the demarcation of public and private domains in Roman houses, Mark Grahame (1997) notes that we should see public and private not as absolutes (i.e., inside is private; outside is public), but as a continuum operating along two dimensions (Figure 2). One interfaces the public world of strangers/visitors with the private world of the inhabitants, while the other interfaces the inhabitants with one another. The degree of privacy is a measure of power in that it controls the level of knowledge that others may have about oneself (Grahame 1997:145). Examination of this phenomenon requires an understanding of how each space is integrated with the rest of the building. This can be achieved using the access graph of a building to calculate the following (see Hillier and Hanson 1984:108–109):

1) *control value (CV)*: measures the degree of control a space exercises over its immediate neighbours. Each space in the building is assigned a value of 1, which is divided among each of the neighbouring spaces to which it is connected. These are totaled to give the control value of each space. The higher the CV, the more controlling the space is.

		ACCESSIBILITY (RA)	
		High	Low
CONTROL (CV)	High	High	Moderately High
	Low	Moderately Low	Low

Figure 3. Presence-availability as determined by control and accessibility (after Grahame 1997:Table 1).

2) *mean depth (MD)*: measures how deep a space is relative to the other spaces in the building.
MD = cumulative depth of each space/p – 1, where p is the number of points in the system.

3) *relative asymmetry (RA)*: measures how accessible a space is from other spaces or how well a space is integrated into the building's structure. The result is a value between 0 and 1 with values approaching 1 indicating lower accessibility.[1]
RA = 2(MD – 1)/k – 2, where MD is the mean depth of the system and k is the number of spaces in the system

According to Grahame (1997:150), the control values and RA values for each space can be used to assess its level of what he calls *presence-availability* – a measurement of the likelihood of people being present in the space and available for social encounters (Figure 3). Based on the work of Anthony Giddens (1984), Grahame (1997:155) suggests that two types of social interactions might be associated with these differing levels of presence-availability. The first type of interaction can be described as *occasions* – these are particular social practices or rituals that tend to be organized as sequenced phenomena. Occasions can vary from the preparation and consumption of food, to more formal religious rituals. *Gatherings*, on the other hand, are more transient in nature, and involve fleeting exchanges (for instance, as people pass in a hallway).

PUBLICITY, PRIVACY AND POWER IN LBA ENKOMI

In order to assess the applicability of these methods to the architecture of LBA Cyprus, I have chosen to

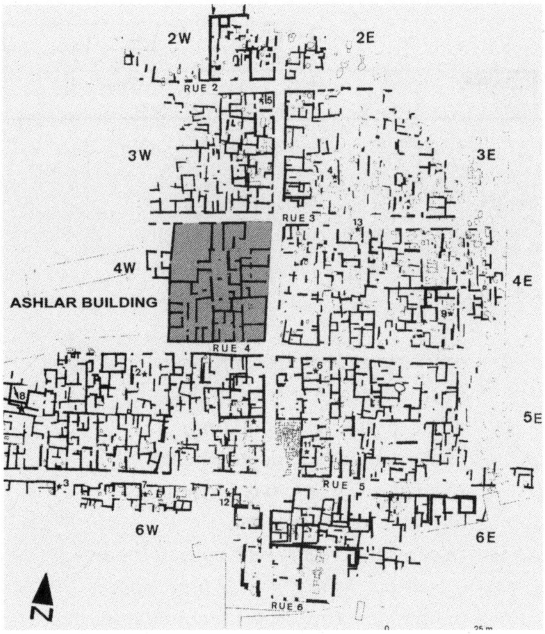

Figure 4. The central part of Enkomi. The Ashlar Building is shaded (modified from Courtois and Legarce 1986:Figure 1).

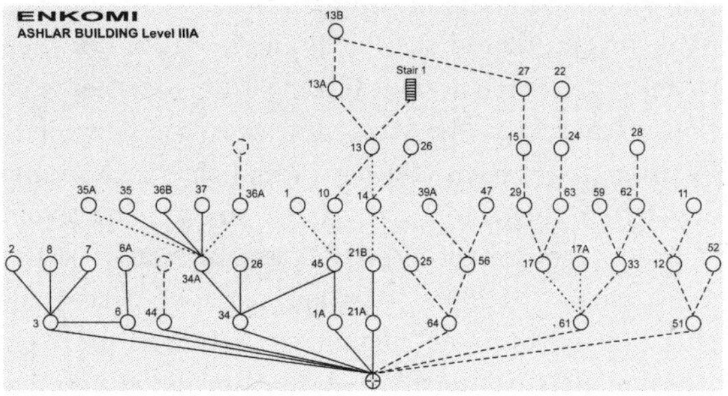

Figure 5. Access graph for Enkomi Ashlar Building, level IIIA.

work with two successive construction phases of a particular building found in the central part of the coastal site of Enkomi (Figure 4). This structure, known as the Ashlar Building for the extensive use of cut-stone masonry in its construction, is an ideal case study in that its large size and complex layout preclude simple visual analysis of its internal arrangements. As well, it has both private residential and "public" uses that might allow us to examine the relationships between the building's inhabitants and those who enter as visitors.

Level IIIA

This building was unquestionably conceived as a monumental structure, measuring nearly 30 m per side and covering much of a city block. Found directly on the city's main north-south axis, the Ashlar Building was, according to the excavator (Dikaios 1969:171–190), initially constructed over the remains of an earlier structure in the Late Cypriot IIIA period shortly after 1190 B.C.E.[2] The official and residential sections of the complex were built mostly of ashlar masonry around a central hall. The southwest section, built mostly of rubble masonry was added shortly after and seems to be the focus of domestic activities in the complex. The monumental nature of the building together with the quality and quantity of items of wealth found within in it testify to its associations with Enkomi's elite.

For this level and the subsequent reconstruction of the building, justified access graphs were drawn (Figures 5 and 6) . In a few instances where doorways were not present (especially in more disturbed parts of the site such as the eastern section), assumptions were made as to their most likely positions based on plans and photographs of the extant walls and the excavator's descriptions. In these cases, connections between spaces are shown by dotted lines on the access graph. Another problem lies in the fact that we know little about the extent and layout of the upper story, although the position of stairwells indicates that one covered at least sections of the building.

Creating the access graphs permitted calculation of the control values of each space within the building (Figure 7). Recognizing that certain spaces are more important than others in structuring space within the building, we can focus on those with particularly high control values. While any space with a CV of 1

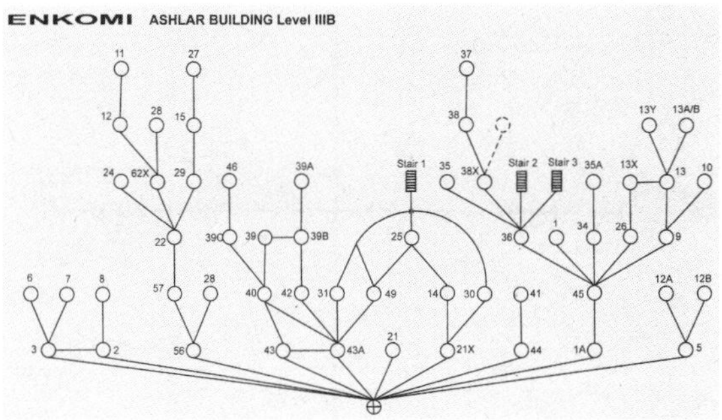

Figure 6. Access graph for Enkomi Ashlar Building, level IIIB.

ENKOMI ASHLAR BUILDING LEVEL IIIA
Control and Accessibility Measures of Nodes

Node	Control Value	Mean Depth	RA
34A	5.2500	3.8367	0.1182
3	3.4444	3.4694	0.1029
46	2.3333	4.1224	0.1301
45	2.2500	3.6327	0.1097
14	2.2500	4.3265	0.1386
13	2.2500	4.5714	0.1488

Node	CV Rank	RA Rank	Depth
34A	1	3	2
3	2	1	1
46	3	4	2
45	4	2	2
14	5	5	3
13	6	6	4

ENKOMI ASHLAR BUILDING LEVEL IIIB
Control and Accessibility Measures of Nodes

Node	Control Value	Mean Depth	RA
36	3.6667	4.5345	0.1240
45	3.0333	3.7586	0.0968
13	2.8333	5.2759	0.1500
3	2.4333	3.8793	0.1010
22	2.3333	4.9828	0.1397
5	2.1000	3.9138	0.1022
43A	2.0167	3.5690	0.0901
39B	2.0000	5.3276	0.1518

Node	CV Rank	RA Rank	Depth
36	1	5	3
45	2	2	2
13	3	7	4
3	4	3	1
22	5	6	3
5	6	4	1
43A	7	1	1
39B	8	8	3

Figure 7. Control value (CV) and relative asymmetry (RA) calculations and rankings.

or more can be described as a controlling space, ones that have a value of 2 or more indicate a space that has an amount of control equivalent to at least two spaces (the space itself and one other, since each space begins with a CV of 1). These spaces are particularly important in providing and controlling access to others and can be referred to as *nodes*. The RA values for these nodes were calculated in order to assess their relationship to the building's spatial structure as a whole. The control and RA values were then ranked and cross-indexed on a simple graph (e.g., Figures 8 and 9) , which could then be interpreted according to the presence-availability table shown earlier (Figure 3). Because the level of presence-availability of any space depends more immediately on its connections to its immediate neighbours, control values get precedence over relative asymmetry (Grahame 1997:150). In addition, recording the depth of each node from the outside can provide some insight into the inhabitant-stranger dimension of privacy by indicating the ease with which someone entering from outside can reach a particular node.

Referring to Figure 8, it is clear that Rooms 34A and 3 have both high control and are relatively accessible and therefore possess a high degree of presence-availability. Rooms 13 and 14, on the other hand, have low control and accessibility relative to the other nodes. Room 46 exhibits the contradictory characteristics of having relatively high control, but with low accessibility. Room 45, on the other hand, has higher accessibility but lower control. I will discuss a few of these rooms in detail in terms of the types of social interaction introduced above. Accessibility is particularly important for occasions in that they often involve a number of individuals, in some cases both inhabitants and visitors. Frequently, more than one space may be required and it might therefore be advantageous to focus particular occasions on a node, such that the spaces controlled by the node can be used for associated activities or the storage of paraphernalia used during the occasion (Grahame 1997:155). Accessibility is also important in facilitating gatherings, and their frequency will be influenced by the number of paths that pass through the space. The control value is an important measure of this.

The areas with the highest presence availability could be locations for both occasions and gatherings (Figure 10). Room 34A is a hallway providing access to

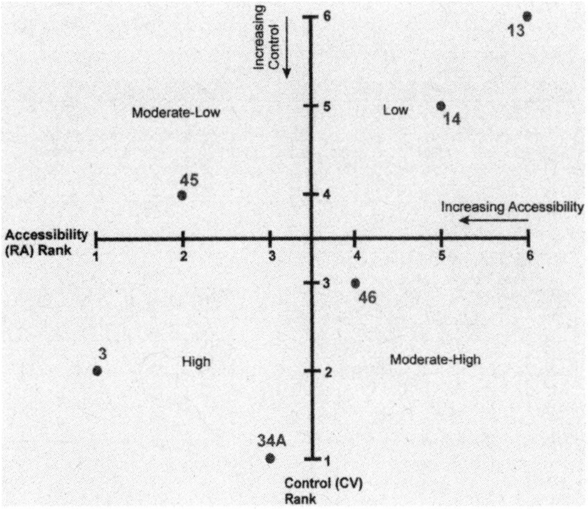

Figure 8. Presence-availability graph of nodes for Enkomi Ashlar Building, level IIIA.

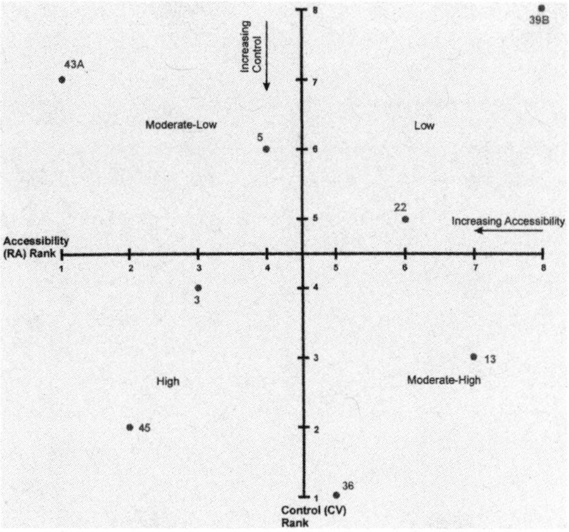

Figure 9. Presence-availability graph of nodes for Enkomi Ashlar Building, level IIIB.

several other rooms and is more likely a place for gatherings. Room 3 is the central court of the lower level of what the excavator described as a residence at the south end of the building (Dikaios 1969:182) The extensive use of finely carved ashlar masonry and finds of luxury items (including an ivory comb, and mould for gold ornaments) would suggest an elite residence. The centrality of this space would indeed promote gatherings among inhabitants of the residence. Its shallowness would also make the space ideal for the informal reception of strangers into the residence.

These areas stand in contrast to Rooms 13 and 14 with low control and low accessibility. Such spaces would most likely be used for occasions, particularly formal ones that would not be subject to the potential interruptions of a room with high control. The fact that these two adjoining spaces are on the path that leads from the building's most impressive entrance (a 30-m ashlar facade with cut door jambs), through a bipartite vestibule marked with non-structural columns, suggests that the occasions might have centred on the formal reception of strangers. Both rooms had the most impressive ashlar walls in the building, consisting of large blocks with drafted margins, and two massive rectangular ashlar columns supporting the roof. Room 14 also contained a formal hearth surrounded by at least three and probably four wooden columns – an arrangement perhaps reminiscent of the central room of a Mycenaean megaron-type palace. The removal of these spaces from everyday activity created a structured environment that reinforced the categorical distinction between inhabitant and visitor (see Grahame 1997:160). These rooms can therefore be seen as reproducing social identities. During occasions they created an environment in which the visitor is continuously reminded of his/her own inferior position vis-à-vis the power of the elite inhabitant(s). This effect could also be enhanced by the appearance of the elite inhabitant from, or withdrawal into, parts of the building not likely accessible to visitors. The staircase leading down into Room 13 from the quarters above might allow for such appearance and disappearance.

The remaining nodes, Rooms 45 and 46, with their higher accessibility and relatively shallow depths might have also served as reception rooms, although on a more informal level. Room 45 with its higher accessibility would likely have promoted gatherings, while 46 might have been used for occasions. Given the presence of large formal hearths in each room,

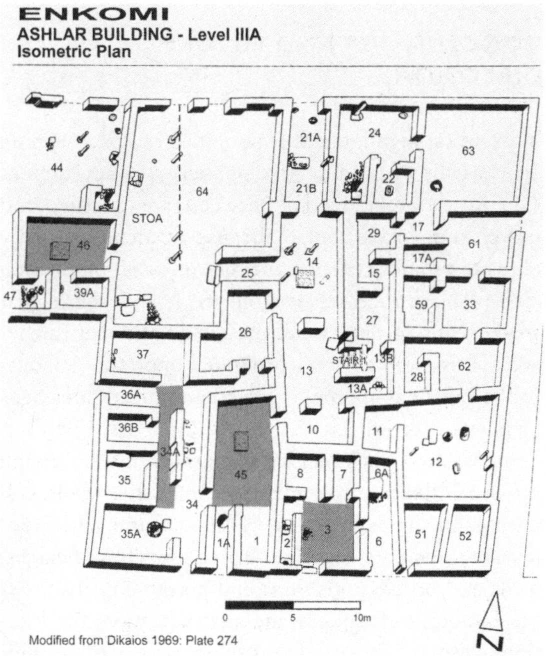

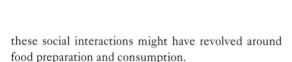

Figure 10. Level IIIA plan with nodes shaded.

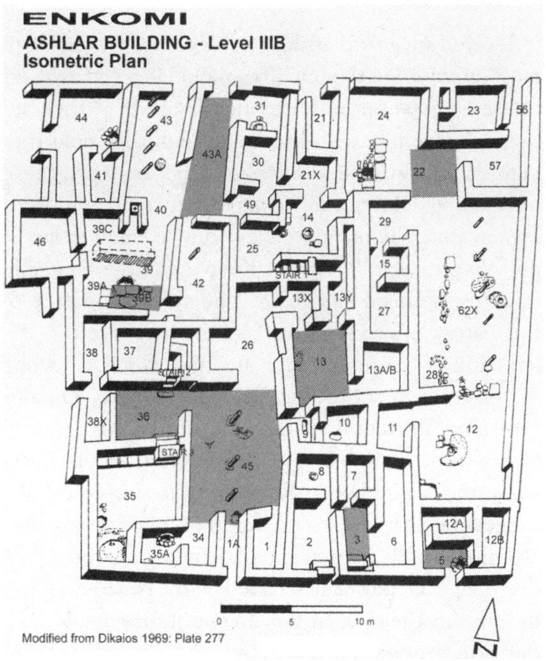

Figure 11. Level IIIB plan with nodes shaded.

these social interactions might have revolved around food preparation and consumption.

Level IIIB

The level IIIA building was destroyed in a great fire around 1160 B.C.E. and soon rebuilt with a number of significant structural changes (Dikaios 1969:191–211) (Figure 11). Part of the reconstructed Ashlar Building functioned as a cult centre, known as the "Sanctuary of the Horned God" after the 54-cm-tall bronze statue found in a pit in Room 10. There is some controversy as to whether or not the statue (which was actually found in the subsequent IIIC level) was in use during the IIIB phase.[3] In any case, the new layout was substantially different with new patterns of accessibility (Figure 7). The IIIA central hall was subdivided and the focus of inhabitant-visitor relations shifted to the southern end of the building, where the new main entrance was located.

In examining the presence-availability of the IIIB reconstruction (Figures 9 and 11), we see that Room 3 once again is a space of both high control and accessibility, suggesting the potential for both occasions and gatherings. Its importance is magnified in this phase by the construction of a new main entrance from the South Street that was marked by the erection beside the stairway of an immense ashlar block re-used from the original structure. The fact that an old entry less than a metre away continued to be used and that a new wall was erected within the building between them is interesting and might suggest an attempt to classify and separate those who entered from outside. Perhaps one entry was for inhabitants (or inhabitants of a certain status?) while the other was for visitors.

Room 45 also has a very high presence-availability. As a possible connection between the high-traffic node Room 36 (a vestibule with stairs) and the South Street, Room 45 may have facilitated casual gatherings. However, it is occasions associated with its function as a node to Rooms 9 and 10 that give Room 45 particular significance. Rooms 9 and 10 (the back of the former great hall) were subdivided and formed the focal point of the building's cultic activities. Room 10 contained a great deal of cult paraphernalia, including an alabaster jug, a bronze knife, and a carved sandstone niche, possibly for the cult statue (if it was in use at this time). A 1.65-m opening was left between Rooms 9 and 10 – oddly with a threshold nearly 50 cm above the floor level.

I would suggest that this opening, much wider than most doorways in the building, should be seen as a sort of viewing portal and attention-focusing device for those in Room 9, with the rather high threshold providing both a real and symbolic barrier between those in Room 9 and those in Room 10. Any ritual proceedings in Room 10 could be viewed by a small group of persons in Room 9 without them actually being able to enter the main cult room. The symbolic nature of this barrier is also suggested by the presence of a 25-cm band of red mud mortar flooring which ran along the inside of Room 10 along the threshold (see Dikaios 1969:196). Furthermore the side of the barrier wall facing those in Room 9 was of dressed ashlar blocks while the facing inside Room 10 was simply rubble, suggesting that those utilizing (i.e., performing rituals) in Room 10 were more concerned with conveying the image of power associated with ashlar masonry to those in Room 9. In this manner those conducting the rituals were manipulating the built environment in order to encode messages of exclusion from direct participation in their activities and hence the esoteric knowledge associated with those activities, to those watching from the viewing room (Room 9). The viewers (possibly lower order elites), unable to participate directly in the activities taking place in Room 10 are reminded physically and symbolically of their less significant place in the social order.

Room 45, in which were found several bulls' skulls, miniature gold bulls' horns and a miniature bronze spear head undoubtedly had role to play in the social occasions associated with the cultic activities in the neighbouring rooms. The placement of a new ashlar doorjamb at the entry to Room 9 marks the significance of movement between these rooms. A clue as to the occasions that took place in Room 45 might be found in the 276 base ring bowls found stacked in Room 10. These together with finds of a bronze knife in Room 10, articulated animal and bird bones in Room 9, and the hearth in Room 45 point to ritual sacrifice and feasting. Room 45 could accommodate a large number of visitors during such feasts, only a limited number of whom would be permitted to enter Room 9 and witness the rituals that took place in Room 10.

CONCLUSIONS AND FUTURE DIRECTIONS

This work highlights the potential of space syntax analysis for examining the publicity/privacy dimension of the relationship between architecture and power and, in particular, the use of architecture by elites to promote particular types of social interaction (or to isolate themselves from it). It also shows that space syntax is not an end unto itself and that further analysis is required to incorporate important elements of the built environment that communicate messages of power nonverbally. As Amos Rapoport (1990) has demonstrated, such messages are transmitted through the use of fixed-feature elements like ashlar walls, columns, thresholds and plastered floors, and semifixed-feature elements such as doors, benches, hearths, wells and other furnishings and portable artifacts.[4] If the buildings of Enkomi are any indication, the location of ashlar masonry seems to be particularly significant, and future work will be directed toward categorizing various types of this stonework and analyzing the potential impact of their locations by examining viewsheds within building interiors.

A study of the Ashlar Building of Enkomi demonstrates that the interplay of these various elements of the built environment was part of an integrated building program designed to encode, transmit and reproduce messages of sociopolitical inequality along the dimensions discussed above: publicity/privacy, segregation/access, and identity/difference. It remains to apply the analytical techniques used here to monumental complexes from elsewhere in Cyprus and the neighbouring regions of the Eastern Mediterranean and Near East in order to examine these building programs in the context of increasing interregional interaction and influence during the LBA. Through such an approach the silent walls of sites like Enkomi might yield new information on LBA sociopolitical dynamics – and if the Cypriot elites still remain nameless, we can at least gain a fuller understanding of the means by which they achieved and maintained their power.

REFERENCES CITED

Courtois, J., J. Lagarce, and E. Lagarce
|1986| *Enkomi et le Bronze Récent à Chypre.* Imprimerie Zavallis, Nicosia.

Dikaios, P.
|1969| *Enkomi: Excavations 1948–1958.* Philip von Zabern, Mainz.

Dovey, K.
|1999| *Framing Places: Mediating Power in Built Form.* Routledge, London.

Giddens, A.
|1984| *The Constitution of Society: Outline of the Theory of Structuration.* University of California Press, Berkeley.

Grahame, M.
|1997| Public and Private in the Roman House: The Spatial Order of the *Casa del Fauno*. In *Domestic Space in the Roman World: Pompeii and Beyond,* edited by R. Laurence, and A. Wallace-Hadrill, pp. 137–164. Journal of Roman Archaeology Supplementary Series No. 22. Journal of Roman Archaeology, Portsmouth, Rhode Island.

Hillier, B., and J. Hanson
|1984| *The Social Logic of Space.* Cambridge University Press, Cambridge.

Karageorghis, V.
|1982| *Cyprus from the Stone Age to the Romans.* Thames & Hudson, London.

Knapp, A. B.
|1986| *Copper Production and Divine Protection: Archaeology, Ideology and Social Complexity on Bronze Age Cyprus.* SIMA Pocket-book 42. Paul Åströms Förlag, Jonsered.
|1988a| Copper Production and Eastern Mediterranean Trade: The rise of Complex Society on Cyprus. In *State and Society: The Emergence and Development of Social Hierarchy and Political Centralization,* edited by J. Glenhill, B. Bender, and M. T. Larsen, pp. 149–169. Allen and Unwin, London.
|1988b| Ideology, Archaeology and Polity. *Man* (N.S.) 23:133–163.
|1990| Production, Location, and Integration in Bronze Age Cyprus. *Current Anthropology* 31:147–176.

Markus, T. A.
|1993| *Buildings and Power: Freedom and Control in the Origin of Modern Building Types.* Routledge, London.

Negbi, O.
|1986| The Climax of Urban Development in Bronze Age Cyprus. *Report of the Department of Antiquities Cyprus,* pp. 97–121.

Rapoport, A.
|1990| *The Meaning of the Built Environment: A Nonverbal Communication Approach.* 2nd ed. University of Arizona Press, Tucson.

Webb, J. M.
|1999| *Ritual Architecture, Iconography and Practice in the Late Cypriot Bronze Age.* SIMA Pocket-book 75. Paul Åströms Förlag, Jonsered.

NOTES

1 For comparison purposes, the RA values of spaces from buildings with different numbers of spaces can be transformed into *Real RA* values by dividing the RA value for a space by its *D-value* provided by Hillier and Hanson (1984:Table 3). Since the RA values here will not be compared directly, this procedure is unnecessary.

2 There is some controversy over the dating of the various levels at Enkomi. While Dikaios (1969) proposes a date for the initial construction of the Ashlar Building during the Late Cypriot IIIA period, others (e.g., Negbi 1986:104) have suggested an initial construction date during the Late Cypriot IIC period. The absolute dates for these periods are also not entirely agreed upon although a starting date for the Late Cypriot IIIA of about 1190 B.C.E. (30 years later than Dikaios proposed) is now widely accepted. For a summarized discussion of these chronological problems, see Webb 1999:91–92.

3 The pit in which the statue was found was dug into debris from the IIIB destruction and clearly belonged to the subsequent IIIC reconstruction. Dikaios (1969:197–199), however, argued that the cult statue was retrieved from the debris after its initial use during the IIIB phase and re-used during the IIIC reoccupation.

4 Rapoport (1990:96–101) also discusses a third element of nonverbal communication: *nonfixed*-feature elements of the built environment, such as the physical and verbal expressions of the building's occupants. These elements are not directly preserved in the archaeological record and are therefore not addressed in the present discussion.

INDIVIDUAL, HOUSEHOLD, AND COMMUNITY SPACE IN EARLY BRONZE AGE WESTERN ANATOLIA AND THE NEARBY ISLANDS

Carolyn Aslan

Carolyn Aslan, Koç University, History Department, Rumeli Feneri Yolu, Sariyer, Istanbul 34450, Turkey.

ABSTRACT

Societies exhibit variation in how they conceptualize and ascribe importance to social categories such as the individual, the household and the community. One way that archaeologists can begin to investigate ancient concepts about social categories is through a study of the arrangement of space. The placement of walls within houses and settlements provides a framework for interactions and negotiations, and the allotment of space should correspond in some degree to social divisions and relationships, or at least ones that the builders chose to mark in a material form. An examination of architectural remains from Early Bronze Age sites in western Anatolia and the nearby island of Lesbos demonstrates how physical boundaries and spatial arrangements can express ideas about the relationship of the individual to larger social categories of an ancient community.

The research behind this study began with the question of how archaeologists might investigate ancient concepts about the individual. Not all present-day societies attribute the same meaning to the individual as a separate social category, and it is likely that significant variation existed in how ancient societies thought about the individual and individual action. Archaeologists are only beginning to investigate how ancient people may have differed in their expression of the individual in comparison with larger social groups. This paper argues that since the category of the individual is socially constructed and variable, both in present and past societies, one needs to be careful about simply transferring present-day ideas of the individual to ancient societies without considering the ancient evidence. One way archaeologists can begin to extract ideas about the individual's relation to larger social categories from ancient material evidence is through an analysis of the spatial arrangements of houses and communities, especially focusing on factors of privacy and segmentation. The architectural remains of two early third millennium sites, namely the site of Troy in Western Anatolia and the site of Thermi on the island of Lesbos, serve as a case study.

CROSS-CULTURAL STUDIES OF INDIVIDUALISM AND COLLECTIVISM

Cross-cultural research reveals that the category of the individual is culturally constructed and variable (Chen et al. 1997; Hofstede 1980; Hui and Triandis 1986; Kagitçibasi 1987, 1989; Kagitçibasi and Berry 1989; Kashima 1987, 1989; Sinha and Verma 1987; Triandis 1987, 1993, 1995; Triandis et al. 1998). Some societies may not think of the individual as a separate social entity that is detached from larger social units such as a family or community. Others may think of society as formed of autonomous individuals, each with a free will and the potential to cause social change through their actions or resistance.

Scholars in cross-cultural psychology employ specific definitions of the terms "individualistic" and "collectivistic" to describe opposing sets of ideas about the individual in society and the corresponding patterns of behaviour (Hui and Triandis 1986; Triandis 1987, 1993). Individualism is defined as a social pattern in which individuals see themselves as independent and place their personal priorities above those of a larger group. Collectivism is a social pattern in which individuals see themselves as interdependent parts of a larger group and their decisions are primarily motivated by group priorities. It should also be noted that individualistic and collectivistic patterns of behaviour can co-exist within a society (Kagitçibasi 1987:96–97; Triandis 1993:162). Any one society is never completely individualistic or collectivistic. There also may be differences based on factors such as age, gender, or class. Nonetheless, when societies are compared cross-culturally, behavior patterns can be grouped according to these general categories.

Researchers have also found that individualism and collectivism can be further subdivided into vertical individualism, vertical collectivism, horizontal individualism and horizontal collectivism (Chen et al. 1997; Singelis et al. 1995; Triandis 1995:44–45). Horizontal collectivism stresses sameness, equality, interdependence and cohesion of the in-group. Vertical collectivism has a hierarchical arrangement of interdependent people who have different obligations to the in-group on the basis of their rank. Horizontal individualism is a system of independent and equal individuals. Vertical individualism also includes the idea of individual independence, but with competition and inequality.

These distinctions could be useful in archaeological considerations of social complexity. It may be possible to differentiate between a society that has a hierarchical system of vertical individualism, in which individuals compete for a position on a hierarchical ladder, from a society with a hierarchical system of vertical collectivism, in which social positions are fixed by hereditary laws and people are encouraged to follow sets of community rules and obligations that serve to maintain the existing vertical structure. It would also be interesting to study how and why societies might change from one pattern to another over time, perhaps as hierarchical structures become more established or even perhaps when threatened.

Some of the attention that the topic of individualism and collectivism has received within cross-cultural psychology can be understood as a response to the globalization and the influence of Western culture (Halman 1996; Kagitçibasi 1987:98–100, 1989:68; Triandis 1993:155, 1995:145–187). Western societies are perceived as highly individualistic (Lukes 1973; Macfarlane 1978, 1979). Mass media and globalization are often seen as spreading individualistic Western values and behaviour to societies with more collectivistic behaviour patterns. Furthermore, ideas of the individual and individualism are embedded deeply in current thinking about political, economic and social organization, and thus are often discussed with a political or moralistic slant. For these reasons, archaeologists need to be especially cautious in inadvertently transferring modern concepts of the individual to interpretations of ancient societies. Yet, since current ideas about the shifting balance between individual and group priorities form a central part of explanations of present-day social change and cultural difference, a consideration of the material expression of the individual can broaden the understanding of ancient social change and cultural difference.

SPATIAL ANALYSIS: PRIVACY AND SEGMENTATION

Since one cannot assume the individual as an important social category, it is necessary to work from the ground up to try to discern the most recognizable social categories in the remains of an ancient culture. Only then can one begin to explore how the material expression of those categories may have operated in the society or changed over time. A study of the placement and position of physical boundaries and the division of space within houses and settlements can lead to an understanding of the social categories operating in ancient communities.

One good reason to focus on houses and the placement of houses within a community is that the home is a primary location where ideas about the individual's relation to larger social units are learned, reinforced and negotiated. For this idea, I am working from Bourdieu's theory (1973, 1977) that the house is an active setting for the formation and maintenance of social structure. The physical features of a house can encourage specific types of behaviour within the setting that conform to expectations of proper social action. The boundaries and spaces formed by walls and furniture transform ideas about social relationships into a material form. In turn, the physical form of the house reinforces the social ideas. The divisions and arrangements within a house can set up hierarchical or other relationships between people, objects, and activities. The daily use or practice within the space helps to maintain and reinforce the social organization.

The house is especially important in establishing and teaching ideas about the relationship of the individual to the family and between the family and the rest of the community (Munro and Madigan 1999; Putnam 1999). The form of the house is related to the way that people think about their individual autonomy, their vertical power relationships with other people in the house, and their horizontal relationships. Furthermore, the arrangement of houses within a community should also be an important indication of social boundaries and social categories.

The placement of physical boundaries in houses and settlements should correspond in some way to conceptual divisions that the builders chose to mark in a material form. Some conceptual divisions may not be manifested in a physical form, or the physical boundaries established may be somewhat flexible or permeable in terms of the actual use of the space. Archaeologists can usually only analyze the most formally expressed divisions within a house. More perishable dividers such as mats or cloth certainly may have been important in partitioning space, but it is usually difficult to retrieve such kinds of evidence from archaeological contexts. Even so, it may be the formalization of divisions through the construction of solid boundary walls that marks an especially significant delineation of spatial organization. Although the placement of walls provides merely a framework for a diversity of social interactions and negotiations, a study of the division of space can begin to describe and define social categories and social boundaries within an ancient community.

There are two aspects of the arrangement of space that emerge as key factors concerning how the individual and other social categories are expressed. These are privacy controls and segmentation. Privacy and segmentation within houses and communities can both be studied with archaeological remains and are thought to relate to the divisions and social categories within a society.

Scholars recognize that privacy mechanisms help control interactions between people, and that privacy varies across cultures (Altman 1977; Lawrence 1990; Moore 1984:12–13; Roberts and Gregor 1971; Sciama 1993). Some scholars interpret increasing privacy as evidence for greater individualism. This interpretation results from the assertion that privacy is necessary for individual self-awareness and development, and to foster a sense of self (Flaherty 1972:viii; Sanders 1990:50; Westin 1968:32–34). Privacy is thought to contribute to feelings of autonomy, self-evaluation, and the development of self-identity. Privacy mechanisms can control interactions at an individual level as well as at the level of the family or community (Sciama 1993:90–97). In some situations, the family may have a great deal of privacy from the rest of the community, but the individual members of the family may have little privacy from each other.

A study of privacy mechanisms within architectural arrangements can help to discern important social categories within the community that are kept private or separate from one another. Donald Sanders (1990) has developed some methods for studying privacy in architectural remains. He defines certain measurable privacy controls, such as walls, the position of doorways and other fixed features, which he used to determine the circulation path through the house and the permeability of a house to the outside. Many divisions in a house may provide a greater opportunity for privacy within the rooms. A house with many rooms has the potential for more privacy for individuals, while a house with only one large room gives little opportunity for privacy.

Doorways and circulation paths are another important indicator of privacy levels. Doorways that lead to the outside of a house are places of access control as well as a point of information leakage between the house and the outside. Doorways inside the house are an indication of the circulation path through the house and the degree of privacy possible within rooms. If the circulation paths in the house mean that one must pass through one room to get to another, only the innermost room will be private. The creation of passage spaces, such as hallways, indicates a greater desire for privacy within each room along the hallway.

Segmentation is another factor that is related to privacy. Susan Kent's (1990, 1991) study of segmentation has shown how societies differ in the degree to which they divide the space within their houses. She also demonstrates that societies with a higher level of social complexity tend to have a greater degree of segmentation. The basic measure of the segmentation of a house is the number of separate rooms. The act of dividing up the space within a house comes out of a much deeper understanding of how the world is ordered and organized. Humans create boundaries in undivided space by building physical features such as walls to enclose or to separate different areas. Space is not segmented arbitrarily; rather it is usually divided in order to separate activities, stored objects or people.

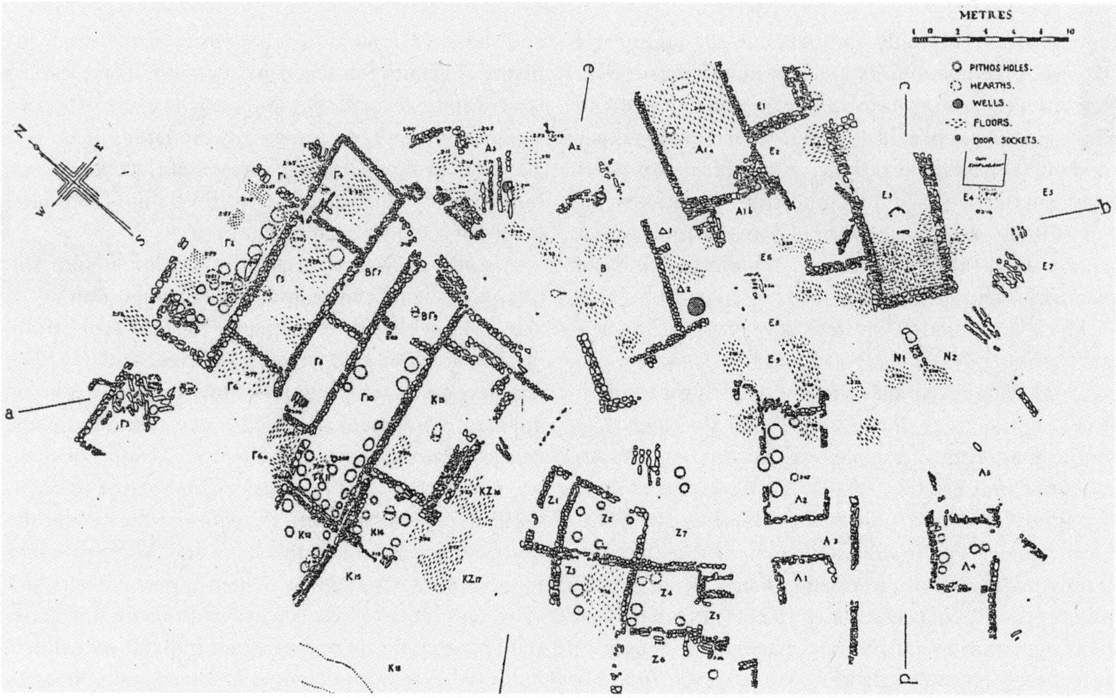

Figure 1. Plan of Thermi I (Lamb 1936:Plan 1, reprinted with permission of Cambridge University Press).

Segmentation is another way to study how different social categories such as the individual are allotted separate space.

Segmentation and privacy controls are factors that can reasonably be studied by archaeologists through examination of house and settlement remains. The way that space is divided and arranged may correspond to how people think about and define the most important social units within the community and how these units are seen in relation to one another. The remains of houses and communities can then inform us about how people who built and lived in the houses thought about and structured their social relations.

CASE STUDY

In the following section, I explain the case study of two communities; the site of Thermi on Lesbos (Lamb 1936) and the site of Troy on the Western coast of Anatolia (Blegen et al. 1950; Dörpfeld 1902; Korfmann 1991, 1992, 1993, 1994). Both of these sites date to the first part of the third millennium B.C. and they share certain cultural features, namely architecture and pottery types that are widely found in Western Anatolia and the nearby islands during this time period. This period in Anatolia is especially interesting to study because different sites exhibit varying patterns of emerging social complexity as they change from rather simple village communities to ones with increasing indications of hierarchy. Some of these experiments are more successful and long-lived than others, while some sites exhibit almost no changes in social complexity during this period.

The two sites I chose for this case study show how two settlements, which are quite similar at the beginning of the third millennium, have very different histories as time progresses. While Thermi shows little change throughout the phases of its occupation, Troy shows a large jump in the level of social complexity between phases I and II. In the earliest phase of both settlements (Thermi phase I, Troy phase I), the two sites share similar features (Figures 1 and 3). The settlements are compact with long houses sharing adjoining walls. It should be noted that both sites are either incompletely preserved or parts of the site are unexcavated in this period, so some of the empty spaces on

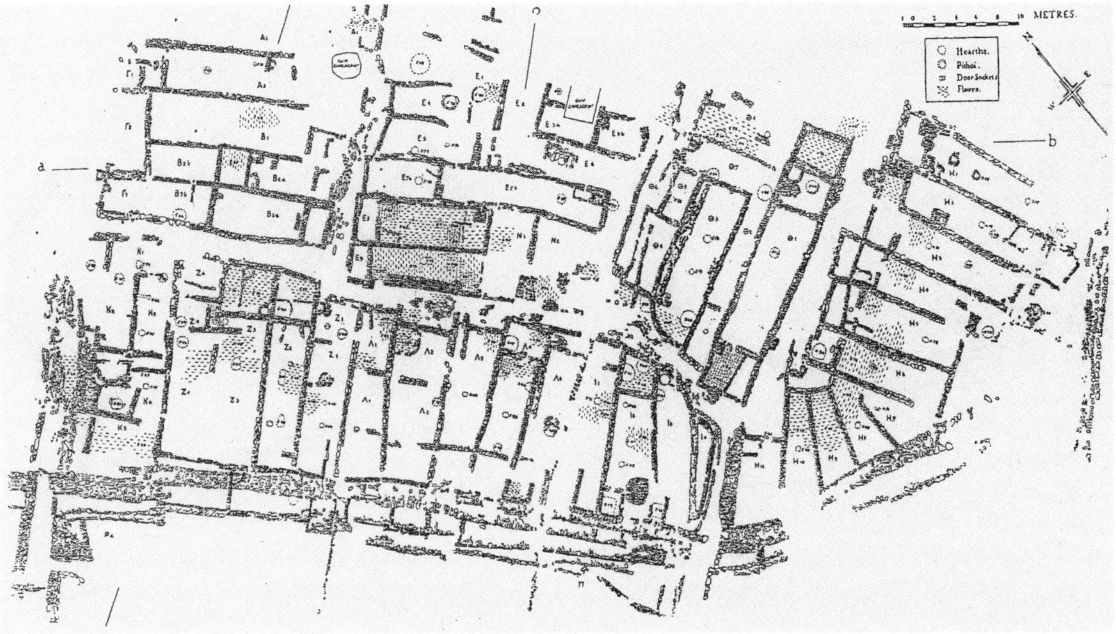

Figure 2. Plan of Thermi V (Lamb 1936:Plan 6, reprinted with permission of Cambridge University Press).

the plans would probably have been occupied by additional houses. The houses show only a small degree of segmentation, with most of the space in the house occupied by one central, large room. Occasionally there are smaller rooms at the front or back of the house. There is little evidence for any differentiation between the houses in terms of size or quality of the finds. Most of the houses in both Thermi and Troy I have an average size of 50–60 m^2.

The settlement at Thermi was rebuilt several times, but the plan remains fairly constant (Lamb 1936). An examination of the settlement plan of the last phase of Thermi (phase V; Figure 2) shows a similar arrangement as before, with long houses sharing party walls. The settlement appears to have a larger number of houses in this level, although this may also be a result of better preservation and more complete excavation of the upper levels of the site. This phase does have evidence for a fortification wall, while the previous levels were probably unfortified.

In contrast to Thermi, Troy exhibits a much larger change between phase I and II . In the Troy II period, the original house form of a long house with one main central room is transformed into a monumental version (Figure 4) (Dörpfeld 1902; Korfmann 1993, Mellaart 1959). In comparison with the average house size in phase I, which was around 60 m^2, the largest building in phase IIc is almost 300 m^2. At the same time as these buildings, there is an increase in trade and luxury goods, including the gold, silver and lapis lazuli objects that were found in the so-called Trojan treasures from this period (Tolstikov and Treister 1996). There is also evidence for the adoption of new feasting practices shown by sets of specialized eating and drinking vessels. During the Troy II period, these monumental buildings show numerous evidence of burning followed by rebuilding, usually along approximately the same lines. These repeated destructions may attest to the instability of this time period, which may also be evidenced by the thick fortification walls found both at Troy, Thermi and at other sites during this period.

A study of the division and arrangement of space within these settlements shows how the inhabitants used spatial arrangements and physical boundaries to express the most important social categories within the community. In the communities within my case study, the category of the individual does not receive

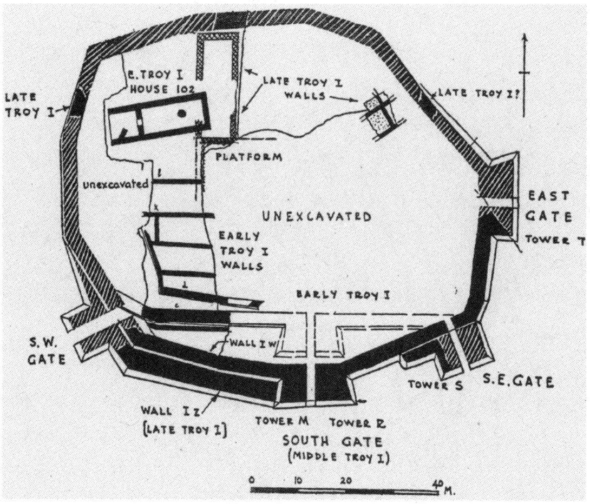

Figure 3. Plan of Troy I (Mellaart 1959:Figure 2, reprinted with permission of James Mellaart).

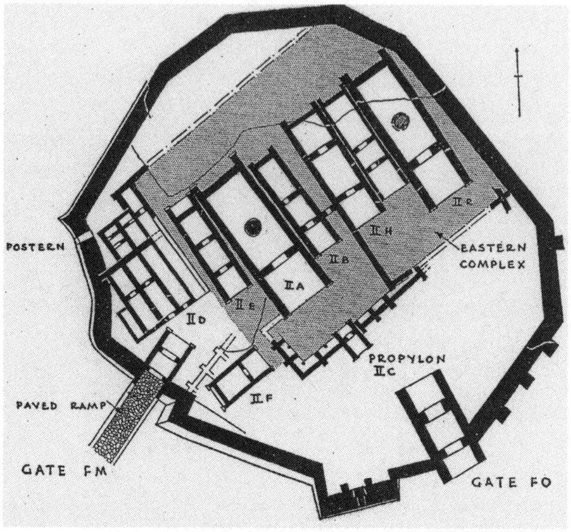

Figure 4. Plan of Troy IIc (Mellaart 1959:Figure 6, reprinted with permission of James Mellaart).

formalized material expression in the architectural remains. Instead other social categories appear to be the primary divisions and probably also primary social forces within those communities.

Starting from the outermost boundary, at both sites the community as a whole is one social category that is delineated by the inhabitants. Troy has recognizable fortification or enclosure walls in all phases (Blegen et al. 1950:38–39; Mellaart 1959). Thermi has an enclosure wall in phase V of the settlement, although, in all phases, Thermi has a dense, compact form that indicates a conceptual boundary, even if not physically marked by a wall in the earlier phases. Although these walls probably had a primarily protective function, they probably aided in fostering a concept of a distinct, enclosed community of inhabitants. The boundary walls may have defined a distinction between habitation and non-habitation areas, and also between members and non-members of the community. Gates control access to the interior of the settlements, and, from there, any strangers could be immediately noticed and monitored.

A second important boundary is around the house units. Each site has segmented units that can be identified as houses. At Thermi (Lamb 1936) and in the Troy I phase (Blegen et al. 1950:36–171; Dörpfeld 1902:42–47, Figure 7; Korfmann 1991:6–10), the houses are fairly equal units in terms of their size and number of rooms. Thermi V has houses that are so similar in size that it is almost as though the inhabitants were deliberately assigning the same amount of space to each house when they rebuilt the settlement (Figure 2). It is likely that this segmentation of the settlement into separate, but equally sized units corresponds to a conceptual division of the community into equal household social groups.

Furthermore, there are privacy controls between the houses, but little privacy within the houses. Often the houses have additional small rooms or a porch near the entrance of the house. These rooms help to shield the main central room. Even though there are privacy mechanisms between the houses of the settlement, the houses are still quite close together, which does reduce the privacy in the settlement. Once one is inside the main central room, however, there was probably little privacy within this room.

In Troy II, the houses represent a different communicative intent in which the buildings are used to display the size and possibly the wealth of the household. At Troy, the equality between the houses that appears in the Early Troy I period is not maintained. Possibly as early as the late Troy I period and certainly in the Troy II period, the house form is transformed into a monumental building (Dörpfeld 1902; Korfmann 1993; Mellaart 1959). Evidence from the finds in these buildings makes it is likely that they would have still served for habitation, although they may have taken on additional functions as places for feasting, storage and other activities of the elites of the community.

In these examples, the individual does not emerge as a significant social category in terms of the allocation of separate space. A consideration of the potential privacy and segmentation levels within the houses and settlements supports the above observation. Privacy levels and segmentation are low. Space was not formally divided to provide separate areas for individuals within the family. There was probably little privacy within houses, which increases the cohesive quality of the group within the house. The settlements are small, and often the houses are so close together that there would have been little privacy within the settlement. Within the houses, there is little space that is physically separated for private use.

This spatial analysis may help us to better understand the nature of the increasing social complexity shown in the Troy II period. James Mellaart (1959), in discussing the Troy II monumental buildings, considers it to be unusual that the ruler of Troy did not receive separate private space, but instead lived in a large, undivided building. Most interpretations of the Troy II period assume an individual in power over a hierarchical arrangement of followers. If this is the case, the separateness of one individual and the hierarchical ordering is not formalized in terms of physical divisions within the building. The inside of the buildings may have expressed the hierarchy through patterns of repeated use, such as reserved areas or hierarchical seating arrangements, yet these arrangements were not formalized through physical walls. This pattern also needs to be considered in light of Susan Kent's cross-cultural study that suggests that more socially complex societies have greater segmentation of architecture. The Troy II buildings may represent either a beginning stage of social stratification when the social forms or hierarchical systems are not cemented into place, or a social system in which the collective unity of a larger group such as a family is an important social force, perhaps more so than one individual leader. The architectural evidence suggests that the elite groups at Troy may have developed as certain families gained power chose to express it through an elaboration of their houses.

As was discussed in the introduction, not all cultures conceptualize or formalize the category of the individual in the same way. At the sites in this study, a separate category of the individual is not expressed through the architecture by setting aside private space for individuals. Instead the most important social categories in the communities that are marked by physical boundaries are the household group and the community as a whole. Within the houses, the space is relatively undivided. There is almost no formalized private space for specific individuals within a house. Thermi and Troy I have a strong emphasis on the collective unit of the community with equal household units. Troy II shows more vertical tendencies, but they seem to be acted out within the realm of collective household or kin units.

REFERENCES CITED

Altman, I.
|1977| Privacy Regulation: Culturally Universal or Culturally Specific? *Journal of Social Issues* 33:66–84.

Blegen, C. W., J. L. Caskey, M. Rawson, and J. Sperling
|1950| *Troy: The First and Second Settlements*. Princeton University Press, Princeton.

Bourdieu, P.
|1973| The Berber House: Swahili Space and Symbolic Markers. In *Rules and Meanings*, edited by M. Douglas, pp. 98–110. Penguin, Harmondsworth.
|1977| *Outline of a Theory of Practice*. Cambridge University Press, Cambridge.

Chen, C. E., J. R. Meindl, and R. G. Hunt
|1997| Testing the Effects of Vertical and Horizontal Collectivism: A Study of Reward Allocation Preferences in China. *Journal of Cross-Cultural Psychology* 28:44–70.

Dörpfeld, W.
|1902| *Troja und Ilion*. Beck and Barth, Athens.

Flaherty, D. H.
|1972| *Privacy in Colonial New England*. University Press of Virginia, Charlottesville.

Halman, L.
|1996| Individualism in Individualized Society? Results from the European Values Survey. *International Journal of Comparative Sociology* 37:195–314.

Hodder, I.
|1982| *The Present Past: An Introduction to Anthropology for Archaeologists*. Batsford, London.
|1991| *Reading the Past*. Cambridge University Press, Cambridge.

Hofstede, G.
|1980| *Culture's Consequences: International Differences in Work-Related Values*. Sage, London.

Hui, C. H., and H. C. Triandis
|1986| Individualism-Collectivism: A Study of Cross-Cultural Researchers. *Journal of Cross-Cultural Psychology* 17:225–248.

Kagitçibasi, Ç.
|1987| Individual and Group Loyalties: Are They Compatible? In *Growth and Progress in Cross-Cultural Psychology*, edited by Ç. Kagitçibasi, pp. 94–103. Swets North America, Berwyn.
|1989| Why Individualism/Collectivism? In *Heterogeneity in Cross-Cultural Psychology*, edited by D. M. Keats, D. Munro, and L. Mann, pp. 66–74. Swets and Zeitlinger, Berwyn.

Kagitçibasi, Ç., and J. W. Berry
|1989| Cross-Cultural Psychology: Current Research and Trends. *Annual Review of Psychology* 40:493–532.

Kashima, Y.
|1987| Conceptions of Person: Implications in Individualism/Collectivism. In *Growth and Progress in Cross-Cultural Psychology*, edited by Ç. Kagitçibasi, pp. 104–112. Swets North America, Berwyn.
|1989| Cultural Conceptions of the Person and Individualism-Collectivism: A Semiotic Framework. In *Heterogeneity in Cross-Cultural Psychology*, edited by D. M. Keats, D. Munro, and L. Mann, pp. 75–81. Swets and Zeitlinger, Berwyn.

Kent, S.
|1990| A Cross-Cultural Study of Segmentation, Architecture, and the Use of Space. In *Domestic Architecture and the Use of Space: An Interdisciplinary Cross-Cultural Study*, edited by S. Kent, pp. 127–152. Cambridge University Press, Cambridge.
|1991| Partitioning Space: Cross-Cultural Factors Influencing Domestic Spatial Segmentation. *Environment and Behavior* 23:438–473.

Korfmann, M.
|1991| Troia – Reinigungs- und Dokumentations-arbeiten 1987, Ausgrabungen 1988 und 1989. *Studia Troica* 1:1–34.
|1992| Troia – Ausgrabungen 1990 und 1991. *Studia Troica* 2:1–41.
|1993| Troia – Ausgrabungen 1992. *Studia Troica* 3:1–37.
|1994| Troia – Ausgrabungen 1993. *Studia Troica* 4:1–50.

Lamb, W.
|1936| *Excavations at Thermi in Lesbos*. Cambridge University Press, Cambridge.

Lawrence, R.
|1990| Public Collective and Private Space: A Study of Urban Housing in Switzerland. In *Domestic Architecture and the Use of Space*, edited by S. Kent, pp. 73–91. Cambridge University Press, Cambridge.

Lukes, S.
|1973| *Individualism*. Harper and Row, New York.

Macfarlane, A.
|1978| *The Origins of English Individualism*. Cambridge University Press, Cambridge.
|1979| The Group and the Individual in History. In *Space, Hierarchy and Society*, edited by B. C. Burnham, and J. Kingsbury, pp. 17–22. British Archaeological Reports International Series 59. British Archaeological Reports, Oxford.

Mellaart, J.
|1959| Notes on the Architectural Remains of Troy I and II. *Anatolian Studies* 9:131–162.

Moore, B. J.
|1984| *Privacy: Studies in Social and Cultural History*. M. E. Sharpe, New York.

Munro, M., and R. Madigan
|1999| Negotiating Space in the Family Home. In *At Home: An Anthropology of Domestic Space*, edited by I. Cieraad, pp. 107–117. Syracuse University Press, Syracuse.

Putnam, T.
|1999| "Postmodern" Home Life. In *At Home: An Anthropology of Domestic Space*, edited by I. Cieraad, pp. 144–153. Syracuse University Press, Syracuse.

Roberts, J., and T. Gregor
|1971| Privacy: A Cultural View. In *Privacy*, edited by J. R. Pennock, and J. W. Chapman, pp. 199–225. Atherton Press, New York.

Sanders, D. H.
|1990| Behavioral Conventions and Archaeology: Methods for the Analysis of Ancient Architecture. In *Domestic Architecture and the Use of Space*, edited by S. Kent, pp. 43–72. Cambridge University Press, Cambridge.

Sciama, L.
|1993| The Problem of Privacy in Mediterranean Anthropology. In *Women and Space: Ground Rules and Social Maps*, edited by S. Ardener, pp. 87–111. Berg, Oxford.

Shanks, M., and C. Tilley
|1987| *Re-Constructing Archaeology*. Cambridge University Press, Cambridge.

Singelis, T. M., H. C. Triandis, D. P. S. Bhawuk, and M. J. Gelfand
|1995| Horizontal and Vertical Dimensions of Individualism and Collectivism: A Theoretical and Measurement Refinement. *Cross-Cultural Research* 29: 240–275.

Sinha, J. B. P., and J. Verma
|1987| Structure of Collectivism. In *Growth and Progress in Cross-Cultural Psychology*, edited by Ç. Kagitçibasi, pp. 123–129. Swets North America, Berwyn.

Triandis, H. C.
|1987| Individualism and Social Psychological Theory. In *Growth and Progress in Cross-Cultural Psychology*, edited by Ç. Kagitçibasi, pp. 78–83. Swets North America, Berwyn.
|1993| Collectivism and Individualism as Cultural Syndromes. *Cross-Cultural Research* 27:155–180.
|1995| *Individualism and Collectivism*. Westview Press, San Francisco.

Triandis, H. C., X. P. Chen, and D. K. S. Chan
|1998| Scenarios for the Measurement of Collectivism and Individualism. *Journal of Cross-Cultural Psychology* 29:275–289.

Tolstikov, V., and M. Treister
|1996| *The Gold of Troy: Searching for Homer's Fabled City*. Harry N. Abrams, New York.

Westin, A. F.
|1968| *Privacy and Freedom*. Atheneum, New York.

PART IV: URBAN SPACES AND CITYSCAPES

BODY, BOUNDARIES, AND "LIVED" URBAN SPACE: A RESEARCH MODEL FOR THE EIGHTH-CENTURY CITY AT COPAN, HONDURAS

Allan L. Maca

Allan L. Maca, Department of Anthropology, Colgate University, Hamilton, New York 13346, U.S.A.

ABSTRACT

The study of site and settlement limits remains a rapidly developing area of study in Maya archaeology. Without critical conceptual tools and new mapping technologies, however, it is difficult to begin to develop hypotheses for indigenous site limits, land use, spatial ideology, and city planning, let alone test them in a fruitful manner. The following proposes a research model for the study of intentional urban planning, site limits, and design at Classic-period (A.D. 300–900) Copan that can be tested through ongoing and future work in the Copan Valley and elsewhere in the Maya area.

CONCEPTUAL BOUNDARIES

The importance of a site-level – or city-based – archaeology of the Classic Maya is the emphasis of this paper, and is seen to be inextricably tied to the issue of boundaries, that is, settlement limits and internal social divisions. Mayanists have scarcely begun to define the boundaries of Classic-period cities, and we still struggle to resolve the issue of whether or not such boundaries ever existed (Maca 2002:18–26). We also have found it difficult to discern internal social divisions of the city that go beyond correlations of rank and status with the size and quantity of visible architecture. Such a gap in research precludes exploring the social dynamics of an urban community.

The lack of site-level analysis in Mayanist archaeology is partly due to the great scale of such an endeavour. Yet it is also due to the simple difficulty of determining what frameworks might be employed to define urban settlement for the ancient Maya, and how to hypothesize meaningful divisions within the social space of urban community. Surely, one must define the unit – however preliminarily and hypothetically – before approaching the inner workings of a city.

Conventional methods for discovering the edges of ancient Maya urban settlement typically rely on drop-offs in architectural density (sensu Willey 1953), or on how and where visible buildings cluster, especially the prominent temples and palaces (sensu Sanders and Webster 1981; Webster et al. 2000). However, every decade we learn more that our understanding of ancient settlement has been coloured: a) by our western way of thinking about cities – as unbridled sprawl; b) by simple gaps in our data due to overly specified objectives and methodologies as well as, frequently, the rigours of research in dense forests (Pyburn 1989); and c) by our attraction to the "striking" and "beautiful" found in the grand centres of the ancient Maya cities (sensu Quilter 2001:764).

At the Classic-period site of Copan in Honduras, these problems are particularly marked, not least because the site has the longest history of research anywhere in the Maya area; thus, some frameworks are so entrenched that they are difficult to move beyond. At Copan, for example, we still employ the "Harvard" typology for visible architecture, which is an ascending 1 to 4 classification based on size and number of surface mounds (see Willey and Leventhal 1979). This scheme hypothesizes that the bigger the architecture, the more prestigious; the smaller, the more common in rank. Architectural typologies like those developed for the Guatemalan Peten are sorely lacking at Copan (e.g., Bullard 1960; Tourtellot 1988).

Moreover, with few exceptions (e.g., Fash 1983), students of the settlement patterns of the ancient Maya city tend not to develop hypotheses based on the spatial cognition, ideologies, and place-making practices of indigenous Maya. Therefore, in the absence of critical theoretical tools, the Maya cities largely remain formless and limitless and, except in the most general sense, they remain internally undifferentiated.

OBJECTIVES

The following sections delineate a proposal based on recent research at Group 9J-5 and in the northern foothills of Copan more generally: I hypothesize that some Maya cities, such as Copan, were characterized at times by distinct settlement boundaries and internal divisions, and that these patterns were socially meaningful and may have been intentionally reinstated at important moments in the history of the city-state; the ninth-century A.D. collapse of the polity is one such moment, addressed below. I show that if we as archaeologists can differentiate formal categories of urban architecture, such as the U-group design seen at Group 9J-5, and if we work to employ indigenous Maya categories for space and place, it is possible to propose hypothetical boundaries and divisions for Classic-period urban life that are eminently testable.

I begin by reviewing some of the concepts involved in the anthropological study of social and spatial boundaries. Then I look cross-culturally at models of spatial structures and boundaries that might inform a study of Maya urban organization, moving in scale from the city down to the human body. I go on to address spatial templates that are specific to the lowland Maya, looking first at ethnographic and then at ethnohistorical data. Finally, my research at Group 9J-5 and in the Copan pocket serves as a case study in which I consider eighth-century city planning as analogous to historic and modern Maya frameworks of spatial definition. Here I briefly outline a model for urban space at Copan that implies the negotiation and the reproduction of explicitly Maya templates for identifying with and living within a large-scale community; these templates arguably were manipulated and elaborated by dynastic authority during periods of instability, especially during the "collapse" of Copan's Classic-period polity.

SOCIAL AND SPATIAL BOUNDARIES: SCALE AND CONCEPT

Over the last thirty five years, in virtually every geographic area, we have seen dramatic advances in anthropological studies of the relationship between spatial boundaries and social organization (e.g., Barth 1969a; Bourdieu 1973; Classen 1993; Coe 1965; Cunningham 1964; Hanks 1990; Hugh-Jones 1979; Humphreys 1974; Levi-Strauss 1963; Lopez-Austin 1988; Moore 1989; Rapoport 1969; Singh and Khan 1999; Sosa 1985; Tambiah 1969; Tuan 1977; Vogt 1976; Waterson 1990; Wheatley 1971). The bodies of theory responding to and shaping these studies have grown in tandem (e.g., Barth 1969b; Bourdieu 1977; Douglas 1982; Foucault 1979; Giddens 1984; Kuper 1972; Levi-Strauss 1963; Turner 1969). The most basic contribution of this research is that anthropologists may now take for granted the great degree to which all cultures classify and distinguish space based on social rules (see e.g., Barth 1969a; Bourdier and Alsayyad 1989; Clarke 1977; Duncan 1981; Gregory and Urry 1985; Hodder 1989; Ingersoll and Bronitsky 1987; Joyce and Gillespie 2000; Kent 1990; Pearson and Richards 1994; Pellow 1996; Stark 1998). These rules include gender, status, age, kinship, public display, sacredness, and ethnicity, to name just a few.

Other organizational principles relate to the classification of the human body, the local landscape, and the solar cosmos, each construed as a spatial entity. Natural facets of the world not only compel social reference, but are actively socialized, politicized, and mythologized within cultural frames; these natural expressions serve as negotiable models for the organization of cultural facets: the home, the agricultural plot, and/or the community. Often we find that structures of meaning, though changeable through time, largely are fixed and scaleable; these may be integrated concentrically, extending, for example, from the human body to the house, the community, the landscape, and to the world or cosmos. These might be expressed as frameworks that are inherent to the human body, brain, or natural environment (up versus down, for example) and/or are integrated and expressed as culture-based ideologies, acted out and negotiated consciously or unconsciously on a daily basis.

Boundaries, whether tangible or invisible, culturally imposed or naturally occurring, serve the cultural classification and division of space. A house or community, therefore, may be classified as distinct by being separated from what is external to it; internally, it may be divided as well, to suit kin, gender, rank or other distinctions. To illustrate these points, I move ahead with a discussion of some salient cross-cultural examples.

CROSS-CULTURAL PERSPECTIVES

City

An urban-level example that will be especially important for my discussion of Copan is found in Constance Classen's (1993) book, *Inca Cosmology and the Human Body*. Classen discusses the degree to which the site planning of Cuzco, the Inka capital city, was imbued with numerous levels and systems of social, political, and religious meaning. She looks specifically at how the ruler, or great Inka, embodied the quadripartite structure of Cuzco and of the Inka Empire as a whole; these concentrically integrated structures – ruler, city, realm – were conceived as bounded, sacred entities, such that what existed outside of them was profane. Areas of Cuzco, as well as specific temples and buildings, were considered to be body parts of the Inka ruler. As well, Classen and other scholars discuss the probability that Cuzco was conceived as and laid out in the form of a puma, the sacred body-double of the ruler (e.g., Classen 1993:100–104; Rowe 1967; but see also Zuidema 1983:68). Thus, for example, parts of the landscape were named after the ruler's puma tail. Moreover, the puma as icon, its sacred image and its power, was held by the Inka people as a manifestation not just of the ruler, but also, of course, of Cuzco and of the empire as a whole – a symbol of Inka identity.

House

The house can be considered a microcosm of the world and closely linked to the experience of the human body. At this level, we can look at the example of Clark Cunningham's (1964) study of the Atoni house in Indonesian Timor. He emphasizes the extent to which the house is not simply a microcosm of the world, but is an integral part of it. The door is oriented away from and in response to the sunrise, and the path of the sun dictates what is left side and what is right. The four cardinal points organize the placement of internal features, such as the sleeping platform and the water jars. So-called mother posts support the house at the intercardinal points, affirming the interior space as female. The mother post at the southeastern corner is called the head. Other features of the house are referred to as parts of the body, for example, the foot and the elbow, demonstrating that the house is also conceived of as a human body, integrated with and reflecting the cosmos (see Pearson and Richards 1994). In general, the roof and the walls maintain a structured, bounded unity, while interior divisions, always changing, negotiate difference at many levels. In this way, boundaries shape and respond to social rules and strategies.

Body

At the core of all experience, and of all social and spatial organization, is the human body. It is the means through which all human beings negotiate and affirm the categories of their surroundings. The physical and social body, consciously and unconsciously, imposes schemata on the world: up, down; past, future; front, back; left, right; sacred, profane; good, evil, and so forth (Hanks 1990:389; Tuan 1977:34–50). The body is the medium for ordering all human experience in space. Such schemata are not necessarily the same from culture to culture, and a study of the variation of body ideologies provides a sense of the global variation, and the universals, inherent in socially constructed space at every scale. I do not go into this here, but it is an important point for emphasizing the centrality of the human body in all spheres of social and spatial cognition.

PRACTICE AND HABITUS

Before moving on to the Maya, I would like briefly to discuss some of the most important studies of the imposition and negotiation of spatial structures. Two of these have been made by the social theorists Anthony Giddens (1984) and Pierre Bourdieu (1977). The structuration theory of Giddens encourages us to see all structures and boundaries as both the media for and the results of social practices, fundamentally based on rules and custom. Spatial organization, then, is not

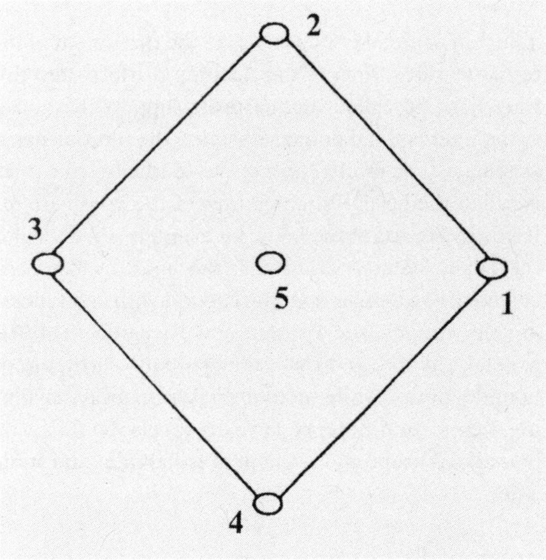

Figure 1. Quincunx (after Hanks 1990:300).

simply something in which social rules take root, but is a medium through which social relations are continually regenerated. In this way, through the routinized actions of the body, social spaces and landscapes are continually remodeled as validations of history and identity.

Bourdieu's practice-based social theory also emphasizes the "actional" element of spatial production in light of prescribed history. His concept of *habitus*, a system of dispositions by which people create and re-create structures includes "both a way of being... [and the] result of an organizing action." It is a "generative principle of regulated improvisations," such that "the 'unconscious' is never anything other than the forgetting of history which history itself produces" (1977:78). Thus, memory and meaning are inscribed in social space, unconsciously or not, by historically and culturally patterned actions.

I cite these theories of social practice to lend a processual, negotiable element to the discussion of boundaries, which are usually explained as static and un-lived. Habitus, especially, is an important concept for thinking about how culture and the body negotiate social relations of all kinds. To provide a means of helping the reader to grasp the notion of habitus, I resort to an anecdote from the anthropologist Roland Fletcher. He does not use the term habitus nor does he discuss Bourdieu or others who have written about "habit." However, his explanation of the locational abilities of the blind girl go a long way in characterizing the social and spatial histories that we all practice and possess:

> In the Dagomba settlement of Gbambaye, there was a blind, presumably effectively mature girl who was able to move around her own house, to negotiate her way through the settlement into other houses and reach the functional location she was seeking. Though she was not quick as her friends, she did not require and did not receive their guidance. Her sense of hearing was very good, and she had identified my presence in the courtyard, but her family had to tell her who and what I was and where I stood. As a child she may have seen the settlement, but its particular form is continually changing. If, consciously or otherwise, she recognized that there was a consistent locational order to the settlement and to each residence unit, then her effectiveness in moving about the structures would be readily explicable. Familiarity with her locational environment would demand the retention of a vast amount of information if the settlement form lacked regularity. It seems to have been the order in her general categories of space which aided her movement. Any specific gap such as a doorway was checked by hand before she attempted to pass through [Fletcher 1977:60].

"LIVED SPACE"

The quincunx: five landmarks for reference and inclusion

William Hanks' study of the Yucatec Maya draws explicitly on the ideas of Bourdieu. Employing a concept he terms "lived space," Hanks' book, *Referential Practice* (1990), is a powerful aid for research on the spatial ideology of the Maya. Through an analysis of the terms, technical aspects, and social contexts of specific, spoken spatial references in Yucatec Mayan language, he is able to render a map of Maya spatial cognition. As other Mesoamericanists have done, Hanks notes that there are five cardinal points in Maya culture, a pattern known as the quincunx (Figure 1). However, Hanks' considerations go beyond others in that he delineates and explicates two cognitive schemata of this cardinal structure: one is fixed and absolute, the other is movable and negotiable (1990:298–304).

The *absolute* cardinal point schema is of special interest for this discussion, especially for its focus on the boundaries and spatial ideologies of fixed units, whether body, house, village, earth, or sky. The absolute cardinal schema is a boundary mechanism *par excellence*. This "enclosing" is enacted partly through circumambulation – especially a ritual circuit – through the four corners to arrive at the centre. Thus, the cardinal places become absolute as their union comes to define an entire region of fixed space. This fixed locale is then characterized by a distinct perimeter, such that the inside is safe and orderly. Without the perimeter, there is no unity and a place is potentially dangerous and uncertain. Moreover, Hanks makes the vital observation that the enclosure is what he calls "definitionally simultaneous" (1990:349), that is, once the five points are established, each one contains all five at once, as a corollary of their being whole.

This cognitive framework arguably is based on the annual movements of the sun, which at middle latitudes appear to give boundaries to the world. The solstitial risings and settings mark the corners, and zenith passage marks the centre of the sky. Zenith passage only occurs in the tropical latitudes. Perhaps because of this, the quincunx and its implied boundary are not inherent in Euro-American language and spatial cognition. Rather, this framework, and its binding potential, is certainly Mesoamerican, particularly Mayan, and wholly indigenous. As such, its basic structure can be inferred for many different epochs in Maya history and for an array of fixed places.

Ethnographic and ethnohistorical data on Maya space frames

Abundant modern and historical evidence explains the ways and settings in which the quincunx frames spatial entities. Altars, for example, are sacralized and bounded by specific types of offerings at the four corners and the centre (e.g., Hanks 1990; Redfield and Villa Rojas 1934). Houses are dedicated, fixed, and bounded by a ritual circuit of offerings at the four corners and centre of the house foundations; this practice unifies the house, giving it life and structure, imbuing it with a type of soul essence, as if it were a body (e.g., Vogt 1976). The protective perimeters of towns, such as modern Yalcobá in Yucatan, are established by the placing of wooden crosses at the town corners, especially along the access or entry points of the community, the points of greatest uncertainty (Sosa 1985:242a). The centre may be marked by a church, a cross, or some other ritually meaningful feature. One type of cross is particularly interesting: often found at a corner place of the town, it is an anthropomorphized tree in the form of an Atlantean, supporting the invisible structure of the world (see Sosa 1985:241a).

In the late colonial period, we see that whole regions of the Yucatan peninsula were conceived within a bounded framework, as seen, for example, in a regional map of northern Yucatan in 1820 (Roys 1939:37, Figure 7). In the early colonial period, as attested by the numerous Chilam Balams of northern and northeastern Yucatan, we read that an entire regional sphere is repeatedly referred to as bounded and divided into quarters, based on the fixed and enclosed spatial frame of the quincunx.

In the middle of the sixteenth century in Yucatan, the Spanish Friar Diego de Landa wrote his account of the town binding ceremonies during the Maya New Year (Landa 1978 [1562]; Tozzer 1941). Michael Coe used this document to draw what is now a well-known diagram of these ceremonies (Coe 1965). He has correctly interpreted the ritual circuit through two cardinal points as effectively engaging the entire perimeter, thereby unifying and purifying the community as a whole. The sixteenth-century account of these New Year's ceremonies also describes the transfer of political offices as well as the offerings placed at the cardinal points where are found the year or sky bearer deities, known as *Bakabs*. *Bakabs* are quadripartite entities; they encompass and support quadrants of the community and the world, and as such they are the pillars of the community as a conceptual house. The *Bakab* in the centre shares duties and cosmic roles with the political and religious officer elected for the following year's term. Just as the one *Bakab* equals the five, the town official becomes the bearer of the community, its order, and its safety. He is the central unifying *Bakab*, the five and the one. This point is key for the case study I discuss below regarding eighth-century Copan.

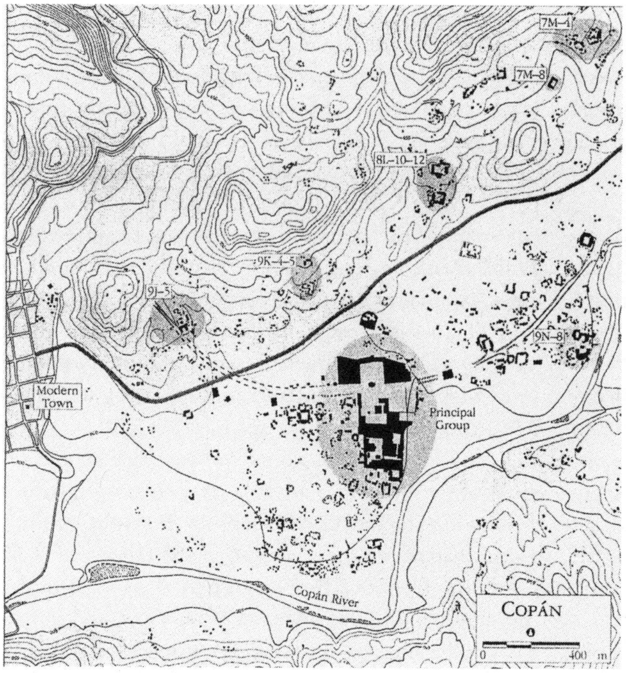

Figure 2. Copan pocket of the Copan Valley, with ancient (arcing) roads, and modern (straight) east-west highway.

EIGHTH-CENTURY COPAN

GROUP 9J-5, NORTHERN FOOTHILLS, COPAN

Despite the fact that the majority of Copan's ruins were preliminarily mapped twenty years ago (Fash and Long 1983) (Figure 2), few excavations have been carried out in the northern foothills and only one published article exists for this area (i.e., Ashmore 1991). For this reason, this area has not contributed to theories on the growth and nature of Copan specifically as a city (though see Fash 1983), and to date has not been considered a part of the city or "urban core" (sensu Sanders and Webster 1981; Webster et al. 2000). More problematic is the fact that these foothill sites lie outside of the current boundaries of the National Archaeological Park, and some have been damaged by landowners and by looters. This, of course, is the context in which, in 1995, William Fash, at the behest of the Honduran Institute of Anthropology and History, initiated excavations at one such threatened site, Group 9J-5. From 1996 to 2001, I was field director of this project, known as PACOM (Proyecto Arqueologico de Comedero, Copan), and am now director of Phase 2. The results of Phase 1 are presented at length elsewhere (Maca 2002).

Group 9J-5 is a monumental "Type 4" site located in the upland Comedero region of the Copan Valley, just five minutes walking from the entrance to Copan's Principal Ruins. During the Classic period this area of the northern foothills was not an outlier nor a marginal terrain. Reflected not least by its monumental architecture and association with a major *sakbe* (Fash 1983), Group 9J-5 was an integral sector of the Classic-period urban sphere at Copan, and PACOM data demonstrate that it was closely linked to elite ceremonial activities on a public and urban scale. In the following section, I explain a new hypothesis regarding the nature of the eighth-century Maya city at Copan that specifically accounts for social and spatial divisions delineated by architectural and stratigraphic data from Group 9J-5. I base this hypothesis on formal similarities between the built forms and site histories of several architectural groups in the Copan Valley. Moreover, I present these ideas in light of the above discussions of the negotiation, practice, and social distinctions of lived space.

U-GROUPS

Figure 3 is a recent (2001) GIS rendering of the visible settlement in the Comedero region of the northern foothills of Copan. The large group is Group 9J-5. In particular, I draw attention to the U-shaped architectural complex, oriented southward. This overlooks the valley and the principal settlements on the valley floor. This U-shaped monument is due west (on the equinox) of another prominent U-shaped monument, that of Group 9N-8, site of the House of the *Bakabs* (Fash 1986; Sanders 1986; Webster 1989; Webster et al. 1986; also referred to as the Scribe House [Fash 2001]). The internal organization of these two groups is dissimilar, and Group 9J-5 was vertically grander and is topographically more elevated. Nevertheless, their surface areas are comparable, and features of their archaeology are related (see Maca 2002). Figure 4 shows their positions in the valley relative to one another, as well as the positions of two other monumental U-groups

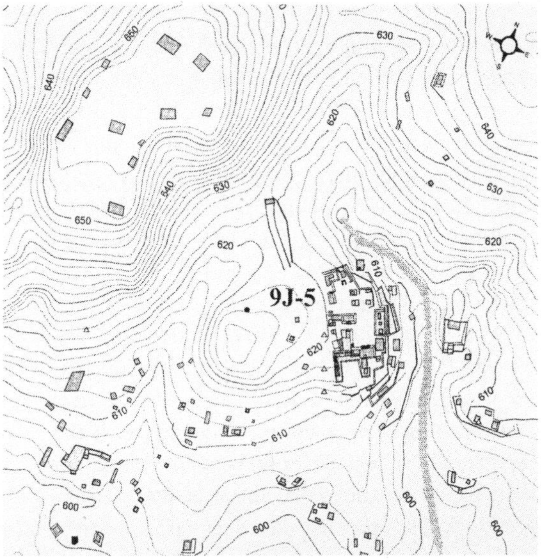

Figure 3. Group 9J-5, Copan. U-shaped monument opens to the southeast.

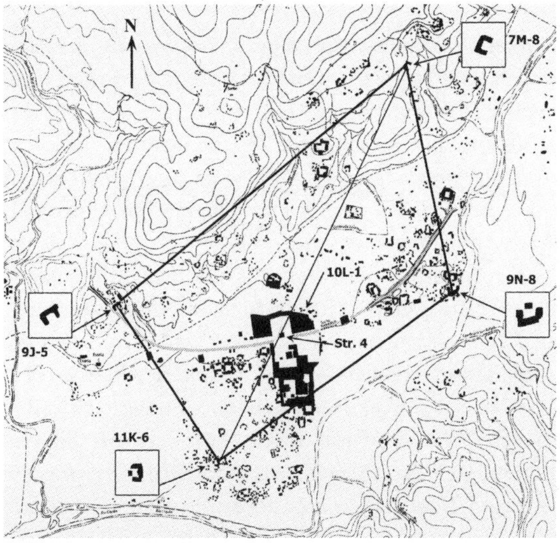

Figure 4. U-group distribution around the central U-group of the Principal Group of Ruins, Copan.

(one of which – Group 7M-8 – currently is designated a Type 2 site). The Fash and Long (1983) survey map shows there are four in total; however, a fifth exists in a prominent yet (ironically) overlooked location. In the centre of this image (Figure 4) we find a much larger U-group, 10L-1, defining the space of the Great Plaza of the Principal Group, at the heart of the tourist core. These are the only U-groups identifiable among the surface architecture at Copan. Together, the five groups therefore create a hypothetical quincunx based on a formal class of architecture.

From a typological standpoint, Gair Tourtellot (1988) has shown that, in the Peten, U-shaped architecture is unequivocally distinct and high status, and thus was a meaningful form, not to be confused with "C-shaped" platform enclosures. All five of the U-groups I highlight overlap chronologically in the final decades of the eighth century. Therefore, I suggest that at some point in the eighth century Copan's U-groups were formally and functionally related units within a system of fixed spatial reference that established the perimeter boundary of the city. Each U-group certainly possessed its own social and architectural history. For example, based on available stratigraphic evidence, the U-groups at Groups 9J-5 and 9N-8 were each made into U-groups at or around A.D. 780; research by Maca (2002) and Webster (1989) attest to this. The framework of the city boundary must have been negotiable and would have required continuous maintenance through both traditional and improvised sociopolitical and religious behavior.

More to the point, I hypothesize that the four smaller "satellite" U-groups framed the perimeter of eighth-century Copan, marking cardinal places that were integrating into an urban design. The central U-group represented the "heart" of the city; it is the place around which the ancient city's identity and design unfold and, because it dates to the reign of the thirteenth ruler (or approximately A.D. 730), it likely served as the model for the coordinated and cross-referencing placements of the four other groups. While I cannot provide the entire argument here, I will briefly discuss several lines of evidence that have led me to this conclusion.

First, one may note the orientations of the respective U-groups. Those of the east and the west each directly refers to the north and the south, respectively; and the north and the south groups are oriented east and west, respectively, towards sunrise and sunset points on the horizon. Thus, in plan, their alignments integrate: a) east and west; b) in and out; and c) foothills and valley floor. Finally, it is interesting that each of the four U-groups opens to a different cardinal direction, and it is intriguing that these directions shift in a clockwise direction as one moves counterclockwise in plan, and vice versa. I suggest some formal logic to the placement of the groups and to their orientations, and this would seem to be supported by the fact that clockwise and counterclockwise movements and relationships are implicit in the way space is defined in indigenous Maya thought and practice.

A second line of evidence is a critical and dynamic set of relationships. It is seen in many cultures throughout the world, including the Maya, and is based on the formal integration of the cultural sphere with the natural, that is, landscape with built environment, as well as elevated terrain with lowlands. One can note the two arcing lines that extend east and west from Structure 4 in the Principal Group; these are reconstructions of the city's two main roads, or *sakbes*. Among the ancient Maya cities and towns across southern Mesoamerica, these are the only *sakbes* known to have been arcing. The western road curves northward and ascends to the foothills, terminating just beyond the U-group at Group 9J-5, and the eastern road extends out along the valley floor, curves northward and terminates just north of the U-group at Group 9N-8. These meet at the central U-group, highlighted by Structure 4; this building arguably integrated the two roads, as well as the upland and the lowland terrains that these access.

Further evidence of this integrating dynamic, which extends as well to the valley's natural spaces, is suggested by the geometry of the U-groups' placement in the valley. As mentioned, the roads link the upper west and lower east parts of the city. A similar type of integration appears to exist for the northern and southern U-groups as well. Relative to one another, these are not aligned to true or magnetic north/south, perhaps due to the valley topography; however, this likely was not a compromise as much as a direct reference and accommodation to the orientations of both the northern ridge of the valley and the river. The ridge dramatically delimits the valley space and its volcanic tuff was the stone used for the construction of the city itself, such that the urban settlement was literally born from this low mountain. One notes as well, not insignificantly, that space is further delimited by the river to the south. In fact, the north and south boundary lines defined by the U-groups (drawn in Figure 4) parallel the natural features of the landscape of the alluvial pocket – the ridge and the river, respectively.

More interesting yet is that a simple line drawn in plan between the northern and southern U-groups passes directly through Structure 4 of the central U-group, a phenomenon that I propose is not mere coincidence. The other two U-groups at Groups 9J-5 and 9N-8 are oriented back into the city. However, the northern and southern groups are each oriented to the outside of the urban boundaries. That Structure 4 is precisely situated along the conceptual line between them points more forcefully to its central integrating role: it linked centre to periphery, and up to down.

Yet a third, and final, line of evidence is Structure 4 itself. It is intimately associated with the central U-group, a feature that spatially defines the Great Plaza and that hosts the majority of the stelae of the thirteenth ruler. Upon closer inspection, one clearly sees that, like the central "U," each of the other two U-groups situated on the valley floor has in its open end a type of isolated structure. This suggests that the U-typology for the valley floor is characterized by additional, meaningful architectural elements. In the two satellite U-groups, the isolated structures for years have been referred to ambiguously as "ritual structures." Structure 4, however, is a well-known class of Maya ceremonial architecture, known as a radial pyramid. It is a cardinally oriented, calendrical monument linked to solar events and the ordering motions of the sun. Stela A, beside it, was erected in A.D. 731, at the same time that Structure 4 was first fashioned as a radial pyramid; these are thus companion monuments (Cheek and Milla Villeda 1983).

One side of Stela A bears an elaborate portrait of the thirteenth ruler. The other sides display a text arranged in four columns of thirteen glyphs each, for a total of 52 glyph blocks, an important number in Maya and Mesoamerican calendrical reckoning. The inscription is famous for citing some type of quadripartitioning rituals that involve the emblem glyphs of four prominent Maya centres of the eighth century, Copan included. It may refer to the Maya realm (e.g., Barthel 1968; Marcus 1976), or to the quadripartite integration of regional and local areas, or all simultaneously (D. Stuart, personal communication 1999). Whatever the case, I believe we can push the limits of our architectural, archaeological, and textual data. Specifically, we may hypothesize structural continuities between the ancient and the colonial and modern periods, such that quadripartite space was integrated concentrically, from the Maya cosmos to the bounded urban community of Copan, down in scale to the body of the ruler himself. This last possibility, that of the ruler's body being expressed through the urban plan, is something I take up in the following section.

The urban Bakab

In an effort to squeeze even more data from the inscription on Stela A, it is worth briefly considering one of the titles cited therein for the thirteenth ruler. He first is named "Holy Lord" (*k'ul ajaw)* of Copan and then he is cited as a "*Bakab*." This *Bakab* title is found in a number of inscriptions at Copan and elsewhere in the Classic Maya area (120+ examples), especially in the context of the seventh and eighth centuries. It seems to suggest a particular function or role that, while perhaps "subordinate" to Holy Lord, is different in kind (Martin, personal communication 2001), suggesting a responsibility or status that is heterarchically ascribed or derived (sensu Crumley 2003).

I argue that this ancient title is the precursor to the Mayan title and deity name used in the early colonial era, which I discuss above for sixteenth-century Yucatan. Few, however, have examined the Precolumbian meaning of *Bakab* in any depth or tried to study it in light of the colonial and modern evidence (but see Love 1986, 1994; Taube 1988, 1992; Thompson 1970). I propose that we model backwards from sixteenth-century sources to eighth-century Copan. We can then hypothesize a range of associations surrounding the *Bakab*, the ruler, Structure 4 and, of course, the central U-group. Through this we can test cognitive and even metonymic aspects of the hieroglyphic texts. I would argue that, citing himself as a *Bakab*, the thirteenth ruler declares himself the four-quartered embodiment of the community. The combination of the text and the quincuntial urban design explained above suggest that the thirteenth ruler employed the *Bakab* title as a way to affirm the relationship between himself and the community, as well as between the limits of his corporeal body and the integrated, quadripartite limits of the city.

Several sets of related data support the existence of the *Bakab* framework at Copan. First is the ubiquitous nature of *Bakabs* in the stone sculpture of eighth-century Copan – from small stone bench supports around the city, to the grand exterior of Temple 11 and the interior of Temple 22 (the first building constructed by the thirteenth ruler). Due to the prominence of *Bakab* imagery at Copan, William Fash has suggested that the *Bakab* was a patron deity of Copan (Fash 1998:256).

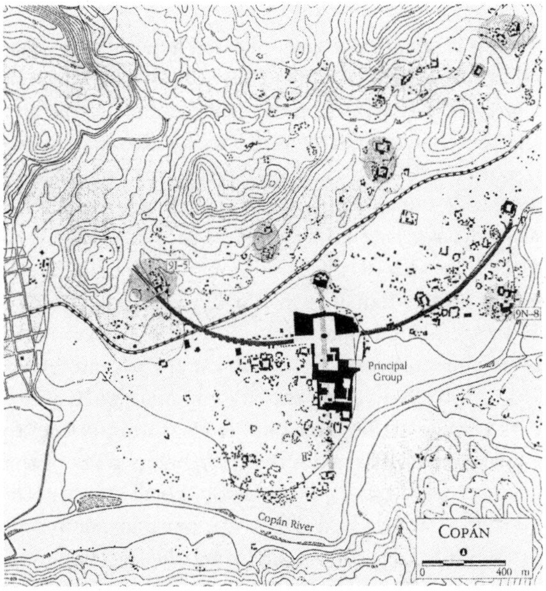

Figure 5. Urban *Bakab* at eighth-century Copan.

I would agree and propose that Copan's relationship with this deity was expressed in ways that drove home its associated ideology every "walking" minute in the lives of ancient Copanecos.

As a second line of evidence, I offer the following consideration (Figure 5). As mentioned, the two main roads at Copan are the only "arcing" roads known for the ancient Maya; they are equal in length and create a pronounced symmetry in plan view. As such, it is perhaps parsimonious to conclude these roads were the raised arms of the city's patron deity, the *Bakab*, and to hypothesize that they were imposed as part of an urban design. To follow this logic, an axis down the length of the Principal Group highlights the body of the *Bakab*; in fact this axis bisects Temple 11, on either corner of which were situated 5-m high *Bakab* statues. The head of the deity is marked by an isolated architectural complex known as the Chinchilla Group, which seems to be an early acropolis with deposits dating back to at least A.D. 100 (Viel, personal communication 2001). Structure 4, of course, is the "heart" of the deity, as well as of the urban community. As a functional and symbolic whole, this *Bakab* design would have grounded the role and responsibility of the ruler as the very embodiment of the city and its inhabitants.

This is admittedly a complicated hypothesis to test, that is, that the city was once laid out in the image of a *Bakab* and that through this deity's ideology, the city and the ruler essentially were conceived as one in spatial, political, social, and religious terms. The (largely non-literate) population of eighth-century Copan would have to have understood this and lived it at every level. The idea may at least be easier to assimilate if one considers that this sort of dynastic embodiment is attested throughout world history. For example, it is documented for mediaeval Europe (Kantorowicz 1957), as well as among the Inka, as mentioned above with respect to the puma form of Cuzco. And closer to Copan, we may consider that indigenous texts of the colonial era cite the precolonial political structure of Yucatan as a giant bird (D. Stuart, personal communication 2001). Therefore, might not the eighth-century Copanecos have walked daily through the body of their ruler and his incarnation as the community-unifying, quadripartite *Bakab*? Though difficult to prove, it is surely possible, and deserves to go on record as one element in the formulation of hypotheses regarding the nature of ancient Maya cities.

Negotiation of design and inclusion: Group 9J-5 and community boundary making

Much of this urban plan – the corner markers and community-wide *Bakab* – must have existed since at least the time of the thirteenth ruler (A.D. 695); after his death (A.D. 738) it would have been periodically re-established and re-negotiated. For its part, Structure 4 was built, and rebuilt, as a radial pyramid only in the eighth century, first with Ruler 13 at around A.D. 730, and later with Ruler 16 at about A.D. 780. The "urban" *Bakab* referenced in the text of Stela 4 and the location and axis marked by Structure 4 would have been elements of the initial design of the thirteenth ruler. This design would have been coordinated with four fixed cardinal places in the valley that defined Copan in terms of its sociopolitical identity, its urban community, and its physical and spatial boundaries. At that time (ca. A.D. 730), however, the four locales outside of the Principal Group almost certainly were not marked by U-shaped architecture (see Webster 1989; Maca 2002). Rather, the urban *Bakab* image and the cardinally placed U-groups were contemporaneous only at the close of the eighth century, just before the rapid decline of centralized rule, and would have served as references to the plan of the Great Plaza of the Principal Group, constructed by the thirteenth ruler. It would not have been until the fateful rulership of Copan's final great dynast, Yax Pasaj, that the framework was remade and the U-forms imposed on the corners and the centre.

Elsewhere (Maca 2002) I discuss the evidence for the history and appearance of the U-group at Group 9J-5. From seventh-century origins as a plaza group, Plaza A was reconfigured as a U-group in a very rapid succession of building construction. This involved numerous structures and probably appeared at or within years of A.D. 781, the dedication on the carved bench at Structure 9N-82, of Group 9N-8 (Stuart et al. 1989). As Webster (1989) shows, the Plaza A mounds at Group 9N-8, the dominant structure of which is Structure 9N-82 (the "Scribe House"), were not configured as a U-group until the final or near final stage of construction, that is, the stage associated with the dated bench. Evidence suggests therefore that the U-shaped plaza at Group 9J-5 and Group 9N-8 each came into to being concurrently as part of the same design. It is possible that this was coordinated by the respective lineage heads, in some manner independent of a central authority or design. However, for several reasons this is not a likely scenario.

First, the amount of labour invested at Group 9J-5, with respect to the terraces, the massive Plaza A platform, the fine-masonry structures, and broad public ceremonial spaces suggests the involvement of authority and resources that exceed those expressed in other facets of the social sphere at Group 9J-5 – for example, the contemporary niche tomb burial discussed elsewhere (Maca 2002:239–242). Second, the presence and distribution of a certain type of jade pectoral ("string-line") may suggest a long association between the inhabitants of Group 9J-5 and Group 9N-8 where two such pectorals have been found. It is interesting as well that a string-line pectoral was also found in a burial at Group 7M-8, site of the northern U-group. Of the dozens if not hundreds of formal graves and cists in the Copan pocket, the string-line jade pectorals only have been found among those at Groups 9J-5, 9N-8, and 7M-8, each of which is defined by a U-group; and each burial context dates to the early seventh century (see Maca 2002). Thus, this type of pectoral may have been some type of badge of honor for duties carried out at one of the four corners of the community – well before they were ever U-groups.

Third, is the evidence from the south superstructural façade of the dominant structure of Plaza A at Group 9J-5. A quasi-mat motif was found in situ, for which there only exists one other example anywhere in the Copan Valley: in Group 9N-8. This design can be seen restored on Structure 9N-67 which is directly north of Structure 9N-82 and is aligned with its central axis. Structure 9N-67 was not built at the same time as the final phase architecture at Group 9N-8 (see Hendon et al. 1990); it predates Structure 9N-82 and the U-group configuration. The dominant structure at Plaza A of Group 9J-5 predates the U-group configuration as well. Thus, we have additional evidence for a processual unfolding of similarities between U-groups and their respective building and site histories that suggests a larger scheme at work, at least larger than the localized spheres of elite lineage heads. I would argue this scheme to have been a framework that was sanctioned and executed by the dynasty, specifically as a means of community regeneration, cosmological renewal, and sociopolitical re-integration. It had to have been done periodically and it is no wonder that its most monumental and unique expression appeared during the dramatic instability of the late eighth century, the period preceding the "collapse" of the Classic-period polity at Copan.

With regard to the social organization of the urban sphere and the internal differentiation of the community, a few brief comments are due. Although the details of the quadripartite model almost certainly changed through time, the paradigm itself may not have, and the existence of quarters, wards, or *barrios* probably were maintained throughout, linked to corner places in the city. In fact, I would suggest that the quincunx and quadripartite community, at every level, were the basis of the habitus of the ancient Maya at Copan. As a central disposition and generative principle for place-making and spatial ordering, it was negotiable through time, and malleable, depending on the exigencies of matter, mind, landscape, and history. Of course, it also would have been a practical tool for domestic sociopolitics and the manipulation of city boundaries and local resources.

CONCLUSION

This paper attempts to advance our thinking about the conceptual limits and the form and meaning of the urban community at Copan. For example, through the conservative ideology of quadripartite space, we can hypothesize the presence of distinct sectors or quarters of the eighth-century city, as linked to the locations of the U-groups. This is readily testable through dirt archaeology and lab studies, for the methods and technologies for such research are at hand.

The study of dynastic-period ceramics at Copan has now reached a point where we can identify meaningful temporal boundaries in the history of settlement (e.g., Bill 1997). Moreover, by moving beyond the Harvard Typology for architecture ("1 to 4") to formal and *emic* categories of space and structure we can begin to examine boundaries and divisions of the urban sphere (Maca 2002). Other avenues of research will lie in the analysis of mitochondrial DNA from burial remains, as well as the typological analysis of architecture and numerous other classes of artifacts. Additionally, ecological analyses and studies of site formation processes are coming of age in Maya archaeology (e.g., Pyburn 1989). Combined, these avenues of research will assist us in delineating the inner workings and organization of ancient indigenous communities, especially those that are near in scale to what we refer to as ancient Maya "cities."

Finally, it is encouraging that cardinally oriented polity boundaries, similar to those I have discussed, recently have been found at the ancient Maya site of La Milpa in Belize (Tourtellot et al. 2000; N. Hammond, personal communication 2001). This research, like that at Group 9J-5 and Comedero, benefited from the use of digital surveying equipment and GIS and GPS technologies. With new methodologies, conceptual frameworks, time, energy, and optimism, a truly urban archaeology of the ancient Maya can intensify. This will be a great contribution to Maya archaeology and ultimately will challenge and strengthen the claims of regional syntheses, cultural evolutionary theory, and other orientations that extend in scale beyond the city sphere.

REFERENCES CITED

Ashmore, W.
|1991| Site-Planning Principles and Concepts of Directionality among the Ancient Maya. *Latin American Antiquity* 2:199–226.

Barth, F. (editor)
|1969a| *Ethnic Groups and Boundaries: The Social Organization of Culture Difference.* Little, Brown, Boston.

Barth, F.
|1969b| Introduction. In *Ethnic Groups and Boundaries: The Social Organization of Culture Difference*, edited by F. Barth. Little, Brown, Boston.

Barthel, T.
|1968| El complejo "emblema." *Estudio de cultura Maya* 7:159–193.

Bill, C. R.
|1997| Patterns of Variation and Change in Dynastic Period Ceramics and Ceramic Production at Copan, Honduras. Unpublished Ph.D. dissertation, Department of Anthropology, Tulane University, New Orleans.

Bourdieu, P.
|1973| The Berber House. In *Rules and Meanings*, edited by M. Douglas. Penguin, Harmondsworth.
|1977| *Outline of a Theory of Practice.* Cambridge University Press, Cambridge.

Bourdier, J. P., and N. Alsayyad (editors)
|1989| *Dwellings, Settlements, and Tradition: Cross-Cultural Perspectives.* University Press of America, Lanham, Maryland.

Bullard, W. R.
|1960| Maya Settlement Pattern in Northeastern Peten, Guatemala. *American Antiquity* 25:355–372.

Cheek, C., and D. E. Milla Villeda
|1983| La Estructura 10L-4. In *Excavaciones en el area urbana de Copan*, Tomo II, edited by W. T. Sanders, pp. 37–91. Instituto Hondureño de antropología e historia, Tegucigalpa.

Classen, C.
|1993| *Inca Cosmology and the Human Body.* Utah University Press, Salt Lake City.

Clarke, D. L.
|1977| Spatial Information in Archaeology. In *Spatial Archaeology*, edited by D. L. Clarke. Academic Press, London.

Coe, M.
|1965| A Model of Ancient Community Structure in the Maya Lowlands. *Southwestern Journal of Anthropology* 21(2):97–114.

Crumley, C.
|2003| Alternative Forms of Societal Order. In *Heterarchy, Political Economy, and the Ancient Maya: The Three Rivers Region of the East Central Yucatan*, pp. 136–146, edited by V. L. Scarborough, F. Valdez, Jr., and N. Dunning. University of Arizona Press, Tucson.

Cunningham, C.
|1964| Order in the Atoni House. *Bijdragen tot de Taal, Land-en Volkenkunde* 120:34–68

Douglas, M.
|1982| *Natural Symbols: Explorations in Cosmology.* Pantheon Books, New York.

Duncan, J. S. (editor)
|1981| *Housing and Identity: Cross-Cultural Perspectives.* Croom-Helm, London.

Fash, W. L.
|1983| Maya State Formation: A Case Study and its Implications. Ph.D. Dissertation, Harvard University. University Microfilms, Ann Arbor.
|1986| La fachada esculpida de la estructura 9N-82: Composicion, forma, e iconografia. In *Excavacions en el area urbana de Copan*, tomo I, edited by W. T. Sanders, pp. 319–382. Instituto Hondureño de antropología e historia, Tegucigalpa.
|1998| Dynastic Architectural Programs: Intention and Design in Classic Maya Buildings at Copan and Other Sites. In *Function and Meaning in Classic Maya Architecture*, edited by S. D. Houston, pp. 223–270. Dumbarton Oaks, Washington, D.C.
|2001| *Scribes, Warriors, and Kings: The City of Copán and the Ancient Maya.* Thames and Hudson, New York.

Fash, W. L., and K. Long
|1983| Mapa de Copan. In *Introduccion a la arqueologia de Copan*, edited by C. Baudez. IHAH, Tegucigalpa.

Fletcher, R.
|1977| Settlement Studies (Micro and Semi-Micro). In *Spatial Archeology*, edited by D. L. Clarke. Academic Press, London.

Foucault, M.
|1979| *Discipline and Punish: The Birth of the Prison.* Vintage Books, New York.

Giddens, A.
|1984| *The Constitution of Society: Outline of the Theory of Structuration.* Polity, London.

Gregory, D., and J. Urry (editors)
|1985| *Social Relations and Spatial Structures.* Macmillan, Basingstoke.

Hanks, W.
|1990| *Referential Practice: Language and Lived Space among the Maya.* University of Chicago Press, Chicago.

Hendon, J. A., R. Agurcia Fasquelle, W. L. Fash, and E. Aguilar Palma
|1990| Excavaciones in 9N-8, Conjunto del Patio B. In *Excavaciones en el area urbana de Copan*, vol. 2, pp. 111–293. Instituto Hondureño de Anthropología e Historia, Tegucigalpa.

Hodder, I. (editor)
|1989| *The Meaning of Things: Material Culture and Symbolic Expression.* Unwin Hyman, London.

Hugh-Jones, C.
|1979| *From the Milk River: Spatial and Temporal Processes in North-West Amazonia.* Cambridge University Press, Cambridge.

Humphreys, C.
|1974| Inside a Mongolian Tent. *New Society* 630:273–275.

Ingersoll, D. W., and G. Bronitsky (editors)
|1987| *Mirror and Metaphor: Material and Social Constructions of Reality.* University Press of America, Lanham, Maryland.

Joyce, R. A., and S. Gillespie
|2000| *Beyond Kinship: Social and Material Reproduction in House Societies*. University of Pennsylvania Press, Philadelphia.
Kantorowicz, E. H.
|1957| *The King's Two Bodies: A Study in Mediaeval Political Theology*. Princeton University Press, Princeton.
Kent, S. (editor)
|1990| *Domestic Architecture and the Uses of Space: An Interdisciplinary Cross-Cultural Study*. Cambridge University Press, Cambridge.
Kuper, H.
|1972| The Language of Sites. *American Anthropologist* 74:411–425.
Landa, D.
|1978|[1562] *Relacion de las cosas de Yucatan*. Edicion Yucateca, Merida.
Levi-Strauss, C.
|1963| *Structural Anthropology*. Basic Books, New York.
Lopez-Austin, A.
|1988| *The Human Body and Ideology: Concepts of the Ancient Nahuas*. University of Utah Press, Salt Lake City.
Love, B.
|1994| *The Paris Codex: Handbook for a Maya Priest*. University of Texas Press, Austin.
|1986| Yucatec Maya Ritual: A Diachronic Perspective. Unpublished Ph.D. dissertation, Department of Anthropology, University of California, Los Angeles.
Maca, A. L.
|2002| *Spatio-temporal Boundaries in Classic Maya Settlement Systems: Copan's Urban Foothills and the Excavations at Group 9J-5*. Ph.D. dissertation, Harvard University, Cambridge. University Microfilms, Ann Arbor.
Marcus, J.
|1976| *Emblem and State in the Classic Maya Lowlands: An Epigraphic Approach to Territorial Organization*. Dumbarton Oaks, Washington, D.C.
Moore, M.A.
|1989| The Kerala House as a Hindu Cosmos. *Contributions to Indian Sociology* 23:169–202.
Pearson, M. P., and C. Richards
|1994| Ordering the World: Perceptions of Architecture, Space and Time. In *Architecture and Order: Approaches to Social Space*, edited by M. P. Pearson, and C. Richards, pp. 1–37. Routledge, London.
Pellow, D. (editor)
|1996| *Setting Boundaries: The Anthropology of Spatial and Social Organization*. Bergin and Garvey, Westport.
Pyburn, A.
|1989| *Prehistoric Maya Community and Settlement at Nohmul, Belize*. British Archaeological Reports International Series 509. British Archaeological Reports, Oxford.
Quilter, J.
|2001| Review of *Stories in Red and Black: Pictorial Histories for the Aztecs and Mixtecs* by E.H. Boone, *Maya Art and Architecture* by M.E. Miller, and *Pre-Columbian Art* by E. Pasztory. *Art Bulletin* 83(4):762–765.
Rapoport, A.
|1969| *House Form and Culture*. Prentice-Hall, Englewood Cliffs, New Jersey.
Redfield, R. and A. Villa Rojas
|1934| *Chan Kom, a Maya Village*. Carnegie Institution of Washington Publication No. 448. Carnegie Institution of Washington, Washington, D.C.
Rowe, J. H.
|1967| What Kind of Settlement was Inca Cuzco? *Ñawpa Pacha* 5:59–76.
Roys, R.
|1939| *The Titles of Ebtun*. Carnegie Institution of Washington Publication No. 505. Carnegie Institution of Washington, Washington, D.C.
Sanders, W.
|1986| Introduccion. In *Excavaciones en el area urbana de Copan*, vol. 1, pp. 11–19. Instituto Hondureño de Antropologia e Historia, Tegucigalpa.
Sanders, W. T., and D. Webster
|1981| Reconocimiento del Asentimiento del Valle de Copán. *Yaxkin* 4(2):85–99.
Singh, J. P., and M. Khan
|1999| Hindu Cosmology and the Orientation and Segregation of Social Groups in Villages in Northwestern India. *Geografiska Annaler* 81(1):19–39.
Sosa, J.
|1985| The Maya Sky, the Maya World: A Symbolic Analysis of Yucatec Maya Cosmology. Unpublished Ph.D. dissertation, Department of Anthropology, State University of New York at Albany.
Stark, M. T.
|1998| *The Archaeology of Social Boundaries*. Smithsonian Institution, Washington, D.C.
Stuart, D., N. Grube, and L. Schele
|1989| A New Alternative for the Date of the Sepulturas Bench. *Copan Notes* 61.
Tambiah, S.
|1969| Animals are Good to Think and Prohibit. *Ethnology* 8:423–459.
Taube, K.
|1988| *The Ancient Yucatec New Year Festival: The Liminal Period in Maya Ritual and Cosmology*. Ph.D dissertation, Department of Anthropology, New Haven, Yale University. University Microfilms, Ann Arbor.
|1992| *The Major Gods of Ancient Yucatan*. Dumbarton Oaks Research Library and Collection, Washington, D.C.
Thompson, J. E. S.
|1970| *Maya History and Religion*. University of Oklahoma, Norman.
Tourtellot, G.
|1988| Peripheral Survey and Excavation Settlement and Community Patterns. Excavations at Seibal, Department of Peten, Guatemala. In *Memoirs of the Peabody Museum of Archeology and Ethnology*, no. 16, edited by G. R. Willey. Harvard University Press, Cambridge.
Tourtellot, G., M. Wolf, F. Estrada Belli, and N. Hammond
|2000| Discovery of Two Predicted Ancient Maya Sites in Belize. *Antiquity* 74:481–482.
Tozzer, A. M.
|1941| *Landa's Relacion de las cosas de Yucatan: A Translation*. Peabody Museum, Cambridge.

Tuan, Y.
|1977| *Space and Place: The Perspective of Experience.* University of Minnesota Press, Minneapolis, Minnesota.

Turner, V.
|1969| *The Ritual Process: Structure and Anti-Structure.* Aldine, Chicago.

Vogt, E. Z.
|1976| *Tortillas for the Gods: Symbolic Analysis of Zinacanteco Rituals.* Harvard University Press, Cambridge.

Waterson, R.
|1990| *The Living House: An Anthropology of Architecture in South-East Asia.* Oxford University Press, Oxford.

Webster, D.
|1989| *The House of the Bacabs.* Dumbarton Oaks, Washington, D.C.

Webster, D., W. L. Fash, and E. M. Abrams
|1986| Excavaciones en el conjunto 9N-8, Patio A (operacion VIII). In *Excavacions en el area urbana de Copan,* tomo I, edited by W. T. Sanders, pp. 155–317. Instituto Hondureño de antropología e historia, Tegucigalpa.

Webster, D. T., N. Gonlin, and A. Freter
|2000| *Copán: The Rise and Fall of an Ancient Maya Kingdom.* Harcourt College Publishers, Fort Worth.

Wheatley, P.
|1971| *The Pivot of the Four Corners: A Preliminary Enquiry into the Origins and Character of the Ancient Chinese City.* Edinburgh University, Edinburgh.

Willey, G. R.
|1953| *Prehistoric Settlement Patterns in the Viru Valley, Peru.* U.S. Government Printing Office, Washington, D.C.

Willey, G. R., and R. Leventhal
|1979| Prehistoric Settlements at Copan. In *Maya Archaeology and Ethnohistory,* edited by N. Hammond, and G. R. Willey, pp. 75–102. University of Texas Press, Austin.

Zuidema, R.T.
|1983| The Lion in the City: Royal Symbols of Transition in Cuzco. *Journal of Latin American Lore* 9(1):39–100.

THE SYMBOLIC SPACE OF THE ANCIENT MAYA SWEATBATH

Mark B. Child

Mark B. Child, 3321 Brampton Lane, Columbia, Missouri 65203, U.S.A.

ABSTRACT

While ancient ideologies can be reconstructed by correlating ethnohistoric and ethnographic beliefs and practices, reconstructing the religious expression of cosmology and ritual within symbolic space is more tenuous. Because sacred space is symbolically defined, the analysis of architecture, iconography, epigraphy and artifact patterns assist in the interpretation of ancient religious behavior. Using the above indicators of religious symbolism, this paper will show how the sacred space of the ancient Maya sweatbath was symbolically expressed and utilized by using a comparative approach that contrasts the past dynamics of the archaeological record to the present statics of sweatbath behaviour.

The sweatbath, commonly found in Maya communities today, serves as a place of healing and ritual. These tightly sealed structures contain a fire hearth where heated stones are sprinkled with water to produce steam. The treatment by moist heat generates therapeutic properties that purge toxins from the body through profuse sweating (Katz 1990:176–178; Orellana 1977:140). It is believed that such practices purify the body from imbalanced corporal and spiritual equilibrium, often at moments of transition and renewal (Logan 1977:89–94; Orellana 1987:37). The sweatbath is especially important to midwives and their patients before, during and after childbirth (Cosminsky 1972:180; Wagley 1949:22). In addition, the process of retreating to the sweatbath is seen as a pinnacle of ritual purification where an individual can emerge as if reborn from the earth (López Austin 1988).

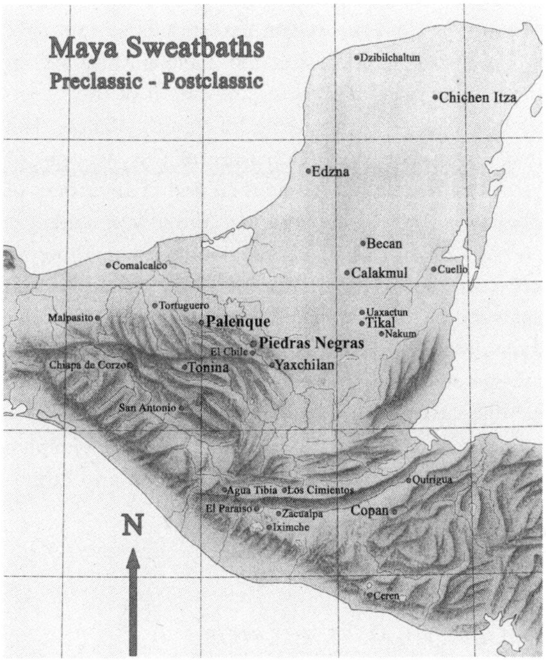

Figure 1. Ancient sweatbath use in the Maya region.

The widespread use of the sweatbath today is not only found among the modern Maya, but also within many indigenous communities of North and Central America (Bucko 1998:24; Groark 1997). Most of these regions have a long-standing tradition of sweatbath use that can be traced back thousands of years in the archaeological record (Alcina Franch et al. 1982). Within the Maya region, sweatbaths have been excavated from the Preclassic to the Postclassic time periods. Although the archaeological record reveals an extensive use of sweatbaths throughout the highlands and lowlands, these structures have yet to be identified at the majority of ancient Maya sites. This insufficient data set has hindered our understanding of

Figure 2. Aztec sweatbath in the Codex Mendoza (after Berdan and Anawalt 1992:3:50).

the religious symbolism of this widespread practice (Figure 1). However, recent excavations of the eight monumental sweatbaths at the ancient Maya site of Piedras Negras – the center and origin of the sweatbath religion – have revealed a wealth of new data that unveils the symbolic nature of this widespread practice. When the architectural and artifact data of Piedras Negras is compared with the monumental expression of the sweatbath religion at its neighboring sites, an archaeological pattern emerges that can be analyzed in light of a historical paradigm of behaviour. Thus, the reconstruction of the symbolic meaning of the sacred space of the ancient Maya sweatbath will be illustrated by using a comparative approach that integrates architectural, epigraphic, and iconographic analyses to a framework of ethnohistoric and ethnographic data.

THEORETICAL FRAMEWORK

The consistency and longevity of the sweatbath tradition reveals its powerful influence in Mesoamerica when considering the religious elements that define its sacred space changed very little in the past 1,500 years regardless of time or region. This pattern makes it possible to reconstruct the religious meaning of how this sacred space was symbolically expressed. At a fundamental level, the sacred space of the ancient sweatbath was symbolically expressed through the following three elements: cosmological valence, supernatural power, and ritual activity.

The first manner in which sacred space is symbolically expressed is through what Eliade refers to as a "cosmological valence; every spatial hierophany or consecration of a space is equivalent to a cosmogony" (Eliade 1959:63). Thus, it is up to the archaeologist to reconstruct how their perception of the universe was symbolically expressed through this sacred space. This also requires the archaeologist to reconstruct the boundaries of the sacred space because "religious and profane life cannot coexist in the same space. If religious life is to develop, a special place must be prepared for it, one from which profane life is excluded" (Durkheim 1995:312). This area has often been referred to as the liminal zone, which symbolizes a threshold where one can communicate or pass to the supernatural world. The liminal zone "is a special and mysterious region with hidden dangers. There are risks of pollution and of failing to comply with the appropriate procedures: ritual washing and cleanliness are therefore emphasized" (Renfrew and Bahn 2000:408). Thus, the reconstruction of symbolic space is generally reflected in the architectural features that reveal cosmological representations of a liminal zone, which is sometimes expressed as sacred geography.

The second mode that sacred space is symbolically expressed through is the public display of supernatural power. The access to this power is always represented in its associated symbol, which "takes the place of the [ideal] thing, and the emotions aroused are transferred to the symbol. It is the symbol that is loved, feared, and respected. It is to the symbol that one is grateful. And it is to the symbol that one sacrifices oneself" (Durkheim 1995:221–222). These symbols "will often relate iconographically to the deities worshiped and to their associated myth. Animal symbolism [of real or mythical animals] may often be used, with particular animals relating to specific deities or powers" (Renfrew and Bahn 2000:409). Thus, it is up to the archaeologist to reconstruct how their access to divine power was publicly displayed, whether it is a representation of a deity in concrete or abstract form.

The third way in which sacred space is symbolically expressed is through ritual action. Because "space is often charged with meaning through events, individual actions define what the space means in relationship to society" (Reese-Taylor and Koontz 2001:10). Thus, each action symbolically expresses sacred space because "the symbol is the smallest unit of ritual which still retains the specific properties of ritual behavior; it is the ultimate unit of specific structure in a ritual context" (Turner 1967:19). In other words, sacred space dictates a symbolic form of ritual that "becomes of factor in social action, a

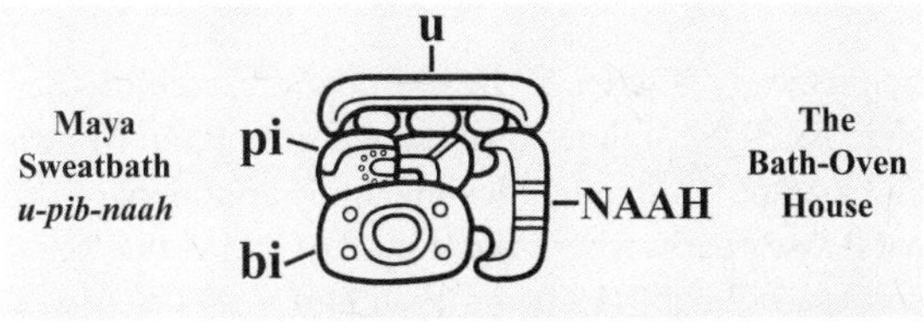

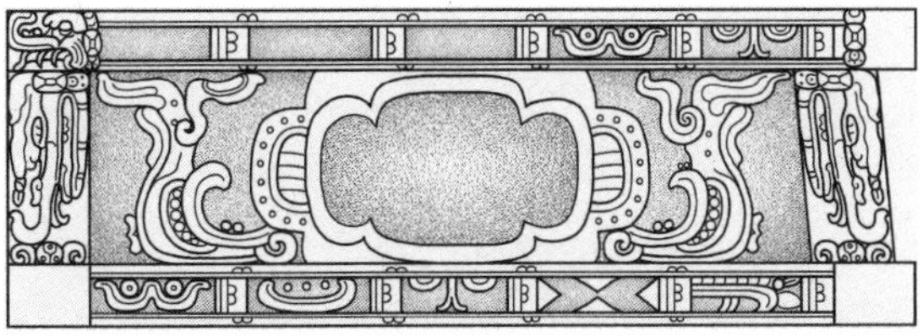

Figure 3. Sweatbath hieroglyph, Tortuguero Monument 6 (after Graham 2002:II-29).

Figure 4. Sanctuary roof entablature, Temple of the Cross, Palenque (after Robertson 1991:Figure 47)

positive force in any activity field...The structure and properties of a symbol become those of a dynamic entity, at least within its appropriate context of action" (Turner 1967:20). Not only is sacred space charged with meaning, but their associated actions must have "the characteristic that they recur periodically" (Durkheim 1995:60). In this way, the archaeologist is obligated to not only reconstruct the ritual activities associated with the sacred space, but also unveil the symbolic meanings that link those practices to that space.

COSMOLOGICAL SPACE

The symbolism that defines the cosmological space of the sweatbath is expressed through sacred geography. Because indigenous communities have always viewed caves and springs as entrances to the underworld, the sacred space of the sweatbath is symbolized as a cave entrance (Bricker 1973:114). The reverse is true as well for the Tzutujil Maya, where caves are sometimes viewed as sweatbaths (Tarn and Prechtel 1986:184). As Sahagún states, "the cave also means place of the dead. Our mothers, our fathers have gone; they have gone to rest in the water, in the cave" (1963:277). This water symbolism is portrayed in many codices by depicting the flow of water from sweatbaths, such as the Aztec example from the Codex Mendoza (Figure 2), which has stated above it, *Temazcalapan*, or "the place of the sweatbath" (Berdan and Anawalt 1992:3:50). In addition, caves were not only viewed as the watery region of the dead, but also were seen as places where newborns came from; hence, the notion of the natal sweatbath (Wagley 1949). Thus, the sweat chamber became a liminal zone where ancestors could be summoned and a place for transformation to the supernatural realm.

There are four lines of evidence that the ancient Maya also expressed the cosmological space of the sweatbath through the symbolic nature of the cave. First, the archaeological record reveals that several sweatbaths have been discovered in various caves throughout Mesoamerica. One example in particular is a non-monumental sweatbath that was recently excavated in the mouth of a cave near Piedras Negras (Child and Child 2001). This small structure was not only tightly sealed with a narrow entrance, but also contained burnt, calcified stones and an artifact assemblage similar to those recovered from the eight monumental sweatbaths in the site core, thus reconfirming the importance of cave symbolism and the ancient Maya sweatbath. Second, the hieroglyphic data from the temples of the Cross Group at Palenque, argued as symbolic sweatbaths (Houston 1996:144), reveal that these structures were represented as caves. The texts from the *alfardas* of these temples refer to their interior sanctuaries as *pib-naahs* (Figure 3), meaning sweatbaths (Stuart 1987:38; Houston 1996:136). This lexical translation is taken from the Motul Maya dictionary, which states that the word p*ib* is a "very hot bath" (Barrera Vásquez 1980:651). The fact that sweatbath glyphs are also referred to as springs and caves at the sites of Palenque and Tortuguero reaffirm the symbolic nature of this sacred space as a cave. Third, the iconographic data on the roof entablatures from the sanctuaries of the symbolic sweatbaths at Palenque portray the cosmological symbolism of the cave (Robertson 1991:36). These cave representations are embodied by the cartouche, a motif commonly seen throughout Mesoamerica, which symbolizes an entrance to the underworld (Figure 4). In addition, the outline created by the drain and benches of the functional sweatbaths

Figure 5. Upper: Temple of the Sun, Palenque; Lower: Structure P-7, Piedras Negras.

at both Palenque and Piedras Negras represent the bottom half of this cartouche, thus reiterating the cave symbolism of the cosmological space of the sweatbath. Fourth, the architectural data from both the functional and symbolic sweatbaths within the Maya lowlands reveal a building style that symbolically expresses the cave. This architectural pattern is expressed when a smaller building with its own roof (a sanctuary) is enshrined within a larger building (Houston 1996:145). The earliest reflection of this architectural enshrinement occurs with the design of the firebox-hearth area within the sweat chambers at Piedras Negras, which arises about A.D. 450 with Sweatbath R-13 (Child and Child 2000). These fireboxes were elaborately built with vaults and stone lintels as symbolic structures enshrined within other buildings. The visual comparison of floor plans between the sweatbaths of the Cross Group at Palenque and the monumental sweatbaths at Piedras Negras demonstrates the similarity of these structures, regardless of their symbolic or functional nature (Figure 5). In addition, this architectural style has been linked to the Maya site of San Miguel on Cozumel through an iconographic argument of the natal sweatbath, where the deity Ix Chel is the "aged goddess of birth" (Houston 1996:146).

The cosmological space of the ancient Maya sweatbath was expressed through the sacred geography of the cave, regardless of its symbolic and functional form. This symbolic space served as a cave entrance and liminal zone where the supernatural was invoked and came forth in birth. Thus, the monumentality of the ancient Maya sweatbath had reached its maximum form of the cosmological expression of cave symbolism by the end of the Late Classic, through patterns of architecture, iconography and epigraphy.

SUPERNATURAL SPACE

The symbolism that defines the supernatural space of the sweatbath is expressed through the public display of power. Because indigenous groups generally associate the display of power with sacred geography such as caves, the supernatural space of the sweatbath is usually symbolized as an aged earth deity, in both concrete and abstract forms. For the Aztecs, this earth deity was a goddess known as Toci, who "was a patroness of midwives and curers" (Miller and Taube 1993:169). She is considered the goddess of filth because she consumes both bodily sickness and spiritual offenses to the gods. This consumption of filth is represented in several codices where her image, which was placed above the doorway of sweatbaths, is depicted with a black ring around her lips, thus representing the purification process (Codex Tudela 1980:62). The Aztecs revered Toci as the grandmother earth deity or the Mother of the Gods, which stemmed from their beliefs that the gods were born in sweatbaths (Duran 1971:229; Sahagún 1969:153–155). Although the Aztecs placed the image of a female earth deity above the doorway of their sweatbaths, the supernatural space of this building was also symbolized by a male counterpart. The Codex Magliabechiano reveals that the Aztec sweatbath was dedicated to Tezcatlipoca, in which this earth deity is sometimes symbolized in abstract form – as the exterior façade of the sweatbath (Nuttall 1903:65). Many Aztec codices that portray sweatbaths depict their façades as an animistic being, whereby the

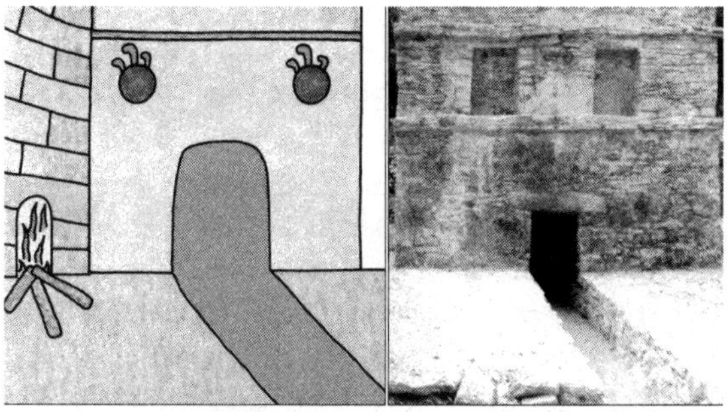

Figure 6. Animistic sweatbath architecture (after Sahagún 1961:Figure 180).

Figure 7. Symbolic sweatbath dedication, Palenque (after Robertson 1991:Figure 286).

two niches above the doorways represent the eyes of this living entity, while the doorway symbolizes the mouth – the entrance to the cave (Figure 6). Although the monumentality of the sweatbath has lost its significance since Spanish occupation, many indigenous groups that still use the sweatbath today symbolize this sacred space as a living entity and give the names of different body parts to the architectural features of their sweatbaths (Katz 1990; López Austin 1988).

The archaeological record of the ancient Maya reveals how the supernatural space of the sweatbath was symbolically expressed in its abstract form of animistic architecture on their exterior façades. This animistic architecture extends as far back as the Classic period for both functional and symbolic sweatbaths of the Maya. An example of this animism is represented on a functional sweatbath at Piedras Negras, known as Structure P7, which is still standing after 1,300 years (Child and Child 2001). Its exterior façade expresses an animistic being, whereby the two niches above the doorway of this structure represent the eyes of the living entity, while the mouth symbolizes the entrance to the cave (Figure 6). An example of animistic architecture for symbolic sweatbaths from Palenque is found on the roof entablatures from both the sanctuary and the vestibule of the Temple of the Cross (Robertson 1991:36). While the animistic façades of these symbolic sweatbaths are not only iconographically represented as earth deities, their associated hieroglyphic texts indicate that these structures were imbued with living souls. The Death Head monument that records the dedication of these symbolic sweatbaths in A.D. 692 (9.12.19.14.12 5 Eb 5 Kayab) reveals the symbolism of introducing a soul, which reads: OCH-K'AK tu-pi-bi-NAAH-li, *och k'ak' t-u-pib-naah-il*, paraphrased as "the fire or soul entered into the sweatbath" (Figure 7). David Stuart (1998:418) makes the case that "by bringing the heat of fire into a building, the space is vivified and invested with its own soul." In addition to giving "the house a soul" as the Tzotzil Maya do today (Vogt 1969:461), the element of fire is also used in many societies throughout the world to symbolically purify the structure for the process of sanctification. Furthermore, epigraphers have pointed out that the verb *och* not only signifies "to enter" in Maya languages, but also means "to become," referring to "changes in states of being" (Stuart 1998:394). Thus, the change that occurred in the symbolic sweatbaths of Palenque on their dedication date not only provided these structures with souls, but also included the sanctification process of purifying these living entities.

In addition to animistic architecture, the ancient Maya symbolically expressed the supernatural space of the sweatbath in more specific forms of aged earth deities. While the ethnohistorical model of this research has illustrated the binary component of a male and female constituent to these aged earth deities, ethnographies of the sweatbath throughout the New World also reveal similar patterns (Bucko 1998; Lipp 1991). Based on archaeological, iconographic and epigraphic data, the following four lines of evidence reveal that God N and Goddess O were the anthropomorphic forms of the aged earth deities for the ancient Maya sweatbath (Child and Child 1999). First, hieroglyphic texts and artifacts from Piedras Negras reveal that Rulers A, 2, and 4 were responsible for the

Figure 8. Piedras Negras sweatbath chronology, with plan views of sweatbaths at Copán, Palenque and Piedras Negras.

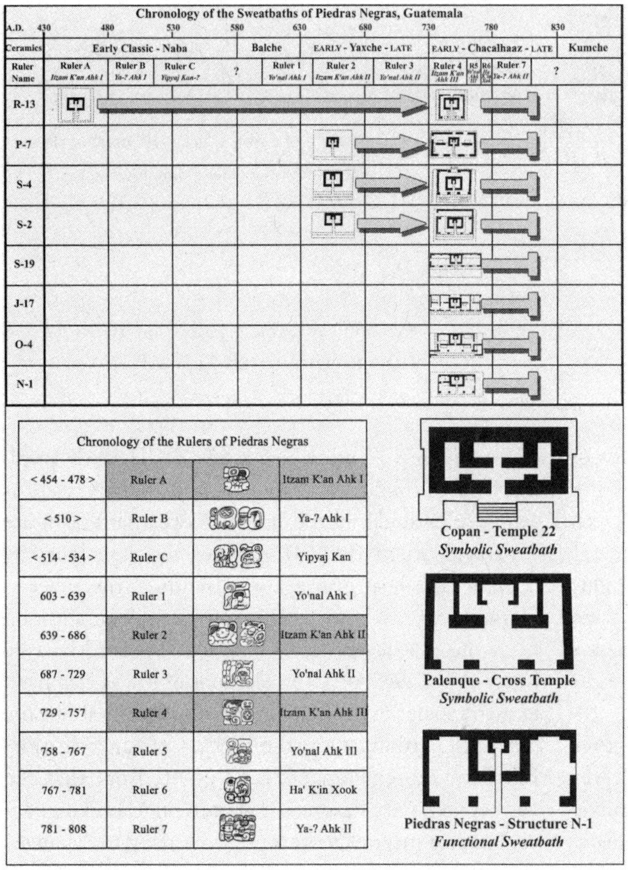
Chronology of the Sweatbaths of Piedras Negras, Guatemala
A.D. 430 480 530 580 630 680 730 780 830
Ceramics
Early Classic - Naba
Balche
EARLY - Yaxche - LATE
EARLY - Chacalhaaz - LATE
Kumche
Ruler Name
Ruler A Itzam K'an Ahk I
Ruler B Ya-? Ahk I
Ruler C Yipyaj Kan-?
?
Ruler 1 Yo'nal Ahk I
Ruler 2 Itzam K'an Ahk II
Ruler 3 Yo'nal Ahk II
Ruler 4 Itzam K'an Ahk III
R5
R6
Ruler 7 Ya-? Ahk II
?
R-13
P-7
S-4
S-2
S-19
J-17
O-4
N-1
Chronology of the Rulers of Piedras Negras
<454 - 478> Ruler A Itzam K'an Ahk I
<510> Ruler B Ya-? Ahk I
<514 - 534> Ruler C Yipyaj Kan
603 - 639 Ruler 1 Yo'nal Ahk I
639 - 686 Ruler 2 Itzam K'an Ahk II
687 - 729 Ruler 3 Yo'nal Ahk II
729 - 757 Ruler 4 Itzam K'an Ahk III
758 - 767 Ruler 5 Yo'nal Ahk III
767 - 781 Ruler 6 Ha' K'in Xook
781 - 808 Ruler 7 Ya-? Ahk II
Copan - Temple 22
Symbolic Sweatbath
Palenque - Cross Temple
Symbolic Sweatbath
Piedras Negras - Structure N-1
Functional Sweatbath

construction and modification of the eight monumental sweatbaths (Figure 8). These three rulers also took upon themselves the name of the aged earth deity – God N, who is portrayed in the Dresden Codex with the iconographic symbols displaying a form of his anthropomorphic name as *Itzam K'an Ahk*. The fact that these three rulers were the only ones to build sweatbaths at Piedras Negras and the only rulers to use the same name as the aged earth deity of God N is not coincidental, especially when coupled with the other three lines of evidence. Second, symbolic sweatbaths expressing enshrined and animistic architecture typically portray zoomorphic forms of an earth deity linked to God N. However, Temple 22 at Copán, which has a similar architectural layout as the symbolic sweatbaths of Palenque and the functional sweatbaths of Piedras Negras, portrays the anthropomorphic form of God N on the portal of the inner sanctum building (Figure 8). The hieroglyphic text of Temple 22 reveals the name of this sanctuary as *k'ahk' y-otoot*, translating as "fire house," which also indicates that this temple represented a symbolic sweatbath. In addition, the animistic façade of this temple represents the open mouth of a zoomorphic earth deity, which is also similar to other symbolic sweatbaths that portray cave entrances to the underworld. The fact that an anthropomorphic form of God N was represented at Copán with the sweatbath pattern of both animistic and enshrined architecture strengthens the argument that the aged earth deity was revered as the male god of the ancient Maya sweatbath. The third line of evidence that links God N to the sweatbath is his association with sweatbath practices, such as birthing. There are numerous examples of iconographic scenes of Classic Maya polychrome vases that portray God N being summoned to aid in the birthing process (Kerr 2000:926). These birthing scenes not only associate God N with the Maya sweatbath, but also link him to the patron deity of midwifery – Goddess O. In addition, the supernatural space of symbolic sweatbaths also links these aged earth deities through the iconographic images of Goddess O that portray her supporting the enshrined architecture of a symbolic sweatbath at San Miguel (Houston 1996:146), which is similar to God N holding up the symbolic sweatbath at Copán. Moreover, the coupling of God N and Goddess O with both their quadripartite expressions on the columns of the Lower Temple of the Jaguar at Chichen Itza, reveal the important association that these aged earth deities share. The fact that God N was summoned at birth, that he was the counterpart to the goddess of midwifery, and that the sweatbath played a primary role in birthing, supports the notion that God N and Goddess O served as the patron deities of the ancient Maya sweatbath. The fourth line of reasoning that points to God N as a Maya sweatbath deity is his association with sweatbath practices, such as purgation. Maya vases that clearly depict enema paraphernalia usually portray the role of God N in these sweatbath rituals (Coe 1978:76–80). Some of these vases that portray God N with enema paraphernalia illustrate sufficient iconographic and hieroglyphic evidence to identify these scenes as a "supernatural sweatbath" (Houston 1996:142). In addition, a few vessels that pertain to purgation portray

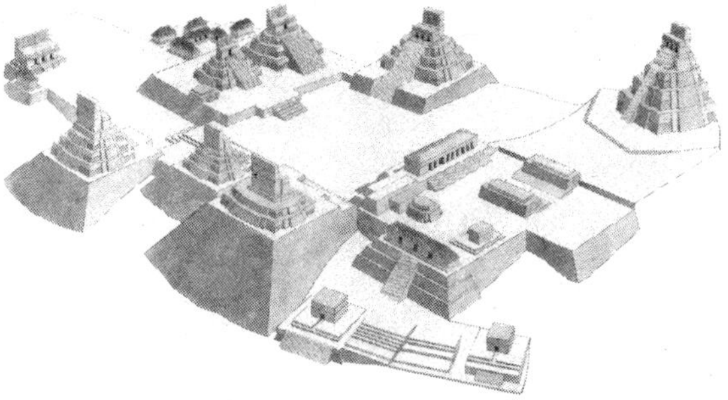

Figure 9. Perspective drawing of the South Group Court, Piedras Negras.

Figure 10. Perspective drawing of the East Group Court, Piedras Negras.

clear scenes of sweatbathing based on essential characteristics, such as an individual crouched in a low and confined space with a heat source (Kerr 1992:378). The fact that God N was summoned during purgation rituals and that the sweatbath played a primary role in purgation strengthens the argument that God N was the anthropomorphic form of the aged earth deity for the ancient Maya sweatbath.

The supernatural space of the ancient Maya sweatbath was expressed through the public display of an earth deity, regardless of its concrete and abstract forms. This symbolic space was represented by both zoomorphic and anthropomorphic forms of the patron deities of the sweatbath – God N and Goddess O. Thus, the monumentality of the ancient Maya sweatbath had reached its maximum form of the supernatural expression of earth deities by the end of the Late Classic, through patterns of architecture, iconography, and epigraphy.

RITUAL SPACE

The symbolism that defines the ritual space of the sweatbath is expressed through the cleansing process of purification. Because of indigenous beliefs that an individual has to be spiritually clean before passing from the profane to the sacred realm, the sweatbath is used to purify the body and the soul for this purpose. Ethnographies reveal the importance of spiritually purifying oneself with the sweatbath before participating in any ceremonial activities, such as ritual dancing (Bucko 1998:82; Lynd 1864:168–171). Ethnohistorical accounts indicate the importance of purifying the soul among the Aztecs when "owners of the sweathouses prayed to her [Toci]...and in her presence confession was made, the heart was open...one recited, and told one's sins" (Sahagún 1970:24). This process is also illustrated in the Prehispanic codices, such as the Codex Nuttall, which portrays the sweatbath as a purification device to cleanse the soul before playing the ball game (Nuttall 1975:16). The practice of praying to a deity during the sweatbath ritual was not only carried out to restore harmony with the gods from being in a state of spiritual disequilibrium, but was also carried out during crucial moments of transition in an individual's life. Many indigenous communities that still use the sweatbath today summon earth deities to purify the pregnant woman because of beliefs that she should be free of sin and filth before delivery (Rodríguez Rouanet 1969:60). In addition, many indigenous groups still use the ritual space of the sweatbath to purify their children during important ceremonies of socialization rites (Katz 1990:180; Servain 1983). Ethnohistorical accounts reveal that the notion of ritual purification for personal rites of passage is a long-standing tradition (Sahagún 1970:22–24). Furthermore, Prehispanic codices confirm the ancient use of the sweatbath for rites of passage, such as puberty, adulthood, and marriage, especially those portrayed in the Mixtec codices from Oaxaca (Bellas 1997:123–125).

The archaeological record of the ancient Maya reveals how the ritual space of the sweatbath was symbolically expressed through the cleansing process of purifying oneself before participating in ceremonial activities. This purification process is evident in the spatial layout of Maya centers in the Western Lowlands during the Classic period. The coupling of sweatbaths and ballcourts located in contiguous plaza

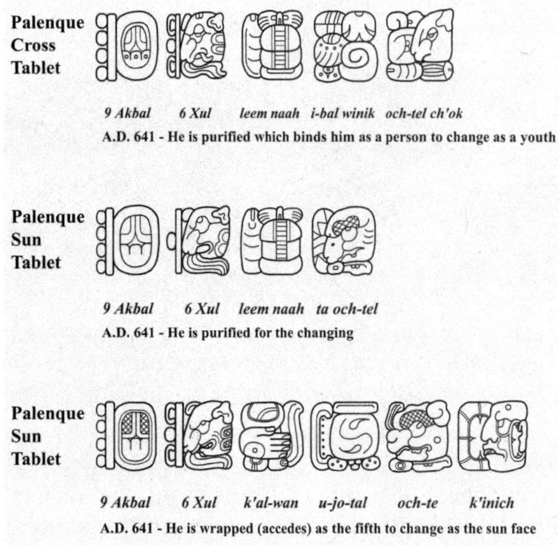
Palenque Cross Tablet
9 Akbal 6 Xul leem naah i-bal winik och-tel ch'ok
A.D. 641 - He is purified which binds him as a person to change as a youth
Palenque Sun Tablet
9 Akbal 6 Xul leem naah ta och-tel
A.D. 641 - He is purified for the changing
Palenque Sun Tablet
9 Akbal 6 Xul k'al-wan u-jo-tal och-te k'inich
A.D. 641 - He is wrapped (accedes) as the fifth to change as the sun face

Figure 11. Tablet of the Cross and Tablet of the Sun text (after Robertson 1991:Figures 9, 95).

space are prevalent at Maya centers, such as Piedras Negras, Yaxchilan and Tonina. This association is clearly demonstrated at the site of Piedras Negras, where two separate complexes were built in the Early Classic and Late Classic periods. Sweatbaths N-1 and R-13 were not only built at the same time with the two ball courts at the site, but were also directly aligned within the same ritual space (Figure 9). In addition to the coupling of ballcourts, Classic Maya sweatbaths were built in association with dance platforms and temples. These ritual spaces were linked to sweatbaths at Western Maya centers, such as Piedras Negras, Palenque, Yaxchilan, Tonina and Copán, for the purpose of purifying the soul before participating in ritual dancing and temple practices (Figure 10).

In addition to participating in ceremonial activities, the ancient Maya symbolically expressed the ritual space of the sweatbath through the cleansing process of purifying oneself before moving on to a new stage in life. At the site of Palenque, these rights of passage were portrayed in the ritual space of the symbolic sweatbath through hieroglyphic and iconographic images. All three of the sanctuary tablets located within the symbolic sweatbaths of the Cross Group portray scenes of the ruler Chan Bahlum II as a 6-year-old child and as a 49-year-old adult. The inner text indicates that this ruler went through certain rites of passage that required the purification process of the sweatbath to transform him to the new stage of puberty and kingship. The Maya inscribed the puberty event of A.D. 641 in the following three forms (Figure 11). The first text is recorded on the inner left of the Tablet of the Cross, which reads: le-ma-WITS-NAAH i-ba-la WINIK OCH-te-le ch'o-ko, *leem wits naah i-bal winik och-tel ch'ok*, which roughly translates as "he is purified in the temple, which binds him as a person, to change as a youth." It is interesting to note that there are over twenty verbs that Maya scribes could have chosen to describe how Chan Bahlum II was introduced or entered the temple. However, the "introduction" verb chosen for this rite of passage deals specifically with purification. The verb expressing this rite of passage *leem*, not only signifies "to introduce" in Yucatec Maya, but also means "to alleviate the cold wind, pain, and sickness from the body" (Barrera Vásquez 1980:445). If the verb *leem* signifies a purification context, then this would be congruent with ethnographic and ethnohistorical accounts that indicate that cold wind and infirmity were alleviated from the body through the ritual practice of the sweatbath. The second text is recorded on the inner part of the Tablet of the Sun, which reads: le-ma-NAAH ta-OCH-te-le, *leem naah / ta och-tel*, which roughly translates as, "he is purified in the temple, for the change." Although the youth glyph *ch'ok* does not directly follow, the preposition *ta* changes the structure of the meaning. In addition, this form uses the previously mentioned *och* verb, which not only signifies to enter, but also means to become, begin or change. It is within this context that the *och* glyph best indicates the connotation of "change." This is also supported by the third text that is recorded on the outer portion of the Tablet of the Sun, which reads: K'AL-wa-ni u-JO-TAL-la OCH-te K'INICH, *k'al-wan u-jo-tal och-te k'inch*, which roughly translates as, "he is wrapped [accedes] as the fifth to change as the sun face." It is interesting to note that the verb used for a ruler's accession, *k'al*, is also used to portray this puberty rite, thus reconfirming the context of transformation in this ritual. When the purification meaning behind the verbs *leem* and *k'al* are coupled with the "changing" verb *och*, it is most likely that the A.D. 641 event is a portrayal of Chan Bahlum II transforming to a new stage of puberty that required the sanctification element of the sweatbath.

The ritual space of the ancient Maya sweatbath was expressed through the cleansing process of purification. This symbolic space was linked to temples, ballcourts and dance platforms in order that their bodies and souls were purified before participating in ceremonial activities and rites of passage. Thus, the monumentality of the ancient Maya sweatbath had reached its maximum form of the ritual expression of purification by the end of the Late Classic, through patterns of architecture, iconography and epigraphy.

CONCLUSION

The widespread use of the Mesoamerican sweatbath provides a comparative framework of ethnographic and ethnohistorical literature for understanding the symbolic space of the ancient Maya sweatbath. The religious meaning of how this sacred space was symbolically expressed is brought to light through the three elements of cosmological valence, supernatural power, and ritual activity.

The cosmological space of the ancient Maya sweatbath was expressed through the sacred geography of the cave. This symbolic space not only served as cave entrance to the underworld, but also functioned as the liminal zone where the supernatural was invoked and came forth in birth. The sweatbath was symbolized as a cave through the interchanging of sweatbath-cave-spring hieroglyphs, through iconographic representations of the cartouche, and through the architectural patterns of inner-sanctum buildings.

The supernatural space of the ancient Maya sweatbath was expressed through the public display of an earth deity. This symbolic space was not only represented by animistic architecture that embodied the zoomorphic form of an earth deity, but was also considered a living entity with its own soul. In addition, this supernatural space was also symbolized through its anthropomorphic form, consisting of a binary component of male and female earth deities, otherwise known as God N and Goddess O – the patron deities of the ancient Maya sweatbath.

The ritual space of the ancient Maya sweatbath was expressed through the cleansing process of purification. This symbolic space was usually located in contiguous plaza space with temples, ball courts and dance platforms for the purpose of ritually purifying oneself before participating in ceremonial activities. In addition, this ritual space was also symbolized in symbolic sweatbaths as rites of passage that required the purification process of balancing one's spiritual and corporeal equilibrium and restoring harmony with the gods before moving on to a new stage in life.

Thus, the comparative approach reveals that the symbolism reflecting the cosmological, supernatural and ritual space of the Mesoamerican sweatbath for the past 1,500 years has fundamentally endured, even in light of Spanish suppression to this practice within the past 500 years. In addition, the comparative approach illustrates that the ethnographic and ethnohistorical data of symbolic space can be aligned with the archaeological patterns of architecture, iconography and epigraphy.

REFERENCES CITED

Alcina Franch, J., A. Ciudad Ruiz, and J. Iglesias Ponce de León

|1982| El "temazcal" en Mesoamerica: evolucion, forma, y funcion. *Revista Espanola de Antropologia Americana* 10:93–132.

Barrera Vásquez, A.

|1980| *Diccionario Maya.* Editorial Porrua, S. A., Mexico, D. F.

Bellas, M.

|1997| The Body in the Mixtec Codices: Birth, Purification, Transformation and Death. Unpublished Ph.D. dissertation, Department of Anthropology, University of California, Riverside.

Berdan, F. F., and P. R. Anawalt

|1992| *The Codex Mendoza.* 5 vols. University of California Press, Berkeley.

Bricker, V. R.

|1973| *Ritual Humor in Highland Chiapas.* University of Texas Press, Austin.

Bucko, R. A.

|1998| *The Lakota Ritual of the Sweatlodge: History and Contemporary Practice.* University of Nebraska Press, Lincoln.

Child, M. B., and J. C. Child

|2000| Los baños de vapor de Piedras Negras, Guatemala. In *XIII Simposio de Investigaciones Arqueológicas en Guatemala, Museo Nacional de Arqueología y Etnología, 1999*, edited by J. P. Laporte, H. L. Escobedo, A. C. Monzón de Suasnávar, and B. Arroyo, pp. 1067–1090. Ministerio de Cultura y Deportes, Instituto de Antropología e Historia, Asociación Tikal, Guatemala.

|2001| The Urban Setting of Monumental Sweatbaths at Piedras Negras, Guatemala. Paper presented at the 66th Annual Meeting of the Society for American Archaeology, New Orleans.

Child, J. C., and M. B. Child
|1999| The Spatial and Temporal Distribution of the Ancient Maya Sweatbaths at Piedras Negras, Guatemala. Paper presented at the 98th Annual Meeting of the American Anthropological Association, Chicago.
Coe, M. D.
|1978| *Lords of the Underworld: Masterpieces of Classic Maya Ceramics*. Princeton University Press, Princeton.
Cosminsky, S.
|1972| *Decision Making and Medical Care in a Guatemalan Indian Community*. Ph.D. dissertation, Brandeis University, Waltham, Massachusetts. University Microfilms, Ann Arbor.
Codex Tudela
|1980| *Codex Tudela*. 2 vols. Ediciones Cultura Hispánica de Instituto de Cooperación Iberoamericana, Madrid.
Duran, Fray Diego de
|1971| *Book of the Gods and Rites and the Ancient Calendar*, translated by F. Horcasitas and D. Heyden. Orion Press, New York.
Durkheim, E.
|1995| *The Elementary Forms of Religious Life*, translated by K. H. Fields from the 1912 edition. The Free Press, New York
Eliade, M.
|1959| *The Sacred and the Profane: The Nature of Religion*. Harcourt Brace, New York
Graham, I.
|2002| Illustration. In *Notebook for the XXVIth Maya Hieroglyphic Forum at Texas - Palenque and its Neighbors*, edited by Simon Martin, Marc Zender, and Nikolai Grube, p. II-29. Maya Workshop Foundation, Austin.
Groark, K. P.
|1997| To Warm the Blood, to Warm the Flesh: The Role of the Steambath in Highland Maya (Tzeltal-Tzotzil) Ethnomedicine. *Journal of Latin American Lore* 20(1):3–96.
Houston, S. D.
|1996| Symbolic Sweatbaths of the Maya: Architectural Meaning in the Cross Group at Palenque, Mexico. *Latin American Antiquity* 7:132–151.
Katz, E.
|1990| El temazcal: entre religion y medicina. Paper presented at the III Coloquio de Historia de las Religiones en Mesoamerica y Areas Afines, Instituto de Investigaciones Antropologicas, Universidad Nacional Autonoma de Mexico, Mexico.
Kerr, J.
|1992| *The Maya Vase Book*, vol. 3. Kerr Associates, New York.
|2000| *The Maya Vase Book*, vol. 6. Kerr Associates, New York.
Lipp, F. J.
|1991| *The Mixe of Oaxaca: Religion, Ritual, and Healing*. University of Texas Press, Austin.
Logan, M. H.
|1977| Anthropological Research on the Hot-Cold Theory of Disease: Some Methodological Suggestions. *Medical Anthropology* 1(4):87–112.
López Austin, A.
|1988| *The Human Body and Ideology: Concepts of the Ancient Nahuas*. 2 vols. Translated by T. and B. Ortiz de Montellano. University of Utah Press, Salt Lake City.
Lynd, J.
|1864| The Religion of the Dakotas. *Minnesota Historical Collections* 2(2):150–174.
Miller, M. E., and K. Taube
|1993| *The Gods and Symbols of Ancient Mexico and The Maya: An Illustrated Dictionary of Mesoamerican Religion*. Thames and Hudson, London and New York.
Nuttall, Z.
|1903| *The Book of the Life of the Ancient Mexicans, Containing an Account of their Rites and Superstitions*, pt. I. University of California Press, Berkeley.
|1975| *The Codex Nuttall: A Picture Manuscript from Ancient Mexico*, introduction by A. G. Miller. Dover Publications, New York.
Orellana, S. L.
|1977| Aboriginal Medicine in Highland Guatemala. *Medical Anthropology* 1(1):113–156.
|1987| *Indian Medicine in Highland Guatemala: The Pre-Hispanic and Colonial Periods*. University of Chicago Press, Chicago.
Reese-Taylor, K., and R. Koontz
|2001| The Cultural Poetics of Power and Space in Ancient Mesoamerica. In *Landscape and Power in Ancient Mesoamerica*, edited by R. Koontz, K. Reese-Taylor, and A. Headrick, pp. 1–27. Westview Press, Boulder.
Renfrew, C., and P. Bahn
|2000| *Archaeology: Theories, Methods, and Practice*. Thames and Hudson, New York.
Robertson, M. G.
|1991| *The Sculpture of Palenque: IV. The Cross Group*. Princeton University Press, Princeton.
Rodriguez Rouanet, F.
|1969| Practicas medicas tradicionales de los indígenas de Guatemala. *Guatemala Indígena* 4(2):51–86.
Sahagún, Fray Bernardino de
|1950–1970| *Florentine Codex: General History of the Things of New Spain (ca. 1578–79)*. Translated by C. Dibble and A. Anderson. School of American Research, Santa Fe.
Servain, F.
|1983| *Les bains de vaoeur en Mesoamerica*. Unpublished masters thesis, University of Paris I, Paris.
Stuart, D.
|1987| *Ten Phonetic Syllables*. Research Reports on Ancient Maya Writing No. 14. Center for Maya Research, Washington, D.C.
|1998| "The Fire Enters His House": Architecture and Ritual in Classic Maya Texts. In *Function and Meaning in Classic Maya Architecture*, edited by S. D. Houston, pp. 373–425. Dumbarton Oaks Research Library and Collection, Washington, D.C.
Tarn, N., and M. Prechtel
|1986| Constant Inconstancy: The Feminine Principle in Atiteco Mythology. In *Symbol and Meaning beyond the Closed Community: Essays in Mesoamerican Ideas*, edited by G. Gossen, pp. 173–184. Studies on Culture and Society, vol. 1. State University of New York, Albany.

Turner, V.
|1967| *The Forest of Symbols: Aspects of Ndembu Ritual.* Cornell University Press, Ithaca.

Vogt, E. Z.
|1969| *Zinacantan: A Maya Community in the Highlands of Chiapas.* Belkap Press of Harvard University, Cambridge.

Wagley, C.
|1949| *The Social and Religious Life of a Guatemalan Village.* American Anthropological Association Memoir No. 71. American Anthropological Association, Menasha, Wisconsin.

SPACE, PLACE, AND THE RISE OF "URBANISM" IN THE CANADIAN ARCTIC

Peter C. Dawson

Peter C. Dawson, Department of Archaeology, University of Calgary, 2500 University Drive N.W., Calgary, Alberta T2N 1N4, Canada.

ABSTRACT

From an archaeological perspective, the rise of urbanism is often seen as a gradual process involving increasing settlement nucleation, and the indigenous development of more complex levels of community organization. In contrast, the creation of permanent nucleated settlements in the Canadian Arctic by the Federal Government in the 1950s and 60s introduced Inuit families to urban life almost overnight. The layout and design of these new Arctic towns was based upon Euro-Canadian concepts of community structure, administrative control, and social cooperation. Roads, utility hook-ups, and building codes replaced cultural values, familial ties, and the requirements of traditional activities in determining the spatial organization of buildings within settlements. Furthermore, the geographical locations of these new communities were selected on the basis of access to air and sea transportation, issues of Canadian sovereignty, or the needs of industry, and sometimes required the relocation of Inuit families to new and unfamiliar regions of the Arctic. In this paper, I compare the location, layout, and design of post-war Arctic towns and hamlets with traditional camps, and examine the effects of planned communities and the rapid shift to urbanism on Inuit culture.

In 1950, V. Gordon Childe published an article in *Town Planning Review* entitled "The Urban Revolution" in which he defined the traits associated with the origins of urbanism in the archaeological record. Among the attributes he outlined was the presence of conspicuous order in the spatial organization of towns and cities. The formalization of building and activity locations within settlements was viewed as evidence for the existence of architects and planners who possessed the power to make decisions regarding where to locate new buildings and facilities. The results of these decisions constituted a form of spatial engineering because they permitted large numbers of people to live together in dense concentrations and moved them about in ways that generated encounters with the providers of essential services.

In the archaeological record, the emergence of urbanism represents the culmination of indigenous cultural processes stretched out over many thousands of years. This stands in vivid contrast to the Canadian Arctic, where during the post-war period urbanism emerged as a product of colonial rather than as indigenous processes. While the term "urbanism" is often used to define aspects of life in large cities, the transition from small remote camps to settled towns and hamlets during the 1950s and 1960s introduced Inuit to communities of a much larger social scale. This transition was encouraged by Canadian Government officials who felt that Inuit families could be better provisioned with health care, education and public services if they were centrally located rather than scattered across the north in small, highly mobile groups. The layout and design of these new Arctic communities was based upon Euro-Canadian concepts of community structure, administrative control and social cooperation. Roads, utility hook-ups and building codes replaced cultural values, familial ties and the spatial requirements of traditional activities in determining the location of buildings within settlements. Out of this emerged the urban grid – a means by which any town becomes a mechanism for generating contact between individuals.

Recent research in the field of space syntax analysis indicates that the spatial configuration of European and

Figure 1. Arial photograph of the community of Arviat.

North American cities generates encounters among inhabitants that create opportunities for social interaction, exchange, and community life (Hillier 1996; Hillier et al. 1993; Peponis et al. 1997). Consequently, the spatial configuration of any community can be seen as a projection of the social relations of its intended inhabitants. If true, then the shaping of space by something other than social factors should have had definite consequences for the Inuit residents living in contemporary Arctic communities. This raises two interesting questions. First, how does the spatial configuration of traditional Inuit settlements differ from the Arctic towns and hamlets of today? Second, if human movement is a culturally variable phenomenon, then what effect have these differences had on Inuit culture? In order to explore these questions, I will begin by comparing the determinants of settlement organization in traditional hunter-gatherer and urban societies. I will then analyze the spatial configuration of two Arctic towns using computer models of urban space. The results of this analysis will then be used to outline the different forms of spatial configuration that characterize contemporary Arctic hamlets and traditional Inuit settlements. Finally, I will speculate on the impact that Euro-Canadian settlement plans may have had on Inuit culture.

DETERMINANTS OF SETTLEMENT ORGANIZATION: HUNTER-GATHERERS AND COMPLEX SOCIETIES

The study of human spatial behaviour has a long history in archaeology and anthropology. While early work by Binford (1978) and others focused on the mechanics of the body and activities as a means of explaining spatial organization in the archaeological record, later research has examined the problem of how movement in space relates to social patterns of communication, interaction, and residential group integration (Rapoport 1982; Hillier and Hanson 1984; Hillier 1996). Out of this has emerged the idea that the spatial organization of any habitation site should mirror or reflect the social organization of the residential group. But how direct is this reflection? Lèvi-Strauss (1963:292) has argued that the relationship between spatial organization and social organization likely varies between cultural groups, making it easy to discover such relationships among some societies and difficult among others. This idea is based on a static perception of space in which the positions of houses and other cultural features on the landscape serve as "attractors" that generate human movement. However, if human movement is a culturally variable phenomenon, then the straight lines of sight and movement that are formed between architectural features and activity areas should provide a more accurate means of measuring how social processes are reflected in space. This is because straight lines of sight and movement provide opportunities for social encounter, and it is through such encounters that culture is reproduced on a daily basis.

THE SPATIAL ORGANIZATION OF TRADITIONAL CAMPS

Among many hunter-gatherer societies, the networks of mutual assistance that are necessary for the organization of labour and the sharing of food require face to face contact which is frequent, regular, and predictable. As a result, hunter-gatherer communities are often laid out in a "clumped" pattern in which groups of dwellings placed in close proximity to one another represent social and/or corporate groups (Whitelaw 1991:158). In these situations, clustered or circular patterns of dwellings represent greater levels of integration and cohesion within the residential group. A classic example of this is the !Kung dry season camp where the circular layout of the camp and the metric distance between huts correlate with the relatedness of camp members. When social stresses increase through population pressure, routing through settlements is often altered to regulate and control physical encounters among inhabitants. This is accomplished by decreasing occupational density, increasing spacing between residences to create spatial buffer zones, and changing the orientations of dwellings so that lines of sight from entrances do not overlap (Whitelaw 1991:158). When settlement density increases to the point at which encounters with others can no longer be effectively managed in these ways, camps are occupied for shorter periods of time and residential units are shuffled between sites (Whitelaw 1991:151).

Figure 2. Arial photograph of the community of Rankin Inlet.

THE SPATIAL ORGANIZATION OF CONTEMPORARY ARCTIC TOWNS

Unlike hunter-gatherer societies, where social factors are principal in determining the spatial configuration of settlements, the layout of Euro-Canadian communities in the Arctic is conditioned primarily by servicing and administrative requirements. The urban grids of these new settlements are configured to balance two tendencies: the need to make the pattern as small as possible to reduce the costs of development and servicing, and the need to separate buildings by at least 12 m in order to control the spread of fire (Strub 1996:92). In most Arctic communities, drinking water is trucked from reservoirs to dwellings and public buildings where it is stored in tanks (Bruce 1969:8; Gerein 1980:91). Likewise, sewage and household refuse are collected from residences and trucked to dump sites located on the outer edges of the community (Bruce 1969:8; Gerein 1980:91). Consequently, the compactness of the urban grid is an important consideration in reducing transportation costs (Gerein 1980:92).

Snow drifting and drainage problems are also paramount concerns in northern community development (Gerein 1980:92; Strub 1996:92). Significant accumulations of snow can block off areas of the settlement, making access difficult for water, sewage and fire trucks. As a solution, street patterns are elongated and paralleled with the prevailing wind direction to keep streets free from snow (Gerein 1980:93). Buildings are oriented in a similar fashion to reduce wind resistance and minimize the accumulation of snow in leeside areas (Strub 1996:94–96). However, the regular placement of street systems and buildings had a tendency to interrupt the existing drainage pattern of the land (Strub 1996:92). This often limited the direction and extent to which settlements could expand. For example, the southward expansion of the hamlet of Arviat, Nunavut, has been conditioned by the combination of an eastern drainage area and drainage via a stream to the south. Easy access to administrative and consumer services is another important determinant for settlement organization in contemporary Arctic communities (Strub 1996:92). This required the central location of facilities such as the community health centre, band office, RCMP headquarters, schools and the cooperative store within the settlement. As we have seen, cross cultural study of hunter-gatherer settlements indicates that traditional Inuit settlements were laid out according to social factors which mediated patterns of communication, interaction and residential group integration. In contrast, the layout of contemporary Arctic communities is determined primarily by functional factors. If human movement is a culturally variable phenomenon, then what effect would living in a town

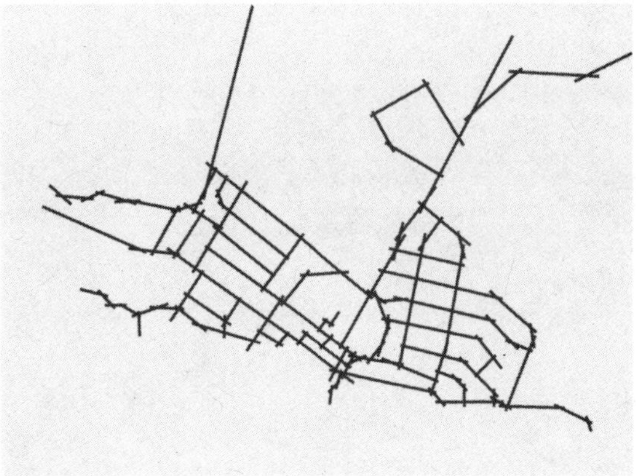

Figure 3. Unprocessed axial map of Arviat.

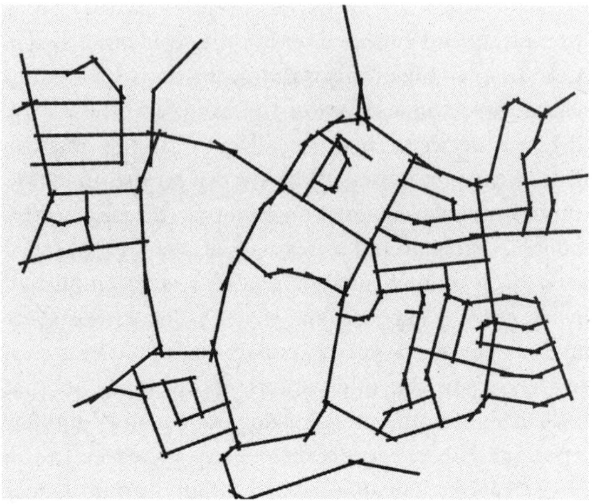

Figure 4. Unprocessed axial map of Rankin Inlet.

spatially configured around the economic practices and cultural values of Euro-Canadians have had on Inuit residents? In order to explore this question, I will analyze the urban grids of two contemporary Arctic communities located on the west coast of Hudson Bay: Arviat – an Inuit community of 2000 people (Figure 1), and Rankin Inlet – an Inuit community of 2500 (Figure 2) .

AXIAL ANALYSIS OF ARVIAT AND RANKIN INLET

Configurational modeling of urban networks has become a major component of space syntax analysis, a theoretical and methodological approach originally developed by Hillier and Hanson (1984). Using this approach, the urban layout of a city or town is broken down into the fewest and longest lines of sight and movement. These axial lines are then described mathematically using a number of statistical measures. By quantifying the configurational properties of community layouts, two or more urban networks can be compared objectively.

Two common measures used in configurational analysis are connectivity and integration. Connectivity simply measures the number of connections each route of movement has to adjacent line segments (Hillier et al. 1993:35). The relationship of each axial line to all other lines in the grid provides an important measure called integration. The most integrated lines in a network are those with the shortest average "trip" lengths to all other destinations within the grid. In contrast, the most segregated lines are those in which trip lengths vary to a much greater degree. In other words, integration measures the mean depth of every axial line in the grid relative to all other lines (Hillier et al. 1993:35).

By examining how integration is distributed throughout the grid within three or more changes of direction, one can develop a sense of how towns and cities with different spatial configurations generate what Hillier (1996) has called "virtual communities." Virtual communities are generated by the physical layout of the grid and constitute patterns of co-presence and co-awareness that arise when others are encountered while moving through a settlement. The more integrated an area is within the grid, the greater the number of encounters, and the larger and more defined the virtual community.

Axman is a computer software package that provides a means of constructing and analyzing axial maps of urban grids. Road systems and paths through the community are first converted into axial lines which define straight lines of sight and movement (Hillier 1996:154). Measurements of connectivity and integration are then taken from the resulting axial map.

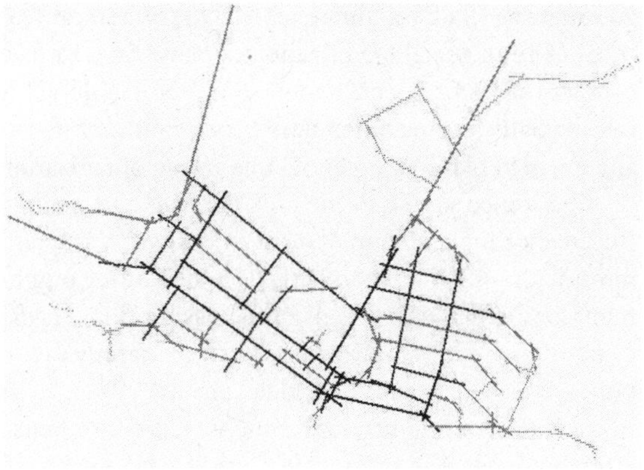

Figure 5. Processed axial map of Arviat. Dark lines indicate highly integrated roads (rad = 3).

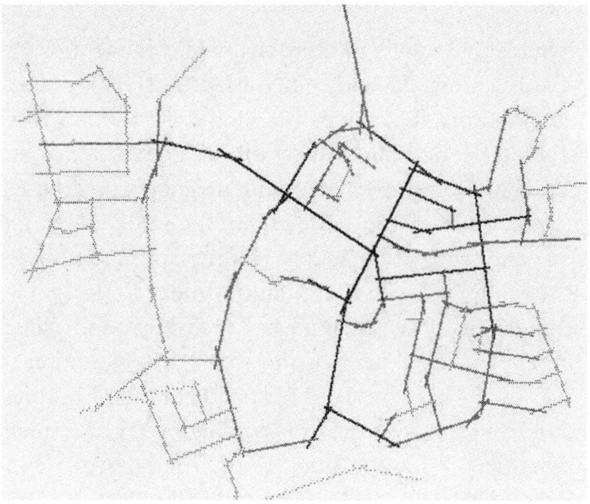

Figure 6. Processed axial map of Rankin Inlet. Dark lines indicate highly integrated roads (rad = 3).

Connectivity measures how connected each axial line is relative to all other lines in the grid (Hillier 1996:129). Integration is measured both at local (small scale) and global (large scale) levels of movement. Local integration calculates how deep or shallow each line is from all other lines within three changes of direction (rad = 3) and is a good predictor of pedestrian movement (Hillier 1996:134). Global integration calculates how deep or shallow each line is from all other lines in the entire grid (rad = n) and is a good predictor of vehicular movement (Hiller 1996:134). High correlations between these two measures provide an indication of how intelligible the urban grid is to the occupants of the community. An intelligible system is one in which the structure of the local grid strongly resembles that of the entire grid (Hillier 1996:129). This makes it possible for an individual to predict the configuration of the entire grid from knowledge of the grid at the local level. Recent space syntax studies have demonstrated that intelligibility is a property that is linked to wayfinding, a term that refers to the route-choice decisions made by people that allow them to move easily through a building or community without becoming lost or disoriented. (Conroy-Dalton 2001). Figures 3 to 6 show the unprocessed and processed axial maps for Arviat and Rankin Inlet. The processed lines are presented here in grey scale so that dark lines indicate highly integrated routes and light grey lines indicate routes with low integration values.

Visual inspection of each axial map reveals that integration is distributed differently within each community. This may relate to the more elongated and regular grid layout of Arviat as compared with the more radial and irregular grid layout of Rankin Inlet. An examination of the processed axial map for Arviat identifies an integration "core" comprised of several long and highly integrated lines that link the eastern and western sections of the community. In contrast, the integration core of Rankin Inlet is sparse, containing few highly integrated lines that are shorter and that do not reach into the peripheral areas of the community.

Table 1. Intelligibility Values for Arviat and Rankin Inlet.

Community	Connectivity vs. Integration (Rad = n)	Intelligibility
Arviat	R^2 = 0.4816	R^2 = 0.7323
Rankin Inlet	R^2 = 0.2566	R^2 = 0.2566

Statistical results indicate that while connectivity is weakly correlated with integration (rad = n) in both communities, R^2 values were lower for Rankin Inlet (Table 1). This shows that well-integrated routes are not always well connected to neighbouring routes. Examination of the correlations for integration (rad = 3) and integration (rad = n) reveal a much higher R^2 value for Arviat than Rankin Inlet (Table 1). The strength of the correlation between local and global integration indicates that the spatial configuration of Arviat is far more intelligible than that of Rankin Inlet. This would suggest that way-finding in Arviat is much easier than in Rankin Inlet. Furthermore, because integration is more locally focused in Rankin Inlet than in Arviat, movement and social interaction are more intensified in the core area of the community rather than in residential sectors.

URBAN GRIDS VERSUS TRADITIONAL CAMPS

As discussed previously, the importance of servicing and administrative requirements as primary determinants of settlement organization result in forms of spatial configuration that differ considerably from those of traditional Inuit camps where spatial configuration is determined primarily by social factors. The spatial configurations of Arviat and Rankin Inlet are characterized by compact grids of regularly spaced dwellings placed in peripheral areas of the community, and the centralization of administrative and servicing facilities in the "downtown" core.

Because many Inuit families continue to engage in traditional activities to varying degrees, this form of spatial organization would appear to represent an inversion of the traditional settlement. Families in Arviat are reliant upon a land-based economy where traditional foods serve to supplement incomes and act as an important source of cultural identity. Outpost camps are maintained by many families and are used to acquire and prepare traditional foods such as caribou, Arctic char, black bears, polar bears, and a variety of shorebirds. Many aspects of traditional Inuit social organization are also in evidence. These include social networks of mutual assistance, the importance of bilateral extended families as the primary economic and social units of production, as well as many aspects of kinship and marriage. The maintenance of these central features of Inuit social organization demand face-to-face contact that is frequent, regular and predictable. This is especially the case for networks of mutual assistance, which plays an essential role in the organization of subsistence activities such as hunting and fishing. Because of high unemployment in many Arctic communities, family members actively pool hunting equipment and labour as a means of increasing their access to traditional foods. Social visits between family members are also frequent. One does not knock on doors in an Inuit community; one simply walks into house after house and is offered tea, traditional food, and conversation. Consequently, because Inuit emphasize regular face-to-face contact among family members and friends to a greater degree than they access government services and retail outlets, then it seems unlikely that the spatial configuration of Arctic communities such as Arviat and Rankin Inlet directly reflect Inuit patterns of movement. Instead, family members distributed throughout the community serve as powerful "attractors" that generate pedestrian movement. However, the centralization of government and commercial services, coupled with housing allocation practices which often place unrelated families in adjacent dwellings, means that most family members end up living in areas of the community that are least integrated. This is especially the case for Rankin Inlet, where the integration core is focused in the centre of the community and does not extend out to residential areas (Figure 6). If we were to turn Arviat and Rankin Inlet "inside out" by centrally locating residences and peripherally locating other types of services, then the spatial configuration of the community would more closely match the social organization of Inuit members of these communities. This would approach the spatial configuration of traditional Inuit communities where members of kin groups were centrally located and lived in close proximity to one another, substantially increasing the probability of encountering members of the kinship group (Whitelaw 1991:158).

The discrepancies in intelligibility that exist between Arviat and Rankin Inlet may also have interesting implications for generating social interactions between residents. The layout of roads and paths according to prevailing wind direction and the optimal routing of essential services, create an urban grid that is almost completely devoid of any social logic. In extreme cases like Rankin Inlet, this significantly reduces the intelligibility of the urban layout, making it difficult to predict who or what one will encounter while moving through the settlement. As a result, encounters with strangers are more random and less controllable. In other studies which have examined the transitions made by hunter-gatherers to life in large, non-traditional communities, the inability to regulate and control interactions with others was found to contribute higher levels of conflict and stressful behaviour, and to the breakdown of traditional values and social systems (Whitelaw 1991:181).

CONCLUSIONS AND DIRECTIONS FOR FUTURE RESEARCH

At the beginning of this paper, I suggested that if human movement was a culturally variable phenomenon, then the spatial configurations of Canadian Arctic communities are likely incompatible with the patterns of movement required to maintain the central features of Inuit social organization. During the summer of 2002, I will be testing the spatial model of Arviat discussed earlier in this paper to see if observed patterns of Inuit movement correlate with the integration values calculated for roads by Axman. Significant correlations between the integration value of an axial line and the amount of pedestrian and vehicular traffic that flows along it have been discovered in studies of Western towns and cities, suggesting that the spatial configuration of an urban network exerts a strong effect on human movement (Hillier 1996; Hillier et al. 1993; Penn et al. 1998; Peponis et al. 1997). If human movement is a culturally variable phenomenon, then Inuit movement patterns should correlate poorly with the integration values of streets in Arviat. Such a result would have important implications for urban planning in the Canadian Arctic.

REFERENCES CITED

Binford, L. R.
 |1978| Dimensional Analysis of Behavior and Site Structure: Learning from an Eskimo Hunting Stand. *American Antiquity* 43:330–361.

Bruce, J.
 |1969| Arctic Housing. *North* 16:1–9.

Childe, V. G.
 |1950| The Urban Revolution. *Town Planning Review* 21:3–17.

Conroy-Dalton, R.
 |2001| The Secret is to Follow your Nose: Route Path Selection and Angularity. Paper presented at the 3rd International Space Syntax Symposium, Atlanta.

Gerein, H. J. F.
 |1980| *Community Planning and Development in Canada's Northwest Territories*. Government of the Northwest Territories, Yellowknife, Northwest Territories.

Hillier, B.
 |1996| *Space is the Machine: A Configurational Theory of Architecture*. Cambridge University Press, Cambridge.

Hillier, B., and J. Hanson
 |1984| *The Social Logic of Space*. Cambridge University Press, Cambridge.

Hillier, B., A. Penn, J. Hanson, T. Grajewski, and J. Xu
 |1993| Natural Movement: Or, Configuration and Attraction in Urban Pedestrian Movement. *Environment and Planning B: Planning and Design* 20:29–66.

Lèvi-Strauss, C.
 |1963| *Structural Anthropology*. Translated by C. Jacobson, and B. G. Schoepf. Basic Books, New York.

Penn, A., B. Hillier, D. Bannister, and J. Xu
 |1998| Configurational Modeling of Urban Movement Networks. *Environment and Planning B: Planning and Design* 25:59–84.

Peponis, J., C. Ross, and M. Rashid
 |1997| The Structure of Urban Space, Movement and Co-presence: The Case of Atlanta. *Geoforum* 28(3–4):341–358.

Rapoport, A.
 |1982.| *The Meaning of the Built Environment: A Non-Verbal Approach to Communication*. Sage, London.

Strub, H.
 |1996| *Bare Poles: Building Designs for High Latitudes*. Carleton University Press, Ottawa.

Whitelaw, T.
 |1991| Some Dimensions of Variability in the Social Organization of Community Space among Foragers. In *Ethnoarchaeological Approaches to Mobile Campsites*, edited by C. S. Gamble and W. A. Boismier, pp. 139–188. International Monographs in Prehistory, Ann Arbor.

ARCHITECTURAL VARIABILITY IN THE MAYA LOWLANDS OF THE LATE CLASSIC PERIOD: A RECENT PERSPECTIVE ON ANCIENT MAYA CULTURAL DIVERSITY

Martin Lominy

Martin Lominy, Department of Education, McCord Museum of Canadian History, 690 Sherbrooke Street West, Montreal, Quebec H3A 1E9, Canada.

ABSTRACT

This experimental work of archaeology is an attempt to compensate for theoretical and methodological shortcomings in the study of Maya architecture. Beginning with the assumption that the different monumental architectures of the Maya lowlands have evolved from a common domestic prototype to reach a peak of complexity and variability in the Late Classic period (A.D. 600–900), it is proposed that the architectural diversification went beyond form and function, and reflects more than regional adaptations and traditions tied to a political-religious system. A structural analysis of the architecture of four regionally important sites (Tikal, Copán, Palenque, Uxmal), combining Chomsky's generative grammar and Lévi-Strauss' structuralism, demonstrates by differences in organizational principles that the variability could also extend to a conceptual structure and reflect deep cultural differences. Moreover, it is suggested that this variability could transfer to other forms of behaviour.

To this day, the study of Maya monumental architecture has mostly focused on its function. Typically Maya architecture has been considered has an adaptive response to an environmental and social context. While some have focused on ecology and systemic analysis suggesting subsistence strategies (e.g., Rathje 1971) and others on energy and quantitative analysis suggesting economic processes (e.g., Abrams 1989, 1994, 1998; Scarborough 1994), most have focused on cosmology and spatial analysis suggesting ideological schemes (e.g., Ashmore 1986, 1989, 1991, 1992; Freidel 1981; Freidel and Schele 1988a, 1988b; Fash 1998; Hansen 1998; Marcus 1973, 1976, 1993; Miller 1998). According to the latter approach, monumental architecture is a material component of a symbolic system and a visual media of social reinforcement of worldview. This political-religious perspective has been applied to other Mesoamerican contexts (e.g., Aveni 1975; Flannery and Marcus 1976; Fritz 1978; Gillespie 1989; Pollard 1991; Sarro 1991). It is through this perspective that ancient Maya architecture has been mostly approached for the past 25 years. Given the number of similarities between the regional architecture and arts of the Classic Maya, it is assumed that the Maya civilization shared a common political-religious system. Although significant regional differences in architecture have always been noted, they have so far remained undefined and set aside as styles to favour a unifying view of Maya culture.

This paper is an overview of my master's thesis (Lominy 2001a; see also Lominy 2001b, 2001c) in which I will briefly discuss my attempt to define the regional differences in Maya monumental architecture in the Late Classic period (A.D. 600–900) and interpret them in a meaningful way. How could these differences be systematically analyzed and what framework could be used to interpret them? Wanting to depart from the political-religious perspective, I have come to realize the underexploited potential of structuralism. This controversial approach, inspired by linguistics and adapted to culture (e.g., Casson 1981; Colby 1975), has been applied to architecture since the 1970s using the concept of grammar (e.g., Hanson and Hillier 1982; Hillier and Hanson 1984) although it has been limited to historical archaeology and domestic architecture (e.g., Carter 1980; Deetz 1977; Glassie 1975; Hugh-Jones 1979; Kent 1984; Sutro and Downing 1988). Applications of this approach to Maya monumental architecture have been rare (e.g., Andrews 1975). Structuralism provides two powerful tools that have been used in this study: a method of analysis

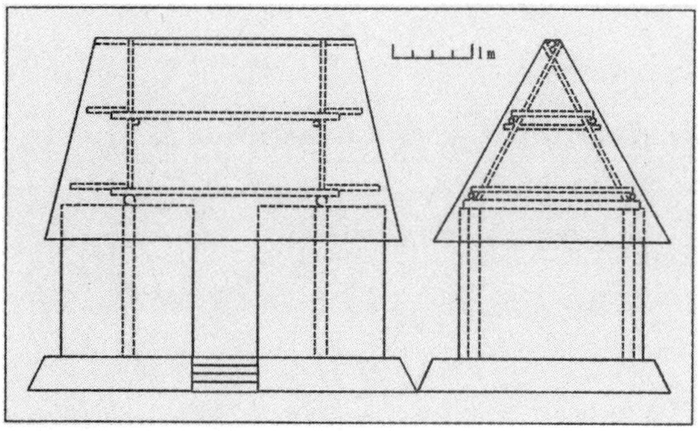

Figure 1. Plans of the Maya hut (showing only the main components).

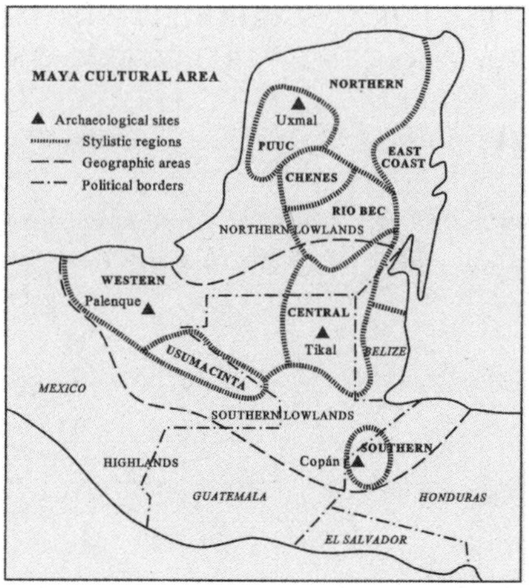

Figure 2. Main stylistic regions of Classic Maya monumental architecture (after Pollock 1965).

(structural analysis) and an interpretive model (culture as structure) allowing inferences about mentality from behaviour. It is assumed that architecture, as a material expression of a form of behaviour, has an underlying conceptual structure that is said to be born from a creative psychological process of categorization and association. Structuralism should not be confused with structuration (e.g., Donley-Reid 1990; Giddens 1979), structural Marxism (e.g., Althusser 1965; Leone 1988) and other forms of structural analysis (e.g., Ashmore 1989, 1991, 1992) whose objective is to interpret power relations rather than cultural structures.

Two studies of domestic architecture have used a peculiar but very promising type of structural analysis combining principles from linguist Noam Chomsky's generative grammar (1965) and anthropologist Claude Lévi-Strauss' structural anthropology (1958). One author, Henry Glassie (1975), analyzed eighteenth-century Virginian architecture by constructing an architectural grammar to account for building rules and then inferred from this grammar a diagram of principles based, using Lévi-Strauss' principle, on binary oppositions and representing decision-making in the mind of the architect. Greatly inspired by this pioneering work, I have modified the method to analyze ancient Maya monumental architecture. While Glassie built a single grammar using Chomsky's principle of basic rules (invariable rules) and transformation rules (dependent upon context) to account for the building process and typological diversity, I have built several grammars to reflect ancient Maya architectural evolutionary process.

According to the prototype theory born from Frederick Catherwood's studies (1844), Maya monumental architecture has followed a multilinear evolution from common domestic prototypes (the hut and the patio group) to reach a peak of complexity and diversity in the Late Classic period. The grammars mentioned in this paper have been designed to reflect this specific evolution. The basic rules are represented by a grammar of the basic architectural form that is the hut (the most simple and ancient form dated to 1100 B.C.) (Figure 1), while the transformation rules are represented by as many grammars as there are styles of monumental architecture. For this analysis I have chosen four well-documented, very distant (250 to 500 km) and contemporaneous sites whose architectural differences are evident and could represent regional trends: Tikal in the central region, Copán on the southern periphery, Palenque on the western periphery, and Uxmal in the northern region (Figure 2). All of these architectures show great similarities pointing to a common root, yet they also show consistent differences that point to something more than aesthetics. This analysis is limited to the two main types of buildings representing both extremes in Maya architecture: the pyramid-temple (a vertical type of building) and the palace (a horizontal type of building). I have used available architectural plans along with descriptive studies, thus limiting our sampling to the major architectural complexes.

THE STRUCTURE

A structure can be defined as the organization of the components of a whole and the system resulting from the interdependence of the components (Pirson 1984:14). We consider two complementary types of structure: a functional structure which is a representation of what is observable (e.g., Hammond 1972:87; Marcus 1973:915) and a conceptual structure which is a representation of what is not observable but has been used to create what is observed (e.g., Glassie 1975:161). In this study, the conceptual structure refers to the concept of culture which must be distinguished from ideology, the former being considered as a generated abstract structure and the latter as a manipulated power structure.

Since I began this analysis with the basic form, I will use it to illustrate the process of analysis. The same process was followed for the regional architectures except where specified. The grammar will be described rather than shown for reasons of space. The grammar of the basic form (or proto-grammar) was divided into three categories: (1) the building components, (2) the annexed components, and (3) the interior components. The building components were then divided into four subcomponents: (A) the platform, (B) the walls, (C) the roof, and (D) the decoration, an added subcomponent in the regional grammars. For each subcomponent a set of rules (a, b, c, etc.) was described according to the organization of the specific components (levels, rooms, doorways, stairways, benches, etc.).

Since I consider both a functional structure and an underlying conceptual structure, I have used the grammar as the former to infer the latter using organizational principles based on binary oppositions. The binary oppositions represent choices in which one polarity is valued over the other (Derrida 1967). I compiled the rules in a table according to the different aspects that they regulate which allowed me to infer six recurring organizational principles (underlined) accounting respectively for arrangement (axes and alignments), form (shape and configuration), surface (area

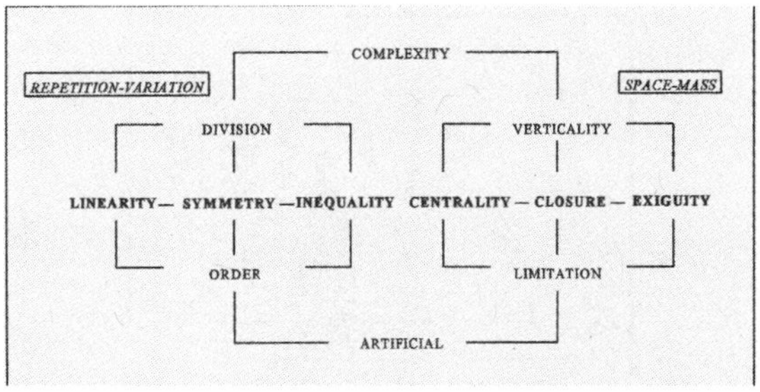

Figure 3. Conceptual structure of the Maya hut as basic architectural form.

and elevation), concentration (space and mass), restriction (accessibility and visibility) and dimension (space versus mass): *linear*/dispersed, *symmetrical*/asymmetrical, *unequal*/equal, *central*/decentred, *closed*/opened, *exiguous*/spacious (Figure 3). The organizational principles and their oppositions were measured using a geometrical logic.

Arrangement (linear or dispersed) was determined by verifying the presence or absence of axes and alignments. A common orientation of components indicates the presence of an axis (a linear arrangement) while different orientations indicate the absence of an axis (a dispersed arrangement). Buildings show a linear arrangement characterized by the presence of perpendicular axes (longitudinal and transverse) with corresponding alignments which translate into perpendicular components and cardinal orientations (north, south, east, west).

Form (symmetrical or asymmetrical) was determined by verifying the shape of the components and the configuration resulting from their combination. This was done by tracing two perpendicular lines through the centre of the shape or configuration and comparing the planes resulting from this division to see if they correspond. A correspondence of the four planes indicates a radial symmetry, a correspondence of the four planes in two pairs indicates a double symmetry, a correspondence of the four planes in two inverted pairs indicates rotational symmetry, a correspondence of two planes indicates bilateral symmetry, and a difference of all four planes indicates asymmetry. Buildings show a double symmetry and their configuration a bilateral symmetry by the transverse axis.

Surface (unequal or equal) was determined by measuring the area and elevation of each component

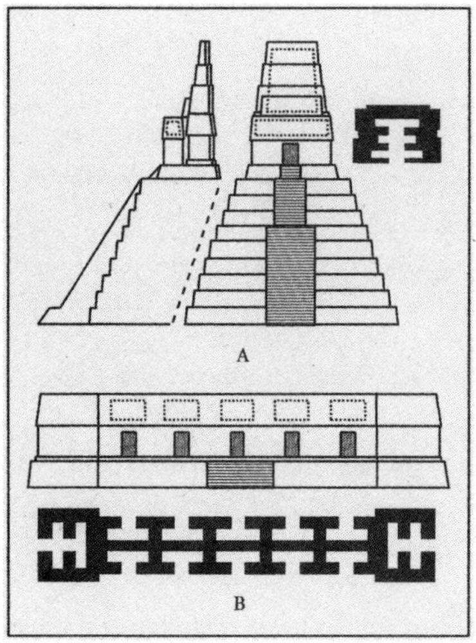

Figure 4. Example of pyramid-temple (A – Temple I) and palace (B – Structure 74) at Tikal, Guatemala.

to see if there is a correspondence between related components. Differences in area or elevation indicate an unequal surface while correspondence indicates an equal surface. Buildings show an unequal surface characterized by differences in both area and elevation. Adjacent components are unequal in elevation while superimposed components are unequal in area progressing by level from the exterior towards the interior following the longitudinal and transverse axes.

Concentration of mass or space (central or decentred) was determined by tracing longitudinal and transverse axes through the centre of each component and compare the axes of the different components to see if they are aligned. A linear alignment of axes with multiple intersections indicates a horizontal centrality (in the case adjacent components), a linear alignment of axes with a single intersection indicates a vertical centrality (in the case of superimposed components), and parallel alignments indicates a lack of centrality (a decentred mass or space). Buildings show linear alignments for adjacent and superimposed components which translates into a horizontal and vertical centrality.

Restriction of space by mass (closed or open) was determined with accessibility and visibility by measuring the ratio between spaces and openings (in the case of accessibility) and the ratio between masses and openings (in the case of visibility). A number of openings (such as doorways and windows) superior to the number of spaces (such as rooms) indicates a great accessibility while an opening area (doorway and window surface) superior to the mass area (wall surface) indicates a great visibility which translate into openness. A number of openings equal to the number of spaces indicates a minimal accessibility while an opening area inferior to the mass area indicates a low visibility which translates into closure. Also, acute angles contribute to closure. Buildings show a closure characterized by a minimal accessibility, a low visibility and the presence of acute angles.

Dimension of space versus mass (exiguous or spacious) was determined by measuring the floor area of spaces and the ratio between space and mass. A space whose floor area is minimal in relation with human proportions can be considered exiguous while a space whose floor area exceeds many times human proportions can be considered spacious. A space whose area or volume is much inferior to the area or volume of the mass can be considered exiguous while a space whose area or volume is much superior to the area or volume of the mass can be considered spacious. Also, insets contribute to make a space exiguous. Buildings that show exiguous spaces are characterized by minimal floor area and the presence of insets progressing bottom-up.

These measurable principles combine in general principles according to two universal interactions in architecture: repetition-variation and space-mass. The interaction between repetition and variation constitutes one block of principles characterized by the combination of symmetry and inequality that create an order by the repetition of planes and a division by a variation within the planes, to which is added linearity that governs the operation of symmetry and inequality by the presence of axes and alignments. The interaction between space and mass constitutes another block characterized by the combination of centrality and closure that create a limitation by establishing strict and tangible limits, to which is added exiguity that creates a verticality by governing the direction of centrality and closure. So verticality is not height but a predominance of height over width resulting from the compensation of the latter by the former.

These general principles (*division*/unity, *order*/disorder, *vertical*/horizontal, *limited*/extensive) in turn combine in global principles inherent to the system and common to other architecture. The order and limitation create an artificial aspect by contrast with the natural environment which exhibits the contrary, while the division and verticality create a complexity by contrast with any simple structure. With these two global principles (*complex*/simple, *artificial*/natural) we get a closed conceptual structure where all principles are interdependent and stratified according to their specificity (Damisch 1964:16–18). By interdependent we mean that a switch of polarities or a change of oppositions would result in a chain reaction creating a different system. By stratified we mean that some of the principles have priority over others when it comes to decision-making, the priority being given to the general principles. We shall see examples of that mechanism with monumental architecture that will show that, although this diagram is quite artificial, it does account for the observed reality.

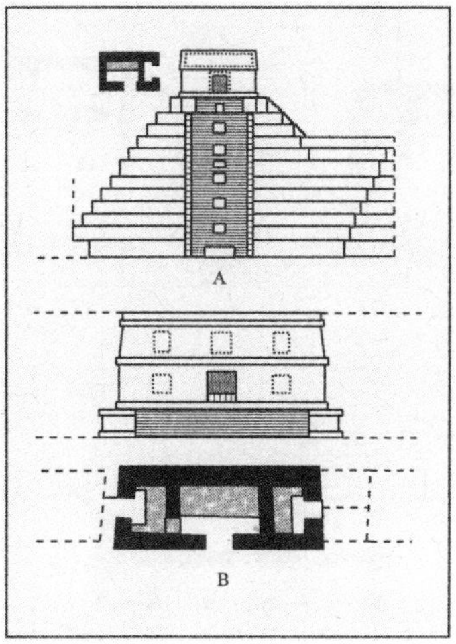

Figure 5. Example of pyramid-temple (A – Pyramid with the Hieroglyphic Stairway) and palace (B – House of the Scribe) at Copán, Honduras.

THE VARIABILITY

The analysis of the architecture of Tikal, Copán, Palenque and Uxmal has allowed us to establish clear differences in organizational principles. While the architecture of Tikal in the central region and Uxmal in the northern region share the same principles as the basic form, the architecture of Copán on the southern periphery and Palenque on the western periphery show differences as inversions of polarity. At Copán, the main inversion is asymmetry valued over symmetry while at Palenque, it is openness valued over closure. Naturally, these inversions involve others in the diagram like a chain reaction.

At Tikal, the formal transformations of monumental architecture from the basic grammar, due to its technical specificity, are quite minor when comparing its basic unit (a masonry vaulted room) with the basic form (a hut). In fact, it seems that techniques such as the corbel vault were specifically developed to maintain the basic form. The massiveness (or predominance of mass over space) of this architecture is typical of the central region. Contrary to western logic, its monumentality does not come from a modification and expansion of space but from an accentuation and multiplication of the basic unit where organizational principles are exaggerated and replicated, thus suggesting that they were highly valued (Figure 4).

At Tikal we can see an example of the exaggeration of principles also showing the stratified quality we have mentioned earlier. As in any other architecture, we can notice exceptional breaches in some organizational principles. This is the case of centrality for the pyramid-temples that have, as an exception, the forward projection of the stairway and the backward position of the roof crest that create a general backward decentering. Considering the extreme verticality of this type of building at Tikal (the extreme predominance of its height over its width), decentering was necessary for some components to be functional, so that the stairway would be possible to climb (60° instead of 70°) and so that the roof crest would not crush the arches (by being placed on the back wall). It would seem that this decentering is a structural compromise in favour of an extreme verticality that would be a predominant principle in the value system of Tikal's architects. Thus we can see how some principles can be exaggerated while others can be compromised, all principles being interdependent and stratified. So could we define, in terms of structural compromise, some traits of the architectural style of Tikal.

At Copán, the principle of asymmetry is an inversion since elsewhere in the Maya lowlands symmetry predominates. This inversion causes major modifications of the basic grammar. Nevertheless, this architecture shares a majority of principles with the architecture

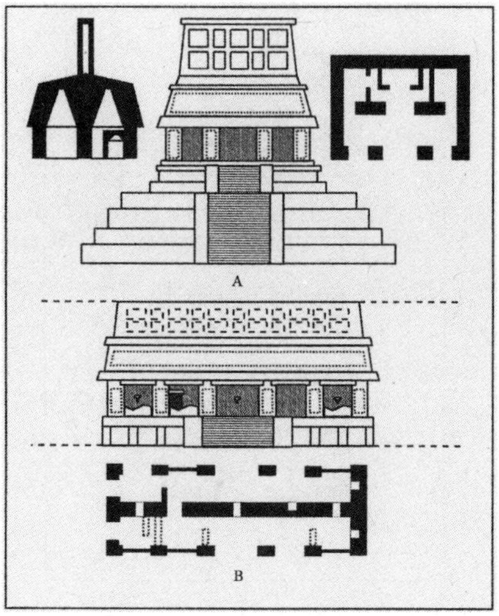

Figure 6. Example of pyramid-temple (A – Temple of the Sun) and palace (B – Building C of the Palace Complex) at Palenque, Mexico.

of Tikal thus suggesting a common prototype. The asymmetry of the components is due to their irregular shape (trapezoid, polygonal or indefinite) and that of their configuration to an imbalance of mass and space characterized by the presence of components (benches, doorways, rooms) that have no counterpart in relation to the building's axis (axis of symmetry) (Figure 5).

It has already been noted that symmetry is not very rigorous in Maya architecture (Kubler 1990:215) but, at Copán, the asymmetry of the components goes beyond calculation mistakes and the asymmetry of their configuration indicates a calculated principle. Hence, the asymmetry of this architecture appears as a lack of interest for the symmetry of components and as a principle that is the asymmetrical assemblage of masses and spaces according to specific and limited rules. While the principle of asymmetry is confirmed by the predictability of the configurations, the lack of interest for symmetry seems to be confirmed by the absence of a polygon model leading us to think that the observed polygons are skewed rectangles, and by the deliberate use of mud as mortar instead of limestone which saves energy but causes a progressive dislocation of joints and, consequently, a deformation of shape.

Within the conceptual structure, the switch to asymmetry causes other switches from order to disorder and artificial to natural. Although these general principles are more debatable, we suggest those changes using in part the observations of others whose studies also qualify this architecture as "flexible" (Gendrop 1974:58–59) and "organic" (Webster 1989:12–13) based on its structure and development.

Like Tikal, we can notice exaggerations and breaches in some organizational principles that exemplify their mechanism. It is again the case of centrality for the palaces that have as an exception the decentering of the floor and interior doorways. Considering the extreme limitation of the rooms created by the benches (that occupy more than half of the space), the floor and the interior doorways had to be decentred to be functional, so that the floor would not be reduced to a narrow central corridor and so that the inner doorways would not be blocked by the benches. It would seem that this decentering is a compromise in favour of an extreme limitation of space. Hence, this limitation would be at Copán what verticality is at Tikal.

At Palenque, the differences in organizational principles are marked by a predominance of openness over closure that also involves major modifications of the basic grammar. It does, however, share a majority of principles with the other regional architectures. It has long since been noted that the distinctive quality of Palenque's architecture is its "airiness" (Gendrop 1974:53) and "lightness" (Kubler 1990:221). In fact, the openness of buildings is due to a great accessibility by a number of doorways greater than the number of rooms (including doorways in the shorter walls) and a great visibility by an opening area superior to the wall area (including the presence of windows) (Figure 6). This principle of openness is expressed by the presence other elements unique to the western region such as aqueducts, underground passages, crypts, numerous niches and decorative perforations.

As we saw previously, the switch of a single principle causes a chain reaction within the conceptual structure. In this case, the switch to openness causes other switches from limited to extensive and artificial to natural. The predominance of these general principles is supported in part by the sculptural style exhibited on the buildings. The sculptural art of Palenque is not limited to specific areas as elsewhere but extended all on buildings as murals. This may explain the apparent lack of interest in stelae, which are absent at the site. It is also very natural in portraying people and activities in a framed style as if looking into a building through a doorway (Miller 2004a).

The openness of buildings involved not only the modification of the basic grammar but also new construction techniques that can be summarized as making the components lighter, such as the roof and its crest, which had to be supported by weaker walls (Gendrop 1974:53). The multiple perforations of the roof crest made it light enough to set it on the central wall, which could not be done at Tikal because of its weight. The double slope and niches of the roof allowed for the reduction of wall thickness and the predominance of room space over wall mass, while at Tikal the weight of the roof required massive walls. Making the roof and its crest lighter allowed for the multiplication and enlargement of openings in the walls and the elimination of some lateral walls to create longer rooms or corridors. In this matter, while Tikal's architects were creating mass, those of Palenque were creating space, reducing mass to a supportive core.

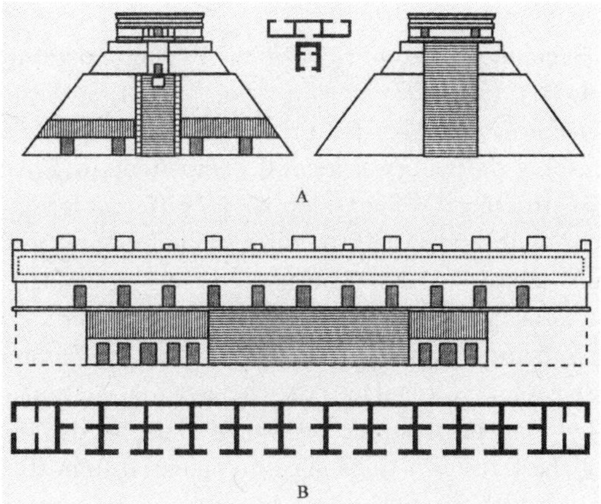

Figure 7. Example of pyramid-temple (A – Pyramid of the Dwarf) and palace (B – Northern building of the Nunnery) at Uxmal, Mexico.

As is the case with Tikal, the architecture of Uxmal is a structural accentuation and multiplication of those principles existing in the basic form with minor grammatical changes due to its functions. However, it has been noticed that the symmetry of Uxmal's architecture was governed by a geometrical assemblage of architectural components (Figure 7). According to Stierlin (1981), this would imply standardization and chain work, thus distinguishing Uxmal's symmetry from the symmetry elsewhere. Nothing more needs to be said about this site for the purposes of this discussion.

DISCUSSION

What do the architectural differences represent in cultural terms? Using structuralist theory, I suggest that these organizational principles expressed in spatial organization part of a mental template regulating many forms of behaviour, like a mindset ordering material culture.

Support for that idea comes from James Deetz (1977) who compared Glassie's architectural principles to other forms of New England material culture and discovered a correlation in spatial organization. Similarly, I have attempted to apply my organizational principles to another level of architecture differing from building structure in constraints and functions: building grouping. If the same principles are found in building groupings as in buildings themselves in spite of such differences, there would be a possibility that they are independent of material and functional factors, and could apply to other forms of behaviour. As a result of this line of inquiry, I found the same principles in building grouping. Although we cannot be certain of the psychological mechanisms involved, I can propose some ideas based on the theories of generative grammar and structural anthropology.

First, we turn to Chomsky's generative grammar (1965, 1968) to suggest a model: competence + context = performance. Competence is the knowledge that an individual possesses, while the context is the conditions in which he uses that knowledge. Performance is the expression of the dialectic between competence and context. The difference between competence and performance can be seen as a distinction between an internal system of knowledge (Goodenough 1971) and an external system of communication (Geertz 1973). Although this model refers to competence and performance as grammar and behaviour, the same principle can be extended to an abstract level considering the conceptual structure as an internal system of knowledge corresponding to the valued principles and as an external system of communication existing in the expression of the grammar. Hence, the conceptual structure would be a system of values acting as a reference in the composition of rules (Hodder 1989a, 1989b) and as a mediator in communication with the outside world (Giddens 1979, 1982).

Second, we turn to Lévi-Strauss' structural anthropology (1958, 1973) to suggest a concept: structural transformation. We use this concept in its general sense as the reorganization of components to create new structures. We consider that for different forms of behaviour conceptual structures would be transformations rather than homologies. Since the principles of our conceptual structures are associated according to architectural grammars, we can imagine a variation of associations to regulate other behavioural grammars. The conceptual structures would thus be dynamic but the transformations must be operated from static units which are the valued principles. These principles would be basis of the conceptual structure until a decision is made to change the values.

Now what do these architectural differences mean in historical terms? Following Glassie's method, we sought the meaning of the architectural variability in the historical record. Using current interpretations of hieroglyphic inscriptions, I have been able to establish some correlations. While the variability can be attributed to a common cause, the structural consequences are site specific.

We know that the architectural diversification occured during a period of unprecedented cultural development visible throughout the material culture of the Maya lowlands. So what motivated the cultural development that led to regional modifications of traditional forms? First, my analysis shows that during the Late Classic period some regional groups adopted new organizational principles, relative to what prevailed elsewhere, which were expressed in architectural innovations and maintained for several generations as inherited traditions. What is interesting is that these groups are located on the periphery suggesting that they were sufficiently close to other cultures or sufficiently distant from the cultural core to develop independent traditions. Second, the historical record shows that during the same period kingdoms were competing for power and engaging in warfare with an increasing intensity (Sharer 1994:211). This correlation between the diversification of architecture and the intensification of warfare suggests a relation of interdependence between political competition and cultural development. It has even been argued that city states and ruling elites developed from competition and warfare (Sharer 1994:143). To illustrate this idea, I will examine the case of Palenque.

At Palenque, the change of principle from closure to openness probably began in the second half of the seventh century with the ruler Pakal, who took over the throne after the city had been destroyed in A.D. 599 and the royal dynasty exterminated in A.D. 611 by attacks from the city of Calakmul. He introduced this principle in the construction of the Palace and the Temple of Inscriptions which together as royal residence and funerary temple became the core of the city. His eldest son Kan Bahlam, who inherited the throne in A.D. 683, maintained the principle in the construction of the Triad, composed of the Temple of the Sun, the Temple of the Cross and the Temple of the Foliated Cross, by which he legitimized his royal position. His brother Kan Chitam inherited the throne in A.D. 702 and perfected the principle with new compositions such as the Palace tower. At the end of the eighth century, construction projects ended permanently as did the royal dynasty and the architectural tradition of Palenque.

What motivated Pakal to establish a new principle? And what motivated his descendants to maintain and even perfect it? Because Palenque was efficiently destroyed, Pakal had the opportunity to recreate it. And because Palenque was repeatedly attacked by other kingdoms threatening its independence, Pakal would have been motivated to consolidate his reign by distinguishing himself and revitalizing the kingdom. The best way to achieve greatness without military success was innovation and the best place to start was monumental architecture. His revolutionary design was probably acceptable there more than elsewhere because of the peripheral location of the city, which might have had more cultural independence. His sons probably maintained the principle to reaffirm the greatness of their father during their reign and perfected it to make their own contribution to what became a tradition.

But why was openness favoured rather than any other principle? We know that Palenque had diplomatic relations with other kingdoms. We can therefore assume that Pakal was aware of other architectural achievements. It is possible that the choice of openness as a dominant principle was influenced by its absence elsewhere. There was no better solution to achieve distinction and revitalization than to create something contrary to what existed elsewhere. In fact, the architecture of Palenque is the perfect opposite of Calakmul which follows the tradition of the central region in its massiveness. Pakal would have achieved his political objective not only by breaking with tradition but also by defying the competition. Since smaller kingdoms often replicated the distinctive features of more successful kingdoms (Kubler 1990:230–231), we can imagine that his revolutionary design would later have been adopted by neighbouring kingdoms, thus explaining architectural similarities at Toniná.

Alternatively, others see environmental factors as an explanation for architectural design. Since the western periphery receives the most rainfall in the lowlands, it has been suggested that longer periods spent indoors inspired the creation of larger spaces (Miller 2004b). This idea implies that the innovations were motivated by comfort and conceived for improvement. However, we see two problems with this idea. First, it assumes that larger spaces were considered to be more comfortable while centuries of architecture demonstrate that exiguity was considered to be ideal. Second, rooms are not larger than elsewhere, it is the walls that are thinner and the doorways that are wider. The openness is a reversal of ratio between space and mass, not a change in dimensions. It also involves an extension of space by elongation and projection rather than enlargement. This is confirmed by the creation of corridors and the use of tarpaulins which extend space while maintaining exiguity. Hence, we consider these innovations as the result of creative expression rather than adaptive improvement.

The idea that the choice of an architectural principle such as openness can be cultural rather than environmental can be further argued. The fact that curtains were used extensively in buildings to close doorways and divide rooms shows that privacy was a neccessity. Curtains were the alternative to compensate for the openness of the buildings thus indicating that the principle was independent of necessity. Since the curtain holders are integrated in the buildings, they were part of the original design. This shows that a balance was established between openness as an architectural ideal and closure as a practical need. So there is no contradiction but a relation of priority. At Palenque, the priority was set on innovation.

However, some features have a purely adaptive origin which can be distinguished. At the end of the Late Classic period, there is a sudden closure in the architecture of Palenque expressed by the closing of doorways and the division of rooms with poorly built walls, so much in fact that the original symmetry was also disregarded in the process. This appears as a reversal of principle but was never part of an architectural design. It happened when the city was in a state of crisis or decline. Hence, this closure is not an architectural principle but an improvised strategy. It was apparently unsuccesful as the city was later abandoned. The same can be said of other lowland sites which show a similar architectural disorder during that period (Harrison 1985:95).

Beyond politics, creativity and achievement, the change of principle from closure to openness probably caused profound cultural changes. First, it could have modified other forms of behaviour in the sense that a change of perception could lead to a new conception of space. An indication of this may be found in the many contemporary artistic innovations (Miller and Martin 2004:199–236). Second, it could have modified communication in the sense that a change of perception could lead to a new interaction with the outside world. The relationship with people and nature would be regulated by this new conception of space. For that matter, it has been suggested that architectural principles could transfer to other forms of behaviour through binary categories of communication such as human/human and human/nature (Glassie 1975:135).

A final issue that must be adressed is the extent of the variability. Since it was observed in monumental architecture, we can assume that it is representative of elite culture. Whether it extends beyond the elite is unknown, but it is reasonable to think that it does not represent the general population. Therefore, the principles that I have described are to be understood in the context of elite behaviour. Also, since I only analyzed the main architectural groups of temples and palaces, it may only be representative of public projects. Nevertheless, this sample was sufficiently homogeneous to argue the predominance of a limited number of principles in a large number of buildings and a variety of functional types.

CONCLUSION

In this paper, we have defined Maya architectural styles as grammatical transformations of a common evolutionary prototype reflecting a variability of structural principles. We suggested that these principles, based on binary oppositions, regulate architectural behaviour sufficiently to distinguish groups of people in terms of spatial concepts. We also considered that these principles could be part of a mental template regulating many forms of behaviour in relation with spatial organization. In the end, we hope to have contributed a mechanism to analyze architecture and its variability along with a theoretical framework to interpret it in terms of mentality, as well as some insights to further understand ancient Maya cultural diversity.

In the perspective of this study, the Classic Maya of the lowlands appear not only as a unified civilization using a common political-religious system and material culture but also as a mosaic of cultural groups with their own structural specificities and particular histories. The main problem of this study resides in the lack of cultural information and the methodology that we were limited to that was imposed upon the data. It is possible that the differences I have suggested reflect no more than Western and Modern criteria. One could wonder what the ancient Maya considered as a significant cultural difference (Harrison 1985:94). "But hypothesis and a bit of scholastic overreaching are better than nothing" (Glassie 1975:117).

REFERENCES CITED

Abrams, E. M.

|1989| Architecture and Energy: An Evolutionary Perspective. In *Archaeological Method and Theory*, vol. 1, edited by M. B. Schiffer, pp. 47–88. University of Arizona Press, Tucson.

|1994| *How the Maya Built Their World: Energetics and Ancient Architecture.* University of Texas Press, Austin.

|1998| Structures as Sites: The Construction Process and Maya Architecture. In *Function and Meaning in Classic Maya Architecture: A Symposium at Dumbarton Oaks*, edited by S. D. Houston, pp. 123–140, Dumbarton Oaks Research Library and Collection, Washington, D.C.

Althusser, L.

|1965| *Pour Marx.* F. Maspero, Paris.

Andrews, G. F.

|1975| *Maya Cities: Placemaking and Urbanization.* University of Oklahoma Press, Norman.

Ashmore, W.

|1986| Petén Cosmology in the Maya Southeast: An Analysis of Architecture and Settlement Patterns at Classic Quiriguá. In *The Southeast Maya Periphery*, edited by P. A. Urban, and E. M. Schortman, pp. 35–49. University of Texas Press, Austin.

|1989| Construction and Cosmology: Politics and Ideology in Lowland Maya Settlement Patterns. In *Word and Image in Maya Culture: Explorations in Language, Writing, and Representations*, edited by W. F. Hanks, and D. S. Rice, pp. 272–286. University of Utah Press, Salt Lake City.

|1991| Site-Planning Principles and Concepts of Directionality among the Ancient Maya. *Latin American Antiquity* 2:199–226.

|1992| Deciphering Maya Architectural Plans. In *New Theories on the Ancient Maya*, edited by E. C. Danien, and R. J. Sharer, pp. 173–184. University Museum, University of Pennsylvania, Philadelphia.

Aveni, A. F.

|1975| Possible Astronomical Orientations in Ancient Mesoamerica. In *Archaeoastronomy in Precolumbian America*, edited by A. F. Aveni, pp. 163–190. University of Texas Press, Austin.

Carter, T.

|1980| Folk Design in Utah Architecture. In *Utah Folk Art: A Catalog of Material Culture*, edited by H. Cannon, pp. 34–59. Brigham Young University Press, Utah.

Casson, R. W.

|1981| *Language, Culture and Cognition.* McMillan Publishing, London.

Catherwood, F.

|1844| *Views of Ancient Monuments in Central America: Chiapas and Yucatan.* London.

Chomsky, N.

|1965| *Aspects of a Theory of Syntax.* MIT Press, Cambridge.

|1968| *Language and Mind.* Harcourt Brace Jovanovich, New York.

Colby, B. N.

|1975| Culture Grammars. *Science* 187:913–918.

Damish, H. (editor)

|1964| *L'architecture raisonnée: extraits du Dictionnaire de l'architecture française / Eugène E. Viollet-le-Duc (1854–1867).* Hermann, Paris.

Deetz, J.

|1977| *In Small Things Forgotten: The Archaeology of Early American Life.* Doubleday, Garden City, New York.

Derrida, J.

|1967| *De la Grammatologie.* Minuit, Paris.

Donley-Reid, L. W.

|1990| A Structuring Structure: The Swahili House, In *Domestic Architecture and the Use of Space: An Interdisciplinary Cross-Cultural Study*, edited by S. Kent, pp. 114–126. Cambridge University Press, Cambridge.

Fash, W.

|1998| Dynastic Architectural Programs: Intention and Design in Classic Maya Buildings at Copan and Other Sites. In *Function and Meaning in Classic Maya Architecture: A Symposium at Dumbarton Oaks*, edited by S. D. Houston, pp. 223–270. Dumbarton Oaks Research Library and Collection, Washington, D.C.

Flannery, K., and J. Marcus
|1976| Formative Oaxaca and the Zapotec Cosmos. *American Scientist* 64(4):374–384.

Freidel, D. A.
|1981| Civilization as a State of Mind: The Cultural Evolution of the Lowland Maya. In *The Transition to Statehood in the New World*, edited by G. D. Jones, and R. R. Kautz, pp. 188–227. Cambridge University Press, Cambridge.

Freidel, D. A., and L. Schele
|1988a| Symbol and Power: A History of the Lowland Maya Cosmogram. In *Maya Iconography*, edited by E. P. Benson, and G. Griffin, pp. 44–93. Princeton University Press, Princeton.
|1988b| Kingship in the Late Preclassic Maya Lowlands: The Instruments and Places of Ritual Power. *American Anthropologist* 90:547–567.

Fritz, J. M.
|1978| Paleopsychology Today: Ideational Systems and Human Adaptation in Prehistory. In *Social Archaeology: Beyond Subsistence and Dating*, edited by C. L. Redman and M. J. Berman, pp. 37–59. Academic Press, New York.

Geertz, C.
|1973| *The Interpretation of Cultures*. Basic Books, New York.

Gendrop, P.
|1974| The Unfolding of Maya Architecture. In *A Guide to Architecture in Ancient Mexico*, pp. 44–82. Minutiae Mexicana, Mexico.

Giddens, A.
|1979| *Central Problems in Social Theory: Action, Structure and Contradiction in Social Analysis*. McMillan, London.
|1982| *Profiles and Critiques in Social Theory*. McMillan, London.

Gillespie, S. D.
|1989| *The Aztec Kings: The Construction of Rulership in Mexican History*. University of Arizona Press, Tucson.

Glassie, H.
|1975| *Folk Housing in Middle Virginia: A Structural Analysis of Historic Artifacts*. University of Tennessee Press, Knoxville.

Goodenough, W. H.
|1971| *Culture, Language and Society*. Addison-Wesley Modular Publishing, Reading, Massachusetts.

Hammond, N. D. C.
|1972| The Planning of a Maya Ceremonial Center. *Scientific American* 226:83–91.

Hansen, R. D.
|1998| Continuity and Disjunction: The Pre-Classic Antecedents of Classic Maya Architecture, In *Function and Meaning in Classic Maya Architecture: A Symposium at Dumbarton Oaks*, edited by S. D. Houston, pp. 49–122, Dumbarton Oaks Research Library and Collection, Washington, D.C.

Hansen, J., and B. Hillier
|1982| Domestic Space Organization. *Architecture and Behaviour* 2:5–25.

Harrison, P. D.
|1985| Ancient Maya Architecture. In *Maya: Treasures of an Ancient Civilization*, edited by F. Clancy, C. Coggins, and T. P. Culbert, pp. 84–96. H. N. Abrams in association with the Albuquerque Museum, New York.

Hillier, B., and J. Hansen
|1984| *The Social Logic of Space*. Cambridge University Press, Cambridge.

Hodder, I.
|1989a| This Is Not an Article about Material Culture as Text. *Journal of Anthropological Aarchaeology* 8:250–269.
|1989b| Post-Modernism, Post-Structuralism, and Post-Processual Archaeology. In *The Meaning of Things: Material Culture and Symbolic Expression*, edited by I. Hodder, pp. 64–78. Unwin Hyman, London.

Hugh-Jones, C. (editor)
|1979| *From the Milk River: Spatial and Temporal Processes in Northwest Amazonia*. Cambridge University Press, Cambridge.

Kent, S.
|1984| *Analyzing Activity Areas: An Ethnoarchaeological Study of the Use of Space*. University of New Mexico Press, Albuquerque.

Kubler, G.
|1990|[1962] *The Art and Architecture of Ancient America: The Mexican, Maya and Andean Peoples*. Yale University Press, New Haven.

Lévi-Strauss, C.
|1958| *Anthropologie structurale*. Plon, Paris.
|1973| *Anthropologie structurale deux*. Plon, Paris.

Leone, M. P.
|1988| The Relationship between Archaeological Data and the Documentary Record: Eighteenth Century Gardens in Annapolis, Maryland. *Historical Archaeology* 22(1):29–35.

Lominy, M.
|2001a| La variabilité architecturale dans les basses terres mayas à la période Classique Récente: analyse structurale de l'architecture monumentale. Unpublished master's thesis, University of Montreal, Montreal.
|2001b| La variabilité architecturale dans les basses terres mayas à la période Classique Récente: une nouvelle perspective sur la diversité culturelle des anciens Mayas. *Altérités* I:2. Electronic document http://www.fas.umontreal.ca/anthro/varia/alterites/n2/lominy.html
|2001c| Maya Architecture: Evolution, Structure and Diversity of a Civilization. Electronic document http://www.mayafiles.com

Marcus, J.
|1973| Territorial Organization of the Lowland Classic Maya. *Science* 180:911–916.
|1976| *Emblem and State in the Maya Lowlands: An Epigraphic Approach to Territorial Organization*. Dumbarton Oaks Research Library and Collection, Washington, D.C.
|1993| Ancient Maya Political Organization. In *Lowland Maya Civilization in the Eighth Century A.D.*, edited by J. A. Sabloff, and J. S. Henderson, pp. 111–184. Dumbarton Oaks Research Library and Collection, Washington, D.C.

Miller, M.
|1998| A Design for Meaning in Maya Architecture. In *Function and Meaning in Classic Maya Architecture: A Symposium at Dumbarton Oaks*, edited by S. D. Houston, pp. 187–222, Dumbarton Oaks Research Library and Collection, Washington, D.C.
|2004a| The Maya Court. Paper presented at the Courtly Art of the Ancient Maya Seminar, Smithsonian Resident Associate Program and National Gallery of Art, Washington, D.C.
|2004b| Daily Life in Motion. Paper presented at the Courtly Art of the Ancient Maya Seminar, Smithsonian Resident Associate Program and National Gallery of Art, Washington, D.C.

Miller, M., and S. Martin
|2004| Palenque: An Exemplary Maya Court. In *Courtly Art of the Ancient Maya*, edited by M. Miller, and S. Martin, pp.199-236. Thames and Hudson, New York.

Pirson, Jean-François
|1984| *La structure et l'objet: (essais, expériences et rapprochements)*. P. Mardaga, Bruxelles.

Pollard, H. P.
|1991| The Construction of Ideology in the Emergence of the Prehispanic Tarascan State. *Ancient Mesoamerica* 2(2):167–179.

Pollock, H. E. D.
|1965| Architecture of the Maya Lowlands. In *Handbook of Middle American Indians*, vol. 2, edited by G. R. Willey, pp. 378–440. University of Texas Press, Austin.

Sarro, P. J.
|1991| The Role of Architectural Sculpture in Ritual Space at Teotihuacan, Mexico. *Ancient Mesoamerica* 2:249–262.

Scarborough, V.
|1994| Maya Water Management. *National Geographic Research and Exploration* 10:185–199.

Sharer, R. J.
|1994| *The Ancient Maya*. 5th ed. Stanford University Press, California.

Stierlin, H.
|1981| *Art of the Maya: From the Olmecs to the Toltec-Maya*. Rizzoli International Publications, New York.

Sutro, L. D., and T. E. Downing
|1988| A Step Toward a Grammar of Space: Domestic Space Use in Zapotec Villages. In *Household and Community in the Mesoamerican Past*, edited by R. R. Wilk, and W. Ashmore, pp. 29–50. University of New Mexico Press, Albuquerque.

Webster, David
|1989| Introduction. In *The House of the Bacabs, Copán, Honduras*, edited by D. Webster. Dumbarton Oaks Research Library and Collection, Washington, D.C.

MAYA READINGS OF SETTLEMENT SPACE

Denise Fay Brown

Denise Fay Brown, Department of Geography/Latin American Studies Program, University of Calgary, 2500 University Drive N.W., Calgary, Alberta T2N 1N4, Canada.

ABSTRACT

Settlement forms and patterns reflect principles of social organization, and therefore potentially speak volumes to the archaeologist about past cultures. In this paper, an analysis of contemporary settlements in the Yucatec Maya region of Mexico is presented in which a local typology of places emerges. The goal is to identify the visible features on the settlement landscape which are meaningful to the present-day Maya, and to understand the basic messages that these features convey. It is argued that these types differ not only in scale, but also in terms of organizational principles. They are nested types but are interdependent in the settlement system. This has important implications for the present debate on the organization of the ancient Maya state.

Analysis of ancient Maya settlements is a routine research focus for archaeologists specializing in the region. This focus has been paramount as they reconstruct the rise of sociopolitical complexity, the emergence of states, the interaction of royal families, the interdependence of regions, the intricacies of ritual belief systems, and the construction of social hierarchies in the Maya region. Settlement systems carry abstract meanings for social scientists, as well as for the inhabitants of the region. They can be envisioned as a "field of power relations" (Gupta and Ferguson 1992:17) and as a key to understanding sociopolitical complexity (Cordy 1985:94), inasmuch as the existence of different settlement types signals the existence of levels of administration and decision-making institutions. It is for this reason that archaeologists are particularly interested in examining settlement differentiation, and the visual or built manifestations of social institutions and organizational principles on the archaeological landscape. Modifications in settlement form reveal changes in settlement function, and potentially societal or regional transformations.

Recently a major debate has erupted in the study of the social and political organization of the ancient Maya: did the Maya state follow a segmentary, lineage/kinship model or a centralized, hierarchical one (see Fox et al. 1996)? Marcus (1998) posits a "dynamic" model in which the social organization vacillates from centralized authority to decentralized, kinship-based organization in distinct times and places. For her part, McAnany (1995) perceives a contestation of powers between "kinship" and "kingship." Gillespie (2000) has opted to skirt the issues by proposing that Levi Strauss's "house" might best approximate the core organizational unit of ancient Maya society. It is proposed here that this debate can benefit from an understanding of present-day settlement systems in the region. What are the organizational principles underlying the settlement system of the Maya today?

The contemporary Yucatec Maya also make observations of settlement patterns in their own areas, and similarly understand social processes and interdependencies. In this chapter, I will attempt to recreate a reading of settlement spaces by some local Maya residents of the central Yucatan peninsula. The objective is to understand their own criteria for deconstructing settlement forms to reveal organizational principles and social systems.

While living in the Yucatec Maya zone of the central Yucatan peninsula, I once filled my van with friends to attend an event in a town approximately an hour's drive away. My intention was to elicit the opinion of my Maya friends about this theatrical show. One individual, Doña Ponciana Canche, however, was more

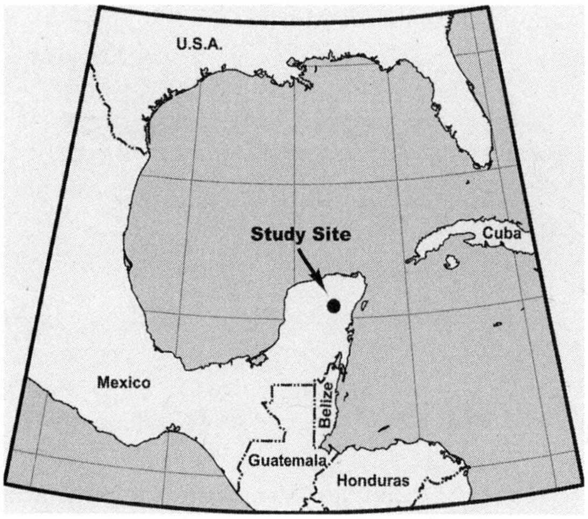

Figure 1. Location of the study site.

impressed with the town itself than the event. As she walked around the grassed central area of the town, she mused, "What a nice town." Doña Ponciana felt that it was like towns should be, she told me. It seemed to her that everyone worked in agriculture, and therefore there was little commercial movement; at the same time, the town felt large and prosperous because it was laid out in a grid pattern with straight streets leading out of a large central space. She remarked that many of the houses were made of stone or *mamposteria*, and that the houselots or *solares* were large, well kept and treed. It was as if she were reading a text. Unintentionally, I had introduced one of my Maya friends into a space which evoked her candid comment on the very theme that I was studying: the social and spatial correlates of settlement. Working back from her reading of this ideal town space, I attempted to understand the meanings of other settlement spaces in this area to the local inhabitant.

It may now be self-evident or banal to say that spaces are culturally constructed. This simply means that spaces encode meanings, and that the same space may evoke different meanings for individuals from different cultures. Research on settlements and settlement systems has often been conducted using criteria of organization and analysis which do not emanate from locally defined categories. In my research into settlement spaces in the Yucatan, I hoped to elicit these local categories, in order to approximate the understanding of these spaces from the Maya viewpoint, and to elucidate the social and cultural structures which generate the patterns observed. If cultural spaces, including settlement spaces, are constructed as in a sentence, I wanted to learn about that language – the morphemes and the semantics. A linguistic approach to the analysis of Maya spaces, particularly domestic spaces, was adopted by William Hanks, who focused on "personal positioning, and body metaphors in the linguistic and conceptual design of spaces" (Hanks 1990:86). While his concern was principles of "micro-organization" (Hanks 1990:88), the understanding of these spaces gleaned in this study seemed to refer to broader social processes and mechanisms. In effect, I wish to answer the question what are some of the "meanings" the settlement system conveys to the Maya of this region? The social and cultural generative structures ("deep structures" for the linguist) have been discussed elsewhere (see Brown 1993, 1994, 1995, 1996a, 1996b) and will only be summarized. This research material was collected in the early 1990s when I lived in the township of Chemax for 18 months to study settlement patterns and their social correlates. It is based on discussions, observations, diagrams and interviews with local inhabitants of diverse ages, genders, ethnic affiliations, occupations and residence, together with a reconnaissance of approximately 100 settlements in the study area. Return visits have provided the opportunity to gather additional details and to test some of the proposals put forth here. It warrants noting that the hypotheses in this document are routinely discussed with interested local people, to determine whether my abstractions have resonance among the people about whom they were written.[1]

THE TYPOLOGY

Chemax is a *cah*, or township, in the central Yucatan peninsula, Mexico (Figure 1). It is in the heartland, and I would argue is one of the last thriving metropoli, of the Yucatec Maya. Today, more than 95 per cent of the population of the municipality of Chemax are mother tongue speakers of Yucatec Maya. The census of Chemax municipality in 1990 documents 157 named settlements with 16,000 inhabitants at the time of the census, spread over an area of 1,000 km^2. The low density of the regional population means that each settlement is a discrete unit in the sense that it is usually separated by several kilometres from the next. The prevalent agricultural practice in the area is slash and burn. In reference to settlements, the people of Chemax showed great consistency in their use of the following terms: *rancho*, *cahtal*, *chan cah* and *cah*.[2] *Rancho* derives from Spanish, and the remaining three from Yucatec Maya. Although these correspond rather closely to size criteria, roughly from smallest to largest in terms of population and settlement area, in fact, they each manifest differences in principles of spatial organization.

Local adults commonly pointed out that the *rancho*s of the study area are of two types: *ranchito* and *rancho fomentado*. Both types of *ranchos* are settlements on private land holdings, which are not prevalent in the region. The local Chemax people, or *Chemaxeños*, recognize a *ranchito* as a cluster of one or two habitable structures, with no spaces defined by fences or walls near the dwellings. The structures are built of wood and palm thatch. *Ranchitos* are thus identifiable to local adults. The other type of *rancho*, the *rancho fomentado*, is also a small settlement comprised of a single or two related families, but manifests some evidence of capital investment, such as fencing, windmills, wells, corrals for animals, and often an arch on the entrance road or path. Another distinguishing characteristic is that the habitable structures of the *rancho fomentado* are constructed of materials more durable than wood and palm thatch, such as stone and mortar. Both types of *ranchos* commonly are involved in raising cattle, activities which leave visible evidence on the landscape, again prompting the identification of these settlement units as *rancho*s. Finally, *rancho*s are always accessed by private feeder paths or roads which enter at right angles from the public road or path. Upon entering, there is no feeling of a distinction between publicly and privately maintained spaces, and, in fact, the outsider feels that access to all spaces is considered to be limited. One would visit only upon invitation. This is private property.

If a local resident refers to a settlement as a *cahtal*, he or she envisages a small settlement with a cluster of habitable structures grouped around a natural well, or *cenote*. The *cahtal* can be permanently or seasonally inhabited by approximately 25 people. It is immediately recognizable by observing the house types and their distribution. The structures are always made of wood and palm thatch, and are distributed without apparent attention to orientation. No fences or stone walls separate the domestic units, although the areas around the dwellings would be expected to be cleared of low vegetation, leaving trees, some planted and some left from the forest. The economic base of the *cahtal* is slash and burn agriculture, so the residents have *milpas* in the community managed forest, or *ejido*, in the vicinity which will require their attention during certain periods of the year only. Therefore, the experienced Chemaxeño would detect changes in a *cahtal* according to the annual calendar. In fact, *cahtal* are the most common settlement type in the study area, but are usually not known or visited by those who do not live there. That is, although access by outsiders to *cahtal* is not formally controlled or limited, they are spaces really familiar only to the agriculturists of the region. Upon approaching the settlement, the Chemaxeño notes the type of access, as he or she "reads" the physical clues. Few *cahtal* are accessible by motorized vehicle, and the entrance is typically via a narrow feeder path which leaves the main path at right angles. Frequently, these path entries are difficult to detect in the forest cover, discernable only by the cognizant. These settlements are not located along the main path, but are accessed by these smaller feeder paths. Some of these paths are a short 50 m to the settlement, while others take the visitor a kilometre or more into the forest. Once arriving, entry to a settlement of this type requires walking through the yards of the residents, which are privately maintained spaces, perhaps to arrive at the *cenote*, or natural well, around which the settlement is organized. The Chemaxeño does normally not visit a *cahtal* unless to call on a friend or relative; otherwise, my experience taught me that these are rather uncomfortable places to visit since there is no defined public space. Where does an outsider with no friends in the settlement go? There is no designated or "appropriate" space, since all of the spaces in the settlement are domestic and privately maintained.

As in the previous example, the morphology of the entrance to the settlement is the first clear distinguishing feature of the *chan cah* settlement types, as compared to the *cahtal*. Here, the entry path leads the visitor to a large and well-defined publicly maintained space. Publicly maintained spaces are those which are not designed for domestic or exclusively family use only, and are not maintained by a single residential or family unit. Rather they are permanent spatial allocations, designed and looked after by means of extra-family organization. The residents of the settlement are responsible for them, and they are spaces in which visitors can be received without an individual or family commitment. In the *chan cah* settlement, the Chemaxeño visitor will note that the habitable structures are made from the same building materials as in the *cahtal*, and the activity areas around them are organized in the same way. However, a separation of the privately designed and maintained spaces from more public ones is notable. In fact, although the *chan cah* normally has a higher population than the *cahtal*, this is not the defining characteristic. The difference rests in the spatial design itself. The *chan cah* settlement manifests a salient morphological distinction over the *rancho* and the *cahtal*. This is a central space. This space represents a significant investment in time and energy by a community group in the delimitation and preparation of a flat central space, or *kiwic*, measuring approximately 60 m by 80 m, and outlined by stone walls of approximately 1.6 m in height. The residential dwellings are constructed around this space, usually facing it, behind the stone wall which separates the central *kiwic* from the yards, or *solares*. These yards typically measure two *mecates*, or 40 m, across the front; thus, approximately eight *solares* face directly onto the *kiwic*. Others are along minor paths running from the *kiwic*. Not all of the yards in the *chan cah* are bordered at the back by other *solares*, nor do they necessarily have a discernible regular shape. Therefore, a formal street layout would be difficult to discern. The visitor simply enters along the entrance path or road, which leaves him or her at the non-private space, the *kiwic*.

In addition to the large central *kiwic*, in the *chan cah* settlements one can expect to find a church or temple structure in the central area, constructed of the same materials as the dwellings, predominantly wood poles and palm thatch. The Chemaxeño's trained eye distinguishes this building from the dwelling structures by its larger size, the fact that it has only one door, and that the door opens from the end, rather from the middle of the long side of the structure, as is the case with houses. The visitor could expect to find school structures, and perhaps one unmarked small "store." Finally, a *chan cah* will have a baseball diamond, often in the *kiwic*. In all cases studied, the baseball diamond had originally been located on the central *kiwic* space. The defining and laying out this large space was the first step in founding a settlement of this type, and there is no confusing a *chan cah* with a *cahtal*, due to this urban planning feature.

The fourth and last settlement type in the region, as recognized by the majority of those interviewed, is the *cah*. Again, this is immediately distinguishable from the other types, and a Chemaxeño might comment, "*tac u pate be cahe*"; "this [settlement] has the form of a town." *Cah* settlements have a grid system layout of streets, which is formalized through the construction of stone walls which demarcate at once the streets and the domestic spaces, or *solares*. One such street funnels traffic and visitors from the outside directly to the main square, or *kiwic*. Here, there is no excuse for a stranger to walk through the *solar*, or domestic space, of a family, because these privately or domestically managed spaces are separated by low stone walls from other such spaces and from street spaces for public use. The *cah* settlement also is characterized by a higher proportion of dwellings constructed of durable materials, such as stone. For the local adult, this is clearly a distinct kind of settlement. The demographic size and type of services offered in the *cah* settlements imply an increase in the number and movement of strangers in the town. Behaviours and expectations are correspondingly different.

The *cah* settlement, as is the case of the *chan cah*, has the characteristic central large flat space called *kiwic*. In this central area also the church and the municipal government buildings are located, both built of more durable materials, relative to similar buildings in the *chan cah* settlements. School buildings are present in the settlement, although they are not always located in the central area. Neither is the baseball diamond, although, again, it was reported that baseball was played on the *kiwic* of all *cah* in the study area until recently. In Chemax, the major *cah* of the area, baseball is now played on a diamond about four blocks from the *kiwic*. The *cah* settlements in the study area are expected to manifest a notable increase in commercial activity of several types. First, there should be more retail commercial activity in the form of small stores dispersed throughout the settlement. Second, it is expected that there would be more commercial outlets, both retail and wholesale, most often run by non-Maya inhabitants. These residents and their activities are segregated to the perimeter of the downtown *kiwic* area (Brown 1995). Third, the *cah* accommodates the regional vendors, in a "moveable marketplace." Trade takes place along the street networks by itinerant vendors, in a form peculiar to the study area (Brown 1981). This type of goods exchange is not common in other settlement types. All of these activities, taking place in their appropriate spaces and characterized by particular spatial behaviours, are evident at first glance to the Maya visitor to the settlement. By observing and understanding settlement features, the Chemaxeño understands the nature of the settlement, and by "reading" this aspect of the landscape, knows the nature of the individuals, goods and services which are available there.

In travelling through the Chemax region with my Mayan colleagues and friends, I realized that each settlement we entered fit into a regional pattern for them; that is, on entering the settlements, the local people understood, on the basis of some of the visible elements discussed above, the place of the settlement and its residents in the overall sociospatial organization of the region. A regional landscape is constructed based on the political, ritual and economic placement of each settlement, and observations of the constructed spaces are meaningful to the local inhabitants in their interpretation of this landscape, at the same time as they corroborate the existence of the social institutions that generated the pattern. That is, in Chemax, the existence of settlement types evokes a complex interregional relationship of people and social institutions.

BRIEF ANALYSIS OF SETTLEMENT TYPES AND SPACES

In keeping with the linguistic metaphor, the preceding section identified some morphemes of settlement in the study area. In this section, some meanings of these morphemes, in their various manifestations, will be proposed. According to local informants, at least five factors of the visible constructed space of a settlement contribute to their "reading" of these places based on simple observation:

(1) means of *access to* and *size* of the settlement unit: paths, roads;
(2) *features*: presence or absence of houses, corrals, schools, plazas, etc.;
(3) the *materials* used in the construction of the features: wood, thatch, stone, cement, cinder blocks;
(4) the relationship between *publicly designed* and maintained spaces and *private* ones: houselots, streets, central squares, baseball fields; and
(5) the "syntax" or *sociospatial organization* of the features themselves.

What might the Maya observer understand about the settlements themselves, their residents, and the social organization of the region from "reading" these features?

Path access, as opposed to road access to a settlement, immediately indicates little commercial movement. All goods must be moved on foot; therefore, no retail outlet would be expected. Access along a narrow footpath which enters at right angles from a wider, more travelled path (called *noh be*, roughly translated as *large path*, in the study area[3]) suggests that only local inhabitants enter, therefore the settlement is expected to be small. A cross, placed at the side of the path, may indicate the crossing of the limits of the settled area, but high vegetation may obscure view of any structures. Local residents recognize a change in the arboreal vegetation, indicating a settlement area, although it may not be immediately known whether the place is settled at the time of observation. If the narrow path begins to dissipate into many, running off in various directions into the forest, then one has entered a *cahtal*. The dwellings would be dispersed around a water source, a single well or a series of wells, or *cenotes*, but it is unlikely that a single path would lead the visitor to this location. Rather the paths lead to the different houses.

The small demographic size of these settlements indicates that they are inhabited by agriculturists who have their fields in the vicinity, with no access within the settlement to goods and commercial services beyond those which are produced on site or brought in by individuals for their own use. The absence of physical dividers between yards or along paths seems to render the settlement a single inhabited space, suggesting a close social relationship among the few residents.[4] In sum, here there is only privately or domestically managed spaces, with a reliance on the family as the social institution charged with their design, organization, use and maintenance. The main economic activities are agriculture and home garden production, and the spaces reveal no apparent social differentiation among the inhabitants. The relative impermanence of the construction materials, wood and palm thatch, suggests impermanence of tenure of the houseplot and of the agricultural fields lying beyond the settlement (and not abject poverty, which is the meaning most frequently ascribed to these house types by outsiders). The *cahtal* settlement is a necessary feature in the settlement system of this region. It signifies the slash and burn agricultural activities that have been the economic mainstay of the region, but require movement over the landscape by the agriculturist. Because of their prior knowledge of the local settlement system, the Chemaxeño probably would assume that the individuals and families that inhabit the *cahtal* live there on a seasonal basis, carrying an affiliation to a township, with a central *cah*, in which they own, or strive to obtain, a more permanent dwelling. The spatial manifestation of this vital connection may be traceable on the physical landscape through the path networks, but otherwise is not discernible from within the settlement space itself.

In contrast, a more direct path that leads to a large public space may access a settlement. Here, the layout of the settlement seems more orderly; that is to say, there is an easily detectable plan. The space to which the path leads requires planning and organizing beyond the domestic or household group – it is a publicly managed space, presuming some level of communal organization and labour input for its design and maintenance. A settlement with these two features would likely be recognized as a *chan cah*. Although the *cenote* as the conventional regional water source is an expected landscape feature in the settlement, in contrast to the *cahtal*, it is not a defining morphological element in the sense that the settlement is built around the square but the square itself was not necessarily planned around this natural formation. As in the *cahtal*, the dwellings are of nondurable materials, which would be understood more by the absence of permanent land tenure than by the impermanence of the settlement itself and its inhabitants, as was the case of the *cahtal*. These are lasting settlement units, with a spatial infrastructure which indicates a level of community organization which transcends family ties. That is to say, social and political structure is more complex than that of the *cahtal*. Outside social institutions may be represented, and manifested visually in a church or school building. However, the local observer would note the absence of certain goods and services needed by the residents of the region. The *chan cah* lacks special public buildings and spaces that speak to local inhabitants of activities and social institutions that are essential in the region, but are only found in a *cah*, the township centre. These features may include such structures and institutions as the men's military *guardia* institution and related space, the annual ritual event and associated space, and the land holding institution and its centre of operation. A *chan cah* resident depends upon the *cah* settlement for these essential services, events, and associations.

A straight and wide entrance road, lined by low stone walls and leading directly to a central *kiwic*, is the first indication that one is entering a settlement of the highest regional order – a settlement which receives goods, information and people from the outside, and mediates delivery of the same from the surrounding region outward. The visitor finds permanently delimited spaces, roads and houselots laid out on a grid pattern. Most local Maya would recognize this settlement as a *cah*. Many structures are of stone and masonry, and the number of house lots and dwellings would suggest that the population is notably larger than in the other settlement types, although these dwellings may only be occupied on a rotating or seasonal basis. The buildings representing the outside institutions, such as the church and municipal government, are monumental in size and constructed of stone. This signifies to Chemaxeños that they are in a permanent settlement with formal land tenure with regard to houselots. This is the nodal town to the regional population – the town in which regional social and cultural institutions are housed. And these regional institutions underlie the regional settlement system. The *cah* settlement depends on the agricultural activities concentrated in the *cahtal* and *chan cah*, just as certain social and cultural institutions upon which the latter two settlement types depend are seated in the *cah*. The impermanence of agriculture and related settlements in the region is counterbalanced by the permanence of the dominant *cah* settlement. In fact, whereas the population of the former fluctuates and is in continual movement across the landscape due to the agricultural activities and technology, the population of the *cah* is relatively fixed; it is essentially comprised of the regional population. All residents of the *rancho*, *cahtal* and *chan cah* settlements must subscribe to the institutions there. Immediately upon entering a *cah* settlement, a Chemaxeño recognizes evidence of these institutions, including: (a) communally organized labour endeavours, particularly in the maintenance of public spaces, including streets and wells; (b) the civil control and protection institution formerly called the *guardia*, which calls on all "neighbours," or *eetcahal*, of the region, and requires their affiliation and cooperation; (c) the regional resource management institution, now called the *ejido*, through which all neighbours from *cahtal*, *chan cah* and *cah* are allocated agricultural plots in the forests annually; and (d) the social institution of *cha'an* which organizes the annual regional celebration held in the *kiwic* of the *cah*. Other institutions frequently represented in the *cah* are the municipal government (the *palacio municipal*), the non-Maya religious institutions (Catholic and/or Protestant churches), and the formal educational institutions (schools). The *cah* thus signifies for the Maya inhabitant of this region. It is the centre of region-wide decision-making institutions. This is the symbolic, ritual, administrative, economic and political centre. It defines the residents of the region, and allows them access to economic resources, ritual resources, protection, services and decision-making participation. All residents of other settlement units must have a township affiliation. Town affiliation means membership in a wider community, a more complex level of sociopolitical and ritual organization, and the Chemax resident is conscious of this.

The *rancho*, *cahtal*, *chan cah* and *cah* are the settlement components of the township – the *cah* in its widest manifestation. They form a system in which the settlements and their residents are interdependent. The large paths in the study area (the *noh be*) lead out from the *cah*, and the feeder paths mentioned earlier (sometimes called *ek be*, or ugly or black paths[5]), diverge from this main path, usually at right angles. Residents of the smaller settlements may also maintain residence in the main *cah* settlement. While they form a hierarchy in terms of their increasing size and social complexity, it is important to emphasize that the smaller settlements are organized through family and kinship principles while the *cah* settlement depends on extra-family principles of social and spatial organization. This means that they are different types of settlement, not simply settlements of different scales.

CONCLUSION

This paper outlines the defining features of a Maya typology of settlement; that is, the visible features on the settlement landscape which are meaningful to the Maya, and the basic messages that these features convey. It is argued that these types differ not only in scale, but also in terms of organizational principles, and that they are interdependent, thus forming a settlement system.

Adopting the urban landscape concept (Smith 1997), urbanization is best understood in context of the total system, and the interrelationship and interdependence of the settlements which comprise this system. The approach is not new, but recent advances do emphasize the nature of the articulation between urban and rural populations. In the Chemax area, it is clear that different settlement types exist in part because of different types of activities, and that distinct kinds of social and spatial organization respond to this. Agricultural settlements scattered in the forest use primarily family and domestic organization for spaces of production and reproduction. However, they are not self-sufficient. These resources are controlled through a centralized institution in the *cah*. At the same time, the *cah* depends for population and agricultural and forest products on the smaller settlements. Does the *cah* predominate? The *cah* hegemony was tested during the rebellions of the nineteenth century. During this conflict, much of the population of the peninsula stayed in the *cahtal* and *chan cah* settlements, abandoning their respective *cah*, each of which lost the political, social and economic basis of its hegemony. With the atrophying of the *cah*, family and kinship became more salient in the social, political and economic organization of the region. As the conflict ended, *cah* townships were restored, along with a kind of regional integration. This important finding in the study area lends support to the "dynamic model" of Maya state formation, recently proposed by Joyce Marcus (1998). A more detailed analysis of the relationship between community and family organizational principles and their role in the social organization of the region has been put forth elsewhere (Brown 1999). However, the evidence provided in this paper supports a model of opposition and balance between the forces of kinship and the forces of community (*cah*) in the social and spatial organization of the region. Segmentary and centralizing forces coexist in opposition, as family/kinship organizational principles confront community/state principles over the control of spaces and resources (Brown 1999).

The settlement system detected through the analysis of the settlement types in the study area throws a new light on some early ethnographic studies in

Yucatec Maya communities, particularly those of Robert Redfield and Alfonso Villa Rojas (Redfield and Villa Rojas 1934, Villa Rojas 1945). Redfield proposed a rural-urban continuum model, which placed distant small-scale Maya settlements in a spatiocultural "folk" setting, whereas the urban settlements represented a "great" tradition. It is interesting to note that the Xcacal Guardia site which represented the "folk" extreme on his continuum (described in detail in Redfield and Villa Rojas [1934]) was arguably a *chan cah* – a *cah* project in the making, rather than the family-based, self-sufficient and homogeneous isolated community needed for Redfield's model. It had a central area, with a ritual building and barracks. This was not a *cahtal*, although it is important to note that a *cahtal* in the region today could not be considered autonomous and family-based either, since it is tied into a settlement system with a *cah* as the hub. In support of this point, recent historical studies have revealed complex ties among the settlements of that region, emerging from the caste war period (Dumond 1997) – these were emphatically not small-scale, self-sufficient, autonomous hamlets. Furthermore, Redfield and Villa Roja's ethnography of Chan Kom purportedly documents a settlement farther along on the continuum towards the "great tradition" of Merida (Redfield and Villa Rojas 1934). However, in light of the results of the analysis presented in this paper, in fact it can be seen to document the self-conscious construction and emergence of a *cah* by a group of "separatists" through appropriation of forest from their original *cah* settlement of Ebtun, and the establishment of spaces and institutions appropriate for a *cah* including the central square, park and "satellite" settlements. That this "village chose progress" is clearly demonstrated by the strategic use of new municipal ordinances and structures to provide a legitimate basis for this *cah* within the formal state legal systems; that is to say, as separate from the Maya *cah* structures of rights and obligations – a hybrid *cah*/municipal capital set up by Maya men and their families. The folk-urban continuum of Redfield and the University of Chicago urban school has long been abandoned in terms of its utility in understanding the Yucatec Maya zone. However, this local typology of *cah – chan cah – cahtal* provides insight into a Maya settlement system that linked agricultural (rural) and institutional (urban) activities into a strong and integrated sociospatial system. It is important to note that this schema oversimplifies the settlement system, especially in terms of the mechanisms that generate and maintain it. Little attention has been paid here to the social and cultural concomitants of the system, with attention focused on material manifestations of the settlements. We have attempted only to explore how settlements convey meaning to local residents.

Doña Ponciana's observations noted at the outset of this paper betrayed a feeling of regret about changes in settlement forms in the region. She reveals a perhaps romanticized image of the towns of her past. Indeed, the last 25 years have seen a dramatic increase in commercial activities, and influx and growth of the non-Maya, or *dzul*, population, characteristically clustered around the main *kiwic* in the Maya towns of this region. This has modified the visual image of the towns in the area – there are more stores and dense buildings around the main squares of the Maya *cah*, obscuring the view of houselots and vegetation from the *kiwic*. Trucks with merchandise, such as Coca Cola, are a common sight. This kind of commercial activity also signals a growth of non-agricultural sources of income. In fact, wage labour has become much more prevalent in the region. Doña Ponciana remembers prosperous agricultural towns. Now she is seeing towns which depend on extra-regional income, much of it from the new tourist city of Cancun at a distance of two hours from the study area. Perhaps a new settlement unit will soon appear on the local typology. Indeed, temporary living in the *cahtal* agricultural settlements has diminished in face of temporary living on the outskirts of Cancun. In a certain way, the arrangement of settlement features in Cancun on the cognitive landscape of the Maya workers resembles that of the *cahtal*. Whatever the case, the importance of *cah* affiliation and subscription to the social, ritual and political institutions which are represented by visual and constructed spatial elements in the *cah* settlements, has not yet been superseded.

Acknowledgments

The research for this paper was partially sponsored by a SSHRC Doctoral Research Grant and the Regents of the University of California. The author would like to thank the people of Chemax township for their continued interest in this research. Comments by editorial readers were much appreciated and improved this paper.

REFERENCES CITED

Brown, D. F.

|1981| Marketing Patterns and Dependence in a Yucatec Mayan Community. Unpublished masters thesis, Department of Anthropology, University of Calgary, Calgary, Alberta.

|1993| Yucatec Maya Settling, Settlement and Spatiality. Unpublished Ph.D. dissertation, University of California, Riverside.

|1994| The Relationship between Space and Place in a Maya Town in Yucatan, Mexico. Paper presented at the 93rd Annual Meeting of the American Anthropological Association, Atlanta, Georgia.

|1995| Ethnicity and Constructed Space in a Maya Town in Yucatan, Mexico. Paper presented at the Annual Conference of the Canadian Association for the Study of European Ideas, Montreal Québec.

|1996a| Familia y comunidad en la definición del paisaje cultural maya yucateco. *Sociológica (Revista de la Universidad Autónoma de México)* 32 (sep–dic).

|1996b| La organización social y espacial de ciudades mayas: aportaciones de la Antropología Social. *Argeitsblatter*, Institut für Ethnologie der Universität, Bern.

|1999| Mayan Family and Community Spaces: An Interdependent Relationship. *Mexican Studies/Estudios Mexicanos* 15(2):91–110.

Cordy, R.

|1985| Settlement Patterns of Complex Societies in the Pacific. *New Zealand Journal of Archaeology* 7:159–182.

Fox, J. W., G. Cook, A. Chase, and D. Chase

|1996| Questions of Political and Economic Integration: Segmentary versus Centralized States among the Ancient Maya. *Current Anthropology* 37:795–801.

Gillespie, S.

|2000| Rethinking Ancient Maya Social Organization: Replacing "Lineage" with "House." *American Anthropologist* 102:467–484.

Gupta, A., and J. Ferguson

|1992| Beyond Culture: Space, Identity and the Politics of Difference. *Cultural Anthropology* 7(1):6–23.

Hanks, W. F.

|1990| *Referential Practice: Language and Lived Space among the Maya*. University of Chicago Press, Chicago.

Marcus, J.

|1998| The Peaks and Valleys of Ancient States: An Extension of the Dynamic Model. In *Archaic States*, edited by G. M. Feinman and J. Marcus, pp. 59–94. School of American Research, Santa Fe.

McAnany, P. A.

|1995| *Living with the Ancestors: Kinship and Kingship in Ancient Maya Society*. University of Texas Press, Austin.

Redfield, R., and A. Villa Rojas

|1934| *Chan Kom, a Maya Village*. University of Chicago Press, Chicago

Smith, M. E.

|1997| The Mesoamerican Urban Landscape from Teotihuacan to the Aztecs. Paper presented at the Conference on the Archaeology of Complex Societies: Centripetal and Centrifugal Forces, University of California, Santa Barbara.

Villa Rojas, A.

|1945| *The Maya of East Central Quintana Roo*. Carnegie Institution of Washington Publication No. 559, Carnegie Institution of Washington, Washington, D.C.

NOTES

1 I am sad to report that Doña Ponciana passed away two years ago, after having carefully guided my discovery of Chemax, and the places and spaces of her culture for 20 years. I hope that she would have recognized some vestiges of her complex understanding in my simple text.

2 Spanish and Yucatec Maya terms and spellings used in this paper follow local usage as closely as possible. Linguistic borrowing has occurred between Spanish and Maya such that terms such as *solar* (frequently occurring as *soral*), derived from the former, are now conventional Maya terms. Spelling of Maya words in this paper follows local usage (Yucatec Maya was transcribed using Spanish conventions early in the colonial period, and these are still followed in the region). For example, the unmarked *k* is the glottalized, while *c* the non-glottalized.

3 The Yucatec Maya term *be* can literally be understood as *path* or *road*, and is a term more generally known because of the identification in the archaeological record of wide, often raised, and frequently paved roadways called *sac be*, or white roads. The term *be* or *bel* is also used metaphorically as life's pathway, and the English question "How are you?" occurs as "*Bix a bel*?", or "How is your path?" The landscape and landscape features such as paths are salient at several levels of abstraction in the study area, as is discussed by Hanks (1990:310–311). The argument presented in this paper, however, limits its focus to material expressions of settlement spatiality and their interpretation.

4 Hanks (1990) provides details of *cahtal* ("*kahtalil*") settlements in his study area, in which he found that the social relations were defined by kinship, and specifically by "nuclear families related by descent

through the males" (Hanks 1990:96). In Chemax, although social relations are assumed to be close, they are not exclusively patrilineal and may not be kinship based.

5 Hanks (1990:311) finds five types of path, including the *noh be* and *ek be*. The others were not salient during the study of settlements in the present research.

SPATIAL ALIGNMENTS IN MAYA ARCHITECTURE

Annegrete Hohmann-Vogrin

Annegrete Hohmann-Vogrin, Faculty of Architecture, Graz University of Technology, Rechbauerstrasse 12/II, A-8010 Graz, Austria.

ABSTRACT

Monumental building groups in the core areas of ancient Maya cities are among the best examples to demonstrate or to understand the space creating function of architecture. Plazas, courtyards and causeways, platforms and terraces, are the constituting elements. An adequate documentation and analysis not only has to cover their specific spatial context, but also the structure of the continuous space created. The interpretation will have various aspects, insofar as the analysis has not been designed to answer only one question.

Thus there are physical aspects and there are cultural aspects concerning the social and symbolical milieu of Maya architecture. My concern in the past years has been on its physical aspects and the symbolical representation. These interpretations are revealing intentions of the ancient Maya behind the way they built their world.

The other intimately related question would be to explore how the built environment could have been perceived and the manner in which it could have affected society. Orientation, alignments, lines of sight, path and goal are most important in this respect. Methods based on a space syntax (Hillier 1996) – developed mainly on the background of the old European city – seem very promising for the analysis and interpretation of space in these "strange cities," as designated by Hillier, but these methods must be adapted and in some parts even invented anew to apply to the cities of the Maya.

> "The human understanding is of its own nature prone to suppose the existence of more order and regularity in the world than it finds" (Francis Bacon, Aphorism XLV, p. 50; cited in Hillier 1996:149).

Figure 1. Perspective reconstruction of the Main Group at Copán (Hohmann and Vogrin 1982).

The monumental building groups to be found in the core areas of ancient Maya cities are among the best examples to demonstrate or to understand the space creating function of architecture. Plazas, courtyards and causeways, platforms and terraces, are the principle constituent elements (Figure 1). Adequate documentation and analysis has therefore to cover not only their specific spatial context, but also the structure of the continuous space created. On that basis an interpretation may cover different aspects as long as the analysis has not been designed to answer only one question. An example of a comprehensive documentation and analysis of Maya architecture has been presented in a monograph on Copán (Hohmann and Vogrin 1982). Later the semiotic analysis has been developed further by the author – on the basis of Norberg-Schulz's *Intentions in Architecture* (1963). One of the results is a graphic representation showing the relations between

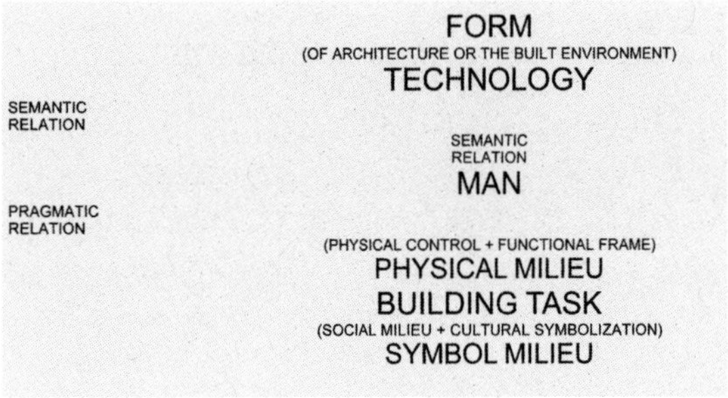

Figure 2. Diagram for a semiotic analysis of architecture.

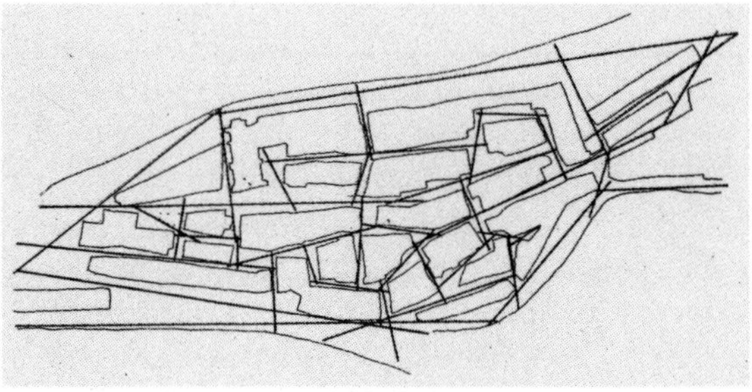

Figure 3. Configuration of urban space shown in an axial map. (Hillier and Hanson 1984:Figure 28).

man, architecture or the built environment, and the intentions creating it or expressed in it (Figure 2).

These intentions contain aspects concerning physical control and aspects of cultural symbolization. Physical control addresses the reaction of the built environment to the specific environmental conditions: heat or cold, flora and fauna, heavy rains, water supply, transportation resistances, and availability of building materials. It could be shown that the specific forms and layout of Maya settlements could be explained to a certain degree only through these facts (Hohmann-Vogrin 1998). In the same way the built environment can be also an expression of cultural symbolization, representing the specific world view of the Maya (Hohmann-Vogrin 2000). Both approaches explore the intentions guiding the activity of building the world in the way the Maya did it, and how this is reflected in the ultimate configuration of that world. In this field my conclusions have been drawn mainly on the basis of structural similarities supported by archaeological, ethnographic and epigraphic sources (Hohmann-Vogrin 2000).

The other intimately related questions address the effect of the built environment, that is, how it could have been perceived at the time when it was in use and if this can tell us something about the functional frame and the social milieu. We may assume that it is again the overall configuration that determines:

- the functional possibilities of a specific area, as this definitely depends on its position in the whole fabric, and
- the social milieu, as this is constituted by the potential of space to generate mutual awareness and encounter.

This approach refers to a theory that has been established in the last decade, known as space syntax (Hillier 1996). Bill Hillier has largely investigated the old European cities, or what he and we would designate as "normal cities." They are defined as variations of the following:

> Buildings are arranged in outward facing blocks so that building entrances continuously open to the space of public access. The space of public access is arranged in a series of intersecting rings that are regularized by a greater or lesser degree of linearization of space to form the – more or less deformed – grid of the town. Through this linearization the larger-scale structure of the town is made intelligible both to the peripatetic individual moving about within the town and to the stranger arriving at its edges. The linear structure links the building entrances directly to a pattern of space which also links closely to the edges of the town. The effect of this control of the linear organization of space is to create a structure in the "axial map" of the town, that is a distribution of local and global "integration," which becomes the most powerful

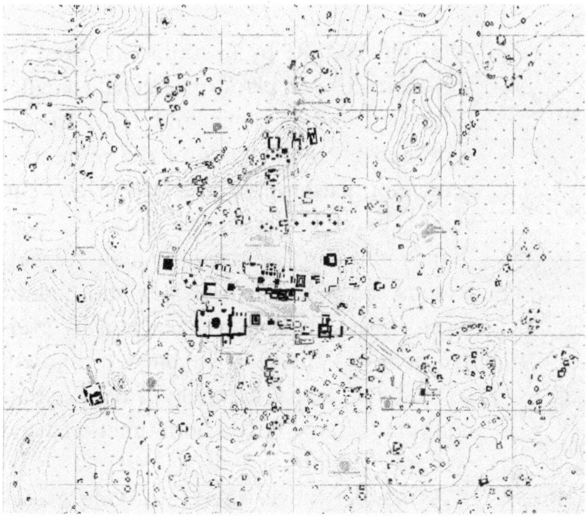

Figure 4. General map of Tikál (Carr and Hazard 1961).

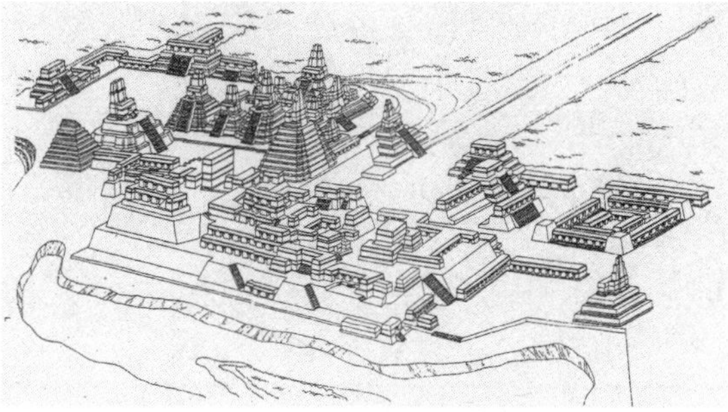

Figure 5. Perspective reconstruction of the Great Plaza at Tikál (Heyden and Gendrop 1975:Figure 112).

> functional mechanism driving first the pattern of movement and, through this, the distribution of land uses, building densities and larger-scale spatial and physical elements such as open spaces and landmarks [Hillier 1996:215].

An "axial map" shows all the horizontal lines of sight that pass the spaces and relate them to the urban structure as a whole (Figure 3). The relationships can be expressed through a value of "integration," which is a measure for the mean distance of a line from all other lines in a system. Hillier then concludes:

> The essence of urban form is that it is spatially structured and functionally driven. Between structure and function is the notion of intelligibility, defined as the degree to which what can be seen and experienced locally in the system allows the large scale system to be learnt without conscious effort. Structure, intelligibility and function permit us to see the town as social process, and the fundamental element in all three is the linear spatial element, or axis [Hillier 1996:215].

Hillier then compares these cities or towns with others that he designates as "strange towns" – cities or towns which do not conform to the rules found for "normal towns" – including amongst them the cities of the ancient Maya. He arrives at the conclusion, that in "strange towns," axes are not instruments but symbols, the spatial configuration therefore being rather more symbolic than functional (Hillier 1996:222). He refers *inter alia* to Teotihuacán with its single axes lined by monumental building complexes including the Pyramid of the Sun and ending at the Pyramid of the Moon. The isolated axes can only be seen as symbols expressing social power through domination and not as instrument guiding movement into the adjacent more profane parts of the city. He links the occurrence of this type of axis to societies "where the needs of social reproduction are dominant over the needs of social production" (Hillier 1996:232).

He refers also to Maya towns or "proto-towns" – following earlier scientific concepts, as Hillier does. Here it is even more confusing from his point of view. No global spatial organization at all seems to be present, apart from some causeways. These causeways never form a main axis, as it is the case in Teotihuacán, though the main groups in Maya towns are also constituted by monumental structures, the more everyday buildings adjacent but not connected. He refers to the map of Tikál (Figure 4) by Robert F. Carr and James Hazard (Carr and Hazard 1961), which indicates only the remains of stone buildings floating on the undulating terrain, shown by means of contour lines – a rough ground plan. For "normal towns" a ground plan might be enough to analyze the spatial structure, as people usually move on street level like in a system

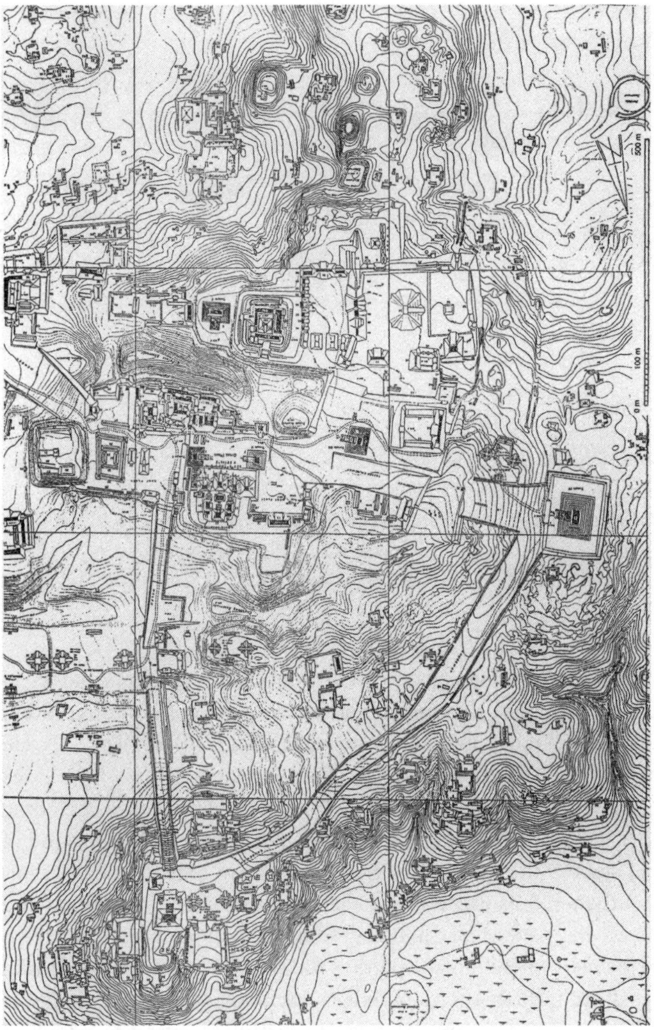

Figure 6. Detail of the general map of Tikál (Carr and Hazard 1961).

of channels confined by vertical elements. For Maya towns or cities using a ground plan alone is far too superficial.

Maya sites are like landscapes, their physical form dependent to a high degree on the environmental conditions of the tropics as I have shown elsewhere (Hohmann-Vogrin 1998). In contrast to "normal towns" there are no streets guiding movement through the city. Open spaces are constituted by plazas, courtyards, terraces and platforms on different levels, while interior space is relatively limited. Access to higher levels was obviously restricted. The stairways become narrower nearer to the top; sometimes they were even blocked off by overbuilding. Step by step, terraces and platforms become smaller (Figures 1 and 5). Sights and views are determined by the altitude of the respective terrace or platform. On the lowest level the sight is limited by walls and platforms taller than the viewer. Accessing higher levels widens the field of vision. On the highest level – presumably never reached by average people – the view becomes unlimited, so to speak. Social hierarchy is demonstrated literally here. This is both functional and symbolic (Figure 5).

As stated above, there are wide causeways mutually connecting groups of monumental architecture – as can be shown in the central part of the map of Tikál (Figure 6) – but they are mostly not confined by walls or buildings which might close off the view, defining lines of visibility. Therefore, they do not necessarily guide movement visually. In effect, in Maya towns or cities, there are no linear spatial elements or axes, which are the main constituents of "normal towns," so important for Hillier's analysis. Can the concept of "space syntax" then be productive at all? How can we start an analysis of these towns, aimed at drawing conclusions regarding functional possibilities or social milieu?

Addressing the question of functional possibilities, we can simply ask for the integration values of the different areas defining convex maps with an appropriate tessellation, to take into account the varying dimensions of the spatial elements (Hillier 1996:96). Considering their different levels would be necessary and would need some extension of the procedure. Analyzing the spatial structure of Copán, the author has made already an attempt to define accessibility and centrality of the different areas in the site's Main Group (Hohmann and Vogrin 1982:91) based on a method proposed by Norman Hammond in his work on Lubaantun (Hammond 1975:78–83).

Regarding the social milieu, questions of intelligibility have to be raised. But axial maps as usual cannot be derived at all as explained above. Intelligibility of the overall pattern, orientation and resulting physical movement are obviously guided by the varied heights of monumental groups which could be seen, and recognized by their specific character, from afar. The horizontal axis leading the flow of people in "normal towns" was probably not so relevant in this context.

Intelligibility was easy to assume, as buildings or masses of buildings usually showed a variety of different faces on each side and, despite the absence of symmetry in spatial arrangements, these faces or facades are often symmetrical, emphasizing a vertical axis with all its symbolic connotations. The absence of spatial symmetry or any other spatial order, which would be easy to recognize, once forced Hasso Hohmann and the author to start the mapping project in the site core of Copán in Honduras using terrestric stereophotogrammetry to get the exact position and shape of buildings (Hohmann and Vogrin 1982). Even though buildings or faces of buildings were frequently changed in time through demolition or overbuilding, continuously altering the way in which they confined the open space (see the comprehensive summary by William Fash in his contribution to the symposium at Dumbarton Oaks in 1994 [Fash 1998]), in one moment in time everything was there that can be seen now. This has to be the base as spatial analysis requires the complete coverage of the area in question. A careful analysis of the resulting site map (Figure 7) has shown that there are interesting spatial relations to be found.

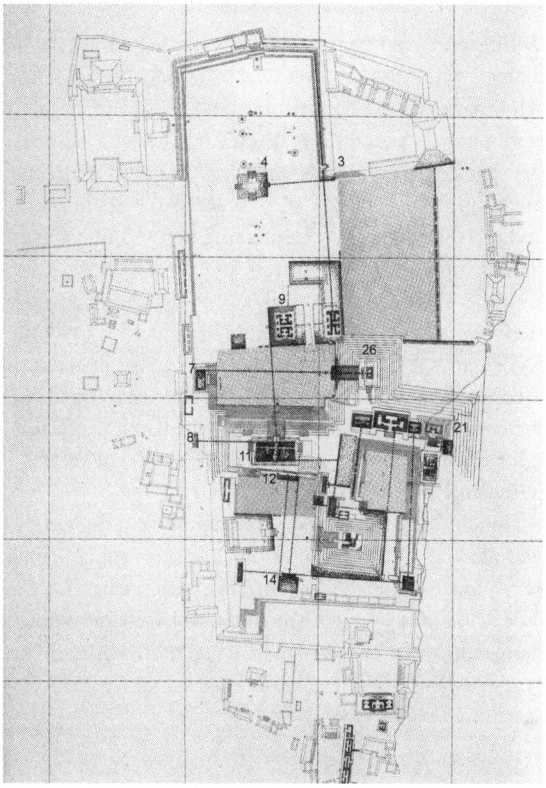

Figure 7. Map of Copán with alignments (Hohmann and Vogrin 1982:Figure 55).

The vertical axes ordering the monumental facades or faces of the masses are often emphasized through alignments with horizontal elements. As an example I would like to point to some of these relations in Copán:

- the edge of the western ball court building, Structure 9, is aligned with the axis of Structure 11;
- the edge of Structure 7 with the axis of the Hieroglyphic Stairway, Structure 26;
- the southern edge of Platform 3 with the centre line of Structure 4;
- the west court also shows interesting alignments between Structure14 and Structure 12, more like a stage but called the "Reviewing Stand," and
- the front wall of Structure 11 is in line with the axis of Structure 8 and of the small building adjacent to Structure 21.

Lines of sight are often established by the edges of buildings, where the outer face of a structure meets the ground. They are to be followed up by the eye to meet the vertical axes or other significant elements. Physical movement is therefore not necessarily governed by that means. The lines are symbolic – such as the one main axis in Teotihuacán. However, in contrast to that site, there is not only one axis or a main axis – there are many different vertical axes and horizontal lines showing a great variety of correlations.

We may conclude that even if axes and alignments here are mostly symbolic, the configuration of the built environment does not show a simple "order" which is usually assumed to characterize the symbolic content. Ordering along straight lines or aligning is a very basic operation that does not require knowledge of abstract concepts of space. It is therefore a very flexible way to constitute meaningful relations in the built environment. To align elements is a suitable means to govern the ordering of successive building phases that produced the aggregations of Maya centres. By alignments a new building or the new face of a building can be set into a relation with the then-existing architecture, the landscape and even with the cosmic realm – and thus communicate intention and meaning (Hohmann-Vogrin 2000). This belongs to the realm of symbolic representation. Regarding the social milieu the configuration of the spaces probably indicates more emphasis on gatherings and encounters in plazas and terraces than movement along defined lines, even though processions are often assumed to have been an integral part in Maya ritual. A comprehensive axial analysis of the spatial configuration could probably reveal, amongst other characteristics, more insights in the interaction of different parts of Maya society. Like the convex map, the axial map would also have to consider the differences in altitude to cover all relevant sights and views.

Concluding, I may state that configurational analysis following the ideas of Hillier's space syntax seems very promising in the field of Maya urbanism. But the procedure of the analysis must be invented anew since their culture is, as this can now be seen, different in every respect.

REFERENCES CITED

Carr, R. F., and J. Hazzard
|1961| *Map of the Ruins of Tikal, El Peten, Guatemala.* Tikal Report No. 11. University Museum, University of Pennsylvania, Philadelphia.

Fash, W. L.
|1998| Dynastic Architectural Programs: Intention and Design in Classic Maya Buildings at Copan and Other Sites. *Function and Meaning in Classic Maya Architecture. A Symposium at Dumbarton Oaks, 7th and 8th October 1994,* edited by S. D. Houston, pp. 223–270. Dumbarton Oaks Research Library and Collection, Washington, D.C.

Hammond, N.
|1975| *Lubaantun, A Classic Maya Realm.* Peabody Museum Monographs No. 2. Peabody Museum of Archaeology and Ethnology, Harvard University, Cambridge, Massachusetts.

Heyden, D., and P. Gendrop
|1975| *Architektur der Hochkulturen Mittelamerikas.* Belser Verlag, Stuttgart.

Hillier, B.
|1996| *Space is the Machine. A Configurational Theory of Architecture.* Cambridge University Press, Cambridge.

Hillier, B., and J. Hanson
|1984| *The Social Logic of Space.* Cambridge University Press, Cambridge.

Hohmann-Vogrin, A.
|1998| Siedlungsform und Klima in den frühen Kulturen Mesoamerikas. *Nachrichtenblatt der Archäologischen Gesellschaft Steiermark (AGST)* 1998(1):49–58.
|2000| El espacio estructurado y la visión del mundo. In *Arquitectura e ideología de los antiguos Mayas: Memoria de la Segunda Mesa Redonda de Palenque,* edited by S. Trejo, pp. 35–54. Instituto Nacional de Antropología e Historia: Consejo Nacional para la Cultura y las Artes, México, D.F.
|2001| Unity in Space and Time, the Maya Architecture. In *Maya Divine Kings of the Rainforest,* edited by N. Grube, pp. 192–215. Könemann, Köln.

Hohmann, H., and A. Vogrin
|1982| *Die Architektur von Copán (Honduras). Vermessung, Plandarstellung, Untersuchung der baulichen Elemente und des räumlichen Konzepts.* 2 Bände. Akademische Druck-u. Verlagsanstalt, Graz.

Norberg-Schulz, Christian
|1963| *Intentions in Architecture.* Universitetsforlaget, Oslo.

ARCHAEOLOGICAL APPROACHES TO ANCIENT MAYA GEOPOLITICAL BORDERS

Gyles Iannone

Gyles Iannone, Department of Anthropology, Trent University, Peterborough, Ontario K9J 7B8, Canada.

ABSTRACT

Archaeologists have employed various theoretical models to determine the location of ancient Maya geopolitical borders (e.g., central-place theory, Thiessen polygons, gravity models, emblem glyphs, marching distances for warfare). The archaeological investigation of border centres has, however, lagged far behind the theoretical approximation of border position. This paper explores the sociopolitical and socioeconomic qualities of border zones. Emphasis is placed on how these geopolitical borders may be recognized on the ground, as well as how they might best be examined through archaeological means. The north Vaca Plateau site of Minanhá is used to illustrate the discussion.

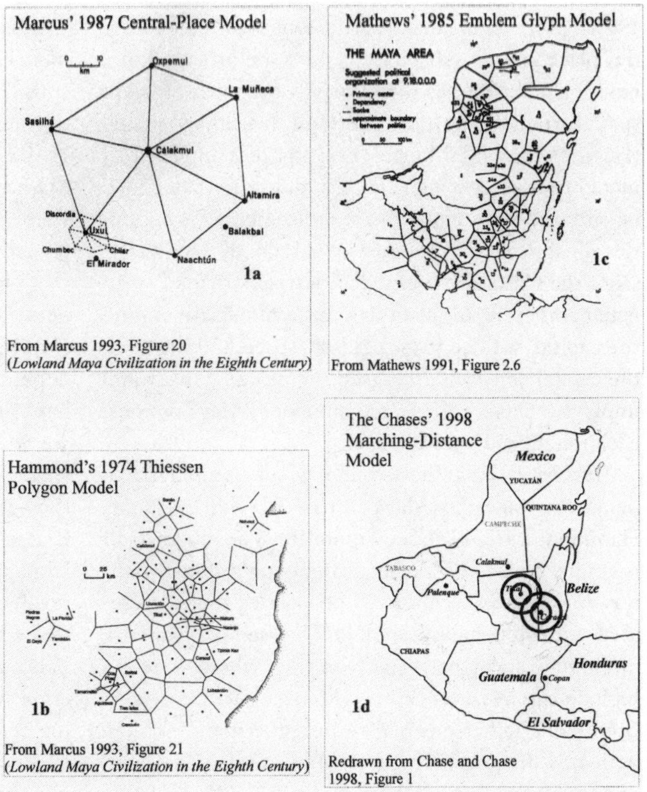

Figure 1. Models for ancient Maya territorial borders.

During the Classic period (A.D. 250–900) the Maya world was comprised of numerous competing polities, each of which would have been separated by a frontier-type border (see also Yoffee 1991:291–292). The size and number of these polities continues to be a topic of debate, with some Mayanists advocating a large number of rather small polities (e.g., Mathews 1985), others a moderate number of regional states (e.g., Adams 1990), and still others a few large "superstates" (Martin and Grube 1995). For obvious reasons, determining the location and character of actual polity borders is critical to the evaluation of polity size and character. This chapter aims to make a contribution to this endeavour by evaluating the models that have been employed to determine border locations, and through an examination of the nature of past borders as suggested by the ethnohistoric and ethnographic records. Using these criteria, the north Vaca Plateau centre of Minanhá will be assessed with respect to its potential role as an ancient Maya border centre.

MODELLING THE LOCATION OF ANCIENT MAYA GEOPOLITICAL BORDERS

To date, Mayanists have employed a variety of models to demarcate the territorial limits of ancient Maya polities. These include: central-place theory, Thiessen polygons, gravity models, emblem glyph distributions, and marching distances for warfare. *Central-place theory* suggests that regions will have a central place that serves the subsidiary settlements within its hierarchy, and which receives in turn goods and labour; the central place is the administrative, religious, and protective or military power for the region (Marcus 1993:153). In an idealized settlement system, the central place and its subsidiary centres are arranged in a hexagonal pattern, as this provides the most efficient spatial arrangement in an "isotropic, featureless plain" (Haggett 1965:49). Marcus (1993:154) has applied this model to the Maya area and has indicated that, based on site-size hierarchies and site distances, Maya polities do appear to fit the hexagonal model. Her analysis of the Calakmul polity demonstrates that subordinate centres are arranged in a uniform pattern around the capital, with centres regularly spaced 30 km from the capital and each other (see Figure 1a). This would imply that there were a large number of Maya polities, each roughly 30 km in radius.

Thiessen polygons have been widely employed to demarcate ancient Maya territorial borders (e.g., Hammond 1972, 1974; see Figure 1b). The model itself is simply based on drawing a right-angle border halfway between two centres. The polities that are created through the application of Thiessen polygons are often quite small, particularly in areas where there is a high density of larger centres (Marcus 1993:155). Aside from being rather unsophisticated, the main problem with this method is that it assumes that polity capitals are of equal power (Hammond 1974:322; 1991:144; Henderson and Sabloff 1993:453; Marcus 1993:155). As a result, some Mayanists have employed *gravity models* to circumvent the shortcomings of traditional Thiessen polygon applications (e.g., Dunham et al. 1989). Gravity models are based on the premise "that larger centres are more attractive than small ones, and therefore [larger centres are] able to maintain their boundaries at greater distances" (Dunham et al. 1989:261; see also Hodder and Orton 1976:73–78). Within gravity model applications both the distances between centres *and* the construction volumes of individual sites are employed to calculate the position of borders. The gravity model is an improvement on the basic Thiessen polygon approach, in that it takes into consideration the differential powers of the centres under investigation (as expressed in construction volumes); however, it still has some inherent weaknesses. For one, it assumes that there is a direct correlation between centre size and political strength – an assumption that may hold true in most instances, but one that cannot be taken as axiomatic.

Mathews (1985) has employed a combination of Thiessen polygons and *emblem glyphs* to demarcate polity borders. Not only is this application of the Thiessen polygon method more sophisticated, it is also more culturally relevant, given that emblem glyphs are considered by many to be one of the few plausible indicators of ancient Maya territorial units (Hammond 1991:276; Stuart 1993:328). The basic premise of the Mathews model is that centres with emblem glyphs were autonomous (see also Hammond 1991:276). Given this assumption, Mathews (1985) has employed the Thiessen polygon method to draw territorial borders between centres exhibiting distinct emblem glyphs. This produces a map with numerous small, independent polities (Figure 1c). Marcus (1993:156–157) has criticized this model, noting that the polities that are formed through the emblem glyph method are too small given ethnohistoric and ethnographic data, and they therefore cannot be accurate representations of Classic-period polities, which would have been even larger. A further criticism of the emblem glyph model revolves around the fact that emblem glyph centres are treated as autonomous centres (Marcus 1993:156–157; Palka 1996). Palka (1996) has recently outlined a situation within which a number of emblem-glyph-bearing centres were allied as one polity. Given this data, Palka (1996:225) concludes that, "emblem glyphs do not appear to be indicators of politically independent Maya centres and local patrilineages." Consequently, there is a possibility that ancient Maya polities were comprised of a number of allied centres, some of which exhibited their own emblem glyphs. With respect to this scenario, Chase and Chase (1998:18) have put forth the possibility that both polity capitals *and* border centres possessed distinct emblem glyphs.

Based on the work of Hassig (1992), Chase and Chase (1998) have recently employed a model for *marching distances* in warfare to determine ancient

Maya territorial size. Hassig (1992, 1999:376) indicates that the marching distance model is based primarily on the transportation costs involved in effectively moving and feeding an army that travels by foot – a key characteristic of Mesoamerican armies. According to Chase and Chase (1998:18), the marching distance model suggests that polity capitals should be situated at least 60 km from each other, if not more. In cases where the 60 km marching distances overlap, the areas of overlap are considered areas of "interpolity conflict." The Chases also note that, within this model, border centres should develop less than 60 km from the capital, and that they should ideally be located around 30 km from the polity capital (Figure 1d). There is some empirical evidence to suggest that this model does have some explanatory value. Webster (1998:331, 1999:347) demonstrates that the average linear distance between antagonists in ancient Maya warfare was 57.5 km. If battles took place in the border zones between polities, as Webster suggests, this would mean that polity borders would have been located roughly 30 km from their respective capitals.

In summary, all of the theoretical models that have been employed to determine ancient Maya territorial size have weaknesses. For one, most fail to factor in the roles that topography and the distribution of natural resources may play in border location (cf. Hammond 1974). In addition, with the exception of the gravity model, all require polity capitals to be centred in their territories with respect to either coequal (Thiessen polygon and emblem glyph models) or subordinate (central-place models) centres. Finally, all of the models are static in application, and thus fail to capture the dynamic nature of past sociopolitical interaction (Marcus 1993:114). Nonetheless, they all serve as valuable heuristic devices which can guide our field research. That is, they provide us with insights as to where to begin looking for past border centres.

As argued by Hammond (1974:322), "The use of Thiessen polygons in defining boundaries is a purely initial one, suggesting where evidence for natural or artificial boundaries may be sought." All of these models can effectively serve this role, and, as long as their usage is restricted to the preliminary identification of potential border regions, they can continue to be employed in our investigations (as will be illustrated in the following case study). One of the key insights to emerge from a number of these analyses is that ancient Maya territorial borders would have been located roughly 30 km from a polity capital. This distance has been arrived at through the application of central-place (Marcus 1993:154) and marching distance models (Chase and Chase 1998:18; Webster 1998:331). Empirical support for this 30-km spacing has been provided by a number of Mayanists (Hammond 1991:278; Harrison 1981; Houston 1993:137; Marcus 1983:463; Webster 1998, 1999). In fact, this pattern appears to be characteristic of city-states in general, with polity borders tending to fall between 10 to 30 km from a capital in most examples (Charlton and Nichols 1997:7). Thus, indications are that ancient Maya polities were of moderate size (ca. 60 km in diameter). They were probably larger than the emblem glyph models suggest, yet smaller than the "super-states" proposed by Martin and Grube (1995). With respect to the latter, it is clear that many centres could have been allied with each other, but there is no indication that there were territorial units this large. Ultimately, the heuristic devices have great utility in that they suggest that we should search out border centres roughly 30 km from the larger, and more powerful, Maya centres that probably served as polity capitals.

ANCIENT MAYA GEOPOLITICAL BORDERS: THE MATERIAL CORRELATES

Bradley (2000:147) has recently pointed out that the archaeological examination of borders has been primarily theoretical in orientation, with actual fieldwork lagging far behind. This statement aptly describes the situation in Maya studies. Although there have been numerous efforts to delimit territorial borders using theoretical models, few projects have been explicitly designed to search for and explore actual borders (e.g., Dunham et al. 1989; Smith 2001). The question remains, therefore, what would an ancient Maya border look like on the ground? Some clues may be gleaned from the ethnohistoric and ethnographic records.

Borders were so important that the Colonial Maya elite kept evidence of their territorial rights in the form of *títulos*: collections "of maps, testaments, deeds, border agreements, and every other scrap of paper referring to land that each community guarded so assiduously" (Farriss 1984:272). The ethnohistoric record includes a number of documents that deal specifically with the settlement of boundary disputes

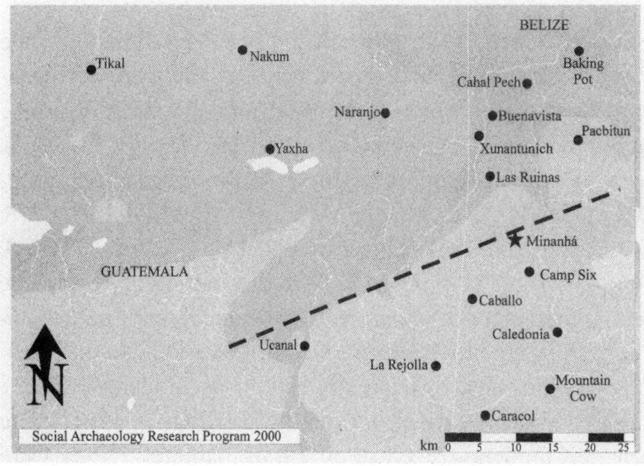

Figure 2. Map showing the location of Minanhá with respect to the Thiessen polygon border between Naranjo and Caracol.

(Farriss 1984:467). In terms of Maya border studies, the 1557 *Land Treaty of Mani* is one of the most intriguing documents (see Roys 1943). Of particular interest is the associated Pepet Tsibil, a Maya map with an outermost ring of towns and natural landmarks that delineates the borders between different polities (Marcus 1993:125–126). The ethnohistoric evidence suggests that, beyond the actual border centres, ancient Maya territorial boundaries were marked similarly to those of the Aztec. That is, borders were mainly signified by natural features such as water sources (*cenotes*, springs, caves with springs, ponds), although stone "boundary mounds" were also employed (Roys 1943:181, 192; see also Marcus 1993:126; McAnany 1995:87; Vogt 1970:43–44).

Not only were borders materially expressed in the Maya area, but there also appears to have been a formal manner through which territorial borders where demarcated (see Roys 1943:185). The ethnohistoric record indicates that borders were often surveyed by community leaders and their subordinates (Roys 1943:181, 192; Marcus 1993:126; McAnany 1995:87), not unlike the ethnographically documented *K'in Krus* ceremony of the Tzotzil Maya (McAnany 1995:87). According to Vogt (1970:43–44), variations on the *K'in Krus* ceremony are conducted by localized lineages (*Snas*), as well as larger "waterhole groups" (comprised of two to thirteen *Snas*). The ceremony consists of a ritual circuit around the territorial lands, the boundaries of which are marked by cross-shrines and stone mounds. Vogt (1970:43) relates that these circuits are aimed at formalizing group boundaries and reaffirming territorial land rights. Interestingly, McAnany (1995:89) proposes that there is evidence from hieroglyphic texts and toponyms to suggest that these ritual circuits were likely employed by the ancient Maya to demarcate their borders.

The ethnohistoric record is also replete with evidence for boundary disputes in the Maya area dating to both the Postclassic (ca. A.D. 900–1525), and colonial periods (Farriss 1984:141; McAnany 1995:87, 89). Prior to the arrival of the Spanish, many of these disputes led to territorial warfare (Farriss 1984:129). Roys (1943:67) notes that during the Conquest period armies often clashed on the roads and trails in the frontier zones between polities (see also Farriss 1984:141, 272). Webster (1999:348) believes that Classic-period territorial warfare also took place in these frontier zones, midway between polity capitals. According to Hassig (1992:99), it was in actuality these frontier lands that were the main focus of territorial warfare. These border zones were also subject to frequent small-scale raids (Hassig 1992:98). In fact, many believe that the vast majority of Maya warfare was restricted to raids into the frontiers just beyond one's own polity (Hammond 1991:281; Schele and Mathews 1991:245). If they were not under attack themselves, it is likely that border centres served as staging areas and resupply points for military excursions into the adjacent frontier (Chase and Chase 1998:18, 25; Webster 1998:331). In sum, given the apparent volatility of Maya polity frontiers, there should be some material residues of conflict in border zones. One of the few indicators of such strife would be the presence of fortifications. Unfortunately, the Maya rarely employed formalized defensive features (Adams 2001:349). Although there is evidence for the use of earthworks, ditches, stonewalls and palisades at some centres, less sophisticated means of defense were much more common, such as the use of hedges of thorny plants, quickly erected barriers on pathways, and naturally defensible locations, such as hilltops (Webster 1998:324–325, 328, 1999:343–344).

In terms of other material correlates for borders, it is often assumed that border zones will exhibit a blending of traits and affiliations (Henderson and Sabloff 1993:466–467). Independent confirmation of this is provided by Smith (2001), who indicates that the communities between Ek Balam and Chichen Itza display a "combination" of traits from both centres. Alternatively, borders may also be characterized by emulation or replication of polity capitals. Hammond (1991:281–282) notes that, during periods of balkanization, the rulers of border centres often solidified their local standing by adopting the symbols employed by polity capitals, such as stelae and public architecture. He goes on to discusses how the border centres around Quirigua built "administrative/elite residential compounds," comprised of multi-roomed range structures on platforms, that are clearly "simpler versions" of those in the polity capital. In another example of replication, Smith (2001:33–34) argues that the ball court at Yaxkukul is a scaled-down version of the Great Ball Court at Chichen Itza. He concludes that this replication is indicative of Yaxkukul's role as a border centre between the Ek Balam and Chichen Itza polities.

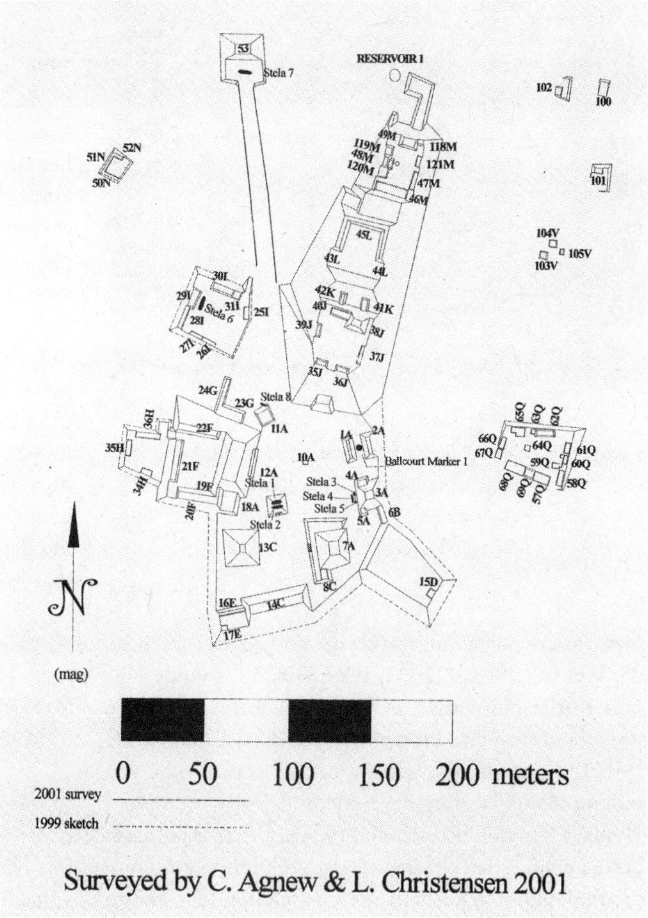

Figure 3. Rectified isometric plan of the Minanhá epicentre.

As should be clear from the previous discussions, there is no well-defined set of characteristics that can be used to isolate borders archaeologically. Some borders may be well demarcated, others may show little evidence for an actual boundary line. Many borders are the setting for hostilities, but this is not true in every instance. Borders may exhibit elaborate fortifications, but they need not. Some borders may display evidence for the mixing of cultural traits and affiliations, others may replicate the traits of one capital. In sum, there are many types of borders, and the character of individual borders is constantly changing. Accordingly, the definitive characteristic of borders is that they are fluid places with potentially highly variable histories. Within hegemonic states, such as that of the Maya, this would have been particularly true. For example, Maya border centres were clearly strengthened by being part of a larger polity, but, as they grew in power, they would have became more difficult to govern (Hammond 1991:281; Hassig 1992:11). The leaders of border centres would have been particularly hard to control, as their distance from the polity capital afforded them a significant level of autonomy (Browman 1997:230). As a result, the leaders of subordinate border centres would have continually fought with their superordinates in the polity capital for power, prestige, and political titles (Webster 1999:346). The struggle for independence and domination is therefore a common theme in border regions (Yoffee 1991:294).

Given their location on the polity frontier, the leaders of Maya border centres would have also been in a strong position to play competing polity capitals against each other, and in the process ally themselves with the polity that provided the best arrangement with respect to enhancing local power structures and institutions. Those border centres that were subject to raiding could also choose to ally themselves with the most dominant polity in a territorial dispute (Hassig 1992:98). In other instances, a border centre could break away altogether and became the capital of its

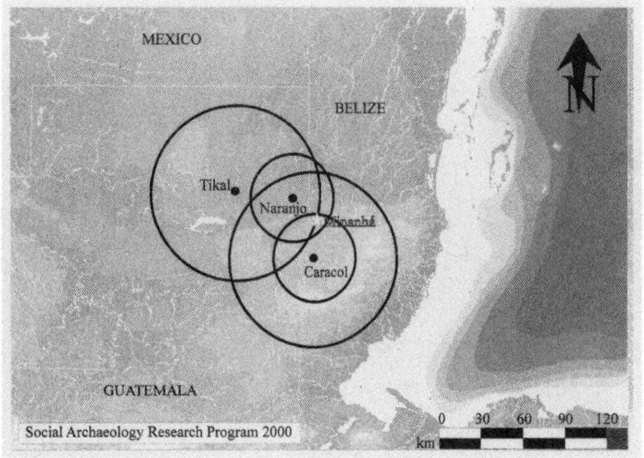

Figure 4. Map showing the location of Minanhá with respect to the Tikal/Caracol 60-km marching distances, and the Naranjo/Caracol 30-km borders.

own independent polity (Chase and Chase 1998:18, 25; Webster 1998:331, 333, 1999:346). This lends support to the postulation that border centres may have possessed their own emblem glyphs (Chase and Chase 1998:18). Specifically, when a border centre achieved independence, it may have adopted its own emblem glyph, a symbol of territorial identity that was maintained even if that centre was later reincorporated into a larger polity. Alternatively, an independent centre may have displayed an emblem glyph prior to ever having been amalgamated into the territory of a more powerful polity. In the end, the picture that emerges with respect to ancient Maya borders is that they were dynamic places, and that the history of a given border centre may provide evidence for numerous conflicts and compromises, victories and defeats.

CASE STUDY: MINANHÁ – WAS IT A BORDER CENTRE?

Given the ideas that I have presented so far, I wish to briefly explore the possibility that the site of Minanhá was a border centre during the Late Classic period. Minanhá is located within the rugged and little explored north Vaca Plateau of west-central Belize (Figure 2). The centre was first discovered in 1922 (Versaval 1922), and the British Museum carried out test excavations there in 1927 (Gann 1927; Iannone 2001; Joyce et al.1927). Having relocated the site in 1998, we initiated a long-term research project there in the summer of 1999. Over the past three years, we have mapped 125 structures within the roughly 39-hectare area that constitutes the site core. The site epicentre is approximately 9.50 hectares in size, and consists of a "court complex" comprised of two major plazas, eight large courtyards, and three smaller patio groups (Figure 3). Excavations indicate that the first high-volume construction was carried out during the Terminal Preclassic (A.D. 100–250), and that the main period of occupation dates to the Middle (A.D. 550–675), and Late Classic (A.D. 675–810) periods. Given its size and degree of elaboration, Minanhá appears to be a strong candidate for secondary centre status. Was it, however, a border centre? Given the criteria outlined above, there is some strong evidence to suggest that it was.

MINANHÁ AS BORDER CENTRE: THE EVIDENCE

In terms of its geographical location, Minanhá appears to satisfy the border criteria put forth by both the central-place and marching distance models, in which Maya territories are proposed to have had a radius of roughly 30 km. Specifically, Minanhá is located roughly 25 km from two of the major antagonists in Classic-period warfare, Naranjo and Caracol (Figure 4). These two primary centres carried out a series of campaigns against each other and each other's affiliates throughout the Middle and Late Classic periods (Martin and Grube 2000:84–115). Minanhá would have been located in the area where the Naranjo and Caracol 30-km borders overlapped. As such, it would have likely been situated in contested territory or, in other words, the "frontier" between the two more powerful centres. Minanhá also satisfies the tenets of the Thiessen polygon model, as a right-angle line drawn midway between Naranjo and Caracol runs just to the north of the Minanhá site core (Figure 2). If the tenets of the gravity model hold true, this would suggest that Caracol and Naranjo were of equal political strength during the Late Classic period. With respect to emblem glyphs, we have recovered no epigraphic materials at Minanhá to date. It is intriguing, however, that there are a number of references to a centre called

B'ital in the epigraphic records from both Naranjo and Caracol. This centre was attacked and burned by Naranjo on two separate occasions (A.D. 693 and 775), and its lord was captured by Caracol in A.D. 800 (Grube 1994:86; Martin and Grube 2000:76, 81, 97). B'ital is postulated to lie somewhere between Caracol and Naranjo (Grube 1994:86), but it has yet to be identified archaeologically. Minanhá's size, complexity and location suggest that it may have indeed been B'ital (Iannone 1999; Minanhá is a name assigned to the site by archaeologists).

According to the ethnohistoric and ethnographic records, the Maya used natural features, such as prominent hills and water sources, as border markers. Both of these criteria are satisfied by Minanhá. The centre itself is situated on one of the highest hilltops in the north Vaca Plateau (ca. 550 m asl). From this vantage point, one can see well into Guatemala to the west, east into Belize's Mountain Pine Ridge, and south, deeper into the plateau. Minanhá is also associated with what once must have been one of the largest natural water sources in the north Vaca Plateau. The recently discovered Mayo Aguada is located ca. 1 km northeast of the site core. Given the paucity of surface water in this karstic environment, this *aguada* would have held considerable importance. The architectural features associated with the *aguada* (formal end walls, large building platforms) suggest that Minanhá put some effort into improving and controlling this water source (Primrose 2001). This seems to confirm McAnany's (1995:87) notion that borders were tied to the control of critical resources, such as water. The *aguada* would have also been an important feature given the projected role that border centres played as resupply and staging areas for Maya warfare (Chase and Chase 1998:18, 25; Webster 1998:331). Seeing as small springs are the most common water source within this part of the Vaca Plateau, the *aguada* would have been a strategic resource, control of which may have been crucial to the success of military campaigns in the region.

Minanhá also displays evidence for the raiding that is suggested to have taken place within polity frontiers. This raiding can be inferred in two ways. First, the site is situated in a highly defensible position. Its hilltop location and position at the junction of some of the major trail systems leading into and out of the Vaca Plateau (Figure 5) indicate that Minanhá was well placed to monitor the movements of malicious groups. Second, the epicentral architecture and the site's top-

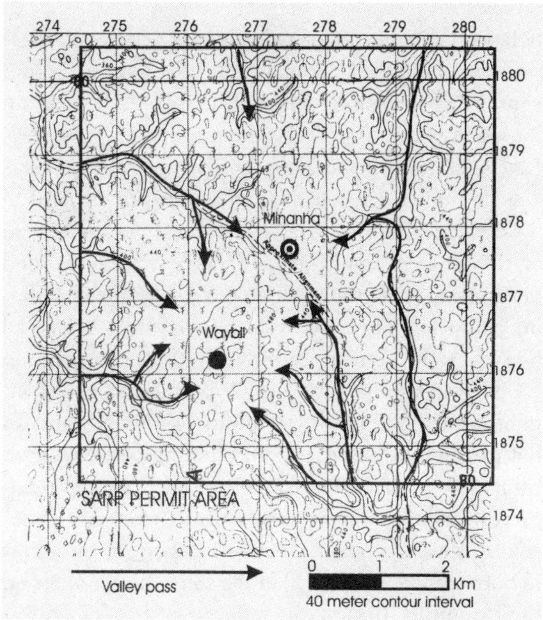

Figure 5. Topographic map showing Minanhá, the subsidiary centre of Waybil, and the major valley passes in the vicinity of both.

ographic position would have combined to provide some level of defense. For instance, the rugged hill slopes surrounding the epicentre would have served to discourage attack. With respect to architecture, the only formal entrance to the site is located in the northwest corner of the epicentre (Figure 3). The rest of the site's perimeter is closed off by architectural features. Ultimately, the combination of topography, architecture, and changes in elevation would have likely created a nested series of highly defensible killing zones. Nevertheless, Minanhá was successfully attacked at least once. Sometime around A.D. 800 both the royal residential compound (Group J), and the monuments associated with the centre's eastern shrine complex (Group A), were destroyed. In sum, although the evidence is still preliminary, Minanhá does appear to have been situated in a hostile, "frontier" environment.

The excavations at Minanhá have yet to produce any evidence for the types of cultural blending that has been suggested to be characteristic of border centres. Minanhá does, however, exhibit some of the replicative qualities of border centres. For one, there is evidence for the replication of stelae and public architecture, a practice which Hammond (1991:281–282) believes to correspond with periods of decentralization and increased autonomy on the part of border centres. For example, although it was destroyed and buried in A.D. 800, indications are that Minanhá's Late Classic royal residential compound (Group J) was a scaled-down version of Caana, the principal royal residence at Caracol. Both compounds are comprised of temples and multi-roomed range structures, and both residential groups sit atop high, terraced building platforms. The eastern shrine complex at Minanhá (Group A) also appears to replicate the eastern shrine complex in Group A at Caracol. Both complexes contain eastern buildings with multiple-entry tombs. In both instances, these eastern buildings were fronted by an axially aligned stela made of slate, with two uncarved compact limestone stelae situated on either side of the basal stair. Finally, the western buildings in both complexes have multiple stelae monuments on their summits. In sum, the replication that is manifest at Minanhá is apparently derivative of Caracol.

Our excavations at Minanhá are too preliminary to ascertain with any degree of confidence whether this site exhibits the varied history that is expected of a border centre. There are suggestions, however, that it does. Beyond the replication of Caracol's royal residential compound and eastern shrine complex, Minanhá also appears to emulate Caracol's ceramic, lithic, and caching patterns. Caracol traits are most prevalent at Minanhá during the Late Classic period (ca. A.D. 675–810). This era of Caracol replication is brought to an end around A.D. 800, with the destruction of Minanhá's royal residential compound, and the breaking of the stelae associated with the eastern shrine complex. Does this destruction represent a raid into Caracol territory by an antagonistic polity such as Naranjo? Or does it reflect the wrath of Caracol itself, who attacked Minanhá and destroyed the symbols that the subordinate centre had adopted during a period of independence? Only future excavations will tell, but the indication is that Minanhá's history will prove to be rife with political intrigue, just the thing one would expect when dealing with a border centre.

CONCLUSIONS

Borders are fluid places with varied histories. Mayanists, like other students of the archaic state, have tended to explore borders through theoretical models, such as Thiessen polygons and central-place theory. Although these heuristic devices have allowed archaeologists to approximate the location of past borders, there have been few concerted efforts to examine these frontiers on the ground. As underscored in this paper, the ethnohistoric and ethnographic records both attest to the importance that borderlands likely held for the ancient Maya. These data sets also provide additional information for use in locating past borderlands. Within this paper the various heuristic devices have been employed, in combination with insights obtained from ethnohistoric and ethnographic sources, to suggest that the ancient Maya centre of Minanhá was a border community located in the frontier between the antagonistic Classic-period polities of Naranjo and Caracol. The relationships that Minanhá had with these competing centres continue to be poorly understood, although it is clear that Caracol was a major source for emulation. Ultimately, it will take many years of concerted research on both the intrasite and interregional scales to fully elucidate the sociopolitical factors involved in Minanhá's emergence as a borderland community, and its subsequent demise. The results of such a study will, however, contribute immensely to our understanding of polity size and political integration in the eastern Maya lowlands.

In broadest terms, this paper asserts that borders are key elements of any state, past or present. These frontiers therefore require the same level of investigation as the capitals of ancient polities. Clearly, an influx of data from the borderlands of ancient Maya polities would enhance our understanding of territory sizes, interpolity interaction, and the changing character of state integration. Undoubtedly, data from the borderlands would also be insightful for scholars studying early states in other parts of the world.

Acknowledgments

I would like to begin by thanking the Institute of Archaeology in Belize for their continued support of our excavations at Minanhá. I am also indebted to all of the staff and students who have contributed to the Minanhá investigations over the years. Funds for this research have been graciously provided by the Social Sciences and Humanities Research Council of Canada, and Trent University. Armando Anaya Hernandez, Peter Mathews, Adam Menzies, Ryan

Primrose, Kathryn Reese-Taylor, Sonja Schwake, Jeff Seibert and Marc Zender provided useful comments on an earlier version of this paper. I am also grateful to the editors for their astute editorial suggestions. The remaining weaknesses are fully attributable to the author.

REFERENCES CITED

Adams, R. E. W.
|1990| Archaeological Research at the Lowland Maya City of Rio Azul. *Latin American Antiquity* 1:23–41.

Adams, R. McC.
|2001| Complexity in Archaic States. *Journal of Anthropological Archaeology* 20:345–360.

Bradley, R.
|2000| *An Archaeology of Natural Places*. London, Routledge.

Browman, D. L.
|1997| Political Institutional Factors Contributing to the Interpretation of the Tiwanaku State. In *Emergence and Change in Early Urban Societies*, edited by L. Manzanilla, pp. 229–243. Plenum Press, New York.

Charlton, T. H., and D. L. Nichols
|1997| The City-State Concept: Development and Applications. In *The Archaeology of City-States: Cross-Cultural Approaches*, edited by D. L. Nichols, and T. H. Charlton, pp. 1–14. Smithsonian Institution Press, Washington, D.C.

Chase, A. F., and D. Z. Chase
|1998| Late Classic Maya Political Structure, Polity Size, and Warfare Arenas. In *Anatomia de una Civilizacion Aproximaciones Interdisciplinarias a la Cultura Maya*, edited by A. Cuidad Ruiz, Y. Fernández Marquínez, J. Miguel Garciá Campillo, M. Josefa Iglesias Ponce de León, A. Lacandena García-Gallo, and L. T. Sanz Castro, pp. 11–29. Sociedad Española de Estudios Mayas, Madrid.

Dunham, P. S., T. R. Jameson, and R. M. Leventhal
|1989| Secondary Development and Settlement Economics: The Classic Maya of Southern Belize. In *Research in Economic Anthropology, Supplement 4*, edited by P. A. McAnany, and B. L. Isaac, pp. 255–292. JAI Press, Greenwich, Connecticut.

Farriss, N. M.
|1984| *Maya Society under Colonial Rule: The Collective Enterprise of Survival*. Princeton University Press, Princeton.

Gann, T.
|1927| *Maya Cities*. Duckworth, London.

Grube, N.
|1994| Epigraphic Research at Caracol, Belize. In *Studies in the Archaeology of Caracol, Belize*, edited by D. Z. Chase, and A. F. Chase, pp. 83–122. Pre-Columbian Art Research Institute Monograph 7. Pre-Columbian Art Research Institute, San Francisco.

Haggett, P.
|1965| *Locational Analysis in Human Geography*. St. Martin's Press, New York.

Hammond, N.
|1972| Locational Models and the Site of Lubaantun: A Classic Maya Centre. In *Models in Archaeology*, edited by D. L. Clarke, pp. 757–800. Methuen, London.
|1974| The Distribution of Late Classic Maya Major Ceremonial Centres in the Central Area. In *Mesoamerican Archaeology: New Approaches*, edited by N. Hammond, pp. 313–334. University of Texas Press, Austin.
|1991| Inside the Black Box: Defining Maya Polity. In *Classic Maya Political History*, edited by T. P. Culbert, pp. 253–284. Cambridge University Press, New York.

Harrison, P. D.
|1981| Some Aspects of Postconquest Settlement in Southern Quintana Roo, Mexico. In *Lowland Maya Settlement Patterns*, edited by W. Ashmore, pp. 259–286. University of New Mexico Press, Albuquerque.

Hassig, R.
|1992| *War and Society in Ancient Mesoamerica*. University of California Press, Los Angeles.
|1999| The Aztec World. In *War and Society in the Ancient and Medieval Worlds: Asia, the Mediterranean, Europe, and Mesoamerica*, edited by K. Raaflaab, and N. Rosenstein, pp. 361–387. Harvard University Press, Cambridge.

Henderson, J. S., and J. A. Sabloff
|1993| Reconceptualizing the Maya Cultural Tradition: Programmatic Concerns. In *Lowland Maya Civilization in the Eighth Century A.D.*, edited by J. A. Sabloff, and J. S. Henderson, pp. 445–475. Dumbarton Oaks, Washington, D.C.

Hodder, I., and C. Orton
|1976| *Spatial Analysis in Archaeology*. Cambridge University Press, Cambridge.

Houston, S. D.
|1993| *Hieroglyphs and History at Dos Pilas: Dynastic Politics of the Classic Maya*. University of Texas Press, Austin.

Iannone, G.
|1999| Rediscovery of the Ancient Maya Center of Minanhá, Belize: Background, Description, and Future Prospects Paper presented at the 64th Annual Meeting of the Society for American Archaeology, Chicago.
|2001| Rediscovery of the Ancient Maya Center of Minanhá, Belize: Background, Description and Future Prospects. *Mexicon* 23:125–129.

Joyce, T. A., J. C. Clark, and J. E. S. Thompson
|1927| Report on the British Museum Expedition to British Honduras, 1927. *Journal of the Royal Anthropological Institute* 57:295–323.

Marcus, J.
|1983| Lowland Maya Archaeology at the Crossroads. *American Antiquity* 48:454–488.
|1993| Ancient Maya Political Organization. In *Lowland Maya Civilization in the Eighth Century A.D.*, edited by J. A. Sabloff and J. S. Henderson, pp. 111–183. Dumbarton Oaks, Washington, D.C.

Martin, S., and N. Grube
|1995| Maya Superstates. *Archaeology* 48(6):41–47.

|2000| *Chronicle of the Maya Kings and Queens*. Thames and Hudson, London.

Mathews, P.

|1985| Maya Early Classic Monuments and Inscriptions. In *A Consideration of the Early Classic in the Maya Lowlands*, edited by G. R. Willey, and P. Mathews, pp. 5–54. Institute for Mesoamerican Studies, Number 10 State University of New York at Albany, Albany.

McAnany, P. A.

|1995| *Living with the Ancestors: Kinship and Kingship in Ancient Maya Society*. University of Texas Press, Austin.

Palka, J. W.

|1996| Sociopolitical Implications of a New Emblem Glyph and Place Name in Classic Maya Inscriptions. *Latin American Antiquity* 7:211–227.

Primrose, R.

|2001| The Water Management System at Minanhá, West Central Belize. Paper presented at the 34th Annual Chacmool Conference, Calgary, Alberta.

Roys, R. L.

|1943| *The Indian Background of Colonial Yucatán*. Carnegie Institution of Washington Publication 548. Carnegie Institution of Washington, Washington, D.C.

Schele, L., and P. Mathews

|1991| Royal Visits and Other Intersite Relationships among the Classic Maya. In *Classic Maya Political History*, edited by T. P. Culbert, pp. 226–252. Cambridge University Press, New York.

Smith, J. G.

|2001| Preliminary Report of the Chichen Itza – Ek Balam Transect Project. *Mexicon* 23:30–35.

Stuart, D.

|1993| Historical Inscriptions and the Maya Collapse. In *Lowland Maya Civilization in the Eighth Century A.D.*, edited by J. A. Sabloff, and J. S. Henderson, pp. 321–354. Dumbarton Oaks, Washington, D.C.

Versaval, A.

|1922| Discovery of Maya City. *Clarion* May 11.

Vogt, E. Z.

|1970| *The Zinacantecos of Mexico: A Modern Maya Way of Life*. Holt, Rinehart and Winston, New York.

Webster, D.

|1998| Warfare and Status Rivalry: Lowland Maya and Polynesian Comparisons. In *Archaic States*, edited by G. M. Feinman, and J. Marcus, pp. 311–351. School of American Research, Santa Fe.

|1999| Ancient Maya Warfare. In *War and Society in the Ancient and Medieval Worlds: Asia, the Mediterranean, Europe, and Mesoamerica*, edited by K. Raaflaab, and N. Rosenstein, pp. 333–360. Harvard University Press, Cambridge.

Yoffee, N.

|1991| Maya Elite Interaction: Through a Glass Sideways. In *Classic Maya Political History*, edited by T. P. Culbert, pp. 285–310. Cambridge University Press, New York.

PART V: LANDSCAPE AND NATURAL ENVIRONMENT

RECONSTRUCTING RITUAL: SOME THOUGHTS ON THE LOCATION OF PETROGLYPH GROUPS IN THE NASCA VALLEY, PERU

Ana Nieves

Ana Nieves, The University of Texas at Austin, Department of Art and Art History, Austin, Texas 78712, U.S.A., and The College of Santa Fe, Art Department, Santa Fe, NM 87505, U.S.A.

ABSTRACT

This article focuses on a group of petroglyphs close to the confluence of the Nasca and Grande Rivers in the Department of Ica, Peru. These petroglyphs, documented in a rock art survey conducted by the author, consist of grooves or channels that run down the inclined sides of boulders. It is proposed that these grooves or channels are evidence of liquid pouring which ultimately may be related to local water sources. Based on a study of the sites' locations, it is suggested that these rock art sites may have indicated points of transition in the landscape.

As Christopher Tilley (1994) argued, the idea of space is a cultural and social construction, its meaningfulness maintained through human activity. Movement through space and interaction with specific, culturally significant places reinforce the meaningfulness of locales to those who use them. The present article focuses on a specific group of petroglyphs in the Nasca valley,[1] part of the Grande River drainage in the Department of Ica, South Coast of Peru (Figure 1). This group of sites, henceforth referred to as the Northern Cluster, contains a high number of sandstone boulders carved with deep grooves or channels. The form and location of these petroglyphs are used to interpret their significance as places of human meaning and interaction within the geographic and cultural landscape of the Nasca valley. I contend that these sites were stops along the paths of travelers and that some of the petroglyphs were receptacles and channels for poured liquids. The form of the grooves indicates that they were intended to receive and direct liquid over each rock's surface. The location as well as the orientation of these petroglyphs indicates a connection to the river and therefore to water. At the same time, the site locations may have also been selected due to the drastic changes in the landscape near the Northern Cluster. Therefore, the sites of the Northern Cluster may have also had a liminal or transitional quality to them.

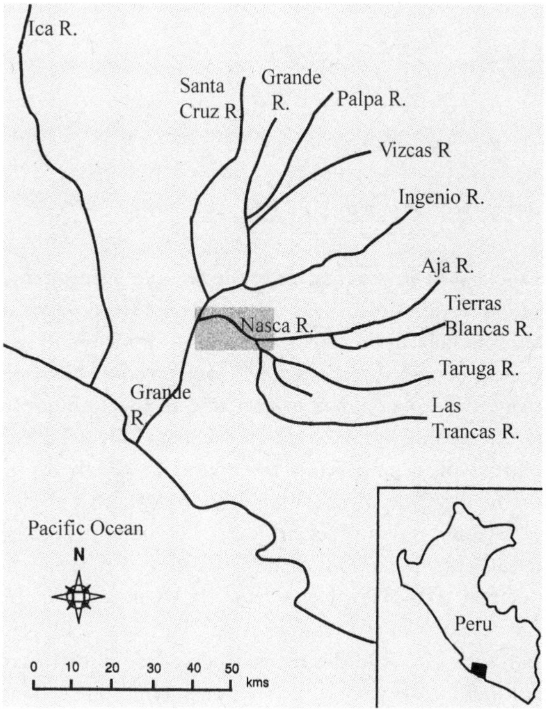

Figure 1. Map showing the Grande River drainage and the Ica River. The petroglyph survey area is indicated in gray (after Kroeber and Collier 1998:35).

Figure 2. Nasca valley, at the juncture with Quebrada Cangana Majuelos.

HISTORY OF RESEARCH

Scholarship on the rock art of the Grande River drainage is scant, since research in the South Coast has been largely limited to the study of other art forms such as ceramics, textiles, and geoglyphs. It is possible that this omission was in part due to the unimpressive size and simple style and iconography of these petroglyphs, compared to the enormous geoglyphs of the nearby *pampas* or the polychrome ceramics of the Nasca civilization. Rock art is also not likely to end up in museum collections, making its study a more complicated affair. However, especially when it comes to the research in the Grande River drainage, the oversight of rock art in the reconstruction of South Coast cultural history may have been due simply to the fact that these sites have remained relatively unknown, in some cases even to the inhabitants of these valleys themselves.

There are a few pioneering studies in the limited historiography of rock art research in this area that are worthy of mention. Former Cuban Ambassador to Peru and rock art enthusiast Antonio Núñez Jiménez (1986) produced a four-volume publication on the petroglyphs of Peru based on fieldwork conducted during the 1970s and 1980s. His study primarily focused on coastal sites, including some located in valleys that are part of the Grande River drainage. His work on this area's rock art, however, is far from thorough since this project was never meant to be a systematic petroglyph survey of any specific area. Regardless of the problems inherent in such a large-scale project, Núñez Jiménez's work proved to be very influential as later work on Peruvian rock art sites was based primarily on his research (Ravines 1986; Guffroy 1999). Specifically within the Grande River drainage, the petroglyphs that subsequently received the most attention were in the Palpa valley. In the 1980s, Giuseppe Orefici produced an analysis of the iconography of eight petroglyph-covered boulders at the Palpa valley site of Chichictara (Orefici and Pia 1982). Later that decade, Peru's Instituto Nacional de Cultura organized a project to register and document all of the 158 engraved boulders at this site in order to make a catalogue of these petroglyphs as well as to make the site more accessible to visitors (Matos Avalos 1987). This was the most detailed documentation of a rock art site in the Department of Ica to this date.

Recent archaeological surveys have also documented the existence of rock art groups in this area, such as the surveys in the Palpa valley by Reindel et al. (1999) and by David Browne (Browne and Baraybar 1988; Browne 1992) and in the Nasca[2] valley by Donald Proulx (1999). In an effort to expand on these archaeological surveys, I conducted a petroglyph survey of the lower portion of the Nasca valley. My petroglyph survey elaborated on the findings of Donald Proulx's 1998 survey of this region, when four petroglyph sites were registered, and resulted in the documentation of 20 more petroglyph groups in the Nasca valley.

THE SURVEY AREA

In order to understand the possible significance of these petroglyph groups, it is important to describe their immediate environment. The South Coast is a desert strip cut by river valleys (Figure 2), not all of which have rivers that carry water year round. Occasionally the fluvial water disappears below ground level, as is the case of the Nasca River (Silverman 1993:9–10). The petroglyph survey was conducted in the lower Nasca valley, close to the union of the Nasca and Grande Rivers, where the Nasca River flows toward the northwest. North and east of this portion of the Nasca River are the *pampas*, or raised flatlands, which are covered with a large number of linear and figural geoglyphs collectively known as the Nasca Lines. During most of the

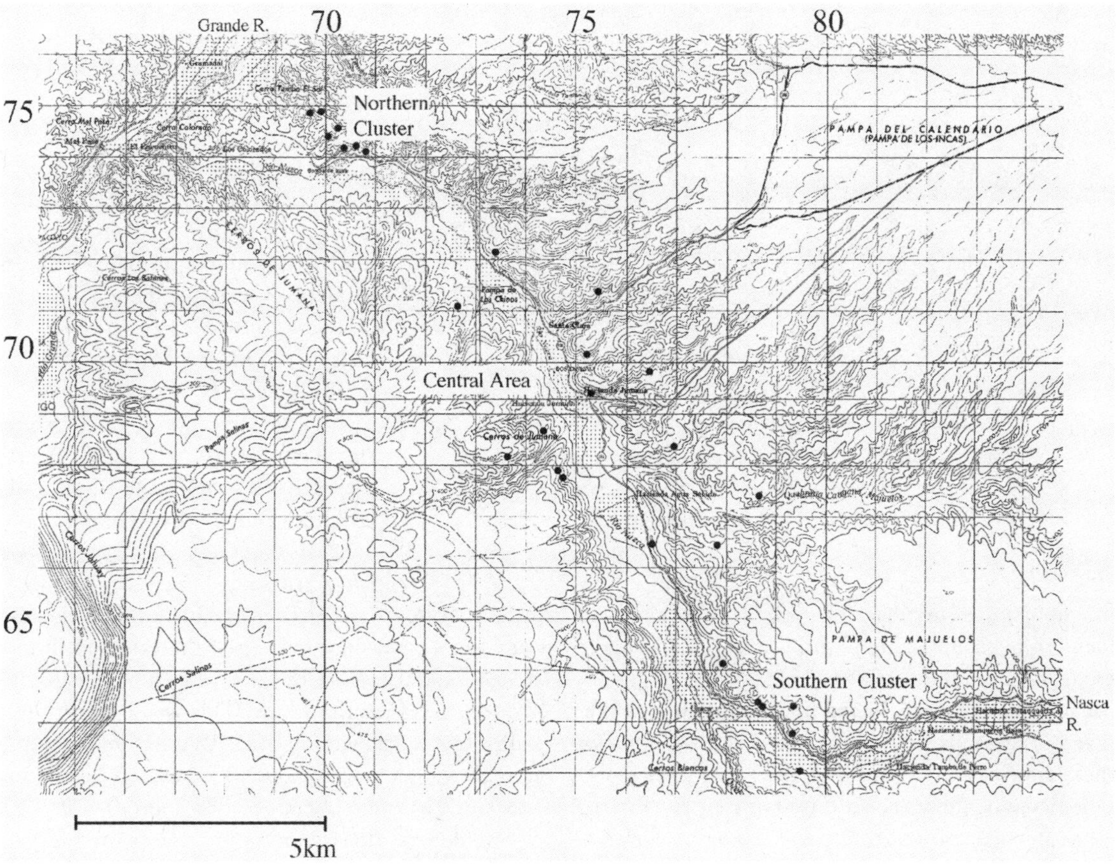

Figure 3. Map of petroglyph survey area showing sites (after maps from Peru's Instituto Greográfico Nacional [1:50,000 series, Edición 1-TPC, Serie J731, Hojas 1841 I–IV]).

year, this portion of the Nasca River shows little to no surface water. Low hills and dry streambeds, also called *quebradas*, flank this valley on both sides. These *quebradas* are much wider and larger on the northeast side, however, where they cut into the geoglyph-covered *pampas*. As one approaches the confluence of the Nasca and Grande Rivers, the valley becomes narrower and the flanking hills become very steep, making it difficult and impractical to cross from one valley to another near this area despite the short distance.

DISTRIBUTION OF SITES AND PETROGLYPH TYPES

Two clusters of petroglyph sites are easily distinguished among the sites documented in the survey (Figure 3). These were named according to their location: the Northern Cluster is located in the northernmost area of the survey, closer to the confluence of the Nasca and Grande Rivers, and the Southern Cluster is next to the Pampa de Majuelos in the southernmost portion of the survey area. The remaining sites constitute the Central Area, which is divided by the Nasca River into northeastern and southwestern sections. These two sections differ in their topography as well as in the types of petroglyph sites found in those locations. Overall the survey revealed a preference for the northeastern side of the valley. The petroglyph sites on the southwestern side of the valley are fewer and considerably smaller than those on the northeastern side .

The petroglyphs found in this survey can be divided into two major types. The first type includes all representational motifs, ranging from geometric designs

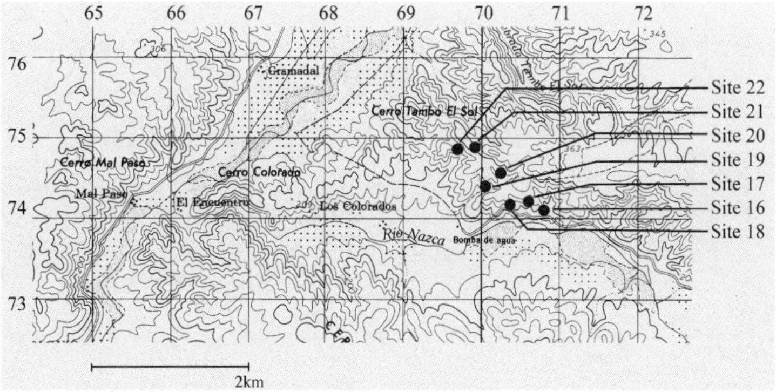

Figure 4. Detail of northern area of petroglyph survey showing Northern Cluster sites (after map from Peru's Instituto Greográfico Nacional [1:50,000 series, Edición 1-TPC, Serie J731, Hoja 1841 IV]).

to figural representations. These figural designs were found throughout the entire survey area.[3] Marks made on the surfaces of the rocks to create these designs are usually not very deep. In addition, the natural erosion that has taken place over centuries has made some of these drawings very difficult to see. None of the representational petroglyphs will be addressed in this article in any depth as their style and iconography necessitates other considerations.

The second type of petroglyph, and the focus of this article, includes carved sandstone boulders that display wide and deep grooves or channels that often run along their inclined upper surfaces as well as their vertical sides (Figures 6 to 11). These grooves are often between 1 and 2 cm deep and are located primarily in the Northern Cluster (Figure 4). All of these grooves or channels were found on the northeastern side of the Nasca valley.

The Northern Cluster is constituted of seven petroglyph sites: Sites 16, 17, 18, 19, 20, 21, and 22. Combined, these sites have 35 engraved rocks, 19 of which have examples of groove or channel petroglyphs. Some of these channels have a circular pit on the highest part of the rock, from which the channel descends (Figures 8 and 9). Most of these are straight, curved or zigzag lines.

GROOVE PETROGLYPHS AND THE IMPORTANCE OF WATER

A formal analysis of these deep grooves is one way of determining their possible function. These grooves tend to be made on the inclined upper surfaces of rocks, although grooves on the vertical sides are also present on some boulders. In some cases a groove continues from the top of a rock to the vertical side and down to the floor. This is the case, for example, of Rock 1 on Site 18 (Figure 10) and Rock 2 of Site 16 (Figure 9). This suggests that these grooves may have served to direct liquid over the rock's surface. Water, or any other liquid, could be poured from a container onto the top of the rock, down the inclined surface along the grooves, and subsequently down the side of the rock. This would in turn explain why the circular pits associated to some of these petroglyphs are made on the most elevated part of the rock surface, at the beginning of a deep groove. The pits would provide a repository for the poured liquid, before it overflowed into the groove.

It is significant that these groove concentrations are found close to the confluence of the Nasca and Grande Rivers. Junctures, especially those involving bodies of water, are important in Andean thought. In addition, there is a particularity to this portion of the Nasca River. It was observed in 1998 as well as in 2000 that even in the driest months of the year, underground water seeps to the surface of the riverbed near the confluence of this river and the Grande River, close to the site of Cerro Colorado (Red Hill). Water starts seeping to the surface below the Northern Cluster, turning what in May and June should be a sandy riverbed into wet soil with considerably more vegetation than the riverbed further south. Helaine Silverman (1993) noted a similar characteristic at the early Nasca ceremonial site of Cahuachi. It seems appropriate that liquid pouring is an action that takes place at a strategic point of the valley where water emerges on the riverbed even in the driest months. The proximity of two water sources and the availability of surface water

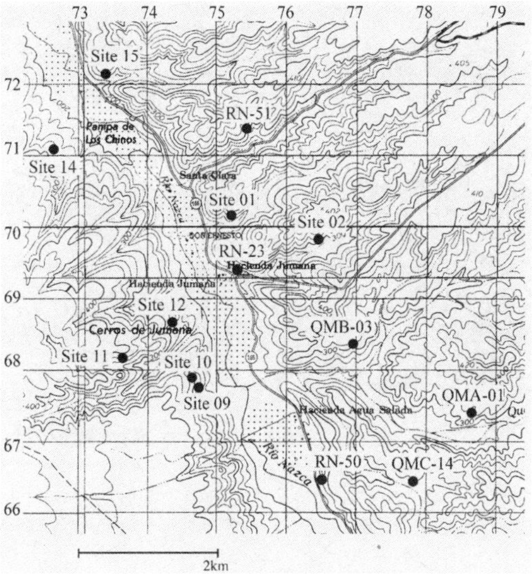

Figure 5. Detail of petroglyph survey area showing the Central Area sites (after maps from Peru's Instituto Greográfico Nacional [1:50,000 series, Edición 1-TPC, Serie J731, Hojas 1841 I–IV]).

Figure 6. Petroglyph Site 21, Rock 8.

add to the importance of liquid, specifically water, to the groove petroglyphs.

The orientation of the surveyed area's petroglyphs also indicates a connection between the rock art and the river. Nearly half of the petroglyphs in the Northern Cluster, the Southern Cluster, and the west side of the Central Area are oriented in the direction of the Nasca River. In the case of Rock 2 of Site 16 (Figure 9), located on a steep hillside above the riverbed, one of the channels continues from the top to the vertical side of the rock facing the river, as if the liquid were to end in the river itself. Symbolically and conceptually, this ties the liquid poured onto the rock to the water of the river. Additionally, the shape of many of these groove petroglyphs echoes the sinuous course of a river valley. The link of the groove petroglyphs with local water sources is therefore made through both location and form.

GROOVE PETROGLYPH SITES AS PLACES OF TRANSITION

Several characteristics of the Northern Cluster sites also indicate that transitions may have been significant in the selection of these locations for the making of groove petroglyphs. Seen in this light, these sites may have been considered thresholds or liminal spaces. Liminality was a concept described by van Gennep (1960) in his analysis of the *rites de passage*, originally published in 1908. According to van Gennep, *rites de passage* may be divided into a pattern of three phases: a pre-liminal phase of separation, a liminal phase of transition, and a post-liminal phase of reincorporation. The liminal state, however, acquires a certain autonomy and is considered a separate entity in its own right. Turner (1967) elaborated on the ideas posited by van Gennep, referring to the liminal state as "betwixt and between," having characteristics of both and of neither, and as being outside of a culturally defined structure. The idea of liminality as applied to physical locations was also addressed by van Gennep. In such a situation, liminality refers to boundaries (or frontiers) and physical thresholds. According to van Gennep, boundaries are marked with significant signs, but these are not made along the entire boundary. Instead, these marks are located at significant locations, "only at points of passage, or paths and crossroads" (van Gennep 1960:17). It is this kind of transitions, boundaries, and liminal spaces that are addressed here.

Figure 7. Petroglyph Site 19, Rock 4.

Figure 8. Petroglyph Site 21, Rock 6.

There are three types of transitions that were noted in the area of the Northern Cluster: the transition from dry to wet, the transition from one valley to another, and the transition from the sandy hills of the Nasca valley to the distinct red hills of Cerro Colorado. The first of these transitions has been discussed above. The reemergence of subsurface water near the sites of the Northern Cluster may have been one of the significant characteristics that were involved in the selection of these sites for the making of petroglyphs and the act of pouring. The availability of surface water marks a considerable change in the landscape, a transition from dryness to wetness. The sites are therefore marking the approximate spot where this change takes place.

The Northern Cluster sites may have also marked the transition from one valley to the other. The hills around the Northern Cluster, especially those directly to the west of the sites, are lower than anywhere else further upriver, giving way to an open area or pass which is the easiest route to take from one valley to the other. In fact, many pathways run through the area of the Northern Cluster. A particularly wide trail goes right next to Rock 1 in Site 20, continues through Site 21, and then heads in the direction of the Grande valley (Figure 11). It is very possible, due to their location and proximity to routes that lead between valleys, that these sites were stops along the way for people in transit between these valleys. If this is the case the liquid offerings were made as one entered or left a valley. A comparable example to this would be the Andean practice of offering stones at *apachetas*, passes on hilltops that were considered thresholds on the routes of travelers (Cobo 1990:24, 45, 119). The area of the Northern Cluster may have been considered the stopping place between these valleys, the boundary one must pass to move from the narrow and relatively dry Nasca valley to the wide and more fertile Grande valley.

It is important to mention as well that the landscape changes considerably near the confluence of the Nasca and Grande Rivers, where Cerro Colorado is located. Cerro Colorado gets its name for the reddish colour of its soil, which contrasts with the sandy tones of other surrounding hills. The Northern Cluster is located in the area of low hills directly upriver from Cerro Colorado, just before the morphology of the landscape changes into the characteristics that make the Cerro Colorado area unique. The importance of distinctive landscape features for the ancient inhabitants of the Grande River drainage is evident in their interaction with such places. At Cerro Colorado, there was an effort to build both on and around this distinctive hill.[4] The importance of the area of the Northern Cluster, therefore, could also reside in its location as a transitional place between the distinctive and important landscape feature, Cerro Colorado, and the rest of the Nasca valley, as well as the transition between Cerro Colorado and the Nasca *pampas* to the east. In fact, in other areas of the survey, rock art sites marked the transition into the geoglyph-covered *pampas*.[5]

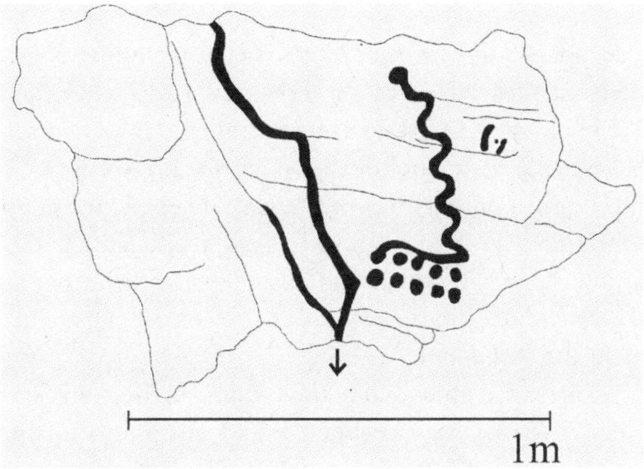

Figure 9. Drawing of the upper portion of Rock 2, Petroglyph Site 16. The arrow indicates that this particular groove continues on the vertical side of the rock, in the direction of the river.

Figure 10. Petroglyph Site 18, Rock 1.

The sites of the Northern Cluster indicate a place of transitions and changes within the landscape. These petroglyph sites indicate the location of boundaries as one walks the pathways that cross this area. Northern Cluster rock art sites are "betwixt and between" culturally significant places. Ancient inhabitants marked this area as special not just through the making of rock art but also through their interaction with the location through the action of pouring liquid onto boulders.

DATING

Petroglyphs are notoriously difficult to date, and the Northern Cluster grooves are no exception.[6] The only diagnostic remains that could provide relative dating for the Northern Cluster sites consist of surface potsherds and other archaeological remains in the vicinity of these petroglyph sites. Surface potsherds at the Northern Cluster sites are very few. Like most petroglyph sites in this valley, the Northern Cluster sites were remarkably clean. Site 18 has fragments of utilitarian pottery and Site 21 has Nasca ceramic fragments (Early Intermediate period, first century B.C. to seventh century A.D.). The nearest habitation sites and cemeteries to the Northern Cluster, as documented in Proulx's (1999) survey of this area, are an urban site (RN-15) with evidence of occupation during the Early Intermediate period and the Late Intermediate period (tenth to fifteenth centuries A.D.) and two cemeteries (RG-1 and RG-2) dating from the Early to the Late Intermediate periods. These sites are located 1 km to the west of the Northern Cluster. There are also an Early Intermediate period habitation site (RN-4) 3.5 km to the southeast (or upriver) and a large, multioccupational cemetery (RN-7) which dates from the Early Horizon (Paracas, eighth to second centuries B.C.) to the Late Intermediate period and possibly even to the Late Horizon (Inca, ca. A.D. 1500), located 2 km south, on the opposite side of the valley. The sites on Cerro Colorado's slopes can be dated to the Late Intermediate period based on surface potsherds, and the sites that surround Cerro Colorado are both from the Early and Late Intermediate periods (see Proulx 1999). Lastly, the only site in the immediate vicinity of the Northern Cluster of sites is a small, undocumented Nasca (Early Intermediate period) cemetery between Petroglyph Sites 16 and 17. The long time span, in which the surrounding sites were used (which could be over 2000 years between Early and Late Horizons), presents a problem. However, the abundance of material from the Early and Late Intermediate periods in this area indicates a greater likelihood that the petroglyphs were made during these particular periods.

Figure 11. Petroglyph Site 20, Rock 1. A wide pathway is visible in the background.

COMPARISONS

Although the location and form of these particular stones indicate their possible function and significance, it is important to point out that acts of liquid pouring are not limited only to the South Coast. The practice, in fact, is widespread throughout the Andean area and has been documented in some colonial documents. In his 1653 account of Inca and contact period ritual practices, Father Bernabe Cobo discussed different types of sacred places as well as ritual offerings performed at those locations. Among the offerings made at sacred sites described by Cobo are acts of liquid pouring. In this case the liquid was specifically *chicha*, or corn beer, which was generously poured over altars and idols (Cobo 1990:116). Evidence of liquid-pouring activities in Precolumbian times also comes in the form of objects that were used as tools in these activities. These objects, called *pacchas*, were containers that had a pouring hole or spout in the lower area of the vessel. Although mainly Inca and Chimu, a few *pacchas* have also been found in the South Coast, including some that are clearly Nasca in style (see Carrion Cachot 1955:lamina XIX, a–c). Interestingly, some *pacchas* have an extension below the spout that serves to catch the liquid poured from the vessel. These extensions sometimes have an engraved zigzag that channels the liquid. Like the Northern Cluster grooves that begin with a circular pit, these *pacchas* also consist of a receptacle and a channel.

Stones with grooves like those found in the Northern Cluster sites have also been found elsewhere in the Andean area. Carrion Cachot (1955) has suggested that large stones with engraved grooves or channels, such as the one at the site of Saywite (Department of Abancay) are larger *pacchas* since they also are tools used for liquid pouring rituals. The Saywite stone is not only covered with deep grooves or channels, but also displays other carvings such as terraces and animals done in relief. Persis Clarkson also mentioned the existence of a rock outcrop covered with grooves and pits too small to have had any functional purpose at Wari (Clarkson 1990:168–169). Although these examples are more elaborate than the Northern Cluster grooves, it would be interesting to investigate the relationship between the rocks at those sites and water sources in order to define whether the same patterns developed in those areas.

CONCLUSIONS

The sites of the Northern Cluster were meaningful locales kept active through human interaction, which in this case took the form of liquid pouring. Although physical evidence of ritual activity is often difficult to find, these grooves or channels present a rare opportunity to see the remains of ritualized actions still present as something tangible. The liquid running through the grooves is symbolically associated to the river. However, the changes in the landscape around the Northern Cluster cannot have gone unnoticed to those who used these petroglyphs. The action of liquid pouring is derived from the immediate environment and at the same time reinforces its importance.

Acknowledgments

The author would like to thank the University of Texas at Austin for providing the financial support that made this research possible in the form of a University Continuing Fellowship. The author is also very grateful to Terence Grieder, Steve Bourget, and Donald Proulx for their support both during the fieldwork and the preparation of this article.

REFERENCES CITED

Browne, D. M.
|1992| Further Archaeological Reconnaissance in the Province of Palpa, Department of Ica, Peru. In *Ancient America: Contributions to the New World Archaeology*, edited by N. Saunders, pp. 77–116. Oxbow, Oxford.

Browne, D. M., and J. P. Baraybar
|1988| Archaeological Reconnaissance in the Province of Palpa, Department of Ica, Peru. In *Recent Studies in Precolumbian Archaeology*, edited by N. Saunders, and O. de Montmollin, pp.299–325. BAR International Series 421. British Archaeological Reports, Oxford.

Carrion Cachot, R.
|1955| *El Culto al Agua en el Antiguo Perú: La Paccha, Elemento Cultural Pan Andino*. Museo Nacional de Antropología y Arqueología, Lima.

Clarkson, P.
|1990| The Archaeology of the Nazca Pampa, Peru: Environmental & Cultural Parameters. In *The Lines of Nazca*, edited by A. Aveni. The American Philosophical Society, Philadelphia.

Cobo, Father B.
|1990| *Inca Religion and Customs*. Translated by Roland Hamilton. The University of Texas Press, Austin.

Guffroy, J.
|1999| *El Arte Rupestre del Antiguo Perú*. Instituto Francés de Estudios Andinos. Lima.

Kroeber, A. L, and D. Collier
|1998| *The Archaeology and Pottery of Nazca, Peru: Alfred L. Kroeber's 1926 Expedition*, edited by P. Carmichael. Altamira Press, Walnut Creek.

Matos Avalos, A.
|1987| *Los Petroglifos de Chichictara*. Submitted to the Instituto Nacional de Cultura, Peru. Copy available from the Museo Regional de Ica, Peru.

Nieves, A.
|2001| *Los Petroglifos de la Cuenca del Río Grande de Nasca, Informe Final*. Submitted to the Instituto Nacional de Cultura, Peru. Copy available from the Instituto Nacional de Cultura, Lima, Peru, Expediente No. 5077-99.

Núñez Jiménez, A.
|1986| *Petroglifos del Perú: Panorama Mundial del Arte Rupestre*. Editorial Científico-Técnica, La Habana.

Orefici, G., and E. Pia
|1982| *Proyecto Nazca-San José. Informe Final*. Submitted to the Instituto Nacional de Cultura, Peru.

Proulx, D.
|1999| *Patrones de Asentamiento y Sociedad en la Costa Sur del Perú: Reporte Final de una Prospección de la Parte Baja del Río Nasca y el Río Grande, 1998*. Submitted to the Instituto Nacional de Cultura, Peru.

Ravines, R.
|1986| *Arte Rupestre del Perú: Inventario General (Primera Aproximación)*. Instituto Nacional de Cultura, Lima.

Reindel, M., J. Isla Cuadrado, and K. Koschmieder
|1999| *Vorspanische Siedlungen und Bodenzeichnungen in Palpa, Süd Peru/Asentamientos Prehispánicos y Geoglifos en Palpa, Costa Sur del Perú*. Beiträge zur Allgemeinen und Vergleichenden Archäologie Band 19. Verlag Philipp von Zabern, Mainz.

Reinhard, J.
|1988| *Las Líneas de Nasca: Un Nuevo Enfoque Sobre su Origen y Significado*. 2nd edition. Editorial Los Pinos, Lima.

Silverman, H.
|1993| *Cahuachi in the Ancient Nasca World*. University of Iowa Press, Iowa City.

Tilley, C.
|1994| *A Phenomenology of Landscape: Places, Paths, and Monuments*. Berg, Oxford.

Turner, V.
|1967| *The Forest of Symbols: Aspects of Ndembu Ritual*. Cornell University Press, Ithaca.

van der Guchte, M.
|1999| The Inca Cognition of Landscape: Archaeology, Ethnohistory, and the Aesthetic of Alterity. In *Archaeologies of Landscape: Contemporary Perspectives*, edited by W. Ashmore, and A. B. Knapp, pp. 149–168. Blackwell Publishers, Malden, Massachusetts.

van Gennep, A.
|1960| *The Rites of Passage*. Translated by Monika B. Vizedon and Gabrielle L. Caffee. University of Chicago Press, Chicago.

NOTES

1 The ideas presented in this article are part of a Ph.D. dissertation currently in progress. Peru's Instituto Nacional de Cultura approved this project in March of 2000, and the fieldwork documents are filed under this institution's Expediente No. 5077.99.

2 The spelling of the name of the Nasca culture as well as the Nasca valley and the city of Nasca varies according to each source. Earlier reports use a "z" instead of an "s" (see, for example, Alfred Kroeber's spelling for the valley and the culture in Kroeber and Collier 1998). Helaine Silverman (1993) proposed using two different spellings: Nasca would refer to the civilization of the Early Intermediate period, while Nazca would refer to both the river and the modern town. At the same time, other scholars still

choose to use a uniform spelling (see Proulx 1999). The names of Nasca and Nazca, however, seem to be used interchangeably in Peru to refer to both geographic features and cultural phenomena (personal observation). In the interest of clarity and consistency, in this article the civilization, the valley and the modern city are all spelled "Nasca."

3 Drawings of the figurative petroglyphs can be found in Nieves (2001). A detailed analysis of the style and iconography of these figurative petroglyphs, as well as a comparison between these and other figurative petroglyphs in the other valleys that constitute the Grande River drainage, will be part of the author's dissertation.

4 This is comparable to what van der Guchte (1999) labeled as the "aesthetic of alterity" of the Incas. A sand-topped mountain near the modern city of Nasca, called Cerro Blanco, presents a similar case. It stands out from the surrounding mountains due to its lighter colouring. Along its slopes, there are scattered potsherds that date from the Early Horizon through the Late Horizon, evidence of centuries of ritual activity. Today, Cerro Blanco is still part of the local mythology and folklore as a source of water and wealth (see Reinhard 1988).

5 The idea that these petroglyph sites indicate a point of transition between spaces may also explain the location of some of the Central Area sites. Sites 02, RN-51, QMB03, QMA01, and QMC14 are all located deep in quebradas (Figure 5), between 1 and 2 km away from the valley itself and any arable land or habitational areas. Although broken pottery is found in the area, there is no architecture, or any other evidence of habitation this deep inside the quebradas. These petroglyph site locations were probably not chosen for practical reasons, or to fulfill the economic needs of Nasca valley inhabitants. These sites also seem to constitute "betwixt and between" places. If these sites also connect significant spaces, the spaces they connect are those of the Nasca valley, along with all its habitational sites and cemeteries, and the geoglyph-covered pampas east of the valley.

6 Some sites in the Central Area have petroglyphs with iconography comparable to works in other media, making it easier to assign possible time frames for those sites.

"WHAT YOU SEE IS WHERE YOU ARE": AN EXAMINATION OF NATIVE NORTH AMERICAN PLACE NAMES

Christine Schreyer

Christine Schreyer, Department of Anthropology, Social Science Centre, University of Western Ontario, London, Ontario N6A 5C2, Canada.

ABSTRACT

This paper discusses aboriginal concepts of space through examination of Native North American place names. The basis of the paper stems from theories of social geography, which explores the connection between social groups and their landscapes. Place names are important guides for hunter-gatherer groups as they travel across and interact with the landscapes around them. This paper specifically examines the ethnographic and archaeological records of various hunter-gatherer societies in North America. Similarities between the groups discussed in the paper include the importance of land to people who live off of it, and the ability of places, and their names to be embedded with cultural meaning. In addition, this paper suggests that there is a relationship between the polysynthetic structure of Native American languages and the descriptive quality of the place names of the languages (Athapaskan, Algonquian, and Apache) that are described. Colonization and globalization have impacted the hunter-gatherer lifestyle causing its decline, and as a result the decline of traditional place names. Finally, the paper concludes by emphasizing the importance of including place names and their embedded cultural meanings into any anthropological study due to the strong relationship that is present between language and culture.

Claude Lèvi-Strauss wrote in his book, *The Savage Mind*, that "space is a society of named places" (Lèvi-Straus 1966:168). This can certainly be said to be true for many different societies which use their languages to describe the area in which they live. In fact, "place names or toponyms comprise a distinct semantic domain in the lexicons of all known languages... [and] have long been objects of anthropological inquiry" (Basso 1990:143). The differences in place names of societies may in fact be the result of the differences in lifestyle and cognition between different groups of people. The reasons behind these differences in place names can be seen in

> a tradition of geographical research [e.g., Gould and White 1974] which sets out from the premise that we are all cartographers in our daily lives, and that we use our bodies as the surveyor uses his instruments, to register sensory input from multiple points of observation, which is then processed by our intelligence into an image which we carry around with us, like a map in our heads, wherever we go [Ingold 1993:155].

The naming of such images results in place names, and as every society has different ways of perceiving their environment, these place names are often distinct not only as a result of perception but due to the languages of the societies as well.

This paper examines place names of hunter-gatherer societies using specific examples from the ethnographic and archaeological record of various Native North American groups. Similarities found between the groups include the importance of the land to people who live off of it, and the ability of places and thus their names to be embedded with cultural meaning. This paper also discusses aspects of place names which are consistent in different hunter-gatherer societies such as the descriptive quality of the place names due to the polysynthetic nature of many Native American languages. Polysynthetic morphology or word formation occurs when words are composed of many morphemes for grammatical and descriptive purposes. In place names these descriptions sometimes specify the area's physical attributes, activities that occur there, historical events, and even the natural resources that occur in an area. This paper will also discuss how place names are a way in which the culture of a group can be transmitted, especially when they are included in narratives. The transformation of culture due to colonization in the past and globalization at present will also be examined in respect to the effect that these processes have had and will have on the culture which is represented by hunter-gatherer place names. Including place names in studies of culture in anthropology today is important to ensure that the cultural aspects that they convey will not be lost and forgotten.

SOCIAL GEOGRAPHY

Basso writes that "geographical landscapes are never culturally vacant... [but rather are] filled to brimming with past and present significance" (Basso 1990:143). Concepts such as this are described as social geography and pervade the study of place names. These concepts must be defined and understood in order to fully understand the significance place names have on a society's impression of their landscape. Margaret Conkey describes social geography as the connection between social groups and their landscape (Conkey 1987:165). This concept is of particular importance to hunter-gatherers, "since such peoples move through their lands with the seasons" (Meyer and Hutton 1998:94). There are strong links between people and the places in which they live, and they are often hard to describe to the people who do not live in the same area, and who do not speak the same language, and hence have different cognitive styles. Archaeologists are able to delve into the complexity of the links between people and place when they are able to see that the landscape is a story. This story has been created by the people who live on the land, and the archaeologists can learn about it not only from their own research, but also by learning how to perceive it properly (Ingold 1993). According to Ingold, "to perceive the landscape is therefore to carry out an act of remembrance" (Ingold 1993:152). The place names of a society are the perfect elements to remember the traditional lifestyles of hunter-gatherer peoples.

HUNTER-GATHERER LIFESTYLE: THE IMPORTANCE OF TRAVEL

Travel is part of every hunter-gatherer society, and consequently the land which is traveled through comes to bear significance in the lives of the hunter-gatherers. The landscape is important as it "is structured in the mind, and becomes a cultural construct" (Ingold 1987:153). For example, the Western Apache believe that it was their ancestors who created the place names that they know because these ancestors had to "travel constantly in search of food, covered vast amounts of territory and needed to be able to remember and discuss many different locations" (Basso 1990:154). The place names then were created as a response to this lifestyle. With the Dene of Fort Good Hope, studies have shown that there is a split between people who live off the land and those who work for wages. The families that spend more time in the bush tend to be monolingual (speaking their native languages) and have a greater knowledge of place naming (Hanks and Winter 1986). This also indicates the connection between hunting and gathering and the knowledge of the land. Similarly, Julie Cruikshank notes in her work with elderly women on place names of the Southern Yukon that the life experiences that are described are often related to travel as the women drive through the areas where they have lived, and name places which are of consequence in their lives (Cruikshank 1990). Lastly, Meyer and Thistle's discussion on the rendezvous sites of the Saskatchewan River area also suggest the importance of travel because the "rendezvous locations were...imbued with considerable sentiment" (Meyer and Thistle 1995:429). Meyer and Thistle suggest that each rendezvous site was connected to a regional band, and that the aggregation site was, for the regional band, "the focus of their world, geographically, socially and culturally" (Meyer and Thistle 1995:435). All of these examples show that travel is important to hunter-gatherers, and that place names help organize their landscapes. Therefore, their lands consist of a "myriad of place names" (Meyer and Hutton 1998:94), which allow for this travel to occur with ease.

ASPECTS OF PLACE NAMES

In their article on the organization of Dene geographical space, Hanks and Winter describe the Dene as using place names as cognitive signs (Hanks and Winter 1986:273). This is interesting in light of the theory of linguistic relativity, which suggests that language affects the way in which people think. The Native American groups mentioned above all speak a specific type of language whose morphology is described as being polysynthetic. As mentioned previously, this means that words are composed of many morphemes that are used not only for grammatical purposes, but also to help create vivid descriptions of objects that are being named. Denny describes words created by polysynthesis as being "sentence-like," and often having "some sort of word internal syntax" (Denny 1989:230). Denny (1989) has examined the "lexical creativity" that occurs in polysynthetic languages, or the ability for morphemes to be strung together to create highly complex words. He writes that members of Algonquian speaking communities have "a high degree of awareness of polysynthetic boundaries, and of the individual components being joined together" (Denny 1989:244). Denny has also studied the classification of the morphemes that make up polysynthetic words, and has discovered that they fall into many different semantic subclasses which describe objects; some of the most common subclasses are for shape and movement (Denny 1979). These semantic categories are means by which to classify the world, and thus they often appear in place names of languages which are polysynthetic.

Examples of the use of the semantic category of movement or lack thereof include the Western Apache names for the places "water flows inward underneath a cottonwood tree" (*t'iis bitl ah tu olii*), "water flows down on top of a regular succession of flat rocks" (*tse bika tu yahilii*), and "white rocks lie above in a compact cluster" (*tseligai dah sidil*) (Basso 1990). These place names are also very descriptive and enable the hearer to picture the places in their minds. Basso describes the words as being "extremely compact yet semantically very rich" (Basso 1990:108). There is a similar intricacy in Athapaskan languages of the Southern Yukon, and "a name is like a picture" because it "encompasses and expresses precise and accurate information about observable features of the landscape" (Cruikshank 1990:55). Examples of this include the place names of *Netadiinlin*, or "current runs down hill through the rocks," and *Hudinlin*, or "water running in against a mountain" (Cruikshank 1990:59). Similar depictions are seen in the Cree place names of the aggregating centers of the Saskatchewan River area. These include the names *misiipaawisitik*, or "a large rapid" (today called Grand Rapids, retaining the original mental picture in English, which is rare), *opaaskeweyaaw*, or "narrows between woods," and the elusive site of *pasquatinow*, or "bald/bare hill" (Meyer and Thistle 1995).

The ability of Native American languages to allow pictures to form in the mind suggests that truly what you see in your head is the place where you are located. Basso writes that, in the case of the Western Apache, "place names implicitly identify positions for viewing these locations, optimal vantage point...from which the sites can be observed clearly and unmistakably, just as their names depict them" (Basso 1990:155). These "optimal vantage points" are the viewpoints from which the entire word picture of the place name can be seen. Usually distance from the place described by the place names is necessary so that it is easier to see. For example, if a person were in the place described by the Western Apache place name *tse bika tu yahilii*, or "water flows down on top of a regular succession of flat rocks," he or she might not be able to see the regular succession of the rocks unless there was enough distance between the observer and the rocks to appreciate it, although the flowing down of the water and the flatness of the rocks might be evident. Similarly, with the Cree name *opaaskeweyaaw*, or "narrows between woods," the narrowing of the woods might not be evident while in the narrow portion. However, when one is away from the narrows it may become more visible. Distance, therefore, is a key to "optimal vantage points" because this is when one is able to step back to see the picture described by the place name. If place names were indeed originally created as guides for travelling, then pictures of places, which can be seen from a distance as a person travels towards a place, would be beneficial. The "optimal vantage point" is what can be observed on the land as one travels through it, and it is also the picture that can be called to the mind's eye when attempting to tell people of travel routes to take or events that occurred in a certain place. This is especially important for hunter-gatherers who travel frequently and who share information from generation to generation through stories.

The majority of the place names in many Native cultures are simply descriptions of the physical attributes of an area but there are place names that depict other things as well. These include activities that were performed near the site, navigational hazards, historical events, mythological names, species of fish or game common there, and changes in vegetation (Basso 1990:110; Cruikshank 1981:79, 1990:59; Hanks and Winter 1986:273; Meyer and Thistle 1995:415). Although not all groups have every kind of place name, these are ones that seem to dominate in the research done on the place names of the Western Apache, Athapaskan, Dene, and Cree communities. Hanks and Winter also discuss how an individual's knowledge "of local place names normally varies with the distance of the place from their base camp" (Hanks and Winter 1986:273). This indicates that the place names which are important to an individual are directly related to the amount of time that they spend in the area being described, and this is related to their ability to picture the place being described more rapidly and with greater ease.

PLACE NAMES AS MORAL LESSONS

According to Casey, the places that are so vividly described by their place names "gather experiences, histories, and even languages and thoughts" as people learn the importance behind them (Casey 1996:23). These experiences, histories, languages and thoughts are sometimes combined together to create rules to live by in the society that holds them in high esteem. Specifically, the Western Apache relate narratives to their place names by "manipulating the significance of local places to comment on the shortcomings of wayward individuals" (Basso 1996:60). It is believed that the wisdom which these places can convey was originally applied to society by the ancestors who first named places and used the land more regularly. However, as the Apaches hunt only on occasion now, the stories are applied to the more mundane aspects of everyday life as ancestral authority (Basso 1996:171). Basso writes that "the most evocative power of place names is...when a name is used to substitute for the narrative it anchors" (Basso 1996:158). The use of just the place name suggests familiarity with the life and rules of the Apache society and the narratives which depict these rules. Outsiders who listen to conversations which mention place names over and over without reference to the associated story will undoubtedly be confused, as they do not have the cultural context of the landscape on which to base the advice of the place name and the story.

The Athapaskan speakers also use place names in stories because they provide a way for the language to be in continued use even when English has become the dominant language (Cruikshank 1990). The place names can still be said in the original language while the rest of the story is in English so that children who only know this language can understand the story. Cruikshank writes that place names are "words which can be isolated, recorded, understood and learned by a non-speaker of the language, and they can remain in English versions of stories. Their use, even by cultural 'outsiders' enhances their value" (Cruikshank 1990:63). This use of place names in the face of a dominant language is a problem which many hunter-gatherer cultures have faced as a result of colonization in the past, and globalization in the present and future.

COLONIZATION AND GLOBALIZATION

Historical documentation suggests that early explorers and travelers across North America relied on Native knowledge to find their way through, as well as to survive in the diverse environments of the land. One such document written in 1890 suggests that:

> to destroy [the Native place names] by substituting words of a foreign tongue is to destroy the natural guides...difficulties should not be increased by changing the picturesque Indian names...the retention of their native names is an excellent medium through which to learn their history [Glave 1890:November 22].

These sentiments were not shared by all, however, and English or French names replaced many Native place names. Evidence for name replacement is found in the Saskatchewan River Valley, where, of the six aggregating centers which were important focal points of the Cree people and named in the custom of polysynthetic languages, four of the centers acquired French names when the French built fur trade posts in the area (Meyer and Thistle 1995:418).

The effects of the fur trade were also felt in areas where the French did not build, such as the rendezvous site of Pasquatinow, a Cree word meaning "bald/bare hill." This site is only a memory for elders of the area. Historically, it is theorized that the significance of the place name has been lost for two factors. These factors were outlined by Meyer and Hutton (1998), who suggested that first an outbreak of the smallpox epidemic in 1781–1782 decreased the Cree population who held knowledge of this place, and then these Crees retreated into other areas. However, Hudson's Bay Company documents and interviews Meyer conducted with members of the Red Earth Cree community suggested continual seasonal use of the land around Pasquatinow. It is believed that this area was a productive site for spring muskrat trapping until "the drought in the mid-1930s [when], the muskrat population declined precipitously, and following 1937 the provincial government terminated muskrat trapping in the Saskatchewan River delta" (Meyer and Hutton 1998:107). Loss of access to the resources in this area occurred, and without access to the area, the place and its name were less frequently used, and became less important to the people who used to travel there to trap (Meyer and Hutton 1998). Only a few elders remembered ever being in the area, and they expressed bitterness about losing a highly productive resource patch. Other members of the community may not have remembered the place explicitly, but conversations between members of the community that Meyer recorded in 1995 showed that perhaps there was a subconscious remembrance (Meyer and Hutton 1998). Meyer and Hutton write of a Cree conversation where elders when asked about Pasquatinow added the grammatical locative (meaning at/on a place) morpheme "–ahk" to the word. Hence, the word Pasquatinow was transformed to Paskwatinahk (Meyer and Hutton 1998). The use of this morpheme suggests that the elders in the conversation knew that the "bald/bare hill" that they were discussing was a specific place. The subconscious addition of yet another morpheme to this polysynthetic word is indicative of knowledge of Pasquatinow as a specific place, possibly from stories told by elders in the past about their travels there.

These changes to "the character and contents of the local landscape...have impacted heavily on the indigenous societies since place is identity" (Turner 1979:6). Related to this is the displacement of Native peoples from their homes to government reserves. With communities separated from the land which holds cultural significance for them, the languages which are connected to these communities no longer bring forth a connection to the environment, "except perhaps in memory, dream, or legend" (Mugerauer 1985:65). At Arviat, Nunavut, there is an increasing loss of familiarity with geographical landmarks, as well as a decline in the use of traditional place names among the Inuit (Hanks and Winter 1986). This has led to "the posting of directional landmarks or signs to help young hunters orient themselves" (Hanks and Winter 1986:275), displaying how the sense of location in place which descriptive place names bring no longer exists. The use of directional landmarks suggests as well that, as it is young hunters who require the man-made landmarks, the culture that was previously embedded in the landscape is no longer being passed down from generation to generation. A sense of place serves to make an area unique to a certain group, and contributes to the group's understanding of the world which surrounds them. In this day of the global world, where all areas are accessible to all people, the Native place names which hold significance for the indigenous people of the land are becoming extinct except as mentioned previously, in the narratives which help their listeners to learn culture.

CONCLUSION

Basso wrote in 1990 that the "study of American Indian place name systems has fallen on hard times. Once a viable component of anthropology...it has virtually ceased to exist, the inconspicuous victim of changing intellectual fashions and large amounts of ethnographic neglect" (Basso 1990:105). Over a decade later, although lessened, there is still neglect in the study of place names, and this is a great pity because the cultural beliefs of hunter-gatherer groups are so often embedded in the names of the places through which they traveled. Information about type of language and semantic categories can also be learned from studies of place names, and this is an invaluable resource in the face of language decline among many Native American communities today. The search for material culture and artifacts is an important task for archaeologists, but learning words that are related to this material culture, especially place names, would be beneficial as well. As Mrs. Annie Ned so aptly summarizes in an interview with Julie Cruikshank, "Now I see what they [archaeologists] are doing. They are looking for *things* and you are looking for *words*" (Cruikshank 1990:58). The combination of these two efforts will lead to a more comprehensive understanding of the culture of hunter-gatherers, as they have unique place names which are often highly descriptive and are intricately connected to their environment. The place names of hunter-gatherers allow you to see in your mind the landscape which is important to them, and truly what you see is where they are, and where we as anthropologists need to be.

REFERENCES CITED

Basso, K.
|1990| *Western Apache Language and Culture: Essays in Linguistic Anthropology*. The University of Arizona Press, Tucson.
|1996| Wisdom Sits in Places: Notes on a Western Apache Landscape. In *Senses of Place*, edited by S. Feld, and K. Basso, pp. 53–90. School of American Research Press, Santa Fe.
Casey, E.
|1996| How to Get from Space to Place in a Fairly Short Stretch of Time: Phenomenological Prolegomena. In *Senses of Place*, edited by S. Feld, and K. Basso, pp.13–52. School of American Research Press, Santa Fe.
Conkey, M.
|1987| L'art mobilier et l'établissement de géographies sociales. In *L'art des objets au paléolithique*, edited by J. Clottes, pp.163–172. Ministère de la Culture, de la Communication, Paris.
Cruikshank, J.
|1981| Legend and Landscape: Convergence of Oral and Scientific Traditions in the Yukon Territory. *Arctic Anthropology* 18(2):67–93.
|1990| Getting the Words Right: Perspectives on Naming and Places in Athapaskan Oral History. *Arctic Anthropology* 27(1):52–65.
Denny, J. P.
|1979| Roots for Rounded Shapes. *Algonquian Linguistics* 4(3):26–27.
|1989| The Nature of Polysynthesis in Algonquian and Eskimo. In *Theoretical Perspectives on Native American Languages*, edited by D. B. Gerdts, and K. Michelson, pp. 230–258. State University of New York Press, Buffalo.
Glave, E. J.
|1890| Our Alaskan Expedition. *Frank Leslie's Illustrated Newspaper* 70:November 22.
Gould, R., and P. White
|1974| *Mental Maps*. Penguin, Harmondsworth.
Hanks, C., and B. Winter
|1986| Local Knowledge and Ethnoarchaeology: An Approach to Dene Settlement Systems. *Current Anthropology* 27:272–275.
Ingold, T.
|1987| *The Appropriation of Nature*. University of Iowa Press, Iowa City.
|1993| The Temporality of the Landscape. *World Archaeology* 25:152–174.
Lèvi-Strauss, C.
|1966.| *The Savage Mind*. University of Chicago Press.
Meyer, D., and R. Hutton
|1998| Pasquatinow and the Red Earth Crees. *Prairie Forum* 23 (1): 93–112.
Meyer, D., and P. Thistle
|1995| Saskatchewan River Rendezvous Centers and Trading Posts: Continuity on a Cree Social Geography. *Ethnohistory* 42:403–444.
Mugerauer, R.
|1985| Language and the Emergence of the Environment. In *Dwelling, Place, and Environment: Towards a Phenomenology of Person and World*, edited by D. Seamon, and R. Mugerauer, pp.51–70. Martinus Nijhoff, Dordrecht.
Turner, J.
|1979| *The Politics of Landscape*. Blackwell, Oxford.

BURIALS AND THE LANDSCAPES OF GOURNIA, CRETE, IN THE BRONZE AGE

Georgios Vavouranakis

Georgios Vavouranakis, Selefkou 10, Nea Ionia 142 32, Athens, Greece.

ABSTRACT

Landscape exists only as meaningfully constructed by human activity. Communities make their landscapes with resources which range from the most material and mundane to the most abstract and symbolic. They create the places wherein they can situate themselves and also the frames through which they can view the rest of the world. People therefore live between a number of landscapes, which include the personal, family, daily, economic, ceremonial, and the exceptional. The boundaries which frame these landscapes are not rigidly fixed but are under constant renegotiation as one landscape is encountered through the inhabitation of another. This paper will examine the application of these ideas to Bronze Age (ca. 3500–1200 B.C.). Gournia, an area on the north coast of the island of Crete, can show how an understanding of funerary activity from a landscape perspective can provide a better understanding of both the material remains and the histories of this area during most of the Bronze Age.

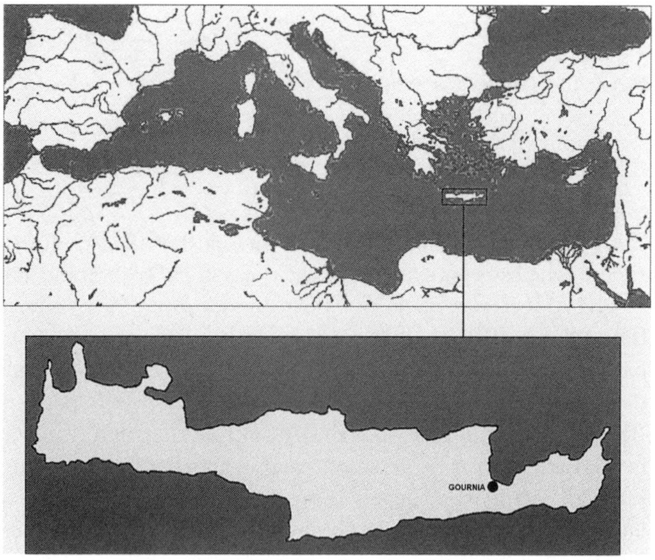

Figure 1. Map of Crete, showing the location of the area of Gournia.

Gournia is a small coastal basin on the north coast of East Crete (Figures 1 and 2). It is surrounded by an inner ring of lowland hills, which might have provided a subsistence basis for the Bronze Age community. The area is also bounded by an outer ring of uplands. A river, which is dry today, might have been perennial in the past and therefore a crucial subsistence resource, as implied by a possible Bronze Age check dam (Watrous et al. 2000:472). A few buildings at the mouth of this river suggest that Gournia might have had a Bronze Age port (Watrous et al. 2000:476–477). Two hills stand within this coastal basin, namely Akropolis and Pera Alatzomouri. This is where most of the archaeology is concentrated .

Akropolis saw a long-lived settlement (Soles 1979). It was founded in the Early Bronze (or Early Minoan) IIA period (ca. early third millennium B.C.), although human presence in the area may be dated back to the Neolithic. Similar developments may be attested throughout the eastern part of the island, e.g., at Mochlos (Soles and Davaras 1996), Myrtos-Phournou Koryphi (Warren 1972), Palaikastro (MacGillivray et al. 1984), Vasiliki (Zois 1976), Zakros (Platon 1999) and Malia (Poursat 1988) (Figure 3). At the same time, the West Court House was built at Knossos, in central

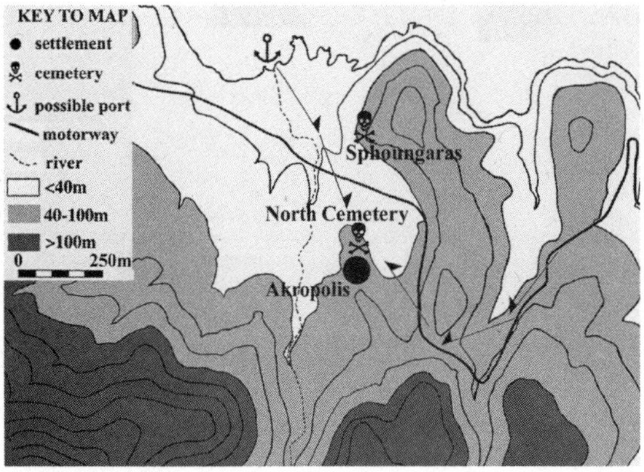

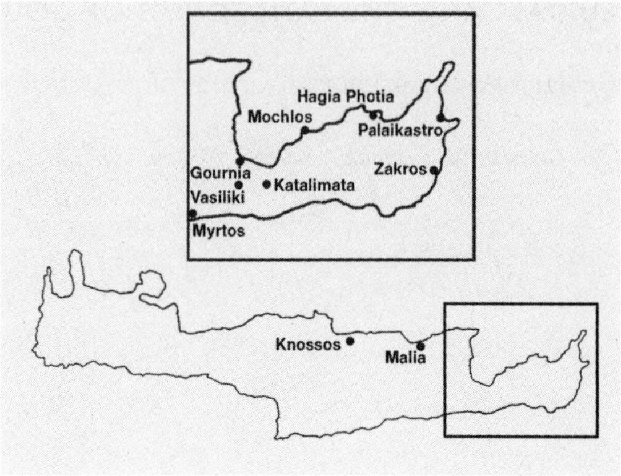

Figure 2. A topographical map of Gournia, indicating main Bronze Age sites and access to the main Bronze Age settlement from land and sea.

Figure 3. Map of Bronze Age sites mentioned in the text.

Crete and was accompanied by the first earthworks, creating the basis for the later palace (Wilson 1994).

The Akropolis settlement was finally destroyed in Late Minoan IIIB (ca. early twelfth century B.C.), as part of a "wave" of destructions of many similar sites that is supposed to herald the end of the Bronze Age. Between Early and Late Minoan IIIB, and particularly in the Late Minoan IA–B period (ca. mid-sixteenth or fifteenth century B.C., depending on high or low absolute chronologies), Akropolis became a complex town. It featured a street grid and a "palace" on top of the hill. Late Minoan I is considered the peak of social complexity in Bronze Age Crete. Such complexity is attested at the well-known "Minoan palaces," smaller but similar buildings, usually dubbed as "villas," and several extended and complex settlements. Other developments include the Linear A script system, the extensive use of seals and the spread of Minoan artistic influence over the Aegean (Rehak and Younger 1998).

The northern tip of the Akropolis hill accommodated the North Cemetery (Soles 1992:3–40, Plan 2, Plates 1–15), which was in use between the Early Minoan IIA and Middle Minoan II periods (ca. nineteenth century B.C.). It has built tombs above ground that imitate domestic architecture (Figures 4 and 5). A stone-built altar possibly comprised a focus of communal ritual activity. This funerary architectural type dominated Early Minoan east Crete. It is also attested in the central part of the island, albeit less frequently. Central, and particularly south-central, Crete features stone-built circular vaults, the so-called tholoi (Branigan 1970b). The pottery from the Gournia tombs included Kamares ware, which is high-standard Middle Minoan pottery (Soles 1992:9–12). Pottery shapes are mainly fruitstands, cups and jugs, which place emphasis on consumption of food and drink during the funerary ritual around the altar .

Another cemetery was placed at the west slope of the Pera Alatzomouri hill, which is called Sphoungaras. The use of this cemetery spans from Early Minoan IIA to the end of Late Minoan IB (Hall 1912). The dead at Sphoungaras were buried in a much simpler fashion than at the North Cemetery, that is, in pits and rock ledges. These were sometimes lined with boulders and were finally backfilled. The dead bodies were accompanied by very few objects, usually for personal adornment (e.g., jewellery and sealstones). No altar has been found. Such a simple burial practice was far less widespread in Early Minoan Crete (only at Malia, with the "Charnier 1"; Poursat 1988; Van Effenterre 1980) than built tombs. It came into fashion in the Middle and Late Bronze Age, when clay body receptacles were introduced, too (Petit 1990). The present paper focuses on the two cemeteries of Gournia. It examines the difference in monumentality between the more prominent built tombs of the North Cemetery

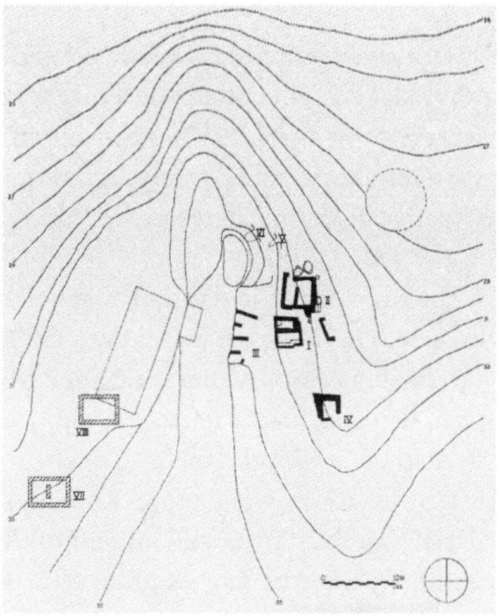

Figure 4. Plan of the North Cemetery at Gournia. Courtesy J. Soles (1992:Plan 2).

Figure 5. Reconstruction of house-tombs I and II at the North Cemetery of Gournia. Courtesy J. Soles (1992:4, Figure 1).

and the less visible underground pits at Sphoungaras. In particular, this paper tries to understand the relationship between funerary monumentality and social structure.

CURRENT UNDERSTANDINGS OF THE ARCHAEOLOGICAL RECORD: A CRITICAL EVALUATION

Before proceeding with a landscape approach to burials, it is useful to present the basic points of current interpretations of Gournia, in order to critically review them and, thus, understand why we need a new landscape approach. Current interpretations see the archaeological record as reflective of social structures, particularly social hierarchy. For example, the Early Minoan finds at North Cemetery and Sphoungaras are supposed to reflect elite and non-elite burials respectively (Soles 1988). The elite reached an apogee of complexity in Late Minoan I (Soles 1991:70–76). Complexity is reflected by the "palace" on top of the Akropolis hill. The palatial magazines stored and thus controlled agricultural surplus. Such politico-economic power was sanctioned through ritual performances around an altar, in the Public Court of the "palace." Finally, the "palace" has several architectural features, such as a Central Hall, residential quarters, banqueting halls, ritual areas, and storerooms, which are arranged so as to make it look like a modest version of the well-known "palaces" at Knossos and Phaistos in central Crete. This resemblance is supposed to indicate that Gournia, as a polity ruled by an elite, was a modest version of the bigger polities in central Crete (Soles 1991:72).

Late Minoan burials are also supposed to reflect the emergence of this polity, as well as a shift from a kinship-based society to a political, urban, and individualistic mode of social organization (Branigan 1970a:178; Rutkowski 1968:235; Soles 1991). Thus, built communal tombs are supposed to have been abandoned for individual burials in clay funerary receptacles in underground pits. These receptacles can be quite different from each other, while they comprise self-contained burials. Once buried under the ground, they were both invisible and inaccessible. It is believed (Branigan 1970a:178; Rutkowski 1968:235) that the lack of visibility and access made any need for accompanying implements and/or funerary ritual redundant. As a result, the rites at the Public Court of the "palace" were allowed to usurp the social importance of funerary ritual.

The above views fail to explain the details of the archaeological record. A closer look at the North Cemetery and Sphoungaras shows that the two might not have been that different. What we see may be purely the result of taphonomic conditions, rather than reflective of past practices. For example, there is strong evidence to suggest that both human remains and artifacts were moved from where they had been initially deposited. For example, a group of Early Minoan II vessels was transferred from tomb III to tomb I in Middle Minoan Ib period, when tomb III had already collapsed (Soles 1992:31). Moreover, we know from other contemporary sites, all over the island, that bones were being rearranged, chopped, burnt, and discarded at a secondary stage of the funeral (Branigan 1987). In addition, the distribution of finds at Sphoungaras suggests that Late Minoan burials cleared away the older Early Minoan ones. This suggestion is based on the spatial distribution of finds. The Early Minoan deposits flank the Late Minoan pithos and larnax burials. It is possible that Late Minoan burials were placed in the middle of a then continuous Early Minoan deposit, thus dividing it into two parts. The above examples indicate that people used the same burial places all the time and interfered with previous deposits in these places, too. Thus, the depositional pattern of the burial record cannot stand quantitative evaluation, let alone support any interpretation about social hierarchy.

On the other hand, there is evidence that the North Cemetery and Sphoungaras might have looked quite similar. Feasting and deposition of prestigious items were not restricted to the North Cemetery. Sphoungaras provides indications for consumption of food and drink, too. The Early Minoan II deposits at areas A and B are comprised of many serving and drinking vessels. In addition, a golden pendant, an ivory seal and a pair of bronze tweezers indicate the presence of prestigious items, similar to those at the North Cemetery. The North Cemetery was not more monumental than Sphoungaras either. Fragments of retaining walls at Sphoungaras would have made the place almost as monumental as the North Cemetery. Tomb III, the only North Cemetery tomb that is contemporary – i.e., Early Minoan II – to Sphoungaras, is not much more monumental than a big rock ledge or crevice, like the ones at Sphoungaras. Tomb III uses the natural bedrock extensively, with a few narrow walls abutting to it in order to create mortuary compartments. On the other hand, the actually monumental "house-tomb" complex with the altar is later, i.e., Middle Minoan, and therefore it cannot be directly compared to the Early Minoan II burials at Sphoungaras.

Finally, Gournia contradicts the idea that the adoption of individual clay receptacles is a direct reflection of the emergence of the Late Minoan urban regime. The North Cemetery house-tomb complex, supposedly an elite manifestation, dates to the Middle Bronze Age when the palatial phenomenon had already been well established, even if it had not reached its Late Minoan apogee. On the other hand, Petit (1990) draws attention to Pacheia Ammos, a site which is very close to Gournia to the east, on the north coast of Crete. Clay receptacles had been adopted there since the last phase of the Early Bronze Age, well before the establishment of any palatial regime. The abandonment of the North Cemetery shortly after its monumental refurbishment is also inexplicable. If the elites needed a cemetery in order to sanction their authority, why did they not maintain the North Cemetery? Late Minoan Knossos, for example, featured the monumental Temple Tomb and the Royal Tomb at Isopata (Niemeier 1994). On the other hand, the supposedly non-elite Sphoungaras is the only cemetery that remained in use at Gournia in the Late Minoan period.

TOWARDS A LANDSCAPE APPROACH TO THE FUNERARY RECORD OF GOURNIA

According to the above critique, any suggestion that the funerary record reflects social processes in a direct manner falls apart. In a similar way the argument about the two cemeteries reflecting two social classes, namely the elite and the rest of the people falls apart, too. The record only tells us about two Early Minoan cemeteries where people were buried in two different ways: in underground tombs at Sphoungaras, and in built tombs above ground at the North Cemetery. In the Middle Bronze Age the North Cemetery becomes more monumental but is abandoned soon after. At the same time, clay receptacles are introduced at Sphoungaras, too, which survives as the only Late Minoan cemetery.

Two questions come out of this picture: a) How did the clay receptacle become a generalized practice? b) How did burials lose their monumentality in the Late Bronze Age? Petit (1990) has tried to argue that the generalized adoption of clay receptacles made funerary architecture and elaborate ritual obsolete. Once the clay coffin that encapsulated the dead body was sealed, there was no need, as well as no way, to interfere with the dead at a secondary stage. Furthermore, the clay coffin was hard and enduring. Therefore, there was no need for a built resting place. The clay coffin simply had to be buried under the ground.

Petit is right to link the two aspects of burials, i.e., clay coffins and architecture. However, there is evidence to suggest that changes hinged upon architecture more than on the introduction of clay coffins. When the North Cemetery was refurbished in the Middle Minoan Ib period, larnakes were introduced there too. The excavator reported the remains of broken "sarcophagi and casellae" in tombs I and II (Soles 1992:8, 21). The case of Gournia is corroborated by other cases in central and southern Crete (Branigan 1993:65–67). They all suggest that it is exactly when burial ritual increases in monumentality and complexity, at the beginning of the Middle Minoan period, that larnakes are introduced as a general trend. Thus, contrary to what Petit suggests, clay coffins cannot explain architectural changes, since they were not mutually exclusive practices.

I would like to propose that in order to explain changes in funerary architecture, we should not focus entirely, as Petit does, on burial contexts. Rather, we have to consider changes in their wider context, i.e., beyond burials and into the landscape. Such a suggestion advocates a landscape approach and should hinge upon the work of many people. For the purposes of the specific arguments that follow, the impact of the following has to be acknowledged: Barrett (1999), Ingold (2000:189–208) and Tilley (1994). From a landscape point of view, changes in the architectural monumentality of Gournia should be considered meaningful. Thus, architecture should be considered as a meaningfully employed tool that gave a formal and permanent expression to previously existing aspects of the social geography of Gournia. For example, maritime contact had been important since the Early Bronze Age. The burial depositions made of bronze, gold, and ivory at Gournia attest to the fact. These raw materials are foreign to Crete. At a more general level, the island is supposed to have been part of a network of maritime interaction with the Cyclades at the time (see Broodbank 2000:276–319 for an update on a long-standing discussion). Nonetheless, it is only in the Late Minoan I period that a port was built at Gournia. People probably used the same catchment areas as a subsistence basis, but it is only during the Late Minoan I that the landscape of subsistence activities became formalized and prominent, as small built installations filled in the landscape of Gournia (Watrous and Blitzer 1999). Architecture selectively emphasized certain aspects of the same, constantly inhabited environment.

Thanks to this selective architectural highlighting, the environment of Gournia acquired a specific shape. For example, during the Early Bronze Age, the landscape of Gournia had two reference points that were fixed with architecture: the cemeteries and the settlement. The inhabitants of Gournia were living in an environment, whose axes operated between the landscape of the living and the landscape of the dead. During the Late Bronze Age, a port, a water dam and individual installations in the countryside were added to the settlement, which became more substantial and complex itself. On the other hand, burials became less prominent. The axis shifts, and it was the landscape of everyday life, economy, and political authority that was prioritized.

It is suggested that architecture shaped human perception of the environment. Architecture was a resource among other resources, ranging from the most practical to the most symbolic. These resources were used as a guide to people's perception of the environment. Resources comprised frames that ordered the Gourniot environment into landscapes. Thus, they helped the Gourniots to make sense of their environment, situate themselves in it, and act.

People did not just live on the land of Gournia. Rather, they lived through a series of meaningfully constructed landscapes, ranging from the personal, familiar, and mundane to the economic, political, ritual, and exceptional. Burial places and funerary activity comprised such a frame and created the funerary landscape. This landscape prompted the overall reproduction of a community after the death of a member. It renegotiated relationships and reallocated roles and resources in everyday life and apportioned the residence of the dead to the realm of ancestral cosmology.

It has to be noted that the life of a community is never interrupted. Death interrupts life, but only at the individual level. As a result, if life is continuous, then the series of landscapes through which life is lived is continuous too. This continuity of movement and life allows one landscape to be approached through another. This observation has two important repercussions. First, each new inhabitation redefines the landscapes that are experienced through it. For example, the daily landscape of social relationships is renegotiated and redefined through the inhabitation of the funerary landscape. This means that the boundaries which frame these landscapes and the prominence of the landscapes within society are not rigidly fixed issues but are under constant renegotiation. Wider social phenomena, such as the rise of elites, do not have a direct impact on social life and, hence, material culture. Rather, people experience the impact of these phenomena, like the rest of social life, through the inhabitation of the landscape upon which the impact of social phenomena is inscribed. In other words, if society is viewed as a dialectic relationship between the agency of people and social structures (Bourdieu 1977; Giddens 1986), the landscape is both the medium and the outcome of it.

Funerary architecture should be seen under the prism of these two repercussions. Architecture might have been an attempt from the part of the inhabitants of Gournia to fix the boundaries of their landscapes and prioritize some of them each time at the expense of others. Social changes affected the monumentality of burials but only through a process that designed, prioritized, and negotiated landscapes. A landscape narrative on burials at Gournia should present changes in funerary monumentality as part of changes in the construction and prioritization of landscapes, which in turn expressed changing relationships between people and social structures.

Hence, the Early Bronze Age landscape of Gournia should be considered as divided between the Akropolis settlement and the two cemeteries. The latter might have been considered important features in the landscape of Gournia for two reasons. First, they were the only places apart from settlements that attained some kind of architectural form, even if that was the few walls at tomb III at the North Cemetery or the enclosure at Sphoungaras. In addition, the deposition of serving and drinking vessels implies consumption of food and drink during the funerary rites. These two features make the cemeteries prominent landmarks that regulated the reproduction of the small Gourniot community, which might have relied on kinship relationships. Although we do not know exactly how big the community was at the time, the Gournia survey has not indicated communities bigger than three to six houses at the area in general (Watrous et al. 2000:474–475). Thus the Early Bronze Age might have prioritized a landscape of ancestral veneration and reproduction of kinship relationships.

This landscape might have affected the perception of other activities and landscapes, e.g., the landscape and seascape of contact with places both within and beyond Crete. Both Sphoungaras and the North Cemetery were at crucial locations for the traffic of exotic goods, many of which were destined to be deposited in the cemeteries (Figure 2). They were along the route from the port to the Akropolis settlement, while Sphoungaras is an obvious navigation landmark for anybody approaching from the west. In other words, the cemeteries were the informal gateways to Akropolis and the filter of any kind of traffic in and out of Gournia.

During the Middle Bronze Age, the landscape of kinship and ancestral veneration maintained its importance within the social geography of Gournia, although its actual meaning might have changed. Burials were still a prominent feature of Gournia, and the refurbishment of the North Cemetery made them even more prominent monuments. Nonetheless, burial activity itself might not have been the centre of attention. The free-standing tombs at the North Cemetery looked a lot like an imitation of the Middle Minoan Ib–II (ca. nineteenth century B.C.) houses in the Akropolis settlement. Foundation techniques, mud brick superstructure with wooden beams, doorways with pivot stones, flat roofing, plaster on the walls, benches in the rooms, shape of the rooms, all these features made the cemetery a miniature of the settlement, rather than a monument of its own (Soles 1979:166). Furthermore, the cemeteries were not the only landmark, either built or non-built, like in the Early Bronze Age. Road systems with watchtowers filled the countryside and small installations appeared too. Sanctuaries on mountain peaks might have gathered communities from wider regions and catered to their ritual needs (Peatfield 1990). The cemeteries were now only one of a series of landmarks.

It seems that the world of everyday life might have started permeating the landscape of funerary ritual. The introduction of clay receptacles meant that the dead became inaccessible. They were restricted inside the tomb or in the ground, while the world of the living started to dominate ritual activity outside the tomb. The strict funerary character of this ritual activity around the kernos at the North Cemetery might not have been clear anymore. The house-tombs made an explicit reference to domestic life. Furthermore, three kernoi in house Aa in the settlement (Soles 1979:152) also attest that ritual might have been more homogeneous in practice, regardless of whether it took place in the cemetery or in a house. Hence, funerary ritual might not have regulated social reproduction any more. On the contrary, rituals on social reproduction might have regulated a great part of burial activity.

This twist in the meaning of burials might be expressive of an attempt to filter social changes through the funerary landscape that the Early Bronze Age had established as prevalent. Middle Minoan east Crete was possibly experiencing wider social forces in operation, beyond the control of a single community. The settlement pattern shows a strong nucleation trend. People might have been displaced, as some settlements were abandoned, while others expanded significantly. Many researchers (e.g., Haggis 1999) hold that this was the result of two factors. The first factor was the ability of certain groups of people to expand their influence and operate as regional elites. The other reason, possibly a consequence of the first reason, was competition and conflict. This is reflected in the reduction of settlements in the area of Gournia (Watrous et al. 2000:475), the establishment of sites on upland naturally defensive locations, like Katalimata (Nowicki 2000:38), and the erection of defensive works, such as the tower at Myrtos-Pyrgos (Cadogan 1992), the bastions at Palaikastro-Roussolakkos (MacGillivray et al. 1984:137), and the possible town wall at the Akropolis of Gournia (Watrous and Blitzer 1999:906) (Figure 5).

The filtering of these social changes through the funerary landscape of kinship and ancestral veneration produced a very specific response. The landscape was transformed into a landscape that reinforced local identity. Some of the communities placed impressive bastions at the entrance of the settlement as at the settlements mentioned above. Others bounded themselves with enclosure walls, like at Hagia Photia-Kouphota (Tsipopoulou 1988). Although the effectiveness and character of the Minoan "defensive works" remains debatable, they certainly comprised impressive public works that marked the entrance to the settlement and thus carved out the boundaries of local communities.

The refurbishment of the North Cemetery might have been another manifestation of this strategy for the reinforcement of local identity. It followed the same principle, namely the placement of a monument at the entrance of the settlement. The cemetery was visible to all visitors coming either from the port, the west, or the east. What happens at Gournia finds parallels at other sites on Crete, like Myrtos-Pyrgos, and Palaikastro-Roussolakkos (see Cadogan 1992; MacGillivray et al. 1984). In both cases, the burials are just outside the bastions. Such a suggestion is supported not only by the strategic location of tombs, but also by architecture. As already mentioned, the North Cemetery looks a lot like an imitation of domestic architecture. The same applies for the tomb at Myrtos-Pyrgos and Palaikastro-Roussolakkos. Both sites have built tombs with a complex plan and, in the case of Myrtos, with an upper storey which is indicated by a central pier in the middle of the main chamber, a paved open area, and a bench. These features again comprise an explicit reference to domestic architecture (for Myrtos, see Cadogan 1992; for Palaikastro, see Soles 1992:179–185).

This Middle Minoan subtle twist of meaning might have provided a springboard for a complete turn towards everyday life in the Late Bronze Age. By that time, it is the politico-economic landscape that is brought to the foreground. Towns become more extensive than before. The whole area of Gournia might have been occupied by houses, although perhaps not continuously. The main settlement at Akropolis might have been as big as four hectares with a population of 400 to 1,200 (Watrous and Blitzer 1999:906). It could now boast a street grid, blocks of houses, and most of all a "palace." The countryside was filled with "villas." Although the character and importance of these buildings is still far from clear, it is certain that they duplicated many of the features of palatial architecture in terms of plan, function of rooms, and architectural elaboration. Thus, they might have operated as regional centres through which political authority was diffused (Tsipopoulou and Papakostopoulou 1997). Furthermore, numerous small installations occupied the countryside, as the Gournia survey indicates (Watrous and Blitzer 1999).

Peatfield (1990) has suggested that the Late Minoan elites might have used the peak sanctuaries too, in order to establish their position. He bases his suggestion on the sharp decrease in the number of sanctuaries – from about 25 down to six. He also points out that the remaining sanctuaries acquire features that are often found in the authoritarian architecture of the "palaces." Such a feature is the tripartite form of the architectural annexes that are added to the sanctuaries. Other features are luxurious and prestigious ritual paraphernalia, such as stone vessels and tables, bronze figurines, and golden jewellery, with many similarities to ritual assemblages from palaces. The palatial link is also corroborated by the discovery of Linear A on peak sanctuaries.

As a result, the Late Minoan period might have seen a landscape of politico-economic power and activity. This landscape was constructed with the meaningful employment of architecture that stressed the world of everyday life and, in particular, places of political authority. Within this landscape the dead had to be accommodated as well. However, their place was not as prominent as in the past, or even as any aspect of Late Minoan daily life. The only cemetery at Late Minoan Gournia was Sphoungaras, which had been in constant use since Early Minoan II. By that time it had probably become a place securely fixed in the history, memory, and topography of Gournia. Although it might have expanded more than ever at the time (Watrous and Blitzer 1999:906), it did not acquire a monumental character. Burials were only made in the form of clay coffins buried underground, without any visible marker. The worlds of the living and the dead seem to have followed opposite trajectories in terms of monumentality. The key to this opposition may be lying in the importance of everyday life. Death, being the opposite, might have withdrawn to a less-conspicuous position.

I would like to suggest that such a withdrawal was enabled thanks to the Middle Minoan shift in the meaning of architecture. It was the Middle Minoan landscape that filtered the emergence of the politico-economic structures. This landscape had been a landscape of local identity. Although it had still been based upon burials, as markers of local identity, its aim was not funerary activity itself. On the contrary, it was everyday life. By placing emphasis on identity, the Middle Minoan landscape managed to disconnect the landscape of the dead from the landscape of the living. As a result, the landscape of the dead was not able to follow up the Late Minoan monumentalization of the landscape of the living. The clay coffins kept the dead body inaccessible and invisible in the tomb, either underground or above ground. On the other hand, funerary ritual took place at a setting greatly resembling that of the domestic sphere because of the kernos and the house-tombs. As a result, and when the landscape was reinterpreted in the Late Minoan period, the burials were pushed to a more subdued position. Although they might have remained important, because death is always important, the funerary landscape was not the main frame that guided the perception of the rest of the landscapes, wherein the Gourniots dwelled.

CONCLUSIONS

This paper has argued that the Bronze Age Gourniots lived in a series of landscapes, ranging from mundane daily life to symbolic funerary ritual. They used architecture as a frame which promoted certain landscapes at the expense of others each time. Architecture created a hierarchy of the Gourniot perception of the world in response to wider changes in social structure. The dead were inserted each time within this world. In the Early Bronze Age they comprised the main landscape. By the Late Bronze Age their place had become more subdued.

Such an interpretation does not imply that the importance of burials decreased through time. In addition, it does not deny the possibility that phenomena of unequal power distribution and/or domination existed; neither does it exclude the possibility that the social importance of these phenomena was expressed through material culture. This paper has argued against seeing material culture as directly reflective of social change. It only doubts the ability of a single social structure to operate as a force that obliged the rest of society, and particularly material culture, to move like balls on a pool table.

Instead, social change has been regarded as being won through a dialectic relationship between people and social structures. Within this dialectic relationship, human agency employed material culture meaningfully. People responded to big social forces by gathering aspects of their life (such as burial and funerary activity) into frames. Architectural monumentality fixed some of these frames and gave them a prominent position. It thus ordered the environment into a landscape. In other words, architecture was a tool that helped the people of Gournia understand their environment and hence the wider social conditions within which they lived. The prominence of certain landscapes affected the rest of the landscapes that comprised the totality of life at Gournia, too. The perception of these other landscapes was filtered through the dominant landscape. As a result, and through architecture, the landscape was both the medium and the outcome of the dialectic relationship between people and social structures. Therefore, changes in the monumentality of burials hinged upon the relationship between people and social structures, as this relationship was channelled through the construction and renegotiation of landscapes.

Such an approach moves away from the question of "why did things happen?" It prefers to understand better how things might have been allowed to happen. It is suggested that the latter research question is more fruitful than the former. The landscape approach avoids the rigorous causality of traditional research in order to bring together different aspects of social life, engulf wider sets of data, and avoid controversies regarding the detail of the archaeological record.

ACKNOWLEDGMENTS

I would like to thank J. Barrett, E. Faber, and E. Nodarou for reading and commenting on the draft versions of this paper. I would also like to thank J. Soles for his kind permission to reproduce Figure 1 and Plan 2 from his 1992 monograph. This paper is part of my Ph.D. research topic, "Funerary Landscapes East of Lasithi, Crete, in the Bronze Age." I have to acknowledge that my arguments have benefited from the supervision of K. Branigan, as well as from discussions with my peers in the Department of Archaeology and Prehistory in Sheffield. Nonetheless, all responsibility regarding the views expressed in this paper stays with me.

REFERENCES CITED

Barrett, J. C.
|1999| The Mythical Landscapes of the British Iron Age. In *Archaeologies of Landscape: Contemporary Perspectives*, edited by W. Ashmore and A. B. Knapp, pp. 253–265. Blackwell, Oxford.

Bourdieu, P.
|1977| *Outline of a Theory of Practice*. Translated by Richard Nice. Cambridge University Press, Cambridge.

Branigan, K.
|1970a| *The Foundations of Palatial Crete: A Survey of Crete in the Early Bronze Age*. Routledge, London.
|1970b| *The Tombs of Mesara: A Study of Funerary Architecture and Ritual in Southern Crete, 2800–1700 BC*. Routledge, London.
|1987| Ritual Interference with Human Bones in the Mesara Tholoi. In *Thanatos, les coutumes funéraires en Égée à l'âge du Bronze: Actes du colloques de Liège (21–23 avril 1986)*, edited by R. Laffineur, pp. 43–51, plates X–XI. *Aegaeum* 1. Université de Liège, Liège.
|1993| *Dancing with Death: Life and Death in Southern Crete c. 3000–2000 BC*. Adolf M. Hakkert, Amsterdam.

Broodbank, C.
|2000| *An Island Archaeology of the Early Cyclades*. Cambridge University Press, Cambridge.

Cadogan, G.
|1992| Myrtos-Pyrgos. In *The Aerial Atlas of Ancient Crete*, edited by J. Wilson Myers, E. Emlen Myers, and G. Cadogan, pp. 202–209. University of California Press, Berkeley.

Giddens, .
|1986| *The Constitution of Society*. Polity Press, Oxford.

Haggis, D. C.
|1999| Staple Finance, Peak Sanctuaries, and Economic Complexity in Late Prepalatial Crete. In *From Minoan Farmers to Roman Traders: Sidelights on the Economy of Ancient Crete*, edited by A. Chaniotis, pp. 53–85. Franz Steiner Verlag, Stuttgart.

Hall, E. H.
|1912| Excavations in East Crete, Sphoungaras. In *The Museum Anthropological Publications VIII*, part 2, pp. 43–73, plates X–XVI. University of Pennsylvania, Philadelphia.

Ingold, T.
|2000| *The Perception of the Environment: Essays in Livelihood, Dwelling and Skill*. Routledge, London.

MacGillivray, J. A., L. H. Sackett, et al.
|1984| An Archaeological Survey of the Roussolakkos Area at Palaikastro. *Annual of the British School at Athens* 79:129–159, plates 8–13.

Niemeier, W.
|1994| Knossos in the New Palace Period (MM III–LM IB). In *Knossos: A Labyrinth of History. Papers in Honour of Sinclair Hood*, edited by D. Evely, H. Hughes-Brock, and N. Momigliano, pp. 71–88. The British School at Athens, Oxford.

Nowicki, K.
|2000| *Defensible Sites in Crete c. 1200–800 BC (LMIIIB/IIIC through Early Protogeometric)*. *Aegaeum* 21. Université de Liège, Liège.

Peatfield, A. D.
|1990| Minoan Peak Sanctuaries: History and Society. *Opuscula Atheniensia* XVIII(8):117–131.

Petit, F.
|1990| Les jarres funéraires du minoen ancien III au minoen récent I. *Aegaeum* 6:29–57, plates VII–XV. Université de Liège, Liège.

Platon, L.
|1999| New Evidence for the Occupation at Zakros before the LM I Palace. In *Meletemata: Studies in Aegean Archaeology Presented to Malcolm H. Wiener as He Enters his 65th Year*, edited by P. P. Betancourt, V. Karageorghis, R. Laffineur, and W.-D. Niemeier, vol. III, pp. 671–681, plates CXLIII–CXLIV. *Aegaeum* 20. Université de Liège, Liège.

Poursat, J.-C.
|1988| La ville minoenne de Malia: Recherches et publications récentes. *Revue archéologique* 61–82.

Rehak, P., and J. G. Younger
|1998| Review of Aegean Prehistory VII: Neopalatial, Final Palatial and Postpalatial Crete. *American Journal of Archaeology* 102:91–173.

Rutkowski, B.
|1968| Apo ten istoria ton Kretikon larnakon (From the History of Cretan Larnakes). In *Pepragmena tou 2ou diethnous Kretologikou Synedriou (Acts of the 2nd International Cretological Conference)*, pp. 234–237. Philologikos Syllogos Chrysostomos, Athens.

Soles, J. S.
|1979| The Early Gournia Town. *American Journal of Archaeology* 83:147–167, plates 18–21.
|1988| Social Ranking in Prepalatial Cemeteries. In *Problems in Greek Prehistory: Papers Presented at the Centenary Conference of the British School of Archaeology at Athens, Manchester, April 1986*, edited by E. B. French, and K. A. Wardle, pp. 49–61. Bristol Classical Press, Bristol.
|1991| The Gournia Palace. *American Journal of Archaeology* 95:17–77.
|1992| *The Prepalatial Cemeteries at Mochlos and Gournia and the House Tombs of Bronze Age Crete.* Hesperia Supplement XXIV. American School of Classical Studies at Athens, Princeton, New Jersey.

Soles, J.S., and C. Davaras
|1996| Excavations at Mochlos 1992–1993. *Hesperia* 65(2):175–230, plates 50–64.

Tilley, C.
|1994| *A Phenomenology of Landscape.* Berg, Oxford.

Tsipopoulou, M.
|1988| Ayia Photia Siteias: To neo evrima (Hagia Photia Seteias: The New Find). In *Problems in Greek Prehistory: Papers Presented at the Centenary Conference of the British School of Archaeology at Athens, Manchester, April 1986*, edited by E. B. French, and K. A. Wardle, pp. 31–47. Bristol Classical Press, Bristol.

Tsipopoulou, M., and A. Papakostopoulou
|1997| "Villas" and Villages in the Hinterland of Petras, Siteia. In *The Function of the Minoan "Villa": Proceedings of the 8th International Symposium at the Swedish Institute at Athens. 6–8 June 1992*, edited by R. Hägg, pp. 215–217. Svenska institutet i Athen, Stockholm.

Van Effenterre, H.
|1980| *Le palais de Mallia et la cité minoenne: Étude de synthèse. Incunabula Graeca LXXVI*, vol. I. Edizioni dell' Ateneo, Rome.

Warren, P.
|1972| *Myrtos: An Early Bronze Age Settlement in Crete.* Thames and Hudson, London.

Watrous, L. V., and H. Blitzer
|1999| The Region of Gournia in the Neopalatial Period. In *Meletemata: Studies in Aegean Archaeology Presented to Malcolm H. Wiener as He Enters his 65th Year*, edited by P. P. Betancourt, V. Karageorghis, R. Laffineur, and W.-D. Niemeier, pp. 905–909, plates CCVIII–CCIX. *Aegaeum* 20. Université de Liège, Liège.

Watrous, L. V., H. Blitzer, D. C. Haggis, and E. Zangger
|2000| Economy and Society in the Gournia Region of Crete: A Preliminary Report on the 1992–1994 Field Seasons of the Gournia Project. In *Pepragmena 8ou Diethnous Kretologikou Synedriou (Acts of the 8th International Cretological Conference)*, vol. A3, edited by A. Karetsou, pp. 471–483. Etaireia Kretikon Istorikon Meleton, Herakleio.

Wilson, D.
|1994| Knossos before the Palaces: An Overview of the Early Bronze Age. In *Knossos: A Labyrinth of History. Papers in Honour of Sinclair Hood*, edited by D. Evely, H. Hughes-Brock, and N. Momigliano, pp. 23–44. The British School at Athens, Oxford.

Zois, A. A.
|1976| *Vasiliki I. Nea Archaiologike Ereuna eis to Kefali plesion tou Choriou Vasilike Ierapetras (Vasiliki I: New Archaeological Investigation at Kefali, close to the Village of Vasiliki at Ierapetra).* Vivliotheke tes en Athenais Archaiologikes Etaireias 83, Athens.

THE ORIGINS OF TRANSHUMANT PASTORALISM IN TEMPERATE SOUTHEASTERN EUROPE

Elizabeth R. Arnold and Haskel J. Greenfield

Elizabeth R. Arnold, Department of Archaeology, University of Calgary, Calgary, Alberta T2N 1N4, Canada.
Haskel J. Greenfield, Department of Anthropology, University of Manitoba, Winnipeg, Manitoba R3T 5V5, Canada.

ABSTRACT

The temporal origins of transhumant pastoralism in temperate southeastern Europe have been debated. Previous hypotheses each propose a different point in time when transhumance would appear, ranging from the advent of the Early Neolithic, to the advent of the Post-Neolithic, and the advent of the Iron Age. This investigation seeks to test for the appearance of transhumance at the Post-Neolithic juncture (ca. 3300 B.C.). Population dispersal, increased areas under cultivation in the low and mid-altitudes and decreased productivity potentials for highland settlements would have resulted in less pasture available for domestic stock in the lowland. Herds would have to be moved farther away from settlements to find sufficient food. Transhumant pastoralism is an efficient response as it encourages exploitation of minimally utilized highland zones less suited for agriculture.

Harvest profiles from mandibular tooth wear and eruption data of remains from three domestic animal taxa (*Ovis/Capra*, *Bos taurus* and *Sus scrofa*) are constructed. It is hypothesized that transhumant pastoralism would appear at the temporal point where complementary culling patterns between highland and lowland sites in the region appear. Several overriding methodological issues hampered this research. As a result, it was not possible to provide strong support for the hypothesis.

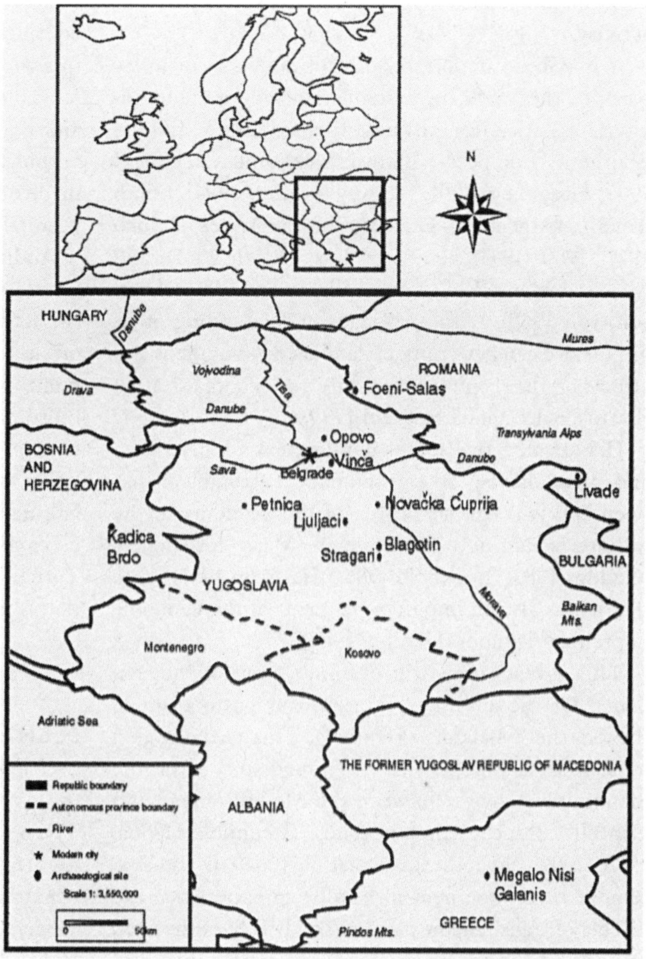

Figure 1. Study area and site locations

Transhumant pastoralism is an economic activity involving the seasonal movement of domestic herds between altitudinally differentiated and complementary pastures (Geddes 1983). Transhumant pastoralism is a form of semi-nomadic pastoralism in which domestic animals play a predominant, but not an exclusive role in the shaping of the economic and cultural lives of the people who depend on them (Galaty and Johnson 1990). It can be further defined as the movement of domestic herds between altitudinally differentiated and/or seasonally complementary pastures. Pastoralism is the predominant activity in the economy but there is a varying emphasis on agriculture as a supplementary activity.

It is still an important form of land use in many parts of the world, in particular in mountainous regions in Africa (e.g., Evans-Pritchard 1940), Europe (southern Europe – Bartosiewicz and Greenfield 1999; Greenfield 2001; Norway – Paine 1994), South America (Argentina – Glatzer 1982; the Andes – Lynch 1971, 1980, 1983), the Near East (Barth 1961), and Asia (Pakistan – Ehlers and Kreutzmann 2000; Tibet – Ekvall 1968). With a stronger understanding of its origins, we can better understand its development and effects on the shaping of a culture's social organization (Bartosiewicz and Greenfield 1999).

Historically, the seasonal migration of herdsmen and their herds, or transhumant pastoralism, has been and is a significant part of the economy in the Mediterranean and the Balkans. Many researchers (Geddes 1983; Greenfield 1986a; Halstead 1981) agree that it was also an important element of the economy in prehistoric times (Harding 2000).

This investigation will examine some of the evidence for the advent of transhumant pastoralism in the Northern Balkans (Figure 1). This is the region of southeast Europe that is immediately over the mountainous divide between the Mediterranean and Central European climatic zones. Greenfield (1986a, 1988, 1999a) hypothesized that this area is the first temperate environment in Europe to experience the effects of transhumant pastoralism. It is hypothesized to occur at the advent of or during an early phase of the Post-Neolithic, specifically either the Chalcolithic (3300–2500 B.C.) or Bronze Ages (2500–800 B.C.). Zooarchaeological data from this region is utilized to test this proposition.

ELEMENTS OF A PASTORAL ECONOMY

Ethnographic research on pastoral societies can provide some general elements of a pastoral economy. The species composition, the age and sex structure of herds are determined by several factors. The biology of the species and geographic conditions are the primary determinates. These same factors will affect whether animals are utilized for primary products (such as meat), or for secondary products (such as wool, milk or traction). Additionally, economic, social, political and cultural factors are also influential (Khazanov 1984).

There are both spatial and temporal components to consider in the mobility of livestock. A variety of factors will affect the distance, timing and location of the movement of livestock. These can include the location and seasonal changes of water and pasture, disease outbreaks, localized drought, the number of people involved in the herd movement and relations with non-pastoral groups (Niamir-Fuller and Turner 1999).

Additionally, the mobility of pastoral groups is not limitless. Constraints, such as geographic knowledge, social contacts and access to resources such as pasture, often result in pastoralists revisiting encampment points on an annual or semi-annual basis. The mobility of livestock does not necessarily correlate with human mobility. The proportion of the human population traveling with the transhumant herds can vary culturally, but also through the influence of political, economic and/or ecological factors (Niamir-Fuller and Turner 1999). This is the element of pastoral societies that is most difficult to establish archaeologically.

ELEMENTS OF A TRANSHUMANT PASTORAL ECONOMY

The most important elements of a transhumant economy are the character of the movements and the pattern of settlement. This involves the examination of three aspects of transhumance:

1) What is the portion of the population traveling with the domestic herds? This is perhaps the most important aspect of transhumance and can vary from movement of the entire community to only the movement of animals under the supervision of professional

shepherds (Rafiullah 1966). It is possible that the same groups in a given society (or subsociety) are occupied with both agriculture and pastoralism, or conversely, there may be specialized groups that devote themselves primarily, or even exclusively, to pastoralism, in conjunction with groups which are primarily occupied with agriculture (Khazanov 1984). The existence of variation is also supported by recent ethnographic investigations, which have shown that in modern transhumant economies, shepherds are wage labourers hired by livestock owners. This is in contrast to modern nomadic pastoral groups, where relatives manage their personal resources. In the Northern Balkans, transhumance was not conducted by specialists. Most transhumant herders were part of village-based agricultural communities. Only a portion, usually the older boys and men, would migrate with the herds (Greenfield 1999a; Halpern 1999).

Figure 2. Mortality profiles of *Sus scrofa dom.* from major temporal periods.

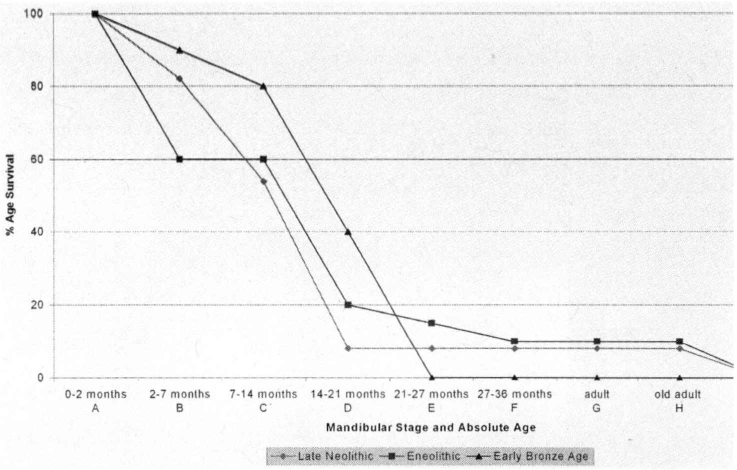

2) What is the organization and number of villages included within transhumant movement? Three variations are recognized. The first pattern is two well-defined villages, one located in the summer pastures and one in the winter pasture. The second pattern consists of multi-village sites. The final pattern is of one well-defined village and a collection of transient settlements (Rafiullah 1966; Walker 1983). Historically, the third pattern was more commonly found in the Northern Balkans.
3) What is the length of the migrations? Transhumant migrations can involve journeys of several hundred kilometres or only a few kilometres and can be a vertical movement between altitudinally different areas or a lateral movement across the landscape (Rafiullah 1966; Walker 1983). In the Northern Balkans, both short and long distance transhumance has been documented (Greenfield 1999a; Halpern 1999; Sterud 1978). However, given the nature of the landscape, with its juxtaposition of highlands and lowlands, most transhumance was probably local in nature.

In arid and alpine environments, the advantages of pursuing transhumant pastoralism are more obvious. Herds are moved to the highland pastures in the summer to escape high temperatures and provide sufficient water and pasturage. But in the temperate environment of the Northern Balkans, the benefits of doing so are not as apparent. Temperature variations in the lowland are not sufficiently extreme during the summer to drive livestock into the mountains in search of grazing and water. Sufficient resources are available year-round in most low and mid-altitude pastures in temperate climatic zones. Additionally, sufficient microenvironments exist, such as marshes, streams, hills and plains, to allow for stock to be safely herded throughout the year in the lowlands. As a result, ecologically, there are fewer incentives for pastoralists from low and mid-altitude settlements in temperate regions to practice transhumance.

Figure 3. Mortality profile of *Ovis/Capra*, Middle Bronze Age Vinča.

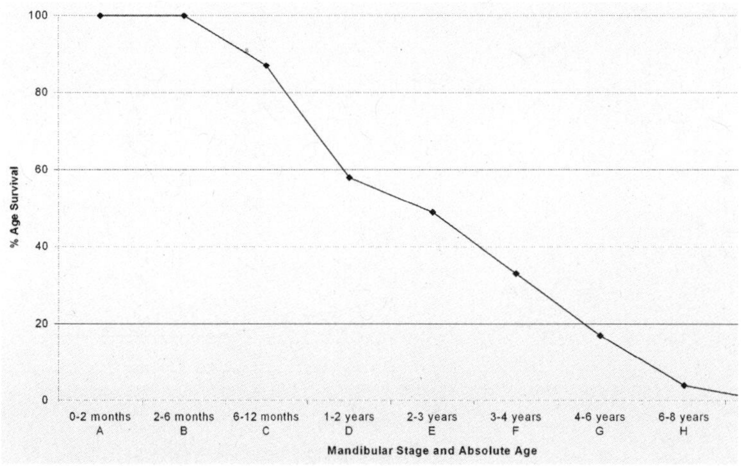

During the Post-Neolithic in the Northern Balkans (ca. 3300 B.C.), archaeological evidence has shown an extensive reorganization of settlement patterns and includes smaller sites, more closely spaced sites, horizontally displaced occupations, lower artifact densities and insubstantial structures. These sites tend not to be located in the same areas as Late Neolithic sites, and there is little evidence for large and internally well-organized communities. This has been interpreted a redistribution of population from one of substantial nucleation, where the regional population is concentrated in a few large settlements, to a new pattern of dispersion where population is distributed into a larger number of smaller and less intensively occupied residential localities (Greenfield 1999a). Additionally, paleoenvironmental data indicates that significant change in the physical, vegetative and micromammalian environments took place at this time (Kordos 1978a, 1978b). The net result was a decrease in the upper altitudinal limit for cultivation, mostly affecting highland communities. This factor, in combination with population dispersal throughout the lower altitudes and increased areas coming under cultivation in these same areas, would have resulted in less pasture available for domestic stock in the lowlands. Herds would have to be moved farther away from settlements in order to find sufficient graze and forage (Greenfield 1999a).

Transhumant pastoralism is an efficient response to the problem of less available and predictable pasture. It encourages exploitation of minimally utilized highland zones, less suited for agriculture. It is likely that the members of the lowland and mid-altitude communities would have been responsible for the colonization of these areas in order to ensure continued access to these new and vital grazing resources for their stock (Greenfield 1999a).

METHODOLOGY

The first step for investigating the originals of transhumant pastoralism, archaeologically, is a sound analysis of the zooarchaeological material of the region in question. Zooarchaeological remains of domestic animals, such as cattle, sheep and goats, are the most relevant data form to test propositions concerning transhumant pastoralism since these are the very species that would be involved in transhumant movements.

The combined cranial and post-cranial material from the northern Balkans has been previously analyzed (Greenfield 1986a, 1986b, 1986c, 1989, 1991, 1994, 1996, 1999a, 1999b, 2001, n.d.; Greenfield and Fowler n.d.) and used to test the above hypothesis (Greenfield 1988, 1991, 1999a, 2001). However, criticisms of these studies have been that they ignore the effect of a variety of taphonomic forces on age distributions. It has been suggested that the mandibular data would be less likely to be affected by such forces (Payne 1973; Lyman 1994). This investigation will specifically examine the mandibles and teeth data for age and season of death information of domestic stock to look for evidence of complementary movement between highland and lowland areas. Harvest profiles (the distribution of age at death for a species [Payne 1973; Hesse 1982]), were created from the analysis of the tooth wear and eruption data from the mandibles of domestic animals, specifically, sheep, goat, cow and pig (Greenfield 1988, 1999a; Payne 1973).

RESEARCH HYPOTHESES

The transhumant movement of domestic stock is predictable. The herd will move into highland pastures in the early spring, soon after lambing/calving occurs and will return to the lowlands during the autumn. Within a subsistence economy, the age groups that are slaughtered in the highlands and the lowlands will be different.

The excess infants and juveniles would be culled from the herds while they are in the highland pastures. Once the herds have returned to the lowlands, the youngest animal is at least 6 months old. In the lowlands, it would be the subadults and adults who would be selected for slaughter. As a result, the age structure within the harvest profiles from highland and lowland settlements should be complimentary (Greenfield 1999a:19).

This hypothesis may be supported if it can be demonstrated that herds were largely absent from the region for part of the year. Conversely, the null hypothesis would be accepted if herds could be shown to have been resident year-round in the highlands.

However, a major complicating factor to this general hypothesis will be the economic usage or herding strategy of the domestic herds. Production strategies, that is, whether the domestic animals were utilized for primary products, such as meat, or whether they were utilized for secondary products, such as milk, traction, wool or hair, will be reflected in the harvest profile derived from the data (Greenfield 1991, 1999a; Payne 1973). The harvest profile will reflect the different exploitation strategies (Payne 1973), as "the different age and sex groups will be slaughtered by herders according to the type of products they wish the herd to produce" (Greenfield 1991:170).

Earlier research by Greenfield (1986a, 1988, 1989, 1991) showed that secondary products exploitation of domestic animals became a major feature of European subsistence in the early Post-Neolithic. As the advent of transhumance is hypothesized to occur at roughly the same time as this shift to secondary products, this diversified economic focus will complicate the general hypothesis for the origins of transhumant pastoralism in southeastern Europe. Consideration of the use of secondary products of these herds is a factor, which cannot be ignored in this region.

Greenfield (1999a) has broken down the general hypothesis presented above into two main hypotheses with several sub-hypotheses in an effort to examine the origins of transhumance utilizing zooarchaeological data and to distinguish between the different production strategies. These hypotheses are detailed in Greenfield 1999a. However, discussion in this investigation focuses solely on movement issues of domestic herds; as a result, only a general hypothesis need be presented. As a result, the major hypothesis can be stated as follows: if transhumant pastoralism was present in southeastern Europe during the Post-Neolithic, then a complementary culling pattern will be seen in settlements from this period between highland and lowland sites.

A minor hypothesis is: if transhumant pastoralism was present in southeastern Europe during the Post-Neolithic, there will be complementary age groups among young animals were slaughtered between highland and lowland sites with those ages slaughtered in highland sites missing from lowland sites and vice versa. The expected patterns for the lowland, mid-altitude and highland sites for each species are summarized in Table 1.

Table 1. Expectations for Transhumant Movement

Ovis/Capra	Age Class		
	0-2 months	2-6 months	6-12 months
Lowland	Present	Absent	Present
Mid-altitude	Absent	Present	Absent
Highland	Absent	Present	Absent
Bos taurus	Age Class		
	0-1 months	1-8 months	8-18 months
Lowland	Present	Absent	Present
Mid-altitude	Absent	Present	Absent
Highland	Absent	Present	Absent

Figure 4. Mortality profile of *Ovis/Capra*, Early Bronze Age Novačka Ćuprija.

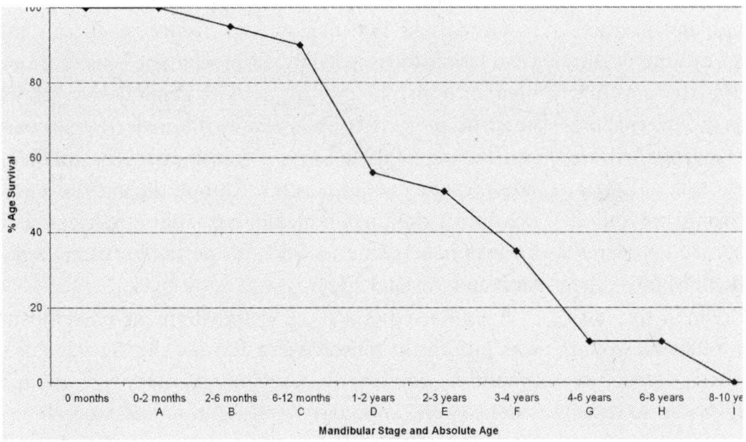

DATA DESCRIPTION

The tooth wear and eruption data consists of mandibular remains from an original sample of 17 sites. However, it was necessary to eliminate several sites due to small sample size. As a result, the final number of sites was 11. Ten of the sites are from the Northern Balkan region, and one site, Megalo Nisi Galanis (Kozani, in Greek Macedonia), is from the Southern Balkan region.

The Northern Balkan region can be divided into lowland, mid-altitude and highland areas. Lowland sites include Foeni-Salaş, Livade, Novačka Ćuprija, Opovo, Stragari and Vinča. Mid-altitude sites are Blagotin, Ljuljaci and Petnica. The sample of highland sites is limited to Kadica Brdo. It is hypothesized that the mid-altitude sites will show harvest profiles most similar to the highland sites in the transhumant movement of herds.

In order to avoid statistical issues such as the influence of sample size on the quantitative distribution of remains, only mandibular and loose tooth samples with ten or more elements per species and per period were considered in the final analysis (Shennan 1988). Sample sizes lower than ten were considered too small to provide accurate harvest profiles.

RESULTS

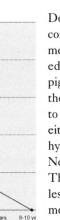

Domestic pig can be considered a control for the transhumant movement of herds. It would be expected that the exploitation patterns of pig should not change over time as these animals were not subjected to the transhumant movement of either cattle or sheep/goat that is hypothesized to occur at the Late Neolithic/Post-Neolithic juncture. This is due to the fact that pigs are less suited to the types of movement that is required of transhumant herds. Although some researchers have noted that pigs are capable of such movement, like the driving of herds long distances to market (Halpern 1999), this tends to be a one-time movement that should not be equated to the regular movements expected in transhumance. As predicted, the harvest patterns do not change over time. All the profiles can be characterized as showing a high mortality of animals between the ages of 2–7 months and 27–36 months. Virtually all animals are slaughtered before reaching adulthood. A summary of the harvest profiles of pig for the major temporal periods is shown in Figure 2. Statistical analysis of sites of the major periods indicates no statistically significant changes. Most importantly, there is no difference in the exploitation patterns of domestic pig between highland and lowland sites either before or after the Late Neolithic/Post-Neolithic juncture or at any other time.

For *Ovis/Capra*, the Middle Bronze Age site of Vinča is the only site where the expectations of the hypotheses are met and there is some suggestion of transhumant pastoralism (Figure 3). As Vinča is a lowland site, the expectations of the hypotheses would be evidence of the 0–2 and 6–12 months age classes and absence of 2–6 months age classes if transhumance is occurring. The harvest profile from Vinča does display these absences. However, the Early Bronze Age site of Novačka Ćuprija is also a lowland site, so it should show the same pattern in a transhumant economy (Figure 4). In contrast, while the Novačka Ćuprija harvest profile shows an absence of the youngest age group (0–2 months), both the 2–6 months and 6–12 months age groups are present. The 0–2 months age class is missing at both sites, in accordance with the major hypothesis. The absence of this age class may not be surprising in these sites and may be a function of assemblage attrition, given the lack of sieving at Vinča (Greenfield 1986a). The slightly older age classes should be less affected (cf. Munson 2000). A problem arises with the presence of the 2–6 months classes at Novačka Ćuprija that is not in accordance with the expectations for a lowland site involved in the transhumant movement of herds. The profiles of Early Bronze Age Novačka Ćuprija and Middle Bronze Age Vinča are very similar. There are no statistically significant differences between the profiles of these sites. It would seem that the evidence for transhumance from this period is somewhat mixed. One site may be interpreted to be part of a transhumant system, and the other may not. However, the lack of significant statistical differences between the profiles, with one supporting the hypotheses, and the other not, makes this evidence for a transhumant movement of *Ovis/Capra* domestic herds unconvincing.

Figure 5. Mortality profile of *Bos taurus*, Late Bronze Age Livade.

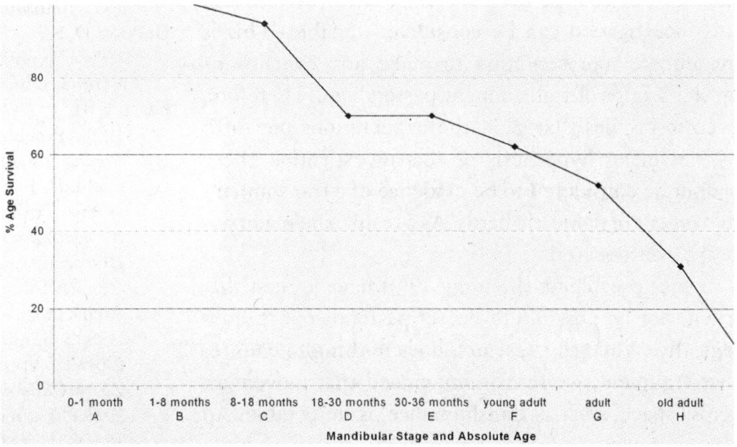

The only site that provides the suggestion of the transhumant movement of herds for *Bos taurus* is the Late Bronze Age site of Livade (Figure 5). The absence of the 1–8 months group is expected in the lowland site assuming a transhumant movement of the domestic herds. The presence of the next age group, 8–18 months, also fits with the expectations of a transhumant movement. As such, it seems that the data implies that animals are being moved in a transhumant fashion. However, acceptance of this profile as strong evidence of transhumance is limited by two taphonomic factors. There was no sieving included in excavation methods at Livade, and very high rates of weathering were present in shallow deposits (Greenfield 1986a). These two factors are most destructive to the youngest age groups (Lyman 1994; Munson 2000).

CONCLUSIONS

The tooth wear and eruption data examined within this investigation does not adequately demonstrate a transhumant movement of domestic herds. It was expected that both *Bos taurus* and *Ovis/Capra* would show the transhumant pattern within each site. However, only two sites fit the expectations of the hypotheses for transhumant movement while only one species per site conforms to the expectations, *Ovis/Capra* from Vinča and *Bos taurus* from Livade. As a result, there is minimal evidence for the transhumant movement of domestic herds in the Northern Balkans based on the tooth wear and eruption data.

Several overriding methodological issues hampered this research. First, sample size was the major limitation of the investigation. Small sample size did not allow for the examination of every domestic species of interest, in each period, and at each site. Second, taphonomic issues, notably the extent of sieving and differential preservation of the age classes due mainly to weathering, were a major contributing factor to the small sample size. Third, the sample was also limited by a lack of highland sites from the earliest periods of the Post-Neolithic, specifically the Eneolithic and the Early Bronze Age. Only one site was considered to be a true highland site (Kadica Brdo).

Shennan (1988) maintains that samples of mandibles less than 15 to 20 should be considered too small to provide accurate harvest profiles. The minimum sample size should be 40 mandibles. As a result, less than 20 per cent of the harvest profiles produced in this investigation can be considered reliable. This is inadequate representation to make any conclusions on the origins of transhumant pastoralism. Therefore, even in profiles that show the expectations put forth by the major hypothesis of this investigation these cannot be considered to be evidence of a transhumant movement of domestic herds. As a result, the major hypothesis is rejected.

Some researchers (Fleming 1971) have argued that it will not be possible to detect pastoralism archaeologically. While this research does nothing to counter that argument, we remain convinced that movement across space, such as transhumance, is detectable. An alternative methodology for examining this problem would be dental cementum analysis. At this time, we are preparing to extend our investigation in this direction, which will hopefully shed further light on the problem.

REFERENCES CITED

Barth, F.

|1961| *Nomads of South Persia. The Basseri Tribe of the Khamseh Confederacy*. Waveland Press, Prospect Heights, Illinois.

Bartosiewicz, L., and H. J. Greenfield.

|1999| Preface. In *Transhumant Pastoralism in Southern Europe: Recent Perspectives from Archaeology, History, and Ethnography*, edited by L. Bartosiewicz, and H. Greenfield, p.7. Series Minor 11. Archaeolingua Publishers (Academy of Sciences), Budapest.

Ehlers, E., and H. Kreutzmann.

|2000| High Mountain Ecology and Economy: Potential and Constraints. In *High Mountain Pastoralism in Northern Pakistan*, edited by E. Ehlers, and H. Kreutzmann, pp. 9–36. Erdkundliches Wissen Heft 132. F. Steiner, Stuttgart.

Ekvall, R. B.

|1968| *Fields on the Hoof: Nexus of Tibetan Nomadic Pastoralism*. Holt, Rinehart and Winston, New York.

Evans-Pritchard, E. E.

|1940| *The Nuer: A Description of Modes of Livelihood and Political Institutions of a Nilotic People*. Clarendon Press, Oxford.

Fleming, A.

|1971| Territorial Patterns in Bronze Age Wessex. *Proceedings of the Prehistoric Society* 27:138–66.

Galaty, J. C., and D. L. Johnson.

|1990| Introduction – Pastoral Systems in Global Perspective. In *The World of Pastoralism: Herding Systems in Comparative Perspective*, edited by J.G. Galaty, and D.L. Johnson, pp. 1–67. Guilford Press, New York.

Geddes, D. S.

|1983| Neolithic Transhumance in the Mediterranean Pyrenees. *World Archaeology* 15:52–66.

Glatzer, B.

|1982| Processes of Nomadization in West Afghanistan. *Studies in Third World Societies* 18:61–86.

Greenfield. H. J.

|1986a| *The Paleoeconomy of the Central Balkans (Serbia). A Zooarchaeological Perspective on the Late Neolithic and Bronze Age (ca. 4500–1000 B.C.)*. British Archaeological Reports International Series 304(i). British Archaeological Reports, Oxford.

|1986b| Summary Report on the Vertebrate Fauna from Nova ka uprija, Serbia (Eneolithic-Late Bronze Age). *Zbornik Radova Narodnog Muzeja* 12:63–74.

|1986c| Fauna: Ki menjaci. In *Ljuljaci: Naselje Protovatinske I Vatinske Kulture*, edited by M. Bogdanovi , pp. 75–78. Narodni Muzej, Kragujevac, Yugoslavia.

|1988| The Origins of Milk and Wool Production in the Old World. *Current Anthropology* 29:573–748.

|1989| Zooarchaeology and Aspects of the Secondary Products Revolution: A Central Balkan Perspective. *Zooarchaeologia* 3:191–200.

|1991| Fauna from the Late Neolithic of the Central Balkans: Issues in Subsistence and Land Use. *Journal of Field Archaeology* 18:161–186.

|1994| Faunal Remains from the Early Neolithic Star evo Settlement at Bukova ka esma, *Starinar: Journal of the Archaeological Institute* 43–44:103–114.

|1996| Sarina Medja, Vrbica, and Ve ina Mala: The Zooarchaeology of Three Late Bronze Age/Early Iron Age Transition Localities near Jagodina, Serbia. *Starinar: Journal of the Archaeological Institute* 45–46:133–142.

|1999a| The Origins of Transhumant Pastoralism in Temperate Southeastern Europe. In *Transhumant Pastoralism in Southern Europe: Recent Perspectives from Archaeology, History, and Ethnography*, edited by L. Bartosiewicz, and H. Greenfield, pp.15–36. Series Minor 11. Archaeolingua Publishers (Academy of Sciences), Budapest.

|1999b| Introduction. In *Transhumant Pastoralism in Southern Europe: Recent Perspectives from Archaeology, History, and Ethnography*, edited by L. Bartosiewicz, and H. Greenfield, pp. 9–12. Series Minor 11. Archaeolingua Publishers (Academy of Sciences), Budapest.

|2001| Transhumant Pastoralism and the Colonization of the Highlands in Temperate Southeastern Europe. In *On Being First: Cultural Innovation and Environmental Consequences of First Peopling*, edited by J. Gillespie, S. Tupakka, and C. de Mille, pp. 471–492. Chacmool Archaeological Association, University of Calgary, Calgary, Alberta.

|n.d.| Re-analysis of the Vertebrate Fauna from *Hajdu ka Vodenica* in the Danubian Iron Gates of Yugoslavia: Subsistence and Taphonomy from the Early Neolithic and Mesolithic. In *New Perspectives on the Iron Gates*, edited by C. Bonsall, V. Boronean , and I. Radovanovi . British Archaeological Reports, Oxford, in press. Ms. 2000.

Greenfield, H. J., and K. Fowler.
|n.d.| Megalo Nisi Galanis and the Secondary Products Revolution in Macedonia. In *Proceedings of the First International Conference on the Zooarchaeology of Greece: Recent Advances*. British School of Archaeology, Athens, in press. Ms. 1999.

Halpern, J. M.
|1999| The Ecological Transformation of a Resettled Area, Pig Herders to Settled Farmers in Central Serbia (Šumadija, Yugoslavia) During the 19th and 20th Centuries. In *Transhumant Pastoralism in Southern Europe: Recent Perspectives from Archaeology, History and Ethnology*, edited by L. Bartosiewicz, and H.J. Greenfield, pp. 79–98. Series Minor 11. Archaeolingua Publishers (Academy of Sciences), Budapest.

Halstead, P.
|1981| Counting Sheep in Neolithic and Bronze Age Greece. In *Patterns of the Past: Studies in Honour of David Clarke*, edited by I. Hodder, G. Isaac, and N. Hammond, pp. 307–339. Cambridge University Press, Cambridge.

Harding, A. F.
|2000| *European Societies in the Bronze Age*. Cambridge University Press, Cambridge.

Hesse, B.
|1982| Slaughter Patterns and Domestication: The Beginnings of Pastoralism in Western Iran. *Man* 17: 403–417.

Khazanov, A.M.
|1984| *Nomads and the Outside World*. Cambridge University Press, Cambridge.

Kordos, L.
|1978a| Changes in the Holocene Climate of Hungary Reflected by the Vole-Thermometer Method. *Kulonnyomat A Foldrajzi Kozlemenyek* 1–3:222–229.
|1978b| A Sketch of the Vertebrate Biostratigraphy of the Hungarian Holocene. *Kulonnyomat A Foldrajzi Kozlemenyek* 1–3:144–160.

Lyman, R. L.
|1994| *Vertebrate Taphonomy*. Cambridge University Press, Cambridge.

Lynch, T. F.
|1971| Preceramic Transhumance in the Callejon de Huaylas, Peru. *American Antiquity* 36:139–147.
|1980| *Guitarrero Cave: Early Man in the Andes*. Academic Press, Toronto.
|1983| Camelid Pastoralism and the Emergence of Tiwanaku Civilization in the South-Central Andes. *World Archaeology* 15:1–14.

Munson, P. J.
|2000| Age-Correlated Differential Destruction of Bones and its Effect on Archaeological Mortality Profiles of Domestic Sheep and Goats. *Journal of Archaeological Science* 27: 391–407.

Niamir-Fuller, M., and N. Turner.
|1999| A Review of Recent Literature on Pastoralism and Transhumance in Africa. In *Managing Mobility in African Rangelands: The Legitimization of Transhumance*, edited by M. Niamir-Fuller. Food and Agriculture Organization of the United Nations, Rome.

Paine, R.
|1994| *Herds of the Tundra: A Portrait of Saami Reindeer Pastoralism*. Smithsonian Institution Press, Washington, D.C.

Payne, S.
|1973| Kill-Off Patterns in Sheep and Goats: The Mandibles from A van Kale. *Anatolian Studies* 13:281–303.

Rafiullah, S. M.
|1966| *The Geography of Transhumance*. Aligarh Muslim University, Aligarh.

Shennan, S.
|1988| *Quantifying Archaeology*. Edinburgh University Press, Edinburgh.

Sterud, Eugene
|1978| Prehistoric populations of the Dinaric Alps. In *Social Archaeology: Beyond Subsistence and Dating*, edited by Charles L. Redman, M. J. Berman, E. V. Curtin, W. T. Langhorne, Jr., N. M. Versaggi, and J. C. Wanser, pp. 381–408. Academic Press, New York.

Walker, M. J.
|1983| Laying a Mega-Myth: Dolmens and Drovers in Prehistoric Spain. *World Archaeology* 15:37–50.

CLOVIS PROGENITORS: FROM SWAN POINT, ALASKA TO ANZICK SITE, MONTANA IN LESS THAN A DECADE?

C. Vance Haynes, Jr.

C. Vance Haynes, Jr., Departments of Anthropology and Geosciences, P. O. Box 210030, University of Arizona, Tucson, AZ 85721, U.S.A.

ABSTRACT

With the recent over emphasis of a coastal migration route for the first Americans to the near exclusion of an ice-free interior route, there is a need for rationality. The purpose of this exercise is to show that the latter is still a viable working hypothesis.

Clovis-site geochronology correlates with northern hemisphere climate changes of the Pleistocene-Holocene transition. Deglaciation chronology and paleoecological evidence from Alaska and Canada can reasonably be correlated with the same paleoclimate data. These indicate that a rapid movement of Nenana explorers from the Yukon Plateau along the Interior Plains of Canada to the Anzick site in Montana may have been possible during Allerød time. The development of fluted projectile points by Clovis progenitors may have occurred as live mammoths were first encountered south of Lake Peace. The initial journey of discovery and subsequent expansion of the Clovis technocomplex may have occurred in less than a century. And extinction of the Pleistocene megafauna at the onset of Younger Dryas also may have occurred in less than a century, suggesting that human impact was only one of several factors causing the extinction.

Here I present a conjectural interpretation of the migration of Clovis progenitors, the Clovis discovery of North America, and the relation of these events to the extinction of Pleistocene megafauna. This interpretation is based upon what I consider the best (most compelling) available evidence. The peopling of America is viewed in the light of North American climate change and its effect on the geologic record. It is assumed that Clovis progenitors, though primarily hunters, were opportunistic generalists exploring a rapidly changing environment (Kelly and Todd 1988; Hoffecker et al. 1993; Webb and Rindos 1997), initially with essentially no competition from other humans and with no concept of what lay ahead. They were pioneers as well as explorers in every sense of the word, discovering new foods, discovering new lithic sources, and dealing with rapid climate changes, as well as landscape changes, some perhaps catastrophic.

CLOVIS-SITE GEOCHRONOLOGY AND CLIMATE CHANGE

Buried stratigraphic evidence of the Clovis occupation of the conterminous United States is confined to very localized alluvial channel deposits, to intermittent pond deposits and to buried land surfaces, commonly erosional, adjacent to the channels and depressions (Haynes 1984). Uncalibrated radiocarbon ages of this period range from approximately 11,600 to 11,000 B.P. (Taylor et al. 1996), essentially during the Allerød warm period of northern hemisphere climate as seen in laminated ice cores and paleolake records (Patterson and Hammer 1987; Stuiver et al. 1995). In the American West, part of the Clovis period may have been a time of drought (Haynes 1991; see Holliday 2000 for an alternative view). With a few equivocal exceptions, no compelling evidence of the presence of humans in North America has been found in older strata. Exceptions may be Cactus Hill, Virginia (McAvoy and McAvoy 1997) and the Hebior and Schaefer mammoth sites in Wisconsin (Overstreet and Stafford 1997).

Sediments deposited directly upon the Clovis age landscape commonly are wet-meadow soils in alluvium and loess ("black mats") or intermittent pond deposits that are stratigraphic manifestations of Younger

Dryas climate and imply higher water tables (Haynes 1998). Archaeological associations include Folsom-Midland, Plainview-Goshen, Agate Basin, and Dalton technocomplexes. Throughout the United States, no extinct megafauna remains other than bison and no in situ Clovis artifacts have ever been found within the Younger Dryas deposits or black mats; no Folsom artifacts have ever been found in situ in underlying strata or in conclusive association with mammoth. The Pleistocene termination of the megafauna appears to have been geologically instantaneous on a land surface that forms the stratigraphic contact between the Younger-Dryas- and Allerød-age deposits.

CLOVIS PROGENITORS

The best candidate for Clovis progenitors appears to be the Nenana complex of Alaska, as Goebel et al. (1991), Hamilton and Goebel (1999), and Yesner (1998) have claimed, or perhaps the American Early Beringian Complex if Nenana-Denali represent essentially the same people, as suggested by West (1996) (see Bever 2001 for a review). There are significant differences from Clovis artifacts but, considering the environmental differences between central Alaska and the Great Plains with its abundant megafauna, the corridor filter, and the time factor, significant changes are to be expected.

As Fiedel (2000a) indicated, the timing is reasonable. The earliest Nenana radiocarbon dates so far are 11,800 B.P. at Walker Road (Goebel et al. 1996) and 11,700 B.P. at Swan Point (Yesner 1996), and the earliest Clovis ages are 11,590 ± 90 B.P. at the Aubrey site in north central Texas (Ferring 1995) and 11,550 ± 60 B.P. for the Anzick Clovis burial (Stafford et al. 1991; T. W. Stafford, personal communication 1998). Is 250 years (more or less depending on calibration and actual ages) enough time for Clovis progenitors to go 6,000 km? That is about 10 generations at an average rate of 20 km per year. As discussed later, this is probably a gross underestimate of their rate of travel.

Webb and Rindos (1997:245) made a convincing argument that the initial Paleoindian populations "were highly mobile generalized foragers who opportunistically hunted a familiar, but comparatively rare" big-game fauna and who did not stay in any given area long enough to have become fully aware of all of the local resources. They carried desirable raw material over considerable distances as finished artifacts in light, highly transportable tool kits "determined by the unfamiliarity in detail...with the territory through which they moved" (Webb and Rindos 1997:245). Their "explorative mode" was an extractive one that "maximized movement over unfamiliar territory" (Webb and Rindos 1997:245). Further, Surovell (2000a) has devised a mathematical model for Clovis mobility and expansion that suggests it is easier (cheaper) to raise children with more frequent camp moves than with staying put for extended periods.

NORTH AMERICAN DEGLACIATION AND CLIMATE CHANGE

There can be little doubt that global climate is the major control or driving force behind deglaciation. Recent research on the geochronology of climate change of the northern hemisphere in relation to American archaeology has been reviewed by Fiedel (1999). Comparing the record of deglaciation and the limited archaeological record to the ice-core records and those of paleolakes (Patterson and Hammer 1987; Stuiver et al. 1995), some pertinent correlations exist that may not be completely fortuitous. The rapid and uninterrupted retreat of the Laurentide ice between 13,000 and 12,000 B.P. is probably in response to the warm Bølling climatic period preceded and ended by brief cold periods, Oldest and Older Dryas, which appear to have had little or no effect in retarding deglaciation. From about 12,000 to 10,800 B.P., the fluctuating warm Allerød period, with an Inter-Allerød Cold period (IACP), furthered deglaciation. In North America, the Two Creeks interstade (TCI) more or less coincides with the Allerød of Europe. Kaiser (1994) has shown by dendrochronology that the TCI lasted at least 252 years between 12,050 and 11,750 B.P.

After its inception about 11,700 B.P., Lake Agassiz attained an area of approximately 134,000 km^2 and drained to the Mississippi system before rapidly draining to the Atlantic Ocean via the Great Lakes and the Saint Lawrence Valley about 10,900 B.P. (Leverington et al. 2000). West of Lake Agassiz, between 12,000 and 10,700 B.P., a dynamic complex of 18 rapidly changing meltwater spillways existed across the northern Great Plains; these were the result of catastrophic

Fluted point and site distribution:
● = Clovis point
= other fluted point finds
= Nenana site
= Clovis sites

Radiocarbon age distribution:
= large mammal bone > 11,500 B.P.
= large mammal bone 11,500–11,000 B.P.
= mammoth bone ≥ 11,500 B.P.
= mammoth bone < 11,500 B.P.
= Arctic ground squirrel bone or nest > 11,500 B.P.
= wood

Localities:
1 = Broken Mammoth, Swan Point and Mead sites, Alaska
2 = Healy Lake area, Alaska
3 = Tangle Lakes area, Alaska
4 = Dawson-Klondike area, Yukon Territory
5 = Charlie Lake Cave, British Columbia
6 = Birch Hills, Alberta
7 = Upper Pembina Valley, Alberta
8 = Vermillion Lake site, Alberta
9 = Sibbald Flat, Alberta
10 = St. Mary Lake, Alberta
11 = Kyle mammoth, Saskatchewan
12 = Boon Lake, Alberta
13 = Locknore Creek, Fraser River Valley, British Columbia
14 = Kluane Lake, Yukon Territory
15 = Portage Mountain Dame tusk locality, British Columbia
16 = Clover Bar gravel pit, East Edmonton, Alberta
17 = Anzick site, Montana
18 = Indian Creek site, Montana
19 = Simon site, Idaho
20 = Richey-Roberts site, east Wenatchee, Washington

Winter camps:
A = Frances Lake, Yukon Territory
B = Toad River, British Columbia
C = Beaton River, British Columbia
D = Grande Prairie, Alberta
E = Drayton Valley, Alberta
F = Patricia, Alberta
G = Coal Bank, Montana
H = Ringling, Montana

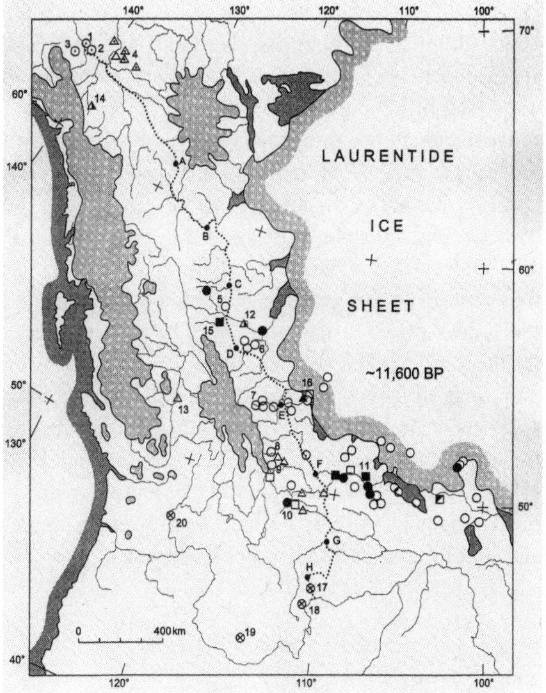

Figure 1. Generalized map of an ice-free passage at approximately 11,600 B.P. in relation to the distribution of fluted points, pertinent radiocarbon ages and proposed winter camps (modified after Dyke and Prest 1987; Jackson and Duk-Rodkin 1996; Kehew and Teller 1994; Lemmen et al. 1995; Morlan et al. 1999; Smith 1994).

floods draining 13 large ice-dammed lakes (Kehew and Teller 1994). Some of these events may have been witnessed by Clovis progenitors.

Deglaciation began in the Great Lakes region with the retreat of Port Huron ice, and reached a maximum retreat at the height of the TCI, just before the Two Creeks forest bed drowned around 11,800 B.P. The forest was drowned by a rising Lake Michigan as ice of the Two Rivers lobe readvanced and blocked the straits of Mackinac and the Cheboygan outlets (Fullerton 1980; Hansel et al. 1985). Post-Clovis fluted point makers appear to have occupied the Great Lakes areas soon after the Two Rivers advance and during the time Lake Algonquin existed (Deller and Ellis 1988; Gramly 1988; Storck 1988), essentially during the Younger Dryas cold period, a rapid return to glacial conditions that lasted about 1,000 years.

AN ICE-FREE PASSAGE

The potential significance of an ice-free corridor to the peopling of the New World was proposed by Johnston (1933) without benefit of chronological control. It was revived (Haynes 1964) when renewed radiocarbon dating of the Two Creeks forest bed (Broecker and Farrand 1963) indicated that the major glacial retreat of the Two Creeks interstade was earlier than the radiocarbon ages of Clovis sites (Haynes 1980).

After reviewing the current status of knowledge regarding the prospects for an ice-free passage and plotting the location of fluted point finds in deglaciated areas as well as pertinent radiocarbon ages on bone, wood and ground squirrel nests (Figure 1) (Haynes 2004; Morlan et al. 1999; Wilson and Burns 1999), it is apparent that the earliest time for pertinent deglaciation of the Yukon Plateau and the western Interior Plains of Canada is 12,000 B.P. However, the passage of humans and animals would depend upon whether environmental conditions such as muskeg, runoff, catastrophic floods and wind chill factors would have allowed it. A recently opened corridor would have been a formidable environment for people to penetrate, one characterized by proglacial lakes, catastrophic floods, and ever-changing drainages (Teller and Kehew 1994), as well as stagnant ice and hummocky ground moraine (Mandryk 1996). However, eventually muskeg, lake and floodwater would have given way to herb- and shrub-dominated vegetation, steppe grassland and riparian areas (MacDonald and McLeod 1996) as drainages became integrated. With the eastern part of the corridor being a land of proglacial lakes (Teller 1995), waterfowl would have been abundant during summer months (Fiedel 2000b). Evidence of the first occupants of the corridor necessarily would be extremely rare, but might be found under aeolian sediments blanketing uplands and the earliest terraces formed during degradation and integration of the drainages. However, as Wilson and Burns (1999) state, some evidence could be deeply buried.

Burns (1996), after evaluating the radiocarbon ages of vertebrate bones in the corridor, proposes that a mammoth steppe environment, as per Guthrie (1982), was established there at least by 11,600 B.P. He further proposes that the lag time between deglaciation and faunal recolonization probably was on the order of hundreds of years rather than thousands. Wilson (1996) described the Alberta part of the corridor as having open poplar woodlands with major patches of grassland, with *B. bison antiquus* as far north as Peace River at least by 11,500 B.P.

From the upper Yukon drainage to Medicine Hat, Alberta, Morlan et al. (1999) show eight localities of mammal bones dating between 11,500 and 11,000 B.P. Considering that at least some of the bone ages could be minimum values because of bone's notorious reputation for younger contamination (Haynes 1967; Taylor 1987), it appears that an ice-free passage was open and passable to people and game animals at least by 11,600 B.P. and, therefore, at the time of occupation of Central Alaska by Paleoindians between 11,800 and 11,300 B.P. (Hamilton and Goebel 1999; Yesner 1998).

Sometime between 12,000 and 11,000 B.P., essentially during the Allerød warm period, there appear to be no significant barriers to ingress and egress via a passage free of glacial ice south of the Mackenzie Mountains (Figure 1). Recently deglaciated areas, initially proglacial lakes and wetlands, soon became open prairies veined with riparian habitats (White et al. 1985), even though some areas of stagnant ice may have remained (Mandryk 1996).

Recent geological work in northwestern Canada by Jackson and Duk-Rodkin (1996) indicates, that although a Peel Valley route to the Mackenzie Valley opened soon after 13,000 B.P., passage southward along the east side of the Mackenzie Mountains (Figure 1) was blocked by glacial Lake Mackenzie until ca. 11,000 B.P. (Lemmen et al. 1995). This is too late for Clovis progenitors to pass that way on dry land (Mandryk 2001). On the other hand, Smith (1994) shows positions of Laurentide ice retreating about 500 years earlier than Lemmen et al. (1995), who state that they present the most conservative position. In any case, the rapidly changing fluviolacustrine conditions in the Mackenzie corridor probably discouraged travel in that area.

Jackson and Duk-Rodkin's map (1996:Figure 14.2) for the period 12,000 to 11,000 B.P. shows a potential route through the Yukon Plateau west of the Mackenzie Mountains via the Tintina Trench and the Pelly River to the upper Liard River. Passage depends on this route being deglaciated by between 11,800 and 11,600 B.P. Jackson and Duk-Rodkin (1996) describe the northern Cordillera as a complex of stagnating ice and ice-dammed lakes before 13,000 B.P. The maps of Morlan et al. (1999) show the area between the St. Elias Mountains and the Mackenzie Range as deglaciated by 12,000 B.P. Therefore, it seems possible, if not likely, that people could have traversed the Pelly and upper Liard valleys by 11,600 B.P. This would bring them into the Interior Plains at Nelson Forks (Figure 1).

THE EXPLORATION OF NORTH AMERICA 11,600–11,592 B.P.

Since the models of Haynes (1966) and Martin (1967; Mosimann and Martin 1975), periodically there have been new models of the colonization of the New World. Examples are Hassan 1981, Hoffecker et al. 1993, Meltzer 1995, Webb and Rindos 1997, Anderson and Gillam 2000, and Steele et al. 2000, to name a few. Some of these are summarized in Haynes (2004). As Anderson and Gillam (2000) conclude, the modeling possibilities are boundless.

In the model that follows, I consider that part of the founding population of interior Alaska were adventurous pioneers who seasonally explored new ground by following river valleys southeastward, observing active deglaciation and taking advantage of new discoveries: new plants, new foods, new lithic sources and new vistas. The ever present question would have been "When and where are we to meet other people?"

The routes taken are derived from maps showing detailed relief data. Distances are determined by doubling valley lengths to estimate actual kilometres traveled. This is more conservative than the 1.5 factor used earlier (Haynes 2004). The rate of travel is assumed to be 10 km per day over familiar ground in the first year and 5 km per day while exploring unfamiliar areas. Travel each summer is from 1 May to sometime in August, September, or October (104 to 170 days). Winter camps last from 195 to 261 days (Table 1). This may be too conservative, considering that travel over northern wet lands is much easier in winter than summer (R. D. Guthrie, personal communication 2001).

The Nenana occupation of Central Alaska began at least by 11,800 B.P. The Broken Mammoth, Mead and Swan Point sites occur in the Tanana River Valley, which leads headward to the divide with the upper Yukon River basin. Arctic ground squirrel nests in the Klondike District (Figure 1, locality 4) with radiocarbon ages between 13,350 and 11,170 B.P. (Morlan et al. 1999) indicate arctic steppe conditions in the region Nenana people would cross in moving up the Yukon Valley or the Pelly Valley, into the deglaciated Yukon Plateau. Over a generation or two, Nenana people may have explored the steppic grassland of the Yukon Plateau as far south as the upper Liard Valley, and annually witnessed the retreat of valley glaciers in the Selwyn and St. Elias Mountains under the influence of relatively warm, dry summer climate (MacDonald and McLeod 1996) during Allerød warming. Each summer, they may have explored farther to the south while subsisting on big game, rumen, fish and waterfowl along lakes and rivers no longer draining from stagnating ice and retreating valley glaciers. Base camps may have shifted farther south every year or so. At the same time, conditions on the Interior Plains continued to improve as Laurentide ice retreated. Lakes and rivers could be traversed by boat and on ice in winter, and dogs may have been used as pack animals (Henderson 1994). After eight years (11,600 to 11,592 B.P.) they may have made a winter camp near Ringling, Montana, 40 km north of the Anzick site (Figure 1, locality 17). A hypothetical scenario as to how this movement might have taken place follows, with the itinerary shown in Table 1.

Table 1: Migration Itinerary of the First Americans from Swan Point, Alaska, to Indian Springs, Montana, via the Anzick Site.

Leg	From	To	Valley Distance (km)	Distance Traveled (km)	Cumulative Distance (km)	Days at 10 km/day[a]	Days at 5 km/day	Cumulative Days	Cumulative Months
1	Swan Point	Healy River	70	70	70	7		7	May
2	Healy River	Dot Lake	55	55	125	6		13	1
3	Dot Lake	Cathedral Rapids	40	40	165	4		17	
4	Cathedral Rapids	Tetlin Junction	60	60	225	6		23	
5	Tetlin Junction	Middle Ladue	60	60	285	6		29	
6	Middle Ladue	White River	70	70	355	7		36	June
7	White River	Yukon River	50	50	405	5		41	2
8	Yukon River	Coffee Creek	40	40	445	4		45	
9	Coffee Creek	Isaac Creek	30	30	475	3		48	
10	Isaac Creek	Fort Selkirk	60	60	535	6		54	
11	Fort Selkirk	Pelly Crossing	50	50	585	5		59	
12	Pelly Crossing	Tintina Trench	110	110	695	11		70	July
13	Tintina Trench	Faro	80	80	775	8		78	3
14	Faro	Ross River	60	60	835	6		84	
15	Ross River	Finlayson Lake	110	110	945	11		95	August
16	Finlayson Lake	Frances Lake	85	85	1030	9		104	4
A[b]	First winter camp, 12 August, year 1 (11,600 B.P.) to 30 April, year 2 (11,599 B.P.) = 261 days								5–12
17	Frances Lake	Tuchitua	55	110	1140		22	387	May 13
18	Tuchitua	Watson Lake	95	190	1330		38	425	June 14
19	Watson Lake	Contact Creek	60	120	1450		24	449	July 15
20	Contact Creek	Fireside	60	120	1570		24	473	August 16
21	Fireside	Liard River	70	140	1710		28	501	September 17
22	Liard River	Toad River Post	65	130	1840		26	527	October 18
B	Second winter camp, 9 October, year 2 (11,599 B.P.) to 30 April, year 3 (11,598 B.P.) = 203 days								19–24
23	Toad River Post	Beaver River	60	120	1960		24	754	May 25
24	Beaver River	Nelson Forks	40	80	2040		16	770	June 26
25	Nelson Forks	Kwigana River	60	120	2160		24	794	July 27
26	Kwigana River	Fort Nelson	70	140	2300		28	822	August 28
27	Fort Nelson	Fontas	85	170	2470		34	856	September 29
28	Fontas	Beaton River	110	220	2690		44	900	October 30
C	Third winter camp, 17 October, year 3 (11,598 B.P.) to 30 April, year 4 (11,597 B.P.) = 195 days								31–36
29	Beaton River	Altona	70	140	2830		28	1123	May 37
30	Altona	Fort St. John	80	160	2990		32	1155	June 38
31	Fort St. John	Dawson Creek	75	150	3140		30	1185	July 39
32	Dawson Creek	Beaverlodge	80	160	3300		32	1217	August 40
33	Beaverlodge	Grande Prairie	60	120	3420		24	1241	September 41
D	Fourth winter camp, 23 September, year 4 (11,597 B.P.) to 30 April, year 5 (11,596 B.P.) = 219 days								42–48
34	Grande Prairie	Calais	90	180	3600		36	1496	May 49
35	Calais	Fox Creek	95	190	3790		38	1534	June 50

Table 1. Migration itinerary of the First Americans from Swan Point, Alaska, to Indian Springs, Montana, via the Anzick Site.

36	Fox Creek	Whitecourt	85	170	3960	34	1568	July 51
37	Whitecourt	Drayton Valley	115	230	4190	46	1614	August 52 September 53
E	Fifth winter camp, 29 September, year 5 (11,596 B.P.) to 30 April, year 6 (11,595 B.P.) = 213 days							54–60
38	Drayton Valley	Red Deer	130	260	4450	52	1879	May 61
39	Red Deer	Drumheller	120	240	4690	48	1927	June 62 July 63 August 64
40	Drumheller	Patricia	110	220	4910	44	1971	September 65
F	Sixth winter camp, 21 September, year 6 (11,595 B.P.) to 30 April, year 7 (11,594 B.P.) = 221 days							66–72
41	Patricia	Medicine Hat	105	210	5120	42	2234	May 73
42	Medicine Hat	Manyberries	75	150	5270	30	2264	June 74
43	Manyberries	Wild Horse	60	120	5390	24	2288	July 75
44	Wild Horse	Havre	70	140	5530	28	2316	August 76
45	Havre	Big Sandy	50	100	5630	20	2336	September
46	Big Sandy	Coal Bank	20	40	5670	8	2344	77
G	Seventh winter camp, 29 September, year 7 (11,594 B.P.) to 30 April, year 8 (11,593 B.P.) = 237 days							78–84
47	Coal Bank	Eagle Buttes	25	50	5720	10	2567	May
48	Eagle Buttes	Judith River	40	80	5800	16	2583	85
49	Judith River	Ware	70	140	5940	28	2611	June 86
50	Ware	Judith Gap	60	120	6060	24	2635	July 87
51	Judith Gap	Harlowton	35	70	6130	14	2649	August 88
52	Harlowton	Martinsdale	35	70	6200	14	2663	September
53	Martinsdale	Ringling	55	110	6310	22	2685	89
H	Eighth winter camp, 5 September, year 8 (11,593 B.P.) to 30 April, year 9 (11,592 B.P.) = 237 days							90–96
54	Ringling	Anzick	40	80	6390	16	2938	May
55	Anzick	Yellowstone River	35	70	6460	14	2952	97
56	Yellowstone River	Livingston	10	20	6480	4	2956	June
57	Livingston	Bozeman	40	80	6560	16	2972	
58	Bozeman	Three Forks	50	100	6660	20	2992	98
59	Three Forks	Sappington	30	60	6720	12	3004	July
60	Sappington	White Hall	40	80	6800	16	3020	
61	White Hall	Twin Bridges	50	100	6900	20	3040	99 August
62	Twin Bridges	Sheridan	15	30	6930	8	3046	100

[a] The journey from Swan Point to Frances Lake is assumed to have been done before so they travel at a rate of 10 km per day. They go into winter camp at Frances Lake 12 August, 104 days from Swan Point, a month and a half early, in order to scout ahead and prepare for about five months of travel at an average rate of 5 km per day during each summer.

[b] Letters designating winter camps are shown on Figure 1.

SWAN POINT TO ANZICK IN EIGHT YEARS: A FANCIFUL YET POSSIBLE JOURNEY

Having already explored the Yukon Plateau over several summers, a band of two dozen explorers might average about 10 km per day over familiar territory (Table 1). Hypothetically, they depart Swan Point (Figure 1, locality 1) on 1 May, 11,600 B.P. and go up the Tanana Valley to Tetlin Junction where they cross the divide with the White River Valley, descend Ladue Creek, and reach White River on 5 June. They go down White River to the Yukon River and up the Yukon Valley as far as the mouth of the Pelly River, camping near Fort Selkirk on 23 June. From previous summer explorations, they know the best way to the Liard Valley is via the Pelly Valley rather than the Yukon Valley. They follow the Pelly Valley to Ross River via Pelly Crossing, Earn Lake and the Tintina Trench to Faro, and reach Ross River on 23 July. From here to Finlayson Lake, 11 sleeps, they leave the Yukon drainage basin and enter the catchment of the Liard River. The Finlayson and Frances River valleys guide them to Frances Lake (Figure 1, winter camp A) where, on 12 August, they go into winter camp early so they can explore ahead before heading to the unknown in the spring.

While in winter camp, parties explore tributary valleys, as well as down the Frances River as far as Tuchitua. Women in camp prepare for the coming winter by gathering firewood, drying meat, making pemmican and preparing storage rooms in the permafrost. Others prepare and repair equipment and clothing during the winter. Subsistence is on deer, elk, caribou, moose, fish and fowl for meat, and on rumen for plant food. Bison (*B. priscus*) are rare but occasionally taken. Experiences and discoveries of their trek are recounted around the camp fire, and in ceremony, the gods are honoured and thanked for the successful journey.

In spring of the second year, 11,599 B.P., they follow the Frances Valley, at a reduced rate of 5 km per day (Table 1), to its junction with the Liard River near Watson Lake, arriving on 29 June. They explore the Liard Valley to the junction with Toad River, British Columbia (Figure 1, winter camp B), where they go into their second winter camp on 14 September. A small group makes a reconnaissance downriver and becomes the first humans ever to see the vast Interior Plains of Canada. The western edge of Laurentide ice can be seen in the far distance with proglacial lakes along the ice front. Along the mountain front, there appears to be a belt of ice-free and vegetated terrain extending southward as far as the eye can see.

This vista dominates the winter conversations. Band leaders' curiosity and thirst for knowledge of the beyond leads to a decision to go as far southward as possible and not return to a base camp as winter approaches. It is decided that six people will return in the spring to the main tribal encampment in the upper Tanana Valley to inform others of their findings and to encourage them to follow. The return journey takes much less time than the outward one because it is over familiar ground without side trips to explore areas missed earlier. It is agreed that the pioneering band will continue southward and mark their trail with stone cairns or decorated poles.

In mid-April 11,598 B.P. the six couriers start their return trip, and the main band continues down the Liard Valley on 1 May, reaching Nelson Forks on 9 June. The next morning they exit the Liard Valley by heading southeast up the Fort Nelson River. Having seen no evidence of other humans since leaving the Yukon Plateau, they pass the mouth of the Kwigana River on 3 July, reach Fort Nelson at the end of July, and pass the Fontas River on 3 September. They follow Conroy Creek to a winter camp at Beaton River on 17 October (Figure 1, winter camp C).

In early spring of year four, 11,597 B.P., the band descends the Beaton River between the Clear Hills and the Rocky Mountain foothills. They discover Lake Peace and camp near Fort Saint John on 29 June. Forays along the shore indicate no end to the lake eastward, and a way around to the west involves crossing a not-so-peaceful Peace River. A water crossing is inevitable. Many tepee hides are sacrificed to make bull boats. After crossing Lake Peace near the mouth of the river, they continue southeastward along the mountain front for 30 sleeps, reaching the Dawson Creek area on 29 July. In passing between the foothills and the Saddle Hills, they find buffalo spoor, and near Beaverlodge on 30 August they discover a large herd of bison (*B. antiquus*). They follow and observe the herd for several days and notice that they differ from the bison they know from farther north. After several failed attempts to kill a buffalo, they succeed, using spear throwers and Chindadn spears, to bring down a young female near Grande Prairie in early September.

In the meantime, the six couriers make it back to Swan Point by the end of August. A month later they, along with 24 others, head for Toad River and, by continuing through the winter, reach the Toad River camp site by February. They pick up the well-marked trail and continue down the Liard and on to the Plains. At a rate of 10 km per day, they overtake the initial band in winter camp in October 11,597 B.P. near Grande Prairie (Figure 1, winter camp D). This results in great jubilation and celebration by all.

Still they find no people, and there are bison in greater numbers than they have ever seen. They continue to perfect their bison hunting weaponry after going into winter camp near Grande Prairie on 23 September. Bison hides, being nearly twice as large as elk hides, reduce the number needed for covering a tepee, but they require thinning by much scraping. This process is perfected by the women as men perfect their bison hunting skills. One adult bison provides as much meat as two elk or one and a half large moose. They know that bison horns make good scoops and ladles. They are becoming a bison-oriented hunting society.

Before the first snow, a hunting party discovers dry boules of dung that can only be from the very large animals, mammoths, that they know about only from legends handed down by their elders and from skeletons they occasionally found in central Alaska. This find generates great excitement. Scouting parties, in searching for live mammoths, find trails along the Smokey River with tracks that can only be those of mammoths. No fresh tracks appear after snow falls, so the search is abandoned until spring. During their winter camping, there is much discussion of how they might bring down a mammoth.

The band departs the Grande Prairie camp with great anticipation on 1 May of year five, 11,596 B.P. They head eastward to Smokey River, follow a mammoth trail up Simonette Creek, and discover a herd of mammoths near Calais on Lake Sturgeon on 5 June. They follow the herd at a distance while considering attack strategies. From a ravine, they ambush a young female on the edge of the herd. Several spears make good hits but fail to adequately penetrate the hide. A large female, the matriarch, charges the hunters as other mammoths mill about in a state of confusion. The matriarch does not follow through and leads the herd away at a trot.

The band continues southeasterly following Losegun Creek and hunting bison. On 16 July, after passing Fox Creek, they cross a divide, enter the valley of the Athabasca River, and follow it between the foothills and Swan Hills, reaching Whitecourt on 16 August. Following mammoth trails, which are easy to travel, they proceed up the McLeod River, pass Chip Lake, cross the Pembina River, and make a winter camp on the North Saskatchewan River near Drayton Valley (Figure 1, winter camp E) on 29 September, having made several more unsuccessful attempts to kill a mammoth. Larger, stouter weaponry is required. Large cobbles of chert are found by prospecting outwash gravels. From these, large bifacial spear points are made and thinned by removing several short longitudinal flakes from the base. But one band member finds that, with careful platform preparation, he is able to remove larger, longer longitudinal blade-like flakes and thereby reduce the thickness of the centre of the biface for a distance approaching or exceeding the width of the base. This greatly facilitates firmly seating the point in the end slot of a foreshaft, previously meant for Chindadn points, and cementing it in place with resin. The shaft is completed by tightly wrapping with wet sinew and streamlining it with a thin veneer of resin after the sinew dries. Also, heftier spear throwers are constructed to accommodate the more robust spears. After much practice throwing, they are ready to try out the new projectiles. Before any big snows, the new weaponry is tried on bison with spectacular success. They look ahead to a successful mammoth hunt in the spring.

On 1 May of year six, 11,595 B.P., they take a southeasterly course past Buck Lake and into the foothills following a mammoth trail. In descending Blindman Creek, they encounter a small herd of mammoths and follow it for several days. Near Red Deer, they find two young adult male mammoths so intent on their sparring that they are unaware of their surroundings. When one is attacked by the hunters from both sides (Figure 2), the other runs for the herd. The hunters bring down the young mammoth by spearing it first from one side and then from the other as it turns its attention from one source of danger to the other. After it falls, a spear is thrust to the heart with the full weight of the hunter behind it. As life ebbs from the mammoth, the hunters immediately start the butchering process. The rest of the band comes up and makes camp nearby. This day, 21 June 11,595 B.P., is a special

Figure 2. A Clovis mammoth kill as depicted by artist Donald Cox of Bisbee, Arizona. (By permission of the artist).

day, one that results in several days of feasting, celebrating, and paying homage to the gods. However, as always, there is a certain degree of anxiety as to when they will encounter other people.

Continuing their southeasterly trek, they follow the Red Deer Valley, reach Drumheller on 8 August, Dinosaur Park on 19 September, and make winter camp near Patricia on 21 September 11,595 B.P. (Figure 1, winter camp F). There is much discussion and excitement about the fossil bones exposed in the badlands. They are strange, rock hard, and heavy. Uncertain of their meaning they move out of the Red Deer Valley and make their winter camp about 10 km to the south. There is much discussion about the prospects of finding living examples of these strange animals somewhere ahead. However, one band member believes these are a form of animal that no longer exists because the gods were not happy with it.

From Patricia on 1 May of year seven, 11,594 B.P., they move overland, following mammoth trails to Medicine Hat passing near Ralston and Bowell. From Medicine Hat on 12 June, they head for the Cypress Hills and explore the western end in late June and early July before camping near Manyberries on 11 July. From Manyberries, they take a southwesterly heading toward the Sweetgrass Hills in Montana, visible in the far distance. On 30 July, they intersect the Milk River and follow it southeasterly, camping near Wild Horse 4 to 5 August. They then go up the Big Sandy Valley, over a divide, and down the Little Sandy Valley to the Missouri River near Coal Bank (Figure 1, winter camp G), where they make winter camp on 29 September. During the winter they explore up the Missouri Valley toward Fort Benton and downriver opposite the White Cliffs as far as Arrow Creek. Downstream appears to be the best choice for moving on in the spring.

A catastrophic flood takes the life of the leader and his son during their exploration of the Missouri Valley near Fort Benton. On their way back to the winter camp, the son's body is found among boulders on an exposed river bar. Near the winter camp at Coal Bank, the body was placed on a scaffold with great but solemn ceremony. The remains will be taken with them in the spring to be kept on temporary scaffolds until defleshed. They will eventually be interred with red ochre and grave goods when an appropriate location is found.

They depart at the beginning of May, pass Eagle Buttes on 10 May, and proceed up Arrow Creek, which eventually heads toward the Little Belt Mountains. Not wanting to enter the high country, they go back to the Missouri, follow it past Missouri Bench and camp at the mouth of the Judith River 20 May. Via the Judith Valley, they reach Ware 23 June and follow Ross Fork to Judith Gap, camping there 17 July. Next day, they take a southerly course, crossing Roberts Creek and following Antelope Creek to its junction with the Musselshell River near Harlowton two weeks later. The Musselshell Valley leads them upstream to near Martinsdale 14 August, where they take the South Fork to a divide between the Castle Mountains to the north and Reservation Mountain to the south. They go into a winter camp near Ringling (Figure 1, winter camp H) at the junction of Sixteen Mile Creek with Lost Creek on 5 September of year eight, 11,593 B.P. The realization that they may be the only people in this vast and bountiful land is awesome.

During the winter, they make exploratory trips up Lost Creek and down Potter Creek to the Shields River, where they find a niche under a prominent sandstone hill at the Anzick site (Lahren 2001) that will be the burial place of the chief's son in the spring. In the winter camp, the best artisans in stone make superb grave goods using fine tool stones found during prospecting trips far and wide. Red ochre is prepared, and antler rods are made that fitted together form a long slender lance socketed to a stout cane shaft. The lance is for thrusting into the heart of a mammoth, to administer the *coup de grâce*, once it is brought down.

After breaking camp in the spring, the band reaches the Anzick site (Figure 1, locality 17) on 16 May of year nine, 11,592 B.P. They inter the bones and artifacts packed in red ochre with great ceremony.

From Anzick, they follow the Shields Valley to the Yellowstone River and camp near Livingston on 30 May. Over the next decade, they explore up and down the Yellowstone Valley and eventually split into two bands, one going westerly to the Indian Creek area (Figure 1, locality 18) and beyond, the other following the Yellowstone out onto the Great Plains. They plan to rendezvous at the mouth of the Big Horn River on a yearly basis.

DISCUSSION

By this scenario, it took them eight years to travel 6,390 km from the upper Tanana Valley to the Anzick site, estimated by multiplying valley lengths on maps by a factor of two to estimate actual kilometres traveled. If they continued traveling at 5 km per day during the winters, instead of making winter camps, the journey would have taken 3.5 years. Even if they traveled at 1 km per day, the trip could have been made in 18 years.

Hundreds to perhaps as many as 2,000 campsites, depending on summer-only or all-year travel, should have been left behind between the Tanana Valley and the Shields Valley of Montana. Discovery of the physical evidence of such a journey by the first group will be a very rare serendipitous event, but so are all Paleoindian site discoveries.

A similar scenario can be invoked for the spread of Clovis people across the United States by doubling the straight-line map distances to account for meandering kilometres and exploration, and assuming a rate of only 2 km per day while hunting and exploring new ground. Scouting parties may have used hide-covered canoes to explore rivers and lakes. Eventually, bands would have broken away from the main group to explore in new directions, with agreement to rendezvous every year or so. Small groups may have returned to Alaska to pass on the good word about the newly discovered land of abundance.

From Anzick via North Platte, Nebraska, to the Aubrey Clovis site near Denton, Texas, is about 1,900 km; it would take about 5.2 years to go twice the distance. Anzick to Clovis, New Mexico, at a distance of 1,550 km, would take about 4.2 years; Anzick to East Wenatchee (Figure 1, locality 20) about two years; Anzick to Kimmswick, Missouri, about five years; and about three more years to reach the Williamson site in Virginia. One band may have reached the Simon site (Figure 1, locality 19) in southern Idaho in less than two years and gone on to Borax Lake, California, and the Pacific coast in about two years. Near East Wenatchee, Washington (Figure 1, locality 20), a band came under an ash fall of the Glacier Peak eruption about 11,200 B.P. (Mehringer and Foit 1990). As day turned into night, the shaman may have ordered offerings of the most magnificent Clovis artifacts ever known (Gramly 1993; Mehringer 1989) in order to appease the gods.

As North America became better known, rates of movement would likely have at least doubled when going from one known point to another via familiar territory. Movements were undoubtedly planned to periodically visit known lithic source areas, known habitats of megafauna and patches of desirable vegetation at the proper time of year. As bands proliferated, tribal rendezvous would likely have been annual events to exchange information, and trade items and genes. Band populations probably increased significantly under favourable conditions, but may have declined during times of drought. As the net decline of water tables during Allerød warming caused spring discharge and traditional watering places to dry up, megafauna under stress became especially vulnerable to hunters when concentrated around water holes. When water tables reached their lowest level, the climate suddenly reversed and became glacially cold during the Younger Dryas. Prolonged winter deep freezes may have further denied access to water for the megafauna. Mammoth, horse, camel, dire wolf, American lion, all but bison, were terminated at the onset of Younger Dryas. Reduced numbers of bison survived in favourable areas perhaps because of their greater numbers. Human population may also have declined because most Folsom evidence does not appear at the base of the immediately overlying stratum at most Folsom sites. Instead, as at the Blackwater Draw Clovis site, it is a few centimetres above the basal contact of the host stratum, that is Stratum D, the Diatomaceous Earth, of Younger Dryas age at Blackwater Draw (Haynes 1998).

CONCLUSIONS

The hypothetical scenarios presented here indicate that the peopling of North America south of the glacial margins could have occurred in much less time than the multiple centuries traditionally allowed for it. Five circumstances support, but do not necessarily prove, the conclusion that a band of hunter-gatherers in Central Alaska at least by 11,700 B.P. could have moved through an ice-free route and into the Interior Plains of Canada by 11,600 B.P. These are: (1) Allerød global warming from 11,800 to 11,000 B.P.; (2) Nenana folk in the upper Tanana Valley in Alaska at the same time; (3) the appearance of mammoth steppe biome over an ice-free route at least by 11,600 B.P.; (4) the Two Creek interval lasting at least 252 years between 12,050 and 11,750 B.P.; and (5) Clovis folk in Montana and central Texas by 11,550 B.P. and throughout the conterminous United States over the next five centuries. During the early Allerød warming peak at 11,700 B.P., the journey to Montana could have been accomplished in eight summer seasons, or less if they continued southward during the winters. Imagine the excitement if Clovis folk or their successors met other people, perhaps of the Western Stemmed Tradition in the Great Basin, people who had arrived along the West Coast via a coastal route (Mandryk et al. 2000; Surovell 2000b).

While the scenario presented here proves nothing, it does show how the peopling of North America by Clovis progenitors could have taken place in decades rather than centuries or millennia. The average rate invoked here is probably the fastest of the possible range. The scenario also shows that an interior ice-free route is as viable as it ever was, if not more so. This does not preclude a coastal route, so both possibilities need to be kept and tested as multiple working hypotheses.

Acknowledgments

A very preliminary version of this paper was presented at the Clovis and Beyond Conference, Santa Fe, New Mexico, October 1998, and will appear in the upcoming conference volume (Haynes 2004). I thank Robson Bonnichsen and Forest Fenn for organizing that excellent and successful gathering of professional and avocational archaeologists and geoarchaeologists. Support for my research has been provided by the National Geographic Society, the National Science Foundation (grants DBS–9119834 and SBR–9725044), and the Regents Professor research fund of the University of Arizona. Various versions of this paper have been read by Dale Guthrie, Bruce Huckell, Richard Morlan, Stuart Fiedel, Larry Lahren, and Todd Surovell. Their comments and suggestions are appreciated as are those of four anonymous reviewers. Expert word processing was provided by Barbara Fregoso and Mary Stephenson, and technical editing was provided by Carol Gifford, all of the Department of Anthropology, University of Arizona. The map of Figure 1 was processed by Jim Abbott.

REFERENCES CITED

Anderson, D. G., and J. C. Gillam
|2000| Paleoindian Colonization of the Americas: Implications from an Examination of Physiography, Demography, and Artifact Distribution. *American Antiquity* 65:43–66.

Bever, M. R.
|2001| An Overview of Alaskan Late Pleistocene Archaeology: Historical Themes and Current Perspectives. *Journal of World Prehistory* 15:125–191.

Broecker, W. S., and W. R. Farrand
|1963| Radiocarbon Age of the Two Creek Forest Bed, Wisconsin. *Geological Society of America Bulletin* 74:795–802.

Burns, J. A.
|1996| Vertebrate Paleontology and the Alleged Ice-Free Corridor: The Meat of the Matter. *Quaternary International* 32:107–112.

Deller, D. B., and C. J. Ellis
|1988| Early Palaeo-Indian Complexes in Southwestern Ontario. In *Late Pleistocene and Early Holocene Paleoecology and Archeology of the Eastern Great Lakes Region*, edited by R. S. Laub, N. G. Miller, and D. W. Steadman, pp. 251–263. Bulletin of the Buffalo Society of Natural Sciences 33. Buffalo Society of Natural Sciences, Buffalo, New York.

Dyke, A. S., and V. K. Prest
|1987| Late Wisconsin and Holocene History of the Laurentide Ice Sheet. *Géographic physique et Quaternaire* 61:237–263.

Ferring, C. R.
|1995| The Late Quaternary Geology and Archaeology of the Aubrey Clovis Site, Texas: A Preliminary Report. In *Ancient Peoples and Landscapes*, edited by E. Johnson, pp. 273–281. Museum of Texas Tech University, Lubbock, Texas.

Fiedel, S. J.
|1999| Older Than We Thought: Implications of Corrected Dates for Paleoindians. *American Antiquity* 64:95–115.

|2000a| The Peopling of the New World: Present Evidence, New Theories, and Future Directions. *Journal of Archaeological Research* 8:39–103.

|2000b| Quacks in the Ice: Waterfowl, Paleoindians, and the Discovery of America. In *Abstracts of the 65th Annual Meeting of the Society for American Archaeology, Philadelphia*, p. 124. Society for American Archaeology, Washington, D.C.

Fullerton, D. S.

|1980| *Preliminary Correlation of Post-Erie Interstadial Events (16,000–10,000 Radiocarbon Years Before Present), Central and Eastern Great Lakes Region, and Hudson, Champlain, and St. Lawrence Lowlands, United States and Canada.* U.S. Geological Survey Professional Paper 1089. U.S. Government Printing Office, Washington, D.C.

Goebel, T., W. R. Powers, and N. H. Bigelow

|1991| The Nenana Complex of Alaska and Clovis Origins. In *Clovis Origins and Adaptations*, edited by R. Bonnichsen, and K. Turnmire, pp. 49–79. Center for the Study of the First Americans, Oregon State University, Corvallis.

Goebel, T., W. R. Powers, N. H. Bigelow, and A. S. Higgs

|1996| Walker Road. In *American Beginnings*, edited by F. H. West, pp. 356–363. University of Chicago Press, Chicago.

Gramly, R. M.

|1988| Palaeo-Indian Sites South of Lake Ontario, Western and Central New York State. In *Late Pleistocene and Early Holocene Paleoecology and Archeology of the Eastern Great Lakes Region*, edited by R. S. Laub, N. G. Miller, and D. W. Steadman, pp. 265–280. Bulletin of the Buffalo Society of Natural Sciences 33. Buffalo Society of Natural Sciences, Buffalo, New York.

|1993| *The Richey Clovis Cache.* Persimmon Press, Buffalo.

Guthrie, R. D.

|1982| Mammals of the Mammoth Steppe as Paleoenvironmental Indicators. In *Paleoecology of Beringia*, edited by D. M. Hopkins, J. V. Matthews, Jr., C. E. Schweger, and S. Young, pp. 307–329. Academic Press, New York.

Hamilton, T. D., and T. Goebel

|1999| Late Pleistocene Peopling of Alaska. In *Ice Age Peoples of North America*, edited by R. Bonnichsen, and K. L. Turnmire, pp. 156–199. Center for the Study of the First Americans, Oregon State University, Corvallis.

Hansel, A. K., D. M. Michelson, A. F. Schneider, and C. E. Larson

|1985| Late Wisconsinan and Holocene History of the Lake Michigan Basin. In *Quaternary Evolution of the Great Lakes*, edited by P. F. Karrow, and P. E. Calkin, pp. 39–53. Geological Association of Canada Special Paper 30. Geological Association of Canada, St. John's, Newfoundland.

Hassan, F. A.

|1981| *Demographic Archaeology*. Academic Press, London.

Haynes, Jr., C. V.

|1964| Fluted Projectile Points: Their Age and Dispersion. *Science* 145:1408–1413.

|1966| Elephant-Hunting in North America. *Scientific American* 214(6):104–112.

|1967| Bone Organic Matter and Radiocarbon Dating. In *Proceedings of a Symposium on Radioactive Dating and Method of Low-Level Counting*, pp. 163–168. International Atomic Energy Agency, Vienna.

|1980| The Clovis Culture. *Canadian Journal of Anthropology* 1:115–121.

|1984| Stratigraphy and Late Pleistocene Extinction in the United States. In *Quaternary Extinctions: A Prehistoric Revolution*, edited by P. S. Martin, and R. G. Klein, pp. 345–353. University of Arizona Press, Tucson.

|1991| Geoarchaeological and Paleohydrological Evidence for a Clovis Age Drought in North America and its Bearing on Extinction. *Quaternary Research* 35:438–450.

|1998| Geochronology of the Stratigraphic Manifestations of Paleoclimatic Events at Paleoindian Sites. In *Abstracts of the 63rd Annual Meeting of the Society for American Archaeology, Seattle.* Society for American Archaeology, Washington, D.C.

|2004| Clovis, Pre-Clovis, Climate Change and Extinction. In *Paleoamerican Origins: Beyond Clovis*, edited by R. Bonnichsen, D. G. Steele, D. Stanford, B. T. Leper, R. Grumman, and C. N. Warren. Texas A & M Press, College Station, in press.

Henderson, N.

|1994| Replicating Dog Travois Travel on the Northern Plains. *Plains Anthropologist* 39:145–159.

Hoffecker, J. F., W. R. Powers, and T. Goebel

|1993| The Colonization of Beringia and the Peopling of the New World. *Science* 259:46–53.

Holliday, V. T.

|2000| Folsom Drought and Episodic Drying on the Southern High Plains From 10,900–10,200 ^{14}C Yr. B.P. *Quaternary Research* 53:1–12.

Jackson, L. E., Jr., and A. Duk-Rodkin

|1996| Quaternary Geology of the Ice-Free Corridor: Glacial Controls on the Peopling of the New World. In *Prehistoric Mongoloid Dispersals*, edited by T. Akazawa, and E. J. E. Szathmary, pp. 214–227. Oxford University Press, New York.

Johnston, W. A.

|1933| Quaternary Geology of North America in Relation to the Migration of Man. In *The American Aborigines: Their Origin and Antiquity*, edited by D. Jenness, pp. 9–45. University of Toronto Press, Toronto.

Kaiser, K. F.

|1994| Two Creeks Interstade Dated Through Dendrochronology and AMS. *Quaternary Research* 42:288–298.

Kehew, A. E., and J. T. Teller

|1994| History of Late Glacial Runoff along the Southwestern Margin of the Laurentide Ice Sheet. *Quaternary Science Reviews* 13:859–877.

Kelly, R. L., and L. C. Todd

|1988| Coming into the Country: Early Paleoindian Hunting and Mobility. *American Antiquity* 53:231–244.

Lahren, L. A.

|2001| The Ongoing Odyssey of the Anzick Clovis Burial in Park County Montana (24PA506): Part 1. *Archaeology in Montana* 42:55–59.

Lemmen, D. S., A. Duk-Rodkin, and J. N. Bednarski
|1995| Late Glacial Drainage Systems along the Northwestern Margin of the Laurentide Ice Sheet. *Quaternary Science Reviews* 13:805–828.
Leverington, D. W., J. D. Mann, and J. T. Teller
|2000| Changes in the Bathymetry and Volume of Glacial Lake Agassiz Between 11,000 and 9300 ^{14}C Yr. B.P. *Quaternary Research* 54:174–181.
McAvoy, J. M., and L. D. McAvoy
|1997| *Archaeological Investigations of Site 44Sx202, Cactus Hill, Sussex County Virginia.* Virginia Department of Historic Resources Research Report Series No. 8. Virginia Department of Historic Resources, Richmond.
MacDonald, G. M., and T. K. McLeod
|1996| The Holocene Closing of the "Ice-Free" Corridor: A Biogeographical Perspective. *Quaternary International* 32:87–95.
Mandryk, C. A. S.
|1996| Late Wisconsinan Deglaciation of Alberta: Processes and Paleogeography. *Quaternary International* 32:79–85.
|2001| The Ice-Free Corridor (or Not?): An Inland Route by Any Other Name is Not So Sweet nor Adequately Considered. In *On Being First: Cultural Innovation and Environmental Consequences of First Peopling*, edited by J. Gillespie, S. Tupakka, and C. de Mille, pp. 575–588. Chacmool Archaeological Association, University of Calgary, Calgary, Alberta.
Mandryk, C. A. S., H. Josenhans, D. F. Fedje, and R. W. Matthews
|2000| Late Quaternary Paleoenvironments of Northwestern North America: Implications for Inland versus Coastal Migration Routes. *Quaternary Science Reviews* 20:301–314.
Martin, P. S.
|1967| Prehistoric Overkills. In *Pleistocene Extinctions: The Search for a Cause*, edited by P. S. Martin, and H. E. Wright, Jr., pp. 75–120. Yale University Press, New Haven.
Mehringer, P. J., Jr.
|1989| Of Apples and Archaeology. *Universe* 1:2–8.
Mehringer, P. J., Jr., and F. F. Foit, Jr.
|1990| Volcanic Ash Dating of the Clovis Cache at East Wenatchee, Washington. *National Geographic Research* 6(4):495–503.
Meltzer, D. J.
|1995| Clocking the First Americans. *Annual Reviews of Anthropology* 24:21–45.
Morlan, R. E., A. S. Dyke, and R. N. McNeely
|1999| Mapping Ancient History. Web page: http://www.geoserv.org.
Mosimann, J. E., and P. S. Martin
|1975| Simulating Overkill by Paleoindians. *American Scientist* 63:305–313.
Overstreet, D. F., and T. W. Stafford, Jr.
|1997| Additions to a Revised Chronology for Cultural and Non-Cultural Mammoth and Mastodon Fossils in the Southwest Lake Michigan Basin. *Current Research in the Pleistocene* 14:70–71.
Patterson, W. S. B., and C. U. Hammer
|1987| Ice Core and Other Glacial Data. In *North America and Adjacent Oceans during the Last Deglaciation*, edited by W. F. Ruddiman, and H. E. Wright, Jr., pp. 91–109. Geological Society of America Decade of North American Geology Project Vol. K-3. Geological Society of America, Boulder, Colorado.
Smith, D. G.
|1994| Glacial Lake McConnell: Paleogeography, Age, Duration, and Associated River Deltas, Mackenzie River Basin, Western Canada. *Quaternary Science Reviews* 13:829–843.
Stafford, T. W., Jr., P. E. Hare, L. A. Currie, A. J. T. Jull, and D. Donahue
|1991| Accelerator Radiocarbon Dating at the Molecular Level. *Journal of Archaeological Sciences* 18:35–72.
Steele, J., C. Gamble, and T. Sluckin
|2000| Estimating the Velocity of Paleoindian Expansion into South America. In *People as an Agent of Environmental Change*, edited by R. Nicholson and T. O'Connor. Symposia of the Association for Environmental Archaeology No. 16. Oxbow, Oxford.
Storck, P. L.
|1988| The Early Palaeo-Indian Occupation of Ontario: Colonization or Diffusion? In *Late Pleistocene and Early Holocene Paleoecology and Archeology of the Eastern Great Lakes Region*, edited by R. S. Laub, N. G. Miller, and D. W. Steadman, pp. 243–250. Bulletin of the Buffalo Society of Natural Sciences 33. Buffalo Society of Natural Sciences, Buffalo, New York.
Stuiver, M., P. M. Grootes, and T. F. Braziunas
|1995| The GISP 2 ^{18}O Climate Record of the Past 16,500 Years and the Role of the Sun, Ocean, and Volcanoes. *Quaternary Research* 44:341–354.
Surovell, T. A.
|2000a| Early Paleoindian Women, Children, Mobility, and Fertility. *American Antiquity* 65:493–508.
|2000b| Can a Coastal Migration Explain Monte Verde? In *Abstracts of the 65th Annual Meeting of the Society for American Archaeology, Philadelphia*, p. 324. Society for American Archaeology, Washington, D.C.
Taylor, R. E.
|1987| *Radiocarbon Dating: An Archaeological Perspective.* Academic Press, Oxford.
Taylor, R. E., C. V. Haynes, Jr., and M. Stuiver
|1996| Clovis and Folsom Age Estimates: Stratigraphic Context and Radiocarbon Calibration. *Antiquity* 70:515–525.
Teller, J. T.
|1995| History and Drainage of Large Ice-Domed Lakes along the Laurentide Ice Sheet. *Quaternary International* 28:83–92.
Teller, J. T., and A. E. Kehew
|1994| Introduction to the Late Glacial History of Large Proglacial Lakes and Meltwater Runoff along the Laurentide Ice Sheet. *Quaternary Science Reviews* 13:795–799.

Webb, E., and D. Rindos
|1997| The Mode and Tempo of the Initial Human Colonization of Empty Landmasses: Sahul and the Americas Compared. In *Rediscovering Darwin: Evolutionary Theory and Archaeological Explanation*, edited by C. M. Barton, and G. A. Clark, pp. 233–250. American Anthropological Association Archaeological Paper No. 7. American Anthropological Association, Arlington, Virginia.

West, F. H.
|1996| Beringia and New World Origins: The Archaeological Evidence. In *American Beginnings: The Prehistory and Paleoecology of Beringia*, edited by F. H. West, pp. 537–559. University of Chicago Press, Chicago.

White, J. M., R. W. Mathews, and W. H. Mathews
|1985| Late Pleistocene Chronology and Environment of the "Ice-Free Corridor" of Northwestern Alberta. *Quaternary Research* 24:173–186.

Wilson, M. C.
|1996| Late Quaternary Vertebrates and the Opening of the Ice-Free Corridor, with Special Reference to the Genus *Bison*. *Quaternary International* 32:97–105.

Wilson, M. C., and J. A. Burns
|1999| Searching for the Earliest Canadians: Wide Corridors, Narrow Doorways, Small Windows. In *Ice Age Peoples of North America*, edited by R. Bonnichsen, and K. L. Turnmire, pp. 213–248. Center for the Study of the First Americans, Oregon State University, Corvallis.

Yesner, D. R.
|1996| Human Adaptations in the Pleistocene-Holocene Boundary (c. 13,000 to 8,000 Yr. B.P.) in Eastern Beringia. In *Humans at the End of the Ice Age: The Archaeology of the Pleistocene-Holocene Transition*, edited by L. G. Straus, B. V. Eriksen, J. M. Erlandson, and D. R. Yesner, pp. 255–276. Plenum Press, New York.
|1998| Human Colonization of Eastern Beringia and the Question of Mammoth Hunting. Paper presented at the International Conference on Mammoth Site Studies, University of Kansas, Lawrence, Kansas.

IMPACTS OF IMPERIALISM: NABATAEAN, ROMAN, AND BYZANTINE LANDSCAPES IN THE WADI FAYNAN, SOUTHERN JORDAN

Graeme Barker, Patrick Daly, and Paul Newson

Graeme Barker, School of Archaeology and Ancient History, University of Leicester, Leicester LE1 7RH, UK.
Patrick Daly, Institute of Archaeology, University of Oxford, 36 Beaumont Street, Oxford OX1 2PG, UK.
Paul Newson, School of Archaeology and Ancient History, University of Leicester, Leicester LE1 7RH, UK.

ABSTRACT

The Wadi Faynan Landscape Survey is an interdisciplinary investigation of settlement and land use history in the desertic Wadi Faynan, from the beginning of the Holocene to the present day, as a contribution to understanding processes of desertification and environmental degradation in arid lands. The wadi is now used only by pastoralists on a seasonal basis, but its rich archaeological record indicates that the locality has also been the focus at different times in the past not just for pastoralism but also for sedentary settlement, intensive floodwater farming, and copper and lead extraction and processing on a major scale. The paper focuses on the Nabataean and Roman/Byzantine periods (ca. 300 B.C.–A.D. 700), to illustrate how an integrated program of landscape archaeology and environmental science is defining changing patterns of arable, pastoral, and industrial activity in classical antiquity, and how Roman imperialism transformed the landscape, with effects that still impact on the lives of the present-day Bedouin pastoralists.

Many dryland regions of the world have archaeological remains suggesting that once upon a time there must have been intensive phases of settlement in what are now dry and degraded environments. How did past societies in these marginal environments learn to cope with risk? What solutions did they develop, and how successful were they? Why did they take the choices they took? To what extent did their actions affect their landscape, and for good or ill? Such questions have been much debated by archaeologists, historians, and geographers from the perspectives of their individual disciplines (e.g., Fantechi and Margaris 1986; Le Houerou 1996; Millington and Pye 1994), with simple models of climatic change or human impact generally being proposed. However, contemporary ecological and anthropological studies emphasize the complexity of potential interactions between people and deserts today, and hence of their likelihood in the past (Barker and Gilbertson 2000; Beaumont 1993; Mortimore 1998; Spellman 2000; Thomas and Middleton 1994;

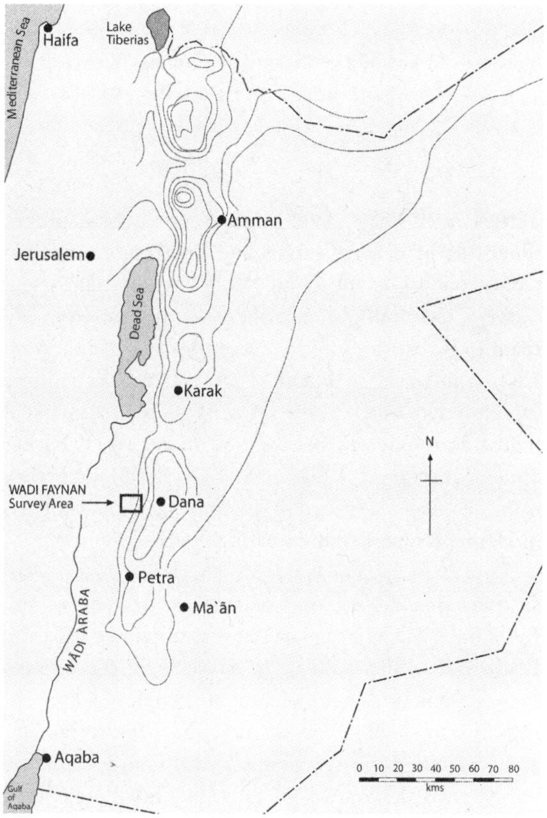

Figure 1. The Levant, showing the location of the Wadi Faynan survey area.

Figure 2. Looking north across the Wadi Faynan. Khirbet Faynan is the prominent hill in the middle distance. Field walls of the ancient field system WF4 are visible in the foreground.

Tiffen et al. 1994). To advance these debates about processes of desertification and environmental degradation in arid lands, the Wadi Faynan Landscape Survey has brought together an interdisciplinary team to investigate the landscape history of the Wadi Faynan in southern Jordan (Figure 1) within a single integrated research framework. The five seasons of fieldwork took place between 1996 and 2000 (Barker 2000; Barker et al. 1997, 1998, 1999, 2000), and work is now actively advanced in the preparation of the final monograph report (Barker et al. 2003).

The Wadi Faynan is one of a series of major wadi systems that dissect the western escarpment of the Jordanian plateau and flow westwards down into the Wadi Arabah rift valley. The climate on the escarpment is semi-arid, with an annual rainfall of some 200 mm, so the villages there practice Mediterranean-style farming, growing cereals, olives, vines, and so on, whereas the Wadi Faynan, only a few hours' walk down the escarpment, is rainless for most of the year and sparsely vegetated. Today the wadi is used entirely for seasonal grazing, partly by nomadic Bedouin pastoralists who live year-round in the Wadi Arabah and partly by transhumant Bedouin who come down into the wadi from plateau settlements on a seasonal basis.

At the center of the wadi, where a series of tributaries joins to form the main channel, there is a major settlement called Khirbet Faynan (the "Ruin of Faynan") of Hellenistic (ca. 300 B.C.–A.D. 1), Nabataean/Early Roman (ca. A.D. 1–150), and Late Roman/Byzantine (ca. A.D. 250–650) date (Figure 2). Nearby, on the other side of the main channel, are an aqueduct, reservoir, and water mill as well as a substantial cemetery, broadly contemporary with the main settlement. The hillslopes around these remains are black with slag, the residues of ancient smelting, and the surrounding hills are honeycombed with ancient mineshafts, for the area is rich in copper and lead ores. The history of mining and metal-working in the Faynan region has been the subject of intensive study by a team from Bochum Mining Museum, who have demonstrated that industrial activity began in the Chalcolithic ca. 5000 B.C. and expanded in scale in the following millennia to climax in Nabataean, Roman, and Byzantine times (Hauptmann 1989, 1992, 2000; Hauptmann et al. 1992). Khirbet Faynan is commonly identified as the settlement or town of Phaino mentioned in classical sources as the regional control center of copper and lead extraction in Roman times, and there are references to Christian slaves from Palestine and Egypt being consigned to work its mines (Athenasius, *Historia Arianorum ad Monarchos* 60, 765–766; Eusebius, *Martyrs of Palestine* 5.2, 7.2, 13.1–4). Extending for some 5 km to the west of Khirbet Faynan is a substantial field system demarcated by hundreds of drystone walls (Figures 2 and 3), its surface pottery indicating primary use contemporary with the settlement. Clearly, these abundant archaeological remains imply that patterns of settlement and land use in the Wadi Faynan were very different in classical antiquity than those of today.

METHODOLOGIES

The first component of the project was a program of geomorphological mapping and palynological analysis, with the primary aim of establishing the climatic and environmental frameworks of human settlement in the study area. However, we also hoped it would provide insights into the nature and scale of the impacts on the landscape of people (and/or their animals) at different times in the past – for example, from evidence of vegetation clearance and for phases of accelerated erosion that could not be readily explained in terms of changes in climatic regimes. Allied to this, we employed geochemical analysis (EDMA – energy dispersive X-ray microanalysis) to measure the nature and scale of environmental pollution caused by the copper and lead mining and smelting; the mining waste produced pollutants that were washed out into the landscape by water flow, and the smelting threw out pollutants into the atmosphere that in due course were also incorporated into sediments.

Another major component of the project was systematic archaeological survey of all visible archaeological remains. We focused on the central sector of the Wadi Faynan, where we defined an area measuring just over 30 km^2 (Figure 3). This survey area was defined in particular to encompass both the ancient field systems flooring the wadi, dominated by the continuous series of over 1,000 fields along the southern side of the Faynan channel classified as WF4, and typical terrain at higher elevations on either side. The eastern and southern boundaries of the survey area were roughly along the lower edge of the escarpment, but in the northeast sector, the survey area was extended into the mountains so that it encompassed one of the major zones of ancient mining and also part of the upper Dana valley, one of the major routes down from the plateau to the Faynan. In this way, we believed that the designated survey area would be large enough to yield a representative series of archaeological data for past arable, pastoral, and industrial activities, whilst also being small enough to be amenable to systematic and intensive study by the field team.

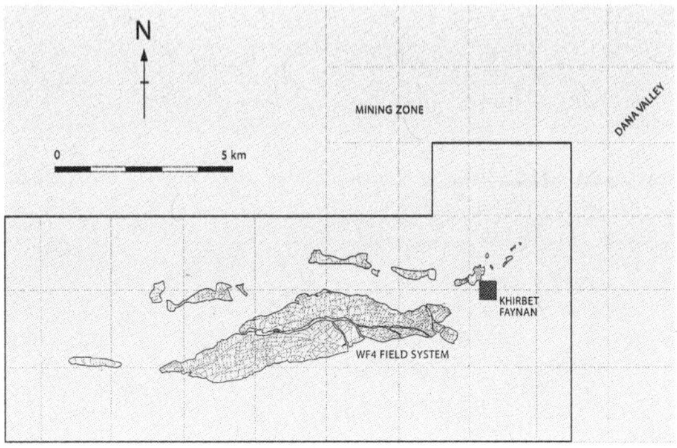

Figure 3. The survey area of the Wadi Faynan Landscape Survey, showing also the location of the ancient field systems classified as WF4 in the survey gazetteer.

The archaeological survey had two distinct elements in terms of the techniques employed for mapping the archaeology within and outside the field systems. Reconnaissance survey had indicated that the densities of archaeological material lying on the surface of the field systems (mainly fragments of pottery, but also lithics, fragments of slag, occasional fragments of glass, etc.) were extraordinarily high, far higher, for example, than those encountered by archaeological surveys in other parts of the Near East and in the Mediterranean. Hence we adopted a survey methodology for the field systems whereby teams of archaeologists traversed each field, walking in parallel lines 10 m apart. All the material visible on the surface was collected by the first walker along their traverse (a 2-m strip of terrain along the direction of walk), and the pottery and lithics in the next four traverses were recorded by clicker counters. The procedure was repeated if necessary according to the size of the field. This method therefore gave us accurate information about densities of different kinds of material in the collected sample that could also be scaled up to give us general indicators of changing densities of pottery and lithics across the field system as a whole. A separate search of the field was made by the team for any key diagnostic sherds to provide a separate "grab" sample to complement the "pick" sample obtained from the systematic walking.

Alongside the field-walking, every exposed face of every wall in the field system was recorded systematically in terms of its constructional details, and from this a typology of wall types was established. This process also recorded constructional elements that were identified as likely to have a function in terms of capturing and/or guiding the direction of flow of floodwater. Three main types were identified: "sluices" – narrow gaps constructed in walls so that floodwater could either flow through naturally or be blocked by some form of simple obstacle such as a wooden board; "spillways" – staircase-like constructions where water could not be blocked but would flow downslope from one field to another without gullying and undermining the wall; and "parallel channels" – systems of parallel walls built to channel floodwaters along the ground (commonly over distances of 100–200 m), to guide them from a wadi channel into a set of fields, or from one set of fields to another.

Any other archaeological structures within the field systems were also recorded as part of the other major mapping program in the archaeological survey, which focused on the archaeology beyond the fields. The

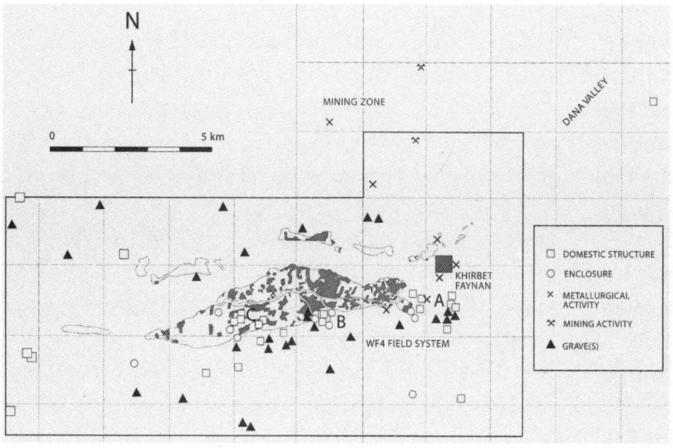

Figure 4. The Nabataean/Early Roman landscape of the Wadi Faynan, ca. 300 B.C.–A.D. 150. The grey shading shows the principal distributions of Nabataean/Early Roman pottery in the WF4 field system.

entire survey area was divided into 500 by 500 m units. Field teams first carried out a "pick" survey of a series of 2-m wide transects running north-south along the western and eastern boundaries of the squares, but excluding the field system zones, in order to provide density figures on the distributions of pottery and lithics outside the field system to compare with those inside. The archaeology of each square was then recorded by teams criss-crossing its terrain systematically. This archaeology included a very wide variety of stone structures interpreted variously as domestic structures such as buildings, enclosures, pens, tent footings, and so on, and funerary structures of varying degrees of constructional complexity. There were also scatters or clusters of surface material without evidence of associated structures, such as pottery, lithics, fragments of slag and mining processing debris, and also rock engravings and inscriptions. The surface material associated with structures was collected, either with the "pick" and "grab" system used in the fields in the case of the larger structures or with total "grab" collections at the smaller ones. Over 1,000 "sites" were identified and described on pro forma sheets, and recorded by photography and measured sketches, and a representative series of the major categories was then revisited for detailed planning. Systematic studies were also made of the very large collections of artifactual material resulting from these survey activities, notably pottery and chipped lithics but also fragments of glass and lamps, coins, smelting slags, stone grinders, architectural fragments, and so on.

The final component of the project was an ethnographic and ethnoarchaeological study of the present-day societies using the Wadi Faynan. These include landless goat herders, 1940s refugees from Israel, who live all year round in the Faynan and Arabah lowlands; various transhumant Bedouin groups who spend part of the year on the plateau and part of the year in the Wadi Faynan; and groups who farm on the plateau but who graze flocks in the Wadi Faynan on a seasonal basis. This ethnographic research was designed to establish insights into present-day links between social forms and subsistence activities in the survey area. We also conducted detailed ethnoarchaeological surveys of abandoned campsites, interviews with the former inhabitants of the more recently abandoned examples, and a program of geoarchaeological analysis of sediments from new and old abandoned campsites, to try to establish the "archaeological signatures" of arable and pastoral activities, and of different seasonal or all-year-round occupations.

The entire data set collected by these approaches was then used to construct an integrated geographical information system (GIS). The rest of the paper presents some of the preliminary results of these methodologies, focusing on the centuries of classical antiquity from the beginning of the Hellenistic period to the end of the Byzantine world and the coming of Islam, a period of almost 1,000 years. Because the primary dating of the archaeology is based on pottery and associated artifacts, it is not possible to divide the survey data neatly into before and after the Roman annexation of the province in A.D. 106. Instead, we have to group the majority of the classical settlement evidence into two major episodes: a "Nabataean/Early Roman" phase from ca. 300 B.C. to ca. A.D. 150; and a "Late Roman/Byzantine" phase from ca. A.D. 250 to ca. A.D. 650. The program of geomorphology and palynology indicates that the climate throughout this period was not significantly different from that of today and that there was a steppic vegetation in Nabataean/Early Roman times, but that by the end of the Byzantine period the landscape was extremely degraded.

THE NABATAEAN/EARLY ROMAN LANDSCAPE, CA. 300 B.C.–A.D. 150

For the last three centuries B.C. and the first century A.D., the Wadi Faynan was part of the Hellenistic kingdom of the Nabataeans, whose capital was at Petra some 40 km to the southeast on the plateau. Wadi Faynan and its surrounding hills were its key source of metal. The settlement system in Wadi Faynan was certainly dominated by Khirbet Faynan, but our survey has shown there were also many smaller domestic settlements and enclosures (Figure 4). The former were mostly rectangular in form, built of coursed masonry with well-fashioned corners and doorways defined by dressed stone orthostats. Some of these structures consisted of a single room, but most consisted of a few rooms round a courtyard. What we defined as enclosures were commonly oval or circular but sometimes rectangular, in the latter case usually well built like the rectangular domestic structures. The enclosures were mostly empty but sometimes had one or two small rooms built against the enclosure wall.

Near the WF4 field system, most of the Nabataean/Early Roman domestic structures and enclosures are in distinct clusters, which we believe represent farmsteads related to agricultural units within the field system. The largest cluster (A in Figure 4) was around the eastern end of the WF4 field system, on low hills immediately overlooking it. The next cluster (B) is 1 km to the west, with outliers beyond. The third dense cluster (C) is 1 km to the west of the second one, but situated inside rather than overlooking the WF4 field system. Both rectangular domestic sites and enclosures of this phase were also located in the hill country away from the field systems, especially on the southern side, but there are also examples of rectangular structures to the northwest and a single outlier in the Dana valley to the northeast.

The survey record also included a wide range of funerary structures, especially simple undifferentiated circular or oval cairns and circular or oval cairns with cists or chambers of vertically set stone slabs, with or without clearly delimited kerbs. There were also a few more elaborate rectangular structures of well-coursed masonry. Many of these structures were types used in both prehistoric and classical times, and sometimes later. Most of those of Nabataean/Early Roman date were either along low ridges overlooking the field system, especially adjacent to the settlement clusters, or in the hill country to the north and south.

Evidence for metallurgical activities such as on-site smelting was found at a few Nabataean/Early Roman domestic structures at the eastern end of the WF4 field system, but especially on the slopes around Khirbet Faynan. In the mining zone, we recorded two locations with evidence for smelting, and two with mining evidence of this period. Studies of charcoal from mining sites by the Bochum team indicate that the Nabataean/Early Roman landscape was sufficiently wooded for the miners to be able to collect local fuelwood for their smelting (Engel 1993; Hauptmann 1992), evidence that chimes with our palynological samples indicating a steppic vegetation in the survey area at this time.

If the distributions of Nabataean/Early Roman pottery in the WF4 field system can be taken as indicators of areas manured by household rubbish, a common interpretation of surface pottery spreads in Levantine and Mediterranean field surveys (Wilkinson 1982, 1989), then there would appear to have been a series of discrete agricultural units or "estates" at this time, separated by unenclosed land. The distribution of these "estates" correlates broadly with the distribution of the main clusters of domestic settlements. At the eastern end of the field system, one set of fields was laid out immediately below the water mill near Khirbet Faynan, with another to the south, both close to Settlement Cluster A. Further west, there was an area of dense land use on almost flat terrain fed by the same tributary wadis, with another area to its south on more steeply sloping land, both overlooked by Settlement Cluster B. There was another agricultural unit in the central sector of the WF4 field system, laid out by its southern margins, in the midst of which was Settlement Cluster C.

The analysis of the walls within these "estates" indicates that the Nabataean/Early Roman farmers concentrated their fields on either side of steeply sloping gullies or channels that would have been well supplied by storm waters from the extensive gravel slopes to the south. They built check dams across these channels at right angles to the direction of water flow, so that the stormwaters could be diverted into the systems of terraced fields laid out on either side. Sluices and slipways were built at key locations in the field walls so that the flow of floodwaters down through the system of terraced fields could be controlled: water could be

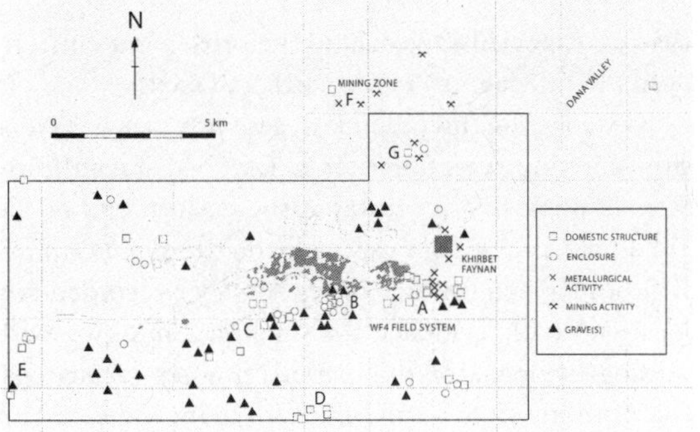

Figure 5. The Late Roman/Byzantine landscape of the Wadi Faynan, ca. A.D. 250–650. The grey shading shows the principal distributions of Late Roman/Byzantine pottery in the WF4 field system.

trapped in a particular field or allowed to flow through it to the field below. In the case of the two farm units "belonging to" Settlement Cluster A, water was fed from the higher fields down to the lower system by means of a narrow channel formed of two parallel walls 1–2 m apart.

Our palynological samples indicate that, by using these simple but effective systems of floodwater farming to overcome the aridity of their landscape, Nabataean/Early Roman farmers were able to grow cereals and tree crops such as olives and vines in the Faynan estates (Barker et al. 1998:21–23). At the same time, the close association between domestic structures and enclosures in the settlement clusters suggests that the floodwater farmers probably also engaged in pastoralism, presumably grazing their animals inside the field system (on the stubble after the harvest, for example) as well as further afield. The scale of the archaeological record created by these people, including the construction of well-built domestic complexes and large numbers of field walls, implies that this integrated system of arable and pastoral land use based on floodwater farming sustained year-round settlement. The small-scale domestic sites in the hill country at a distance from these farms may present more seasonal settlements, perhaps pastoral-based communities who spent part of the year also on the plateau – the nature of settlement and land use at the different categories of site is currently being investigated by the analysis of biological and botanical residues in the floor sediments. However that may be, the lack of clear spatial differentiation in the various forms of Nabataean/Early Roman graves, and the location of these graves both beside the wadi-floor farms and in the hill country along with the domestic sites and enclosures there, implies that, as today, people belonging to broadly similar social and ethnic groups practiced different lifestyles. One would seem to have been more arable based and sedentary, the other more pastoral based and more mobile.

THE LATE ROMAN/BYZANTINE LANDSCAPE, CA. A.D. 250–650

With the formal annexation of the region by Rome in A.D. 106, Wadi Faynan became a major focus of the Roman copper and lead industry supplying the eastern Mediterranean and the Levant, the large number of mine workers and ancillary workers being coordinated by the garrison community at Khirbet Faynan (Phaino). The survey has revealed remarkable transformations to the landscape in response to the impact of Roman imperialism on the region (Figure 5). The field system was considerably enlarged to include both the hillslopes and the almost flat floor of the main wadi, and, on the evidence of the surface pottery, the separate blocks of irrigated land of the Nabataean/Early Roman period were now incorporated into a single large agricultural unit or estate encompassing most of the WF4 field system. Floodwaters entering the system from the eastern and southern tributary channels were transported considerable distances from one set of fields to another by ingenious systems of parallel walls which excavation has shown are the aboveground evidence of well-built channels. Floodwaters egressing from a channel into a farmed zone were distributed from field to field by means of carefully sited sluices and slipways (Figure 6). Our GIS modeling of water flow indicates that the use of water resources was coordinated down the length of the field system. The center of Wadi Faynan had become a highly organized imperial estate, with extensive field systems carefully managed and farmed to feed the industrial workers operating the mines and the smelting works.

There continued to be small-scale domestic settlement beyond Khirbet Faynan (Figure 5), but there are indications of changes in their use. The numbers of domestic structures sites in Settlement Cluster A at

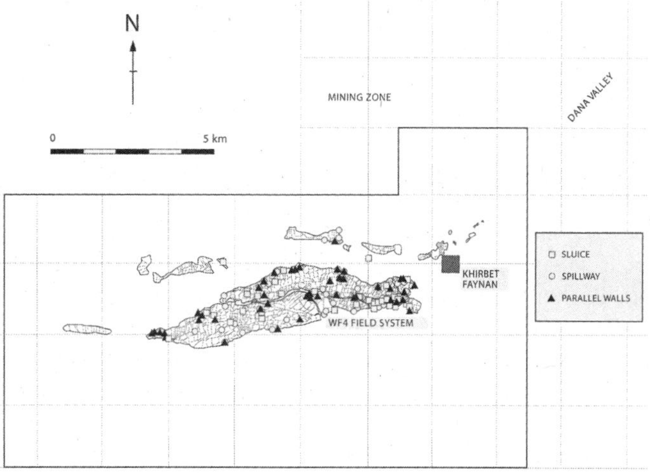

Figure 6. The distribution of water management technologies, which enabled the entire WF4 field system to be managed as a single agricultural estate in the Late Roman/Byzantine period.

the eastern end of the field system increased from eight to ten. The concentration of evidence for metallurgical activity in the vicinity of these structures suggests strongly an industrial role for this complex – it was immediately adjacent to the rotary mill, which was probably used for crushing ore. The structures in Settlement Cluster A also have examples of heavy hand-held crushing stones which are quite different from normal grain rubbers; for this reason, we suspect they were part of the ore crushing process prior to smelting. One of the new structures has a distinct barrack-like appearance, suggesting some kind of control or surveillance role. Settlement Cluster B stayed the same size as before, with five sites and six enclosures. This complex overlooked three tributary channels that supplied much of the floodwater to the central and lower system, and so was critically located for observing and controlling floodwaters. At Settlement Cluster C, three of the five domestic structures within the boundaries of the field system went out of use, and some new structures and enclosures were built instead just beyond its edge to the south. This central-southern part of the field system is very different from the rest, consisting of rubble-strewn terraces at a relatively high elevation. It is possible that this zone was particularly important for tree crops such as olives, with Settlement Cluster C focused on their management.

Several more settlements were established in the hill country in the Late Roman/Byzantine period (Figure 5), especially a village-like cluster high above the field system at the foot of the main escarpment at the southern edge of the survey area (D), and another near the southwest corner (E). Both of them lack enclosures, and both have numerous examples of the heavy crushing stones found at Settlement Cluster A, so seem to have been part of the industrial landscape, perhaps being served by the Roman-period mines that it is known were operating in the hills to the south of them. Two sets of structures (F and G in Figure 5) were also built in the northern mining zone, both with evidence for associated metallurgical activity and near mines with evidence for contemporary use.

One very large cemetery, termed the South Cemetery, was established about 1 km southeast of Khirbet Faynan, and seems to have served its population. It consists of hundreds of graves, mostly inhumations in deep slots with single stones as grave markers. At the same time, the traditional forms of cairn graves continued to be built on prominent locations in the hill country, especially south of the field system, their numbers double those of the Nabataean/Early Roman phase. Perhaps these burials signify the presence in the Late Roman/Byzantine landscape of people living the traditional way, pastoralists using Faynan on a seasonal basis despite being increasingly marginalized by the imperial estate and its industrial activities.

THE IMPERIAL LEGACY

The remarkable agricultural landscape supporting the industrial workforce controlled by the Khirbet Faynan garrison seems to have collapsed more or less in its entirety by the closing centuries of the Roman empire, the formerly marginalized mobile pastoralists reclaiming the landscape thenceforwards. There is striking evidence that the demise of intensive agriculture was directly related to the intensity of the Roman exploitation of the locality: the geoarchaeological and paleoecological studies indicate that the Late Roman/

Byzantine landscape was progressively and massively eroded, degraded, and polluted.

The pollen record from sediments that accumulated behind a barrage at Khirbet Faynan shows that the landscape rapidly developed after the Nabataean/Early Roman period into the extremely degraded and desertic environment of Wadi Faynan today (Barker et al. 1998:21–23). The charcoal residues collected by the Bochum team from mining sites demonstrate that fuelwood now had to be brought down from the plateau because the Faynan landscape had been stripped bare of timber (Engel 1993). Erosion made the floodwater farming systems increasingly difficult to sustain as gullying lowered the depth of water flow below many diversion walls, especially on the upper slopes. The EDMA geochemical studies indicate extraordinarily high levels of heavy metal pollutants in the Khirbet Faynan barrage sediments in the Roman and Byzantine centuries, many times higher than modern safe limits (Barker et al. 1999:262–269; Pyatt, Barker, Birch, Gilbertson, Grattan, and Mattingly 2000). The fact that today the biomass and cover values of barley plants growing in the wadi increase significantly with distance from these contamination "hot spots" suggests that metal pollution would also have been affecting the productivity of the crops being grown in the field system (Pyatt, Gilmore, Grattan, Hunt, and McLaren 2000). The very high levels of Roman/Byzantine pottery and other settlement debris strewn over the fields may indicate increasingly desperate attempts to maintain soil fertility by intensive manuring, though in fact this activity simply served to carry metallurgical slags further out into the fields. The heavy metals would certainly have entered the human food chain: even the small amounts of pollution at the top of the Khirbet Faynan barrage sediments, far lower than those of classical times, result in significant levels of copper pollution in the milk of the Bedouin flocks that graze on the vegetation there today.

CONCLUSION

The arguments presented in this paper can only be regarded as provisional given that the field research by the Wadi Faynan Landscape Survey has only recently been completed, and analysis of the very rich data sets is in progress. Nevertheless, the combination of landscape archaeology and environmental science employed by the project has succeeded in elucidating the principal features of the Holocene landscape history of the study area. This paper has focused on the thousand years of classical settlement in this story, from ca. 300 B.C. to ca. A.D. 700, when the Wadi Faynan passed from being within the kingdom of the Nabataeans to being part of Roman Arabia. The indications are that the relations between arable, pastoral and industrial activities in the wadi were very different in the two periods. The central settlement of Khirbet Faynan was probably the focus of copper and lead mining for the Nabataeans, but the survey suggests that the rest of the landscape was used by communities integrating floodwater farming for cereals and tree crops with pastoralism, though the relationship between them and the Khirbet Faynan community is unclear. Under the Roman empire, Faynan's rich metal sources were mined on a massive scale, and a huge investment was made in the agricultural sector so that the industrial workforce could be fed from local produce. The barracks-like buildings around Khirbet Faynan suggest that the agricultural workforce, like the miners and their ancillary workers, were kept under careful surveillance. It is likely that the valley continued to be used by pastoralists operating on the fringes of the imperial landscape, people who in due course were able to reclaim the landscape when the mines and field systems were abandoned. The environmental sciences within the project's multidisciplinary methodology suggest strongly that Wadi Faynan is a startling example of humanly induced desertification: the Roman imperial economy impacted on a marginal landscape in ways that created a desert, along with a legacy of pollution for future generations to come.

REFERENCES CITED

Barker, G.
|2000| Farmers, Herders, and Miners in the Wadi Faynan, Southern Jordan: A 10,000-Year Landscape Archaeology. In *The Archaeology of Drylands: Living at the Margin*, edited by G. Barker and D. Gilbertson, pp. 63–85. One World Archaeology 39. Routledge, London.

Barker, G., and Gilbertson, D.
|2000| Living at the Margin: Themes in the Archaeology of Drylands. In *The Archaeology of Drylands: Living at the Margin*, edited by G. Barker and D. Gilbertson, pp. 3–18. One World Archaeology 39. Routledge, London.

Barker, G., O. H. Creighton, D. Gilbertson, C. O. Hunt, D. J. Mattingly, S. J. McLaren, and D. C. Thomas
|1997| The Wadi Faynan Project, Southern Jordan: A Preliminary Report on Geomorphology and Landscape Archaeology. *Levant* 29:19–40.

Barker, G., R. Adams, O. H. Creighton, D. Gilbertson., J. P. Grattan, C. O. Hunt, D. J. Mattingly, S. J. McLaren, H. A. Mohammed, P. Newson, T. E. G. Reynolds, and D. C. Thomas.
|1998| Environment and Land Use in the Wadi Faynan, Southern Jordan: The Second Season of Geoarchaeology and Landscape Archaeology (1997). *Levant* 30:5–26.

Barker, G., R. Adams, O. H. Creighton, D. Crook, D. Gilbertson., J. P. Grattan, C. O. Hunt, D. J. Mattingly, S. J. McLaren, H. A. Mohammed, P. Newson, C. Palmer, F. B. Pyatt, T. E. G. Reynolds, and R. Tomber
|1999| Environment and Land Use in the Wadi Faynan, Southern Jordan: The Third Season of Geoarchaeology and Landscape Archaeology (1998). *Levant* 31:255–292.

Barker, G., R. Adams, O. H. Creighton, P. Daly, D. Gilbertson, J. P. Grattan, C. O. Hunt, D. J. Mattingly, S. J. McLaren, H. A. Mohammed, P. Newson, C. Palmer, F. B. Pyatt, T. E. G. Reynolds, H. Smith, R. Tomber, and A. Truscott
|2000| Archaeology and Desertification in the Wadi Faynan: The Fourth (1999) Season of the Wadi Faynan Landscape Survey. *Levant* 32:27–52.

Barker, G., D. Gilbertson, and D. Mattingly (editors)
|2003| *Archaeology and Desertification: the Landscape Archaeology of the Wadi Faynan, Jordan.* Manuscript on file, Council for British Research in the Levant, London.

Beaumont, P.
|1993| *Drylands: Environmental Management and Development.* Routledge, London.

Engel, T.
|1993| Charcoal Remains from an Iron Age Copper Smelting Slag Heap at Feinan, Wadi Arabah (Jordan). *Vegetation History and Archaeobotany* 2:205–211.

Fantechi, R., and N. S. Margaris (editors)
|1986| *Desertification in Europe: Proceedings of the Information Symposium in the EEC Programme on Climatology Held in Mytilene, Greece, 15–18 April 1984.* D. Reidel, Dordrecht.

Hauptmann, A.
|1989| The Earliest Periods of Copper Metallurgy in Feinan, Jordan. In *Archaemetallurgie det Alten Weltt/Old World Archaeometallurgy*, edited by A. Hauptmann, E. Pernicka, and G. A. Wagner, pp. 119–136. Beiheft 7, Der Anschnitt. Deutsches Bergbau-Museum, Bochum.
|1992| Feinan/Wadi Feinan. *American Journal of Archaeology* 96:510–512.
|2000| *Zur frühen Metallurgie des Kupfers in Fenan/ Jordanien.* Beiheft 11, Der Anschnitt. Deutsches Bergbau-Museum, Bochum.

Hauptmann, A., E. Begemann, E. Heitkemper, E. Pernicka, and S. Schmitt-Strecker
|1992| Early Copper Produced at Feinan, Wadi Araba, Jordan: The Composition of Ores and Copper. *Archaeomaterials* 6:1–33.

Le Houerou, H. N.
|1996| Climate Change, Drought, and Desertification. *Journal of Arid Environments* 34:133–185.

Millington, A., and K. Pye (editors)
|1994| *Environmental Change in Drylands: Biogeographical and Geomorphological Perspectives.* John Wiley and Sons, Chichester.

Mortimore, M.
|1998| *Roots in the African Dust: Sustaining the Drylands.* Cambridge University Press, Cambridge.

Pyatt, F. B., G. Barker, P. Birch, D. Gilbertson, J. P. Grattan, and D. J. Mattingly
|2000| King Solomon's Miners – Starvation and Bioaccumulation? An Environmental Archaeological Investigation in Southern Jordan. *Ecotoxicology and Environmental Safety* 43:305–308.

Pyatt, F.B., G. Gilmore, J. P. Grattan, C. O. Hunt, and S. J. McLaren
|2000| An Imperial Legacy? An Exploration of the Environmental Impact of Ancient Metal Mining and Smelting in Southern Jordan. *Journal of Archaeological Science* 27:771–778.

Spellman, G.
|2000| The Dynamic Climatology of Drylands. In *The Archaeology of Drylands: Living at the Margin*, edited by G. Barker and D. Gilbertson, pp. 19–41. One World Archaeology 39. Routledge, London.

Thomas, D. S. G., and N. J. Middleton
|1994| *Desertification: Exploding the Myth.* John Wiley and Sons, Chichester.

Tiffen, M., M. Mortimore, and F. Gichuki
|1994| *More People, Less Erosion: Environmental Recovery in Kenya.* John Wiley and Sons, Chichester.

Wilkinson, T. J.
|1982| The Definition of Ancient Manured Zones by Means of Extensive Sherd-Sampling Techniques. *Journal of Field Archaeology* 9:323–333.

Wilkinson, T. J.
|1989| Extensive Sherd Scatters and Land Use Intensity: Some Recent Results. *Journal of Field Archaeology* 16:31–46.

PART VI: IN TRANSIT: THE ARCHAEOLOGY OF TRANSPORTATION

COMPARING LANDSCAPES OF TRANSPORTATION: RIVERINE-ORIENTED AND LAND-ORIENTED SYSTEMS IN THE INDUS CIVILIZATION AND THE MUGHAL EMPIRE

Heather M.-L. Miller

Heather M.-L. Miller, Department of Anthropology, University of Toronto, 3359 Mississauga Road North, Mississauga, Ontario L5L 1C6, Canada

ABSTRACT

Through the comparison of two disparate transportation systems, I discuss factors affecting the choices made during movement through a landscape, and thus the entire transportation system. One case is the Indus Civilization (third millennium B.C.E), where transport systems are reconstructed as river-oriented, based largely on the riverine-focused settlement pattern. In contrast, transport systems of the Mughal empire (early 1500s to 1850s C.E.) are represented in historical records as primarily land transport by pack animal caravans. Factors affecting these markedly different transportation systems, operating in the same region of South Asia at different time periods, include both changes in the natural environment and in the cultural context, as well as possible biases in the different types of data used (archaeological versus textual). Aspects of the cultural context discussed here are cultural affiliations and landscape ideals, location of political centres of control, and changes in transportation technology, but many other aspects remain to be explored in this potentially profitable approach to the comparative study of social systems.

THE ARCHAEOLOGY OF TRANSPORTATION

The papers in this section begin to create an archaeology of transportation, looking at the past from a perspective of *movement through a landscape*. We draw on examples from around the world, using a spectrum of techniques and approaches, including spatial perspectives from settlement pattern analysis, connections across regions from provenience studies, and perceptions of landscape from landscape archaeology. We employ these approaches from a distinctive outlook, seeing landscapes from the perspective of movement, rather than the perspective of settlement.

Transportation systems provided conduits of access and modes of integration, both physical and ritual. They channeled and symbolized economic flows, ceremonial paths, and political power. Many of these papers (Gates 2005; Ng and Cackler 2005; Walker 2001) creatively explore such a range of uses for one of the most important types of transportation system: roads (see also Keller 2001 and Snead 2002, versions of which were presented in this conference session). In addition to traces of the roads themselves, these authors employ linguistic and historical data, associated architectural and artifactual distributions, and settlement pattern studies. Other papers use provenience studies to reconstruct routes and methods of transportation (Law 2005; Schwartz and Hollander 2005). They note the utility of determining the relative quantity and type of material moved in reconstructing the types of transportation systems employed.

My own contribution takes a very large-scale approach, examining entire transportation systems comparatively. During the third millennium B.C.E, transport systems of the Indus civilization are reconstructed as largely river-oriented, based primarily on the riverine-focused nature of the settlement system. In contrast, transport systems of the historic Mughal empire (ca. early 1500s to 1850s C.E.) are characterized by land routes, as represented in historical records of large caravans of pack animals. What are the reasons for these markedly different transportation systems within the same landscape?

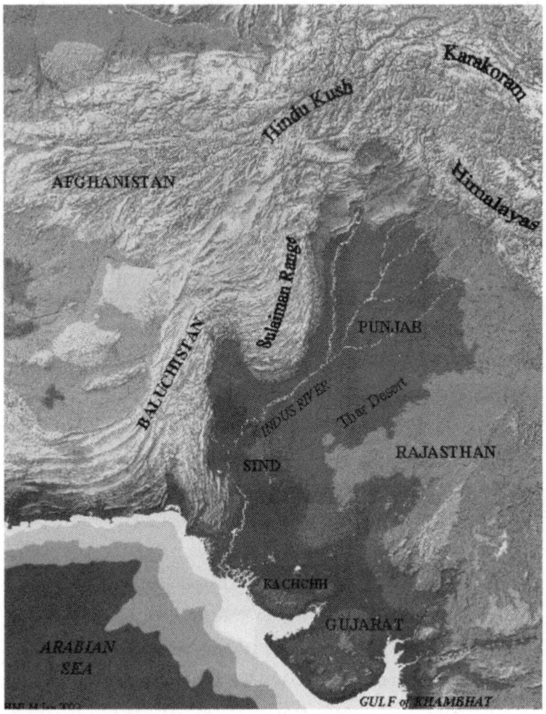

Figure 1. Topographic map indicating locations mentioned in the text (courtesy R. W. Law).

While these particular systems are quite interesting, I want to also generalize this discussion to look at broader aspects of the archaeological analysis of transportation systems. I will first provide a brief overview of the physical landscape and some details of my two examples, then move to a comparative discussion of particular conditions affecting these transportation systems. The factors in transportation choice presented here are: aspects of the natural environment; a variety of issues relating to cultural context, from political structure to group identity; changes in transportation technology; and potential biases in the data.[1] Other papers in this section examine these and other factors, and the ways such factors play out in their particular cases. For example, Walker (2001) discusses possible political reasons for the construction of multiple causeways between settlements, and Ng and Cackler (2005) look at temporal changes in the functions and meanings of roads and canals originally built for logging transport. With the discussion and organization of such factors in transport choice, we begin to outline a general approach to archaeological transportation systems.

BACKGROUND

Physical landscape

The location for my discussion is the Punjab of Pakistan and India, and surrounding areas (Figures 1 and 2) . The majority of the Punjab is a flat, silty, riverine floodplain drained by five rivers, which merge into the Indus River at the border between the Punjab and Sind to the south. The Indus Valley, including the Punjab, is a massive semi-arid plain composed entirely of silty clay, with no particles larger than sand sized for well over 100 km. With water, this is an extremely fertile area, and the Punjab has been an agricultural centre throughout history, wheat and cotton being the premier crops.

The rivers of the Punjab are both obstacles to be crossed and pathways in themselves, depending on the destination. They are navigable by small boat most times of the year, and by larger boats (60–100 tons) during the wetter seasons of March to October (Habib 1986). These rivers are highly variable in their water and silt content at different seasons and in different years, and this affects both navigation and crossings. Fords can be used in some seasons, but at other times ferries or bridges must be employed. Permanent bridges were not common in the plains until the colonial period (Deloche 1984), a point to which I will return. Instead, fords, ferries, and boat bridges were by far the most common river-crossing methods.

Surrounding these plains to the north are resource-rich foothills that lead up into the Himalayan, Karakorum, and Hindu Kush mountain ranges, barring the way to Kashmir, China, northern Afghanistan and Central Asia. To the west are the lower but drier Sulaiman Range and other Baluchi ranges, also mineralogically rich, which funnel the land routes into southern Afghanistan and Iran. All of these ranges had to be entered and crossed through passes, a constraint guiding the reconstruction of land transport routes for any period.

To the east of the Punjab is a small region of raised plain and foothills, and beyond that the great Gangetic Valley, another enormously productive agricultural region set in riverine floodplains. To the southeast and south are the Thar Desert and sparsely populated semi-arid regions of Rajasthan. Beyond this is Gujarat, composed of the marshlands of Kachchh (or Kutch), the peninsula of Saurashtra, and a coastal strip east of the Gulf of Khambhat (or Cambay), an important destination during both of the periods I will discuss.

The Indus civilization

My first example of a transportation system is that of the Indus civilization, at its greatest extent ca. 2600 to 1900 B.C.E., contemporaneous with early states in Egypt and Mesopotamia (see Kenoyer 1998 for an overview of the Indus, or Harappan, civilization). Indus settlements are spread across a very large area, including all of the floodplains of the Indus river system (both in the Punjab and Sind regions), the lowlands of Baluchistan to the southwest, and most of Gujarat to the southeast (Figures 1 and 2). This is an area the size of all of the west coast states of the United States, or the size of ancient Mesopotamia and Egypt combined. The Indus civilization must therefore have had a highly efficient transportation and communication system to allow the degree of uniformity we see in the material culture spread across this region, whether this uniformity represents an exchange of actual objects, or of conceptions and techniques.

Because of their settlement pattern, which is heavily oriented to the rivers and coasts, it has been assumed that the Indus civilization primarily employed riverine transport. While we have no preserved boat fragments, there are a few depictions of Indus boats and one proposed terracotta model (Kenoyer 1998; Rao 1979–1985). It is somewhat surprising that there are so few boat depictions, given the number of terracotta models of carts and furniture found, but perhaps model boats were made of perishable materials, especially if flotation was desired.

Some portion of Indus transport must have been by land. We know that they had carts, not only because we find many clay models of a variety of types, but also from the cart ruts found in the streets of the ancient city of Harappa (Kenoyer 1998:89). Pack animals were probably also very important, as discussed below. Nevertheless, there are no depictions of animals bearing loads or pulling carts in the admittedly small corpus of Indus figurative materials, which are primarily scenes on seals and tokens. Neither do any of the terracotta animal figurines appear to be carrying packs.

Overall, unlike other early Old World states, the existing Indus pictorial depictions and figurines are of limited use in investigating the Indus transportation system. The Indus writing is not yet deciphered, and the preserved examples consist of very short inscriptions in any case. So it is not surprising that there has been little discussion of the process of transport and travel by Indus people, whether by water or by land. For the most part, it has been assumed, probably correctly, that the major routes in the Indus period would have been quite similar to those of the historic period, especially for long distance land routes over the mountain passes to procure various raw materials (e.g., Ratnagar 1981). This assumption has not been contested or affirmed, due to the relative lack of precise research into Indus exchange patterns. Only recently has detailed proveniencing research begun to allow more precise reconstructions of Indus trade routes (e.g., Blackman and Vidale 1992; Méry 1996, Law 2005).

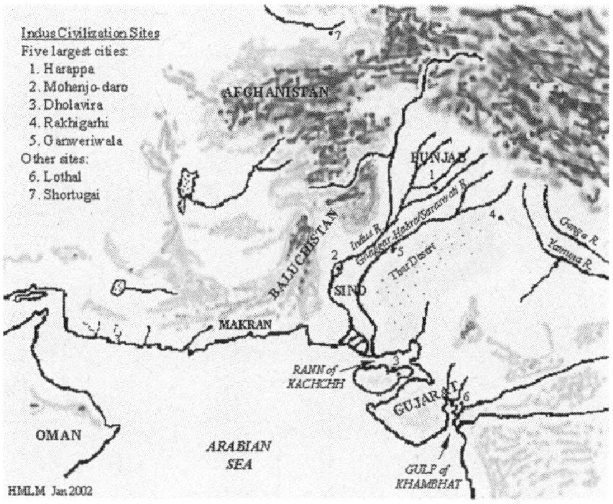

Figure 2. Map of Indus Civilization region, showing ancient double river system.

The Mughal empire

My second transportation system, focused on land routes, is that of the medieval period in this region, particularly the system under the Mughal empire, from the early sixteenth century to the middle of the nineteenth century (1500s to 1850s C.E.) (see Richards 1993 for an overview of the Mughal empire). However, many of these patterns were begun at least several centuries earlier, particularly for the Punjab (Dar 1994, 1999; Deloche 1993; Levi 2001). The area of influence of the Mughal empire was even larger than that of the Indus civilization, but only partially overlapped the

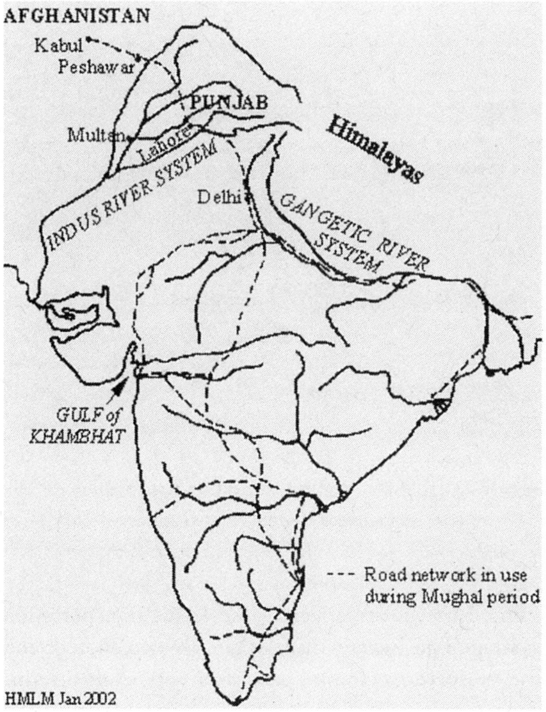

Figure 3. Map showing road system in use during Mughal period (after Deloche 1993).

Indus region (Figures 1, 2 and 3). The Mughal centre of power was between the Gangetic Valley and the Punjab, and at its height the empire controlled most of peninsular India to the south, and into Central Asia to the west. But it only nominally included the lower Indus River Valley (Sind) south of Multan.

Historical accounts emphasize the importance of the caravan trade routes in the medieval period, particularly the Grand Trunk Road, which extended from the Gangetic Valley through the Punjab via Delhi and Lahore, then on into Afghanistan and Central Asia (Figure 3) (e.g., Dar 1994, 1999; Deloche 1968, 1993; Levi 2001). Numerous caravans of camels, horses, and (in the plains) bullocks and ox carts traversed these routes, and improvements were made to the land transport system by the imperial government, by members of the court, and by local elites. Such improvements included the construction of way-stations with amenities for caravans, known as *qâfilah* (Arabic) or *caravanserai* (Persian); the placement of regularly spaced road markers or *kos minar*; and even the paving of at least parts of the Grand Trunk Road through the Punjab (Dar 1994, 1999; Deloche 1968, 1993; Hameed 1980). Horse-riding messengers of the official government communications system also operated along these routes, and government posting stations for these messengers and other government agents were often located within or near the caravan way-stations.

In contrast, much less emphasis was placed on riverine transport during this period. River boats were certainly used during this period, and Habib (1986) even indicates the seasonal navigability of rivers in his atlas of the Mughal empire. But very few major Mughal sites are found along the rivers, except for sites near river crossings along primary trade routes, such as those at the northern crossings of the Indus River on the road to Peshawar. Another such exception is the city of Multan, located near the crossing for the southern confluence of several Punjab rivers and a staging point for the routes through the passes to southern Afghanistan. However, it is perhaps equally significant for its prominent place in the Mughal road system that Multan was also a paramount pilgrimage site for both Muslim and Hindu sects. Pilgrimage was and is a significant aspect of most of the South Asian religions, and pilgrims have formed a sizable proportion of travelers for as long as we have records. Many of the way-stations were specifically dedicated as acts of piety, to aid religious pilgrims and other travelers (Deloche 1993; Richards 1993).

FACTORS IN TRANSPORTATION CHOICES

Rather than reconstruct these transportation systems in more detail individually, I want to focus on why such different transport systems were emphasized during these two periods. Using these two examples, the Indus civilization and the Mughal empire, I will briefly address this question via a number of factors we might investigate for *any* study of archaeological transportation: the natural environment, cultural context, changes in transportation technology, and data bias. This is by no means an exhaustive list of the possible factors involved in transportation choices, as can be seen in other papers in this volume, but they are major factors for this particular comparison.

The type of connection between the Punjab and the Gulf of Khambhat region of Gujarat is a useful comparative case, as these regions were of similar importance during the Indus and Mughal periods

(Figures 1, 2 and 3). The Punjab plains were premier agricultural regions and centres of wealth during both periods. In the Indus period and later, Gujarat was the major source of the high-quality agate, including carnelian, used for the Indus and historic period bead-making industries (Kenoyer 1998). And for centuries if not millennia before the Mughal period, the Gulf of Khambhat was a major shipping region for the Arabian Sea, and also a major textile production area. However, routes and apparently methods of transport between these regions were quite different.

In 1968, Jean Deloche proposed that there were major differences in the primary Indus period and historic transportation routes (Figure 4); note especially the change in the route between the Punjab plains and the Gulf of Khambhat region. The environmental changes in the river and coastal systems discussed below played a role in this change in transportation flow, but I think the main reason for this change was a rearrangement of political and cultural interaction systems. Surprisingly, in spite of great claims related to the introduction of the camel and horse soon after the Indus period, changes in transportation technology between the Indus and Mughal periods were of minimal importance for this and most other routes. Biases in the different types of data for these two periods may be a serious issue, however, and one that only additional field and archival research can address.

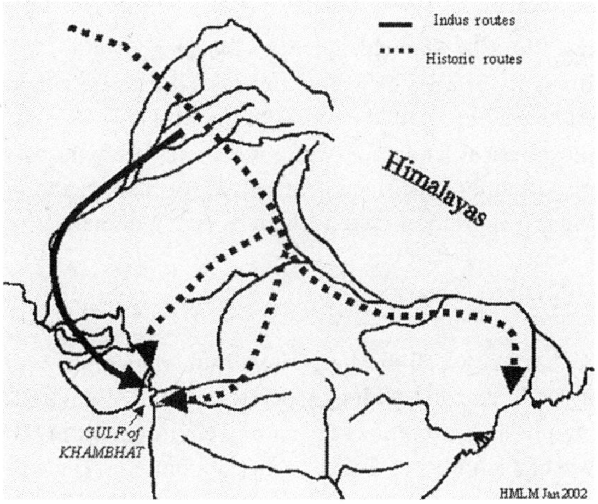

Figure 4. Indus and historic routes to Gujarat, as proposed by Deloche (after Deloche 1968).

Natural environment

A major aspect of any transportation system will be the natural environment through which people are traveling. This includes, for example, the features of the landscape, climate, and seasonal changes. Even though I am looking at the same general location, there have been significant changes in the natural environment in the four thousand years between the two time periods discussed. Any changes in climate would change the flow rates of rivers that had to be navigated or crossed, as well as affecting the frequency of rains (and thus road mud) both absolutely and seasonally. Any climatic temperature changes would affect the length of time that mountain passes were open to Afghanistan and beyond. So dealing with the seasonality of transport systems would have been one of the most essential aspects of their operation in this region. At this point, our climatic data are simply not refined enough to reconstruct the Indus period system in detail, and so no serious comparative analysis can be made.

Our knowledge of changes in landscape features is slightly better, and several landscape features changed dramatically between the Indus and Mughal periods. At the time of the Indus civilization, a seasonal or a perennial second river system ran parallel to the Indus River (Figure 2, Ghaggar-Hakra/Saraswati River), emptying either into the extended Indus delta or into the shallow saline waters of the Rann of Kachchh. The Rann of Kachchh, a seasonally marshy area by the medieval period, was once navigable water for at least part of the year, but has gradually filled with silts. The current region of Kachchh was thus at least seasonally an island at various times in the past. The changes in the geography of this region, particularly its navigability by boat, are thus especially important for the changing nature of contacts between the Punjab region and Gujarat, including Kachchh and the Gulf of Khambhat (Figure 4).

The Indus civilization transport along this route would have been primarily by boat, down the rivers of the Indus system and along the coast at least to Kachchh, if not all the way to the Gulf of Khambhat. In contrast, Mughal period routes passed along the road from Lahore to Delhi, then overland across northwestern India to the Khambhat ports (Figure 4), employing a variety of carts and pack carriers as described in the transportation technology section below. However, while the second river system and the Rann of Kachchh were no longer navigable, the Indus River itself as well as the coastal passage would still have been viable options for the Mughals, as far as the physical landscape was concerned. Other factors played a more decisive role in this route change, and in the transportation system changes more generally.

Cultural context

As has been well discussed in cultural geography and in landscape archaeology studies, the human environment is as important as the natural environment in the use of a landscape. This human environment, the cultural context of decisions about landscape use, includes everything we refer to as culture: political, economic, social, and ideological system components of all types. Unfortunately, our current knowledge of the Indus civilization is entirely dependent on relatively sparse archaeological data, so it is difficult to unravel these various strands contributing to the overall cultural approach to landscape use by Indus peoples. Here, I will focus on the general attitudes towards landscapes for these two periods, particularly preferred settlement locations, to examine broad effects of cultural systems on transportation. In the next section, I give an example of the effect on transportation system of a specific aspect of cultural context, changes in technology.

In the Indus period, Sind was strongly a part of the Indus civilization, if not its heartland, and the core of the Indus civilization was oriented along the length of the rivers in the greater Indus Valley floodplains (Figure 2). Particularly with the double river system and the navigability of the Rann of Kachchh, transport by boat would have been an easy route to Kachchh and the Saurashtran peninsula of Gujarat. From there, Indus sites such as Lothal on the Gulf of Khambhat could have been reached either overland, or continuing by boat around the coast of Gujarat. In contrast, land routes from Punjab to the east and southeast were less certain – the Indus people seem to have had trading relations with the inhabitants of inland northwestern India, but no strong settled presence.

Furthermore, Indus external trade definitely had a strong maritime component, at least to Oman. The Indus settlements along the Makran coast and the Indus finds in Oman (e.g., Méry 1996), indicate that boats or ships were sailing across the Gulf and touching at points along it. Whether these boats were operated by Indus or by Omani sailors is not clear. Overland, the question of Indus external trade to Afghanistan and Central Asia is still equivocal, due to lack of research, but it seems more likely that they participated in down-the-line exchange rather than setting up trading colonies (see also Law 2005). The Indus site of Shortugai, near the Oxus River, is the only reported Indus settlement in this region, and seems to have been an isolated traders' outpost, although additional research in this area would be extremely welcome.

In contrast, the centre of the Mughal empire was not along the Indus, but across the northern plains of the Punjab and the Gangetic plain. This region spanned the floodplains of two different sets of unconnected rivers, and so rivers were not useful as a continuous transportation path (Figure 3). However, by placing their imperial capitals between these two river systems, the Mughals were in a good position to control both of the major agricultural floodplains of the north. The southern Indus Valley was no longer a core of the transport system, and Sind (south of Multan Province) was not a politically or economically significant region by the Mughal period. Instead, throughout the historic period, land routes were used to Gujarat and the Gulf of Khambhat, passing through northwestern India. The land route to Gujarat was shorter and easier than the riverine route down the Indus, because the region around Delhi was the centre of economic and political power, rather than the Indus Valley.

Continuing by land along the east-west line of the Mughal centres of control, the land route to Central Asia was of special importance for the Mughals (and earlier polities), as Central Asia was not only an important source of trade revenue, but also the historic homeland of the ruling class. The peoples of Afghanistan and Central Asia were not "foreigners" to the Mughals, but ancestral kin with cultural ties. The Mughals had a strong sense of spatially based cultural identity, tied to this geographic homeland.

Geographic homelands are not the only aspect of spatially based cultural identity at issue in this example. The Indus and Mughal peoples may have preferred different types of landscape for their cities, just as their cities are quite different in layout and architectural design (Jansen 1993, Kenoyer 1998 for the Indus; Asher 1992, Richards 1993 for the Mughals). Unlike the floodplain-oriented Indus people, the Mughals seemed to have preferred the foothills and uplands. Additionally, historic records repeatedly indicate the Mughals' preference for transport and military engagement by land rather than by boat, something that hampered them in later trading competition with the Europeans, and perhaps relates to their mythological harkening to a Central Asian nomadic lifestyle, as reflected in their architecture.

However, unlike a number of recent archaeological landscape studies, this is certainly not a case where the built landscape of the Indus was incorporated and given new meaning in the landscape of the Mughals nearly five thousand years later, except perhaps to be noted as some of the many ruins of earlier times. In general, the Indus civilization was remarkably unrecognized as a distinct past society, even in the folklore of local peoples, due perhaps to the great time depth involved and especially the lack of Indus monumental structures, other than the cities themselves. In both periods, though, there were doubtless some aspects of historicity, in that earlier roadways and other transport features would have influenced the placement of later features.

In sum, the landscape was different during these two periods not only because of actual differences in landscape features or environment. The configuration of the political system, the geographical centres of power, and historic cultural ties can be just as important in perceptions of a transportation landscape. These cultural landscapes play out practically as well as conceptually. Travelers and especially traders had to take into account the differential distributions of travel amenities as well as tolls when planning a route. They also had to consider regional security risks, since banditry was a serious issue, as well as helpful kin networks. The type of transport employed was another culturally influenced choice.

Transportation technology

Changes in the transportation technology often have major effects on transportation systems. However, technology is a part of the cultural system, not somehow outside of it. The adoption of new transportation technologies is not necessarily automatic, and even if adopted, new technologies do not necessarily have the same effects when introduced into a different cultural context.

An example of this is seen in the land transport system of this region. The addition of the horse and the camel from Central Asia is always cited as a major change in the animal assemblage during the second millennium B.C.E., just after the Indus period, precisely because of their transportation value. However, it is not clear that these new animals were adopted in any great numbers until much later. Historically, the horse was always a precarious inhabitant of this region, and was often kept more for prestige than for general transport usefulness. The exception to this was the horse's great ability for swift movement, which was essential in the government communication system and for certain types of military maneuvers. The camel, however, was the quintessential caravan animal in the historic period, given its tolerance for aridity and its large carrying capacity. Once introduced, camels carried the bulk of objects taken from the Indian subcontinent to Afghanistan and Central Asia. Law (2005) discusses the size-limited carrying capacity of herds of goats, the probable pack animal of choice for mountain crossings before the camel became available in this region.

The camel was thus a significant addition to the transportation choices for arid regions, especially Afghanistan, Central Asia, and even Baluchistan. But for the plains, especially in the Punjab, there was an indigenous animal already present that was very useful as a pack animal – the zebu or humped cattle. Pack zebu bullocks were very common in historic times, and were likely used extensively in the Indus period.[2] Punjab breeds of cattle were famed for their strength and speed (Deloche 1993). Furthermore, zebus could plow, thresh, and drive water wheels, as well as drawing carts, making them a useful multipurpose animal. Bullock-drawn carts were a common means of transportation during the historic as well as the Indus periods, for goods as well as people. This was very different from the Middle East, particularly Persia.

During the Mughal period, foreign travelers commented with amazement on the plethora of transportation types in South Asia (Deloche 1993:255). Besides carts and pack animals such as bullocks and camels, human porters were a major source of transport power well into the historic period, especially in the hills and in southern India. Both men and women acted as porters, carrying individuals and objects of amazing weights. Deloche (1993) provides comparative measures of carrying weights for humans, animals, and carts, and distances which could be traversed. He also illustrates a number of important devices, such as carrying frames that allowed large numbers of human porters to carry massive objects like stone blocks or

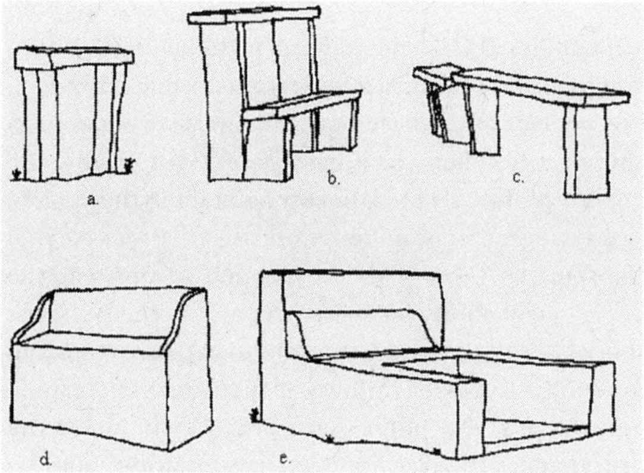

Figure 5. Porter's rests: (a), (b) and (c) are made from granite slabs; (d) and (e) are brick benches (after Deloche 1993).

statues across difficult country, with the weight distributed across many poles. For archaeologists trying to trace porters' routes, Deloche (1993) provides valuable notes about the construction of load rests (Figure 5), which were stone crossbeams or brick benches set at waist height for back-carried packs and at head height for head-carried packs. The stone crossbeam types are deceptively similar to "ritual" structures made from large stone slabs, a monument type known from many parts of the world.

In sum, the camel would have been an important introduction for larger-scale long-distance trade to Afghanistan and Central Asia, and perhaps for regional trade in areas like Baluchistan and the Thar Desert, altering the possible scale of transportation across all of these arid regions. But for trade within the plains of Punjab, Sind, and northwest India, and in the surrounding foothills, pack bullocks and carts were probably more important than camels even in the historic period. And the value of human porters should not be underestimated.

Similarly, in spite of developments in architecture and great governmental interest in improving the long-distance routes across this region since before the medieval period, we do not see much change in the technologies used for crossing rivers, even during the Mughal period. While some permanent bridges were built during the Mughal period, fords, ferries and boat bridges continued to be of primary importance in the plains, and rope suspension bridges and wooden plank bridges in the hills (Deloche 1984). Boat bridges, composed of a row of lashed boats overlaid with a plank road, could be more easily adjusted to the seasonal fluctuations in water than most solid bridges. Such bridges would raise and lower with the seasonal rise and fall of the river, and could be expanded or contracted in breadth with the addition or removal of extra boats as needed. Boat bridges would be especially useful in this region of frequently shifting river courses, as they could be moved wholesale to a new riverbed, unlike permanent bridges.

More importantly, boat bridges were more effective than permanent bridges from a military standpoint in those times of constant warfare. The boat bridge could be disassembled when the enemy advanced, but quickly reassembled when desired. Significantly, Deloche (1984:19, footnote 3) notes that no permanent bridges were built over the Yamuna River near the Mughal capitals, only massive boat bridges. It is noteworthy, however, that the places where Mughal arched bridges were constructed followed the two major Mughal trade routes – the portion of the Grand Trunk Road from the Gangetic Plain through the Punjab to Peshawar, and the route from Delhi to the Gulf of Khambhat (Deloche 1984). But near the frontier, even on the Grand Trunk Road, boat bridges were employed. Even the very important crossing over the Indus River at Attock consisted until 1883 of a boat bridge, which was in use seven or eight months of the year (Deloche 1984:1, footnote 1).

Overall, it is important to consider the choices involved in technological changes. Travelers and merchants adopted such transport systems as suited their needs. For example, the greater efficiency of a cart versus a pack animal would depend on the areas crossed, the load to be carried, and the speed requirements, not to mention the traveler's budget. Such choices might be different in different seasons, depending on drought, floods, snow, and mud. Kin or religious relationships might influence the choice of particular routes, freight haulers, or caravan groups. In building bridges, governments and regional elites weighed the encouragement of increased travel (and thus increased tolls) against security issues. New aids to transport were of use for specific tasks and environments, but they were not necessarily adopted wholesale. While we have more information about these choices for the Mughal period, they also serve as reminders that the situation in the Indus period may have been equally complex.

Data-source bias

Finally, in this particular case, it is imperative to consider whether these apparent differences in transportation emphasis are biased by the approach to reconstruction. The Indus civilization is known entirely from archaeological data, which is less complete than for many areas of the world. Our reconstruction of its riverine orientation is based primarily on the concentration of settlements along river systems. However, this settlement pattern does not necessarily reflect the transportation system, but may be heavily influenced by the agricultural system, if this was primarily dependent on river water. A further complication to the interpretation of the Indus settlement pattern is that many locations that would be likely candidates for overland trade route stops were inhabited in later periods. So we simply do not know if there are Indus period settlements buried beneath the enormous mounds of the historic and modern settlements. This is an essential question to answer for assessing the relative importance of agricultural- versus trade-based wealth for the Indus.

In contrast, the Mughal period is known primarily from historical records. Archaeological documentation of structures has been hampered by lack of personnel and funds, and only a few regional surveys have been made, most in the past decade and most with a multi-period focus (e.g., Ali 1999; Dar 1994, 1999; Franke-Vogt et al. 2000; Mughal 1997; Rehman et al. 1998). The historical record strongly reflects the interests of the government and the elite, who desired the wealth available from the long-distance trade to Central Asia. In contrast, regional and local trade in lower-cost goods, probably already controlled by regional leaders and so less available to the Mughal imperial elite, may have often made use of river transport.

In fact, I might propose an alternative scenario to the riverine Indus transport system versus the land-based Mughal system. It is possible that during *both* periods, internal trade in lower-cost local goods was chiefly by riverine transport, while external trade in higher-priced goods was largely overland. We know that the external trade of the Mughal period was more prominent in historical records, as the elite and the government had both an economic and a political interest in it. Perhaps only the lack of translated records saves us from the same sort of bias in the Indus period, and they also used overland routes for high-priced goods sponsored and consumed by elites. While I find this second scenario unlikely, particularly given the lack of evidence for Central Asian goods in the Indus, and the huge scale of bulk goods like wheat and cotton moved overland during the medieval period (Levi 2001), it is a reasonable alternative which must be considered. For the Mughal period, at least, targeted scrutiny of the documentary evidence for local as well as long-distance trade should be able to address the relative importance of riverine transport. Archaeological research on historic period settlement patterns will also be helpful, and my colleagues and I hope to begin such a project in the near future.

CONCLUSION

Data bias, while a serious issue, can only be a portion of the story. There is no question that there are some major differences in the transportation flows and systems of these two societies. During the Indus period, there is definitely a strong linear interaction along the Indus river system, a configuration not seen during the medieval period. Instead, the Mughal empire is interested in trade throughout the northern region of the subcontinent, and on into Central Asia. The Gulf of Khambhat region is important in both periods, but reached by entirely different routes (Figure 4).

The reasons for these differences include changes in environmental factors, and especially changes in cultural affiliations, political centres of control, and perhaps preferred modes of transport and landscape ideals. The addition of the camel was probably increasingly important for trade with Afghanistan and Central Asia, but transport within the Indian subcontinent would not have been much affected. Biases in the types of data available for these two time periods may be an issue for the determination of the relative importance of riverine versus land travel for local trade routes. Data biases may also be masking differences in the relative importance of trade-based versus agriculturally based wealth during these two periods, particularly with regards to settlement location choice. Any such differences in wealth sources may in turn be related to climate change, increasing specialization and globalization of economies, and/or the addition of new elite classes from outside the subcontinent. This is not a simple problem. That is what makes the archaeology of transportation such a potentially useful field for further endeavor.

REFERENCES CITED

Ali, T.

|1999–2000| Baolis, Bridges and Caravan Sarais along the Grand Ancient Trunk Road in N.W.F.P. *Ancient Pakistan* 13:69–108.

Asher, C. B.

|1992| *The Architecture of Mughal India.* The New Cambridge History of India, vol. I.4. Cambridge University Press, Cambridge.

Blackman, M. J., and M. Vidale

|1992| The Production and Distribution of Stoneware Bangles at Mohenjo-Daro and Harappa as Monitored by Chemical Characterization Studies. In *South Asian Archaeology 1989*, edited by C. Jarrige, pp. 37–44. Prehistory Press, Madison, Wisconsin.

Dar, S. R.

|1994| Caravanserais along the Grand Trunk Road in Pakistan – A Central Asian Legacy. *Journal of Central Asia* 17(1–2):15–31.

|1999| Caravanserais and Related Buildings in Pakistan: System and Structures. *Journal of Asian Civilizations* 22(1):104–125.

Deloche, J.

|1968| *Recherches sur les routes de l'Inde au temps des Mogols. (Étude critique des sources).* Publications de l'École Française d'Extréme-Orient Vol. LXVII. École Française d'Extréme-Orient, Paris.

|1984| *The Ancient Bridges of India.* Sitaram Bhartia Institute of Scientific Research, New Delhi.

|1993| *Transport and Communications in India Prior to Steam Locomotion. Volume 1: Land Transport.* French Studies in South Asian Culture and Society, vol. 7. Translated by J. Walker. Updated with additions by the author, from the original French edition of 1980. Oxford University Press, Delhi.

Franke-Vogt, U., S. Shams Ul-Hag, and M. H. K. Khattak

|2000| Archaeological Exploration in the Kanrach Valley (Las Bela, Balochistan). In *South Asian Archaeology 1997*, vol. I, edited by M. Taddei, and G. De Marco, pp. 189–213. Istituto Italiano per l'Africa e l'Oriente (IsIAO), Rome and Istituto Universitario Orientale, Naples.

Gates, J.

|2005| Hidden Passage: Graeco-Roman Roads in Egypt's Eastern Desert. In *Space and Spatial Analysis in Archaeology*, edited by E. C. Robertson, J. D. Seibert, D. C. Fernandez, and M. U. Zender, pp. 315–322. University of Calgary Press, Calgary, Alberta.

Habib, I.

|1986| *An Atlas of the Mughal Empire.* Reprint with corrections of 1982 edition. Oxford University Press, Delhi.

Hameed, A. (photographer)

|1980| Image ID IHP0042, Grand Trunk Road. Aga Khan Visual Archives, Massachusetts Institute of Technology (MIT). http://bloom.mit.edu/agakhan/info/index.html. Associated text refers to: Farooque, A. K. M. 1977 *Roads and Communications in Mughal India.* Idarah-i Adabiyat-i, Delhi.

Jansen, M.

|1993| *Mohenjo-Daro: City of Wells and Drains. Water Splendour 4500 Years Ago. (Stadt der Brunnen und Kanäle. Wasserluxus vor 4500 Jahren).* Frontinus-Gesellschaft e.V., Bergisch Gladbach.

Keller, A.

|2001| Finding the Way: Identifying Directed Movement at the Late Classic Maya Center of Xunantunich, Belize. Paper presented at the 34th Annual Chacmool Conference, Calgary, Alberta.

Kenoyer, J. M.

|1998| *Ancient Cities of the Indus Valley Civilization.* Oxford University Press, Karachi.

Law, R. W.

|2005| Moving Mountains: The Trade and Transport of Rocks and Minerals within the Greater Indus Valley Region. In *Space and Spatial Analysis in Archaeology*, edited by E. C. Robertson, J. D. Seibert, D. C. Fernandez, and M. U. Zender, pp. 301–313. University of Calgary Press, Calgary, Alberta.

Levi, S. C.

|2001| *The Indian Diaspora in Central Asia and its Trade, 1550–1900.* E. J. Brill, Leiden.

Méry, S.

|1996| Ceramics and Patterns of Exchange across the Arabian Sea and the Persian Gulf in the Early Bronze Age. In *The Prehistory of Asia and Oceania*, edited by G. Afanas'ev, S. Cleuziou, J. R. Lukacs, and M. Tosi, pp. 167–179. ABACO, Forli, Italy.

Miller, L. J.

|2003| Secondary Products and Urbanism in South Asia: The Evidence for Traction at Harappa. In *Indus Ethnobiology: New Perspectives from the Field*, edited by S. A. Weber, and W. R. Belcher, pp. 251–325. Lexington Books, Landham, Maryland.

Mughal, M. R.

|1997| A Preliminary Review of Archaeological Surveys in Punjab and Sindh: 1993–95. *South Asian Studies* 13:241–249.

Ng, O., and P. R. Cackler

|2005| The Life and Times of a British Logging Road in Belize. In *Space and Spatial Analysis in Archaeology*, edited by E. C. Robertson, J. D. Seibert, D. C. Fernandez, and M. U. Zender, pp. 293–300. University of Calgary Press, Calgary, Alberta.

Rao, S. R.

|1979–1985| *Lothal: A Harappan Port Town (1955–1962).* 2 volumes. Archaeological Survey of India, New Delhi.

Ratnagar, S.

|1981| *Encounters: The Westerly Trade of the Harappan Civilization.* Oxford University Press, Delhi.

Rehman, S.-U., G. M. Khan, M. Hassan, and M. Afzal Khan
|1998| *Survey Report of Archaeological Sites and Monuments in Punjab. Volume 1 (Lahore and Kasur Districts).* Department of Archaeology and Museums, Ministry of Culture, Government of Pakistan, Lahore.

Richards, J. F.
|1993| *The Mughal Empire.* The New Cambridge History of India, vol. I.5. Cambridge University Press, Cambridge.

Schwartz, M., and D. Hollander
|2005| Boats, Bitumen and Bartering: The Use of a Utilitarian Good to Track Movement and Transport in Ancient Exchange Systems. In *Space and Spatial Analysis in Archaeology*, edited by E. C. Robertson, J. D. Seibert, D. C. Fernandez, and M. U. Zender, pp. 323–330. University of Calgary Press, Calgary, Alberta.

Snead, J. E.
|2002| Ancestral Pueblo Trails and the Cultural Landscape of the Pajarito Plateau, New Mexico. *Antiquity* 76:756–765.

Walker, J. H.
|2001| Building Connections in the Bolivian Amazon. Paper presented at the 34th Annual Chacmool Conference, Calgary, Alberta.

NOTES

1 A longer paper, examining these two transportation systems in more detail, is in preparation for publication elsewhere. This longer paper elaborates further on the factors in transportation choice presented here: natural environment, cultural context, changes in transportation technology, and data bias. Additional factors only mentioned in this paper, such as the role of religious pilgrimage and security-military considerations, are also covered.

2 Although there is currently no evidence for the use of zebu as pack animals in the Indus period, zooarchaeological studies of evidence for the use of zebu for traction and haulage may provide future insights into this question (L. J. Miller 2003, and dissertation in progress, Anthropology Department, New York University).

THE LIFE AND TIMES OF A BRITISH LOGGING ROAD IN BELIZE

Olivia Ng and Paul R. Cackler

Olivia Ng, Department of Anthropology, University of Pennsylvania, 325 University Museum, Philadelphia, Pennsylvania 19104, U.S.A.
Paul R. Cackler, Department of Anthropology, University of Colorado at Boulder, Boulder, Colorado 80309, U.S.A.

ABSTRACT

The evolution of built space is explored in the life of a British logging road in northwestern Belize. Abandoned earlier this century, the roads are now used in a variety of ways unrelated to logging. The roads are much more than just abandoned features from a previous era, as archaeologists use them to access sites, and present local inhabitants use them to access natural resources. Drawing upon documentary materials and observation of contemporary practices, this paper uses the life history of logging roads as an interpretive tool to illustrate the ongoing dialectic between people and their landscapes.

Logging roads snake across lush jungle floors in double-rowed ruts, proclaiming the past presence of British loggers in the northwestern corner of Belize. Abandoned earlier in the twentieth century, these roads are now used in ways unrelated to logging. Archaeologists use them to access sites, while present local inhabitants use them to extract natural resources. To describe these features solely as abandoned logging roads is to ignore the ongoing dialectic between people and their landscapes. More specifically, the roads to be discussed are part of a regional logging system based out of Hillbank, a colonial settlement on the New River Lagoon. This analysis utilizes documentary materials, results of archaeological fieldwork, and personal observations of contemporary practices to consider the many uses and identities of logging roads through time.

Logging roads can be viewed simply as a means of getting from one point to another, but these roads are also the material remains of a particular social and economic system that tethered Belize to Europe and the United States. A popular model for exploring global economies in archaeology has been world systems theory (Wallerstein 1974, 1980). It depicts a parasitic European world economy with colonies in the New World as dependent peripheries that experience underdevelopment as a result of institutionalized exploitation. Logging, an extractive economy typical of colonial interactions, led to underdevelopment and lack of infrastructure in Belize, which further compounded a reliance on imported goods (Ashcraft 1973).

The archaeology of world systems and colonialism tends to focus on establishing links between artifacts at specific sites (see Lyons and Papadopoulous 2002). Models of trade networks are constructed by tracing imported goods, such as glass bottles, to their point of origin (Baugher-Perlin 1982; Schuyler 1974). Even though the transportation networks between components of the world system are crucial in establishing a model, the routes do not always lend themselves to archaeological investigation. However, much of Belize's logging network is preserved in the landscape, and can provide insights about the colonial system responsible for its creation and perpetuation.

Drawing upon the work of British landscape archaeologists enhances our consideration of roads and their changing identities. Bradley's (1993) concept of the "afterlife of monuments" is one useful approach. The concept refers to the way people interact with monuments that have fallen out of active use, though perhaps in ways different from those originally intended. With the passage of time, monuments are often relocated, reinterpreted, and recycled. Bradley applied the concept of an "afterlife" specifically to monuments, but this idea is useful for interpreting all facets of material culture, including the built landscape. It is easy to dismiss logging roads as abandoned, but they are only abandoned in the sense that loggers no longer use

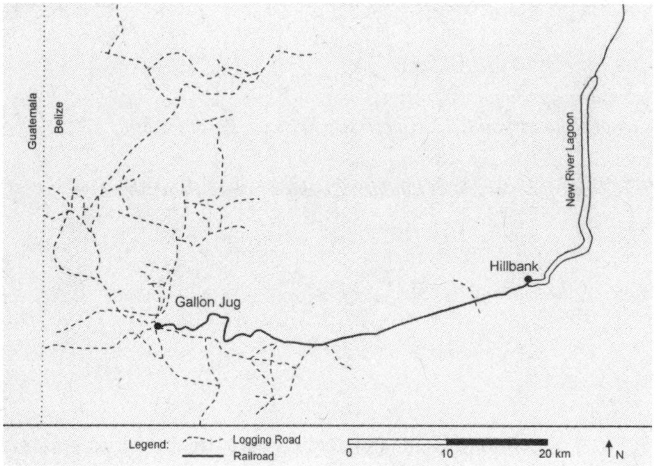

Figure 1. Map of the Hillbank logging system.

them. To call them abandoned is to ignore the successive generations that continue to use the roads for their own purposes, redefining them and contributing to the "afterlife" of these logging roads in the process.

This discussion also draws upon Barrett's (1999) ideas about the nature of archaeological remains and constructs of archaeological time. He argues against conceptualizing historical phases as static periods characterized by a particular pattern of material remains. This traditional practice sees change in the archaeological record as a series of discrete transformations and implies isolation of people from their past. Rather, people constantly incorporate and ideologically manipulate remnants of the past to construct their world. In Barrett's words, "each generation can be regarded as having to confront its own archaeology as the material remains of its past piled up before it" (1999:257). In our study, logging roads may be regarded as a diagnostic feature of the presence of previous logging operations. However, that is not their only role, as we demonstrate below.

Focus on the ongoing life of logging roads is more than an academic attempt to elaborate our understanding of transportation systems. Archaeological finds are rarely pristine; almost no sites are hermetically sealed between their deposition and their recovery. Aside from the effects of bioturbation, they are frequently affected by the daily activities of modern populations, sometimes to the point of significant alteration. Therefore, knowledge of the modern context of archaeological remains – in this case, present day Belize – is essential. In turn, knowledge of logging is essential to understanding modern Belize, formerly the colony of British Honduras until 1981. Logging was one of the main reasons for Western settlements in the region, and has continued to play a major role in the development, or underdevelopment, of the economy and infrastructure. The following brief discussion of the background and operations of Belizean logging will focus on the aspects most pertinent to archaeological interest.

HISTORICAL BACKGROUND AND OPERATIONS OF LOGGING IN BELIZE

Initially, British settlers in the colony, known also as the Baymen, focused on the logwood tree. Its dye was in great demand, and its proximity to rivers and relatively small size made for easy transportation. Only small teams, comprising a few settlers and their slaves, were necessary to locate and process the wood. However, the introduction of a synthetic dye substitute at the end of the eighteenth century caused the European logwood market to plummet. Baymen consequently turned to the mahogany tree, which, because of its hardness and beauty, was favoured for making ships and furniture. In contrast to logwood, mahogany required large work groups of slaves (Finamore 1994). Mahogany trees are much larger and scattered individually in the jungle further inland (Figure 1). As a result, settlers needed to acquire huge tracts of land to better their chances of an adequate mahogany yield (Bolland 1988:16–19). Once a tract of land was acquired, experienced slaves known as hunters were sent out into the jungle to locate the trees. They were followed by mahogany gangs, commonly consisting of around nineteen slaves led by a foreman. Mahogany gangs built scaffolding around a tree to cut it down. The scaffolding, commonly known as a barbeque, supported the axemen 2–3 m from the ground, allowing them to cut the tree above the flaring buttresses of the root system. After it was cut, its limbs were trimmed and it was hauled to the closest water to ship out from a point known as the Barquadier (Gibbs 1883:120–124; Morris 1883:47–48).

Life could be difficult for slaves, and some ran away to neighbouring Spanish territories, which encouraged the movement as a way of retarding British logging and expansion (Craig 1969:60). Although slaves were officially emancipated in the British West Indies by 1838, their standard of living in British Honduras did not improve. Through the 1840s, the continuing rise in the mahogany trade intensified the monopolization of land (Bolland and Shoman 1977). Under control of a small elite group, land prices were too high for freedmen to purchase. Since the majority of the population had no land with which to support themselves agriculturally, they were forced to continue working in poorly paid mahogany gangs. The timber industry also bound its labor force through an advance system, in which workers were paid a cash advance right before the holiday season. The workers almost invariably spent it celebrating with family and accumulated debts to their employers. As the logging season progressed out in the remote jungle, workers fell further into debt through the truck system. Items for daily use were trucked in by the employers and available only at marked up prices. The inevitable outcome of these conditions was a population that had neither the money nor opportunity to build an agricultural base for subsistence, thus perpetuating a reliance on imports. This trend of exploitation and underdevelopment held steadily into the late twentieth century.

One physical effect of this trend was the preservation of vast tracts of forest, which still have not been converted to agricultural land. However, the nature of these preserves has changed. Instead of providing timber to benefit a wealthy minority, these holdings exist to conserve Belize's natural resources for everyone in the nation. Today, much of these lands, including the site of Hillbank, are owned and maintained by Programme for Belize (PfB), a non-profit conservation group.

Until the 1920s, logs were either rolled or pulled on skids to the river. There, workers prepared the logs for shipping down the river by "manufacturing" them, which involved stripping the trunks of their limbs and squaring the trunks. In later techniques, cattle or oxen were used in place of skids, until they were replaced by the internal combustion engine crawler tractor. All of these methods were slow. Their speed was described as "around walking pace" (Anderson 1958:28). Their advantage lay in requiring relatively little work in the way of bush clearing. All woodcutters had to do was clear a main road, or artery, off which trails were opened to mahogany trees. Once cut, the trees were hauled through the trails to the main artery and down to the waterway. Each season, a new area was identified for harvesting, so that arteries and their trails quickly disappeared back into the jungle. As a result, logging roads from this era can be difficult to detect. The advent of the tractor in the 1920s only exacerbated the situation (that is, for archaeologists wishing to investigate traces of logging) as it allowed for more logs to be hauled in less time, and the logging season shortened from eleven to six months (Leslie 1997:76). As a consequence of the shortened season, roads from this period were used for shorter amounts of time and became even more ephemeral. They would be difficult to locate on the ground today.

The 1930s witnessed the advent of the *camión*, which are multi-wheeled logging trucks. Since these trucks were capable of larger loads than the tractors, loggers were willing to invest more effort in an area. Consequently, more permanent logging roads were established. Instead of creating new roads each season, they could return to the same road for several years, extending it further each season. Such roads are more substantial than ones cut in earlier phases of logging. In some parts of Belize, the logging roads were substantial enough to be appropriated by the government and turned into general vehicular roads (Anderson 1958). Presumably, the logging roads currently used by archaeologists to access sites are more likely to date from this era onward. The introduction of various forms of logging equipment and their impact on roads is an illustration of technology's effect upon transportation systems (see Miller 2005).

The logging system based out of Hillbank is an excellent example of a transportation system designed to extract natural resources from a large geographic area (Figure 1). From at least the mid-nineteenth century, Hillbank was an important logging settlement in British Honduras (Antochiw and Breton 1992). Located on the New River Lagoon, it quickly became a regional hub for loggers. Mahogany logs could be floated down the lagoon to the Caribbean Sea via the New River, from where they would be shipped to Britain or the United States. Hillbank's importance is affirmed by the construction of a railroad during the 1920s between it and Gallon Jug, approximately 40 km further inland to the west (Figure 2). Loggers moved further inland as the supply of

Figure 2. Mahogany log being loaded onto the narrow gauge that ran between Hillbank and Gallon Jug. (Courtesy Belize National Archives, Belmopan, Belize)

mahogany close to the rivers dwindled, as demonstrated by the development of the landlocked Gallon Jug station. A need to increase production was the driving force behind the railroad's construction. The transportation components of the Hillbank regional logging system included logging roads, a railroad, and the waterway represented by the New River Lagoon. Other aspects of the system included primary and satellite settlements, and heavy equipment, such as steam engines and steam tractors. Logging roads are the focus of this discussion, but other components are also subject to the idea of multiple uses and various "lives," articulated by Bradley (1993) and Barrett (1999). Such details are discussed further below.

LOGGING ROADS AND ARCHAEOLOGISTS

Archaeologists working in Belize and surrounding regions benefit from an awareness of the impact of logging upon the landscape. Nineteenth-century descriptions suggest logging was a widespread practice. As stated previously, loggers had to canvass huge areas because of the individual patterning of mahogany distribution. The archaeologist Millet Cámara (1984), working from this premise, has proposed that some features identified as Precolumbian irrigation canals in the Campeche region of Mexico may in fact be logging channels from the eighteenth and nineteenth centuries. A canal at Hillbank was clearly used in historic times, as evidenced by wooden poles with ceramic insulators along the length of the canal (Figure 3). The exact function of the canal and the circumstances of its construction have not been determined yet, but it links the lagoon with timber resources.

These examples illustrate the prevalence of logging in the region, and highlight the point that few, if any, archaeological sites and features exist in a vacuum insulated from time. The colonial inhabitants of Hillbank clearly observed Maya archaeological features, occasionally modifying them and perhaps even collecting artifacts. British loggers trenched through ancient Maya mounds when constructing the rail lines at Hillbank, exposing Precolumbian pottery sherds, lithics and human remains (Albert Tucker, personal communication 2002). Our own excavations in historic contexts at Hillbank have also yielded occasional examples of Maya pottery and lithics. Similarly, it is difficult to consider prehistoric sites as being "discovered" after long centuries of undisturbed slumber when there is a logging road running through the main plaza. The site of Calakmul in Campeche is such an example. In these instances, logging roads serve as a reminder of the inextricable link between archaeological materials and their modern context.

These are examples of Barrett's (1999) concept that people engage remnants of the past in constructing their worlds. The loggers must have noticed the Precolumbian ruins at Hillbank and Calakmul as they laid down their roads, whether these mounds were viewed as obstructions or reference points in their way. These possibilities recall Bradley's (1993) idea about the afterlife of monuments, as neither of these functions was intended by the builders of the mounds. Presumably, the mounds and buildings of the main plaza at Calakmul were constructed with civic purposes in mind, while the mound at Hillbank was probably residential. Centuries later, it is doubtful that British loggers regarded these same monuments in the same spirit as their Precolumbian originators intended.

Of greater certainty is the fact that these objects were treated differently. They were mounds to be trenched through, stone ruins seen as navigational reference points in the construction of roads to transport timber. In turn, the logging roads themselves were not intended to function the way we are using them right now, as an interpretive tool. There are also other roles, intended or not, that roads play for archaeologists.

While archaeologists may dread the presence of logging roads near a site because it implies a higher probability that it has been disturbed in recent times, some archaeologists have chosen to incorporate the roads into their investigations. Generally, archaeologists use logging roads for transportation to sites. One particular logging road in the Hillbank system, known primarily by its proximity to the Maya site of Ma'ax Na, has been used by a couple of research teams (Barnhart and Barry n.d.; Cackler et al. 2001).

This road was utilized by survey teams led by Ed Barnhart to facilitate access to an otherwise remote and inaccessible region of PfB in 1996. Initially, Barnhart used the road to speed foot access into the area. The bulldozers used in the construction of the logging road had cut reduced grades up the multiple steep escarpments that were otherwise difficult to climb. Reopening the logging road, first to foot access and subsequently to four-wheel drive vehicles, greatly aided the discovery and preliminary mapping of the site of Ma'ax Na (Barnhart and Barry n.d.). Transects were cut off the logging road in a preliminary survey effort. The road was then used not only to access the structures, but as a reference point to map them as well. The latest team, led by Kathryn Reese-Taylor, researched the relationship between watershed management and Maya political boundaries (Cackler et al. 2001). In addition to using this particular road for access, they used other roads in the area for reference points while conducting reconnaissance. In this context, logging roads are being used in yet another way unintended by their builders, to provide a means of extracting archaeological information.

The extractive potential of roads is nothing new to archaeologists. In one case, archaeologists have even constructed roads to transport artifacts out of sites. Starting in 1930, J. Alden Mason built such a road at Piedras Negras, located in the dense growth around the Usumacinta River in Guatemala (Danien 2001). Over thirty miles long, its description resembles that of early logging roads: "merely a cleared, unsurfaced

Figure 3. Historic canal near Hillbank at the south end of the New River Lagoon.

trail for the most part, graded only where necessary, swamp areas made passable with logs laid down to create a roadbed, and all of it usable only in the dry season" (Danien 2001:43). This striking similarity in construction and purpose prompts an exploration into the relationship between a road's form and function.

In their initial construction and life, logging roads had an economic purpose that determined their direction and permanence. They snaked through the jungle to connect lone mahogany trees to the closest water source. Their maintenance comprised just enough clearing to drag a log through dense growth, with more effort invested if there happened to be more mahogany to extract from the area. Consequently, it was not uncommon for them to be reabsorbed into the jungle. Logging roads can be contrasted with Classic Maya *sacbe*, particularly those of Xunantunich (Keller 2001). Those roads, primarily political, were constructed by elites. Straight, elevated and shining white, they were meant to be noticed, to convey a message of power and highlight social relationships to viewers (Keller 2001). A significant amount of effort went into *sacbe* construction, and it is not surprising that they are still visible after hundreds of years. Likewise in South America, it has been hypothesized that raised earthen causeways served social functions (Walker 2001). These causeways connect raised residential locations by spanning low-lying flooded areas used for subsistence activities. Walker (2001) argues that the investment of multiple causeways connecting the same areas suggests that the

Figure 4. Historic steam tractor in front of Hillbank lodgings.

causeways served to conspicuously display and reinforce social relationships.

The juxtaposition of logging roads, *sacbe*, and earthen causeways suggests that the original function can impact the form of a road, which in turn influences how the road subsequently functions. Archaeologists continue to use logging roads in an extractive capacity, although they seek data rather than mahogany. At the same time, it is important to keep in mind that the reuse of logging roads by new actors in a different temporal context can lead to new meanings for logging roads.

LOGGING ROADS AND THE LOCAL POPULATION

The archaeologists' extraction of information is paralleled by the local population's extraction of natural resources. Like archaeologists, the local population also uses the road for transportation. As mentioned previously, some logging roads from the *camión* era of hauling were substantial enough for the government to appropriate and turn into general vehicular roads. The particular road in the PfB region that we have been discussing has not achieved this status, since, among other reasons, it is in the middle of a conservation area. However, archaeologists have had occasion to observe local workers from PfB collecting natural resources off the road.

Workers used the road to harvest thatch palms used in roofing structures. The logging road facilitated much greater access to the natural resource, since it allowed a tractor and trailer to transport both workmen and the harvested palm leaves. Logging roads are also used to extract other types of resources. A road close to the Hillbank station is used to gain access to an abandoned logging camp and sawmill. Our survey and excavation at the camp indicates that the site was probably abandoned fairly recently, perhaps as late as the 1970s. The road is currently used to mine a very large deposit of mahogany sawdust and chips. The chips are recycled at the Hillbank station in their environmentally friendly composting toilets (Henry Langsworth, personal communication 2002).

Other components of the Hillbank logging system act as illustrations of the views presented by Barrett (1999) and Bradley (1993), once abandoned and now gaining new meanings unanticipated by their initial users. After the railway ceased operation sometime in the late 1970s, a number of rails were removed from their earthen bed and laid side by side to create the floor and supports of a shed. Most notably, giant machines of the railway, including steam engines and tractors, are dispersed throughout the forestry station at Hillbank. The steam engine in particular has been moved to a prominent location in front of guest housing, and currently acts as a tourist attraction (Figure 4). Instead of being perceived as mostly functional, utilitarian objects by the loggers, these large machines now symbolize a rich and at times contentious aspect of Belize's colonial heritage. It might be considered ironic that this train equipment, which by definition was expected by loggers to constantly be in motion, now is expected to remain in place for viewing purposes. However, one common thread runs between the two states of movement and stillness – making money – in the past, by exporting mahogany, in the present, by drawing more tourism. In addition to the network of roads, Hillbank's train rails and large equipment are constant reminders of the past that have been reincorporated, and in some cases, redefined in the current environment.

The relationship between the local population and the remnants of Belize's once dominant timber industry is complicated. On one hand, logging roads may be seen as convenient transportation and a way for the local population to extract material resources, and old logging equipment may be symbols of a colourful past. However, the history of logging is fraught with class tension (Bolland and Shoman 1977), suggesting that feelings about associated roads may not be so simply positive. When the Baymen bought large parcels of jungle to log mahogany, they effectively monopolized Belizean land for the next few centuries. As a result, most of that land was never developed for agriculture or public use. Many of the people that use logging roads to access resources, as described above, do so because they have little access to land for subsistence farming.

The suppression of agriculture and subsequent underdevelopment of the country is roundly denounced in Belizean textbooks (Leslie 1997). While the logging industry provided the government with roads that could be developed for general use, mahogany logging and its monopolization of land has been blamed for the lack of an adequate national infrastructure (Anderson 1958). The historical resentment against the industry is aggravated by the recent decision of the financially troubled government to award logging concessions in the Toledo area of Belize. Such a measure threatens the livelihood of current Maya inhabitants. Conceivably, negative attitudes toward the industry could be extended to its roads. At the same time, however, Belizeans have also found ways to benefit from remnants of the timber industry. They use the roads to reach natural resources, display old pieces of equipment to attract more tourist money, and protect their environment by recycling mahogany sawdust in composting toilets.

CONCLUSION

In this exploration of the many lives of British logging roads, we have discussed the original function of the roads within their economic context, and examined how both their meaning and use have changed through time. Originally, these logging roads were the imprint of a colonial extractive economy on the Belizean landscape. Vast tracts of land were concentrated in the hands of few foreign owners to be monopolized for logging, and never developed for agricultural purposes. Because these historical circumstances prevented the land from being subdivided, the effect is still visible in the large contiguous landholdings of Programme for Belize. The PfB nature conservancy preserves the logging roads as historical artifacts, a visible reminder of why the land was first set aside.

When discussing the evolution of the landscape, we have drawn upon the concept of the "afterlife of monuments," referring to the way people interact with monuments that have fallen out of active use, though perhaps in ways different from those originally intended (Bradley 1993). In a related vein, Barrett (1999) cautions against the traditional practice of seeing the archaeological record as a series of discrete, static periods characterized by particular patterns of material remains. People are not isolated from material remnants of the past; rather they constantly incorporate these remnants into their worlds and imbue them with new meaning. Moreover, such concepts are not limited to traditional monuments, but also apply to more mundane elements such as logging roads. At first glance, they are simply abandoned logging roads. A more careful scrutiny reveals that they are not quite abandoned nor primarily used for the purpose of logging. To the contrary, some are in active use today in ways never imagined by the loggers who created them. To the Baymen they served, they represented capitalism, progress and wealth. To the Belizean working class, past and present, these roads are simultaneously a means to support themselves and representations of a rich history, social oppression, and economic underdevelopment. To archaeologists, they are access to sites, reference points, reminders of the unavoidable stamp of the present on the past, and of the past on the present. Throughout the plethora of possible identities, one message remains clear: this is not just an abandoned logging road.

REFERENCES CITED

Antochiw, M., and A. Breton
|1992| *Cartographic Catalog of Belize (1511–1880).* Translated by T. Papworth. Bureau Regional de Cooperation en Amerique, San Jose, Costa Rica.

Anderson, A. H.
|1958| *Brief Sketch of British Honduras.* Printing Department, British Honduras.

Barnhart, E., and B. Barry
|n.d.| Ma'ax Na Mapping Project – 1996 Report. Manuscript on file, Programme for Belize (PfB) Archaeological Project, Department of Anthropology, University of Texas, Austin.
Barrett, J.
|1999| Mythical Landscapes of the British Iron Age. In *Archaeologies of Landscape*, edited by W. Ashmore, and A. B. Knapp, pp. 253–265. Blackwell, Oxford.
Baugher-Perlin, S.
|1982| Analyzing Glass Bottles for Chronology, Function, and Trade Networks. In *Archaeology of Urban America: The Search for Pattern and Process*, edited by R. S. Dickens, Jr., pp. 259–290. Academic Press, New York.
Bolland, N.
|1988| *Colonialism and Resistance in Belize: Essays in Historical Sociology*. Society for the Promotion of Education and Research, Belize City, Belize.
Bolland, N., and A. Shoman
|1977| *Land in Belize 1765–1871*. Institute of Social and Economic Research, University of the West Indies, Jamaica.
Bradley, R.
|1993| *Altering the Earth: The Origins of Monuments in Britain and Continental Europe*. Society of Antiquaries of Scotland Monograph Series 8. Society of Antiquaries of Scotland, Edinburgh.
Cackler, P. R., K. Reese-Taylor, M. Zender, D. Fernandez, O. Ng, and M. Rich
|2001| Identifying Maya Political Boundaries: Watersheds, Ideologies and Politics in Northwestern Belize. Paper presented at the 34th Annual Chacmool Conference, Calgary, Alberta.
Craig, A.
|1969| Logwood as a Settlement Factor of British Honduras. *Caribbean Studies* 9(1):53–62.
Danien, E.
|2001| Chicken Soup and Canvas Bags: Advice for the Field. *Expedition* 43(3):41–45.
Finamore, D.
|1994| *Sailors and Slaves on the Wood-Cutting Frontier: Archaeology of the British Bay Settlement, Belize*. Ph.D. dissertation, Boston University. University Microfilms, Ann Arbor.
Gibbs, A. R.
|1883| *British Honduras: An Historical and Descriptive Account of the Colony from its Settlement, 1670*. Sampson, Low, Marston, Searle & Rivington, London.
Keller, A.
|2001| Finding the Way: Identifying Directed Movement at the Late Classic Maya Center of Xunantunich, Belize. Paper presented at the 34th Annual Chacmool Conference, Calgary, Alberta.
Leslie, R. (editor)
|1997| *A History of Belize: Nation in the Making*. Cubola Productions, Benque Viejo de Carmen, Belize.
Lyons, C. L., and J. K. Papadopoulous (editors)
|2002| *The Archaeology of Colonialism*. The Getty Research Institute. Los Angeles.
Miller, H. M.-L.
|2005| Comparing Landscapes of Transportation: Riverine-Oriented And Land-Oriented Systems in the Indus Civilization and the Mughal Empire. In *Space and Spatial Analysis in Archaeology*, edited by E. C. Robertson, J. D. Seibert, D. C. Fernandez, and M. U. Zender, pp. 281–291. University of Calgary Press, Calgary, Alberta.
Millet Cámara, L.
|1984| Logwood and Archaeology in Campeche. *Journal of Anthropological Research* 40:328–342.
Morris, R.
|1883| *The Colony of British Honduras: Its Resources and Prospects; With Particular Reference to its Indigenous Plants and Economic Productions*. E. Stanford, London.
Schuyler, R. L.
|1974| Sandy Ground: Archaeological Sampling in a Black Community in Metropolitan New York. *Papers of the Conference on Historic Sites Archaeology* 7(2):12–52.
Wallerstein, I.
|1974| *The Modern World-System. Vol. 1: Capitalist Agriculture and the Origins of the European World-Economy in the Sixteenth Century*. Academic Press, New York.
|1980| *The Modern World System. Vol 2: Mercantilism and the Consolidation of the European World-Economy, 1600–1750*. Academic Press, New York.
Walker, J.
|2001| Building Connections in the Bolivian Amazon. Paper presented at the 34th Annual Chacmool Conference, Calgary, Alberta.

MOVING MOUNTAINS: THE TRADE AND TRANSPORT OF ROCKS AND MINERALS WITHIN THE GREATER INDUS VALLEY REGION

Randall Law

Randall Law, Department of Anthropology, University of Wisconsin–Madison, 5240 Social Science Building, 1180 Observatory Drive, Madison, Wisconsin 53706, U.S.A.

ABSTRACT

The prehistoric urban center of Harappa is located in the middle of the Punjab plain of northwestern South Asia. There are no stone resources of any kind nearby, only sand and silt. Yet a great diversity of rock and mineral types are present at the site. This paper first examines Harappa's rock and mineral assemblage from the perspective of the greater Indus Valley's complex geology. The subsequent section will consider the *scale* – both quantity and bulk size – of the materials that were transported to Harappan cities. Next, the *distance* one would have to travel to acquire certain materials will be examined from the standpoint of the lack of stone resources around Harappa and the nature of the materials themselves. An outline of the several possible modes by which the physical *movement* of lithic commodities took place will follow. I conclude with a discussion of the differing *motivations* behind the acquisition and transport of rock and minerals in the greater Indus Valley region.

In this paper, I will present observations regarding the acquisition and the transportation of rock and mineral commodities to Harappa and other Indus Civilization sites from source areas located in the highlands (piedmont and mountains) of the greater Indus Valley region. Dependable access to sources of raw materials (including rocks and minerals) is essential for the growth and functioning of urban settlements and thus was a necessary precondition for the development of early state-level societies (Kenoyer 1991:343–344). However, past studies attempting to define these important resource areas for the Indus Civilization (Fentress 1977; Lahiri 1992) have relied too heavily on data from outdated, noncomprehensive geologic overviews and the limited information in century-old British district gazetteer summaries. In order to produce the most accurate model of the extensive lithic exchange networks in the prehistoric Indus Valley, a project has been initiated that utilizes the vast body of contemporary geological literature, personal field observations, collection of raw rock and mineral samples from source areas, and geochemical comparisons of source materials to archaeological samples from the site of Harappa. The observations presented below regarding transportation systems are derived from recent fieldwork in Pakistan and India that marked the completion of the first phase of this project.

The Indus or Harappan Civilization (ca. 2600–1700 B.C.) encompassed over 680,000 km^2 (Kenoyer 1998:17) – more than twice the area occupied by its contemporaries in Egypt and Mesopotamia. Harappan sites across this great expanse shared many remarkable similarities in terms of their material culture, iconography and settlement pattern, and it was not uncommon for early investigators to speak of the Indus Civilization's cultural "uniformity" (Piggott 1950:140). Although regional variations have been defined (Mughal 1992), the geographical extent of the Harappan phenomenon demonstrates the presence of well-developed and far-reaching communication and transportation networks that bound its "various social groups as a distinct cultural entity" (Shaffer 1988:1316). The material assemblage at Harappa, the second-largest urban center and type-site of the Indus Civilization, reflects this enormous interaction system – especially in regard to its rock and mineral artifacts. A wide range of material types, from the comparatively common (such as quartzite and limestone) to the semiprecious (lapis lazuli and agate), is present at the site. However, Harappa lies in the center of a broad alluvial plain, hundreds of kilometres from any

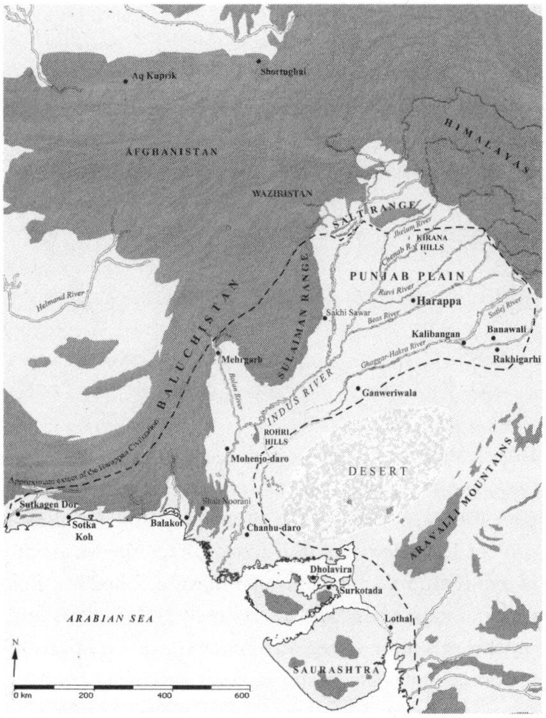

Figure 1. Sites and physical features of the greater Indus Valley region.

significant stone sources. All lithic materials found at the site, down to the smallest pebble, had to have been *transported* there by some human activity from the surrounding highland areas. Hypotheses regarding potential modes and avenues of transportation and the groups involved in them can be generated by considering the nature of Harappa's lithic assemblage, the material types themselves, and the physical aspects of the greater Indus Valley region.

In the first section of this paper, I will discuss the *diversity* of the rock and mineral assemblage at Harappa, and how it is a reflection of complex geology of the greater Indus Valley region, the city's position at a nexus of numerous trade routes, and the social composition of Harappan society. The subsequent section will consider the *scale* – both quantity and bulk size – of the materials that were transported to Harappan cities. Next, the *distance* one would have to travel to acquire certain materials will be examined from the standpoint of the lack of stone resources around Harappa and the nature of the materials themselves. An outline of the several possible modes by which the physical *movement* of lithic commodities took place will follow. I will conclude with a discussion of the differing *motivations* behind the acquisition and transport of rock and minerals in the greater Indus Valley region.

DIVERSITY

A five-period chronology (Table 1; Meadow and Kenoyer 2001) has been established at the Indus Valley site of Harappa extending from its foundation ca. 3300 B.C. through its long urban phase extending from 2600 B.C. to approximately 1900 B.C.. Although quantification of the rock and mineral assemblage through each phase at Harappa is still in progress, the greatest diversity of material types appears to be found, not

Table 1. Harappa Chronology.

Period	Phase	Dates
Period 1	Ravi Phase	> 3300 B.C. – ca. 2800 B.C.
Period 2	Kot Diji (Early Harappa) Phase	ca. 2800 B.C. – ca. 2600 B.C.
Period 3A	Harappa Phase A	ca. 2600 B.C. – ca. 2450 B.C
Period 3B	Harappa Phase B	ca. 2450 B.C. – ca. 2200 B.C.
Period 3C	Harappa Phase C	ca. 2200 B.C. – ca. 1900 B.C.
Period 4	Harappa/ Late Harappa Transitional	ca. 1900 B.C. – ca. 1800 B.C.
Period 5	Late Harappa Phase	ca. 1800 B.C.? – < 1300 B.C.

Note: After Meadow and Kenoyer 2001.

surprisingly, in period 3 – when the Indus Civilization was at its greatest extent (Figure 1). Over 30 rock and mineral types have been identified from this period through various means including visual comparison, petrography, X-ray diffraction, and electron microprobe analysis (Kenoyer and Vidale 1992; Law 2001; Vats 1940; Vidale and Bianchetti 1997). Within certain material categories such as steatite, chert, and stone for grinding purposes (sandstone, quartzite), there are recognizable subvarieties present, indicating the utilization of multiple source areas (Law 2004). Geologic source provenance studies currently in progress of lead ore, alabaster, limestone, and agate-carnelian are expected to reveal that more than one source may have been used to obtain these materials. Similarly, varied rock and mineral assemblages have been described at other Harappan settlements including Mohenjo-Daro (Marshall 1931), Lothal (Rao 1985), and Chanhu-Daro (Mackay 1938a).

On one level, the variety of rock and mineral types present at Harappan cities is a reflection of the rich geology of the greater Indus Valley region. The Indian subcontinent's collision with the Asian Plate beginning approximately 55 million years ago (Powell 1979:16) is the ultimate source of this richness. Enormous beds of sedimentary detrital rock (sandstone and shale), carbonates (limestone and dolomite), and sulfide evaporates (gypsum and anhydrite) developed in the shallow Tethys Sea that existed prior to and during the convergence of the two continental plates (Bender 1995:11–13). As the Indian Plate subducted beneath Asia, these beds were folded, raised and exposed in massive sequences along the northern and western margins of the Indus Valley (Farah et al. 1984:161–163). Another product of this subduction was the development of volcanic island arcs and their associated rocks (basalt, rhyolite, andesite, etc.), which eventually were emplaced between the sutured continental margins (Shams 1995:131–133). Similarly, large fragments of oceanic crust (ophiolites – composed of basalt, gneiss, etc. and containing radiolarian cherts) were obducted onto the continental crust (Asraullah and Abbas 1979). Pressure and stress from the collision altered existing rock in myriad ways and brought to the surface highly metamorphosed rock from as deep as the earth's mantle (Shams 1995). East of the Indus Valley, some of the oldest rocks on the earth, the Indian basement complex, rise in the form of the Aravalli Mountains and are rich in metals and metamorphic minerals (Wadia 1975:94–95). Finally, gem varieties of agate and carnelian erode from the basalts of the Deccan Traps that extend into Gujarat and the Saurashtra Peninsula southeast of the Indus Valley (Merh 1995).

It should come as no surprise that the lithic assemblages of Indus Valley settlements, surrounded by areas with such extreme geologic diversity, might reflect this diversity. The city of Harappa, located in the center of the Punjab plain (Figure 1), was especially well placed in terms of direct access to multiple resource zones and/or other large urban centers that could provide rocks and minerals indirectly from more distant areas. To the west of Harappa are the Sulaiman Mountains and passes leading into Northern Baluchistan and Afghanistan. Moving clockwise, to the north are found the Salt Range and the routes into the remote valleys and mountains of Kohistan and the Hindu Kush. Continuing clockwise, one only needed to follow the rivers of the Punjab northeast to their sources in Kashmir and the greater Himalaya region to access the rich resources there. Lying east of Harappa are the settlements (including the large urban site of Rakhighari) of the eastern Punjab and Haryana that would have provided indirect access to the resources of the northern Aravalli Mountains. To the south, the city of Ganweriwala and other sites along the now dry Ghaggar-Hakra River system are points where interaction with the ancient nomads of the Cholistan desert (Mughal 1994) would have made available the resources the southern Aravallis and northern Gujarat. Finally, the route following the Indus River southwest towards Mohenjo-Daro, the largest Indus city, would have been a supply route for the raw material sources of the Rohri Hills, Sindh Kohistan, and southern Baluchistan.

The composition of Harappan society would have also influenced the site's diverse rock and mineral assemblage. The current state of research suggests that Harappa and other Indus cities were likely occupied and/or utilized by peoples of different communities, classes, and ethnicities (Kenoyer 1998:126–127). Although Indus cities lacked the temples, palaces, and ostentatious burials that are considered indicators of elite status in other state-level societies, clear evidence that a high degree of social stratification and differentiation did exist is found in many forms, including the possession of items of personal adornment that would have been inaccessible to all members of Harappan society (Kenoyer 1992). Power and social standing could

Figure 2. Harappan ringstone. (Courtesy Dr. J. M. Kenoyer, Harappa Archaeological Research Project, photographer)

have been created and maintained through control of the raw material sources for these status-marking ornaments, as well as other critical resources including land and livestock (Kenoyer 1997). There is ample evidence that craft activities such as agate and steatite bead-making took place simultaneously in several different areas of Harappa (Kenoyer 1997:269) indicating more than one elite group took part in and/or controlled these activities. Competing elites would have certainly found it beneficial to maintain access to as many reliable sources as possible. This might have been achieved through ties with kin or clan relations (Kenoyer 1989) or via interaction with nomadic communities and other migrating ethnic groups. Given the complex geologic setting of the greater Indus Valley, such ties and interactions with peoples from distant parts of the Harappan realm should naturally be reflected in the rock and mineral assemblage of the city itself.

SCALE

When discussing the transportation of rock and mineral resources, it is necessary to consider the scale – both quantity and bulk size – of the materials being moved. From a qualitative standpoint, the amount of stone transported to Harappa would appear to be quite significant. Grindingstones (querns and mullers), most often composed of sandstone or quartzite, make up the majority (by weight) of all lithic material types identified at Harappa. The nearly 2600 examples that have been recovered since excavations in resumed in1986 collectively weigh 15,500 kg. A preliminarily source provenance study of these grindingstones indicated that the vast majority derived from sources that were located 200 km or more from Harappa (Law 2001). In terms of the number of individually tabulated artifacts (n = 20,125), however, chert is by far a more common lithic material than grindingstone. Based on the appearance, uniformity, and quality of the material, the extensive beds of the Rohri Hills of Sindh are generally acknowledged to be the primary chert source for Harappa during Period 3 (Kenoyer 1995:218–219). Although ratios of grindingstone and chert in relation to the volume of excavated strata are still being calculated, the abundance of these materials in all periods and habitation areas at Harappa suggests that they were transported to the site in large quantities to supply the needs of a densely populated urban settlement.

At the Indus Civilization city of Dholavira (Bisht 2000), which is located directly adjacent to building stone sources, limestone slabs (some perhaps weighing up to several tons) were used as elements in a variety of constructions including gateways and drains. Most Indus settlements, however, are found on the alluvial plains and were generally constructed of baked or mud brick. All stone had to be transported to them from often very great distances. Therefore the size of stone artifacts at plains sites can be revealing in terms of the labour spent on their transportation. The very largest and heaviest artifacts recovered at Indus Civilization cities located on the plains are perforated stone rings. These "ringstones" are usually made of limestone or calcareous sandstone. Interpretations of these enigmatic objects have ranged from Shivite "yoni" stones (Marshall 1931:158–160), to astronomical "calendar stones" (Maula 1984), to ceremonial stones associated with cultic tree-worship (During-Caspers and Nieskens 1992:94), to decorative bases for wooden columns (Kenoyer 1998:53). The largest ringstone found at Harappa weighs 135 kg. So while Harappa did contain monumental structures (walls, platforms, etc.), the largest materials used in their creation (if indeed ringstones were used for architectural purposes) do not appear to have exceeded a size that would have required more than two people to carry (Figure 2). Some debitage associated with the manufacture of ringstones has been identified at Harappa (J. Mark Kenoyer, personal communication 2002); however the quantity of it suggests that material was brought to the site in a rough-out form close the final size of the finished ringstone, rather than as large unworked boulders. Nevertheless, a significant expenditure in energy would have been involved in transporting stone of this size. A recently completed provenance study of ringstone fragments from Harappa indicated that certain varieties of limestone used in their creation derived from sources over 800 km away (Law and Burton 2004).

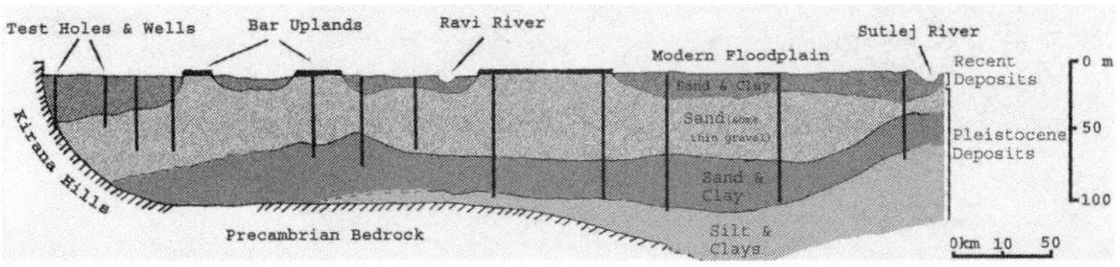

Figure 3. Alluvial deposits of the Punjab plain (after Kazmi and Jan 1997).

Steatite (talc) artifacts have been found at almost every excavated Harappan site. This easily carveable material was used by Indus craftsmen not only for the production of common items, such as ornamental disc beads, but also for the manufacture of objects with political and/or economic value such as seals and tablets. Wafer-like steatite disc beads are so common that their presence alone could almost be considered a marker of the Harappan character of a site (Vidale 1989:29). The large-scale use of steatite at the city of Harappa is suggested by the fact that this material is found during all periods and in most excavated areas of the site. However, in terms size the scale of use was apparently much smaller. The square unicorn seal recovered during the 1999 excavations at Harappa is one of the largest (5.2 by 5.2 cm) examples of these rare objects ever found (Meadow and Kenoyer 2001:32). The largest steatite object found at any Indus site is the famous "Priest King" bust from Mohenjo-Daro (Marshall 1931:356–357, Plate XCVIII). At 17.5 cm in height, this rare example of Harappan statuary is extremely small compared to the life-size and larger figures that became common in South Asia starting in the Early Historic period (Chakrabarti 1995:251–252). All evidence indicates that although steatite was an important and widely used material, it would not have been necessary to transport it in blocks larger than a single individual could carry.

In summary, although stone was utilized on a large scale during the Harappan period, the individual portions transported to sites on the Indus Valley plains were generally small in scale. This is in stark contrast to other early Old World states such as Egypt, where the long-distance transportation of large monolithic blocks of stone for statuary and architectural purposes would have necessarily required the labour of numerous individuals (Arnold 1991). In South Asia this did not occur until the Mauryan Period – ca. 185 B.C.–A.D. 320 (Jayaswal 1998).

DISTANCE

If you lived at Harappa and you needed stone for a tool, what distance would you need to travel to find one? The site is located in the middle of the vast alluvial plain known as the Punjab – Land of the Five Rivers. The alluvium of the Punjab has been accumulating since at least the early Pleistocene (Kazmi and Jan 1997:267) and cross sections based on tube well logs indicates its great depth (Figure 3). With the exception of sporadic beds of thin gravels (Kazmi and Jan 1997:267) and pedogenic carbonate nodules, or *kankar* (Amundson and Pendall 1991:18), the alluvial strata of this part of the Indus basin are composed entirely of sand, silt, clay and loess. The nearest rock sources to Harappa begin at the Kirana Hills, located 120 km to the north-northwest. These Precambrian outcrops related to the Indian Shield are the only rocks to penetrate the deep alluvium of the Punjab plain. The alluvium becomes progressively deeper as one moves west toward the Sulaiman Range. There are no other known subsurface rocks formations in the Punjab that might have been exposed during the Harappan period some 4,000 years ago. Therefore, except for the Kirana Hills, all rocks and minerals found at Harappa must have come from the foothills and ranges surrounding the Indus Basin or beyond.

Several scholars have proposed that certain lithic materials could be acquired from riverbeds in and near the mountain ranges west of the Indus Valley, thus making it unnecessary travel to the actual geologic sources of those materials (Inizan and Lechevallier

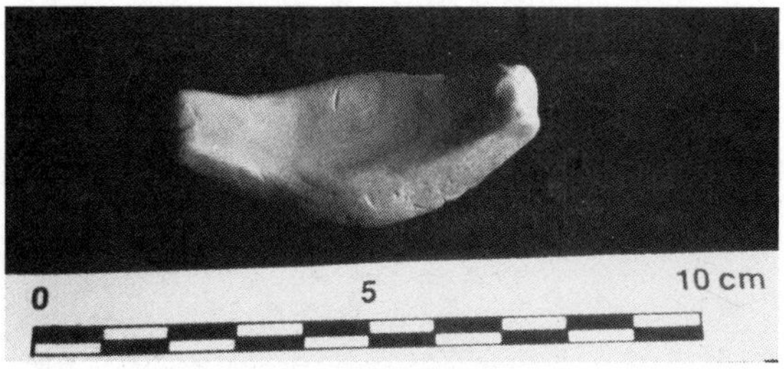

Figure 4. Terracotta boat model from Harappa. (Courtesy Dr. J. M. Kenoyer, Harappa Archaeological Research Project, photographer)

1990:51–52; Kenoyer 1998:35; Khan et al. 1987:102). However, it is important to determine if river deposits could actually have served as sources for many or all of the stones found in the mountains that they drain. River-borne sediments undergo rapid fining through abrasion, chipping, splitting, cracking, and chemical weathering as they are moved downstream (Werrity 1992). Rocks such as granitoids and limestones suffer slower attrition than others like sandstone (Werrity 1992:343), allowing larger clasts of those materials to be acquired at greater distance from formations that they occur in. A resident of Harappa seeking a grindingstone would have needed only to travel to one of the massive alluvial fans at the base of the Sulaiman Range to get a suitable cobble rather than into the mountains themselves. However, to obtain a material like chert, which easily becomes chipped and fractured as it is carried downstream, or steatite, which quickly disintegrates, it was probably necessary to travel to the actual source or very close to it. While further study is needed, preliminary observations of the movement of radiolarian chert down the Tochi River from its source in the Barzai region of Waziristan indicate that this material becomes highly fractured and rare at the point the river reaches the plain some 70 km away. Similar examinations were made of drainages in Northern Baluchistan confirming Inizan and Lechevallier's observations of chert in the Bolan River near Mehrgarh (Inizan and Lechevallier 1990:52), which suggested that finding good quality (unfractured) chert is quite rare at locations far from source areas. While it is certainly true that slope gradient and river discharge may have changed since prehistoric times, thus altering and/or obscuring the composition of drainages that once contained good material, it is much more likely that then, as now, the best quality chert or steatite was obtained at or near the formation from which they originated.

MOVEMENT

A central question in the study of Indus Valley rocks and mineral exchange system is how these materials were physically moved to lowland sites like Harappa from their highland sources. Heather Miller (2005) notes that because the settlement pattern of the Indus Civilization was oriented toward the river systems and coastal zones of northwestern South Asia it has been commonly assumed that boats were a primary mode of transportation. Shaffer (1988) points out that while boats are an important means of transportation and communication in other riverine civilizations like Egypt and Mesopotamia, it need not be automatically assumed this was true for the Harappans. Like so many other aspects of the indigenously developed Indus Civilization, its systems of exchange and interaction along with primary modes of transportation may have been fundamentally different than that of its contemporaries to the west.

In all likelihood, however, some degree of transportation and communication within the Indus Valley region did take place by boat. While no physical remains of watercraft from the Harappan period have been found in the Indus Valley, there are three depictions from Mohenjo-Daro: one on an unfired seal (Mackay 1938b:Plate LXXXIII, 30); one as graffiti on a potsherd (Mackay 1938b:Plate LXIX, 4); and one on a terracotta tablet (Dales 1968:39). These depictions feature high-prowed, flat-bottomed boats quite similar in appearance to the ones still used on portions of the lower Indus River today (Greenhill 1972). A terracotta model of a flat-bottomed boat was excavated at Harappa in 1989 (Figure 4; J. Mark Kenoyer, personal communication 2002). Evidence for seagoing vessels is indirectly provided by the existence of sites like Lothal, Dholavira, Sotka Koh and Sutkagen Dor that are located along what would be important coastal trade routes and, in the case of Lothal, have port facilities and ample evidence of trade with cultures across the Arabian Sea in present-day Oman (Rao 1979). One complete and four fragmentary terracotta models of boats were also found at Lothal (Rao 1985:505). Finds at Ra's al-Junayz, Oman, of bitumen fragments with reed bundle impressions and barnacles still attached appear to be caulking material for some type of seagoing craft (Cleuziou and Tosi 1994). Although chemical analysis indicated that the bitumen was of Near Eastern origin (Cleuziou and Tosi 1994:756), many fragments were found in association with Harappan materials including a copper stamp seal (Cleuziou and Tosi 1994:748). Harappan-period traders, as the above evidence makes clear, were at the very least familiar with large river- and ocean-going vessels, if not experienced users of such craft themselves.

Certainly some form of watercraft, like the rafts of inflated bullock hides employed to ford the Kabul River during the Mughal period (Verma 1977:71), had to have existed so that land travelers could cross the Indus and its tributaries. Assurance that rivers could be reliably forded would have been of vital importance to any ancient group involved in seasonal migration or long-distance trade. Historically, the control of ferry points in South Asia has shifted between the state and specialized groups (Deloche 1993:126–128). Today, traders and pastoralists who seasonally cross the Indus near Mohenjo-Daro supply the local fisher-ferrymen who move them with goods such as grain and livestock (Begum 1987:184). Such specialization and interdependence of social groups, common in South Asia today (Dumont 1980:92), is argued to have had its origins deep in the prehistoric period (Kenoyer 1998:43). In this social milieu, the groups who traveled by land, although relying on specialists to assist in crossing the region's many wide rivers, were perhaps the most instrumental in terms of transporting rock and mineral commodities during the Harappan period.

While there is some limited evidence that Harappans had knowledge of both the domesticated horse and camel (Shaffer 1988), the presence of these animals in South Asia clearly did not become common until after the Harappan period (Meadow 1987:51–54). The primary mode of material transport on the plains and plateaus of the greater Indus Valley region during the third millennium B.C. almost certainly would have been zebu cattle (var. *Bos indicus*), or Indian ox, either pulling a cart or carrying an individual load. Small terracotta models of carts (Figure 5) are found in abundance at Harappan sites, including Mohenjo-Daro (Mackay 1938b:568–569), Harappa (Vats 1940:451–452) Lothal (Rao 1985:225), Surkotada (Joshi 1990:282), Banawali (Bisht 1983:119), Kalibangan (Thapar 1973:89) and Shortugai (Francfort 1984:302) to name a few. No other vehicle in the ancient world was depicted in such abundance. While miniature models of humans, animals, and other objects are sometimes created as children's toys or used for decorative purposes, in South Asia they are also important symbols for economic or ritual activities (Jayaswal 1984). From this perspective the cart was clearly a significant aspect of Harappan culture. Figurines of humped cattle are equally common at Harappan sites (Figure 6). While there are no depictions of zebu actually pulling carts, the rapid size diminution of early domestic cattle that you see in Europe, the Middle East, and peninsular India is not apparent in cattle varieties at Indus Valley sites (Meadow 1988). This is possibly indicative of a conscious effort by Harappan and pre-Harappan peoples to maintain cattle size for draft purposes (Meadow 1988:207). Single animals of good breeds can carry upwards of 150 kg 20 km per day (Deloche 1993:241–246).

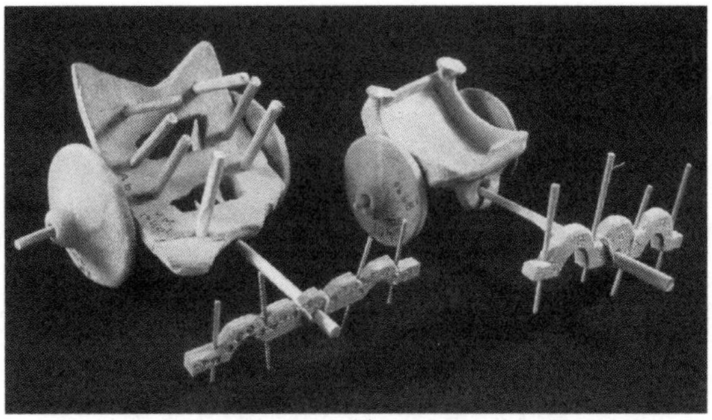

Figure 5. Two cart models from Harappa. (Courtesy Dr. J. M. Kenoyer, Harappa Archaeological Research Project, photographer)

Zebu cattle, with or without carts, probably would not have fared well, however, on the steep, rocky trails and talus slopes of the mountains where many of the materials found at Harappan sites are located. How then were minerals transported from those sources to the points where they could be loaded onto zebu carts or boats? One possibility to be considered is the use of sheep or goats as pack animals. In highland Asia, the use of these animals for transporting goods is still practiced today (Fisher 1986:89; Minhas 1998:73), and it has been suggested (Shaffer 1988) that they were used for this purpose in the prehistoric period as well. Evidence from Aq Kuprik (Dupree 1972) and Mehrgarh (Meadow 1993) indicates that goats were domesticated by the seventh millennium B.C., if not earlier in the Baluchistan-Afghanistan highlands. Sheep and goat dominate the faunal assemblages of highland

Figure 6. Zebu figurine and modern zebu at the Harappan site of Balakot.

sites throughout the prehistoric period (Meadow 1982). While none of this proves that these animals were used to carry stone commodities from mountain sources, it can be argued that, of all the animals utilized by the inhabitants of the highland regions during this period, sheep and goats would have been the most capable of performing this difficult task. These animals evolved in highland settings and thus can move across landscapes inaccessible to other pack animals due to the rugged terrain, and/or water and fodder requirements. Although a single large goat can only carry a few dozen kilograms at most (Mionczynski 1992), an entire herd could potentially move a great deal of stone.

Human porterage of rock and mineral commodities should also be considered. The use of bamboo frames and dozens of porters to transport large masses of quarried stone, statuary and other cargo in and out of the mountains of North India was once common (Deloche 1993:208–210). Depending on the altitude, gradient, individual and wage, single porters transporting goods in the mountains reportedly could carry anywhere from 30–100 kg on their heads or backs (Deloche 1993:210–212). In the absence of animals for transport, prehistoric peoples of the greater Indus highlands could realistically have transported stones, in the amounts and sizes discussed in this paper, from their sources to the point where they could have been loaded onto zebu-drawn carts or river transport.

MOTIVATIONS

The motivations behind acquiring rocks and minerals and transporting them over long distances are varied. The simplest ones are need-based and involve obtaining materials necessary for day-to-day utilitarian uses. At the other end of the spectrum would be the motivation to control access to and distribution of semiprecious materials that were important status markers. Consumption of such wealth items is necessary to maintain hierarchical social stratification, and it is strict control of these materials that partly characterizes state-level societies (Kenoyer 1991:345). It is ease of access (dependent on distance and abundance), as well as the technological modifications required to craft usable items, which imbues raw materials with differing degrees of value, provides the possibility of control, and allows individuals and groups to establish and maintain social power (Kenoyer 2000; Vidale and Miller 2000).

At sites like Harappa where all stone is nonlocal, even the supply of comparatively mundane materials like chert and quartzite would appear to have been controlled to some degree. The widespread distribution and standardization of chert blades produced at the Harappan quarry-factories in the Rohri Hills (Allchin 1979; Biagi 1995; Biagi et al. 1995) point to the existence of some form of an organized large-scale distribution network for this material (Inizan and Lechevallier 1990, 1997:79). The dominance of sandstone-quartzite from the Sulaiman Range in the lithic assemblage at Harappa perhaps indicates the existence of organized procurement of this material as well. While the Indus Civilization encompassed sources for these and many other materials, it was primarily composed of lowland settlements poor in stone commodities. Highland sites did exist, most notably in the Harappan settlements of the southern Baluchistan region (Franke-Vogt et al. 2000). However, materials not found within the alluvial areas would have had to been obtained by direct long-distance exploitation by Harappans themselves or through interaction with non-Harappan highland groups.

Harappans themselves certainly could have journeyed to regions outside of their realm to collect rock and mineral commodities. The distant Harappan outpost of Shortugai in Northern Afghanistan (Francfort 1984) might be representative of just such an activity. However, in order to procure the materials they sought in these areas, Harappans would have needed the sanction and/or assistance of local populations. Shaffer's overview of the prehistoric cultures of Baluchistan led him to conclude that the "primary procurer/carrier of raw materials" in the greater Indus Valley region was probably the pastoralist (Shaffer 1978:153). As seasons change, pastoral peoples are compelled to move where their herds can find adequate water and pasturage. In northwestern South Asia a pattern of wintering on the plains and spending summers in the highlands surrounding still exists (Bozdar et al. 1989; Nagy et al. 1989), and a symbiotic relationship with the settled cultures on the plains has developed. This allows pastoral peoples to obtain agricultural products that they lack (Khazanov 1994) and provides the plains dweller a way to access the resources of the highland regions. Because of their migration patterns, pastoralists would have been intimately familiar with both the sources of materials in the highlands and the people who would wish to acquire them on the plains. Most importantly pastoralists had the animals to transport the materials between the two.

Beyond internally organized trade, direct long-distance procurement and interaction with pastoral groups, materials may have been passed along through what Possehl (1999:15) describes as itinerant specialists who engage in a variety of craft, labour or entertainment activities. Another avenue of transportation that has deep historical roots in South Asia is the movement of goods in tandem with the movement of pilgrims traveling to and from sacred places. One arm of the great pilgrimage to the tomb of Saidi Ahmad at Sakhi Sawar and other shrines in the foothills of the Sulaiman Range (Diack 1898:51–56) passes directly next to the mounds at Harappa. Sacred spots such as these serve as seasonal gathering places of people from different regions (Nolan 1994). Pilgrims often return with charms or medicinals of mineral origin. Vidale and Shar (1990) have documented steatite carvers from throughout Pakistan who are among those making the annual pilgrimage to the shrine of Shah Bilwal Noorani in southern Baluchistan. Also making the journey are the Mengel tribesmen who mine steatite. After performing anniversary prayers (urs) at the saint's tomb, the steatite carver returns to his city with 50 kg or so of material – enough stock until the following season. Shah Noorani is deep in the southern Baluchistan highland region, and the many Buddhist and Hindu shrines in the area testify to pilgrimage activities having a long history in this region (Minchin 1907:35–44).

CONCLUSION

While utilizing a large quantity of diverse rocks and minerals, Harappans did not appear to have needed to move massive blocks of those materials over long distances. This, however, is not to imply that Harappans could not or did not move large amounts of material. The scale of Harappan lithic transportation system might best be described as extensive but not necessarily labour intensive in regard to single loads. The alluvium of the Indus basin is extremely deep, nearly devoid of rocks and minerals, and does not appear to have obscured any rock outcrops in the past 4,000 years that might have been close to cities like Harappa. Cobbles of tough rocks could be acquired at the base of mountain ranges. Other material such as chert could have been collected from riverbeds downstream from source areas, but for reliable quantities of good quality stone, one would have needed to travel directly to or close to the source. Sheep or goat and/or human porters would have been necessary to move lithic commodities out of mountain source areas that were too rugged or remote for other pack animals. Once on the plains, bullock carts and boats were, perhaps, a primary method of transportation. Mineral commodities could either have been obtained directly by Harappans themselves or via trade with highland groups. While organized procurement and transportation networks appear to have existed, other avenues of material exchange such as the migrations of pastoral peoples, the movement of itinerant specialists, and pilgrimage routes may have also played a vital role in the transmission of rocks and mineral commodities to and from the Harappan settlements of the greater Indus Valley.

Acknowledgments

Financial support for this work was provided by the Harappa Archaeological Research Project, the American Institute of Pakistan Studies and the Fulbright Foundation. I wish to thank Dr. Richard Meadow and Dr. J. Mark Kenoyer, co-directors of the Harappa Archaeological Research Project, for permission to study the lithic materials at Harappa. Thanks also to Saeed-ur Rehman, Director General, Department of Archaeology and Museums, Government of Pakistan, for allowing me to study the Department's extensive collections in Karachi and to carry out analyses of materials in Islamabad and Peshawar. Thanks to Dr. Ihsan Ali and Dr. Farooq Swati at the Department of Archaeology, University of Peshawar, and Shah Nasr Khan and Nidoula Sarai at the Museum of Archaeology and Ethnology, University of Peshawar. Special thanks to Prof. Dr. Syed Hamidullah at the Center of Excellence in Geology, University of Peshawar; without his expertise I could not have accomplished half of what I did. I most gratefully acknowledge the help of Dr. Syed Baqri at the Pakistan Museum of Natural History; Dr. Akhtar Kassi, Dr. Khalid Mahmood, and Mehrab Baloch at the Center of Excellence in Mineralogy, University of Baluchistan; and Dr. Imran Khan and Asif Rana at the Geological Survey of Pakistan, Quetta. Finally, thanks to Dr. Heather Miller for suggesting the title of this paper and for organizing the session it was presented in.

REFERENCES CITED

Allchin, B.
|1979| Stone Blade Industries of Early Settlements in Sind as Indicators of Geographical and Socio-Economic Change. In *South Asian Archaeology 1977*, vol. 1, edited by M. Taddei, pp. 173–211. Istituto Universitario Orientale, Naples.

Amundson, R., and E. Pendall
|1991| Pedology and Late Quaternary Environments Surrounding Harappa: A Review and Synthesis. In *Harappa Excavations 1986–1990: A Multidisciplinary Approach to Third millennium Urbanism*, edited by R. H. Meadow, pp. 13–28. Prehistory Press, Madison, Wisconsin.

Arnold, D.
|1991| *Building in Egypt: Pharaonic Stone Masonry*. Oxford University Press, New York.

Asraullah, Z., and S. G. Abbas
|1979| Ophiolites in Pakistan: An Introduction. In *Geodynamics of Pakistan*, edited by A. Farah, and K. A. De Jong, pp. 181–192. Geological Survey of Pakistan, Quetta.

Begum, S. S.
|1987| Boats on the Indus. In *Reports on Field Work Carried Out at Mohenjo-daro, Pakistan, 1983–84*, vol. 2, edited by M. Jansen, and G. Urban, pp. 183–184. IsMEO-Aachen University Mission, Rome.

Bender, F. K.
|1995| Geological Framework. In *Geology of Pakistan*, edited by F. K. Bender and H. A. Raza, pp. 11–62. Gebruder Borntraeger, Berlin.

Biagi, P.
|1995| An AMS Radiocarbon Date from the Harappan Flint Quarry-Pit 862 in the Rohro Hills (Sindh-Pakistan). *Ancient Sindh* 2:81–84.

Biagi, P., C. Ottomano, A. Pessina, and N. Shaikh
|1995| The 1994 Campaign on the Rohro Hills (Sindh-Pakistan): A Preliminary Report. *Ancient Sindh* 2:13–40.

Bisht, R. S.
|2000| Urban Planning at Dholavira: A Harappan City. In *Ancient Cities, Sacred Skies: Cosmic Geometries and City Planning in Ancient India*, edited by J. M. Malville, and L. M. Gujral, pp. 11–23. Aryan Books International, New Delhi.

Bozdar, N., J. G. Nagy, G. F. Sabir, and J. D. H. Keating
|1989| Animal Raising in Highland Balochistan. *International Centre for Agriculture in the Dry Areas Research Report* 50:1–27.

Chakrabarti, D. K.
|1995| Post-Mauryan States of Mainland South Asia (c. BC 185–AD 320). In *The Archaeology of Early Historic South Asia*, edited by F. R. Allchin, pp. 274–326. Cambridge University Press, Cambridge.

Cleuziou, S., and M. Tosi
|1994| Black Boats of Magan: Some Thoughts on Bronze Age Water Transport in Oman and Beyond from the Impressed Bitumen Slabs of Ra's al-Junayz. In *South Asian Archaeology 1993*, vol. 2, edited by A. Parpola and P. Koskikallio, pp. 707–714. Suomalainen Tiedeakatemia, Helsinki.

Dales, G. F.
|1968| The South Asia Section. *Expedition* 11(1):38–45.

Deloche, J.
|1993| *Transport and Communications in India Prior to Steam Locomotion*. French Studies in South Asian Culture and Society 7. Oxford University Press, Delhi.

Diack, A. H.
|1898| *Gazetteer of the Dera Ghazi Khan District*. "Civil and Military Gazette" Press, Lahore, Pakistan.

Dumont, L.
|1980| *Homo Hierarchicus: The Caste System and its Implications*. University of Chicago Press, Chicago.

Dupree, L. (editor)
|1972| *Prehistoric Research in Afghanistan 1959–1966*. The American Philosophical Society, Philadelphia.

During-Caspers, E. C. L., and P. J. M. Nieskens
|1992| The "Calendar Stones" from Mohenjo-daro Reconsidered. In *South Asian Archaeology 1989*, edited by C. Jarrige, pp. 83–96. Prehistory Press, Madison, Wisconsin.

Farah, A., R. D. Lawrence, and K. A. De Jong
|1984| An Overview of the Tectonics of Pakistan. In *Marine Geology and Oceanography of Arabian Sea and Coastal Pakistan*, edited by B. U. Haq, and J. D. Millman, pp. 161–176. Van Nostrand Reinhold, New York.

Fentress, M. A.
|1977| Resource Access, Exchange Systems and Regional Interaction in the Indus Valley: An Investigation of Archaeological Variability at Harappa and Moenjo Daro. Unpublished Ph.D. dissertation on file, Department of Oriental Studies, University of Pennsylvania, Philadelphia.

Fisher, J. F.
|1986| *Trans-Himalayan Traders: Economy, Society, and Culture in Northwest Nepal.* University of California Press, Berkeley.

Francfort, H.-P.
|1984| The Harappan Settlement of Shortugai. In *Frontiers of the Indus Civilization*, edited by B. B. Lal, and S. P. Gupta, pp. 301–310. Books and Books, New Delhi.

Franke-Vogt, U., S. Ul-Haq, F. A. Shams, and M. H. K. Khattak
|2000| Archaeological Explorations in the Kanrach Valley (Las Bela, Balochistan). In *South Asian Archaeology 1997*, edited by M. Taddei, and G. de Marco, pp. 189–213. IsIAO, Rome.

Greenhill, B.
|1972| *Boats and Boatmen of Pakistan.* Great Albion, South Brunswick.

Inizan, M.-L., and M. Lechevallier
|1990| A Techno-Economic Approach to Lithics: Some Examples of Blade Pressure Debitage in the Indo-Pakistani Subcontinent. In *South Asian Archaeology 1987*, edited by M. Taddei, and P. Callieri, pp. 43–59. IsMEO, Rome.
|1997| A Transcultural Phenomenon in the Chalcolithic and Bronze Age Lithics of the Old World: Raw Material Circulation and Production of Standardized Long Blades: The Example of the Indus Civilization. In *South Asian Archaeology 1995*, edited by B. Allchin, and R. Allchin, pp. 77–85. Oxford and IBH, New Delhi.

Jayaswal, V.
|1984| Interpretation of Terracotta Figurines from Archaeological Sites: An Ethnographic Approach. *Jijnasa: A Journal of the History of Ideas and Culture* III(Part I):105–110.
|1998| *From Stone Quarry to Sculpturing Workshop: A Report on the Archaeological Investigations Around Chunar, Varanasi, and Sarnath.* Agam Kala Prakashan, Delhi.

Joshi, J. P.
|1990| *Excavations at Surkotada 1971–72 and Exploration in Kutch.* Archaeological Survey of India, New Delhi.

Kazmi, A. H., and Q. Jan
|1997| *Geology and Tectonics of Pakistan.* Graphic, Karachi.

Kenoyer, J. M.
|1989| Socio-Economic Structures of the Indus Civilization as Reflected in Specialized Crafts and the Question of Ritual Segregation. In *Old Problems and New Perspectives in the Archaeology of South Asia*, edited by J. M. Kenoyer, pp. 183–192. Wisconsin Archaeological Reports Vol. 2. Department of Anthropology, University of Wisconsin–Madison, Wisconsin.
|1991| The Indus Valley Tradition of Pakistan and Western India. *Journal of World Prehistory* 5(4):331–385.
|1992| Ornament Styles of the Indus Tradition: Evidence from Recent Excavations at Harappa, Pakistan. *Paléorient* 17(2):79–98.
|1995| Interaction Systems, Specialized Crafts and Culture Change: The Indus Valley Tradition and the Indo-Gangetic Tradition in South Asia. In *The Indo-Aryans of Ancient South Asia: Language, Material Culture and Ethnicity*, edited by G. Erdosy, pp. 213–257. Indian Philology and South Asian Studies Vol. 1. W. DeGruyter, Berlin.
|1997| Trade and Technology of the Indus Valley: New Insights from Harappa, Pakistan. *World Archaeology* 29(2):262–280.
|1998| *Ancient Cities of the Indus Valley Civilization.* Oxford University Press, Karachi.
|2000| Wealth and Socio-Economic Hierarchies of the Indus Valley Civilization. In *Order, Legitimacy and Wealth in Early States*, edited by J. Richards, and M. Van Buren, pp. 90–112. Cambridge University Press, Cambridge.

Kenoyer, J. M., and M. Vidale
|1992| A New Look at Stone Drills of the Indus Valley Tradition. In *Materials Issues in Art and Archaeology, III*, edited by P. Vandiver, J. R. Druzik, G. S. Wheeler, and I. Freestone, pp. 495–518. Materials Research Society, Pittsburgh.

Khan, F., J. R. Knox, and K. D. Thomas
|1987| Prehistoric and Protohistoric Settlements in Bannu District. *Pakistan Archaeology* 23:99–148.

Khazanov, A. M.
|1994| *Nomads and the Outside World.* University of Wisconsin Press, Madison, Wisconsin.

Lahiri, N.
|1992| *The Archaeology of Indian Trade Routes Up to c. 200 BC: Resource Use, Resource Access and Lines of Communication.* Oxford University Press, Delhi.

Law, R. W.
|2001| Appendix 5: Recent Investigations and Analyses of Rocks and Minerals from Harappa. In *Harappa Archaeological Research Project: Harappa Excavations 2000 and 2001*, edited by R. H. Meadow, J. M. Kenoyer, and R. P. Wright. Report submitted to the Director-General of Archaeology and Museums, Government of Pakistan, Karachi.
|2004| Source Provenance Studies of Rocks and Minerals from Harappa – Part One. In *Proceedings of the Sixteenth International Conference on South Asian Archaeology, Paris, 2–6 July, 2001*, edited by C. Jarrige. CERNS, Paris, in press.

Law, R. W., and J. H. Burton
|2004| A Technique for Determining the Provenance of Harappan Banded Limestone "Ringstones" Using ICP-MS. Paper presented at the 34th International Symposium of Archaeometry, Zaragoza, Spain.

Mackay, E.
|1938a| Excavations at Chanhu-daro by the American School of Indic and Iranian Studies and the Museum of Fine Arts, Boston. *Smithsonian Report for 1937* 3473:469–478.
|1938b| *Further Excavations at Mohenjodaro.* Government of India, New Delhi.

Marshall, S. J.
|1931| *Mohenjo-daro and the Indus Civilization.* A. Probsthain, London.

Maula, E.
|1984| The Calendar Stones of Moenjodaro. In *Reports on Fieldwork Carried Out at Mohenjo-Daro, Pakistan, 1982–1983 by the IsMEO-Aachen University Mission*, edited by M. Jansen, and G. Urban, pp. 159–170. IsMEO-Aachen University Mission, Rome.

Meadow, R. H.
|1982| Pre- and Protohistoric Subsistence in Baluchistan and Eastern Iran. In *Information Bulletin*, vol. 2, pp. 56–61. International Association for the Study of the Cultures of Central Asia, Moscow.
|1987| Faunal Exploitation in the Greater Indus Valley: A Review of Recent Work to 1980. In *Studies in the Archaeology of India and Pakistan*, edited by J. Jacobson, pp. 43–64. Aris and Phillips in cooperation with American Institute of Indian Studies, Warminister, England.
|1988| Faunal Remains from Jalilpur, 1971. *Pakistan Archaeology* 23:203–220.
|1993| Animal Domestication in the Middle East: A Revised View from the Eastern Margin. In *Harappan Civilization: A Recent Perspective*, edited by G. L. Possehl, pp. 295–320. Oxford and IBH, New Delhi.

Meadow, R. H., and J. M. Kenoyer
|2001| Recent Discoveries and Highlights from Excavations at Harappa: 1998–2000. *Indo-Koko-Kenkyu [Indian Archaeological Studies]* 22:19–36.

Merh, S. S.
|1995| *Geology of Gujarat*. Geological Society of India, Bangalore.

Miller, H. M.-L.
|2005| Comparing Landscapes of Transportation: Riverine-Oriented And Land-Oriented Systems in the Indus Civilization and the Mughal Empire. In *Space and Spatial Analysis in Archaeology*, edited by E. C. Robertson, J. D. Seibert, D. C. Fernandez, and M. U. Zender, pp. 281-291. University of Calgary Press, Calgary, Alberta.

Minchin, C. F.
|1907| *Las Bela*. Government of India Baluchistan Gazetteer Series. Gosha-e-Adab, Quetta.

Minhas, P.
|1998| *Traditional Trade and Trading Centers in Himichal Pradesh*. Indus, New Delhi.

Mionczynski, J.
|1992| *The Pack Goat*. Pruett, Boulder.

Mughal, M. R.
|1992| The Geographical Extent of the Indus Civilization during the Early, Mature and Late Harappan Times. In *South Asian Archaeology Studies*, edited by G. L. Possehl, pp. 123–143. Oxford and IBH, New Delhi.
|1994| The Harappan Nomads of Cholistan. In *Living Traditions: Studies in the Ethnoarchaeology of South Asia*, edited by B. Allchin, pp. 53–68. Oxford and IBH, New Delhi.

Nagy, J. G., G. F. Sabir, and J. M. Stubbs
|1989| Descriptive and Diagnostic Studies of Sheep and Goat Production in the Farming Systems of Upland Balochistan. *International Centre for Agriculture in the Dry Areas Research Report* 28:1–23.

Nolan, M. L.
|1994| Seasonal Patterns of Christian Pilgrimage. In *Pilgrimage in the Old and New World*, edited by S. M. Bhardwaj, G. Rinschede, and A. Sievers, pp. 37–56. Dietrich Reimer Verlag, Berlin.

Piggott, S.
|1950| *Prehistoric India*. Penguin, Harmondsworth.

Possehl, G. L.
|1999| *Indus Age: The Beginnings*. Oxford and IBH, New Delhi.

Powell, C.
|1979| A Speculative Tectonic History of Pakistan and Surrounding: Some Constraints from the Indian Ocean. In *Geodynamics of Pakistan*, edited by A. Farah, and K. A. DeJong, pp. 5–24. Geological Survey of Pakistan, Quetta.

Rao, S. R.
|1979| A "Persian Gulf" Seal from Lothal. In *Ancient Cities of the Indus*, edited by G. L. Possehl, pp. 148–152. Vikas, New Delhi.
|1985| *Lothal: A Harappan Port Town (1955–62)*, vol. 2. Memoirs of the Archaeological Survey of India 78. Archaeological Survey of India, New Delhi.

Shaffer, J. G.
|1978| *Prehistoric Baluchistan*. B & R Publishing, Delhi.
|1988| One Hump or Two: The Impact of the Camel on Harappan Society. In *Orientalia Iosephi Tucci Memoriae Dicata*, edited by G. Gnoli, and L. Lanciotti, pp. 1315–1328. IsMEO, Rome.

Shams, F. A.
|1995| Igneous and Metamorphic Rocks. In *Geology of Pakistan*, edited by F. K. Bender, and H. A. Raza. Gebruder Borntraeger, Berlin.

Thapar, B. K.
|1973| New Traits of the Indus Civilization at Kalibangan: An Appraisal. In *South Asian Archaeology*, edited by N. Hammond, pp. 85–104. Duckworth, London.

Vats, M. S.
|1940| *Excavations at Harappa*. 2 vols. Government of India Press, Delhi.

Verma, H. C.
|1977| *Medieval Routes to India*. Mustafa Waheed, Lahore.

Vidale, M.
|1989| A Steatite-Cutting Atelier on the Surface of Moenjodaro. *Annali* 49:29–51.

Vidale, M., and P. Bianchetti
|1997| Green Stones from Pakistan: XRD Identification of Ethnographic and Archaeological Samples of "Steatite" and Other Rocks. In *South Asian Archaeology 1995*, edited by B. Allchin, pp. 947–953. Oxford and IBH, Bombay.

Vidale, M., and H. Miller
|2000| On the Development of Indus Technical Virtuosity and its Relation to Social Structure. In *South Asian Archaeology 1997*, edited by M. Taddei, pp. 115–132. IsIAO, Rome.

Vidale, M., and G. M. Shar
|1990| Zahr Muhra: Soapstone-Cutting in Contemporary Baluchistan. *Annali* 50:61–78.

Wadia, D. N.
|1975| *Geology of India*. Tata McGraw-Hill, New Delhi.

Werritty, A.
|1992| Downstream Fining in a Gravel-Bed River in Southern Poland: Lithological Controls and the Role of Abrasion. In *Dynamics of Gravel-Bed Rivers*, edited by P. Billi, R. D. Hey, C. R. Thorne, and P. Tacconi, pp. 337–346. John Wiley and Sons, New York.

HIDDEN PASSAGE: GRAECO-ROMAN ROADS IN EGYPT'S EASTERN DESERT

Jennifer E. Gates

Jennifer E. Gates, Kelsey Museum of Archaeology, University of Michigan, 434 S. State Street, Ann Arbor, Michigan 48109, U.S.A.

ABSTRACT

Trade routes are often passed over in discussions of trade networks in favour of the sites that they connect. The archaeological oversight of these intermediate spaces reflects the notion that roads and trails are sterile, transient and unimportant archaeologically. The road itself, however, contains information about the political and cultural situation which shaped the trade network, as well as conceptual interactions with place. The study of ancient landscapes challenges us to include all aspects of the natural and constructed environment and, in so doing, to access patterns of behaviour including movement through the landscape. The system of regional trade routes in Egypt's Eastern Desert exemplifies the potential that road networks have to inform social behaviours in environmentally marginal areas with relatively few preserved archaeological sites. During the Ptolemaic and Roman periods (ca. 323 B.C.E. to sixth century C.E.) a complex series of roads and trails were established that connected major sites on the Red Sea Coast with those in the Nile Valley. This paper presents an overview of the archaeological evidence for these roads and considers the challenges of extracting cultural inferences from a deliberately unelaborated road network.

The roads of Egypt's Eastern Desert are a confounding puzzle. They look nothing like the elaborate Roman roads of Italy and North Africa, nor the Hellenistic routes of western Asia. Snaking through the wadis, a road is often no more than a simple track or stretch of sand marked by cairns and graves, a faint trace on the shifting sands of the rocky desert. Yet these roads were an integral part of a trade network established in the early years of the Ptolemaic rulers and used well into the later years of the Roman Empire and early Islamic period. Precious commodities such as elephants, gold, cloth, pepper and valuable stones were transported across the rocky mountains and sandy flats to the Nile or northward along the Red Sea coast. The major ports of Berenike, Myos Hormos, 'Abu Sha'ar and a smaller installation at Marsa Nakari supplied Egypt and more distant parts of the Mediterranean with commodities imported from the Indian Ocean, and precious minerals were extracted from the Eastern Desert itself.

These roads were created at the impetus of the Ptolemaic monarchs and the Roman emperors and were part of a larger system of conscribing the resources of Egypt for the aggrandizement of a larger political whole. Yet the roads exhibit none of the elaborations that an imperial or kingly imperative might demand. Since these roads offer the archaeologist none of the political capital that is so apparent in Inca, Mayan, Roman and Mughal roads (Keller 2001; Miller 2005; Walker 2001), how can they be interpreted? Their scant traces indicate that an alternative system of landscape utilization and organization may have been at work in the Eastern Desert, one that favoured a road structure closely integrated with the natural surroundings and deliberately designed to minimize the presence of outside elements in the desert landscape.

The study of roads and movement falls largely under the rubric of archaeological landscape analysis (Trombold 1991:1). Landscape, once the exclusive purview of historical geographers, is increasingly recognized as a repository for social memory and a dynamic reflection of and participant in the human experience (Bender 1993:1–17; Knapp and Ashmore 1999:1–8; Layton and Ucko 1999:1–2). The landscape is both a physical and conceptual entity which interacts with the human observer on many levels. For the archaeologist, understanding the larger context of sites

Figure 1. Looking south in Wadi Sikait. Note ruins in the foreground and standing building on the saddle across the wadi. Excavation tents are in the distance.

and artifacts is crucial since the landscape holds clues not just to settlement and subsistence, but to a more comprehensive ideological framework.

How is such meaning located in the landscape? Meaning cannot necessarily be correlated with "obtrusively marked, archaeologically detectable" actions (Knapp and Ashmore 1999:2). Meaning is nested in the patterns and expressions of social relationships which leave sometimes slight and subjective marks on the landscape (Baker 1992:5; Evans 1999:452; Thomas 1993:26). Individual *experiences* of landscape may be beyond the ken of archaeological inquiry (Craik 1986:51; Knapp and Ashmore 1999:5), but landscape studies do allow us to see "real actors in the past" (Keller 2001:1) since interactions with landscape can be gleaned from the patterns of archaeological remains, however subtle, distributed across the landscape. Roads are an integral, if often neglected, part of the archaeological material that falls between sites, monuments and other natural foci on the landscape. Roads, trails and paths cross the spaces between sites and are indicators of how movement and interactions with the landscape looked in actual practice.

The study of roads from an archaeological standpoint is challenging. Environment, preservation and the long-term use of a road or path network can make understanding and interpreting road traces very difficult. In addition, there are challenges of perspective. Particularly in historical periods, the study of roads via landscape makes it necessary to step outside the historical assumptions surrounding a particular period and learn to see the landscape as both an inherent and a material entity. In his essay "Exploring Everyday Places and Cosmologies," Peter van Dommelen states:

> Any landscape...represents a product of specific historical and local conditions that is continuously open to reinterpretation and subject to reproduction. In this perspective, the *unity* of natural and cultural features is emphasized and attention is focused on the ways in which a particular landscape has taken shape [1999:278; emphasis in original].

Roads and pathways built during historical periods are sometimes pushed into a model of economy and spatial organization derived from textural sources and clues to a conceptual understanding of the landscape are not explored. Roads and landscape also offer a means of accessing groups who did not participate in the writing of history and for seeing activity for which there is very little historical or ethnographic attestation (Bender 1993:2). The shape of roads may also inform the "conceptual strategies" at work in their construction and allow us to see perceptions of a landscape or attitudes towards a region which might otherwise be completely absent from historical documents (Snead 2002).

The Eastern Desert of Egypt offers an opportunity to read conceptual approaches in the characteristics of a road network that is more notable for its *lack* of construction than for its overt manipulation of the natural environment. The Eastern Desert is uniquely situated at the margins of Egyptian social and cosmological conceptions and yet, during the Graeco-Roman period, was the focus of intense economic exploitation. It is located east of the Nile, between the Nile Valley and the Red Sea. To the north, it is bordered by the Delta and Sinai, and to the south, the deserts of Nubia, in modern Sudan. It is an arid, desert region, very mountainous and dry, receiving on average less than 100 mm of rainfall per year (Wright and Herbert 2003). The stony mountain ranges and gravel cliffs are traversed by sandy wadis (dry stream beds), which direct the occasional seasonal flash flood (Figure 1).

This remote desert was an economically important place throughout Egyptian history. In the Pharaonic period, the desert was used sporadically exploited as a source for minerals and stone and as a conduit to lands further south (Hikade 2001:36-46; 58-60). The desert's role shifted somewhat in later periods and royal interest in the resources of the desert was formalized through the exploration, settlement and elaboration of a series of ports and roads that facilitated domestic and foreign trade. Gold and war elephants were the primary goods moving along these routes during the Ptolemaic period as gold was ferried from Nubia and from mines in the Eastern Desert itself (Sidebotham and Wendrich 2001–2002:41; Sidebotham and Zitterkopf 1995:40; Young 2001:27). In the Roman period, the range of goods moving along these roads was much greater. Marble, beryl, gold and amethyst were quarried in the Eastern Desert at mining sites scattered along the various trade routes (Klemm and Klemm 1994, Maxfield and Peacock 2001; Peacock and Maxfield 1997; Rivard et al. 2002). From the Red Sea ports, wine, beads, cloth, pottery and spices were carried to the Nile by pack animal and draught (Sidebotham and Wendrich 1995, 1996, 1998, 1999, 2000).

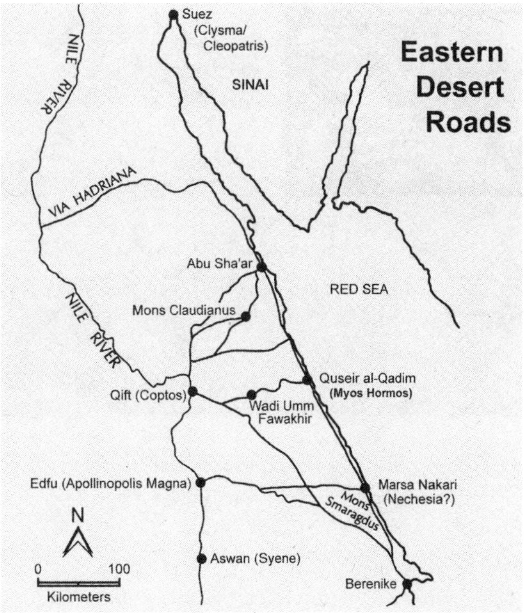

Figure 2. Major routes in the Eastern Desert (adapted from Sidebotham and Wendrich 2001–2002).

As shown in Figure 2, the primary routes through the desert connected Berenike, the largest and most important port city founded by the Ptolemies and maintained by the Romans, to settlements on the Nile. These Nile cities acted as distribution points and goods were shipped from these centers towards the Mediterranean and the major cities in the Delta. Apollinopolis Magna (modern Edfu) and Coptos (modern Qift) were two of the most important economic hubs in the southern Nile Valley and the principal roads through the desert connected these cities with Berenike. The more southerly route, which connected Berenike to Edfu, appears to be the older of the two routes, since it preserves substantial Pharaonic period remains, as well as a large numbers of Ptolemaic sites (Sidebotham and Zitterkopf 1995:40; Wright and Herbert 2003).

The Berenike–Coptos route is populated with sites dating to the Ptolemaic and early Roman periods, but also a proportionally higher number of later Roman sites, suggesting that the trade pattern shifted to the more northerly route after Roman involvement became more pronounced (Sharon Herbert and Henry Wright, personal communication 2002). This is a potentially important change, since it may indicate internal alterations to trade patterns by the new Roman rulers or perhaps a local response to a dynamic regional situation (for other explorations of the relationship between political shifts and road construction and use, see Keller 2001; Miller 2005; Walker 2001). Exclusively Roman period routes also connected Kainopolis further north to 'Abu Sha'ar on the coast by way of the stone quarries at Mons Porphyrites and Mons Claudianus (Peacock and Maxfield 1997; Maxfield and Peacock 2001), while the Via Hadriana ran north along the coast from Berenike to Antinoë on the Nile (Sidebotham et al. 1991:572). Supplies and nourishment would undoubtedly also have moved from the Nile valley to these remote settlements along the same roads.

Settlements pepper the routes and range from complex, well-preserved communities (Figure 3) to rock shelters and pottery scatters without associated architecture. The relationship between Ptolemaic and Roman settlements in the region is still being explored, but the Ptolemaic settlements in the desert are in general less numerous and more transient. Ptolemaic interest in the region was more ephemeral than the emphatic presence of the Roman military and the Roman remains are accordingly much more extensive. Hydreuma or water stations (Figure 4) are known from both periods, although the Roman forts are much larger and more numerous. Other settlements with different architectural characteristics are known but they are of indeterminate function. Most have some sort

Figure 3. Standing structure at Roman settlement in Wadi Shenshef.

Figure 4. Roman fort with round corner towers at Dweig.

of interior well or cistern indicating that part of their function was to provide a water source for residents and travelers. These forts and stations would have provided security and sustenance to small caravans moving goods in either direction (the range of settlement form and types is too great to be covered here in detail; for examples, see Reddé and Golvin 1987; Rivard et al. 2002; Sidebotham 1996; Sidebotham and Wendrich 1995, 1996, 1998, 1999, 2000; Sidebotham and Zitterkopf 1995; Sidebotham et al. 1991; Wright and Herbert 2003; Zitterkopf and Sidebotham 1989).

But what of the physical evidence for the roads themselves? The survey projects undertaken in the Eastern Desert have most often plotted the road courses based on the location of sites discovered in closely spaced linear sequence and connected by wadis that acted as natural conduits; road traces are noted when present, but not analyzed as a facet of the archaeological landscape on par with the sites they connect. This relative neglect may be a function of the fact that the roads are not, in fact, easy to find or understand, as well as the tendency to focus on sites and ignore the seemingly empty spaces between. The Eastern Desert roads largely defy comparison to other Graeco-Roman road systems. They are as remarkable for their lack of defining features as Roman roads in other parts of North Africa and the Near East are for their use of milestones, frequent inscriptions and straight courses (Chevallier 1997:250–252; Millar 1993:138-139; Raven 1993:66–70).

The "constructed" stretches of roads in the Eastern Desert are most often simply tracks of varying width, sometimes as much as 20 m wide, cleared of surface rubble and boulders (Figure 5) (Sidebotham 1999:683–684; Sidebotham and Zitterkopf 1995:42; Sidebotham et al. 1991: 581, 597; Young 2001:45). Road sections were occasionally, although rarely, built up to create revetted causeways and elaborate ramps (see Maxfield and Peacock 2001:210–211 for examples). These ramps, like the one seen by the author at Middle Sikait in the Eastern Desert (Figure 6) or recorded at the Mons Porphyrites quarries are largely intrasite constructions and do not often appear along open stretches of road between settlements. Road ruts are common along the Kainopolis–'Abu Sha'ar road and the Via Hadriana, but seem to be associated almost exclusively with the quarrying activities at Mons Claudianus and Mons Porphyrites and not with the Red Sea trade that shaped the southerly routes (Young 2001:45–46).

The complete lack of milestones along these roads is astonishing. The local and imperial road markers that constituted a statement of military power for the Roman rulers and local officials who established roads in other parts of the empire are completely lacking. The Eastern Desert seems to be one of very few, if not the only place where a Roman period road is not marked by frequent course markers or inscriptions (Sidebotham and Zitterkopf 1995:42). A Ptolemaic inscription, however, from the site of Bir 'Iayyan records the activity of a Ptolemaic official during the reign of Ptolemy II (Bagnall et al. 1996:320–323) along

Figure 5. Section of cleared road between Wadi Abu Greiya and Berenike. (Courtesy S. Sidebotham, photographer)

Figure 6. The Roman ramp to the emerald mines at Sikait. (Courtesy B. Foster, photographer)

the Berenike–Edfu road, indicating that inscriptions mentioning local officials were present at certain sites during the Ptolemaic period. Likewise, inscriptions and testimonials to Roman emperors seem to have been concentrated at the forts and watering stations that dotted the desert during the Roman period.

For example, a recently discovered inscription dating to 76/77 C.E. records the names of local officials and their activities in the ninth year of Vespasian's reign (Sidebotham 2002:365, 377). This massive inscription in local stone was mounted over the main gate of the hydreuma at Siket near Berenike. This inscription and others at forts in the Eastern Desert of comparable date act as a kind of surrogate marking system, although the emphasis is strikingly shifted away from the road course itself to the forts and settlements. This change in treatment of the road almost certainly reflects a hesitancy to claim the road tracks and surfaces as controlled, familiar spaces. The impression created by such a system is one of forts and stations as islands linked by unmarked and possibly dangerous, transgressive spaces.

The roads themselves were marked with more passive elements that were significantly less intrusive on the landscape. Small cairns, usually between 3 and 5 feet in height and made of local stone, were placed along the sides of the wadi or road bed or occasionally along a mountain ridge, marking a route in a wadi below (Figure 7). These cairns appear in both round and square forms and are essentially undateable except on the basis of pottery and other material scattered around their bases. Towers, which look very much like large cairns, also appear along ridges and denote the course of the road aligned below (Figure 8) (Zitterkopf and Sidebotham 1989:160).

Looking at this region from the perspective of movement requires approaching the roads not just as a means of getting from site to site and water-station to water-station, but as part of a system of interacting with the landscape and understanding one's relation to the natural environment. On some level, the road articulates a conceptual dynamic in a way that a single site along the road cannot, especially given the fact that these desert sites are almost entirely unexcavated. Yet what is to be made of such a system—a palimpsest of periods and constructions interacting across a vast landscape? The empirical data for these Graeco-Roman roads is still in early stages of collection, and it is difficult to understand the complex ideational factors which may have shaped the road network. Yet there are some patterns which emerge. The Eastern Desert roads were essentially "natural constructions," if it possible to describe such a thing. Their courses were largely determined by the orientation of the wadis and the routes themselves were simple in the extreme – unpretentious cleared segments, marked by unobtrusive cairns built of local materials, ramps and revetments occurring rarely outside of industrial sites and large settlements.

How should these features be interpreted? Did the ad-hoc nature of first Ptolemaic (Bagnall et al. 1996:323–327) and later Roman administration not demand standardization or elaboration of the Eastern Desert roads? This is contradictory to the Roman

Figure 7. Stone cairn on a mountain ridge marking a path in the valley below. (Courtesy B. Foster, photographer)

Figure 8. Watch tower on a mountain ridge near Sikait. (Courtesy B. Foster, photographer)

treatment of other provincial road systems (Chevallier 1997) and the standardized appearance of the desert forts themselves suggests that the Roman military's settlement of the desert was as rigorous and organized as it was in other parts of the empire. Was paving simply unnecessary? The deep sand in many of the wadis argues that it would not have been impractical, although seasonal floods would have made maintenance labour-intensive.

It may be that purely functional or historical approaches overlook another possible explanation: that these roads were deliberately "hidden" in the landscape. Throughout the Graeco-Roman period, the rulers of Egypt were in a constant state of negotiation with other local population elements, groups who actually lived in the desert and competed with traders, soldiers and officials for precious resources (Gates 2004; Wright and Herbert 2003). The desert roads and settlements intruded in this landscape and were a visible reminder of the passage of "outside" forces through this space. Perhaps these roads were deliberately minimalized so as not to overtly rework the natural landscape and draw attention to a vulnerable population. Were "outside" impacts on the land visually restricted in order to lessen conflicts with local groups? For the Ptolemaic rulers, who consistently demonstrated a willingness to adapt and modify existing administrative structures (Bagnall et al. 1996), this kind of pragmatism seems an entirely reasonable explanation. Yet the Roman military presence in the Eastern Desert, based on the numbers of forts and the documentary evidence from Berenike, is sufficiently intense that one quite reasonably expects to find a system of marking and delineating space that conforms to patterns in other *limes*. Why is the Eastern Desert frontier different?

The deliberate linkage between the roads and the natural ruggedness of the landscape argues for a much more subtle reading of the Eastern Desert environment in both the Roman and Ptolemaic periods. In the Egyptian cosmology, desert was the "red land," the center of chaos and the edge of the Egyptian universe (Richards 1999:85–91). The intentionally unconstructed nature of the Eastern Desert roads did not challenge the essential form of this cosmologically unpredictable desert landscape; in fact, the lack of formalized roads and trails could be interpreted as an acknowledgment of the conceptualization of the desert as a dangerous and unpredictable place, which in point of fact, it was.

Viewed this way, the road network is less surprising. The landscape is not subjugated by a system of regular roads and trails, rather the forts and settlements are the primary manifestation of a Graeco-Roman presence. They are the provisions that allow one to survive in the desert environment and thus become the markers and delineators of the road course, standing in as nodes of cultural and physical comfort in a landscape that requires one to tread lightly for political as well as cosmological reasons. Deliberately inconspicuous, the in-between spaces are the polar opposite of the elaborate New World and Roman road systems that were marked with such explicit symbols of order and power. The Eastern Desert presents the case of a very different interaction, one in which the landscape was a dynamic participant in shaping human activity, not just in terms of environmental constraints, but by bestowing a general social meaning and determining a spatial ordering which influenced the way people thought, understood and traveled through the landscape around them.

REFERENCES CITED

Baker, A. R. H.
|1992| Introduction: On Ideology and Landscape. In *Ideology and Landscape Historical Perspective*, edited by A. R. H. Baker, and G. Biger, pp. 1–14. Cambridge Studies in Historical Geography 18, A. R. H. Baker, J. B. Harley, and D. Holdsworth, series editors, Cambridge University Press, Cambridge.

Bagnall, R. S, J. G. Manning, S. E. Sidebotham, and R. E. Zitterkopf
|1996| A Ptolemaic Inscription from Bir 'Iayyan. *Chronique d'Égypte* 71:317–330.

Bender, B.
|1993| Landscape – Meaning and Action. In *Landscape: Politics and Perspectives*, edited by B. Bender, pp. 1–17. Berg, Oxford.

Chevallier, R.
|1997| *Les voies romaines*. Picard, Paris.

Craik, K. H.
|1986| Psychological Reflections on Landscapes. In *Landscape Meanings and Values*, edited by E. C. Penning-Roswell, and D. Lowenthal, pp. 48–64. Allen and Unwin, London.

Evans, C.
|1999| Cognitive Maps and Narrative Trails: Fieldwork with Tamu-Mai (Gurung) of Nepal. In *The Archaeology and Anthropology of Landscape: Shaping your Landscape*, edited by P. J. Ucko, and R. Layton, pp. 439–457. Routledge, London.

Gates, J. E.
|2004| Most Necessary Things: Ptolemaic Desert Settlements on the Southern Red Sea Trade roads. Paper presented at the Annual Meeting of the American Research Center in Egypt, Tucson, Arizona.

Hikade, T.
|2001| *Das Expeditionswesen im ägyptischen Neuen Reich*. Heidelberger Orientverlag, Heidelberg.

Keller, A.
|2001| Finding the Way: Identifying Directed Movement at the Late Classic Maya Center of Xunantunich, Belize. Paper presented at the 34th Annual Chacmool Conference, Calgary, Alberta.

Klemm, R., and D. D. Klemm
|1994| Chronologisher Abriß der antiken Goldgewinnung in der Ostwüste Ägyptens. *Mitteilungen des Deutschen Archäologischen Instituts* 50:189–222.

Knapp, A. B., and W. Ashmore
|1999| Archaeological Landscapes: Constructed, Conceptualized, Ideational. In *Archaeologies of Landscape: Contemporary Perspectives*, edited by W. Ashmore, and A. B. Knapp, pp. 1–8. Blackwell, Oxford

Layton, R., and P. J. Ucko
|1999| Introduction: Gazing on the Landscape and Encountering the Environment. In *The Archaeology and Anthropology of Landscape: Shaping your Landscape*, edited by P. J. Ucko, and R. Layton, pp. 1–20. Routledge, London.

Maxfield, V. A., and D. P. S. Peacock
|2001| *The Roman Imperial Quarries: Survey and Excavation at Mons Porphyrites 1994–1998*. Egypt Exploration Society, London.

Miller, H. M.-L.
|2005| Comparing Landscapes of Transportation: Riverine-Oriented And Land-Oriented Systems in the Indus Civilization and the Mughal Empire. In *Space and Spatial Analysis in Archaeology*, edited by E. C. Robertson, J. D. Seibert, D. C. Fernandez, and M. U. Zender, pp. 281–291. University of Calgary Press, Calgary, Alberta.

Peacock, D. P. S., and V. A. Maxfield
|1997| *Mons Claudianus: Survey and Excavation, 1987–1993*. Institut Français d'Archéologie Orientale, Cairo.

Raven, Susan
|1993| *Rome in Africa*. 3rd ed. Routledge, London.

Reddé, M., and J.-C. Golvin
|1987| Du Nil à la Mer Rouge: documents anciens et nouveaux sur les routes du Désert Oriental d'Égypte. *Karthago* 21:5–64.

Richards, J. E.
|1999| Conceptual Landscapes in the Egyptian Nile Valley. In *Archaeologies of Landscape: Contemporary Perspectives*, edited by W. Ashmore and A. B. Knapp, pp.83–100. Blackwell, Oxford.

Rivard, J.-L., B. C. Foster, and S. E. Sidebotham
|2002| Emerald City. *Archaeology*, 55(3): 36–41.

Sidebotham, S. E.
|1996| Newly Discovered Sites in the Eastern Desert. *The Journal of Egyptian Archaeology* 82:181–192.
|1999| Roman Forts in Egypt. In *Encyclopedia of the Archaeology of Ancient Egypt*, edited by Kathryn A. Bard, pp. 682–684. Routledge, London.
|2002| The Roman Empire's Southeasternmost Frontier: Recent Discoveries at Berenike and Environs (Eastern Desert of Egypt) 1998–2000. In *Limes XVIII: Proceedings of the XVIIIth International Congress of Roman Frontier Studies*, edited by P. Freeman, J. Bennett, Z. T. Fiema, and B. Hoffmann, pp. 361–378. BAR International Series 1084. Archaeopress, Oxford.

Sidebotham, S. E., and W. Wendrich
|1995| *Berenike 1994. Preliminary Report of the 1994 Excavations at Berenike (Egyptian Red Sea Coast) and the Survey of the Eastern Desert.* Centre of Non-Western Studies, Leiden.
|1996| *Berenike 1995. Preliminary Report of the 1995 Excavations at Berenike (Egyptian Red Sea Coast) and the Survey of the Eastern Desert.* Centre of Non-Western Studies, Leiden.
|1998| *Berenike 1996. Report of the 1996 Excavations at Berenike (Egyptian Red Sea Coast) and the Survey of the Eastern Desert.* Centre of Non-Western Studies, Leiden.

|1999| *Berenike 1997. Report of the 1997 Excavations at Berenike (Egyptian Red Sea Coast) and the Survey of the Egyptian Eastern Desert, Including Excavations at Shenshef.* Centre of Non-Western Studies, Leiden.

|2000| *Berenike 1998. Report of the 1998 Excavations at Berenike and the Survey of the Egyptian Eastern Desert, Including Excavations in Wadi Kalalat.* Centre of Non-Western Studies, Leiden.

|2001–2002| Berenike: Archaeological Fieldwork at the Ptolemaic-Roman Port on the Red Sea Coast of Egypt 1999–2001. *Sahara* 13:23–50.

Sidebotham, S. E., and R. E. Zitterkopf

|1995| Routes through the Eastern Desert of Egypt. *Expedition* 37(2):39–52.

Sidebotham, S. E., R. E. Zitterkopf, and J. A. Riley

|1991| Survey of the 'Abu Sha'ar–Nile Road. *American Journal of Archaeology* 95:571–622.

Snead, J.

|2002| Ancestral Pueblo trails and the cultural landscape of the Pajarito Plateau, New Mexico. *Antiquity* 76:56-65.

Thomas, J.

|1993| The Politics of Vision and the Archaeologies of Landscape. In *Landscape: Politics and Perspectives*, edited by B. Bender, pp. 20–48. Berg, Oxford.

Trombold, C. D.

|1991| An Introduction to the Study of Ancient New World Road Networks. In *Ancient Road Networks and Settlement Hierarchies in the New World*, edited by C. D. Trombold, pp. 1–9. Cambridge University Press, Cambridge.

Van Dommelen, P.

|1999| Exploring Everyday Places and Cosmologies. In *Archaeologies of Landscape: Contemporary Perspectives*, edited by W. Ashmore, and A. B. Knapp, pp. 277–285. Blackwell, Oxford.

Walker, J.

|2001| Building Connections in the Bolivian Amazon. Paper presented at the 34th Annual Chacmool Conference, Calgary, Alberta.

Wright, H., and S. C. Herbert

|2003| Preliminary Report on the University of Michigan/University of Assiut Archaeological Survey in the Eastern Desert of Egypt. In *Excavations at Coptos (Qift) in Upper Egypt, 1987–1992*, edited by S. C. Herbert and A. Berlin, JRA Supplement 53. JRA, Portsmouth, Rhode Island.

Young, G. K.

|2001| *Rome's Eastern Trade: International Commerce and Imperial Policy, 31 B.C.–A.D. 305.* Routledge, London.

Zitterkopf, R. E., and S. E. Sidebotham

|1989| Stations and Towers on the Quseir–Nile Road. *The Journal of Egyptian Archaeology* 75:155–189.

BOATS, BITUMEN AND BARTERING: THE USE OF A UTILITARIAN GOOD TO TRACK MOVEMENT AND TRANSPORT IN ANCIENT EXCHANGE SYSTEMS

Mark Schwartz and David Hollander

Mark Schwartz, Department of Anthropology, Grand Valley State University, 1 Campus Drive, Allendale, Michigan 49401, U.S.A.

David Hollander, College of Marine Science, University of South Florida, St. Petersburg, 140 Seventh Avenue South, St. Petersburg, Florida 33701, U.S.A.

ABSTRACT

Any study of ancient exchange must involve a determination of the geographic source of trade goods and their movement in the exchange system. In current analyses of the fourth millennium B.C. Mesopotamian colonial trading system known as the Uruk expansion, the prestige goods that were involved are extremely rare in archaeological deposits and hard to source chemically. To remedy this, our research has focused on analyses of bitumen, a utilitarian petroleum tar which is abundant in archaeological contexts, is chemically sourceable, and also serves as a secondary marker for other trade goods. Stable carbon and stable hydrogen isotope analyses in addition to molecular data have helped to detail the organization of exchange of the Uruk expansion. In addition, spatial-functional analyses have yielded new information on early boat technology and the early riverine transport of exchange goods on the Euphrates River. The site of Hacinebi, a local Anatolian site in southeast Turkey which had a Mesopotamian enclave in its latter history, revealed several bitumen artifacts that appear to have been the remnants of a coating placed on early reed boats to waterproof them. The oldest pieces are the earliest fragments (3800 B.C.) from this area of the Near East, demonstrating the antiquity and widespread use of this transport technology. While many of the trade goods are missing from the sites involved in the Uruk expansion, the material used to both seal and move these goods is present and provides an opportunity to study several different aspects of the archaeology of transportation simultaneously.

This article was written for the *In Transit* conference session on ancient transport systems and discusses the archaeology of transportation from the perspective of ancient exchange. Many of the methods presented in this symposium have a great deal to contribute to the study of ancient exchange. Landscape patterns can hint at trade routes, ancient roadways and trading posts or caravanserai (Gates 2005). The analysis of prestige goods and their role in an exchange system can help identify the participants in the economic network (Law 2005). Finally, technological analyses of certain artifacts can suggest different modes of transport employed by ancient people in a trading system (Miller 2005). However, if these sources of data or artifact assemblages are absent, it can be extremely difficult or impossible to reconstruct the inner workings of ancient exchange. This is particularly noticeable in the fourth millennium B.C. colonial trading system in the Near East known as the Uruk expansion. This paper attempts to address this problem by examining an archaeological proxy for ancient exchange goods. With this proxy material, one can track the movement of trade goods through chemical analyses, examine changing patterns of trade over time and reconstruct the ancient transportation technology used to transport these trade goods. With this data one can then address larger theoretical questions concerning the Uruk expansion.

THE URUK EXPANSION

The ancient Near East is one of the best areas to investigate the nature of trade in early complex societies because the rise of states in Mesopotamia is linked closely to long-distance, cross-cultural trade with emerging complex societies in Anatolia and Iran. The southern alluvium of Iraq and southwestern Iran was the setting of major cultural advancements in the fourth millennium B.C. During the period between 3100 and 3700 B.C., the world's first urban centers grew dramatically, most noticeably at the 250-hectare site of Uruk from which the period gets its name (Nissen 1988; Pollock 1992; Wright 1986; Wright and Johnson 1975). The rise of these cities was parallel to the appearance of early administrative/writing systems, social stratification, kingship, warfare, and other key elements of early states (Nissen 1988; Pollock 1992; Stein 1999). The complex political economy of the region was based on the abundant agricultural resources of the region, the mobilization of surplus, and the control of craft specialists (Pollock 1992; Wright and Johnson 1975).

However, while arable land, livestock and bitumen were plentiful, vital resources such as metals, stone and timber were completely absent in the region. This is seen by some as the impetus for the establishment of intensive trade with neighboring regions. The presence of Uruk-style artifacts and architecture in distant areas of southeast Turkey, Syria and Iran during the Late Uruk period has been interpreted by some to be evidence of trading colonies (Algaze 1989, 1993). Spanning an area of approximately 5500 km^2, this trading empire, known as the Uruk expansion, is regarded by many as the world's earliest colonial trading system.

The Uruk expansion provides archaeologists with the opportunity to examine the economic, political and social impact of state level societies from Mesopotamia on smaller, emerging complex societies in the foothills of the Taurus and Zagros mountains. Guillermo Algaze, a leading researcher on the Uruk expansion, contends that trade with Mesopotamian colonies produced and economic overspecialization in local communities focused on trade related activities, making their economies inflexible, unstable and prone to collapse with the end of the Uruk expansion (Algaze 1989, 1993). Using the principles of world systems theory, Algaze believes that the core state societies of Mesopotamia extracted surplus from the less complex peripheral societies of Turkey, Iran and Syria. This research attempts to address this view with material from an ideal site to test these issues, Hacinebi Tepe.

THE STUDY AREA: HACINEBI TEPE

Hacinebi Tepe is an ideal site to explore this ancient exchange system and anthropological issues of interregional interaction because its stratigraphic sequence allows a diachronic study of the Uruk expansion. The 3.3-ha, fortified, Late Chalcolithic Anatolian settlement is located on the Euphrates River at the historic east-west crossing point of the Euphrates (Dilleman 1962:135; Oates 1968:7) and the head of the main north-south riverine trade route along this river (Chesney 1850:45; Great Britain 1916:167; Idrisi 1840, II:137). The earliest sequence at the site (Phase A [ca. 4100–3800 B.C.] and B1 [ca. 3800–3700 B.C.]) dates to the early fourth millennium B.C., before the Uruk expansion and is referred to as the "Pre-Contact period." The later phase (Phase B2, ca. 3700–3300 B.C.) consists mainly of a continuation of this local occupation with what appears to be a small Mesopotamian enclave in the northeast corner of the site (Stein 1999; Stein and Misir 1994; Stein et al. 1996). The stratigraphic sequence of the ancient community permits one to examine the effect Mesopotamians had on the organization of exchange, subsistence and administrative activities of the Anatolians by examining the artifactual material from levels before and during Mesopotamian contact.

PRELIMINARY RESULTS: GEOCHEMICAL ANALYSES OF UTILITARIAN GOODS

The major problem in detailing the exchange system at Hacinebi and the Uruk expansion in general is the rarity of trade goods in archaeological deposits. Textiles, grain and timber are all perishable materials. Copper artifacts are rare at Hacinebi and hard to source. Provenience studies on obsidian at Hacinebi have detailed some exchange linkages, but since obsidian sources lie only in Anatolia, obsidian cannot serve as a marker for trade with Mesopotamia (Stein 1999). One of the most promising avenues of research, then, lies with bitumen analysis, because this utilitarian petroleum tar is abundant in archaeological contexts, is chemically sourceable, and is a secondary marker for other trade goods.

Bitumen, a natural petroleum tar available from a variety of seepages in the Near East, could be considered the plastic of its day. It was used primarily in Mesopotamia as a waterproofing material for pottery, reed matting and baskets, and as a mastic used in the production of objects such as the royal standard of Ur (Forbes 1936). In this form, bitumen was likely used as a packaging material for other trade goods. Finds of bitumen blocks (Pollock 1990) and textual records from later periods indicate that Mesopotamians traded bitumen as a utilitarian good in the periods after the Uruk expansion, if not earlier.

The unique properties of bitumen make it possible to source specific artifacts back to their point of origin. Different bitumen seepages in the Near East have different geologic histories and their chemical signatures reflect these differences (Waples 1987). Bitumen, like all petroleum products, is composed of hydrocarbons – molecules made up of carbon and hydrogen derived from prehistoric marine and terrestrial life. Different types of organisms will have unique ratios of carbon and hydrogen isotopes. These heavier isotopes, ^{13}C and deuterium (^{2}H) do not degrade over time and are thus termed "stable" in contrast to radioactive isotopes such as ^{14}C. Because these stable isotopes were present in different proportions in various forms of simple prehistoric life, the oil derived from these organisms will share this isotopic signature (Waples 1987). Therefore, different bitumen seepages with different geologic histories will have their own distinct chemical "fingerprint." This fundamental principle lies as the basis for our ability to draw site to source correlations of bitumen.

Because the processes involved in carbon and hydrogen isotope enrichment (selection for heavier isotopes) are different from one another, a specific carbon isotope ratio will not be automatically paired with a specific hydrogen isotope ratio (Waples 1987). To put it another way, two samples with the same carbon isotope ratio will not necessarily have the same hydrogen isotope ratio. Thus, combining stable carbon and stable hydrogen isotope analyses will help discriminate source groups with overlapping stable carbon isotope values. Stable carbon isotope ratios have provided a means of comparing archaeological samples to source material. We have performed stable carbon isotope analyses by themselves, but these analyses on their own did not provide us with the statistical power needed to accurately source the archaeological material from Hacinebi. For our pilot project we remedied this by performing detailed gas chromatography-mass spectrometry analyses to "fingerprint" five archaeological and two source samples (Schwartz et al. 1999). The analytical methods of gas chromatography mass spectrometry and compound-specific isotope analysis are the same ones employed by UN inspectors to determine if tankers in the Persian Gulf are illegally carrying Iraqi oil (Becker 2000). While very effective, these analyses are too costly and time consuming to be performed on a large data set.

Archaeologists studying obsidian artifacts have realized that it is preferable to trade accuracy for a more representative sample size. For example, in the analysis of obsidian from the Neolithic Italian site of Filiestru, an early study of four samples yielded the following results for the sources used: 50 per cent SA, 25 per cent SB, 25 per cent SC. A later analysis using 86 samples gave vastly different results: 10 per cent SA, 49 per cent SB, 41 per cent SC (Tykot 2003). It was then decided that bulk stable isotope analysis was best suited for this research because of the lower labor investment needed when compared to more detailed analyses such as gas chromatography-mass spectrometry and compound specific isotope analysis. Currently, the authors of this paper are involved in a large-scale sourcing project utilizing over 500 bitumen samples from Hacinebi and over 200 source samples, samples from archaeological proxies and contemporaneous archaeological sites. This large data set will allow us to look at overall patterns of exchange instead of accurately sourcing only a handful of samples with little representative value. The data presented here in this paper are preliminary results from the stable carbon and stable hydrogen analyses of a small number of test samples (Figure 1). The ellipses represent hypothesized groupings based on clear visual discriminations between artifacts.

To this date, previous molecular data suggests that there was Mesopotamian material at Hacinebi during the Uruk period, and that this Mesopotamian bitumen was chemically distinct from Anatolian bitumen (Schwartz and Hollander 2000; Schwartz et al. 1999). Recent stable carbon and stable hydrogen isotope analyses seem to confirm that samples from the site of Hacinebi from Uruk Mesopotamian archaeological contexts clearly match material from the southern Mesopotamian site of Kish (Figure 1). This bivariate plot also shows the clear chemical distinction between

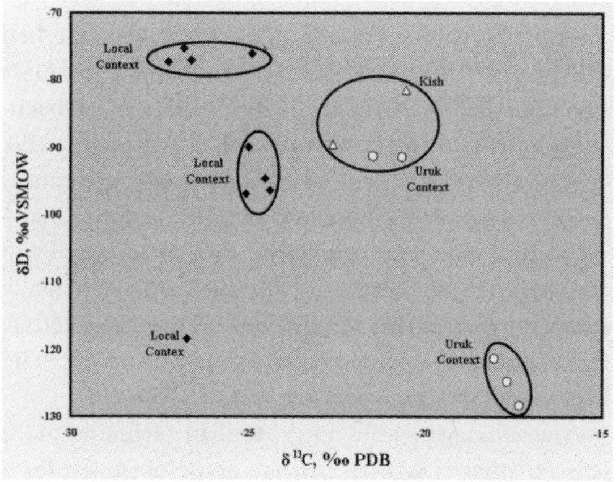

Figure 1. Cross plot of bulk stable carbon and stable hydrogen isotope ratios of bitumen artifacts from the site of Hacinebi and from the southern Mesopotamian site of Kish.

bitumen from Mesopotamia and Anatolia archaeological contexts from the site of Hacinebi, hinting at chemical distinctions between bitumen from these two geologic source areas. Initial results also imply that Mesopotamian trade goods were coming from multiple, culturally distinct areas of Mesopotamia as one can see from the two distinct elliptical areas of Uruk context artifacts from Hacinebi.

From the data on Anatolian context bitumen at Hacinebi, it is also clear that multiple local non-Mesopotamian bitumen sources were utilized by the local population (Figure 1). There are at least three if not more local Anatolian sources represented in the Hacinebi assemblage that were used by the local population. The evidence of multiple Anatolian bitumen sources present at Hacinebi serves as further proof of the existence of exchange networks with different areas of Anatolia in the Pre-Contact phase of the site and supports the scenario of Hacinebi as part of a developing, socially complex culture before contact with Mesopotamia. If Hacinebi was engaged in long-distance Anatolian trade networks before Mesopotamian contact, it would be consistent with the idea that the Mesopotamians set up a colony at Hacinebi to tap into already existing, extensive trade networks in Anatolia (Stein 1999). This is a logical conclusion considering the strategic location of Hacinebi on the Euphrates and its possible function there.

BITUMEN ARTIFACTS AND ANCIENT TRANSPORT TECHNOLOGY

Besides chemical analyses, spatial functional analyses have yielded very different kinds of data. Recent analyses have generated new information on early boat technology. Several pieces from Hacinebi appear to be the remnants of coating placed on early reed boats to waterproof them. From the largest piece and its associated latex cast (Figure 2a), one can clearly see the impressions of reed bundles lashed together with rope, similar to archaeological and ethnographic patterns of reed boats and unlike the impressions of waterproofed basketry and reed mats that also appear at Hacinebi. This largest and earliest of the fragments, dated by stratigraphically associated radiocarbon samples to 3800 B.C., is approximately 20 cm by 20 cm and weighs.66 kg. While they are not the earliest reed boat fragments in the world, these are the earliest fragments from this area of the Near East, demonstrating the early and widespread use of this technology.

The world's earliest reed boat fragments date to the sixth millennium B.C. and are from the H3 site on the Subiya coastal plain in Kuwait (Carter and Crawford 2001). These pieces and the fragments from Hacinebi are identical to bitumen artifacts which were identified as fragments of reed boats from 2500–2200 B.C. from the site of Ra's al-Junayz in Oman (Tosi and Cleuziou 1994). The perpendicular construction of reed and rope and the presence of barnacles on the reverse side, demonstrate that the Ra's al-Junayz artifacts were exposed to salt water for an extended period of time as a waterproofing layer on a reed material (Tosi and Cleuziou 1994). These reed bundles were lashed together to form vessels that were either boat-shaped rafts, whose buoyancy relied on the reeds themselves, or actual boats which had the ability to displace water (Johnstone 1980; Thesiger 1964:126–127, Plate 41). This technique of construction (illustrated in Figure 2b), is the most efficient way to construct riverine craft using only reed and rope (Heyerdahl 1979:15–19) and has been noted historically and ethnographically in areas of the world ranging from Lake Titicaca in Peru to New Zealand and Australia to the marshes of southern Iraq to Lake Chad in the Sudan (Hornell 1946:39–60; Johnstone 1980:7–17; Ochsenschlager 1992:67). While modern reconstructions of ancient reed boats including the one from Ra's al-Junayz have accurately depicted these vessels

(Vosmer 2000), bitumen was rarely used on the full-scale working replicas, making them prone to become waterlogged and/or rotten, (Heyerdahl 1979:24; Tzalas 1995). The fourth millennium inhabitants of Hacinebi, however, had access to *Phragmites australis* (Cav.) Trin. Ex Steud., the common reed (Brown 1979), and several Anatolian bitumen sources (Lebkuchner 1969; Schwartz et al. 1999).

The prehistoric and historic use of reed boats in the Near East is well documented by several different lines of evidence besides these early bitumen fragments. Ethnographic material hints at what ancient boats must have looked like and usually focuses on the Marsh Arabs of southern Iraq, who constructed and waterproofed reed rafts and boats up until the middle of the twentieth century (Ochsenschlager 1992:67; Thesiger 1964:126–127, Plate 41). There are also mentions of the use of reed boats in the nearby regions of the Sudan, Greece, Kuwait, and Iran (Hornell 1946). Accounts from nineteenth-century British explorers in Mesopotamia describe the construction of reed and bitumen boats in detail and demonstrate the incredible ingenuity of humans in utilizing the simple materials around them.

Once such description is by F. R. Chesney (1850) who himself attempted to navigate the Euphrates from the region around Hacinebi Tepe, Turkey to the Persian Gulf in 1835. Chesney witnessed the construction of a 20-ton reed boat by Arabs in southern Mesopotamia near the bitumen source of Hit, which was one of the major, if not the major source of bitumen in Mesopotamia in antiquity and the recent past (Forbes 1936). The vessel was constructed in one day using only an axe, a saw, and a ladle for the molten bitumen and a roller for smoothing it. These craft were waterproofed both inside and out and drew only 22 inches of water when laden and 6 inches when empty (Chesney 1850). It seems obvious that these boats were quite capable of transporting trade goods down the Euphrates and that ancient boats were similarly adept at this.

Glyptic evidence from fourth millennium B.C. Mesopotamian tablets (Figure 2d and 2e), as well as Neo-Assyrian reliefs (Figure 2c), show that ancient boats did indeed share the characteristic reed bundle technique of construction. Even boat symbols from Mesopotamian seal impressions that do not show these striations still have high upturned prows and sterns and shallow hulls, another marker of reed boats

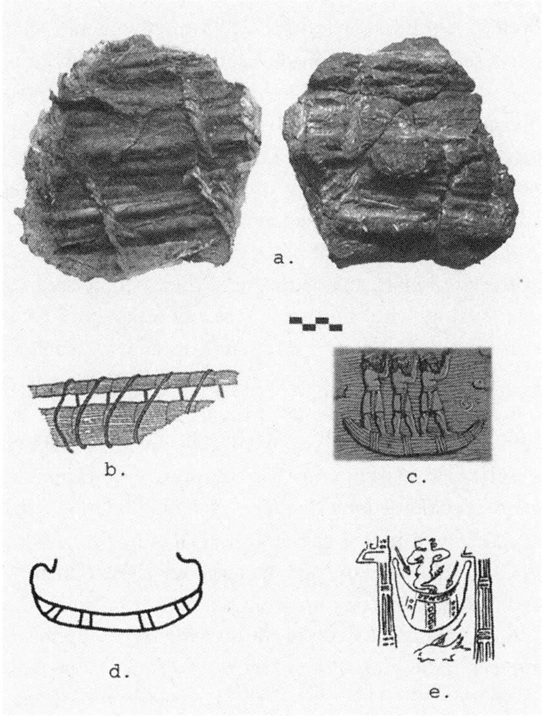

Figure 2. (a) Reed boat remains from Hacinebi Tepe dated to 3800 B.C. The original bitumen waterproofed coating is on the right with its modern latex cast on the left; (b) An illustration of reed boat construction technique (after Heyerdahl 1979); (c) reed boats depicted in an Assyrian relief from the palace of Sennacherib (after Layard 1853); (d–e) 2 examples of fourth millennium B.C. Mesopotamian glyptic depictions of reed boats: (d) southern Mesopotamia (after Bass 1972), and (e) south west Iran (after Amiet 1980).

(Potts 1997). It is likely that these impressions are of waterproofed reed boats which would not have had their reed bundles exposed (Johnstone 1980).

Ancient Mesopotamian texts further strengthen the argument that archaeological remains of waterproofed reed bundles are most likely from some sort of watercraft. Numerous Ur III texts describe the use of reed for boatbuilding while texts from Ur III, Old Babylonian and Neo-Babylonian periods describe the use of bitumen for caulking boats (Potts 1997). Fifth millennium B.C. clay models of bitumen-covered reed boats from the site of Eridu in southern Mesopotamia (Safar et al. 1981) and from the site of Tell Mashnaqa in northern Syria (Weiss 1994) further attest to the antiquity and wide geographic range of this form of transport. Now, the discovery of these boats in Anatolia adds to our understanding of the site of Hacinebi.

The oldest reed boat piece dates to the early phases of the site before any evidence of this specific trading relationship with southern Mesopotamia. Non-local items dating to before Mesopotamian contact, such as copper, shell and chlorite, suggests that local Anatolian trade existed at the site in earlier periods (Stein 1999:137–138). The presence of boats adds further weight to the argument that the people of Hacinebi were developing long-distance exchange relationships on their own before the arrival of Mesopotamians to the site. This area of Anatolia has been known historically as an important crossing point of the Euphrates and as a region of riverine traffic lying on a number of ancient trade routes (Herodotus 1973, vol. I:194–198; Stein 1999:117–118). Thus, the presence of early waterproofed boats provides a more complete picture of the ancient exchange economy of Southeast Anatolia.

CONCLUSIONS

While historic records can provide some glimpse into prehistoric trade routes, there is much to be gained from analyses of utilitarian goods. If trade goods are absent archaeologically, it may be impossible to determine the trade participants, origins of trade goods, and trade routes of the exchange system. In addition anthropological questions concerning the economy of early trading partners may be impossible to address. Combined sourcing and archaeological analyses of simple utilitarian goods can provide much information that would be impossible to gain otherwise. The research at Hacinebi has used chemical analyses to look at the source of the packaging material used on trade goods to determine the participants in the trade network and the trade routes used.

Preliminary results hint at some of the dynamics of this trading system through the distinguishing of artifacts according to their geologic source. These results demonstrate that stable carbon and stable hydrogen isotope analyses can distinguish between bitumen artifacts from Anatolia versus Mesopotamia. In addition, with the limited number of samples in this study, one can see that trade goods were coming from multiple Mesopotamian and Anatolian sources. The key problem for future research will be to identify any change in the proportion of these sources in local contexts both before and during the Uruk expansion in order to track any economic changes in the local Anatolian community. The initial results of this study suggest that this is possible. With an expansion of the data set through analyses of all archaeological materials from Hacinebi, I can identify patterns of exchange and reconstruct changing trade patterns. I will also be able to correlate artifacts from a specific source with other archaeological information such as their distribution in the site, their function and their role as finished products or production debris. This will allow me to look at patterns of production and test the validity of a World Systems Model for the Uruk expansion by determining if local Anatolians were producing specifically for the Mesopotamians at the site.

Initial functional analyses of bitumen artifacts have also hinted at what types of riverine vessels were used to transport trade goods in the Uruk expansion. The location of Hacinebi downriver from an important copper source, combined with the presence of reed boats and bitumen from at least two areas of Anatolia suggest that the site was an important regional exchange center prior to the Uruk expansion. The reed boat artifacts discovered at Hacinebi are in fact the earliest evidence of riverine boats in the Near East and perhaps the world, and attest to the antiquity and wide spread distribution of this ancient technology. The identification of early reed boats at Hacinebi has therefore added a new dimension to our study of indigenous trade before contact with the states of Mesopotamia.

Thus, while many of the actual trade goods are missing from the site of Hacinebi, the material used to both seal and transport these items is present and provides a powerful methodological tool in the reconstruction of ancient trade roots and trade technology. With many of the trade goods absent archaeologically, bitumen artifacts serve as an excellent proxy for these items and also provide additional economic information on production and exchange. Preliminary analyses presented here give a glimpse into the ancient exchange patterns and modes of transport of the Uruk expansion. Employing these methodological techniques on a larger set of artifacts in the future should provide sufficient data to determine the economic impact the state societies of Mesopotamia had on the merging complex societies of Anatolia in the fourth millennium B.C.

ACKNOWLEDGMENTS

The authors would like to thank first and foremost, Gil Stein, director of the Hacinebi Tepe Excavations, for his unceasing help with this project. Special thanks must be given to Lisa Pratt, Simon Brassell, Arndt Schimmelmann, Steve Studley and Jon Fong from the Biogeochemistry Lab at the Department of Geological Sciences, Indiana University, for their help with the project's geochemical analyses. Serge Cleuziou, Robert Carter, Harriet Crawford and Edward Ochsenschlager provided invaluable advice on the reed boat remains. Finally, the people who provided bitumen source materials are too numerous to name here, but the authors want to acknowledge their help in building a library of bitumen artifacts.

REFERENCES CITED

Algaze, G.
|1989| The Uruk Expansion: Cross-Cultural Exchange in Early Mesopotamian Civilization. *Current Anthropology* 30:571–608.
|1993| *The Uruk World System*. University of Chicago Press, Chicago.

Amiet, P.
|1980| *Glyptique Mesopotamienne Archaique*. Edition du centre national de la recherché scientifique, Paris.

Bass, G. F.
|1972| *A History of Seafaring Based on Underwater Archaeology*. Thames and Hudson, London.

Becker, E.
|2000| U.S. Seizes Russian Tanker Said to Carry Oil From Iraq. *New York Times* 4 February.

Brown, L.
|1979| *Grasses: An Identification Guide*. Houghton Mifflin, Boston.

Carter R., and H. E. W. Crawford
|2001| The Kuwait-British Archaeological Expedition to As-Sabiyah: Report on the Second Season's Work. *Iraq* 63:1–20.

Chesney, F. R.
|1850| *The Expedition for the Survey of the Rivers Euphrates and Tigris Carried on by the Order of the British Government in the Years 1835, 1836, and 1837: Preceded by Geographical and Historical Notices of the Regions Situated Between the Rivers Nile and Indus*. Longman, Brown, Green and Longmans, London.

Dilleman, L.
|1962| *Haute Mesopotamie Orientale et Pays Adjacents*. Librarie Orientaliste Paul Geuthner, Paris.

Forbes, R. J.
|1936| *Bitumen and Petroleum in Antiquity*. E. J. Brill, Leiden.

Gates, J.
|2005| Hidden Passage: Graeco-Roman Roads in Egypt's Eastern Desert. In *Space and Spatial Analysis in Archaeology*, edited by E. C. Robertson, J. D. Seibert, D. C. Fernandez, and M. U. Zender, pp. 313-320. University of Calgary Press, Calgary, Alberta.

Great Britain
|1916| *A Handbook of Mesopotamia*. Admiralty War Staff Intelligence Division.

Herodotus
|1973| *The Histories*. Translated by Aubrey de Sélincourt. Penguin Books, Harmondsworth, U.K.

Heyerdahl, T.
|1979| *Early Man and the Ocean*. Doubleday, New York.

Hornell, J.
|1946| *Water Transport: Origins and Early Evolution*. Cambridge University Press, Cambridge.

Idrisi, al
|1840| *Géographie d'Edrisi*. Translated by P. Amédée Jaubert. Imprimerie Nationale, Paris.

Johnstone, P.
|1980| *The Sea-Craft of Prehistory*. Harvard University Press, Cambridge.

Law, R.
|2005| Moving Mountains: The Trade and Transport of Rocks and Minerals within the Greater Indus Valley Region. In *Space and Spatial Analysis in Archaeology*, edited by E. C. Robertson, J. D. Seibert, D. C. Fernandez, and M. U. Zender, pp. 299–311. University of Calgary Press, Calgary, Alberta.

Layard, A. H.
|1853| *The Monuments of Nineveh; Including Bas-reliefs from the Palace of Sennacherib and Bronzes from the Ruins of Nimroud. From Drawings Made on the Spot, During a Second Expedition to Assyria*. John Murray, Albemarle Street, London.

Lebkuchner, R. F.
|1969| Occurrences of the Asphaltic Substances in Southeastern Turkey and Their Genesis. *Bulletin of the Mineral Research and Exploration Institute of Turkey (Ankara, Foreign Edition)* 72:74–96.

Miller, H. M.-L.
|2005| Comparing Landscapes of Transportation: Riverine-Oriented And Land-Oriented Systems in the Indus Civilization and the Mughal Empire. In *Space and Spatial Analysis in Archaeology*, edited by E. C. Robertson, J. D. Seibert, D. C. Fernandez, and M. U. Zender, pp. 281–291. University of Calgary Press, Calgary, Alberta.

Nissen, H.
|1988| *The Early History of the Near East: 9000–2000 B.C.* University of Chicago Press, Chicago.

Oates, D.
|1968| *Studies in the Ancient History of Northern Iraq*. Oxford University Press, London.

Ochsenschlager, E.
|1992| Ethnographic Evidence for Wood, Boats, Bitumen and Reeds in Southern Iraq: Ethnoarchaeology at al-Hiba. In *Trees and Timber in Mesopotamia*, edited by J. N. Postgate, and M. A. Powell. Bulletin on Sumerian Agriculture 6. Eisenbrauns, Warsaw, Indiana.

Parpola, A., and P. Koskikallio (editors)
|1993| *South Asian Archaeology 1993*. AASF Ser B 271, Helsinki.

Pollock, S.
|1990| Political Economy As Viewed From the Garbage Dump: Jemdet Nasr Occupation At The Uruk Mound, Abu Salabikh. *Paléorient* 16(1):57–75.
|1992| Bureaucrats and Managers, Peasants and Pastoralists, Imperialists and Traders: Research on the Uruk and Jemdet Nasr Periods in Mesopotamia. *Journal of World Prehistory* 6:297–336.

Potts, D. T.
|1997| *Mesopotamian Civilization: The Material Foundations*. Cornell University Press, Ithaca.

Safar, F., M. A. Mustafa, and S. Lloyd
|1981| *Eridu*. Republic of Iraq, Ministry of Culture and Information, State Organization of Antiquities and Heritage, Baghdad.

Schwartz, M., and D. Hollander
|2000| Annealing, Distilling, Reheating and Recycling: Bitumen Processing in the Ancient Near East. *Paléorient* 26(2):83–91.

Schwartz, M., D. Hollander, and G. Stein
|1999| Reconstructing Mesopotamian Exchange Networks in the 4th Millennium BC: Geochemical and Archaeological Analyses of Bitumen Artifacts from Hacinebi Tepe, Turkey. *Paléorient* 25(1):67–82.

Stein, G.
|1999| *Rethinking World-Systems*. The University of Arizona Press, Tucson.

Stein, G., and A. Misir
|1994| Mesopotamian-Anatolian Interaction at Hacinebi, Turkey: Preliminary Report on the 1992 Excavations. *Anatolica* 20:145–189.

Stein, G., R. Bernbeck, C. Coursey, A. McMahon, N. F. Miller, A. Misir, J. Nicola, H. Pittman, S. Pollock, and H. Wright
|1996| Uruk Colonies and Anatolian Communities: An Interim Report on the 1992–1993 Excavations at Hacinebi, Turkey. *American Journal of Archaeology* 100:205–260.

Thesiger, W.
|1964| *The Marsh Arabs*. Longmans, Green and Co., London.

Tosi, M., and S. Cleuziou
|1994| Black Boats of Magan: Some Thoughts on Bronze Age Water Transport in Oman and beyond from the Impressed Bitumen Slabs of Ra's al-Junayz. In *South Asian Archaeology 1993*, edited by A. Parpola, and P. Koskikallio, pp. 745–761. AASF Ser B 271, Helsinki.

Tykot, R.
|2003| Determining the Source of Lithic Artifacts and Reconstructing Trade in the Ancient World. In *Written in Stone: The Multiple Dimensions of Lithic Analysis*, edited by P.N. Kardulias, and R. Yerkes. Lexington Books, Lanham, Maryland.

Tzalas, H. E.
|1995| On the Obsidian Trail: With a Papyrus Craft in the Cyclades. In *Tropis III: 3rd International Symposium On Ship Construction in Antiquity*. Hellenic Institute for the Preservation of Nautical Tradition, Athens.

Vosmer, T.
|2000| Ships in the Ancient Arabian Sea: The Development of a Hypothetical Reed Boat Model. *Proceedings of the Seminar for Arabian Studies* 30:235–242.

Waples, D. W.
|1987| *Introduction to Petroleum Geochemistry*. Society for Sedimentary Geology, Tulsa.

Weiss, H.
|1994| Archaeology in Syria. *American Journal of Archaeology* 98:111–112.

Wright, H.
|1986| Evolution of Civilizations. In *American Archaeology Past and Future*, edited by D. Meltzer, D. Fowler, and J. Sabloff, pp. 323–365. Smithsonian Institution, Washington, D.C.

Wright, H., and G. Johnson
|1975| Population, Exchange and Early State Formation in Southwestern Iran. *American Anthropologist* 77:267–289.

PART VII: TEXTUAL AND ICONOGRAPHIC APPROACHES

WEAVING SPACE: TEXTILE IMAGERY AND LANDSCAPE IN THE MIXTEC CODICES

Sharisse D. McCafferty and Geoffrey G. McCafferty

Sharisse D. McCafferty, Department of Archaeology, University of Calgary, 2500 University Drive N.W., Calgary, Alberta T2N 1N4, Canada.
Geoffrey G. McCafferty, Department of Archaeology, University of Calgary, 2500 University Drive N.W., Calgary, Alberta T2N 1N4, Canada.

ABSTRACT

Mixtec pictorial manuscripts from Late Postclassic Oaxaca represent textiles as costume but also in relation to both the natural and built environments. This paper relates these apparently anomalous images to accounts of the mythical weaving of sacred landscapes. Weaving metaphors become important for interpreting emic concepts of the sacred landscape and, based on the engendered quality of costume elements and of spinning and weaving as stereotypically female practice, add a gendered worldview to Mixtec ideology. We suggest that by representing the natural landscape as "woven," the Mixtec brought it into the cultural realm, and therefore claimed control over natural forces.

Pictorial manuscripts from late pre-Conquest and early Colonial Oaxaca, Mexico – known as Mixtec codices after the cultural group that produced them – contain important historical as well as cultural information. Most scholarly interpretations of these manuscripts focus on their genealogical information as a means of constructing culture histories (e.g., Anders et al. 1992; Caso 1979), or the continuity of ideas into modern folk traditions (e.g., Jansen 1990; Jansen and Pérez Jiménez 2000; Monaghan 1990). More archaeologically oriented research considers the activities of the codex actors as a window onto past cultural behaviour, and the objects depicted as contextually meaningful material culture (e.g., McCafferty and McCafferty 1994). At the 2000 Chacmool Conference we adopted this latter perspective in a costume analysis of over 3,100 individuals as a step toward inferring such social identities as gender, occupation and ethnicity (McCafferty and McCafferty 2000). That analysis included not only a typology of the clothing items themselves, but also a detailed catalogue of the design elements used on each clothing category.

In the course of that analysis, we began to notice textiles and textile patterns that were used in non-costume situations, particularly as design elements on the façades of buildings and on elements of the natural environment (e.g., hills). In this spin-off of the initial study, we will characterize the use of textile imagery in these situations, and suggest what this may reveal about the emic conceptualization of the built and natural environments by the Postclassic Mixtec.

"Mixtec" describes a cultural group that speaks an Oto-Manguean language, Mixtec, and occupies the western portion of the modern state of Oaxaca, as well as sections of the adjoining states of Guerrero and Puebla. The Mixtec region extends from Pacific coastal tropics to high mountains with many small, temperate valleys in which, during the Postclassic period (ca. 900–1520 C.E.), numerous autonomous city-states existed (Byland and Pohl 1994; Spores 1967). The few Mixtec codices that survive relate mythological and historical details of the Postclassic period (Jansen 1992; Troike 1978). Archaeological investigations, primarily in the form of settlement pattern surveys (e.g., Byland 1980; Spores 1972), provide additional information. Unfortunately, little excavation of Postclassic architecture has occurred, so archaeological support for the codical patterns is scarce. Michael Lind (1979) did expose architectural decoration associated with elite residential structures in the Nochixtlan Valley. Outside of the Mixteca, the Valley of Oaxaca site of Mitla features standing architecture with possible textile patterns in stone mosaic on the building façades (Hamann 1997; Pohl 1999).

The Mixtec codices provide a wide range of imagery, including marriage scenes, births, military

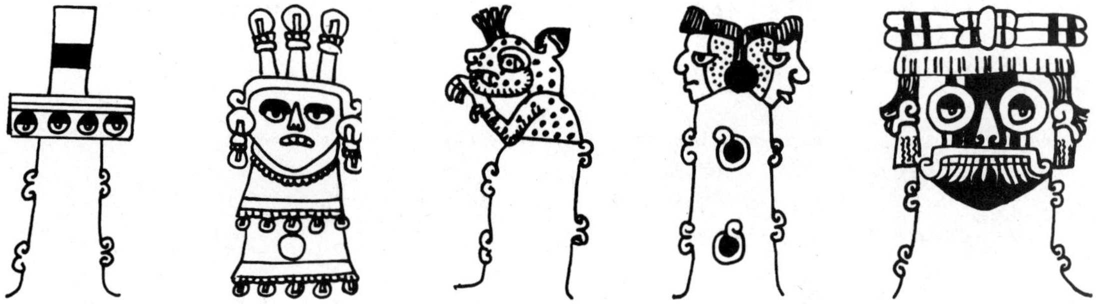

Figure 1. Hills in the *Codex Vindobonensis* (1992:9–10): (a) hill with star band; (b) hill with jewelled woman; (c) hill of jaguar; (d) hill with dual faces; (e) hill with storm god.

Figure 2. (a) Anthropomorphic hill with pregnant belly and arms (*Codex Nuttall* 1992:82); (b) anthropomorphic hill beating drum (*Codex Nuttall* 1992:73).

campaigns, religious rituals and political machinations, among others. Interspersed among these actions are landscape elements, both natural and artificial, such as hills, plains, rivers, temples and ball courts. Often these feature iconographic elements used as toponyms to name the place of the social action. Standardized symbols, described by Mary Elizabeth Smith (1973), provide identifying traits for the geographic features. Further elements serve to name the sites. For example, in the *Codex Vindobonensis* (1992:9–10) a range of twelve hills are decorated with naming elements, including human and animal heads, a fully clothed mannequin with mask, and a storm god face (Figure 1).

On numerous occasions, places in the natural environment are identified with anthropomorphic traits. For example, in the *Codex Nuttall* (1992:82) there is a hill that features bent arms and legs, and a distended abdomen suggesting pregnancy (Figure 2a). Again in the *Codex Nuttall* (1992:73) a hill with head, hands and feet sings while beating a drum and holding a rattle (Figure 2b). Anthropomorphic landscapes complement the many zoomorphic elements also found throughout the codices, suggesting a conceptualization of the natural landscape as having lifelike qualities. This is discussed in detail in John Monaghan's ethnographic studies (1995), where the people of Nu'yoo in the Mixteca Alta recognize a range of anthropomorphic earth spirits, known as *ñuhu*.

In addition to the zoomorphic and anthropomorphic elements that appear on landscape elements, other patterns are typically used, including interlocked diamonds and dots, and groupings of perpendicular lines. These are characteristic textile patterns, suggesting that some aspects of the natural landscape were conceptualized metaphorically as woven. Weaving was considered a female task in many pre-Columbian cultures (McCafferty and McCafferty 1991), and was also linked metaphorically to sexual reproduction (Sullivan

Figure 3. (a) Diamond-and-dot pattern on hill with cave (*Codex Selden* 1964:1); (b) diamond-and-dot pattern on hill with architectural feature (*Codex Egerton/Sanchez Solis* 1994:31).

Figure 4. Woman's skirt with diamond-and-dot pattern (*Codex Egerton/Sanchez Solis* 1994:13).

1982). The process of transforming raw materials such as cotton or maguey into a highly cultured good (i.e., cloth) was an important symbol of "civilization," and distinction between clothed and unclothed was used by the Aztecs to critique their barbarian cousins from the wild north. We suggest that by clothing the landscape, Mixtecs were bringing it into the domain of culture.

The interlocked diamond-and-dot pattern is known to weavers as the "point twill" motif, defined as "a straight twill that reverses direction at intervals" (Strickler 1991:25). In the codices it usually occurs on mountains or plains. For example, in the opening scene of the *Codex Selden* (1964:1) a cavernous mountain (with a head in the cave) is covered by the diamond-and-dot pattern (Figure 3a). This pattern occurs often in the *Codex Egerton/Sanchez Solis* (1994), usually with an architectural element on top of the hill (Figure 3b). It is also the most common decorative motif on women's skirts in the *Codex Egerton/Sanchez Solis* (Figure 4). In fact, in our costume analysis (McCafferty and McCafferty 2000) this motif only occurs on female costume elements such as skirts and upper body garments such as *huipiles* and *quechquemitls*.

Patricia Anawalt (1990, 1998) identifies a blue variant of this motif in relation to Toltec identity, and infers its use by later Aztec nobles as a symbolic claim to Toltec ancestry and, thereby, legitimacy. The pattern occurs on a wide variety of objects, including ceramic vessels in the Nahua *Codex Borgia* of the Puebla-Tlaxcala region, where the pattern might better be interpreted as simply implying preciosity (Chadwick and MacNeish 1967), perhaps relating to the jade *chalchihuites*. The restricted use in Mixtec manuscripts suggests that this meaning should not apply to our case.

Panels of interlocking half diamonds (i.e., triangles), often with dots or small squares, are a common motif especially in the *Codex Nuttall* (1992). The motif

Figure 5. Lord 7 Lizard on hill decorated with plaited twill motif (*Codex Selden* 1964:11–3).

Figure 6. Tree birth scene with plaited twill motif on trunk (*Codex Vindobonensis* 1992:37–2).

occurs alone to indicate a plain, or as a panel on hill glyphs. It is also a common element on architectural façades, to be discussed below. The panel of interlocking triangles is identified by Smith (1973:38–39) by the Mixtec term *ñuu*, meaning "city" in much the same way as the Nahuatl *tollan*. On costumes, the pattern occurs as a decorative border element on men's upper body garments.

The second textile pattern that shows up often on the natural landscape consists of groupings of parallel lines that abut at right angles, or nearly right angles, with others. This pattern is known as a "plaited twill," defined as "a weave in which opposing diagonal lines seem to interlace or braid with each other" (Strickler 1991:100). In the Mixtec codices it appears on mountains, plains, and even in the water and on a flowering tree depicted as part of a supernatural birth. For example, in the *Codex Selden* (1964:11–3) a man named 7 Lizard sits on the lower slope of a hill glyph identified by a long thin textile, probably a male loincloth. The body of the hill is decorated with the plaited twill pattern (Figure 5). The same pattern occurs where two individuals sit in a body of water bounded by a feathered serpent (*Codex Selden*1964:1–2). Note that parallel scenes appear in the *Codex Nuttall* (1992) and *Codex Vindobonensis* (1992) but without the plaited twill pattern, suggesting that the pattern is not necessary to the story (the plaited twill does appear in other contexts in these codices).

A famous scene from the *Codex Vindobonensis* (1992:37–2) depicts a split tree, whose base is in the form of a female head (Figure 6). Two individuals are using hafted tools to score the tree trunk, which is split open and a naked man emerges from the split. The tree trunk is decorated with the plaited twill pattern, and further elaborated with arrows on the right side and perforated disks, perhaps spindle whorls, on the left. Elsewhere we have discussed the structural equivalence linking male weapons and female weaving tools (McCafferty and McCafferty 1989).

The use of textile patterns to represent the natural landscape may relate to a Zapotec origin myth in which the landscape was created when supernatural twins stole the weaving tools of the old goddess and threw them down to create mountains in order to obstruct pursuers (Parsons 1936:*222–223*, 324–328; see also McCafferty et al. 1994). A woven landscape is also an important concept among the Huichol, where Stacy Schaefer has observed loom parts that represent landmarks on the peyote pilgrimage (1990). Weaving tools such as battens, spindles and whorls are often carried by powerful women as symbols of their authority over the female domains of creation and procreation (McCafferty and McCafferty 1989, 1991), as

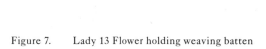

Figure 7. Lady 13 Flower holding weaving batten and spindle (*Codex Nuttall* 1992:19).

Figure 8. Temple with plaited twill motif on façade (*Codex Nuttall* 1992:78–3).

demonstrated in the representation of Lady 13 Flower in the *Codex Nuttall* (1992:19), where the goddess associated with sexuality and textile production carries a spindle with whorl and spun thread along with a batten (Figure 7). Spinning and weaving tools were also important components of Tomb 7 at Monte Albán and Tomb 1 at Zaachila, where the highly ornamented carved bones served as effigy tools as well as symbols of female power (Hamann 1997; McCafferty and McCafferty 1994).

Textile patterns also occur as decorative elements on the façades of buildings. In some cases they are similar to the motifs already discussed, such as the plaited and point twills. For example, in the *Codex Nuttall* (1992:78–3) a temple with a long staircase features the plaited twill pattern in red and white on the pyramidal base, and also on two levels of the temple wall (Figure 8). The base also has three gold-coloured disks in a horizontal line. Two solid-coloured bands with a third band of alternating black and white appear both at the top and bottom of the base. This border is very typical of woven garments in the codices, with the alternating black-and-white panel representing the fringe at the base of a woven textile where the warp strings are tied off (e.g., *Codex Nuttall* 1992:12–1; *Codex Vindobonensis* 1992:12–1). Another fringe element appears around the roof of the temple. As mentioned previously, the plaited twill pattern is a consistently female design element, as are the fringe styles.

The diamond-and-dot/point twill motif is less common as an architectural design (e.g., *Codex Nuttall* 1992:19a). On the other hand, the interlocked triangles that represent half diamonds are quite common. In the *Códice Alfonso Caso* (1996:36) a sacrificial victim stands on a small platform with *talud-tablero* construction (Figure 9). The vertical *tablero* features interlocked triangles within a frame of two coloured bands. A staircase in the centre of the platform features a balustrade on either side, painted with red lines on a white background. The red-on-white pattern is often reproduced on costume cloth, for example in the *Codex Vindobonensis* (1992:9), where a woman sits spinning with a skirt of identical pattern.

The *Codex Selden* features two complex place signs that incorporate a motif of a large dot surrounded by smaller dots, a pattern that is also found on priestly upper body garments. In the *Codex Selden* (1964:2–1) a man and woman sit on a woven mat in front of a temple in a walled courtyard (Figure 10). The courtyard is depicted with the dot motif and a red swirl motif that may represent a spring or a well. In the *Codex Selden* (1964:9–3) a temple with a sweatbath rests on a hill with a cave monster. The background, probably representing the floor of the temple compound, uses the

Figure 9. Sacrificial victim on temple platform decorated with interlocked triangles of point twill motif (*Códice Alfonso Caso* 1996:36).

Figure 10. Man and woman in courtyard decorated with concentric dot motif (*Codex Selden* 1964:2–1).

Figure 11. a) Lord 10 Monkey wearing upper body garment with concentric dot motif (*Codex Selden* 1964:14–3); b) mountain impersonator wearing cloth decorated with concentric dot motif (*Codex Nuttall* 1992:15–2).

Figure 12. a) Temple with cloth decorated with flint knife motif (*Codex Vindobonensis* 1992:9); b) Lady 8 Movement's skirt with flint knife motif (*Codex Nuttall* 1992:35–2).

Figure 13. a) Stepped fret motif on the Temple of the Ascending Serpent (*Codex Nuttall* 1992:15–2); b) stepped fret motif on priestly cloak (*Codex Nuttall* 1992:25–2); c) male loin-cloth decorated with triangle and hatch marks (*Codex Nuttall* 1992:79–4).

dot pattern. An example of this pattern on costumes includes Lord 10 Monkey, who wears a priestly upper body garment decorated with the dot pattern while incensing a divine bundle at a temple at Jaltepec in the *Codex Selden* (1964:14–3; Figure 11a). Similar priestly garments appear in *Codex Nuttall* 25–1 and 25–2 (1992). The pattern also occurs on a cloth covering for a mountain impersonator in *Codex Nuttall* 15–2 (1992), where Lady 3 Flint Shell Quechquemitl offers incense and holds a weaving pick (Figure 11b).

Other architectural features with costume elements include a temple in the *Codex Vindobonensis* (1992:9) with a "garment" hung from the back wall like a cape (Figure 12a). The garment is decorated with flint knife motifs, coloured bands, and a fringe with more knives. Flint knives appear on both male and female costumes, as on the skirt of Lady 8 Movement in the *Codex Nuttall* (1992:35–2; Figure 12b).

The temple roof in *Codex Nuttall* 26–3 (1992) is decorated with a panel of curved frets. The stepped fret, known as a *xicalcoliuhqui*, appears as a panel on the lower portion of the Temple of the Ascending Serpent in *Codex Nuttall* 15–2 (1992; Figure 13a). A similar fret pattern appears on a priestly cloak in *Codex Nuttall* 25–2 (1992; Figure 13b). The *xicalcoliuhqui* motif probably represents the profile of a cut conch shell, and was the symbol of the wind god Ehecatl, an avatar of Quetzalcoatl. This temple also features the half-diamond-and-dot motif and a panel of concentric circles, another pattern which occurs on the borders of female and male costumes. The balustrade of the staircase has another red-on-white decoration, as discussed above. The *tablero* at the top of the balustrade features a red triangle surrounded by small hatch marks, a pattern found on male loin cloths such as that of 4 Jaguar in *Codex Nuttall* 79–4 (1992; Figure 13c).

DISCUSSION

Elements of the natural and built environment are decorated with textile patterns and decorative motifs identical to those found on human costumes. Major design elements such as the twill patterns are embellished with specific designs, and contextualized as costume through the addition of border and fringe elements. In *Codex Nuttall* 79–3 (1992) two males kneel on a temple platform that is shown frontally with decoration including borders and fringes and even a neck hole as if the entire structure was arrayed in clothing (Figure 14).

Pyramids were conceptualized as artificial mountains, as at Cholula where the Great Pyramid is known literally as Tlachihualtepetl, "man-made mountain" (McCafferty 2001). Maya pyramids were known as *witz*, again the name used to indicate mountains. In Nahuatl, the language of the Aztecs, pyramid platforms were known as *cue*, a derivative of the word for skirt, *cueitl*. The slopes of a mountain are known in

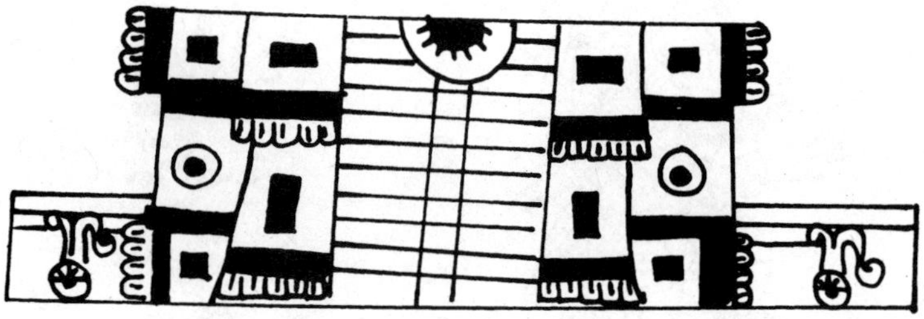

Figure 14. Temple platform with costume-like borders, fringes and neck hole (*Codex Nuttall* 1992:79–3).

Mexican Spanish as the *faldas*, or skirts, and one of the major mountains of the Puebla area, now known as La Malinche, was originally called Matlalcueye, "lady of the blue-green skirt," because of the forested slopes below the tree line. The use of textile patterns to cover the slopes of mountains and pyramids in the Mixtec codices continues this metaphoric description of natural and constructed space.

Recent anthropological studies of the Mesoamerican worldview indicate a belief that the natural environment was alive, and that through dedication rituals the built landscape could also be imbued with symbolic life (Mock 1998). By dressing the landscape, its lifelike characteristics were recognized. Moreover, by clothing it in textiles, it was incorporated into the cultural world, and was therefore subject to control. For Mesoamerican nobility the claim of control over natural and supernatural forces was an important condition of their legitimacy. Specialized knowledge such as calendrical systems to control time and predict weather was among the distinguishing factors that separated nobles from commoners. The construction of artificial mountains was used to establish a centre as an *axis mundi*, a symbolically charged site from which the nobles exerted control. The Mixtecs characterized mountains and temples using textile metaphors that animated them, bringing these elements into the cultural domain under the control of the nobility. Finally, since textiles and their production were culturally perceived as gendered goods, the practice of clothing the built and natural landscape may be seen as engendering space by emphasizing the female practice of bringing order to nature (see Klein 1982; McCafferty and McCafferty 1996).

REFERENCES CITED

Anawalt, Patricia R.
|1990| The Emperor's Cloak: Aztec Pomp, Toltec Circumstance. *American Antiquity* 55:291–307.
|1998| Knotted and Netted Capes: Colonial Interpretations vs. Indigenous Primary Data. *Ancient Mesoamerica* 7:187–200.

Anders, F., M. Jansen, and A. G. Pérez Jiménez
|1992| *Crónica mixteca: El rey 8 Venado, Garra de Jaguar, y la dinastía de Teozacualco-Zaachila.* Sociedad Estatal Quinto Centario, Spain, Akademische Druck-und Verlaganstalt, Austria, and Fondo de Cultura Económica, Mexico.

Byland, B. E.
|1980| *Political and Economic Evolution in the Tamazulapan Valley, Mixteca Alta, Oaxaca, Mexico.* Ph.D. dissertation, Pennsylvania State University. University Microfilms, Ann Arbor.

Byland, B. E., and J. M. D. Pohl
|1994| *In the Realm of 8 Deer: The Archaeology of the Mixtec Codices.* University of Oklahoma Press, Norman.

Caso, A.
|1979| *Reyes y reinos de la mixteca, vol. II: Diccionario biográfico de los señores mixtecos.* Fondo de Cultura Económica, Mexico, D.F.

Chadwick, R., and R. S. MacNeish
|1967| *Codex Borgia* and the Venta Salada Phase. In *The Prehistory of the Tehuacan Valley: Environment and Subsistence*, vol. 1, edited by D. S. Byers, pp. 114–131. University of Texas Press, Austin.

Codex Egerton/Sanchez Solis
|1994| *Codex Egerton.* Facsimile with introduction and commentary by M. Jansen. Akademische Druck-und Verlagsanstalt, Austria, and Fondo de Cultura Económica, Mexico.

Codex Nuttall
|1992| *Códice Zouche-Nuttall.* Facsimile with introduction and explanation by F. Anders, M. Jansen, and G. A. Pérez Jiménez. Sociedad Estatal Quinto Centenario, Spain, Akademische Druck-und Verlaganstalt, Austria, and Fondo de Cultura Económica, Mexico.

Codex Selden 3135 (A.2)
|1964| *Codex Selden.* Facsimile with commentary by A. Caso. Sociedad Mexicana de Antropología, Mexico.

Codex Vindobonensis
|1992| *Códice Vindobonensis.* Facsimile with introduction and explanation by F. Anders, M. Jansen, and G. A. Pérez Jiménez. Sociedad Estatal Quinto Centenario, Spain, Akademische Druck-und Verlagsanstalt, Austria, and Fondo de Cultura Económica, Mexico.

Códice Alfonso Caso
|1996| *Códice Alfonso Caso: La vida de 8-Venado, Garra de Tigre (Colombino-Becker I).* Facsimile with introduction by M. L. Portilla and interpretation by A. Caso. Patronato Indígena, AC, Mexico, D.F.

Hamann, B.
|1997| Weaving and the Iconography of Prestige: The Royal Gender Symbolism of Lord 5 Flower's/Lady 4 Rabbit's Family. In *Women in Prehistory: North America and Mesoamerica*, edited by C. Claassen, and R. A. Joyce, pp. 153–172. University of Pennsylvania Press, Philadelphia.

Jansen, M.
|1990| The Search for History in the Mixtec Codices. *Ancient Mesoamerica* 1:99–112.
|1992| Mixtec Pictography: Conventions and Contents. In *Handbook of Middle American Indians, Supplement 5*, edited by V. R. Bricker with the assistance of P.A. Andrews, pp. 20–33. University of Texas Press, Austin.

Jansen, M., and G. A. Pérez Jiménez
|2000| *La dinastía de Añute: Historia, literature, e ideología de un reino mixteco*. Research School of Asian, African and Amerindian Studies (CNWS), Leiden University, Leiden.

Klein, C. F.
|1982| Woven Heaven, Tangled Earth: A Weaver's Paradigm of the Mesoamerican Cosmos. In *Ethnoastronomy and Archaeoastronomy in the American Tropics*, edited by A. F. Aveni, and G. Urton, pp. 1–35. Annals of the New York Academy of Sciences, vol. 385. New York Academy of Sciences, New York.

Lind, M. D.
|1979| *Postclassic and Early Colonial Mixtec Houses in the Nochixtlan Valley, Oaxaca*. Vanderbilt University Publications in Anthropology No. 23. Vanderbilt University, Nashville.

McCafferty, G. G.
|2001| Mountain of Heaven, Mountain of Earth: The Great Pyramid of Cholula as Sacred Landscape. In *Landscape and Power in Ancient Mesoamerica*, edited by R. Koontz, K. Reese-Taylor, and A. Headrick, pp. 279–316. Westview Press, Boulder, Colorado.

McCafferty, S. D., and G. G. McCafferty
|1989| Weapons of Resistance: Material Metaphors of Gender Identity in Postclassic Mexico. Paper presented at the 88th Annual Meeting of the American Anthropological Association, Washington, D.C.
|1991| Spinning and Weaving as Female Gender Identity in Post-Classic Central Mexico. In *Textile Traditions of Mesoamerica and the Andes: An Anthology*, edited by M. Schevill, J. C. Berlo, and E. Dwyer, pp. 19–44. Garland, New York.
|1994| Engendering Tomb 7 at Monte Albán, Oaxaca: Respinning an Old Yarn. *Current Anthropology* 35:143–166.
|1996| As the Whorl Turns: Spinning and Weaving as Metaphors for Female World-View. Paper presented at the 95th Annual Meeting of the American Anthropological Association, San Francisco.
|2000| Tricky *Traje*: Mixtec Costume as Symbolic Communication. Paper presented at the 33rd Annual Chacmool Conference, Calgary, Alberta.

McCafferty, G. G., S. D. McCafferty, and B. Hamann
|1994| Powerful Women of Pre-Columbian Oaxaca. Paper presented at the 93rd Annual Meeting of the American Anthropological Association, Atlanta, Georgia.

Mock, S. B.
|1998| Prelude. In *The Sowing and the Dawning: Termination, Dedication, and Transformation in the Archaeological and Ethnographic Record of Mesoamerica*, edited by S. B. Mock, pp. 3–18. University of New Mexico Press, Albuquerque.

Monaghan, J.
|1990| Sacrifice, Death, and the Origins of Agriculture in the *Codex Vienna*. *American Antiquity* 55:559–569.
|1995| *The Covenants with Earth and Rain: Exchange, Sacrifice, and Revelation in Mixtec Society*. University of Oklahoma Press, Norman.

Parsons, E. C.
|1936| *Mitla: Town of the Souls and Other Zapotec-Speaking Pueblos of Oaxaca, Mexico*. University of Chicago Press, Chicago.

Pohl, J. M. D.
|1999| Lintel Paintings of Mitla and the Function of the Mitla Palaces. In *Mesoamerican Architecture as a Cultural Symbol*, edited by J. Kowalski, pp 176–197. Oxford University Press, Oxford.

Schaefer, S. B.
|1990| Loom and Time in the Huichol World. *Journal of Latin American Lore* 15(2):179–194.

Smith, M. E.
|1973| *Picture Writing from Ancient Southern Mexico*. University of Oklahoma Press, Norman.

Spores, R.
|1967| *The Mixtec Kings and Their People*. University of Oklahoma Press, Norman.
|1972| *An Archaeological Settlement Survey of the Nochixtlan Valley, Oaxaca*. Vanderbilt University Publications in Anthropology No. 1. Vanderbilt University, Nashville.

Strickler, C. (editor)
|1991| *A Weaver's Book of 8-Shaft Patterns: From the Friends of HANDWOVEN*. Interweave Press, Loveland, Colorado.

Sullivan, T.
|1982| Tlazolteotl-Ixcuina: The Great Spinner and Weaver. In *The Art and Iconography of Late Post-Classic Central Mexico*, edited by E. H. Boone, pp. 7–36. Dumbarton Oaks, Washington, D.C.

Troike, N. P.
|1978| Fundamental Changes in the Interpretation of the Mixtec Codices. *American Antiquity* 43:553–568.

ENGENDERING ROMAN SPACES

Penelope M. Allison

Penelope M. Allison, School of Archaeology and Anthropology, Australian National University, Canberra, ACT 0200, Australia.

ABSTRACT

This paper introduces a research project which is contributing to a more gendered understanding of Roman space. Two types of sites – Roman houses and Roman military forts – provide the archaeological contexts for two different case studies. The project engages with feminist theory to provide frameworks for contextualizing gender roles within Roman spaces. The main theoretical perspective is that the material conditions (i.e., architectural and other forms of material culture) facilitate the negotiation of gender, age and status distinctions. The archaeological record provides the spatial signatures of these processes, recognized in the organization and characteristics of the material remains. This paper samples some of the results from Pompeian houses and from the military fort of Vetera I on the Lower Rhine.

This paper addresses the theoretical and methodological frameworks for a research project entitled "Engendering Roman Spaces." The objective of the project is to contribute to a gendered history of the Roman world through the analysis of its material-cultural remains. This means using archaeological approaches to Roman material culture for a more holistic understanding of the nature and functioning of Roman society in its relationship to space. It also means a closer engagement with feminist scholarship for studies of Roman space, and more critical analyses of the use of ancient written sources to provide processes for contextualizing gender roles within space.

With a tradition of scholarship founded on nineteenth-century concepts of empire and colonialism (Freeman 1997; Hingley 2000), investigations of the Roman world have conventionally been concerned with the representation of masculine power. The biases of ancient authors and of past investigators, both predominantly male elites, have also had a major impact on the types of research into this world. The visual impact of the physical remains of Roman architectural and engineering feats, of Roman roads, armies and trading networks have fuelled the concentration of much archaeological scholarship on the "maleness" of this world. This, in turn, has led scholars in other disciplines to conceptualize a Roman world which epitomizes "manliness" and "masculine values and virtues, those of the military man and the administrator" (Lefebvre 1991:249).

Roman historians, notably Australian ones (Dixon 1988, 1992, 2001; Rawson 1986, 1991; Rawson and Weaver 1997), have been concerned with redressing the balance, and with focusing on Roman women and families towards more rounded views of Roman society. The most widely used evidence for such research is representations of women in ancient texts – texts that are predominantly written from a male viewpoint. More recently, inscriptions and works of art, particularly sculpture and papyri, have also been used as less biased resources (Fantham et al. 1994; Kleiner and Matheson 1996; Koloski-Ostrow 1997; Phang 2001). However, attempts to use a wider range of contextualized Roman material culture (e.g., architecture, pottery, household objects) for more engendered perspectives of Roman society have generally been untheorized, using material-cultural evidence as the setting for the textual, rather than as independent information.

One of the principal issues for the archaeological discipline, more broadly, is the gender-marking of activities that once took place in the material conditions, now represented by the archaeological record. The main theoretical perspective of my project is that these material conditions facilitate the negotiation of gender, age and status distinctions. The archaeological record provides the spatial signatures of these historical processes, recognized in the organization and the characteristics of these material remains.

The combination of the written and material evidence from the Roman world provides a much richer resource than is available for most other branches of the archaeological discipline. A principal significance of this project is its demonstration that much can be learnt about past societies through more theorized and sophisticated approaches to their material culture and to the relationships between history and archaeology (see Dyson 1995; Storey 1998). While written sources can assist in the reading of material culture, they are not always the appropriate tools with which to direct that reading. Material culture is both an indicator of social behaviour and an active agent in social relations. Gender relations may be played out as spatial distinctions between activity areas, rights of access, and the orientation and distribution of people in private and communal gatherings. Written texts predominantly project the male, usually elite, voice. Females and non-elite males were also both viewers and active participants in the production and utilization of material culture and space.

To quote Bernard Knapp (1998:32), "[A]n archaeology informed by feminism...looks critically at theories of human action and uses archaeological data to challenge existing structures of knowledge." An engagement with feminist theory "can help to balance objectivism against extreme relativism, and to realize a more encompassing archaeology that acknowledges contexts, contingencies and ambiguities" (Knapp 1998:34). Much work has been carried out in other branches of archaeology to engender the past (e.g., Bacus et al. 1993; Gilchrist 1999). However, there has been criticism that few so-called feminist archaeological publications have engaged directly with feminist theory (Engelstad 1999). Shelby Brown (1997:14) noted that "classical archaeologists continue to avoid feminist theory" and Louise Zarmatti (1994:773) observed the lack of articles on classical archaeology in Bacus et al. (1993). While art-historical studies of the classical world have developed more feminist approaches, little attention has been paid to a rigorous engendering of the kinds of remains found in archaeological contexts of the Roman period (although see Scott 1999 for infant burials).

Fundamental to the theoretical design of this project is that it is grounded in the aspects of feminist scholarship that are appropriate to its objectives and to its dataset. Of particular importance is the awareness that gender has been theorized as a social construct, that it is not inherent in archaeological data (Roberts 1993:16), and that a feminist perspective is not a more objective reconstruction of the past but rather an alternative perspective.[1] Awareness that twentieth- and twenty-first-century perspectives have their own biases is equally important.

The basic premise that gendered relations are constituted in historically specific ways means that particular categories of material cannot be assumed to have always carried a particular engendered value without detailed consideration of the assumptions being deployed in that reasoning. Consequently, this project operates on four levels:

- to critically evaluate cross-cultural assumptions normally used to assign gender values to particular categories of Roman material culture;
- to establish the relevant evidence from the sources and to use each source to critically interrogate the other, rather than simply to confirm one another;
- to establish the procedures needed to use architectural organization and material residues from a large number of different archaeological contexts to investigate for the spatial patterning of behaviour;
- to critically evaluate the extent to which regional distinctions cross-cut more general empire-wide trends of engendered identities and the extent to which such regional processes disrupt attempts to integrate the various kinds of evidence.

The samples used in this paper concern the first three levels.

PROCEDURES AND METHODOLOGIES

The excavated remains of two types of sites that are emblematic of Roman spaces provide the archaeological contexts for different case studies. These are domestic space and military space.

Principal concerns are the archaeological and historical visibility of the roles of women in these institutions, as well as the roles of other groups who are also less evident in more traditional readings (e.g., children, slaves, non-soldiers, etc.). The project takes a critical approach to the interrelationships of textual remains and the archaeological record, concentrating on the ways in which activities are both segregated and integrated spatially. This highlights the fluidity of gender relationships in a world that was male dominated in theory but more complex in practice. The rich textual and artistic resources from the Roman world render these approaches more complex for Roman archaeology than for prehistoric and early historical archaeology, but at the same time more rewarding. A rigorous, engendered analysis of the evidence for the spatial and gender distribution of activities in Roman archaeology provides useful cross-cultural analogies for gendering such activities in other past societies.

The main datasets for this project are excavation reports, but also Roman authors, inscriptions and works of art with relevant iconography. As the principal concern is the engendering of material culture, the project involves a critical approach to the way in which activities and gender contexts have been ascribed to Roman material culture in past scholarship. It uses an understanding of the range and nature of material culture found in archaeological contexts, together with those contexts themselves, as the basis from which to investigate relevant textual information on spatial and gender distribution of activities. By this process, these archaeological remains are investigated for the expression of the roles of women and other occupants in the patterning of material culture across the various spaces within these sites.

An essential issue in this project is a comprehension of the concepts of "public" and "private" space in the Roman world, a set of relationships which is inadequate for a more critical perspective on Roman physical remains and social behaviour (see Riggsby 1999:557). Roman houses and military forts are places where people both lived and worked. The language of a dichotomized public/private, in the modern sense, is not appropriate here. This project takes a differently structured approach, investigating ranges of accessibility and inaccessibility, and concepts of gender-marked, status-marked, and unmarked spaces.

CASE STUDIES

Domestic Space

Previous studies of domestic space, particularly, have used material culture, but often merely to illuminate the written sources (e.g., George 1997; Wallace-Hadrill 1994, 1996). Rather than analyzing the relationships between the historical and archaeological records, many studies use the extant remains of Roman dwellings to house analogical, and often anecdotal, literary references. In addition, analogies with the modern world (e.g., Hingley 1993; cf. Gilchrist 1999:especially 34, 113) are often used to produce dichotomies (e.g., public/private, male/female, inside/outside) that are not necessarily appropriate for Roman houses.

For example, Andrew Wallace-Hadrill (1994:11) emphasized Vitruvius' obsessive concerns with social rank and divided the Roman house along public/private and grand/humble axes. To add weight to such divisions he used analogies with houses of the nobility in eighteenth-century France. This analogy is interesting in its potential elucidation of ancient written information on domestic differentiation, but it does not employ the material remains of Roman houses in this elucidation. Rather, it uses the weight of Vitruvius' authority, and behaviour in the French *ancien régime*, to explain behaviour in Roman houses. Such analogies can best be used to explore relationships between modern and ancient behaviours rather than to explain them. Indeed, the physical remains of Pompeian houses – the arrangements of their courtyards, the distribution of wall and floor decoration, the locations for food-preparation and storage, and the distribution patterns of the contents – point to much more complex spatial integration of domestic activities (see Allison 1997a, 2004:124–158; Dunbabin 1995:390).

Since the attention paid to engendering Roman domestic space by other scholars has focused on Pompeian houses (e.g., Laurence and Wallace-Hadrill 1997), this project has commenced with a case study of Pompeian houses. Also, the material remains from Pompeii are useful for assessing the veracity of ascribing gender categories to particular classes of material and to particular spaces, as found in other contexts. For example, mirrors and combs are generally associated with toilet activities and have been "symbolically associated with women" since Greek times (Kampen

1996:22). However, they were also used by males (see Wyke 1994:especially 135–138) and found in assemblages with razors in Pompeii (Rhea Berg, personal communication 2001).

Pompeian Houses

My investigations of artifact assemblages and their spatial distribution in thirty Pompeian *atrium* houses have involved the analyses and collation of old excavation reports to produce computerized catalogues of household artifacts and room assemblages (e.g., Allison 1994, 1995, 1997a, 1997b, 2004, n.d.a). Some 6,000 artifacts from over 800 rooms in thirty Pompeian *atrium* houses have been studied. These datasets were analyzed and interpreted through material-cultural approaches and their relationships to any textual evidence on the use of space in Roman houses assessed. That is, the interpretations of the use of space in Pompeian houses were not driven by the textual evidence, as is more common in Roman archaeology and history (see Allison 2001). Rather these interpretations commenced with a contextual study of the material culture and the results were then examined in relation to textual evidence, which is largely analogical as few texts survive that refer directly to Pompeian houses (although see Pirson 1997:especially 168, 179).

Important to a gendered study of Roman domestic space is an understanding of what can be considered female material and female activities. An industry that is relevant in this regard is cloth production. Gender and status separation of cloth producers and of locations for cloth production in the Roman world has traditionally been based on whether or not the cloth was for household or commercial use (see Ling 1997:180). The term *textor* (e.g., Martial, *Ep.* 12, 59.6; Juvenal, *Sat.* 9, 30) indicates that weaving was an activity engaged in by men as well as by women. However, there is little reason to assume that male involvement was for commercial purposes, taking place in specialist workshops, and that female participation was for domestic purposes only, taking place within the household context (see Dixon 2001:117–125). Evidence from Pompeii appears to indicate that women, whether slave or free, worked in commercial weaving workshops (see Dixon 2001:122). Thus, evidence for weaving is not, of necessity, evidence of the activities of women, but evidence for spinning and perhaps needlework can probably be more securely used as documentation of the presence of female activities, at least within the household (e.g., Deschler-Erb 1998:136–137; Treggiari 1976:82; cf. Allason-Jones 1995:28).

Material evidence for cloth production in Pompeian houses occurred in the form of loom weights, combs and warp-beaters, spindles and spindle whorls, and bronze and bone needles. In the sample of thirty *atrium* houses cloth production-related artifacts occurred in nearly every house (Allison 2004:146–148), their distribution indicating that there were 46 possible locations for this activity throughout these houses (Allison 2004:Table 6.9a). The majority of the evidence was found in the front hall, or *atrium*, but cloth-production artifacts also occurred in small closed rooms off it, the so-called *cubicula*. The evidence in the front hall consisted mainly of that for weaving and that weaving took place in this area. For example, 56 loom weights found in the front hall of House I 10,8 no doubt indicated that a warp-weighted loom had been in use here. Sometimes, however, loom weights were also stored in this area (e.g., in a cupboard in the front hall of the Casa del Sacello Iliaco). Spinning and needlework equipment tended to be found in so-called *cubicula*, the small closed rooms off front halls. This equipment was likely to have been stored in these rooms for use in better lit front halls or possibly garden areas. While cloth-production items were remarkably absent from main garden areas themselves, there was a notable pattern for the presence of weaving, spinning and needlework items in the small closed rooms off them (Allison 2004:Table 6.9a). Such material also occurred in the upper levels and in the areas of the ground floor away from the main front hall-garden axis, but less frequently. Thus, the most likely location for all types of cloth production had been the front hall or *atrium* area, with some perhaps occurring in the garden, but less on upper floors or in what are considered to have been the service areas of the house. This suggests that it had been a highly visible activity and therefore an important part of the "public" activities in the household.

What is not discernible from this study is any distinction between cloth production destined for household use or for distribution outside. Simpson noted (1997:35) that weaving is the task of every household in the Roman world and thus that loom weights give no indication of the economic basis of a site. Ling suggests (1997:180, especially no. 22) that the quantity of loom weights found in the front hall of House I 10,8 was excessive for a domestic loom but, comparable quantities occur in other Pompeian houses (e.g., in the Casa di Principe di Napoli and in House VI 16,26) and are consistent with the presence of a single loom (Wild 1970:61, plates Xa–b, Table M no. 28). There seems little reason to assume that the weights found in the front hall represent anything other than normal domestic activity, at least some of which was likely to have been carried out by women, whether slave or free. In combination with the evidence for spinning and needlework, this suggests that women were actively involved in cloth-production in this most public part of the house.

Also important to a study of gender in Pompeian houses are notions of the dichotomies public /private: male/female, which seem to pervade studies of the ancient world. Such notions can be shown to apply to Greek houses, where female household members could be separated from male guests (Nevett 1999:18–20, 174). Assumptions that Roman houses were organized along similar lines are unvalidated, however. For example, based in Vitruvius' description of a Roman town and country houses (Book VI, 3–7), the front hall, or *atrium*, of a Pompeian house is believed to be a public space, a largely empty and spacious reception area, reserved for the *paterfamilias* to receive his male clients in the mornings (see Leach 1993). Conversely, the colonnaded garden, further into the house, is assumed to be a more private, family, space and the small rooms opening of both these spaces, the so-called *cubicula*, more private still (see Wallace-Hadrill 1994:especially 17). Artifact distribution studies demonstrate that such dichotomies do not adequately explain domestic behaviour in Pompeii. Rather relationships between gender and space in Pompeian houses are more complex. For example, instead of being furnished only with display furniture to impress the visitor, as assumed by most scholars (e.g., Dwyer 1982:113–115), the front hall can be found to have been filled with a great range of household paraphernalia. In particular, most of the thirty houses in the sample had cupboards and chest filled with domestic material (although interestingly not cooking apparatus), as well as evidence for commerce, in the form of amphorae, and for household industries, notably weaving (Allison 2004:65–70). The consistency of this pattern across a number of Pompeian houses demonstrates that the front hall was not the reserve of the male owner and his male visitors, but rather that it was frequented by all who needed to use household equipment, or were involved in activities such as weaving or supplying produce to the house. Rather than being like the foyer in an elite Georgian house, Pompeian front halls were the centre for many household activities and space where all household members could enter and congregate for these activities (see Allison 1997a:349–350). Indeed, both Virgil (*Aeneid* 7:377–389) and Lucretius (4:400–404) depicted children playing in the *atrium*. It may have been the most "public" part of the house, with direct access to the street, but Pompeian householders did not hide their other activities and utilitarian domestic materials, or their women and their children, from the public eye nor prohibit them from using this more public space.

The artifact distribution in the rear garden areas of Pompeian houses is, perhaps surprisingly, similar to that in the front halls. Again, cupboards and chests with domestic contents were found against the walls of the ambulatories. Unlike the assemblages in the front hall area, however, there is evidence that this area was used for eating, and also for cooking in front of the diners (Allison 2004:87–90). While these gardens might be considered to have been more private than the front halls, in that they were further inside the house, the assemblages in these garden areas indicate that they were used by the householders themselves in much the same manner as the front halls. Indeed Vitruvius stated that uninvited people could also enter the peristyles, as well as the front part of the house (Book VI:1, 5).

One aspect of both the front hall and colonnaded garden areas indicates that these public and display areas were also very much part of the more utilitarian functioning of the house. In most Pompeian houses, water could only be collected from these open areas, from well-heads that led to cisterns underneath (see Allison 2004:especially Tables 5.3a, 5.9b). This water was used for display features, particularly in the garden, but most members of the household would have needed to collect water from well-heads in both the garden area and the front hall. This included slaves for utilitarian domestic activities and other household members for their ablutions. Again, the need for access to water by most household members would have meant that they must all have frequented these courtyard areas.

The small rooms off both the front hall and the main garden area, the so-called *cubicula*, were found to contain a higher proportion of more personal items, such as washing equipment and small glass bottles, so-called *unguentaria*, thought to be perfume bottles (see Allison 2004:especially 71–76, 94–98, Table 4.3). However, there is no specific reason to assume that many of the personal items and toiletries were associated with women. For example, the *unguentaria* could have been used by men to take oils to the bath, or for the storage of substances needed for medical treatments (Jackson 1988:especially 74). It is sometimes possible to use association to ascribe them to women, however. In room 2 in the Casa del Fabbro in Pompeii, possibly in a chest, three such bottles were found with two spindles and a bone spoon, suggesting a women's collection (Allison 2004:companion website). In this particular case there would indeed seem to be a link between a more private space and female activity but this specific association pattern is not apparent across the sample. In combination with the evidence in the more open and public courtyard areas, the material evidence suggest rather that women did not have their own spaces or areas of the house (see Allison 2004:156–157; cf. Wallace-Hadrill 1994:9). There is little reason to suggest that the dichotomies public/private: male/female were operative in Pompeian houses.

Laurence has argued (1994:122–132) that there was a temporal distribution of occupancy of Pompeian houses which was based on a binary male/female separation. He argued that the front hall would have been a male space in the early morning and left very much as a female space for the remainder of the day. Certain members of the household undoubtedly vacated it during parts of the day, particularly the *paterfamilias* in his civic and public roles and servants involved in industrial and commercial activities outside the household. The temporal engendering of these spaces needs closer scrutiny. However, such scrutiny is probably not possible through analysis of the material remains, but rather through a critical re-examination of the textual evidence. It seems more reasonable to envisage that the overlap of activities, documented by material remains found particularly in the front halls and in the colonnaded gardens, bore witness to considerable overlap between the various activities which took place there, and also to the simultaneous presence of various household members and outsiders, of diverse ages, gender and status, who performed these activities. To separate the people and the household activities, along the lines suggested by Laurence and without good textual evidence, is to apply nineteenth-century separate spheres' (see e.g., Vickery 1993) ideologies to Roman households. Rather, the evidence suggests that Pompeian houses functioned in a much more integrated fashion than is widely assumed. Feminist readings of ancient authors and of inscriptional evidence indicate that women, both free and slave, were involved in a range of commercial activities outside the home (see Kampen 1981; Dixon 2001:113–132). They also indicate that both men and women were involved in cooking (Foss 1994:47–50), that both men and women dined together (see e.g., Yardley 1991:151–152) and that children could be important members of the household (Rawson 2003).

By adopting a more critical and theorized approach to contextual and gender associations of household material culture, this project demonstrates that the first step in understanding gender relations within Pompeian houses is to investigate the material-cultural patterning. Any mismatch between interpretation of that patterning and current perspectives should not be interpreted as the unreliability of the archaeological remains. Rather it should encourage a re-examination of the origins of such perspectives which often tend to draw too heavily on modern analogy before fully interrogating the contemporary evidence, both the material and the textual.

Military Space

Roman military studies have concentrated on the expression of forts as a male domain, a combat unit at the edge of the civilized world. Studies of the archaeology of Roman military forts have concentrated on the evidence that these forts provide for strategic military constructions and to document Roman power, especially its chronological spread and its relationships with native populations (e.g., Groenman-van Waatringe 1997; Jones 1997:90). However, these sites were both habitation and administrative spaces, involving a whole frontier community. In recent years, therefore, more attention has been paid to the presence of non-military personnel at these sites, particularly in settlements often found outside the fortifications, the so-called *vici* or *canabae* (e.g., Bowman 1994; Goldsworthy and Haynes 1999). Certain textual and inscriptional material has been used as evidence for living conditions (e.g., gravestones and the Vindolanda tablets), and Lindsay Allason-Jones (1989:59, 1995,

1999) has combined skeletal and inscriptional evidence with other artifacts and with spatial arrangements to provide more information on these communities. In general, studies of artifact from within military forts have largely concentrated on military equipment (e.g., Bishop and Coulston 1993; Southern and Dixon 1996:89–126). Pat Southern and Karen Ramsay Dixon (1996:3) noted that pottery "can illustrate the quality of mundane life" but that it is generally employed only as dating evidence. However, some recent studies have concentrated on specific classes of material from forts to document the presence of families, such as the range of sizes of leather shoes (van Driel-Murray 1995). What is largely lacking from all these studies is a more comprehensive contextual analysis of the archaeological record for its documentation of the complexity of army life and of the interactions of its personnel.

Again, feminist critique of current research of Roman military space and archaeological approaches to material-cultural patterning provides a basis for a rigorous investigation of the activities of all occupants of these forts. The data from Roman military sites is being used to assess for similarities and differences of material-cultural patterning within the various architectural spaces of a fort and between forts. In the first instance, the differences that can result from different site formation processes (e.g., rapid abandonment or slow decay), different dates for the excavation, or chronological or geographical differences between sites are assessed. Once such anomalies have been accounted for, relationships between the structural remains and the artifact assemblages are investigated for information on the range and distribution of the activities documented at each site. Thus, this project takes a critical approach to relationships between artifacts and their contexts within these forts, and the range of social activities and social actors with which they may have been associated.

An important issue in this study is the relationship between these material-cultural patterns and the changing laws permitting legal marriages for ordinary soldiers at the end of the second century C.E. (see Phang 2001). Prior to that date, only officers had been permitted to be accompanied by their wives and children while on military duty (see Allason-Jones 1989:50–69). Therefore, only the wives, families and households of officers were thought to have inhabited or frequented the inside of a military fort. All commercial or entertainment activities, in which other women partook, are traditionally believed to have been transacted in the settlement outside the fort proper (see Allason-Jones 1989:60, 81). It is still assumed that, even after ordinary soldiers were permitted to marry their families would have also lived in the *vicus* or *canabae* (see Phang 2001:18, 35, 122–124). Thus, an important question for this project is whether this change of law was reflected in a change in the distribution of material within military forts. That is, does the distribution of material definitively associated with women's presence and women's activities, such as certain types of *fibulae* (brooches), cloth-working artifacts, and jewellery (see Allason-Jones 1995), support van Driel-Murray's evidence for women's and children's shoes within the soldiers' barracks of first- and second-century forts? With the exception of officers' households, therefore, can women be found to have been present within the fort prior to the end of the second century C.E. and if so, where and what were they doing there?

This case study has commenced with well-excavated and rapidly abandoned military forts in the western provinces, particularly on the Rhine and Danube frontiers. For example, the recent publication of the artifacts excavated from the double legionary fort of Vetera I in the Lower Rhine region (Hanel 1995) has provided useful material for spatially mapping artifact distribution at this site (Allison n.d.b; Allison et al. n.d.).

Vetera I

Vetera I was probably founded ca. 10 B.C.E., substantially rebuilt in stone ca. 43 C.E., and then destroyed and abandoned during revolutionary upheavals in 68/69 C.E. Only the central part of the fort has been excavated so little of the ordinary soldiers' barracks are known but the central administrative buildings, two legates' palaces and possibly six other officers buildings have been excavated, as well as many other buildings whose identification is less clear, along the principal cross street, the *via principalis*. Being a first-century fort one would expect to find evidence for the presence of women predominantly within the officer's residences. This could also apply to the quarters of the petty officers, the centurions (Phang 2001:130–132), which were often found at the ends of barrack blocks. Unfortunately, no such centurions' quarters have been identified at Vetera I.

It was possible to assign gender categories to some 700 of the 11,000 artifacts recorded from Vetera I. These are predominantly items related to dress and various crafts and other activities. In some cases it is possible to assign a specific gender category to certain artifacts. For example, hair pins, spinning items and some *fibulae* and jewellery, have been classified as definitively "female" while other *fibulae* and activities such as combat or stone-working are classified as definitively "male." In other cases, such as certain types of *fibulae*, bone pines and beads, the classification is less certain so a number of possible categories are included. These are: "male?," "female?," "male?/female?" and "female?/child?." For the reasons given above, most toilet items were classified as "male?/female?." Food-preparation items may also, potentially, be classified as possibly female. As van Driel-Murray has noted (1997:55), the technological difference between handmade cooking vessels and other artifacts (e.g., weaponry) found within military forts should make us question whether cooking was being carried out by soldiers themselves, as is traditionally believed, or by local women within the camp. However, this is a complex issue and so is not included in this current study.

On the bases of the above gender classifications, GIS mapping capabilities were used to plot the spatial distribution of these gender categories across the excavated area of Vetera I and then these plots were analyzed. They showed that the central administrative buildings contained a wealth of items related to male activities, especially combat activities, but also to administrative activities such as writing. In contrast, personal activities, such as dress (excluding combat dress), toilet activities, and leisure activities (e.g., gaming), whether male, female or unassigned, were comparatively less well represented in these buildings than they were in buildings identified as the officers' residences and in buildings along the *via principalis*. Similarly, items which could be identified as women's, or possibly women's and children's, were almost non-existent in the administrative buildings but relatively predominant in the officers' residences. In addition to this expected pattern, though, there was also a relative concentration of women's and children's material in the central open area of the fort, believed to have been the market area (Hanel 1995:311–312; Pseudo-Hyginus 12), as well as in the east gateway of the *via principalis*, and in the smaller buildings lining this street. The high proportion of possibly female and children's items in these parts of the fort may point to the equal, or even greater, numbers of women and children passing along and frequenting these public and relatively commercial areas as the officers' private residences. This includes a noted concentration of dress-related items in the buildings lining the main street, believed to have been shops (Lehner 1930:39). The numbers are extremely small but, if the quantity women's and children's items in the officers' residences documents their habitation there, then the quantity and nature of the artefacts in these so-called shops might also document female habitation. Thus the evidence from Vetera I hints that women and children may have been as prevalent in the commercial parts of the forts as in the officer's residences. Interestingly, a concentration of food-preparation items and tableware was also found in these areas (Allison n.d.b). It is therefore, tempting to suggest that this distribution pattern indicates that women were involved in feeding the troops from these more public spaces and supplied them with required merchandise.

This evidence supports that identified on inscribed wooden tablets found in the rubbish dump of the first century C.E. fort of Vindonissa, in Switzerland. Some of these wooden tablets have house numbers, which have been identified as belonging to buildings within the fort, and these same tablets refer to women who worked in these establishments as barmaids and innkeepers (Speidel 1996:55,186–187). Thus, these documents, likewise, suggest that women were involved in providing services to soldiers, including food and drink. However, it has been assumed that such women would only have worked within the fort during the day and resided in the settlement outside. It is difficult to imagine how a female innkeeper would have operated, had she not also inhabited her place of work.

Thus, analysis of the distribution of gender-marked artifacts at Vetera I adds further weight to the growing perception that Roman military forts in the first and second centuries C.E. were far from exclusively male zones. Rather, a range of women and families were likely to have been involved in activities within fort and may also have been domiciled there. As well as the officers' households, these included women involved in supplying various needs of the soldiers, within the fort and as well as in the settlement outside. It is not possible, from the Vetera or the Vindonissa evidence, to establish the relationships of such women to ordinary soldiers but the presence of children's items could support an argument for some co-habiting arrangement. Given such evidence, it is not, as Carol van Driel-Murray has stated (1997:61), a question of whether the women were within the forts, but how we use the archaeological record to provide more information on their presence and their activities.

REMARKS

This project involves a more self-reflexive approach to the construction of archaeological knowledge about the Roman world and more critical perspectives in our understanding of the nature and the complexity of gender relations in Roman society. In this, it contributes to understandings of the intrinsic nature of theorized gender in the discipline of archaeology more generally. In addition, it contributes to a gendered history of the western world and to more informed perspectives on issues relating to the continuity of social structures from ancient to modern worlds.

Issues concerning the social use of space in the Roman world have wider ramifications for humanities and social science research, as well as architectural and engineering research of the built environment, which often draw on the Roman world for explanations of social behaviour (e.g., Lefebvre 1991). A project which takes a more critical perspective on the relationships between gender and space in the Roman world can provide an important resource for social theorists and philosophers who explore the ancient world for concepts of continuity in attitudes to sexuality and gender relations (see McNay 1992:especially 49–50, 62; Spencer-Wood 1999).

Acknowledgments

This paper was first presented at the Australasian Association of Classical Studies 2001 Conference, Adelaide, February 2001. Discussions with Haijo Westra at that conference led to my participation in the 2001 Chacmool Conference. I would like to thank Haijo for his collegiality and for masterminding my trip to Canada. I am also grateful to the organizers of 2001 Chacmool Conference for contributing to my travel costs. In addition, I am indebted to John Barratt, University of Sheffield, for his support and encouragement in the inception of this project, and I am grateful to the Australian Research Council for the QE II Fellowship and research grant to it carry out. The presented paper has been substantially altered for this published version.

REFERENCES CITED

Allason-Jones, L.
|1989| *Women in Roman Britain*. British Museum Publications, London.
|1995| "Sexing" Small Finds. In *Theoretical Roman Archaeology: Second Conference Proceedings*, edited by P. Rush, pp. 22–32. Worldwide Archaeology Series No.14. Avebury, Aldershot.
|1999| Women and the Roman Army in Britain. In *The Roman Army as a Community*, edited by A. Goldsworthy and I. Haynes, pp. 41–51. Journal of Roman Archaeology Supplementary Series No. 34. Journal of Roman Archaeology, Portsmouth, Rhode Island.

Allison, P. M.
|1994| *The Distribution of Pompeian House Contents and its Significance*. Ph.D. dissertation, University of Sydney. University Microfilms, Ann Arbor.
|1995| Pompeian House Contents: Data Collection and Interpretative Procedures for a Reappraisal of Roman Domestic Life and Site Formation Processes. *Journal of European Archaeology* 3(1):145–176.
|1997a| Artefact Distribution and Spatial Function in Pompeian Houses. In *The Roman Family in Italy: Status, Sentiment and Space*, edited by B. Rawson, and P. Weaver, pp. 321–354. Humanities Research Centre, Canberra and Clarendon Press, Oxford.
|1997b| Why Do Excavation Reports Have Finds' Catalogues? In *Not So Much a Pot, More a Way of Life*, edited by C. G. Cumberpatch, and P. W. Blinkhorn, pp.77–84. Oxbow, Oxford.
|2001| Using the Material and the Written Sources: Turn of the Millennium Approaches to Roman Domestic Space. *American Journal of Archaeology* 105:181–208
|2004| *Pompeii Households: Analysis of the Material Culture*. Cotsen Institute of Archaeology at UCLA Monograph 42. Cotsen Institute of Archaeology, University of California, Los Angeles. Companion website – www.stoa.org/pompeianhouseholds/.
|n.d.a| *The Insula of the Menander in Pompeii, Vol. 3: The Finds in Context*. Oxford University Press, Oxford, in press.
|n.d.b| Mapping Artefacts and Activities within Roman Military Forts. *Proceedings of the XIXth International Congress of Roman Frontier Studies (Pécs 2003)*, in press.

Allison, P. M., A. S. Fairbairn, S. J. R. Ellis, and C. W. Blackall
|n.d.| Extracting the Social Relevance of Artefact Distribution in Roman Military Forts. *Internet Archaeology*, in press.

Bacus, E. A., A. W. Barker, J. D. Bonevich, S. L. Dunavan, J. B. Fitzhugh, D. L. Gold, N. S. Goldman-Finn, W. Griffin, and K. M. Mudar (editors)
|1993| *A Gendered Past: A Critical Bibliography of Gender in Archaeology*. University of Michigan Museum of Anthropology, Ann Arbor.

Bishop, M. C., and J. C. N. Coulston
|1993| *Roman Military Equipment: From the Punic Wars to the Fall of Rome*. Batsford, London.

Bowman, A. K.
|1994| *Life and Letters on the Roman Frontier: Vindolanda and Its People*. British Museum Publications, London.

Brown, S.
|1997| "Ways of Seeing" Women in Antiquity. In *Naked Truths: Women, Sexuality, and Gender in Classical Art and Archaeology*, edited by A. O. Koloski-Ostrow, and C. L. Lyons, pp. 12–42. Routledge, London.

Deschler-Erb, S.
|1998| *Römische Beinartefakte aus Augusta Raurica: Rohmaterial, Technologie, Typologie und Chronologie*. Forschungen in Augst Band 27/1. Augst, Römerstadt Augst

Dixon, S.
|1988| *The Roman Mother*. Croom Helm, London.
|1992| *The Roman Family*. Johns Hopkins University Press, Baltimore.
|2001| *Reading Roman Women*. Duckworth, London.

Dunbabin, K. M. D.
|1995| Houses and Households of Pompeii. *Journal of Roman Archaeology* 8:387–390.

Dwyer, E.
|1982| *Pompeian Domestic Sculpture: A Study of Five Pompeian Houses and their Contents*. Georgio Bretschneider, Rome.

Dyson, S. L.
|1995| Is There a Text in this Site? In *Methods in the Mediterranean: Historical and Archaeological Views on Texts and Archaeology*, edited by D. B. Small, pp. 25–44. E. J. Brill, Leiden.

Engelstad, E.
|1999| The Archaeology of Gender and Feminist Theory. Paper presented at 5th Women in Archaeology Conference, University of New South Wales, Sydney.

Fantham, E., H. P. Foley, N. B. Kampen, S. B. Pomeroy, and H. A. Shapiro
|1994| *Women in the Classical World: Image and Text*. Oxford University Press, New York.

Foss, P.
|1994| *Kitchens and Dining Rooms at Pompeii: The Spatial and Social Relationship of Cooking to Eating in the Roman Household*. Ph.D. dissertation, University of Michigan. University Microfilms, Ann Arbor.

Freeman, P. W. M.
|1997| Mommsen Through to Haverfield. In *Dialogues in Roman Imperialism*, edited by D. Mattingly, pp. 27–50. Journal of Roman Archaeology Supplementary Series No. 23. Journal of Roman Archaeology, Portsmouth, Rhode Island.

George, M.
|1997| Repopulating the Roman House. In *The Roman Family in Italy: Status, Sentiment, Space*, edited by B. Rawson, and P. Weaver, pp. 299–319. Humanities Research Centre, Canberra and Clarendon Press, Oxford.

Gilchrist, R.
|1999| *Gender and Archaeology: Contesting the Past*. Routledge, London.

Goldsworthy, A., and I. Haynes (editors)
|1999| *The Roman Army as a Community*. Journal of Roman Archaeology Supplementary Series No. 34. Journal of Roman Archaeology, Portsmouth, Rhode Island.

Groenman-van Waateringe, W. (editor)
|1997| *Roman Frontier Studies 1995: Proceedings of the XVIth International Congress of Roman Frontier Studies*. Oxbow, Oxford.

Hanel, N.
|1995| *Vetera I: Die Funde aus den römischen Lagern auf dem Fürstenberg bei Xanten*. Rheinische Ausgrabungen 35. Rheinland Verlag, Cologne.

Hingley, R.
|1993| Attitudes to Roman Imperialism. In *Theoretical Roman Archaeology: First Conference Proceedings*, edited by E. Scott, pp. 23–27. Worldwide Archaeology Series 4. Avebury, Aldershot.
|2000| *Roman Officers and English Gentlemen: The Imperial Origins of Roman Archaeology*. Routledge, London.

Jackson, R.
|1988| *Doctors and Diseases in the Roman Empire*. British Museum Publications, London

Jones, G. D. B.
|1997| From *Brittunculi* to Wounded Knee. In *Dialogues in Roman Imperialism*, edited by D. Mattingly, pp. 185–200. Journal of Roman Archaeology Supplementary Series No. 23. Journal of Roman Archaeology, Portsmouth, Rhode Island.

Juvenal
|1970| *Satires*, edited by J. D. Duff. Cambridge University Press, Cambridge.

Kampen, N. B.
|1981| *Image and Status: Roman Working Women in Ostia*. Mann, Berlin.

Kampen, N. B. (editor)
|1996| *Sexuality in Ancient Art: Near East, Egypt, Greece, and Italy*. Cambridge University Press, Cambridge.

Kleiner, D. E. E., and S. B. Matheson (editors)
|1996| *I Claudia: Women in Ancient Rome*. Yale University Art Gallery, New Haven, distributed by the University of Texas Press, Austin.

Knapp, A. B.
|1998| Boys will be Boys: Masculinist Approaches to a Gendered Archaeology. In *Redefining Archaeology: Feminist Perspectives*, edited by M. Casey, D. Donlon, J. Hope, and S. Wellfare, pp. 32–36. Department of Prehistory, Research School of Pacific Studies, The Australian National University, Canberra.

Koloski-Ostrow, A. O.
|1997| Violent Stages in Two Pompeian Houses. In *Naked Truths: Women, Sexuality, and Gender in Classical Art and Archaeology*, edited by A. O. Koloski-Ostrow, and C. L. Lyons, pp. 243–266. Routledge, London.
Laurence, R.
|1994| *Roman Pompeii: Space and Society*. Routledge, London.
Laurence, R., and A. F. Wallace-Hadrill (editors).
|1997| *Domestic Space in the Roman World: Pompeii and Beyond*. Journal of Roman Archaeology Supplementary Series No. 22. Journal of Roman Archaeology, Portsmouth, Rhode Island.
Leach, E. W.
|1993| The Entrance Room in the House of Iulius Polybius and the Nature of the Roman Vestibulum. In *Functional and Spatial Analysis of Wall Painting: Proceedings of the 5th International Congress of Ancient Wall-Painting, Amsterdam 1992*, edited by E. Moormann, pp. 23–33. Bulletin Antieke Beschaving Annual Papers in Classical Archaeology Supplement 3. Stichting BABESCH, Leiden.
Lefebvre, H.
|1991| *The Production of Space*. Translated by D. Nicholson-Smith. Blackwell, Oxford.
Lehner, H.
|1930| *Vetera: Die Ergebnisse der Ausgrabungen des Bonner Provinzialmuseums bis 1929*. Römisch-Germanische Forschungen 4. Römisch-Germanische Forschungen, Frankfurt.
Ling, R.
|1997| *The Insula of the Menander in Pompeii, Vol. 1: The Structures*. Clarendon Press, Oxford.
Lucretius
|1986| *De rerum natura*, vol. 4, translated by J. Godwin. Aris and Phillips, Warminster.
Martial
|1957| *Epigrammata*, translated by W. C. A. Ker. William Heinemann, London and Harvard University Press, Cambridge, Massachusetts.
McNay, L.
|1992| *Foucault and Feminism: Power, Gender and the Self*. Polity Press, Cambridge.
Nevett, L.
|1999| *House and Society in the Ancient Greek World*. Cambridge University Press, Cambridge.
Phang, S.
|2001| *The Marriage of Roman Soldiers (13 BC–AD 235): Law and Family in the Imperial Army*. Brill, Leiden
Pirson, F.
|1997| Rented Accommodation at Pompeii: The *Insula Arriana Polliana*. In *Domestic Space in the Roman World*, edited by R. Laurence, and A. Wallace-Hadrill, pp. 165–181. Journal of Roman Archaeology Supplementary Series No. 22. Journal of Roman Archaeology, Portsmouth, Rhode Island.
Pseudo-Hyginus
|1994| *De munitionibus castrorum*. In *Polybius and Pseudo-Hyginus: The Fortification of the Roman Camp*, edited and translated by M. C. J. Miller and J. C. De Voto, pp. 59–102. Ares Publisher, Chicago.
Rawson, B. (editor)
|1986| *The Family in Ancient Rome: New Perspectives*. Croom Helm, London.
|1991| *Marriage, Divorce and Children in Ancient Rome*. Humanities Research Centre, Canberra, Clarendon Press, Oxford and Oxford University Press, New York.
|2003| *Children and Childhood in Roman Italy*. Oxford University Press, Oxford and New York.
Rawson, B., and P. Weaver (editors)
|1997| *The Roman Family in Italy: Status, Sentiment, Space*. Humanities Research Centre, Canberra and Clarendon Press, Oxford.
Riggsby, A. M.
|1999| Integrating Public and Private. *Journal of Roman Studies* 12:555–558.
Roberts, C.
|1993| A Critical Approach to Gender as a Category of Analysis in Archaeology. In *Women in Archaeology: A Feminist Critique*, edited by H. du Cros and L. Smith, pp. 16–21. Department of Prehistory, Research School of Pacific Studies, The Australian National University, Canberra.
Scott, E.
|1999| *The Archaeology of Infancy and Infant Death*. Archaeopress, Oxford.
Simpson, C. J.
|1997| *The Excavations of San Giovanni di Ruoti. Volume II: The Small Finds*. University of Toronto Press, Toronto.
Southern, P., and K. R. Dixon
|1996| *The Late Roman Army*. Yale University Press, New Haven.
Speidel, M. A.
|1996| *Die römischen Schreibtafel von Vindonissa*. Veröffentlichungen der Gesellschaft Pro Vindonissa Band XII. Gesellschaft Pro Vindonissa, Brugg
Spencer-Wood, S.
|1999| The World Their Household. In *The Archaeology of Household Activities*, edited by P. M Allison, pp. 162–189. Routledge, London.
Storey, G.
|1998| Archaeology and Roman Society. *Journal of Archaeological Research* 7(3):203–248.
Treggiari, S.
|1976| Jobs for Women. *American Journal of Ancient History* 1:76–104.
van Driel-Murray, C.
|1995| Gender in Question. In *Theoretical Roman Archaeology: Second Conference Proceedings*, edited by P. Rush, pp. 3–21. Worldwide Archaeology Series No.14. Avebury, Aldershot.
|1997| Women in Forts? *Jahresbericht der Gesellschaft Pro Vindonissa*:55–61.
Vickery, A.
|1993| Historiographical Review: Golden Age of Separate Spheres? A Review of the Categories and Chronology of English Women's History. *The Historical Journal* 36.2:383–414.
Virgil
|1977| *Ad Aeneid*, books 7–8, edited by J. D. Christie. Oxford University Press, Oxford.

Vitruvius
|1985| *De Architectura*, translated by F. Granger. William Heineman, London and Harvard University Press, Cambridge, Massachusetts.
Wallace-Hadrill, A. F.
|1994| *Houses and Society in Pompeii and Herculaneum*. Princeton University Press, Princeton.
|1996| Engendering the Roman House. In *I Claudia: Women in Ancient Rome*, edited by D. Kleiner, and S. Matheson, pp. 104–115. Yale University Art Gallery, New Haven, distributed by the University of Texas Press, Austin.
Whitley, D. (editor)
|1998| *Reader in Archaeological Theory: Post-Processual and Cognitive Approaches*. Routledge, London.
Wild, J. P.
|1970| *Textile Manufacture in the Northern Roman Provinces*. Cambridge University Press, Cambridge.
Wyke, M.
|1994| Woman in the Mirror. In *Women in Ancient Societies: An Illusion of the Night*, edited by L. J. Archer, S. Fischler, and M. Wyke, pp. 134–151. Macmillan Press, London.
Yardley, J. C.
|1991| The Symposium in Roman Elegy. In *Dining in a Classical Context*, edited by W. J. Slater, pp. 149–155. University of Michigan Press, Ann Arbor.
Zarmatti, L.
|1994| Review of *A Gendered Past: A Critical Bibliography of Gender in Archaeology*, edited by E. A. Bacus, A. W. Barker, J. D. Bonevich, S. L. Dunavan, J. B. Fitzhugh, D. L. Gold, N. S. Goldman-Finn, W. Griffin, and K. M. Mudar. *American of Journal Archaeology* 98:773–774.

NOTES

1 See Whitley (1998:7, and especially 301) on the question of the existence of an objective reconstruction of the past.

A STAR OF NARANJO: THE CELESTIAL PRESENCE OF GOD L

Michele Mae Bernatz

Michele Mae Bernatz, University of Texas at Austin, 7495 Robinson Road, Arcade, New York 14009, U.S.A.

ABSTRACT

The text and imagery of Maya art show a relationship between Classic-period warfare and the positioning of celestial bodies in cosmic space. While the nature of this correlation remains unclear, earlier research has attempted to characterize a general scheme for a Venus-regulated warfare by comparing the synodic cycle of the planet with calendrical information from across the Maya region. This paper focuses on the lowland site of Naranjo, and on battles fought in the seventh and eighth centuries A.D. In contrast to data that links a majority of Venus war events to the evening star phase of this planet, the pattern of aggression at Naranjo during the reign of K'ak' Tiliw reveals an apparent preference for timing military attacks under the auspices of inferior conjunction and Venus as morning star. The highly successful martial record of K'ak' Tiliw may have been attributed to the proper timing of warfare and the patronage of the mythical deity called God L. Evidence links the representation of this being to the conjunction of Venus, the sun and moon on specific dates occurring within the lifetime of K'ak' Tiliw. The depiction of God L may address the fluctuating power of this supernatural being and illustrate the importance of prognostication in the planning of military strikes.

Beginning with Floyd G. Lounsbury's (1982) article on the use of astronomical knowledge at Bonampak, various scholars (Carlson 1993; Milbrath 1999; Nahm 1994; Schele and Freidel 1990; Sprajc 1998) have alleged a strong connection between the cycles of the planet Venus and the timing of Maya warfare. To test the assertion, this paper examines Venus cycles in relation to warfare undertaken at the site of Naranjo during the seventh and eighth centuries A.D. of Classic Maya history. I focus on the reign of K'ak' Tiliw Chan Chaak, who ruled Naranjo from A.D. 693 to at least A.D. 728. Although the evidence does not confirm a strict correlation between Venus cycles and the pattern of aggression at Naranjo, two hypotheses lend peripheral support to the idea of Venus-regulated warfare: 1) during the reign of K'ak' Tiliw, there was an apparent preference for timing military action within inferior conjunction and the morning star phase of Venus; and 2) the prominence of God L on ceramic wares created at Naranjo may relate to the Venus cycle and the military success of K'ak' Tiliw. My hypotheses are based on the reconstruction of the military record through Long Count dates inscribed on various monuments and the comparison of data with the timing of Venus cycles. This hypothetical reconstruction is augmented by contextual information derived from hieroglyphic inscriptions and the visual representations of related works of art.

VENUS AND THE MAYA

Many scholars acknowledge the significance of astronomical cycles to the development of Maya cosmology (Aveni 2001; Carlson 1993; Closs 1979; Kelley 1980; Malmström 1997; Milbrath 1999; Schele and Freidel 1990; Sprajc 1998). The elaborate Long Count and Tzolkin calendars are based on careful observation of the solar system and the seasonal changes that directed community activities during ancient times. While the sun and moon likely carried the highest regard of ancient people, stellar and planetary phenomena were also important. The movement of Venus, in particular, was tracked with great care and the accumulated knowledge of its cycles was recorded in sacred books

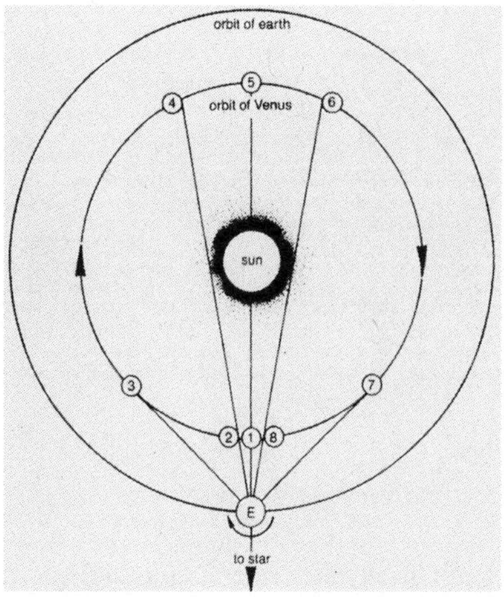

Figure 1. The motion of Venus (after Aveni 2001:82, fig. 36, diagram by P. Dunham).
1. Inferior conjunction
2. Heliacal rise as "morning star" on eastern horizon
3. Greatest western elongation
4. Disappearance during superior conjunction
5. Superior conjunction
6. First appearance as "evening star" on western horizon
7. Greatest eastern elongation
8. Disappearance during inferior conjunction

Table 1. Mean Position of Selected Points in the Venus Cycle, Measured from Inferior Conjunction (after Closs 1979:154).

Position in cycle	Venus day count
Superior conjunction	-292
Heliacal rising after superior conjunction	-269 to -257
Greatest eastern elongation	-72
Greatest brilliancy as evening star	-37
Beginning of retrograde motion	-22
Heliacal setting before inferior conjunction	-4
Inferior conjunction	0
Heliacal rising after inferior conjunction	+4
Termination of retrograde motion	+22
Greatest brilliancy as morning star	+37
Greatest western elongation	+72
Heliacal setting before superior conjunction	+257 to +269
Superior conjunction	+292

like the Dresden Codex, a late Postclassic document thought to originate in the Yucatan region of Mexico. This information may have served the Maya in the prognostication of beneficial or detrimental times for planting, warfare, and the ascension of new kings. According to Aveni (2001:83), "The first annual morning or predawn appearance of Venus ... termed its *heliacal* rising ... was probably the most important single event in Maya astronomy."

The ancient Maya were most concerned with the *synodic* cycle of Venus: the interval between successive identical configurations of the planet relative to the sun (Aveni 2001:83–84). Modern astronomers assign approximate day-counts to the various phases of the planet (Figure 1 and Table 1) . During the average 584-day cycle, Venus spends about eight days hidden in the sun's luminosity at inferior conjunction, and then rises in the east as morning star for a mean period of 263 days. Afterwards, Venus disappears for an average of 50 days at superior conjunction before it rises again for 263 days, this time on the western horizon during its evening star phase. While astronomers generally ascribe 584 days to the cycle of Venus, there is fluctuation from year to year in this figure. Venus actually follows a symmetrical sequence in regard to the day-count of its cycle (e.g., 587, 583, 580, 583, 587, etc.) and repeats its synodic patterning every eight years (Milbrath 1999:51). Similarly, the count assigned to each of its four stations can vary up to 16 days depending on the cycle in question (Schele and Grube 1997:104). The Postclassic Maya certainly understood this variation: the Dresden Codex includes base date corrections to account for the cyclic shift (Milbrath 1999:170–173; Schele and Grube 1997:97–138).

Much like modern astronomers, the ancient Maya assigned mean figures to the anticipated day-counts for each of the four Venus stations. The Maya used eight as the approximation of days for inferior conjunction. However, in contrast to modern theory, the Maya allocated values of 236, 90, and 250 respectively for the stations of morning star, superior conjunction, and evening star. Researchers do not yet understand this differentiation from canonical figures, but Aveni (2001:84) suggests it may be due to the tracking of Venus relative to the moon rather than the sun. Regardless, the motion of Venus above the horizon was a subject of great concern in ancient Mesoamerica and knowledge of the projected actions of this planet served in the prognostication of future events.[1]

Scholars have attempted to determine an overall pattern of wartime activity, but it remains unclear exactly how the Maya understanding of Venus cycles may have guided military behaviour. For example, Schele and Freidel (1990:130–131) argue that a cult of Tlaloc-Venus warfare began in the Maya region around A.D. 378 with the intrusion of forces from Teotihuacan. Combat gear like the *atlatl*, mosaic helmet, back-attached mirrors and coyote tails – as well as symbols such as the "Tlaloc goggles" and Venus-star hieroglyphs – represent this new battle format (Schele and Freidel 1990:130–164; Stone 1989). Lounsbury (1982) was the first to associate Venus with Maya warfare. His data indicates that military aggression was frequently linked to the first visibility of Venus in the morning or night sky and during its disappearance at inferior conjunction. Citing Aveni and Hotaling's (1994) research in regard to the timing of war, Milbrath (1999) finds that 70 per cent of "star war" dates correspond to the evening phase of Venus. Of these dates, 84 per cent align with the first appearance of the evening star. Milbrath (1999:196) also suggests that the period of invisibility at superior conjunction was avoided and that military excursions frequently took place during the dry season, presumably because the dryness facilitated access to passable roadways or coincided with a time when agricultural chores were less demanding on the population. Sprajc (1998:41–126) agrees that the Classic Maya, like a majority of the various Mesoamerican cultures he studied, were more interested in Venus as evening star. In contrast to inscriptional data from the Classic period, however, the Venus pages of the Dresden Codex illustrate that the Postclassic Maya emphasized the morning star phase of the planet. The shift of emphasis over time raises the possibility that the Maya focused on diverse aspects of Venus at different times in their history (Aveni 2001:166). It is also plausible in my opinion that alternative phases of Venus were considered favourable depending on the given epoch, the specific site in question and the ruler in power.

THE MILITARY RECORD OF NARANJO

Contrary to arguments that claim a prevalent correspondence between Classic-period warfare and evening star Venus, ruler K'ak' Tiliw of Naranjo appears to have favoured the auspices of Venus at inferior conjunction or in its rise as morning star.[2] Located southeast of Tikal, the polity developed a special alliance with the site of Dos Pilas and depending on the era in question, was both an ally and foe of Calakmul. Inscriptions record numerous battles between Naranjo and the smaller polities that populated the surrounding region, but Calakmul, Caracol and Tikal were its most outstanding adversaries over the course of the polity's 500-year history (Martin and Grube 2000:68–83). In fact, Naranjo's most contentious relationship with its political rivals coincides with the reign of K'ak' Tiliw. The Naranjo sovereign was born January 3, A.D. 688 and his ascension into kingship occurred under the supervision of his mother, Lady Six Sky (Martin and Grube 2000:74–75). A daughter of B'alaj Chan K'awiil, the breakaway ruler whose newly established Dos Pilas kingdom threatened giant Tikal for a time, Lady Six Sky arrived in Naranjo in A.D. 682 to reinvigorate the dynastic lineage of this battered polity. Though it is rare to find a Maya woman in such a powerful position, Lady Six Sky brought Naranjo out of its slump and into a new phase of prosperity through the rededication of sacred architecture and the elevation of her son into kingship. While Lady Six Sky may have been responsible for the timing of Naranjo's successful war effort, it was in the name of K'ak' Tiliw that history

Table 2. Naranjo Victories under K'ak' Tiliw[a].

Adversary	Long count	Julian equivalent	Venus count
K'inichil Kab'	9.13.1.4.19	June 17, A.D. 693	-4
Tuub'al	9.13.1.9.5	September 11, A.D. 693	+83
B'ital	9.13.1.13.14	December 9, A.D. 693	+172
Tikal	9.13.2.16.10	January 29, A.D. 695	+1
Dotted Ko	9.13.4.1.13	March 27, A.D. 696	-155
Eared Skull	9.13.5.4.13	May 2, A.D. 697	+265
K'inichil Kab'	9.13.6.4.17	May 20, A.D. 698	+41
Ucanal	9.13.6.10.4	September 4, A.D. 698	+148
Yootz	9.13.14.4.2	March 24, A.D. 706	-13
Yaxha	9.13.18.4.18	March 19, A.D. 710	+276
Sakha'	9.14.2.15.7	September 23, A.D. 714	+172
? Site	9.14.4.7.5	April 3, A.D. 716	+147

[a] Long-count dates and hieroglyphic interpretations after Martin and Grube 2000.

would record these events.

To reveal the pattern of warfare, the aggressive middle period (ca. A.D. 680 to A.D. 720) of Naranjo history requires further scrutiny (Table 2). Stela 22 records the ascension as well as the first eight victories of this reinvigorated polity. K'ak' Tiliw acceded to the throne on May 28, A.D. 693, less than three weeks before Venus conjoined with the sun in its inferior stage. The initial conflict of the young lord's reign took place just 20 days later, during the brief disappearance of the planet that signaled the beginning of a new cycle. This preliminary battle is described as the "bringing down" (*jub'uy*) of an *ajaw* named K'inichil Kab' (Martin and Grube 2000:76–77). K'ak' Tiliw's first victory was quickly followed by another success on September 11, A.D. 693 at a site thought to be near Lake Peten-Itza called Tuub'al (Martin and Grube 2000:76–77). This second event, marked with a hieroglyph signifying "burning" (*puluy*), took place approximately 80 days into the morning star rise of Venus and close to its greatest western elongation. A third triumph (another *puluy*) against an enemy camp called B'ital, which was located between Naranjo and Caracol, occurred another 90 days later on December 9, A.D. 693 (Martin and Grube 2000:76–77), a date falling within the same morning star phase.

A little over a year after the encounter with B'ital, the military forces of K'ak' Tiliw attacked again imitating the earlier pattern of action, perhaps to once more exploit the auspices of a new Venus cycle. Allied with Calakmul in this effort, Naranjo fought an important battle on January 29, A.D. 695 against giant Tikal within one day of an inferior conjunction. The clash was another success for K'ak' Tiliw, who captured a Tikal lord named S'iyaj K'awiil (Martin and Grube 2000:76–77). Naranjo boasts four more military raids against neighbouring territories from A.D. 696 to A.D. 698 (Martin and Grube 2000:76–77). Of these, one took place under evening star Venus, one during the heliacal setting of the morning star before superior conjunction, and two solidly within the morning star phase. After a seven-year hiatus, conflict returned in A.D. 706 with an aggression against the city of Yootz (Martin and Grube 2000:76–77). For a third time K'ak' Tiliw, now a seasoned commander, entered into battle much as he had in his initial conflict some 12 years earlier: very close to inferior conjunction and a new cycle of Venus. The following decade brought only occasional warfare to Naranjo, which was now reasonably secure against adversaries in the region (Martin and Grube 2000:76–77). Of the three incidents between A.D. 710 and A.D. 716, two more coincide with the morning star cycle.

In a review of the 12 wartime events of K'ak' Tiliw's reign, three occurred near or within the inferior conjunction of Venus just prior to beginning a new cycle; six happened at various points within the morning star phase of Venus; two battles came either during the last morning visibility or when Venus had entered into superior conjunction; and one took place under the evening star.[3] Thus, a majority of battles recorded at the site of Naranjo under ruler K'ak' Tiliw coincide with the new phase inferior conjunction or rise of Venus as morning star. Such regularity in the timing of warfare implies that the position of Venus was a crucial element in military planning. Yet if battle maneuvers were timed according to a preferred station of Venus, the Maya scribes who recorded Naranjo's victories did not highlight this celestial contingency. Rather than to construct narrative that acknowledges the force of Venus (e.g., to use the "star war" hieroglyph that includes a Venus sign), Naranjo scribes most frequently employed the verbs *jub'uy* (to "bring down"), *puluy* (to "burn"), and *chukaj* (someone "captured"). Further study of the ideology of warfare is needed to determine whether the cycles of Venus were important in all military endeavours or only those marked by the still unreadable "star war" hieroglyph.

The pattern revealed is interesting, but this information does not prove that Naranjo warfare was deliberately timed according to Venus cycles. However, the case gains strength when examined within the context of Naranjo history and the life of its reigning king. One must consider the apparent urgency with which Lady Six Sky acted when placing her young son into kingship and beginning a military campaign in his name. K'ak' Tiliw was just five years of age when he took the throne, and it was only 20 days after his ascension that Naranjo's aggression began. A decade had already passed since Lady Six Sky's arrival in Dos Pilas, time that could have been used to build up resources and prepare soldiers for battle. Besides the obvious military preparation, it must have been important in Classic times to go to war in the name of a legitimate king. This was probably at least part of the reasoning behind the decision to accede a child so young to the throne. Regardless, these events point to a strong resolve in the planning of Naranjo's new war effort,

Table 3. Naranjo Warfare under Other Rulers[a].

Adversary	Long count	Julian equivalent	Venus count
			Prior to K'ak'Tiliw:
Caracol (indecisive)	9.9.13.4.4	May 25, A.D. 626	+24
Caracol (indecisive)	9.9.13.6.4	July 4, A.D. 626	+64
Caracol (Naranjo defeat)	9.9.14.3.5	May 1, A.D. 627	-219
Calakmul (Naranjo defeat)	9.9.14.3.5	December 24, A.D. 631	-264
Caracol (Naranjo victory?)	9.12.7.12/13.?	February A.D. 680	-188 to -216
			After K'ak' Tiliw:
Tikal (Naranjo defeat)	9.15.13.11/12.?	February, A.D. 744	-166 to -195
B'ital (Naranjo victory)	9.17.4.?.?	A.D. 775	+1 to +292?
Yaxha' (Naranjo victory)	9.17.8.2/3.?	February, A.D. 799	+62 to +90

[a] Long-count dates and hieroglyphic interpretations after Martin and Grube 2000.

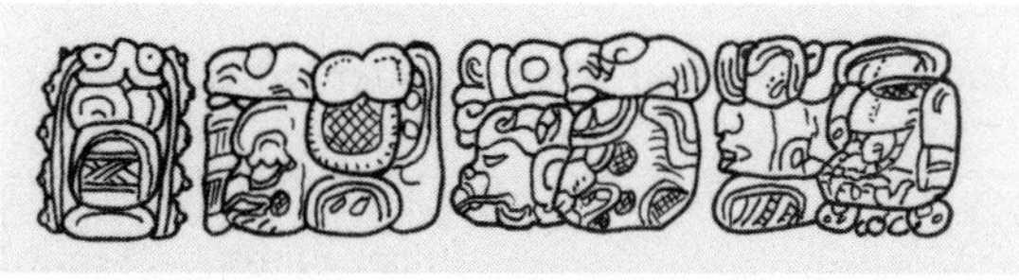

Figure 2. "Star war" defeat of Naranjo on December 24, A.D. 631, Naranjo Hieroglyphic Stairway (redrawn by author after Martin and Grube 2000:106).

and careful strategizing such as this might also have included the selection of appropriate dates for the initiation of enemy attacks.

If K'ak' Tiliw were to contrive an allegiance to new phase and morning star Venus, his acclamation may have been based on the military successes and failures of his predecessors (Table 3). After the seemingly prosperous reign of the thirty-fifth ruler Aj Wosal (regal dates A.D. 546 to at least A.D. 615) the affluence of Naranjo plummeted early in the seventh century A.D. (Martin and Grube 2000:70–72). It was the thirty-sixth lord who faced a significant threat from two powerful rivals: Caracol located to the south and Calakmul to the north (Martin and Grube 2000:72–73). The first aggression came in three episodes recorded together in the inscriptions beginning with an intrusion by Caracol on May 25, A.D. 626 that was followed by a second raid 40 days later (Martin and Grube 2000:72–73, 91–92). The written record denotes these events with the word *jub'uy* (to "bring down"), and both assaults against Naranjo took place under Venus as morning star. The incursions were undoubtedly somewhat detrimental, but they must not have equaled utter defeat because 10 months later, Caracol felt the need to repeat their attack on Naranjo (Martin and Grube 2000:72–73, 91–92). The inconclusiveness of the first two adversarial offensives may have contributed to a belief in the protective support that morning star Venus could lend to the polity of Naranjo.

In contrast to these indecisive battles, it appears that evening star assaults brought certain victory to Naranjo's adversaries. For example, a regrouped Caracol launched its third offensive against Naranjo on May 1, A.D. 627 (an evening star date) and this time captured a prisoner from Tzam, a probable tributary of Naranjo. This unfortunate captive was apparently sacrificed in a ballgame ritual that took place three years later (Martin and Grube 2000:72–73, 92, 106; Schele and Freidel 1990:176–177). However, the most devastating blow of Naranjo's early period came during a "star war" with Calakmul on December 24, A.D. 631 (Figure 2). According to Martin and Grube (2000:16), the "star war" hieroglyph "marks only the most decisive of actions, the conquest of cities and the fall of dynasties." This final collision took place as Venus reappeared after superior conjunction and entered the evening star phase. It resulted in *k'uxaj*, the horrific death of Naranjo's thirty-sixth ruler, who was tortured and possibly eaten after the conflict (Martin and Grube 2000:72–73, 92, 106). It would be 50 long years before Naranjo regained the glory lost in this stinging defeat.

A final Naranjo battle took place prior to the arrival of Lady Six Sky and the ascension of K'ak Tiliw. In February of A.D. 680, the thirty-seventh ruler launched his own "star war" against Caracol, perhaps in reprisal for the death of his predecessor in the *k'uxaj* of A.D. 631 (Martin and Grube 2000:73). It is unclear whether this evening star clash was a firm victory for Naranjo. A recently uncovered portion of the Caracol conquest stairway records Naranjo's defeat of Oxwitza' ("Three Hill Water"), an ancient name of Caracol. But Martin and Grube (2000:73) posit that still missing text likely records a victorious Caracol retribution after February A.D. 680 that eventually led to the total destruction of the ruling dynasty at Naranjo and the subsequent makeover that took place with Lady Six Sky's arrival in A.D. 682.

Moving now to the eighth century and the military record of K'ak' Tiliw's successors, the inscriptions denote one major Naranjo loss along with two war victories. In February A.D. 744 Naranjo was again the victim of a "star war," this time launched by the Tikal polity. The details of the battle are inscribed on a wooden lintel at Tikal's Temple 4 (Figure 3). The text recounts the sacking of Wak Kab'nal ("Six Earth Place"), the city of the "Square-nosed Beastie" (nickname for the mythical founder of Naranjo) and the capture of a personal god effigy of ruler Yax Mayuy Chan Chaak (Martin and Grube 2000:70, 78–79). As in the losses of A.D. 627 and A.D. 631, the enemies of Naranjo delivered this crushing defeat under the auspices of Venus as evening star. In contrast, two lords reigning in the later part of the eighth century celebrated military successes. K'ak' Ukalaw Chan Chaak, the son of K'ak' Tiliw, reportedly burned the city of B'ital in A.D. 775. The specific date of this victorious event is not known, but with a new Venus cycle beginning around January 1, A.D. 775, it is probable the conflict

Figure 3. "Star war" defeat of Naranjo in A.D. 744, Temple 4 at Tikal (redrawn by author after Martin and Grube 2000:79).

Figure 4. *Rabbit Vase.* Roll-out of vessel from Naranjo, K1398, circa A.D. 710 (after Kerr 1989, Volume 1:81, photo copyright Justin Kerr).

happened during the rise of the morning star. Later, the grandson of K'ak' Tiliw, a man named Itzamnaaj K'awiil, successfully raided three satellite settlements of Yaxha (February A.D. 799). The sovereign initiated these assaults during morning star Venus.

To summarize the close-to-200-year history here recounted, there is a noticeable pattern of achievement in war for Naranjo during inferior conjunction and the morning star phase of Venus. Conversely, failure and defeat were more often the case in military struggles timed during superior conjunction and the evening star phase of the planet. This evidence diverges from previously cited observations regarding the predominance of evening star Venus in the timing of Classic-period warfare. More research is required to determine whether the positioning of celestial bodies was a factor in all types of military campaigns or only those marked by the "star war" hieroglyph. In its deviation from the statistical majority, the military record of Naranjo suggests that the timing of warfare and its perceived correspondence to a favoured celestial arrangement may have varied with location, era, and ruler.

GOD L, VENUS AND THE SITE OF NARANJO

In terms of military success, it is the reign of K'ak' Tiliw that stands out from all other Naranjo rulers. His era as lord is decorated with an impressive list of victories and more than thirty years of freedom from outside oppression. Whether the result of luck or military prowess, the persistent triumph of this king must have been recognized both by the ruler himself as well as his followers. It is conceivable that in the mindset of the ancient Maya, the efficacy of K'ak' Tiliw might have been attributed at least in part to the proper timing of aggression. Good fortune in war may have also been conceptualized as the bestowal of an imaginary guardian who oversaw the polity or a particular segment of cosmic time. We know from the inscriptional record of the conflict between Tikal and Naranjo in A.D. 744 that military assaults sometimes involved the capture of a ceremonial litter and god effigy (Martin and Grube 2000:79). If K'ak' Tiliw's military success were tied to the patronage of a beneficent deity, perhaps it was the mysterious God L, a mythical being related to both Classic-period warfare and Venus.

God L adorns the painted surface of three ceramic vessels created for Naranjo kings.[4] K'ak' Tiliw was surely familiar with the deity as is evidenced by the painted narrative and text on the so-called *Rabbit Vase* (Figure 4) : the Primary Standard Sequence of this vessel indicates it was his personal drinking cup. The hieroglyphic inscription that accompanies the sequence of actions is not entirely understood, but scholars believe the scene represents the humiliation or fleecing of God L (Dütting and Johnson 1993; Stuart 1993). The beginning scene portrays a large balloon-eared rabbit holding the owl hat and staff of the aged deity, who stands humbly below having been relieved of his regalia and/or tribute. Next God L speaks to the enthroned sun god and complains about the theft of his clothing. Responding to the contrite God L, the sun god denies knowing the whereabouts of the rabbit-thief who is sitting alongside him.

Figure 5. *Vase of Seven Gods*. Roll-out of vessel from Naranjo, K2796, circa A.D. 750-800 (after Reents-Budet 1994:64, photo copyright Justin Kerr).

Figure 6. Naming phrase for Spear-thrower Owl (redrawn by author after Martin and Grube 2000:31).

The full meaning of this curious episode is currently beyond our reach, but it must have held some special significance as the personal vessel of a dynastic lord. Taken within the context of K'ak' Tiliw's reign, it is plausible the vase was made to pay tribute to supernatural beings while presenting a parody of real life events. Milbrath (1999:214) suggests that the vase depicts the actions of astronomical bodies, specifically the sun, moon and Venus. Using the correlation figure of 584, 283[5] and the Calendar Round date of 13 Ok 18 Wo (shown at the top of left interior column), Milbrath calculates a possible date of March 21, A.D. 700 (Gregorian), assuming the event in question took place during the lifetime of K'ak' Tiliw. Venus was a morning star on this date, but more interesting is the fact that there was a conjunction between Venus and the waning moon. Milbrath hypothesizes that the reversal of attributes in the scene represents the conjoined characteristics of the two astronomical bodies: the rabbit holds God L's regalia with a human hand while God L appears to have a rabbit paw. The 7 Ak'b'al date painted in the right column of hieroglyphs tells us that the second episode (God L kneeling before the sun god) took place 33 days later. The morning sky on this day, now the Gregorian date of April 23, A.D. 700, shows the moon conjoining with the sun. According to Milbrath, this could explain why the lunar rabbit is seen hiding just behind the sun god's knee.

Although not addressed in depth by Milbrath, the hieroglyphic text[6] supports her reading of this scene. One inscription (Figure 4, left interior column) tells us about an action that happened in a sacred setting visited or overseen by the divine being named *b'olon okte' k'uh*.[7] This location is poetically described as the "white (?) place, the five flower ocelot place." A second incident (Figure 4, right interior column) occurred at a "mountain watery (?) sky cave" where a jaguar throne (?) was possibly overturned during a military scrimmage.[8] The meaning of these literary phrases is largely obscure, but the text points to the possibility of aggressive events taking place at sacred and perhaps historical locations. At the same time the text could metaphorically refer to celestial settings and the convergence of adversarial divinities. For example, one would expect a solar deity to inhabit the cosmic realm. Similarly, some authors hypothesize that the "13 Sky" *(XIII-chan)* emblem attached to the owl on God L's hat may denote the portion of the cosmos where the war owl resides (Schele and Grube 1997:47). In the unusual first-person conversations that take place between the actors in this narrative, the participants refer to each other as *mam*, a Maya word signifying "ancestor" and "the relationship between grandparent and grandson" (Stuart et al. 1999, 2:47–48). This could mean that each of the beings represented, whether rabbit, aged deity or sun god, is related in a mythical kinship and interacts in the same cosmic space. Hence, it is plausible that at one level of interpretation all three figures represent celestial entities.

Milbrath's observations are credible, but the meaning of the narrative may reach beyond the representation of astronomical events. A viewer watching the real life conjunction would see the moon pass in front of Venus, in between it and the sun, effectively shadowing the planet's reflective light and metaphorically stealing its power. Because Venus is always close to the sun, rising before it as morning star and setting after it as evening star, the planet could be imagined in a mythological sense as the sun's elder brother and underworld guardian (Aveni 2001:80; Milbrath 1999:34–36). The passage of the moon between the two celestial companions interrupts the power created by the amalgamation of Venus and the sun in the morning and evening sky. In support of this argument, the dialog presented in the inscription focuses on the loss of the headdress, staff, and backrack (?) or tribute of God L,[9] and the type of clothing worn or tribute offered in ritual are symbolic of both status and authority in Maya ideology. Thus, the *Rabbit Vase* may be a metaphorical statement about strength that is distributed or taken away during rituals performed or the passing of deities through the celestial sectors of the Maya universe. Moreover, the contrition of God L prior to his rise as potent morning star Venus would not be an inappropriate subject for a drinking vessel made for a boy-king – after all K'ak' Tiliw would have been just 12 years old by this date. Perhaps the message to the young lord was to be mindful of the ebb and flow of power or the necessity of paying proper tribute to the gods.

If the narrative of the *Rabbit Vase* is about the celestial action of Venus, the sun and moon as suggested by Milbrath (1999:214), the apparent lack of Venus symbolism on the ceramic vessel presents a challenge to this hypothesis. While God L appears prominently among the Venus deities of the Postclassic Dresden Codex, Classic-period iconography does not express a clear relationship between God L and Venus (Taube 1992:79). An indirect connection occurs on the *Vase of Seven Gods* (Figure 5), which was created in the Naranjo region ca. A.D. 750, after the reign of K'ak' Tiliw. This representation includes Star (Venus?)-Earth bundles apparently to be guarded or dispersed by the supernatural beings that are gathered together on the mythical 4 Ajaw 8 Kumk'u date of this narrative. The positioning of God L as the leader of the group implies his authority to determine when and how the bundles will be handled. Because of his superior ranking amongst the deities who guard the Star (Venus?)-Earth bundles, one might question whether God L and Venus intersect on the *Rabbit Vase* too.

The companion *kuy* owl and occasional weaponry of God L in Classic-period imagery link this deity to warfare, but not directly to the planet Venus according to our current understanding of Maya iconography. If the idea of Venus-regulated warfare proves viable as research on this issue develops, then the owl hat worn by God L and prominently shown confiscated by the rabbit in Figure 4 may be a symbol both of Venus and his military capability. It is possible the owl symbolism along with the ideology of a Venus-regulated warfare originated in the Maya area ca. A.D. 378 when inscriptions record the "arrival" of a contingent led by a figure called Spear-Thrower Owl (Figure 6). The nature of this exchange and the origin of the characters involved are still very much in contention (Braswell 2003); however some authors argue the "foreigners" came from Teotihuacan (Martin and Grube 2000:28–36; Schele and Freidel 1990:144–153; Stone 1989; Stuart 2000). Whether Spear-Thrower Owl was indeed of central Mexican origin or not, new symbols of military prowess like the shell mosaic helmet, back-mounted mirror, dangling coyote tails and the visually powerful combination of the owl and *atlatl* that form his hieroglyphic naming phrase, grew more prevalent in the Maya region after the purported Early Classic arrival.

Figure 7. Record of "star war" between Tikal and Calakmul in January A.D. 657, Dos Pilas Hieroglyphic Stairway (redrawn by author after Martin and Grube 2000:109).

The new ideology of warfare including the owl motif and Venus-star iconography was certainly known in Lady Six Sky's home site of Dos Pilas (Grube and Schele 1994). During her father's reign, Dos Pilas allied with Calakmul against Tikal and a January A.D. 657

Figure 8. Detail of Dos Pilas Stela 9. Note the kuy owl atop the back rack of B'alaj Chan K'awiil (drawing by Linda Schele, © David Schele, courtesy Foundation for the Advancement of Mesoamerican Studies, Inc., www.famsi.org).

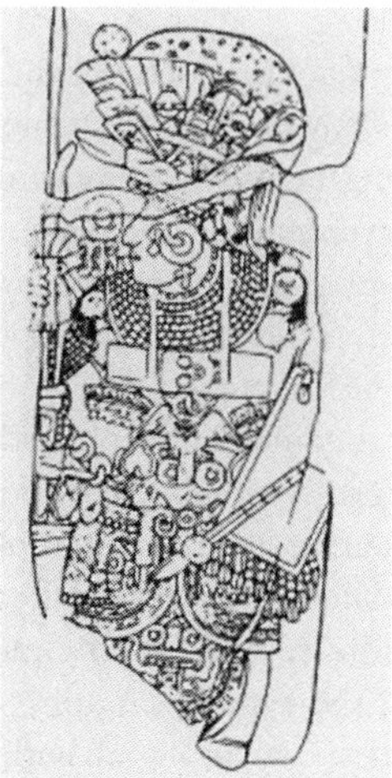

Figure 9. Detail of Dos Pilas Stela 2. From STAR GODS OF THE MAYA: ASTRONOMY IN ART, FOLKLORE AND CALENDARS by Susan Milbrath, Copyright © 1999. By permission of the University of Texas Press.

"star war" attack on the giant Tikal was recorded on the hieroglyphic stairway in celebration of the victory (Figure 7). Whereas the "star war" attacks on Naranjo by Tikal came under the evening star, the A.D. 657 event took place during the morning star phase of Venus (+111 to +141). In the portrait of B'alaj Chan K'awiil, appearing on Dos Pilas Stela 9 and dated to A.D. 682, a *kuy* owl sits atop the ruler's royal backrack (Figure 8). In addition, a later ruler of Dos Pilas (Ruler 3, reign A.D. 727 to A.D. 741), whose life span overlaps with that of Lady Six Sky, used an owl pectoral in order to visually highlight his warrior status (Figure 9). On Stela 2, even the owl itself (Figure 10) wears a Mexican-style Venus emblem around its neck, linking it to the idea of Venus warfare (Carlson 1993:206). The separation of God L from his owl companion in the *Rabbit Vase* scene could therefore indicate the loss of his military strength, a power that may be endowed by the positioning of Venus.

Another possible iconographic link between God L and Venus may be the dotted ring that encircles the stolen regalia on the *Rabbit Vase.* The ring with its two long trailing ends resembles the streams of dots on either side of the "star-over-Seibal" hieroglyph (Figure 11) recorded by Lounsbury (1982:Figure 2c). The stream of dots, replaced by water stacks in other "star war" hieroglyphs (Figures 2 and 3), refers to some type of liquid (water or blood?). A textual reference to water appears within the second scene of the *Rabbit Vase*: the phrase *uwitzil pipha' chan ch'een* ("mountain of the lake or watery? sky cave") may describe the location of the illustrated event. Moreover, the symbol denoting God L in the Dresden Codex (Figure 12) makes an allusion to water with its *imix* (water lily) sign (Taube 1992:84) and imitates the dripping liquid of the "star-war" hieroglyph. Unfortunately, the reading of this Postclassic name phrase resists complete decipherment. Although strictly conjecture, it is conceivable the water symbolism refers to the nautical horizon to the east and west of Mesoamerica where celestial bodies could be seen to arise and disappear in their daily circuit. The Dresden Codex proves that by the Postclassic era the Maya believed the power of the morning star passed from one deity to another as Venus cycles progressed through time (Schele and Grube 1997:97–138). Perhaps the ring of dots around God L's stolen clothing on the Classic-era ceramic signifies that his dominance of the morning star had receded or was soon to be restored.

That God L represents a Venus deity of the Classic period is certainly possible. As stated earlier, the iconography of the *Vase of Seven Gods* (Figure 5) establishes a relationship between the deity and Star (Venus?)-Earth bundles as early as the eighth century.

Figure 10. Detail of War Emblem Owl pectoral, Dos Pilas Stela 2 (redrawn after Carlson 1993:206, figure 8.2c [listed as detail of Stela 16]).

Figure 11. Star-over-Seibal hieroglyph. From STAR GODS OF THE MAYA: ASTRONOMY IN ART, FOLKLORE AND CALENDARS by Susan Milbrath, Copyright © 1999. By permission of the University of Texas Press.

His prominence in the Dresden Codex proves that by the Postclassic era God L was considered a dangerous entity when associated with the first station of Venus. While it is uncertain the meaning of God L remained consistent throughout the Classic to Postclassic eras, a comparative analysis of the timing of warfare at Naranjo and the information presented in the Venus tables of the Dresden Codex produces some interesting parallels.

In the Dresden Codex, 20 different Venus gods are named, each passing through various stages of activity. Representations of God L occur on the first and fifth pages of the almanac (pp. 46 and 50). These pages trace Venus movements during the first and last cycles of the five-part series that completes the inventory of Venus tracks and interlocks these cycles with the 365-day *haab* calendar (5 Venus cycles = 8 vague years). The fifth cycle sets into place the beginning of a new eight-year round, which returns a reader to cycle one and the repetition of the entire process. God L appears in the columns of p. 50 that mark the course of Venus through the 90-day superior conjunction and 250-day evening star phases. The final column stands for the 8-day inferior conjunction before the rise of a renewed Venus. The hieroglyphic text says that in his position moving towards and through the evening star phase, God L "was tied to the West" and "is fed in the West" (Schele and Grube 1997:115–117). Hence, the last evening star phase before inferior conjunction depicts a time of restraint and then regeneration for some Venus deities. With the start of a new cycle on p. 46 (Figure 12), God L emerges with the full force of his power as the ruler of this station and in the guise of a warrior. He is armed with darts with which he stabs the K'awiil below him. The augury predicts that when God L is "tied to the East" as morning star, there will be profound negative aspects for people, for the Maize God, and for rulers and rulership (Schele and Grube 1997:121–122).

Choosing this time for warfare, especially when the goal was to reestablish a fallen dynasty, would add psychological strength to a polity's military force (as long as one believed the power would not work against him). In fact, Naranjo instigated the first war in A.D. 693 during the changeover from a fifth station inferior conjunction to a first station morning star: the exact timeframe of God L's mythical dominance of Venus in the Postclassic document. According to Maya mythology, the base date of the Venus count in the Dresden Codex and the first mythical morning star rise of Venus occurred on 12.19.13.16.0, 1 Ajaw 18 K'ayab, a date 2,200 days before the inaugural appearance of the sun (Dütting 1984:8). My calculations (Table 4) show that 2,385 Venus cycles had passed since the

Figure 12. God L in Dresden Codex, page 46 (redrawn by author after Schele and Grube 1997:113).

Table 4. Venus Day-Count Calculation Since Dresden Codex Base Date.

Inferior conjunction of June 21, A.D. 693 (Gregorian) = Julian date	1,974,348
Mythical first rise of Venus on August 4, 3120 B.C. (Gregorian) = Julian date	-581,694
	1,392,654
Average length of Venus cycle	1,392,654
Total Venus cycles completed since base date August 4, 3120 B.C.	÷583.92
	2,385.0082

base date of the Dresden almanac, which correlates to a fifth to first station changeover. Therefore, if an almanac similar to the Dresden Codex existed during the Classic period, it would show that the initial attack of Naranjo's middle-period campaign fell under the auspices of God L in his Venus war guise. Moreover, the 12 Kawak Tzolk'in count that corresponds to the attack on January 17, A.D. 693 would be just one day before 13 Ajaw, a date the Maya predicted as a first station morning star rise (Schele and Grube 1997:109, Dresden 50, T8).

If a Venus almanac like the Dresden Codex did exist in the Classic period, it could help explain the narrative of the *Rabbit Vase.* The scene can be viewed as a parody of the rise of God L from a place of humble frailty to the awesome strength of a warrior endowed with the mythical power of Venus. Using the dates provided by Milbrath for the two episodes (Gregorian dates March 21, A.D. 700 and April 23, A.D. 700) places the narrative within the morning star phase of a new fifth station at the day-counts +126 and +159 respectively. At this point in the fifth station God L is weak; it is not until the Maya 90-day superior conjunction (+236) and evening star phase (+236 and +90) that he regenerates when "tied to the West" and "fed in the West." Continuing this speculative line of thought, the *Rabbit Vase* could then recount the deficiency of the pre-ascent period and the gradual accumulation of God L's prowess. Note that the first scene depicts God L wearing nothing but his smoking cap[10] while in the second episode he possesses a small backrack, two feathers extended above his forehead, and a noticeably large penis. The phallus could also present an iconographic link to Venus. According to Carlson (1993:225), male symbolism signifies Venus and the directional south, whereas female elements equate with the moon and north. If Carlson's assessment of gender symbolism is correct, the penis may insinuate Venus and its actual location in the southeast sector on March 21, A.D. 700.

CONCLUSIONS

It is clear from the text and imagery of Classic-period art and documents like the Postclassic Dresden Codex that the movement of celestial bodies was a topic of great importance to the ancient Maya. With this in mind, several authors have proposed that Maya warfare was timed according to cycles of the planet Venus. Research on this topic produced the assertion that Classic-period combat predominantly occurred during the evening star station. In contrast to this hypothesis, the timing of military events at Naranjo during the reign of K'ak' Tiliw Chan Chaak indicates a preference for aggression during inferior conjunction and the morning star phase of Venus. While the pattern of aggression during Naranjo's middle period suggests the possibility that military excursions were deliberately planned in accordance with Venus cycles, most of the conflicts are not recorded with specific reference to Venus but described with verbs like *jub'uy* (to bring down), *puluy* (to burn), and *chukaj* (someone captured). Further study of the ideology of warfare is needed to determine whether the cycles of Venus were important in all military endeavours or only those marked by the still unreadable "star war" hieroglyph. The data from Naranjo imply a deliberate pattern, but it remains inconclusive whether the position of Venus was actually a factor in military planning. The broad correspondence of dates could just as easily result from some other factor or perhaps even chance. Until we know more about the logistics and mechanisms of Maya warfare, this question will remain unanswered. One important point that surfaced with this research is the frailty of asserting an overall scheme for ancient warfare. If celestial positioning was indeed an element in the timing of military strikes, the favourability of a particular Venus station may have depended upon the site in question, ruler in power or era of military conflict.

It is conceivable that the tremendous success of K'ak' Tiliw may have been attributed to the proper timing of military campaigns or even the benevolence of a supernatural guardian. Appearing on three ceramic vessels made for Naranjo kings, including the personal drinking cup of K'ak' Tiliw, God L was apparently given special reverence at this site. The owl companion of God L links this deity to the new mode of warfare that surfaced in the Maya lowlands after the early Classic arrival of so-called "foreigners," a time that is marked by inscriptions naming Spear-Thrower Owl. God L prominently appears in the Venus pages of the late Postclassic Dresden Codex, but a specific relationship to Venus in Classic-period mythology, although possible, is not well established at present. The correlation of Naranjo's middle-period aggression within the fifth to first station changeover of Venus, the exact timeframe of God L's mythical power in the Dresden Codex, establishes an interesting parallel between the two eras. The iconography of many painted ceramics from the Classic period communicated at once a complex and multilayered mythology. One level of meaning that may be expressed by the narrative scene on the *Rabbit Vase* is the passage and conjunction of the sun, moon and Venus during the year A.D. 700. Another intention may have been to remind its owner of the ebb and flow of power as well as the continued need for ritual and prognostication to ensure the prosperity of Naranjo.

Acknowledgments

I gratefully acknowledge the assistance given by the 2001 Chacmool editorial committee. Their suggestions regarding the content of this paper helped to improve the quality and accuracy of my text. I also extend my gratitude to David H. Kelley (personal communication 2001) for his comments on various aspects of my research, and to Clive L. N. Ruggles (personal communication 2001), who introduced me to the work of John Carlson (1993) on the subject of Mesoamerican astronomy.

REFERENCES CITED

Aveni, A. F.
|2001| *Skywatchers*. University of Texas Press, Austin.

Aveni, A. F., and L. D. Hotaling
|1994| Monumental Inscriptions and the Observational Basis of Maya Planetary Astronomy. *Archaeoastronomy* 19: S21–S54.

Braswell, G. E. (editor)
|2003| *The Maya and Teotihuacan: Reinterpreting Early Classic Interaction*. University of Texas Press, Austin.

Carlson, J. B.
|1993| Venus-Regulated Warfare and Ritual Sacrifice in Mesoamerica. In *Astronomies and Cultures*, edited by C. L. N. Ruggles and N. J. Saunders, pp. 202–252. University Press of Colorado, Niwot.

Closs, M. P.
|1979| Venus in the Maya World: Glyphs, Gods and Associated Astronomical Phenomena. In *Tercera Redonda de Palenque*, vol. IV, edited by M. G. Robertson, pp. 147–165. Pre-Columbian Art Research Institute, San Francisco.

Dütting, D.
|1984| Venus, the Moon and the Gods of the Palenque Triad. *Zeitschrift für Ethnologie* 109(1): 7–74.

Dütting, D., and R. E. Johnson
|1993| The Regal Rabbit, the Night Sun and God L: An Analysis of Iconography and Texts on a Classic Maya Vase. *Baessler-Archiv* 41:167–205.

Grube, N., and L. Schele
|1994| Kuy, the Owl of Omen and War. *Mexicon* 16:10–17.
Harris, J., and M. Harris
|1993| Maya Calendrics. Maya Calendar Program Version 3.02.00.
Kelley, D. H.
|1980| Astronomical Identities of Mesoamerican Gods. *Archaeoastronomy* 2:S1–S54.
Kerr, J.
|1989| *The Maya Vase Book*, vol. I. Kerr Associates, New York.
|2003| Kerr Archives, Maya Vase Data Base. http://www.famsi.org/mayavase.
Lounsbury, F. G.
|1982| Astronomical Knowledge and its Uses at Bonampak, Mexico. In *Archaeoastronomy in the New World*, edited by A. F. Aveni, pp. 143–168. Cambridge University Press, Cambridge.
Malmström, V. H.
|1997| *Cycles of the Sun, Mysteries of the Moon*. University of Texas Press, Austin.
Martin, S., and N. Grube
|2000| *Chronicle of the Maya Kings and Queens*. Thames and Hudson, London.
Milbrath, S.
|1999| *Star Gods of the Maya: Astronomy in Art, Folklore, and Calendars*. University of Texas Press, Austin.
Nahm, W.
|1994| Maya Warfare and the Venus Year. *Mexicon* 16:6–10.
Reents-Budet, D.
|1994| *Painting the Maya Universe: Royal Ceramics of the Classic Period*. Duke University Press, Durham and London.
Schele, L., and D. Freidel
|1990| *A Forest of Kings*. William Morrow, New York.
Schele, L., and N. Grube
|1997| *The Proceedings of the Maya Hieroglyphic Workshop: The Dresden Codex, March 8–9, 1997*. Transcribed and edited by P. Wanyerka. University of Texas, Austin.
Sprajc, I.
|1998|[1996] *Venus, lluvia y maíz: simbolismo y astronomía en la cosmovisión mesoamericana*. Instituto Nacional de Antropología e Historia, México, D. F.
Stone, A.
|1989| Disconnection, Foreign Insignia, and Political Expansion: Teotihuacan and the Warrior Stelae of Piedras Negras. In *Mesoamerica after the Decline of Teotihuacan, A.D. 700–900*, edited by R. A. Diehl and J. C. Berlo, pp. 153–172. Dumbarton Oaks Research Library and Collections, Washington, D.C.
Stuart, D.
|1993| Breaking the Code: Rabbit Story. In *Lost Kingdoms of the Maya*, edited by G. S. Stuart, and G. E. Stuart, pp. 170–171. National Geographic Society, Washington, D.C.
|2000| "The Arrival of Strangers": Teotihuacán and Tollan in Classic Maya History. In *Mesoamerica's Classic Heritage*, edited by D. Carrasco, L. Jones, and S. Sessions, pp. 465–513. University of Colorado Press, Boulder.
Stuart, D., S. Houston, and J. Robertson
|1999| *The Proceedings of the Maya Hieroglyphic Workshop: Classic Maya Language and Classic Maya Gods, March 13–14, 1999*. Transcribed and edited by P. Wanyerka. University of Texas at Austin.
Taube, K. A.
|1992| *The Major Gods of Ancient Yucatan*. Dumbarton Oaks Research Library, Washington, D.C.
Thompson, J. E. S.
|1972| *A Commentary on the Dresden Codex*. American Philosophical Society, Philadelphia.
Wald, R., and M. D. Carrasco
|2004| *Rabbits, Gods, and Kings: The Interplay of Myth and History on the Regal Rabbit Vase*. Public presentation at the 2004 Maya Meetings at Texas, University of Texas at Austin.
Walker, J.
|2000| Home Planet. Release 3.1 for Windows 95/98. Software for planetary observations, http://www.fourmilab.ch/homeplanet/homeplanet.html, accessed September 2001.

NOTES

1 See Aveni (2001:80–94) for a detailed description of the celestial characteristics of Venus and the extraordinary correspondence of its cycles with the ancient Maya calendar. Because the reasoning behind the day-count assigned by the Maya is not understood, I use the canonical figures 8, 263, 50, and 263 in my reconstruction of ancient Venus cycles.

2 To calculate Venus positions at Naranjo, I employed the coordinates 17° 7' 30" N and 89° 13' 30" W. Home Planet software (Release 3.1, January 2000) by John Walker allowed me to simulate planetary positions for specific Long Count dates. All dates given in this paper are Julian dates unless otherwise stated. I utilized the Mark Harris and John Harris Mayan Calendrics program (Version 3.2.00; December 24, 1993; conversion base 584,285 and Gregorian calendar) to generate dates from Long Count inscriptions, which were then changed into the Julian format. Obviously, the value of my data is dependent upon the accuracy of the augmented Goodman-Martinez-Thompson correlation figure used here. Any significant change in this figure would throw the calculation of Venus cycles off mark. In this regard, I acknowledge the criticism of David H. Kelley (personal communication 2001), who disagrees with the currently accepted correlation numbers. In order to judge the validity of Kelley's criticism, I await the opportunity to review his as yet unpublished data on this question. To some degree, the correctness of data also relies on the authority of recorded dates. Because of political or ideological concerns the rulers

who presumably commissioned monumental stelae may have provided a falsified record of history. Even if inscriptional dates are unreal, however, the events and dates recorded may reflect a significant pattern that is culturally important.

3 The day-count figures given in Tables 2 and 3 are estimates based on the calculations of the John Walker program. As noted earlier in this essay, actual day-counts may vary up to 16 days from the approximated count due to the normal fluctuation of the synodic cycle (Schele and Grube 1997:104).

4 Figures 4 and 5 illustrate two of these vessels. The third, which is sometimes titled the *Vase of Eleven Gods*, is not included here due to limited space, but can be viewed at the Maya Vase Data Base (Kerr 2003:No. 7750).

5 I used the Goodman-Martinez-Thompson (+2) correlation figure of 585,285 for the calculation of Venus cycle dates, however, the two-day differentiation between this and the alternate figure (584,283) does not significantly alter the impact of my argument. Even if placed two days earlier, the war dates in question would fall within the Venus stations I have presented.

6 The transcription of the various segments of the *Rabbit Vase* text given in the paragraphs below are derived from the following published sources: Dütting and Johnson 1993; Stuart et al. 1999:44–49; as well as personal communications with epigraphers Michael D. Carrasco, Kerry Hull and Robert Wald in 2000 and 2001. My work on this vessel was part of a seminar project at the University of Texas during the spring of 2000, developed jointly with Penny Steinbach and under the supervision of Nikolai Grube. Further revisions to the text were made before publication of this essay based on the March 2004 Texas Meetings presentation by Robert Wald and Michael D. Carrasco (2004).

7 *Oxlajuun ok/waxaklajuun ik'kát/k'in?/nich'amaw/ nikuyte'?/yit/b'olon okte'/k'uh/uhtiiy/sak 'aj?/nal/ho nik* or *nichte'/b'olaynal...* {13 Ok/18 Wo/[is the] day?/I took or received/my owl? headdress/his accompaniment/9 or many pillars? or handles?/god/it happened/ [at the] white?/place/the five flower/ocelot place...}.

8 *Huk ak'b'al/uhtiiy/k'in/u-/witzil/pipha'?/chan ch'een/ hiin/pat-/b'uniiy/b'alam? tz'am?/te' b'a(j)/tok' b'a(j)...* {7 Ak'b'al/it happened/[on that] day/[at] its/mountain/lake or watery?/sky cave/I/turned it face down/ jaguar throne?/wood strikes/flint strikes...}.

9 In scene two, for example, God L says: *uch'amaw/ niye'te'/nib'uhk/nipat* {he took/my staff or display pole?/my clothes/my tribute or backrack?}. Wald and Carrasco (2004) favour the gloss "display pole" for *niye'te'*. Stuart et al. (1999:47) prefer "tribute" (rather than "backrack") for the word *pat*.

10 There appears to be a Kab'an glyph attached to God L's cap. Perhaps it represents the day following 1 Kib', which is predicted as the final date of an inferior conjunction in the fourth station, row 8 of the Dresden Codex (Schele and Grube 1997:109, Dresden 49, P8).

PERFORMING COATEPEC: THE RAISING OF THE BANNERS FESTIVAL AMONG THE MEXICA

Rex Koontz

Rex Koontz, Department of Art, 100 Fine Arts, University of Houston, Houston, Texas 77204, U.S.A.

ABSTRACT

The Mexica solar year festival Panquetzalitzli (Raising of the Banners) stood at the centre of Mexica definition of military might. This paper examines the mythological and ritual foundations of that definition, and how these were communicated to the populace during the festival period. I define a range of goods and power that circulated during the festival, isolating three elements: sacrificial human bodies, the body of the deity, and war banners. I propose that the movement of sacrificial human bodies from the captor's compound to the central religious precinct of Tenochtitlan was analogous to other movements toward the centre during these festivities. I hypothesize that the various banners of the Mexica warrior units were also brought to the centre and deployed during these rites. After the sacrificial bodies and war banners were assembled in the centre, the state then produced and shared the body of the patron deity, Huitzilopochtli, during the climax of the rites. The circulation of these three ritual goods created reciprocal relationships between warrior and state, and patron deity and people, which were performed and reaffirmed annually in the Raising of the Banner rites.

This essay examines one series of rites, that of Panquetzalitzli or "Raising of the Banners," and its accompanying backdrop of mythic space, as it was practiced by the Mexica in Central Mexico at the time of the Spanish Conquest. The goal of this investigation is to provide relevant information on the elements, uses, and power effects of the rites. I argue that the Raising of the Banners rituals stood at the centre of an economy of sacred martial power. Over the course of the festival, military groups were allied to the Mexica state through the sharing of the patron deity's body. Further, the festival commemorated a primordial war carried out by the patron deity, anchoring the contemporary circulation of power in that foundational event. Because of the concentration on the festival as it took place in Tenochtitlan, I use Mexica to designate the people of that city and their close allies in Tlatelolco, as opposed to the more popular term Aztec, which may embrace Nahuatl speakers of the entire Valley of Mexico and beyond.

The Raising of the Banners was one of 18 solar year festivals that organized the Mexica ritual calendar. These festivals were the chief public Mexica ritual performances (Quiñones Keber 2002:12–13). As a key festival of Mexica identity, the Raising of the Banners centred on the main temple of Tenochtitlan's sacred precinct (Templo Mayor). The relevant part of this temple was defined by the Mexica as Coatepec, the mountain where their patron deity was born and their first war was waged and won under the tutelage of the deity (León-Portilla 1987). In several sources this space was directly associated with Tollan (Place of the Bulrushes), the primordial city for the Mexica and the original seat of urban civilization. Tollan may be seen as the template for Mexica urban civilization, and indeed the Mexica followed its outline in executing the ceremonial centre of their urban capital, Tenochtitlan, where the banner raising rites were performed.

Much of the above is well rehearsed, due largely to the discovery of the "Coyolxauhqui Stone" during the late 1970s, underneath central Mexico City (Matos Moctezuma 1988). The iconography of the stone illustrates one well-attested aspect of the Coatepec tale, that of the dismemberment of Coyolxauhqui at the foot of Coatepec. The monument's placement at the foot of the south side of the Templo Mayor pyramid leaves no doubt that the Mexica conceived of this part of their central pyramid as Coatepec, as brilliantly analyzed by Matos Moctezuma (1988), León-Portilla (1987), and others. Beyond the simple iconographical identification, these same scholars linked the Coyolxauhqui monument to the performance of Panquetzalitzli, or the Raising of the Banners, staged annually at the foot of the Templo Mayor. Before this find, scholars had relied almost exclusively on the written documents produced after the fall of Tenochtitlan to recreate the rituals enacted in the centre of the city during its apogee. To find a monument that was directly associated with major rites made available the archaeological context of those rites as they were practiced in early sixteenth-century Tenochtitlan. The archaeological in formation revealed the actual ritual space and physical accoutrements that the early Colonial descriptions of the rites could not provide. This level of detail for an imperial Mexica festival simply did not exist previous to the excavations of the late 1970s, and was the source for a mass of publications on the festival and its context (Broda et al. 1987; Gutiérrez Solana 1989; León-Portilla 1987; Matos Moctezuma 1988).

COATEPEC/TOLLAN: IDEAL SPACE

The annual Mexica Banner rites took place in a well-defined time and space: that of Coatepec, or Hill of the Serpent. Much of the information about this primordial place comes from the migration cycle of the Mexica, where Coatepec was a stop on the way to founding their capital, Tenochtitlan (Smith 1984). Durán (1994:26) described Coatepec's importance like this: "The place [Coatepec] became filled with aquatic flowers and cattails... The Aztecs were so contented here, although it was no more than a model, no more than a pattern, of the promised land." More than just a stop on the migration trail, Coatepec was the indigenous Mexica model of central urban space, as is clearly indicated from the quote above. While the place is referred to as "no more than a model," Durán's informants are here making the point that Coatepec was not the final destination for the Mexica, but a preliminary glimpse of what was to be their urban capital, Mexico-Tenochtitlan. As model, however, the Coatepec episode sets the meaning for central urban space that is realized in the later capital.

For the student of Mesoamerican urban ceremonial space and its meanings, the idea of exploring the indigenous model over the physical reality of the capital has its advantages: instead of the copious laundry list of buildings we are given of the actual ceremonial precinct of Tenochtitlan (Sahagún 1950–1982, 2:165–180), or the detailed information found in the recent archaeological investigations of the most central part of the precinct (Gutiérrez Solana 1989; López Luján 1993), in the Coatepec descriptions the centre is stripped of its complexity and revealed in its most basic architectural configuration. The architecture is explained in terms of several fundamental mythic tropes, including the mountain/pyramid dedicated to the deity, the ball court below, and the centre of the ball court as the Itzompan, or place of the skull and decapitation sacrifice. The basic template is laid out and then utilized in these primordial texts, serving, as Durán noted, as models for later building at Tenochtitlan. Moreover, Coatepec is associated in time and space with Tollan. Sahagún (1950–1982, 2:1) states specifically that Coatepec is "near Tula" while Durán (1994:214) places it "in the province of Tula," thus making Coatepec a part of the larger Tollan complex. If we recall that Tollan is the figure of urban civilization for the Mexica, then it follows that the Coatepec episode, so closely linked to Tollan and the first migration stop to be described mainly in terms of constructed urban space, is the first revelation of this urban paradigm.

Two sixteenth-century manuscript groups deal specifically and at length with the Mexica image of Coatepec. Of these, the most detailed is the "Crónica X" group of Durán and Tezozomoc (Barlow 1945). All the important descriptions have the following in common (Figure 1):

1) A temple is built for the patron deity, Huitzilopochtli, on Coatepec itself;
2) A ball court is built at the foot of the mountain, and;
3) The people and their temples distribute themselves around these two central structures.

Figure 1 illustrates the temples mentioned by Tezozomoc (Alvarado Tezozomoc 1949:32).

The first Coatepec passage found in Sahagún (1950–1982, 3:1–5) is important for its detailed description of the supernatural events that occur on the mountain (see also Alvarado Tezozomoc 1944:12–14, 1949:30–

37; Durán 1994:25–28). These events define the fundamental importance and meaning of the space, for it will be these events that are commemorated by the Panquetzalitzli rites. The story may be summarized as follows.

Coatlicue (She of the Serpent Skirt), the mother of the 400 Southerners, is sweeping at the top of Coatepec when something like a ball of feathers descends on her. With these she is impregnated, which angers her innumerable sons and her one daughter (the latter is called Coyolxauhqui). The sons and daughter vow to kill their mother in order to relieve their shame at her pregnancy. Just as her offspring are going to commit matricide, Huitzilopochtli, the patron deity of the Mexica, is miraculously born to Coatlicue at the summit of Coatepec. He immediately makes war on his half-siblings. He defeats and sacrifices them on Coatepec, breaking the body of his half-sister Coyolxauhqui into pieces as he rolls her down the mountain.

In an important Crónica X variant (Alvarado Tezozomoc 1949:35), Coyolxauhqui is decapitated in the ball court at the foot of the mountain. In Durán (1994:25–28) and Tezozomoc (1949:32–36) this ball court plays a central role in the story, as Huitzilopochtli commands that it be built at the foot of Coatepec soon after the Mexica arrival. The patron deity then assures the irrigation of the crops through water bursting forth from a dammed canyon (Alvarado Tezozomoc 1949:34), or from a well in the centre the ball court itself, called the Iztompan or "place of the skull" (Alvarado Tezozomoc 1944:12; see Leyenaar and Parsons 1988:100–101).

Synthesizing these materials, Coatepec is the place where the patron deity first appears "in the flesh" and immediately makes successful war. It is the "place of portents" in the words of Miguel León-Portilla (1987:22), in that several characteristics glimpsed at Coatepec will become fundamental to Mexica society. This is especially true of the martial power of the patron deity, proven by his defeat of the 400 half-siblings, and its manifestation in the Mexica themselves, proven later by their ability to construct the empire. The plan of the central urban space contained in the tale is also portentous, in that it will manifest itself fully in the future Mexica capital, Tenochtitlan. Further, the ideal of urban civilization in all its aspects is contained in the concept of Tollan, to which Coatepec was attached through geography and conceptualization.

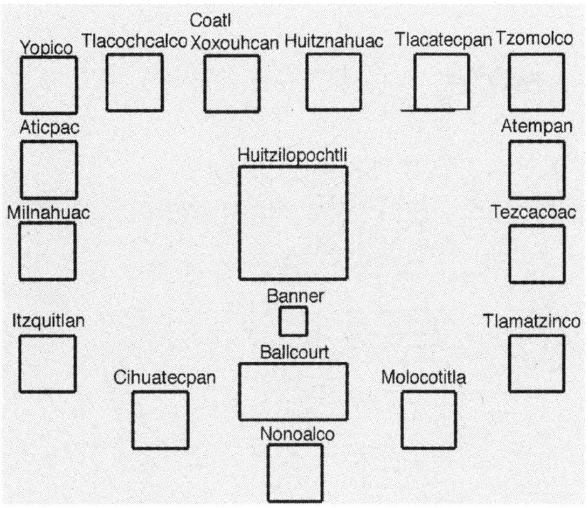

Figure 1. Schematic rendering of the Mexica settlement at Coatepec as described by Alvarado Tezozomoc 1944, 1949 (drawing by the author).

COATEPEC/TOLLAN: LIVED RITUAL

While the Coatepec/Tollan tales may contain many of the basic relations of symbols and space, that information will not tell us how the meaning was proclaimed by elites and lived by audiences (Low 2000:122). For that, we must turn to the performances that enlivened the space and reaffirmed the basic meanings attributed to the space in the foundational narratives. In this context Elizabeth Boone (1991) has shown that the migration stories were constructed along the lines of ritual performance. The migration "performance," which Boone (1991:122) compares to the monthly ceremonies such as the Panquetzalitzli festival, ends by transforming the Mexica from an unimportant wandering group to world conquerors. It is a classic rite of passage, with Coatepec as a central transformational moment. Further, the rites allow the Mexica elite to perform certain relations of military power, by bringing goods and symbols into the centre and deploying them in ritual contexts. These rites not only replicate the actions of the patron deity, but at the same time illustrate the hegemony of the Mexica elite who orchestrated these performances, as I argue below.

Given this close relationship between the migration tales and the festival that commemorated them, it is

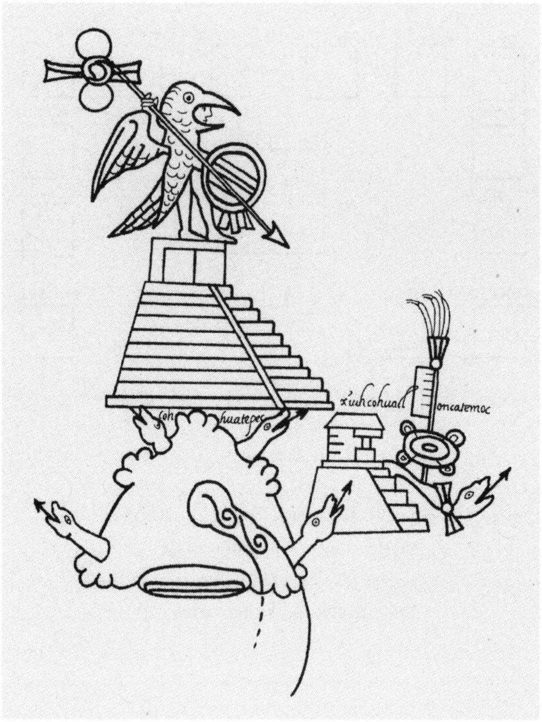

Figure 2. Codex Azcatitlan, p. 11, detail (drawing by Daniela Medeiros Epstein, courtesy of the artist).

interesting to note that none of the major texts used to describe the events at Coatepec mention banners in any form, although they become the major motif of the festival celebrating the Coatepec events. For evidence of banners at Coatepec during the migration epic, we must turn to the early pictorial manuscripts that illustrate the migration tale. In the Codex Azcatitlan (Barlow 1949), the Coatepec events are summarized on page 11 (Figure 2). Here we see the newly born patron deity, Huitzilopochtli, poised on the top of a temple, with his full hummingbird costume. In his right hand he holds a long spear, and in the left his shield, both emblematic of the war that immediately followed his birth. Below the temple is the sign for Coatepec, while to the side of this glyph is a smaller temple emitting a serpent with a banner emerging from its back. The banner form matches several war banners carried on the back of Mexica war captains, as illustrated in the Codex Mendoza (Berdan and Anawalt 1997:139, folio 67r). Although the overall shape and the rectangular flag element near the top are diagnostic of many Mexica war banners, the black disk midway up the shaft seems to be unique to this object. The associated text names the serpent as xiuhcoatl, "fire or turquoise serpent," a being mentioned in various related texts as accompanying the patron deity to war during his defeat of the 400. At times it serves him as his atlatl, or dart thrower, but here the serpent functions as carrier of the war banner of the patron deity. Although the texts do not mention this original banner, it is clear from this illustration that the Mexica were referencing the raising of the deity's war banner during their annual banner rites. Given the image above and the emphasis on banner manipulation in the annual Coatepec rites, it appears that banners were central to the performance of the Coatepec narrative.

FESTIVAL OF PANQUETZALIZTLI OR RAISING OF THE BANNERS

The Raising of the Banners festival took place inside the solar calendar round of festivals described for the Mexica, and indeed variations of this same festival cycle can be found throughout Post-Classic Mesoamerica. These always consist of 18 twenty-day "months" followed by a period of five days of an inauspicious nature. Each of the 18 months (often called *veintenas*) was associated with a particular deity or deities. Caso (1971:343) notes that the festival proper was celebrated on the last day of the month, when the deity or numinous power was especially venerated.

The documented details of the Panquetzalitzli rites are many (Caso 1971:339–343; Graulich 1999; Kubler and Gibson 1951:32–33). For our purposes, an outline with the fundamental actions will serve as an introduction and reference point for a later discussion of specific elements. I give below a general outline of the rites as they were practiced in Tenochtitlan, culled mainly from Sahagún (1950–1982, 2:130–138), the most detailed description of Contact-era practice extant.

1) Priests fasted for 80 days preceding the festival. They laid fir branches on all mountaintops and circular altars while remaining nude during this entire time. On the first day of the month they processed with shell trumpets while carrying fir branches.
2) Beginning on the first day of the

month, and continuing for the 20 days, the state prostitutes danced.

3) The old men from each ward gathered water from a sacred spring inside a cave, brought it to the foot of the Templo Mayor (Coatepec), and sprinkled each of the "bathed ones" (sacrificial victims captured in war or purchased for this festival) in a ritual purification. They gave each victim paper clothing, then painted the victims' bodies with blue and yellow striping, and gave them a nose piece in the shape of an arrow and reed and feather headdresses. The owners (the people who captured or paid for the victims) then returned home, each to his ward, and began to dance with their spouses.
4) Four days of fasting for the participants was followed by an elaborate nighttime "snake dance," where the dancers simulated the undulating movement of the serpent.
5) The next day was the last, and thus the true feast day of the month. At dawn, the sacrificial victims took leave of their captors, they "went singing as if they were hoarse." The victims' dress was again laid out for them, and "quite of their own will they arrayed themselves." The victims then danced in the central ceremonial courtyard of the ward that "owned" them.
6) All the city wards then delivered the victims to the central ceremonial courtyard of Tenochtitlan, directly in front of the Templo Mayor. The victims climbed the stairs, processed around the sacrificial stone in front of the Temple of Huitzilopochtli, and then came down again. They each ran back to the various wards that owned them. Here, an all-night vigil was given in their honor. The victims were given *pulque* and food. At midnight, their heads were shaved, the owners keeping the hair. Then, all over the city, the common people (*macehuales*) sat down to a meal of amaranth dough tamales. These tamales were not broken with their hands, but with the maguey thorns of sacrifice. Every common person in Tenochtitlan then went to sleep on the ground.
7) Just before dawn, the *ixiptla* (the physical manifestation) of Huitzilopochtli, which was embodied in a statue, descended from the Templo Mayor, carried by a god impersonator. When the deity arrived at the ball court at the base of the temple, four of the victims were slain, and their bodies are dragged around the court so that "it was if they painted it with the victims' blood."
8) The *ixiptla* of Huitzilopochtli was then processed around the Valley of Mexico. Runners carried him to sacred spots, and at each of these victims were slain.
9) At the same time that the image of Huitzilopochtli was being processed around the valley, back at the Templo Mayor a ritual battle pitted the sacrificial victims against impersonators of the 400 Southerners. When the *ixiptla* of Huitzilopochtli returned from the procession, the ritual officiants cried "Mexicans, now indeed he cometh! Now already the lord cometh! Enough!"
10) Meanwhile two seasoned warriors processed two of the most sacred war banners of the Mexica. These banners were called "devices for seeing," a reference to their ability to scry or otherwise divine. They took these banners to the top of the Temple of Huitzilopochtli, where another image of the god was waiting for them. This image was made of the same amaranth dough that went into the making of the commoner's tamales the night before. The two warriors threw the banners on the deity image, thus the quote "capturing" their patron deity. They then fell to the ground in front of this image; a priest cut their ears, to bleed and revive them. They sprang up and grabbed the amaranth dough image of their god, and then brought it in front of the Mexica king. A priest called Quetzalcoatl then killed the image by piercing it with a flint-tipped dart (Clavigero 1964:169–170; Sahagún

1950–1982, 3:6). The king then divided the image into two pieces, one for the residents of Tenochtitlan and one for their main allies, the people of Tlatelolco. The Mexica portion was then divided into four pieces, one for each ward of the city. The king and his councilors ate a portion of the body of their deity, and then the rest was distributed, in minute portions, to every Mexica male, who also devoured a portion of the body of the patron deity. The Mexica called this *teocualo*, "to eat god."

11) The victims were made to circle the temple one time. The Xiuhcoatl then descended from the top of the temple, just as the first fire serpent did on Coatepec. "It was just like a blazing pine firebrand. Its tongue was made of flaming red feathers" (Sahagún 1950–1982, 2:136). The priest who carried the serpent then pointed it at the four world directions, re-creating space and time at that moment. Then they burned the serpent.

12) The *ixiptla* of Huitzilopochtli was brought down for a second time. Then the victims were brought to the top of the Temple, and there they were sacrificed one by one and subsequently rolled down the temple stairway to the bottom.

13) Four days later the paper vestments of the victims were burned, and the ashes scattered. This signals the arrival of the victims in Mictlan, the place of the dead. Everyone then took a ritual bath. Here ends the festival of Panquetzalitzli.

Earlier analyses of the Panquetzalitzli rites have focused on the stunning dramatization of the original Coatepec story (León Portilla 1987; Matos Moctezuma 1988), and I have nothing to add to that essential literature. Instead, I wish to focus on the circulation of captives (or sacrificial bodies), the body of the god, and the movement of war banners as forming a systematic exchange. This exchange creates an economy of power moving through the Mexica populace over the course of the rites. In referring to an economy of ritual goods and power, I follow Johanna Broda (1979:74), who has discussed analogous movements for other Mexica rituals. Davíd Carrasco (1987:148) has also pointed out that the Templo Mayor was "the symbolic instrument for the collection and redistribution of wealth and goods from all over the empire," a definition that also alludes to the creation of an economy of power in that central space, in that the wealth and goods were intimately bound up with the distribution of power.

Beginning with #3 above, the rites focus most closely on the "bathed ones," captives who have been taken in war or purchased for the purpose. While the purchase of captives by merchants and their eventual incorporation into the banner rites is an important element of the festival, a full discussion is beyond the scope of this paper, which has as its focus the sacrificial victims captured in war. These captives were closely associated with their captors at the beginning of the festival cycle: they were taken to the centre where they were ritually purified and given the vestments for their role, then they were brought back to their captor's ward where they were the centre of festivity and ritual over several days (events #3–5). Finally on the main feast day these captives leave the ward of their captor to move to the centre, where the most public rites were held (event #6). Here their Mexica captors, who up to this point held ownership and oversaw most of the rituals surrounding these captive bodies, gave the victim up to the central rites. These rites include the eventual sacrifice of the captive at the Templo Mayor/Coatepec. All these rites were grounded in the slow movement of the captive from captor to state, from ward deity to Huitzilopochtli, and from peripheral temple to the central temple/mountain of Coatepec. Thus the economy of warfare sacrifice, evidenced in the captive's bodies, may be seen as a tribute system, where the captor's produce is eventually claimed by the state. In other instances, sacrificial victims brought to the centre by vassals were literally part of the tribute paid the empire (Durán 1994:329).

At dawn of the feast day (event #7), the ritual reenactment of the Coatepec episode began. Four of the captives were made to impersonate the enemies of Huitzilopochtli and were slain in the ball court at the base of Coatepec, echoing the Tezozomoc description of Coyolxauhqui's decapitation cited above. A battle involving the captives and some Mexica warriors was then joined around the temple, echoing the battle waged by Huitzilopochtli at Coatepec. Huitzilopochtli himself was processed around the Valley in what was described as a circuit of homage for the deity. Although the places visited do not strictly conform to the central imperial area (Hodge 1996:18), the circuit took in 15 km (Clavigero 1964:190) and may have also functioned as a definition of the heart of empire for Mexica society.

After the procession of Huitzilopochtli around the valley and the mock battle at the centre, a curious thing happened: the Mexica ruler "captured" an amaranth dough statue of the deity, and then distributed the god's body to the population (event #10). This was done with the aid of two sacred war banners of the Mexica, called "devices for seeing." These are described as "sprays of feathers, with a hole in their midst" (Sahagún 1950–1982, 2:135). Two seasoned warriors processed the banners through the Eagle Portal to the top of the Templo Mayor, where they were thrown upon the amaranth dough statue of Huitzilopochtli. The patron deity is now referred to as "captured," and Sahagún recounts how the amaranth dough image was taken home and eaten. Clavigero (1964:170) states that the amaranth dough statue was kept until the next morning, when a solemn ceremony took place with only the king and several high-ranking priests in attendance. The statue was "killed" by an arrow shot, after which the statue's heart was removed and given to the king to eat. Only then was the statue divided up, a tiny piece to be given to every Mexica male. While one wonders how this may have been done, the basic symbolism is clear: the males were to share in the patron deity's martial exploits through this rite. This ceremony was called *teocualo*, or "eating god."

The directionality of human sacrificial bodies and the "captured" amaranth dough body of the patron deity is clear: as the sacrificial bodies move toward the centre and become the property of the patron deity, the body of the god goes out, with the centre serving as the central node of redistribution. As David Carrasco (1987:153) has pointed out, Mexica sacrificial rites were not only a "feeding" of the god, but also "a ritual re-creating Aztec dominance and power established in their sacred history." Certainly this is the case with foreign guests who were invited to sacrificial rites for the express purpose of inspiring awe and fear in them (Durán 1994:328–336). At the same time, these rites afforded the Mexica governing class the space to proclaim hegemony over the Mexica people. Sahagún (1950–1982: Book 9:65) states that during Panquetzalitzli the commoners were allowed into the sacred precinct to watch these festivities. The participation of the populace is never clearer than in the Panquetzalitzli rites, where the foundational martial power of the god, established in their sacred history, is literally distributed to the (male) population through the distribution of the deity's amaranth dough body. The debt payment in exchange for this circulation of divine power is a captive or slave to be sacrificed at Huitzilopochtli's altar, a rite clearly controlled by the Mexica state.

While the circulation of human bodies is described in the great majority of sources on the fiesta, what of the banners that give the festival its name? The commentator on Codex Vaticanus A states that the festival was so named because everyone put a small paper banner on top of the house to honor "this god of battles" (Anders et al. 1996:233), and it is possible that the name of the festival descends from this practice or the use of small paper banners in Mexica ritual sacrifices. There is extensive evidence, however, that the festival concerns the manipulation of Mexica war banners. We have already seen how the mythical underpinning of the rites – Huitzilopochtli's victory at Coatepec – contained illustrations of a war banner being raised at the foot of the mountain (Figure 2). The Templo Mayor, which became a re-creation of Coatepec during these rites, was found with banner bearers cached along the foot of the pyramid on axis with Huitzilopochtli's shrine during one of the earlier stages of the building (Matos Moctezuma 1988:73). Further, the image of Huitzilopochtli that decorates codical references to the Panquetzalitzli rites routinely holds a Mexica war banner in one hand. Codex Vaticanus A is an especially telling example, because the banner held by Huitzilopochtli that announces the rites (page 49v) is very similar to the illustrations of high-ranking Mexica warriors with banners in the same codex (page 58v; see Anders et al. 1996). Tovar (Kubler and Gibson 1951:32) suggests that Panquetzalitzli was the special feast of the Mexica war captains, and that a war banner was set up in the middle of the courtyard to mark the occasion. Let us recall that Mexica captains wore the banners during battle, suggesting that they also donned the banners during their festival. Sahagún (1950–1982, 2:132) mentions the participation of "those who would carry the banners," but it is unclear if this passage alludes to the two carriers of the sacred banners already mentioned, or to other banner bearers. Taken together, the above details strongly suggest that Panquetzalitzli involved war banner manipulation, as its name would imply, but the Spanish preoccupation with the festival's sacrifices caused them to ignore much of the martial symbolism and organization. Indeed, much of the information on banners comes from the indigenous drawings and recently excavated archaeological materials, as we have seen.

While we may have identified Mexica war banner manipulation during the Panquetzalitzli rites, we have not defined the meaning and function of the war banner itself. The chief method for identifying Mexica military units was through the use of these banners (Hassig 1988:57–58). These standards were tied tight to wearers and placed in the centre of the military group, as the physical sign of that group. Normally, the head of the unit wore the standard (Clavigero 1964:226). If the banner was taken or destroyed, the entire unit fled. If the military commander or king lost their banner, then the entire army retreated (Hassig 1988:58–59). It is clear that these banners were the physical embodiment of the military group, lovingly protected, with their loss feared above almost all else (Freidel et al. 1993:295). These are the instruments that would have been manipulated during the Raising the Banners festival, if one accepts my arguments above. To bring these banners into the centre of the city over the course of the festival may be seen as indicative of the control of military might by the Mexica state, in that the gathering of banners was a sign of military allegiance, just as it was when the army organized itself around these banners in actual battle (Hassig 1988:96–97). To hypothesize further, the array of banner bearers at the foot of the temple would have been the place of important banner placement, perhaps of the chief military divisions of Tenochtitlan. While this is certainly speculative, it would echo elegantly the patron deity's banner raising at the foot of Coatepec during the primordial war, as illustrated in the codices and discussed above.

This ability of the Mexica centre to attract to itself military insignia, and thus military power, has a further analogue in the Coatepec narratives. After the defeat of his enemies at Coatepec, Huitzilopochtli strips the defeated of their insignia. Sahagún (1950–1982, 3:5) states "he assumed them [the insignia] as his due, as if taking the insignia to himself." Davíd Carrasco (1999:63–64) has discussed the deposition of several thousand foreign ritual items by the Mexica at the Templo Mayor as the same sort of action. Like Huitzilopochtli appropriating the insignia of the defeated, the Mexica would take the ritual items of subjugated cultures, eventually depositing them in the foundation of the Templo Mayor/Coatepec. Thus the building calls to itself the ritual power of the tributaries through the deposition of their ritual objects in the building itself. If one accepts my argument for the circulation of war banners above, then they too are part of this centripetal motion over the course of the festival: the banners are brought into the centre and raised, echoing Huitzilopochtli's banner raising during the war on Coatepec. By replicating the patron deity's act, the Mexica war captains are at the same time putting themselves in the service of those who govern in the name of Huitzilopochtli.

CONCLUSIONS

The festival of Panquetzalitzli created an economy of supernatural and martial power, carefully controlled by the Mexica state. The marketplace for this economy was the ritual area in front of the Templo Mayor/Coatepec. It is not metaphorical to say that the goods obtained by the state – war captives and banners, indices of the allegiance of the military groups – were fundamental to Mexica might. In exchange, the state produced the primordial supernatural martial power. Let us recall that this was the feast in the annual round that celebrated the military prowess of the Mexica patron deity, and by direct extension Mexica military might. Military insignia were gifted out by the king himself during another of the solar year festivals, Ochpaniztli, which was celebrated less than three months before the Raising of the Banners (Broda 1979:53–54; Sahagún 1950–1982, 2:114–116). These insignia were brought back to the centre during Panquetzalitzli, which now may be seen as a physical manifestation of the military alliances that undergirded Mexica governance. Further, the banners were able through this movement towards the centre to replicate the original banner raised by Huitzilopochtli on Coatepec (Figure 2).

In this way the Raising of the Banners festival allowed the Mexica elite to orchestrate a performance of certain power relations, especially as they involved the military. By bringing the captives into the centre in celebration of the state's rites, the bodies were treated as tribute, and in other contexts were demanded as such. The immediate reciprocal gift from the state was the body of the patron deity, created through ritual and embodied in an amaranth dough statue that was shared among the male Mexica. I have suggested here that war banners were circulated during the festival in much the same way as sacrificial bodies, where the banners of the war captains were brought into the centre, under the aegis of the patron deity and hence the state. Through the reenactment of the original banner raising, the Mexica elite were able to assemble, and hence control, the martial groups that served as the basis of Mexica might.

REFERENCES CITED

Alvarado Tezozomoc, F.
|1944| *Crónica Mexicana*. Editorial Leyenda, México, D.F.
|1949| *Crónica Mexicayotl*. Translated by Adrian León. Imprenta Universitaria, México, D.F.

Anders, F., M. Jansen, and L. Reyes García
|1996| *Religión costumbres e historia de los antiguos mexicanos*. Fondo de Cultura Económica, México, D.F.

Barlow, R. H.
|1945| La crónica X: Versiones coloniales de la historia de los méxica-tenochca. *Revista Mexicana de Estudios Antropológicos* 7(1–3):65–87
|1949| Codex Azcatitlan. *Journal de la Société des Americanistes* 38:101–135

Berdan, F. F., and P. R. Anawalt
|1997| *The Essential Codex Mendoza*. University of California Press, Berkeley, California.

Boone, E. H.
|1991| Migration Histories as Ritual Performance. In *To Change Place: Aztec Ceremonial Landscapes*, edited by Davíd Carrasco, pp. 121–151. University of Colorado Press, Niwot, Colorado.

Broda, J.
|1979| Estratificación social y ritual mexica: Un ensayo de Antropología Social de los mexica. *Indiana* 5:45–82

Broda, J., D. Carrasco, and E. Matos Moctezuma
|1987| *The Great Temple of Tenochtitlan: Center and Periphery in the Aztec World*. University of California Press, Berkeley, California.

Carrasco, D.
|1987| Myth, Cosmic Terror and the Templo Mayor. In *The Great Temple of Tenochtitlan: Center and Periphery in the Aztec World*, edited by J. Broda, D. Carrasco, and E. Matos Moctezuma, pp. 124–162. University of California Press, Berkeley, California.
|1999| *City of Sacrifice: The Aztec Empire and the Role of Violence in Civilization*. Beacon Press, Boston, Massachusetts.

Caso, A.
|1971| Calendrical Systems of Central Mexico. In *Archaeology of Northern Mesoamerica*, pt. 1, edited by G. F. Ekholm, and I. Bernal, pp. 333–348. Handbook of Middle American Indians, vol. 10. University of Texas Press, Austin, Texas.

Clavigero, F. J.
|1964| *Historia Antigua de México*. Editorial Porrua, México, D.F.

Durán, D.
|1994| *The History of the Indies of New Spain*. Translated, annotated, and with an introduction by Doris Heyden. University of Oklahoma Press, Norman, Oklahoma.

Freidel, D., L. Schele, and J. Parker
|1993| *Maya Cosmos: Three Thousand Years on the Shaman's Path*. William Morrow, New York.

Graulich, M.
|1999| *Ritos aztecas: las fiestas de las veintenas*. Instituto Nacional Indigenista, México, D.F.

Gutiérrez Solana, N.
|1989| Diez años de estudios sobre el Templo Mayor de Tenochtitlán, 1978–1988. *Anales del Instituto d e Investigaciones Estéticas* 60:7–31

Hassig, R.
|1988| *Aztec Warfare: Imperial Expansion and Political Control*. University of Oklahoma Press, Norman, Oklahoma.

Hodge, M. G.
|1996| Political Organization of the Central Provinces. In *Aztec Imperial Strategies*, edited by F. Berdan et al., pp. 17–46. Dumbarton Oaks, Washington, D.C.

Kubler, G., and C. Gibson
|1951| *The Tovar Calendar: An Illustrated Mexican Manuscript ca. 1585*. Memoirs of the Connecticut Academy of Arts and Sciences Vol. XI. Connecticut Academy of Arts and Sciences, New Haven, Connecticut.

León-Portilla, M.
|1987| *México-Tenochtitlan: su tiempo y espacio sagrados*. Plaza y Valdés, México, D.F.

Leyenaar, T. J., and L. A. Parsons.
|1988| *Ulama: Het balspel bij de Maya's en Azteken/The Ballgame of the Maya and Aztecs*. Spruyt, Van Mantgem and De Does, Leiden, Holland.

López Luján, L.
|1993| *Las ofrendas del Templo Mayor de Tenochtitlán*. Instituto Nacional de Antropología e Historia, México, D.F.

Low, S. M.
|2000| *On the Plaza: The Politics of Space and Culture*. University of Texas Press, Austin, Texas.

Matos Moctezuma, E.
|1988| *The Great Temple of the Aztecs: Treasure of Tenochtitlan*. Thames and Hudson, London.

Quiñones Keber, E.
|2002| Representing Aztec Ritual in the Work of Sahagún. In *Representing Aztec Ritual: Performance, Text and Image in the Work of Sahagún*, edited by E. Quiñones Keber, pp. 3–20. University Press of Colorado, Boulder, Colorado.
Sahagún, Fray B. de
|1950–1982| *Florentine Codex: General History of the Things of New Spain*, translated by A. J. O. Anderson, and C. E. Dibble. 13 vols. School of American Research and the University of Utah, Santa Fe, New Mexico.
Smith, M. E.
|1984| The Aztlan Migrations of the Nahuatl Chronicles: Myth or History? *Ethnohistory* 31:153–186.

PART VIII: FRAMEWORK FOR THE FUTURE

ARCHAEOLOGY IN THE NEW WORLD ORDER: WHAT WE CAN OFFER THE PLANET

Carole L. Crumley

Carole Crumley, Department of Anthropology, CB #3115, 301 Alumni Building, University of North Carolina, Chapel Hill, North Carolina 27599-3115, U.S.A.

The image of the "blue marble," first seen by humans from space in 1969, brought forth from all who saw it a surprisingly strong and tender response. So lonely, so beautiful, suspended in darkness, our planet was encountered for the first time as a single entity, a system of air and rock and water and living organisms that every one of us calls home. It seemed that by means of the technology that had endeavoured to outdistance her, Gaia, our planet, had found her voice.

I was in Sicily that summer, employed as site architect for excavations of Morgantina, where a famous revolt of slaves against their Roman masters, led by Spartacus, had taken place. So I was down about two metres and back a couple millennia in time. In the trattoria in town we watched the moon landing and I first saw the image. Gaiophilia, love of Earth, swept over me, throughout that summer and to this day.

Certain problems now clearly jeopardize the health of our beautiful planet: the dangers to environmental, political and social security brought on by the global-scale loss of biodiversity, anthropogenic pollution and climate change, war, and other conditions. Since 1969 the purview of my chosen field of archaeology has expanded, increasing information available at many scales. However, on several frontiers – spatial, temporal, cognitive – archaeologists must now be prepared to apply their insights and expertise to important issues that affect our species at a Gaian scale.

Archaeologists have long known that humans alter the environment and environmental change revises human activity, but now the scale of impact is broader than at any time in the human past. Our Pleistocene ancestors affected the success of plant and animal communities, eventually at the regional scale. By 6,000 years ago, human settlement and land use had altered coastlines, soil productivity, and the courses of rivers on every inhabited continent. By 2,000 years ago, ice- and marine sediment-cores, vegetation, and other proxy evidence document the effects of African and Eurasian deforestation which, through agricultural and industrial activities, altered key components of the Earth's atmosphere, affected sea level and global average temperatures, and changed climate at the continental scale (Crumley 1994; Redman 1999).

Humans were, and are, a keystone species: human behaviour affects the evolutionary success of species other than our own. As humanity struggles with huge environmental problems largely of our own making, it has become fashionable to demonize the human role altogether. Yet despite what would seem to be ample evidence to the contrary, archaeologists have documented human modifications to their surroundings that were not always destructive. Until the industrial revolution transformed landscapes, resources, and populations (e.g., intensified urbanization), just the opposite was more common. The majority of humans did not live in cities but in much smaller communities where extraction and consumption patterns were local and regional.

Throughout the world, archaeologists, anthropologists, and others have recorded the strategies and practices that maintain environmental productivity. Based on lengthy and astute observation (referred to as cultural knowledge), many peoples have and do manage complex ecosystems using environmentally sound and organizationally sophisticated solutions. This is not to say that non-industrial and non-urban peoples are by definition Ecologically Noble, but neither must we humans be invariably *Homo devastans* (Balée 1998:16).

For example, a network of water temples – the precolonial means used in Bali to irrigate rice terraces – maintained community values as well as the landscape in which they were embedded; researchers seeking the "most efficient" solution to water management there discovered that their computer model mirrored the traditional temple-based management practice (Lansing 1987, 1991). In the Amazon basin, societies maintain the rainforest as if it were a garden: people encourage or discourage certain species, employ the organic soils found at abandoned settlements, and demonstrably increase biodiversity (Graham 1998; Posey 1998). In contrast, the exponential twentieth-century acceleration in the rate of change attendant on the extraction of fossil fuels has resulted in profound planet-wide economic, social, political and cognitive transformations (industrialization, urbanization, globalization) that pose myriad threats to our planet. Now everyone – archaeologist, Amazon gardener, international industrialist – must fear that damage may already be irreversible. Gaia speaks and we must listen, as inaction is potentially lethal to our species.

RUPTURE AND SYNTHESIS

The bright promise of a pragmatic management science at the dawn of the twentieth century was soon lost to eugenics, diverted by wars, sunk in disciplinary rivalries. A critical collaborative link between the synthetic disciplines of geography and anthropology was broken, eclipsing (among other fields) archaeology. The integrative study of Earth systems was sacrificed to a rivalry over funding among atmospheric, marine, and biological sciences, whose definition of the Earth system excluded humans. By the middle of the century, a second costly and immensely destructive world war in as many decades had left most industrial nations in ruins. Cities on several continents were destroyed, people and landscapes were contaminated, and even the most rudimentary environmental management had been everywhere sacrificed to win the war. In victory, the United States alone enjoyed an expansion of its industrial might and political hegemony. With the aid of military technologies adapted to peacetime and Cold War uses and a G. I. Bill-educated workforce, the 1950s and early 1960s were a time of wide-eyed economic optimism and environmental slumber.

Only Rachel Carson, Robert Oppenheimer and a few others warned of serious anthropogenic threats to health and the environment posed by burgeoning chemical and fossil fuel industries and the unabated production of radioactive materials. As Big Science gave way to budget cuts in the 1980s, the highly technical fields with economic applications competed against one another for government support while integrative projects as well as many field sciences (e.g., botany, zoology) were underfunded. With the fall of the Berlin Wall in 1989, it could be seen that the impoverished Eastern Bloc countries' extraction and manufacturing patterns (if not those of consumption) were worse than but remarkably similar to those in the West. Not only had twentieth-century degradation reached the global scale, but integrative scholarship had been caught napping.

When physicist and novelist C. P. Snow first characterized the chasm between the sciences and the humanities as the "two cultures" (1959), there was much discussion but little urgency to bridge that gap. Now it is imperative that the human use of the earth be understood in an integrated fashion if we are to frame effective environmental policies for the future. It is fortunate that several twentieth-century disciplinary and cross-disciplinary intellectual traditions, while marginalized economically and politically, have continued to contribute to our ability to link the past with the future and the microscopic with the cosmic. Chief among them is archaeology.

Archaeologists have advanced their field in three major areas: *spatial* analysis, *temporal* refinement, and *interpretative* approaches. This work underscores the integrative program of archaeology: spatial and temporal control, primarily the purview of science, is essential to all archaeology, but all archaeological interpretation must address more ideational and cognitive factors such as cultural difference and researcher bias.

SPACE

In a little over 100 years we have built our interpretations on the *artifact* and the *site* (which continue to be rich sources of information), expanding to the *environs of the site* (e.g., 1950s catchment archaeology), then *settlement patterns*, *settlement systems* and *drainages* (1950s through 1970s), and *landscapes* (1980s to the present). Logically we should expect the next step to be the culture history of entire *regions* and *continents*, and eventually the entire planet.

Time

One hundred years ago, only a few places on the planet had roughly accurate chronologies (e.g., Egypt, Mesopotamia); now reasonably good chronologies exist nearly everywhere. They are of course not perfect, but the broad outline of human occupation may be sketched, and in many areas change may be charted across both time and space. This advance gives us the opportunity to compare distant coeval activity and to ask new questions about how human societies respond to hemispheric and planetary-scale environmental change (e.g., the Little Ice Age, the end of the Pleistocene). Now archaeologists can hold space constant and practice "trans-temporal" archaeology (the study of all time periods in their region), tracing changes in a variety of parameters across the landscape. My own work on changing landscapes in east-central France, for example, spans more than 2,800 years of Burgundian history (Crumley and Marquardt 1987; Crumley 1995a, 2000).

Mind

Landscape-based approaches have opened many doors, allowing us to see how previous modifications affected subsequent inhabitants and how our own discipline's temporal and spatial biases have often obscured major cultural shifts which could only seen by examining a variety of temporal or spatial scales. They also have exposed our own discipline's myopia, and we have been beneficially challenged by the postmodern and postprocessual critiques of researcher bias; two examples are gender studies (Gero and Conkey 1991; Zihlman 1997) and the critique of "complexity" as hierarchy. Among other effects, such shifts in archaeological understanding have allowed us to refute Christopher Hawkes' (1954) gloomy assertion that archaeologists could hope to infer very little of the life of the mind in the past. We have been able to investigate paleo-cognition, including perceptions, values, belief, power relations and many other topics hardly imagined 50 years ago.

INTELLECTUAL ARCHITECTURE FOR THE GLOBAL SCALE

Three concepts that draw on intellectual traditions already familiar to many archaeologists could leverage the next stage of integration. They are the *new systems theory*, an alternative form of order termed *heterarchy*, and a revival and expansion of *multiscale ecology*.

New systems theory

Systems theory was a major influence on ecology from the outset, and complex systems have been a focus of research since the 1930s (Bateson 1972; Ellen 1982). The benefits of environmental systems thinking are considerable, but there have also been significant criticisms. Chief among several issues is the charge that systems thinking is inherently reductionist and leads to the study of simpler and simpler systems at more and more minute scales. Just the reverse is required if we are to study our planet, the most complex dissipative system known. Another problem has been the quest by systems ecologists for "pristine" ecosystems to study (that is, ones ostensibly "without human impact") and the tendency to leave time out of their considerations of systemic function and structure. These criticisms have resulted in the search for a framework that draws on the strengths of systems theory, relates myriad anthropogenic and exogenous factors, and integrates every spatial scale from microscopic to global and all temporal scales.

Since its founding in 1984, researchers at the Santa Fe Institute (SFI) have concentrated on understanding the dynamics of complex systems in new ways.[1] They and investigators elsewhere have developed a new candidate idea: self-organization. The governing assumption in self-organization research is holism, the idea that an organism is more than just the sum of its parts. The self-organization researchers are critical of reductionist scientific endeavour, where the basic assumption has been that if the entity (living or not) can be broken down into its constituent parts, its behaviour can be understood.

Briefly they contend that current understandings of evolution force us to see a universe in which randomness alone explains the infinitesimal chance that life could be created out of a chemical soup. In other words, in the evolutionary process the introduction of transmission errors through mutation and the operation of selection do not alone explain the complexity that may be seen in myriad living systems, from fireflies to fiddle players. They argue that a second, more fundamental source of order exists, called *self-organization*. This means that there is a synergy that comes from communication, and that two (or more) communicating entities have different properties than each alone (Jantsch 1982; Kauffman 1993, 1995; Langton 1992; Mithen 1996). The development of communication is important for both the emergence of cognition in human history and the formation of community. The self-renewing, autonomous, reproductive aspect of self-organization (termed autopoiesis) may be related to two varieties of human communication, language and social organization, that persist in collective memory and material culture and are stored and passed on from generation to generation (Crumley 2000; Gunn 1994; McIntosh et al. 2000). This is, of course, an essential definition of culture and a valuable entry point for anthropologists and especially archaeologists.

The Santa Fe scholars and their colleagues do not advocate the abandonment of Darwinian evolution as a central paradigm, but rather the *addition* of self-organization. Together, they argue, selection and self-organization form the structure of the universe; neither alone suffices. Together, Darwinian evolution and self-organization bring order from chaos: self-organization creates new forms, and evolution judges their goodness of fit. Each new stage of organization has the potential for further change, emphasizing the transformative nature of communication.

Key universal features of complex systems thinking are: *integration* (holism), *communication* (self-organization) and *history/initial conditions* (what SFI researchers term chaos). These correspond with key features of *social* systems: integration (culture), communication (language, society), and history/initial conditions (traditions, structures and materials, strategies, habits of mind). This new systems thinking has opened an important door between the social and biophysical sciences, in that systems thinking has been revised to accommodate the results of human cognition (religion, politics, systems of formal knowledge such as science). Archaeologists, already familiar with "old" systems thinking and its critique, can find refreshing potential in complex systems research, which offers a means by which human history and culture can be accommodated in a biophysical framework.

Re-visioning societal order

From earliest human societies to the present day, coupled individual creativity and collective flexibility have met with success. Thus biological diversity has a correlate in human societies: the toleration of difference in individuals and groups and of variety in circumstances increases societal choice and offers a reserve of alternative solutions to problems. Similarly, organizational flexibility – economic, social and political – enables societies to adjust to changed circumstances.

Although there exist several useful vocabularies for discussing the organizational characteristics of society, twentieth-century American archaeology was dominated by one: the framework of band, tribe, chiefdom and state (Service 1971). Using this framework, considerable flexibility was attributed to bands and tribes, but much less to stratified society (chiefdoms and states). The difference was seen primarily in terms of increasing order, manifest in hierarchies of power and their attendant systems of communication. Yet while hierarchical organization characterizes many aspects of state power, hierarchy alone does not capture the full range of state organizational relations. Alternative forms of social order and state power – coalitions, federations, leagues, unions, communities – are just as important to state operation as they are in more egalitarian groups (bands and tribes).

Terming such groupings associations, Service noted their importance. Unfortunately, subsequent archaeological theory disregarded this avenue and concentrated instead on how power pyramids are constructed by elites. Yet as the September 11, 2001 events demonstrate, power flows in many channels (Samford 2000) and can manifest entirely outside the framework of state hierarchies and beyond their control. In self-organization terminology, this is termed *chaos* or surprise (Crumley 2001) and is related to systemic negligence in engaging other dimensions of power.

Hierarchy (the classic, pyramidal organizational form) is a structure composed of elements that on the basis of certain factors are subordinate to others and may be ranked (Crumley 1979:44, 1987b:158). In a control hierarchy each higher level exerts control over the next lower level; the U. S. court system and the army are control hierarchies. By contrast, disturbances at any level in a scalar hierarchy (referring only to the size of the conceptual field) can affect any other scales (Crumley 1995b:2). This is because in control hierarchies, individuals and groups with authority and those with responsibility are isomorphic; information and the means of communicating it becomes a commodity to be hoarded (e.g., literacy). In scalar hierarchies, for better or worse, elements at all scales are in communication with elements at all other scales.

Another way of conceiving of this meshwork of dimensions and levels is as a heterarchy, a term that describes the relation of elements to one another when they are unranked, or when they possess the potential for being ranked in a number of different ways depending on conditions (Crumley 1987b:158).[2] Understood from a heterarchical perspective, sources of power are counterpoised and linked to values, which are fluid and respond to changing situations. This definition of heterarchy and its application to social systems is congruent with Warren McCulloch's research into how the brain works. A strong influence on the self-organizing systems theorist Kauffman (1993, 1995:xx), McCulloch first employed heterarchy in a contemporary context (1945) in the examination of independent cognitive structures in the brain, the collective organization of which he terms heterarchy. He demonstrates that the human brain is not organized hierarchically but adjusts to the re-ranking of values as circumstances change. McCulloch's heterarchical "nervous nets," source of the brain's flexibility, is a fractal (same structure at a different scale) of the adaptability of fluidly organized, highly communicative groups.

For example, an individual may highly value human life in general, but be against abortion rights and for the death penalty (or vice versa). The context of the inquiry and changing (and frequently conflicting) values (Bailey 1971; Cancian 1965, 1976; Crumley 1987b) mitigates this logical inconsistency and is related to what Bateson (1972) terms a "double bind." Priorities are re-ranked relative to conditions and can result in major structural adjustment (Crumley and Marquardt 1987:615–617).

McCulloch's insight about the autonomous nature of information stored in the brain and how parts of the brain communicate revolutionized the neural study of the brain. It also solved major organizational problems in the fields of artificial intelligence and computer design (Minsky and Papert 1972). What McCulloch realized was that information stored in bundles as values in one part of the brain may or may not be correlated with information stored elsewhere, depending on the context; in computer terminology, subroutine A can subsume ("call") subroutine B and vice versa, depending on the requirements of the program. Rather than the "tree" hierarchy of the first computers, those today use an addressing (information-locating) RAM (random access memory) system that is heterarchical, more like a network or matrix.

In summary, heterarchies are self-organizing systems in which the elements stand counterpoised to one another. In social systems, the power of various elements may fluctuate relative to conditions, one of the most important of which is the degree of systemic communication. Hierarchies and heterarchies of power coexist in all human societies, including states. Societal dilemmas in which values are in conflict are resolved by achieving a novel, transcendent state that either ranks competing values relative to one another (hierarchy) or does not allow them to be definitively ranked (heterarchy). At each successive level of integration and over time, new ordering principles come into play. Thus, conflict or inutility leads to suspension of old forms but ensure the preservation of useful elements through communication to provide creative new solutions to challenges (transcendence of older forms). In these novel forms societies retain near-term flexibility, although there is of course no guarantee that the new form is more stable than the old or that tensions will not reappear in another guise (surprise). For example, revitalization movements such as the Ghost Dance or Christianity seek transcendence through individual and collective rededication based on both new information and the retention of selected old values; an example is the "born again" phenomenon, also termed mazeway reformulation (Wallace 1970).

The addition of the term heterarchy as a descriptor of power relations in so-called complex societies (Crumley 1979, 1987b, 1995b) is a reminder that there exist in every society forms of order that are not hierarchical, and that interactive elements in complex systems need not be permanently ranked relative to one another. Although a heterarchical ("egalitarian") form of order has long been recognized in smaller ("simpler") societies, it has been rejected as an appropriate organizational form for states. It is both impractical and inaccurate to exclude such a fundamental adjustment mechanism from the characterization of more populous political forms. The more successfully a society consolidates power and melds distinct hierarchies (e.g., religious, political, economic) into hyperhierarchy or hypercoherence, the less flexibility there is in dealing with surprise. The current theoretical paradigm in archaeology, which falsely assumes that the only form of order is hierarchy, no longer explains data collected in many parts of the world (Ehrenreich et al. 1995). The new systems thinking and the concept of heterarchy can reinvigorate archaeological interpretation.

Revitalizing multiscale ecology

First used by natural scientists in the late nineteenth century, the term ecology (from the Greek *oikos*, dwelling) emphasizes the reciprocal relationships among living and nonliving elements of our world. Growing in concert with systems theory, ecology had emerged as a discipline in its own right by the 1960s. The generation that came of age at about the same time our species first set foot off-planet (1969) could hardly help but note the contrast between American postwar materialism and the growing human, economic, and environmental toll in Viet Nam. They were the first eager students of the new academic discipline of ecology, which became for them a shorthand for the relation of our species to all facets of its *oikos*. That first view of the blue planet and the compelling spirituality of the Gaia hypothesis embraced a definition of ecology – broadly integrative relationships among living organisms and the physical environment – that includes all scales (local to global) of relations among living and nonliving elements, including humans.

The discipline of ecology has since bifurcated, and its emphasis has undergone a scalar shift. Today microecology, with ties through cell and molecular biology and genomics to schools of medicine and public health, dominates the field; macroecology (e.g., wildlife ecology, landscape ecology, Earth systems ecology) trains fewer practitioners and garners fewer research dollars than its larger and better-connected twin. Although Russian scientists pioneered the concept (Budyko 1980), only recently has the West perceived the need for a global-scale ecology. Broader-scale ecologies (e.g., landscape ecology) are increasingly important, but lessons from the social sciences and humanities have been incorporated slowly therein. For example, many landscape ecologists conceive ecosystems as "natural" and human presence there as invariably negative, including the scholarly presence of the research scientists themselves (e.g., Forman and Godron 1986; Naveh and Lieberman 1990). This attitude is slowly beginning to change, as journals such as *Landscape Ecology*, *Ecological Restoration* and *Ecological Applications* offer a forum for integrated approaches and ample opportunity for archaeologists to participate.

The "two cultures" divide between science and the humanities, to which C. P. Snow brought attention, cost twentieth-century ecology not only the insight of multiple spatial scales but also those of time. But it was not just ecology that forgot history in the rush to model process; so too did geography, much of anthropology (including for a time archaeology itself), physics and (even more mystifying) climatology (with the exceptions of Gordon Manley and H. H. Lamb). I recall the open derision of any scientific link between climate and human history from NOAA atmospheric scientists (mostly modelers) as late as a 1992 conference organized by archaeologist Ervan Garrison and applied anthropologist Shirley Fiske. Circumstances have changed in the interim and atmospheric scientists are now more interested in climate history, thanks to the work of some modelers (e.g., John Kutzbach) but much of the burden has rested on historians, geographers, archaeologists and palynologists to demonstrate the utility of historical analogues (e.g., Crumley 1994; Gunn 2000; Hughes 1975; PAGES Newsletter 2000; Pfister et al. 1992, 1999; Redman 1999).

Why might this be so? A journal editor who analyzed reviewers' comments found that scientists consider historians' (mostly qualitative) approaches imprecise and their styles of argumentation histrionic; historians perceive scientific (mostly quantitative) methods to be mechanistic and their findings trivial (Ingerson 1994). While historians rightly concentrate on both intended and unintended consequences of human action and offer convincing examples of the plastic role of history and culture, they usually have less command of the biophysical systems that further condition human activity. For their part, many scientists remain naive about how "natural" systems are shaped by politics, belief and other aspects of society.

This is a powerful moment for anthropology, which trains practitioners to be familiar with both the sciences and the humanities. Anthropologists and especially archaeologists, familiar with ecological theory, ecological applications, and their critiques, are well positioned to make use of this return to an ecology practiced at multiple spatial scales, and to insist that human activity be folded into understandings about the ecosystem of which we are an undeniable part. What our discipline must also ensure is the practice of human ecology at multiple *temporal* scales, in the same sense that the practice of geology is an interpretative dialectic between structure and process.

AN INTERDISCIPLINARY EFFORT

Clearly, humans must respond *both* to global changes that make local differences *and* to local practices that drive global change, employing every means at our disposal. We must search for common ground, in relatively new terrain and on relatively neutral terms. The term *environment* must encompass the built environment, the cultural landscape, and nature wild and tame. The definition of *ecology* must include humans as a component of all ecosystems. The term *history* must include that of the Earth system as well as the social and physical past of our species.

Construction of an integrated framework has proven difficult. One issue has been the scalar incompatibility of human activity with planetary-scale atmospheric phenomena. Patterns of settlement and land use, emissions, and extractive procedures must be investigated at regional and local scales. On the other hand, collective human response to global-scale changes (e.g., climate) must be verified at the macroscale through methods involving parallel change events in widely dispersed regions. Growing scientific understanding of the interconnectivity of the atmosphere, hydrosphere, biosphere and geosphere in the global system provides reasonable background cause-and-effect linkages and cyclicity, but wide-ranging social science theory and methods are needed to document human activity at all temporal and spatial scales and attribute broader systemic causation. But without environmental and cultural information at local and regional scales, there exists no opportunity to test and refine global models; without planetary-scale confirmation of the long-term effects of human activity, arguments over values (embedded in property rights, social justice, environmental policy, and other issues) will continue without action.

Historical ecology explores complex chains of mutual causation in human-environment relations, drawing on concepts from the biological and physical sciences and ecology, and from social sciences and humanities disciplines. The practice of historical ecology draws a picture of human-environment relations over time in a particular place, through the integration of a broad spectrum of evidence from every discipline.[3] Focusing on the unique characteristics of place, historical ecologists identify: (1) extant environmental and cultural evidence for the region in question; (2) the range of current practices likely to be impacted by environmental change; (3) effective responses, found in traditional and innovative adaptive strategies appropriate to the region and to the culture(s) affected, and to the nature and magnitude of the anticipated change; and (4) the means by which such adaptations might be fostered through policy.

The term historical ecology – new to both ecology and history – was chosen in an effort to foster collaboration in two crucial social science disciplines (anthropology and geography) and among several hybrid fields (e.g., environmental history, environmental sociology, landscape ecology) that seek to mend the divide between the two cultures. While environmental history has a distinguished and somewhat parallel development among historians (e.g., Cronon 1983, 1995; Crosby 1986, 1994; Worster 1977, 1993), the more inclusive term historical ecology facilitates intra- and interdisciplinary collaboration in the study of changing human-environment relations.

Of interest to researchers in historical ecology are rules for treating diverse evidentiary categories (e.g., all lines of evidence must initially be treated as independent). Multiple cause-and-effect relationships must be presumed, that provide an important cross-check on physical environmental data and on instrumental records. Other work relates the history of place and the politics of compliance and links scientific and institutional goals with public awareness and participation (Brosius 2001; Johnston 2001). The political and historical study of collaborative schemes for solving differences of opinion on environmental issues is rich: some schemes are matrix organization, collective bargaining, stakeholder participation, the European Union's term *concertation* (meaning dialogue, cooperation). The study of such schemes underscores the formative and transformative aspects of environmental values and perceptions (Poncelet 2001).

The development of an interdisciplinary grammar and the identification of shared concepts and understandings is also well along. For example, the term *landscape* is a unit of analysis in several disciplines (archaeology, geography, ecology, geomorphology, architecture, art, regional planning) and as a concept in scores of others. Broadly defined as the spatial manifestation of the relations between humans and their environment (Marquardt and Crumley 1987:1), landscapes offer several advantages. The study of changes in the temporal and spatial configurations of landscapes (a traditional pursuit of archaeology), in conjunction with work in cognition, offers practical means of integrating the natural and social sciences and the humanities. Landscapes record both intentional and unintentional acts; in its study, *both* humans' role in the modification of the global ecosystem *and* the importance of past events in shaping human choice and action can be assessed. Since cultural understandings undergird decisions about which practices are maintained or modified and which ideas are given substance, landscapes retain the physical evidence of these understandings. Such common terms, especially when their variant meanings stimulate discussion and help integrate diverse evidence.

Perhaps the most important characteristic of historical ecology is that it celebrates *both* the open-mindedness of scientific inquiry *and* the phenomenological intensity of human experience. The historical ecology of any part of the world is always an unfinished manuscript, passed from hand to hand, critiqued, debated, amended, and revised. The approach values historical insights, stimulates creative thinking about the mitigation of contemporary problems, and encourages locally and regionally developed answers to global situations in which sensitive cultural issues play an important part. It is, after all, through reflection upon intended and unintended change that all people are moved to action.

Historical ecology offers an important opportunity for anthropologists, archaeologists, historians, and geographers to demonstrate the relevance of work in which they have been engaged for a century. Such an interdisciplinary approach is traditional for archaeologists, who routinely consult science and humanities colleagues or have training themselves in these disciplines. Archaeology alone provides the temporal and spatial breadth required for long-term ecological analysis.

Several national professional organizations have found utility in historical ecology. For example, the Society for Ecological Restoration (SER) has published an historical ecology handbook for their many members (Egan and Howell 2001). Restorationists must struggle with the political, social, and economic implications of landscape restoration projects; it is then impossible for ecological restorationists to do their job without integrating biotic and social communities at multiple temporal and spatial scales.

Government agencies also benefit from this integrated approach. For example, the National Science Foundation's Long Term Ecological Research (LTER) projects in ecosystem history are now 20 years old and number 22 sites. The newest of these are two urban ecosystems, Central Arizona-Phoenix (headed by archaeologist Chuck Redman) and Baltimore. In them, NSF's LTER project has stepped into the future, as now over half of the world's population lives in cities and that percentage is expected to steadily increase. It is imperative that we learn the historical ecology of cities to learn how they can become part of the global system without permanent damage.

At the global level, international institutions (the International Geosphere-Biosphere Project [IGBP], the World Meteorological Organization, the United Nations' International Council of Scientific Unions [ICSU], United Nations Educational, Scientific, and Cultural Organization [UNESCO], the Scientific Committee on the Protection of the Environment [SCOPE], and the International Union of Biological Sciences [IUBS]) are already searching for the means by which global-scale changes can be related to local- and regional-scale activity. These organizations, through new local and regional "case studies," concur that cultural and biophysical differences among regions preclude the success of top-down models of ecosystemic change (Oldfield 1993, 1996).

Finally, policy makers at every level must address myriad issues (e.g., agricultural and industrial productivity, insurance, health) in which human and environmental conditions are inextricable. Not only must they respond to emergencies but anticipate future crises. The only laboratory available to us is the past, and we must make the best of the analytic resources we have. What is new for policy makers is the realization that both culture (there is no reform without compliance), and scale (there must be a framework to understand changes that occur well beyond their jurisdictions) count (Johnston 2001).

In sum, a powerful array of conceptual and practical tools has been combined into a toolbox termed historical ecology, permitting the integrated investigation of ecosystemic change at global, regional, and local scales. The few-million-year human time frame can be compared with the billions of years of Earth history; local and regional changes can be compared and contrasted with measures that reflect the state of the Earth system as a whole. We have the means by which we can study ourselves as a conscious species in conjunction with the history of our planet.

WHY ARCHAEOLOGISTS AND WHAT'S NEXT?

Archaeologists, who must always place human activity in its environmental context, have pioneered the integration of biophysical data with evidence of human activity. Archaeologists' theoretical and methodological insights may be traced in the history of twentieth-century archaeology; it is then not surprising that the earliest practitioners of historical ecology were archaeologists. What is new for archaeologists is the planetary scale of thinking about the human-environment interface (Tainter 1988).

Archaeology has guarded many useful aspects of anthropology's federative disciplinary structure, drawing important ideas from sister fields. Archaeology has its own sophisticated interpretative framework that integrates many disciplines and works across the "two cultures" divide. Archaeologists are experienced in interdisciplinary project management and employ integrative theoretical and practical techniques drawn from many fields of study (e.g., geomatics). Archaeology has space/time models that include a familiarity with environmental reasoning and research. Archaeologists can model forward and backward; that is, we can use contemporary data to investigate the past and use historical circumstances to illuminate contemporary issues.

Archaeologists also engage in lively and principled debate. Although our debates are sometimes acrimonious, painful and embarrassing (e.g., Kennewick) they are largely open, invariably instructive and more often than not result in action (e.g., legislation, public education) that transmits broad lessons about our species and the planet we call home. A good example is the North American Graves Protection Act (NAGPRA). This and other debates *within* our field have been turned into legislation (e.g., Carl Chapman and Bob McGimsey's successful efforts to protect cultural resources) and public education (see the Society for American Archaeology website http://www.saa.org/Education/index.html) by means of which we can transmit broad lessons. Abiding public interest in archaeology gives us a broader audience than sociologists or economists or cultural anthropologists.

Archaeologists can take action in three ways. First, we can join together with other researchers to understand regional, trans-regional and supra-regional patterns. An example would be to form a "virtual consortium" linking archaeological and paleoenvironmental research at the scale of the circum-Gulf of Mexico region (joining the U. S. Gulf coast with Middle America and the Caribbean); the next broader scale would compare the cultural effects of Gulf climate with other areas governed by the Azores High (temperate Europe, the Mediterranean, northern Africa). In other words, what are the long term effects on human populations of the augmentation or diminution of the power of the Azores High? Since the strength of the Azores High is a function of global average temperature, much could be learned about the effects of global warming on human societies.

Second, we can join up with other societies (e.g., the American Society for Environmental History, the Society for Ecological Restoration) and with international scientific organizations (e.g., ILTERs, IGBP-PAGES). It is easy to learn about the activities of these societies and organizations on the Internet, and to contact individuals for more information. For example, visit IGBP-PAGES at http://www.pages_igbp.org/, choose structure, then scroll down to the Human Impacts on Terrestrial Ecosystems (HITE) initiative. To add to the integrated history of these ecosystems and the global database, HITE palynologists and geomorphologists wish to work with archaeologists who are engaged in trans-temporal regional studies.

Third, we can speak out on lessons from the past that inform the present (e.g., environmental degradation, local knowledge, flexibility, diversity) to administrators, lawmakers, the public. My own work in Burgundy has in recent years focused on the lessons that may be gleaned from a broad time-scale analysis of climate and land use. We have been able to demonstrate the ecological and economic benefits of diversity in crops and livestock, the importance of cultural knowledge, and that climatic variation (hot to cold to wet to dry) is more difficult to manage than consistent extremes (cold, drought).

I have outlined the role archaeology can play in joining the human sciences with research on Earth's physical system, and the urgency with which we must proceed. It is critical that we settle on a flexible research design to address issues that will shape our human future. A scheme such as historical ecology – which itself is yet unfinished and incomplete – can make use of appropriate information, whatever its form and from whatever discipline.

The arrow of causation in the evolution of all systems – including human societies – must be seen to be two ways; that is, we are not inevitably on a rising stair of human accomplishment but can find ourselves in the blink of an eye in a condition much more dire and hopeless than any time in that part of human history red in tooth and claw. As a species like any other, there is no guarantee of progress. Finally, we must review a description of the world that is solely mechanistic, denying spirituality as an essential characteristic of the human species. We have allowed pragmatic arguments to triumph in almost every quarter, and to relegate emotions to a small, closely moderated compartment of our psyche. While they were not the earnest ecologists some have imagined, our human forebearers did at least see that the sun, the heavens, the earth, the waters, their fellow creatures and themselves were all a single system, and held all sacred. While they too made management mistakes, they never lost sight of the integrated nature of the universe. We must attempt to retrieve this lost insight.

REFERENCES CITED

Adams, R. N.
|1988| *The Eighth Day: Social Evolution as the Self-Organization of Energy*. University of Texas Press, Austin.

Bailey, F. G. (editor)
|1971| *Gifts and Poison: The Politics of Reputation*. Basil Blackwell, Oxford.

Balée, W. (editor)
|1998| *Advances in Historical Ecology*. Columbia University Press, New York.

Bateson, G.
|1972| *Steps Toward an Ecology of Mind*. Ballentine, New York.

Bilsky, L. J. (editor)
|1980| *Historical Ecology: Essays on Environment and Social Change*. Kennikat Press, Port Washington, New York.

Brosius, J. P.
|2001| The Politics of Ethnographic Presence: Sites and Topologies in the Study of Transnational Movements. *New Directions in Anthropology and Environment: Intersections*, edited by C. L. Crumley, pp. 150–176. Altamira Press, Walnut Creek, California.

Bryson, R. A., and T. J. Murray
|1977| *Climates of Hunger*. University of Wisconsin Press, Madison.

Budyko, M. I.
|1980| *Global Ecology*. Progress Publishers, Moscow.

Cancian, F.
|1965| *Economics and Prestige in a Maya Community: The Religious Cargo System in Zincantan*. Stanford University Press, Stanford, California.
|1976| Social Stratification. *Annual Review of Anthropology* 5:227–248.

Cronon, W. J.
|1983| *Changes in the Land: Indians, Colonists, and the Ecology of New England*. Hill and Wang, New York.
|1995| *Uncommon Ground: Toward Reinventing Nature*. Norton, New York.

Crosby, A. W.
|1986| *Ecological Imperialism: The Biological Expansion of Europe, 900–1900*. Cambridge University Press, Cambridge.
|1994| *Germs, Seeds, and Animals: Studies in Ecological History*. Sharpe, Armonk, New York.

Crumley, C. L.
|1979| Three Locational Models: An Epistemological Assessment for Anthropology and Archaeology. In *Advances in Archaeological Method and Theory*, edited by M. Schiffer, pp. 141–173. Academic Press, New York.
|1987a| Celtic Settlement before the Conquest: The Dialectics of Landscape and Power. In *Regional Dynamics: Burgundian Landscapes in Historical Perspective*, edited by C. L. Crumley and W. H. Marquardt. Academic Press, San Diego.
|1987b| A Dialectical Critique of Hierarchy. In *Power Relations and State Formation*, edited by T. C. Patterson, and C. W. Gailey, pp. 155–168. American Anthropological Association, Washington, D.C.
|1993| Analyzing Historic Ecotonal Shifts. *Ecological Applications* 3(3):377–384.
|1994| The Ecology of Conquest: Contrasting Agropastoral and Agricultural Societies' Adaptation to Climatic Change. In *Historical Ecology: Cultural Knowledge and Changing Landscapes*, edited by C. L. Crumley, pp. 183–201. School of American Research Press, Santa Fe.
|1995a| Building an Historical Ecology of Gaulish Polities. In *Celtic Chiefdom, Celtic State*, edited by B. Gibson, and B. Arnold, pp. 26–33. Cambridge University Press, Cambridge.

|1995b| Heterarchy and the Analysis of Complex Societies. In *Heterarchy and the Analysis of Complex Societies*, edited by R. M. Ehrenreich, C. L. Crumley, and J. E. Levy, pp. 1–5. Archaeological Papers of the American Anthropological Association No. 6. American Anthropological Association, Washington, D.C.
|2000| From Garden to Globe: Linking Time and Space with Meaning and Memory. In *The Way the Wind Blows: Climate, History, and Human Action*, edited by R. J. McIntosh, J. A. Tainter, and S. K. McIntosh, pp. 193–208. Columbia University Press, New York.
|2001| Communication, Holism, and the Evolution of Sociopolitical Complexity. In *Leaders to Rulers: The Development of Political Centralization*, edited by J. Haas, pp. 19–33. Plenum, New York.

Crumley, C. L. (editor)
|1994| *Historical Ecology: Cultural Knowledge and Changing Landscapes*. School of American Research Press, Santa Fe.
|2001| *New Directions in Anthropology and Environment: Intersections*. Altamira Press, Walnut Creek, California.

Crumley, C. L., and W. H. Marquardt (editors)
|1987| *Regional Dynamics: Burgundian Landscapes in Historical Perspective*. Academic Press, San Diego.

Egan, D., and E. A. Howell (editors)
|2001| *The Historical Ecology Handbook: A Restorationist's Guide to Reference Ecosystems*. Island Press, Washington, D.C.

Ehrenreich, R. M., C. L. Crumley, and J. E. Levy (editors)
|1995| *Heterarchy and the Analysis of Complex Societies*. Archaeological Papers of the American Anthropological Association No. 6. American Anthropological Association, Washington, D.C.

Ellen, R.
|1982| *Environment, Subsistence, System: The Ecology of Small Scale Social Formations*. Cambridge University Press, Cambridge.

Forman, R. T. T., and M. Godron
|1986| *Landscape Ecology*. Wiley and Sons, New York.

Gero, J. M., and M. W. Conkey (editors)
|1991| *Engendering Archaeology: Women and Prehistory*. Basil Blackwell, Oxford.

Goodwin, B.
|1994| How the Leopard Changed its Spots: The Evolution of Complexity. Weidenfeld & Nicholson, London.

Graham, E.
|1988| Metaphor and Metamorphism: Some Thoughts on Environmental Metahistory. In *Advances in Historical Ecology*, edited by W. Balée and C. L. Crumley, pp. 119–137. Historical Ecology Series, W. Balée, and C. L. Crumley, general editors, Columbia University Press, New York.

Gunn, J. D.
|1994| Global Climate and Regional Biocultural Diversity. In *Historical Ecology: Cultural Knowledge and Changing Landscapes*, edited by Carole L. Crumley, pp. 67–97. School of American Research Press, Santa Fe.

Gunn, J. D. (editor)
|1988| *The Years Without Summer: Tracing A.D. 536 and its Aftermath*. British Archaeological Reports S872. British Archaeological Reports, Oxford.

Hawkes, C.
|1954| Archeological Theory and Method: Some Suggestions from the Old World. *American Anthropologist* 56(2):155–168.

Hughes, J. D.
|1975| *Ecology in Ancient Civilizations*. University of New Mexico Press, Albuquerque.

Ingerson, A. E.
|1994| Tracking and Testing the Nature/Culture Dichotomy in Practice. In *Historical Ecology: Cultural Knowledge and Changing Landscapes*, edited by C. L. Crumley, pp. 43–66. School of American Research Press, Santa Fe.

Jantsch, E.
|1982| From Self-Reference to Self-Transcendence: The Evolution of Self-Organization Dynamics. In *Self-Organization and Dissipative Structures: Applications in the Physical and Social Sciences*, edited by W. C. Schieve, and P. M. Allen. University of Texas Press, Austin.

Johnston, B. R.
|1998| Anthropology and Environmental Justice: Analysts, Advocates, Mediators, and Troublemakers. In *New Directions in Anthropology and Environment: Intersections*, edited by C. L. Crumley, pp. 132–149. Altamira Press, Walnut Creek, California.

Kauffman, S. A.
|1993| *The Origins of Order: Self-Organization and Selection in Evolution*. Oxford University Press, New York.
|1995| *At Home in the Universe: The Search for Laws of Self-Organization and Complexity*. Oxford University Press, New York.

Kiel, L. D., and E. Elliott (editors)
|1996| *Chaos Theory in the Social Sciences: Foundations and Applicati*ons. University of Michigan Press, Ann Arbor.

Kontopoulos, K. M.
|1993| *The Logics of Social Structure*. Structural Analysis in the Social Sciences 6. Cambridge University Press, Cambridge.

Lamb, H. H.
|1972–1977| *Climate: Present, Past, and Future*. Methuen, London.
|1995| *Climate, History, and the Modern World*. 2nd ed. Routledge, London.

Langton, C. G. (editor)
|1992| *Artificial Life II: Proceedings of the Workshop on Artificial Life, Santa Fe, NM*. Addison-Wesley, Redwood City, California.

Lansing, S. J.
|1987| Balinese Water Temples and the Management of Irrigation. *American Anthropologist* 89:326–341.
|1991| *Priests and Programmers: Technologies of Power in the Engineered Landscape of Bali*. Princeton University Press, Princeton, New Jersey.

Lewin, R.
|1999| *Complexity: Life at the Edge of Chaos*. 2nd ed. University of Chicago Press, Chicago.

McCulloch, W. S.
|1945| A Heterarchy of Values Determined by the Topology of Nervous Nets. *Bulletin of Mathematical Biophysics* 7:89–93.

McIntosh, R., J. A. Tainter, and S. K. McIntosh (editors)
|2001| *The Way the Wind Blows: Climate, History, and Human Action*. Historical Ecology Series, W. H. Balée, and C. L. Crumley, general editors, Columbia University Press, New York.
Mingers, J.
|1995| *Self-Producing Systems: Implications and Applications of Autopoiesis*. Plenum, New York.
Minsky, M., and S. Papert
|1972| *Artificial Intelligence Progress Report (AI Memo 252)*. MIT Artificial Intelligence Laboratory, Cambridge.
Mithen, S.
|1996| *The Prehistory of the Mind: The Cognitive Origins of Art, Religion and Science*. Thames and Hudson, London.
Naveh, Z., and A. S. Lieberman
|1990| *Theory and Application*. Student ed. Springer-Verlag, New York.
Oldfield, F.
|1993| Forward to the Past: Changing Approaches to Quaternary Palaeoecology. In *Climate Change and Human Impact on the Landscape*, edited by F. M. Chambers. Chapman Hall, London.
|1996| Palaeoenvironmental Narrative and Scenario Science. In *Companion Encyclopaedia of Geography: The Environment and Humankind*, edited by I. Douglas, K. Tuggett, and M. Robinson, pp. 952–964. Routledge, London.
PAGES Newsletter (http://www.pages_igbp.org/)
|2000| Ecosystem Processes and Past Human Impacts. *PAGES Newsletter* 8(3), December.
Pfister, C.
|1999| *Wetternachhersage: 500 Jahre Klimavariationen und Naturkatastrophen (1496–1995)*. P. Haupt, Bern.
Pfister, C., B. Frenzel, and B. Glaser (editors)
|1992| *European Climate Reconstructed from Documentary Data: Methods and Results*. G. Fischer, Stuttgart.
Poncelet, E. C.
|2001| The Discourse of Environmental Partnerships. In *New Directions in Anthropology and Environment: Intersections*, edited by C. L. Crumley, pp. 273–291. Altamira Press, Walnut Creek, California.
Posey, D. A.
|1997| Diachronic Ecotones and Anthropogenic Landscapes in Amazonia: Contesting the Consciousness of Conservation. In *Advances in Historical Ecology*, edited by W. Balée, pp. 104–118. Historical Ecology Series, W. Balée, and C. L. Crumley, general editors, Columbia University Press, New York.
Redman, C. L.
|1999| *Human Impact on Ancient Environments*. University of Arizona Press, Tucson.
Samford, P.
|2000| Power Flows in Many Channels: Pits and West African-Based Spiritual Traditions in Colonial Virginia. Unpublished Ph.D. dissertation, Department of Anthropology, University of North Carolina, Chapel Hill.
Schieve, W. C., and P. M. Allen (editors)
|1982| *Self-Organization and Dissipative Structures: Applications in the Physical and Social Sciences*. University of Texas Press, Austin.
Scott, G. P. (editor)
|1991| *Time, Rhythms, and Chaos in the New Dialogue with Nature*. University of Iowa Press, Ames, Iowa.
Service, E. R.
|1971| *Profiles in Ethnology*. Harper and Row, New York.
Snow, C. P.
|1959| *The Two Cultures and the Scientific Revolution*. Cambridge University Press, New York.
Tainter, J. A.
|1988| *The Collapse of Complex Societies*. Cambridge University Press, Cambridge.
Wallace, A. F. C.
|1970| *Culture and Personality*. 2nd ed. Random House, New York.
Williams, G. P.
|1997| *Chaos Theory Tamed*. Joseph Henry Press, Washington, D.C.
Worster, D.
|1977| *Nature's Economy: A History of Ecological Ideas*. University Press, New York.
|1993| *The Wealth of Nature: Environmental History and the Ecological Imagination*. Oxford University Press, New York.
Zihlman, A.
|1997| *Paleolithic Glass Ceiling: Women in Human Evolution*. Routledge, London.

NOTES

1 If you are interested in reading more broadly on complexity, self-organization and related concepts, here are some introductory references: Goodwin 1994; Jantsch 1982; Kauffman 1993, 1995; Kiel and Elliott 1996; Langton 1992; Lewin 1999; Mingers 1995; Williams 1997. For applications in the social sciences, see: Adams 1988; Kontopoulos 1993; Schieve and Allen 1982; Scott 1991.

2 If you would like to read more about heterarchy and its connection to brain research and artificial intelligence, here are some references: Bateson 1972; Crumley 1979, 1987b, 2001; Crumley and Marquardt 1987; Ehrenreich et al. 1995; Kontopoulos 1993; McCulloch 1945; Minsky and Papert 1972; Mithen 1996.

3 For an overview of historical ecology, see Crumley 1994 and Balée 1998. Don S. Rice attributes first use of the term to the archaeological palynologist Edward S. Deevey, who directed the Historical Ecology Project at the University of Florida in the early 1970s. Historian J. Donald Hughes uses the term environmental history in his1975 book, but, with anthropologists, a human ecologist, an economist, and other historians, contributed to

Historical Ecology: Essays on Environment and Social Change (1981), edited by historian Lester J. Bilsky. Anthropologist Alice Ingerson organized a session on historical ecology at the 1984 American Anthropological Association annual meeting. She sought to address the chasm between cultural (e.g., nature as metaphor) and environmental (energy cycles) studies in anthropology, and to explore political economy and social history approaches. I first used the term as the title of a chapter in *Regional Dynamics: Burgundian Landscapes in Historical Perspective* (1987), edited with William H. Marquardt, and subsequently edited a School of American Research volume entitled *Historical Ecology: Cultural Knowledge and Changing Landscapes* (1994). Since the early 1990s ethnographer and cultural ecologist William Balée has been fostering historical ecology; together we edit the *Historical Ecology Series* for Columbia University Press (Balée 1998; McIntosh et al. 2000). Restoration ecologists Dave Egan and Evelyn A. Howell edit *The Historical Ecology Handbook: A Restorationist's Guide to Reference Ecosystems* (2001). A recent search of websites employing the term found dozens of references representing a variety of projects. Most – although not all – of these sites explicitly address the relation between the environment and human activity.

INDEX

D

E

M

N

O

P

Q

R

S

U

V

W

X

Y

Z